12th Global Wordnet Conference (GWC 2023)

Donositia-San Sebastian, Spain
23-27 January 2023

Editors:

German Rigau
Francis Bond
Alexandre Rademaker

ISBN: 978-1-7138-9088-1

Printed from e-media with permission by:

Curran Associates, Inc.
57 Morehouse Lane
Red Hook, NY 12571

proceedings.com

Some format issues inherent in the e-media version may also appear in this print version.

Printed with permission by Curran Associates, Inc. (2024)

Association for Computational Linguistics
209 N. Eighth Street
Stroudsburg, Pennsylvania 18360

Phone: 1-570-476-8006
Fax: 1-570-476-0860

acl@aclweb.org

Additional copies of this publication are available from:

Curran Associates, Inc.
57 Morehouse Lane
Red Hook, NY 12571 USA
Phone: 845-758-0400
Fax: 845-758-2633
Email: curran@proceedings.com
Web: www.proceedings.com

GWC 2023

Proceedings of the 12th Global Wordnet Conference

German Rigau, Francis Bond, Alexandre Rademaker (Eds.)

23–27 Jan, 2023
University of the Basque Country in Donostia-San Sebastian
Basque Country

Foreword

The 12th Global Wordnet Conference was celebrated in Donostia-San Sebastián two years after the outbreak of the coronavirus pandemic forced the preceding event to take place online. Fortunately, this year the receding threat from the virus and the slow return to pre-pandemic life allowed scholars and researchers from Africa, America, Asia, and Europe to make the journey to the Basque Country. Reunited in person once more, the conference was an opportunity to greet longtime colleagues and forge new acquaintances. Its varied sessions were interspersed with outings to local landmarks and historical spaces, including a visit to the traditional cider house on an unusually frigid and windswept evening.

These activities were organized by this year's host, HiTZ, the Basque Center for Language and Technology. Many of the center's members have long been active participants in the development of WordNet and its related resources. This includes the steady creation of a Basque WordNet, a notable example of the multilingual nature of wordnets globally.

We received fifty-two submissions, two more than the previous edition. The increase points to the continuing strength of WordNet and its critical importance to Natural Language Processing within the current wave of Large Language Models. Among the forty-three submissions accepted and presented during the conference were studies that discussed the use of Wordnet for improving deep learning, methods to connect wordnets to other ontologies and resources, Wordnet extensions, and wordnets for Latvian, Guarani, Cantonese, and Japanese. Our invited speakers provided histories of NLP and WordNet that took us from their origins to the present day and into the future. Christiane Fellbaum, co-founder and co-president of the Global WordNet Association, presented a retrospective overview of WordNet, while José Camacho, Senior Lecturer at Cardiff University's School of Computer Science and Informatics, discussed the open challenges that exist in word embeddings and language models.

We hope the work collected in this volume will not only encourage further research into wordnets and their place within NLP today, but also serve as a bridge to future advances in the field.

Begoña Altuna, Itziar Aldabe, Xabier Arregi, Itziar Gonzalez-Dios, Aritz Farwell, Esther Miranda.

January 2023

Conference Chairs

- German Rigau, HiTZ Center, University of the Basque Country UPV/EHU
- Francis Bond, Palacký University

Local Organising Committee

- Begoña Altuna, HiTZ Center, University of the Basque Country UPV/EHU
- Itziar Aldabe, HiTZ Center, University of the Basque Country UPV/EHU
- Xabier Arregi, HiTZ Center, University of the Basque Country UPV/EHU
- Itziar Gonzalez-Dios, HiTZ Center, University of the Basque Country UPV/EHU
- Aritz Farwell, HiTZ Center, University of the Basque Country UPV/EHU
- Esther Miranda, HiTZ Center, University of the Basque Country UPV/EHU

Program Committee

- Adam Pease, Articulate Software
- Ales Horak, Masaryk University
- Alexandre Rademaker, IBM Research Brazil and EMAp/FGV
- Bolette Pedersen, University of Copenhagen
- Christiane Fellbaum, Princeton University
- Darja Fiser, University of Ljubljana
- David Lindemann, IWiSt, University of Hildesheim
- Diptesh Kanojia, IIT Bombay
- Eneko Agirre, HiTZ Center, University of the Basque Country UPV/EHU
- Ewa Rudnicka, Wrocław University of Technology
- Francis Bond, Palacký University
- Gerard De Melo, Rutgers University
- German Rigau, HiTZ Center, University of the Basque Country UPV/EHU
- Haldur Oim, University of Tartu

- Heili Orav, University of Tartu
- Hugo Gonçalo-Oliveira, Department of Informatics Engineering of the University of Coimbra
- Janos Csirik, University of Szeged
- John Mccrae, National University of Ireland, Galway
- Kadri Vider, University of Tartu
- Kevin Scannell, Saint Louis University
- Kyoko Kanzaki, Otemon Gakuin University
- Maciej Piasecki, Department of Computational Intelligence, Wroclaw University
- Marten Postma, Vrije Universiteit Amsterdam
- Paul Buitelaar, National University of Ireland, Galway
- Piek Vossen, VU University Amsterdam.
- Sanni Nimb, The Danish Society for Language and Literature
- Shan Wang, The Education University of Hong Kong
- Shu-Kai Hsieh, National Taiwan Normal University
- Sonja Bosch, Department of African Languages, University of South Africa
- Thierry Declerck, DFKI, Saarbruecken
- Tim Baldwin, The University of Melbourne
- Tomaž Erjavec, Dept. of Knowledge Technologies, Jožef Stefan Institute
- Umamaheswari Vasanthakumar, Nanyang Technological University
- Valeria de Paiva, Natural Language and AI Research Laboratory of Nuance Communications, Inc.
- Verginica Mititelu, Romanian Academy Research Institute for Artificial Intelligence

Invited Speakers

- Christiane Fellbaum
- José Camacho Collados

Invited talk

Christiane Fellbaum: 35 years of WordNet: Taking stock and looking ahead

We provide a brief behind-the-scenes look at the early days of WordNet, highlighting its initial motivation and its evolution. Examples of WordNet's current and potential future contributions to research in linguistics and psycholinguistics as well as to a wide range of applications are discussed.

Bio Christiane Fellbaum is a Lecturer with Rank of Professor in the Program in Linguistics and the Computer Science Department at Princeton University. She was educated in Germany, France, and the U.S. and received her Ph.D. in Linguistics from Princeton University. She is a co-developer, with George A. Miller, of the lexical database WordNet, and has been active in WordNet-related research and diverse applications. She has published widely on topics in lexical semantics and computational linguistics.

José Camacho-Collados: Contextualized Embeddings, Word Sense Disambiguation and Open Challenges

Embeddings have been one of the most important topics of interest in Natural Language Processing (NLP) for the past decade. Representing knowledge through low-dimensional vectors that are flexible and easily integrable in modern machine learning models has played a central role in the development of the field. Embedding techniques initially focused on words but the attention soon started to shift to other forms. Recently, contextualized embeddings such as those provided by BERT and similar approaches have taken NLP by storm, providing improvements in many downstream tasks. Unlike static word embeddings, contextualized models can dynamically capture the meaning of a word in context. In this talk, I will explain to what extent this is true, showing the main advantages and limitations of current approaches. I will take word sense disambiguation as a proxy to answer these questions, presenting an overview of the field from a language modelling perspective and discussing open challenges.

Bio Jose Camacho-Collados is a Senior Lecturer and UKRI Future Leaders Fellow at Cardiff University, leading the Cardiff NLP group. Before joining Cardiff University, he completed his PhD in Sapienza University of Rome and was a Google AI PhD Fellow. He has worked on different areas of Natural Language Processing (NLP) with a particular focus on semantics. He is the co-author of the "Embeddings in Natural Language Processing" book and is the current Program Chair of *SEM. In addition to semantics, he is interested in lexical resources and multilinguality, and in the last few years he has worked on developing NLP models specialised in social media, such as those included in the recently released TweetNLP platform.

Table of Contents

Probing Taxonomic and Thematic Embeddings for Taxonomic Information

Filip Klubička and **John D. Kelleher**
ADAPT Centre, Technological University Dublin, Ireland
{filip.klubicka, john.kelleher}@adaptcentre.ie

Abstract

Modelling taxonomic and thematic relatedness is important for building AI with comprehensive natural language understanding. The goal of this paper is to learn more about how taxonomic information is structurally encoded in embeddings. To do this, we design a new hypernym-hyponym probing task and perform a comparative probing study of taxonomic and thematic SGNS and GloVe embeddings. Our experiments indicate that both types of embeddings encode some taxonomic information, but the amount, as well as the geometric properties of the encodings, are independently related to both the encoder architecture, as well as the embedding training data. Specifically, we find that only taxonomic embeddings carry taxonomic information in their norm, which is determined by the underlying distribution in the data.

1 Introduction

Research on probing (Ettinger et al., 2016; Shi et al., 2016; Veldhoen et al., 2016; Adi et al., 2017) has gained significant momentum in the NLP community in recent years, helping researchers explore different aspects of text encodings. While its potential for application is broad, there are still many NLP tasks the framework has not been applied to. Specifically, it seems the majority of impactful probing work focuses on analysing syntactic properties encoded in language representations, yet the rich and complex field of semantics is comparably underrepresented (Belinkov and Glass, 2019). One particular semantic problem that has not been explored at all in the context of probing is the distinction between the **taxonomic** and **thematic** dimensions of semantic relatedness (Kacmajor and Kelleher, 2019): words or concepts which belong to a common taxonomic category share properties or functions, and such relationships are commonly reflected in knowledge-engineered resources such as ontologies or taxonomies. On the other hand, thematic relations exist by virtue of co-occurrence in a (linguistic) context where the relatedness is specifically formed between concepts performing complementary roles in a common event or theme.

This distinction informs the theoretical basis of our work, as we wish to explore the tension between taxonomic and thematic representations by examining how their information is structurally encoded. Indeed, the vast majority of pretrained language models (PTLMs) are trained solely on natural language corpora, meaning they mainly encode thematic relations. Consequently, most probing work is applied to thematic embeddings, while taxonomic embeddings remain unexplored. We thus use the probing framework to study and compare taxonomic and thematic meaning representations.

In addition, one aspect of embeddings that has not received much attention is the contribution of the vector norm to encoding linguistic information. We have recently highlighted this gap in the literature and developed an extension of the probing method called *probing with noise* (Klubička and Kelleher, 2022), which allows for relative intrinsic probe evaluations that are able to provide structural insights into embeddings and highlight the role of the vector norm in encoding linguistic information. We find taxonomic embeddings to be particularly interesting for probing the role of the norm, as we suspect that the hierarchical structure of a taxonomy is well suited to be encoded by the vector norm—given that the norm encodes the vector's magnitude, or distance from the space's origin, it is possible that the depth of a tree structure, such as a taxonomy, could be mapped to the vector's distance from the origin in some way[1]. Applying the *probing with noise* method to taxonomic embeddings on a taxonomic probing task could shed some light on this relationship. In order to draw

[1]A hypothesis based on the finding that the squared L2 norm of BERT and ELMo can correspond to the depth of the word in a syntactic parse tree (Hewitt and Manning, 2019).

broader comparisons, we apply the same evaluation framework to taxonomic and thematic SGNS and GloVe embeddings.

2 Related Work

Hypernymy, understood as the capability to relate generic terms or classes to their specific instances, lies at the core of human cognition and plays a central role in reasoning and understanding natural language (Wellman and Gelman, 1992). Two words have a hypernymic relation if one of the words belongs to a taxonomic class that is more general than that of the other word. Hypernymy can be seen as an *IS-A* relationship, and more practically, hypernymic relations determine lexical entailment (Geffet and Dagan, 2005) and form the *IS-A* backbone of almost every ontology, semantic network and taxonomy (Yu et al., 2015). Given this, it is not surprising that modelling and identifying hypernymic relations has been pursued in NLP for over two decades (Shwartz et al., 2016).

While research on hypernym detection has been plentiful, work applying any probing framework to identify taxonomic information in embeddings is scarce, and the existing work does nor probe for it directly, but rather infers taxonomic knowledge from examining higher-level tasks. For example, Ettinger (2020) identified taxonomic knowledge in BERT, but rather than using a probing classifier, BERT's masked-LM component was used instead and its performance was examined on a range of cloze tasks. One of the relevant findings was that BERT can robustly retrieve noun hypernyms in this setting, demonstrating that BERT is strong at associating nouns with their hypernyms. Ravichander et al. (2020) build on Ettinger's work and investigate whether probing studies shed light on BERT's systematic knowledge, and as a case study examine hypernymy information. They devise additional cloze tasks to test for prediction consistency and demonstrate that BERT often fails to consistently make the same prediction in slightly different contexts, concluding that its ability to correctly retrieve hypernyms is not a reflection of larger systematic knowledge, but possibly an indicator of lexical memorisation (Levy et al., 2015; Santus et al., 2016; Shwartz et al., 2017).

Aside from this recent focus on BERT, little work has been done in the space of probing embeddings for hypernym information. However, work on modelling hypernymy has a long history that stretches back before large PTLMs and includes pattern-based approaches (Hearst, 1992; Navigli and Velardi, 2010; Lenci and Benotto, 2012; Boella and Di Caro, 2013; Flati et al., 2014; Santus et al., 2014; Flati et al., 2016; Gupta et al., 2016; Pavlick and Paşca, 2017) that are based on the notion of distributional generality (Weeds et al., 2004; Clarke, 2009), as well as distributional approaches (Turney and Pantel, 2010; Baroni et al., 2012; Rei and Briscoe, 2013; Santus et al., 2014; Fu et al., 2014; Espinosa-Anke et al., 2016; Ivan Sanchez Carmona and Riedel, 2017; Nguyen et al., 2017; Pinter and Eisenstein, 2018; Bernier-Colborne and Barrière, 2018; Nickel and Kiela, 2018; Roller et al., 2018; Maldonado and Klubička, 2018; Cho et al., 2020; Mansar et al., 2021). We highlight the work of Weeds et al. (2014), who demonstrated that it is possible to predict a specific semantic relation between two words given their distributional vectors. Their work is especially relevant to ours as it shows that the nature of the relationship one is trying to establish between words informs the operation one should perform on their associated vectors, e.g. summing the vectors works well for a co-hyponym task. We consider this in §3.

In terms of evaluation benchmarks for modeling hypernymy, in most cases their design reduces them to binary classification (Baroni and Lenci, 2011; Snow et al., 2005; Boleda et al., 2017; Vyas and Carpuat, 2017), where a system has to decide whether or not a hypernymic relation holds between a given candidate pair of terms. Criticisms to this experimental setting point out that supervised systems tend to benefit from the inherent modeling of the datasets in the task, leading to lexical memorization phenomena. Some attempts to alleviate this issue involve including a graded scale for evaluating the degree of hypernymy on a given pair (Vulić et al., 2017), or reframing the task design as Hypernym Discovery (Espinosa-Anke et al., 2016). The latter addresses one of the main drawbacks of the binary evaluation criterion and resulted in the construction of a hypernym discovery benchmark covering multiple languages and knowledge domains (Camacho-Collados et al., 2018).

3 Probing Dataset Construction

Conneau et al. (2018) state that a probing task needs to ask a simple, non-ambiguous question, in order to minimise interpretability problems and confounding factors. While we acknowledge the hypernym discovery framing as an important benchmark, and the cloze tasks used by Ettinger (2020) as an enlightening probing scenario, we suspect neither is suitable for our probing experiments, for which we require a simpler task that more directly teases out the hypernym-hyponym relationship. We thus opt to construct a new taxonomic probing task: predicting which word in a pair is the hypernym, and which is the hyponym. This dataset is directly derived from WordNet (Fellbaum, 1998) and contains all its hypernym-hyponym pairs. Thus each word pair shares only an immediate hypernym-hyponym relationship between the candidate words: a word in a pair can *only* be a hyponym or hypernym of the other.

However, in our experiments we wish to probe both taxonomic and thematic encoders. Given that we are mostly using pretrained thematic and taxonomic embeddings (see §4), their vocabulary coverage might vary dramatically. We wish to mitigate confounders by comparing like for like as much as possible, so to retain a higher integrity of interpretation when comparing models, we prune the dataset to only use the intersection of vocabularies of all the used models—we only include word pairs that have a representation for both candidate words in all the embedding models.

Note here that one of the goals of our work is to use the *probing with noise* method to learn about embeddings and the way they encode different types of information in vector space. We assert that a prediction of the relationship between a pair of words cannot be fairly done without the classifier having access to representations for both words in the pair. Yet, our probe is a classifier which can only take a single vector as input. Informed by the work of Weeds et al. (2014) we considered options such as averaging or summing the individual word vectors, but found that these were not suitable for our framing as they muddled the notion that the classifier is receiving two separate words as input. We instead concatenate the word vectors in question and pass a single concatenated vector to the classifier (similar to approaches used by Adi et al. (2017)). This approach allows us to formulate the task as a positional classification task: given a pair of words, is the first one the hypernym or the hyponym of the other? We can then assign each instance in the corpus a binary label—0 or 1—representing the class of the first word in the pair. The probe can then predict if the left half of the vector is the hyponym (0) of the right half, or whether it is its hypernym (1).

Finally, the inherent tree structure of WordNet means that a smaller number of words will be hypernyms, while a larger number will be hyponyms. We want to avoid the probe memorising the subset of words more likely to be hypernyms, but rather to learn from information encoded in the (differences between) vectors themselves. In an attempt to achieve this, we balance out the ratio of class labels by duplicating the dataset and swapping the hypernym-hyponym positions and labels. Before duplicating, we also define a hold-out test set of 25,000 instances, so as to exclude the possibility of the same word pair appearing in both the train and test split—thus, the probe will be evaluated only on unseen instances. This duplication resulted in a final dataset of 493,494 instances, of which 50,000 comprise the test set and 443,494 comprise the training set. Here are some example instances:

***0**, north, direction*
***1**, direction, north*
***0**, hurt, upset*
***1**, upset, hurt*

4 Experimental Setup

4.1 Chosen Embeddings

In our experiments we probe taxonomic and thematic SGNS embeddings, and make an analogous comparison with taxonomic and thematic GloVe embeddings. Usually pretrained taxonomic embeddings are not as easy to come by as thematic ones, but fortunately we were able to include a set of freely available taxonomic embeddings that are based on a random walk algorithm over the WordNet taxonomy, inspired by the work of (Goikoetxea et al., 2015). In short, the approach is to generate a pseudo-corpus by crawling the WordNet structure and outputting the lexical items in the nodes visited, and then running the word embedding training on the generated pseudo-corpus. Naturally, the shape of the underlying knowledge graph affects the properties of the generated pseudo-corpus, while the types of connections that are traversed will affect the kinds of relations that are encoded in this resource. A Python implementation has been made freely available[2] and the embeddings

[2] `https://github.com/GreenParachute/wordnet-randomwalk-python`

have been shown to encode taxonomic information (Klubička et al., 2019). Ultimately we chose these embeddings as they allow us to be methodologically consistent by creating taxonomic embeddings that employ the same encoder architectures used to obtain thematic embeddings.

word2vec (SGNS) For *taxonomic SGNS* representations[3] we opt for embeddings trained on the pseudo-corpus that yielded the highest Spearman correlation score on the wn-paths benchmark (introduced by Klubička et al. (2020)), i.e. the corpus with 2 million sentences, with the walk going both ways and with a 2-word minimum sentence length. The lack of a directionality constraint provides higher vocabulary coverage and a smaller proportion of rare words, while the 2-word minimum sentence length limit ensures that we only have representations for words that are part of WordNet's taxonomic graph and have at least one hypernym-hyponym relationship, which makes them suitable for this task. For the *thematic SGNS* embeddings we use a pretrained model, and opt for the gensim[4] word2vec implementation which was trained on a part of the Google News dataset (about 100 billion tokens) and contains 300-dimensional vectors for 3 million words and phrases[5].

GloVe To train *taxonomic GloVe* embeddings, we use a popular Python implementation of the GloVe algorithm[6,7] and, importantly, train it on the same 2m-both-2w/s pseudo-corpus as the above taxonomic SGNS was trained on[8]. For the *thematic GloVe* embeddings we use the original Stanford pretrained GloVe embeddings[9], opting for the larger common crawl model, which was trained on 840 billion tokens and contains 300-dimensional embeddings for a total of 2.2 million words.

Note that when we concatenate the two word embeddings required for an instance in the train or test set, they become a 600-dimensional vector which is then passed on as input to the probe.

[3]`https://arrow.dit.ie/datas/12/`

[4]`https://radimrehurek.com/gensim/`

[5]word2vec-google-news-300

[6]`https://github.com/maciejkula/glove-python`

[7]We used the following training parameters: window=10, no_components=300, learning_rate=0.05, epochs=30, no_threads=2. Any other parameters are left as default.

[8]`https://arrow.dit.ie/datas/9/`

[9]`https://nlp.stanford.edu/projects/glove/`

4.2 Probing with Noise

The method is described in detail in Klubička and Kelleher (2022)[10]: in essence it applies targeted noise functions to embeddings that have an ablational effect and remove information encoded either in the norm or dimensions of a vector.

We remove information from the norm (abl.N) by sampling random norm values and scaling the vector dimensions to the new norm. Specifically, we sample the L2 norms uniformly from a range between the minimum and maximum L2 norm values of the respective embeddings in our dataset[11].

To ablate information encoded in the dimensions (abl.D), we randomly sample dimension values and then scale them to match the original norm of the vector. Specifically, we sample the random dimension values uniformly from a range between the minimum and maximum dimension values of the respective embeddings in our dataset[12]. We expect this to fully remove all interpretable information encoded in the dimension values, making the norm the only information container available to the probe.

Applying both noise functions to the same vector (abl.D+N) should remove any information encoded in it, meaning the probe has no signal to learn from, a scenario equal to training on random vectors.

Even when no information is encoded in an embedding, the train set may contain class imbalance, and the probe can learn the distribution of classes. To account for this, as well as the possibility of a powerful probe detecting an empty signal (Zhang and Bowman, 2018), we need to establish informative random baselines against which we can compare the probe's performance. We employ two such baselines: (a) we assert a random prediction (*rand.pred*) onto the test set, negating any information that a classifier could have learned, class distributions included; and (b) we train the probe on randomly generated vectors (*rand.vec*), establishing a baseline with access only to class distributions.

Importantly, while we use randomised baselines

[10]Code available here: `https://github.com/GreenParachute/probing-with-noise`

[11]Thematic SGNS: [0.6854, 9.3121]
Taxonomic SGNS: [2.1666, 7.6483]
Thematic GloVe: [3.1519, 13.1196]
Taxonomic GloVe: [0.0167, 6.3104]

[12]Thematic SGNS: [-1.5547, 1.7109]
Taxonomic SGNS: [-1.8811, 1.7843]
Thematic GloVe: [-4.2095, 4.0692]
Taxonomic GloVe: [-1.3875, 1.3931]

as a sense check, we use the vanilla SGNS and GloVe word embeddings in their respective evaluations as *vanilla baselines* against which all of the introduced noise models are compared. Here, the probe has access to both dimension and norm information, as well as class distributions from the training set. However, given the lack of probing taxonomic embeddings in the literature, it is equally important to establish the vanilla baseline's performance against the random baselines: we need to confirm that the relevant information is indeed encoded somewhere in the embeddings.

Finally, to address the degrees of randomness in the method, we train and evaluate each model 50 times and report the average score of all the runs, essentially bootstrapping over the random seeds (Wendlandt et al., 2018). Additionally, we calculate a confidence interval (CI) to make sure that the reported averages were not obtained by chance, and report it alongside the results.

4.3 Probing Classifier and Evaluation Metric

The embeddings are used as input to a Multi-Layered Perceptron (MLP) classifier, which predicts their class labels. We used the scikit-learn MLP implementation (Pedregosa et al., 2011) using the default parameters[13]. The choice of evaluation metric used to evaluate the probes is not trivial, as we want to make sure that it reliably reflects a signal captured in the embeddings, especially in an imbalanced dataset where the probe could learn the label distributions, rather than detect a true signal related to the probed phenomenon. Following our original approach (Klubička and Kelleher, 2022), we use the AUC-ROC score[14], which is suited to reflecting the classifier's performance on both positive and negative classes.

5 Experimental Results

Experimental evaluation results for taxonomic and thematic embeddings on the hypernym-hyponym probing task are presented in Tables 1 and 2. Note that all cells shaded light grey belong to the same distribution as random baselines on a given task, as there is no statistically significant difference between the different scores; cells shaded dark grey belong to the same distribution as the vanilla baseline on a given task; and all cells that are not shaded contain a significantly different score than both the random and vanilla baselines, indicating that they belong to different distributions.

SGNS				
Model	THEM		TAX	
	auc	±CI	auc	±CI
rand. pred.	.5000	.0009	.4997	.0009
rand. vec.	.5001	.0012	.5001	.0011
vanilla	.9163	.0004	.9256	.0003
abl. N	.9057	.0004	.9067	.0005
abl. D	.5039	.0008	.5294	.0010
abl. D+N	.4998	.0010	.5002	.0009

Table 1: Probing results on SGNS models and baselines. Reporting average AUC-ROC scores and confidence intervals (CI) of the average of all training runs.

SGNS Starting with *thematic SGNS* (THEM), Table 1 shows that the random baselines perform comparably to each other, as would be expected, and their score indicates no ability to discriminate between the two classes. We can see that the vanilla representations significantly outperform the random baselines, indicating that at least some taxonomic information is encoded in the embeddings.

The norm ablation scenario (abl.N) causes a statistically significant drop in performance when compared to the vanilla baseline. In principle, this indicates that some information has been lost. If instead of the norm, we ablate the dimensions (abl.D), we see a much more dramatic performance drop compared to vanilla, indicating that much more information has been removed. Unsurprisingly, the difference in the probe's performance when applying both noising functions (abl.D+N) compared to random baselines is not statistically significant, meaning there is no pertinent information left in these representations. Notably, once just the dimension container is ablated, its performance drops to extremely low levels and approaches random baseline performance, yet it does not quite reach it—as small as it is, the difference is statistically significant, indicating that not all information has been removed in this setting. While significant, given how minor this difference is, one might argue it does not convincingly indicate the norm's role in

[13] activation='relu', solver='adam', max_iter=200, hidden_layer_sizes=100, learning_rate_init=0.001, batch_size=min(200,n_samples), early_stopping=False, weight init. $W \sim \mathcal{N}\left(0, \sqrt{6/(fan_{in} + fan_{out})}\right)$ (scikit relu default). See: `https://scikit-learn.org/stable/modules/generated/sklearn.neural_network.MLPClassifier.html`

[14] `https://scikit-learn.org/stable/modules/generated/sklearn.metrics.roc_auc_score.html`

GloVe				
Model	THEM		TAX	
	auc	±CI	auc	±CI
rand. pred.	.4999	.0011	.4998	.0010
rand. vec.	.5001	.0010	.5001	.0008
vanilla	.9327	.0004	.8824	.0005
abl. N	.9110	.0004	.8435	.0008
abl. D	.5002	.0008	.6621	.0008
abl. D+N	.5000	.0011	.5006	.0011

Table 2: Probing results on GloVe models and baselines. Reporting average AUC-ROC scores and confidence intervals (CI) of the average of all training runs.

encoding taxonomic information.

However, we observe a much crisper signal in the *taxonomic SGNS* (TAX) results. The random baselines perform comparably, while the vanilla baseline significantly outperforms them, while also significantly outperforming the THEM vanilla baseline, confirming that the taxonomic embeddings encode more taxonomic information than thematic embeddings. The norm ablation scenario causes a statistically significant performance drop from vanilla, while ablating the dimension container yields a larger drop, but does not reach the random-like performance achieved when ablating both containers. Here the difference in scores between ablating just the dimensions and ablating both dimensions and norm is also significantly different from random, but notably also an order of magnitude larger than in the THEM example. This indicates that the taxonomic SGNS embeddings use the norm to encode taxonomic information more so than thematic ones.

GloVe In Table 2 we see that *thematic GloVe* (THEM) vanilla performance dramatically outperforms the baselines, but the scores drop when the norm is ablated. After ablating the dimension information, there is a substantial drop in the probe's performance and it is immediately comparable to random baselines with no statistically significant difference. Furthermore, performance does not significantly change after also ablating the norm.

Meanwhile, the *taxonomic GloVe* embeddings tell a different story. Firstly, while vanilla embeddings outperform the random baselines, they perform much worse than THEM vanilla GloVe, indicating an inferior representation for the hypernym-hyponym prediction task, even though they were trained on WordNet random walk pseudo-corpora (we discuss this in §6). Ablating the dimensions causes a significant drop in performance, but it is nowhere near the random performance reached when ablating both dimensions and norm. This is a really strong signal that indicates the norm encodes some hypernym-hyponym information. This echoes the findings on SGNS, showing that taxonomic embeddings tend to use the norm to encode taxonomic information more so than thematic ones.

5.1 Dataset Validation Experiments: Dimension Deletions

Our experimental design is based on the assumption that providing the probe with a concatenated vector of word embeddings would allow it to infer the asymmetric relationship between the words and use that signal to make predictions. While we have taken some steps to ensure this and mitigate lexical memorisation (see §3), there is still a concern that the models could have memorised other regularities encoded in the individual word representations and used that information to make predictions. For example, while many candidate words can indeed be both hyponyms or hypernyms, given the tree structure of the taxonomy and the distribution of edges, the frequencies at which a word takes on a hypernym or hyponym role are still skewed. It is thus more likely that any given word will be a hyponym than a hypernym, and it is possible that the embeddings implicitly encode the frequency at which a word takes on a hypernym role, versus a hyponym role.

To validate that the probe is actually learning a relationship between the candidate words, we run an additional batch of probing experiments to establish another set of baselines specific to this particular probing task. We examine the impact of two scenarios on the probe's performance: given the same labels, a) what if the probe's input was only one word vector, and b) what if the probe's input was only half of each word vector in the pair?

We denote this line of enquiry as *deletion experiments*, given that in practice a) can be seen as deleting half of the concatenated vector, and b) as deleting one half each vector before concatenating. The crucial difference is that in a) the probe can only learn from one word vector without having any access to a representation of the other word, meaning it can only predict whether the candidate word is a hyponym or a hypernym by relying on the probability derived from its frequency. In b) the

SGNS				
Model	THEM		TAX	
	auc	±CI	auc	±CI
rand. pred.	.5000	.0009	.4997	.0009
rand. vec.	.5001	.0012	.5001	.0011
vanilla	.9163	.0004	.9256	.0003
del. ea. 1h	.8929	.0004	.8998*	.0005
del. ea. 2h	.8927	.0004	.9039	.0004
del. ct. 1h	.8496	.0004	.8525	.0004
del. ct. 2h	.8495	.0004	.8523	.0003

Table 3: Probing results on SGNS deletions and baselines. Reporting average AUC-ROC scores and confidence intervals (CI) of the average of all training runs.

GloVe				
Model	THEM		TAX	
	auc	±CI	auc	±CI
rand. pred.	.4999	.0011	.4998	.0010
rand. vec.	.5001	.0010	.5001	.0008
vanilla	.9327	.0004	.8824	.0005
del. ea. 1h	.9120*	.0003	.8727	.0005
del. ea. 2h	.9179	.0004	.8730	.0006
del. ct. 1h	.8522	.0004	.8405	.0004
del. ct. 2h	.8522	.0004	.8406	.0004

Table 4: Probing results on GloVe deletions and baselines. Reporting average AUC-ROC scores and confidence intervals (CI) of the average of all training runs.

probe has a representation for both vectors, meaning it could leverage the relationship between them, but the individual vectors are truncated, meaning that half of the dimensions are gone for each word, making this inferior to the vanilla setting[15].

We ran these experiments for taxonomic and thematic SGNS and GloVe embeddings and when performing deletions assessed the impact of both halves of the vectors. All dimension deletion results are included in Tables 3 and 4, where scenario a) is denoted as *del.ct.1h/2h* (deleted 1st/2nd half of concatenated vector) and scenario b) is denoted as *del.ea.1h/2h* (deleted 1st/2nd half of each vector). When comparing the deletions of the different halves, in cases where there is a statistically significant difference between their scores, the lower of the two scores is marked with an asterisk (*).

SGNS Unsurprisingly, deleting half of the vector in either scenario causes a statistically significant drop in performance when compared to vanilla. We also observe a larger drop in both *del.ct.* settings versus the *del.ea.* settings, which confirms that predicting a word's relationship to an "imaginary" other word is the more difficult task.

However, strikingly, the performance is also significantly above random, which indicates that the probe likely did learn some frequency distributions from the graph. It is possible that this is a reflection of the imbalance inherent to WordNet, given the large number of leaf nodes in the taxonomic graph.

Even still, the significant difference in scores between the two settings demonstrates that having access to both words, even at the cost of half the information in each word's dimensions, is more informative than having a full representation of a single word, *indicating that the probe is inferring the relevant relationship between them.*

GloVe The GloVe deletion results echo the findings on SGNS in most settings. Deleting half of the vector in either scenario causes a significant performance drop, which is largely above random performance, and the drop is larger in the *del.ct.* setting versus the *del.ea.* setting. This provides further indication that, while there is an inherent imbalance in the underlying data, the probe is inferring the relevant relationship between the candidate words when given a concatenation of two word vectors. The probe benefits significantly from having access to a representation of both words, or even just two halves of each representation. Even when it is not explicitly told that it is actually getting two inputs, it is able to pick up on the fact that there is a difference between them which can be helpful in deciding on a label.

6 Discussion

There are a number of points to take away from our experimental results. Firstly, we see that both vanilla thematic embeddings encode taxonomic information and the GloVe vanilla model significantly outperforms the SGNS vanilla model. This is at least partially due to the fact that the pre-trained SGNS and GloVe thematic embeddings were trained on unrelated corpora, which differ in terms of size, topic and coverage: the corpus that GloVe was trained on is over 8 times larger than the one used to train the SGNS model, and belongs to a different, much more varied genre of text data. Thus, word representations derived from

[15]This choice is motivated by a desire to make this setting comparable to a) in terms of dimensionality—had we simply compared it to vanilla, it would have the advantage of having access to twice as many dimensions.

these resources are likely very different and it is possible that due to the broader scope and much larger size of the GloVe corpus, the GloVe representations reflect more taxonomic knowledge.

However, these encoders exhibit the opposite behaviour when trained on the same WordNet random walk pseudo-corpus: expectedly, vanilla taxonomic SGNS scores improve upon its thematic version, yet vanilla taxonomic GloVe scores significantly underperform compared to thematic. While we would expect it to mirror what was observed in SGNS, taxonomic GloVe is in fact our worst-performing vanilla model. Given the significant differences in model architectures, it is possible that this unexpected behaviour is due to an interaction between the architecture and training data[16]. While this may play a role, we suspect that the dominant factor is rather training corpus size. The WordNet pseudo-corpus used for training taxonomic embeddings was only about 9 million tokens in size (which is sufficient to encode taxonomic relations, as shown by Maldonado et al. (2019)), whereas SGNS and GloVe were trained on 100 and 840 billion tokens respectively. It is not surprising that GloVe trained on a small and relatively sparse pseudo-corpus underperforms compared to training on a large natural corpus. If anything, it is encouraging that SGNS trained on a 9-million-token pseudo-corpus outperforms one trained on a 100-billion-token natural corpus.

Another important finding from our experiments is the strong evidence that *word embedding models can use the norm to encode taxonomic information, regardless of what is encoded in the vector dimensions*. We find the clearest example of this in taxonomic GloVe after ablating dimension information, where the score remains as high as ≈0.66, meaning that the difference of 0.16 points is solely due to information in the norm. This is a very large difference given our understanding of the underlying mechanics, where it is well known that dimensions contain most, if not all information relevant for a task (e.g. Durrani et al. (2020, 2022)), and this is much more than has been demonstrated on any of the sentence-level experiments in our previous work (Klubička and Kelleher, 2022). Additionally, this is the only case where deleting half of each word vector yields a significantly higher score (≈0.87) than ablating the norm (≈0.84). This suggests that more information is lost when the norm is ablated than when half of the dimensions are removed. This is a strong indicator that in this case the *norm encodes information that is not at all available in the dimensions*. Certainly, the majority of the information in an embedding is and will always be encoded in the dimensions, but it is striking how much of it is present in the norm in this case.

Generally, when it comes to dimension deletion experiments, it is expected that the performance would drop dramatically in comparison to vanilla embeddings. However, an important takeaway is that in all settings the drop is much smaller than might be expected, being quite close to vanilla performance and largely above random performance. This points to a redundancy within the dimensions themselves, seeing as either half of the vector seems to carry more than half the information required to model the task, indicating that not many dimensions are needed to encode specific linguistic features. This is consistent with the findings of (Durrani et al., 2020), who analysed individual neurons in PTLMs and found that small subsets of neurons are sufficient to predict certain linguistic tasks. Our deletion results certainly corroborate these findings, given how small the drop in the probe's performance is when half the vector is deleted.

For additional insight into the norm, we examine the norm values. We calculate the norms of the individual hypernym and hyponym word vectors in our dataset and present the results in Figure 1. The median norm value shows that the difference between hypernym and hyponym norms seems to be minor in both thematic embedding types (GloVe: 6.26 and 6.24; SGNS: 2.78 and 2.76), whereas the difference is an order of magnitude larger in both taxonomic representations (GloVe: 2.03 and 2.67; SGNS: 5.64 and 5.80). The difference is also quite large between taxonomic GloVe and SGNS, and it seems to be what is reflected in our experimental results, which show that GloVe stores the most hypernym-hyponym information in the norm.

The median norm measurements show that, on average, the norm of hypernyms is larger than the norm of hyponyms. This means that hypernyms, which are higher up in the tree, are positioned further away from the origin of the vector space than hyponyms, which are positioned lower in the tree and are closer to the origin. Notably, this is only

[16]The interested reader might consult Klubička (2022, pages 121-123) for some speculation as to what that interaction might be.

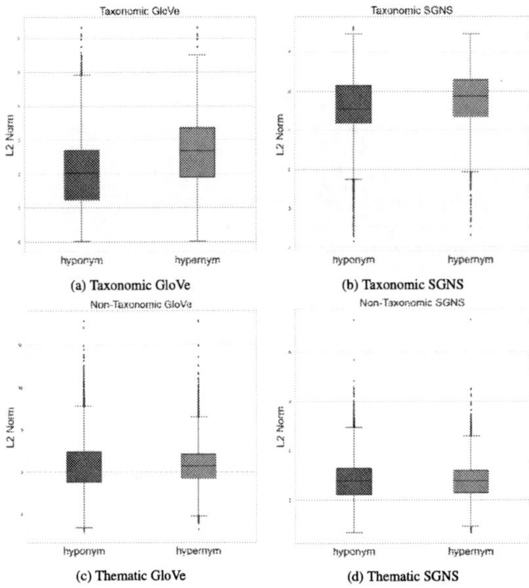

(a) Taxonomic GloVe (b) Taxonomic SGNS (c) Thematic GloVe (d) Thematic SGNS

Figure 1: Box plots depicting the median values of the L2 norm in the different sets of word vectors, separate for hyponyms and hypernyms. There is a marked difference observed between hyponym and hypernym norms in taxonomic GloVe and SGNS, but not in thematic.

true in taxonomic embeddings, but not the thematic ones, indicating that in taxonomic embeddings *there is a mapping between the taxonomic hierarchy and distance from the origin.*

Finally, in spite of the fact that taxonomic GloVe (TAX) is the worst-performing vanilla model, it is interesting that its norm also encodes the most taxonomic information. We base our interpretation of this result on the following: i) in many embeddings there is a high correlation between the norm and word frequency (Goldberg, 2017), and ii) WordNet pseudo-corpora reflect hypernym-hyponym frequencies and co-occurrences. We suspect the principal signal that plays a role in the way taxonomic embeddings encode taxonomic knowledge is precisely these word co-occurrences, which GloVe is designed to capture. In turn, the norm can be seen as analogous to the hierarchical nature of taxonomic relationships and becomes the most accessible place to store this information. The thematic corpora reflect thematic co-occurrences and frequencies and hence GloVe (THEM) does not store taxonomic information in the norm, as such relations are not hierarchical in nature.

7 Conclusion

In this paper we applied the *probing with noise* method to two different types of word representations—taxonomic and thematic—each generated by two different embedding algorithms—SGNS and GloVe—on a newly-designed taxonomic probing task. The overall findings are that (a) both taxonomic and thematic static embeddings encode taxonomic information, (b) that the norm of static embedding vectors carries some taxonomic information and (c) thus the vector norm is a separate information container at the word level. (d) While in some cases there can be redundancy between the information encoded in the norm and dimensions, at other times the norm can encode information that is not at all available in the dimensions, and (e) whether the norm is utilised at all is sometimes dependant on training data, not just the encoder architecture.

We also show that in the case of SGNS, taxonomic embeddings outperform thematic ones on the task, demonstrating the usefulness of taxonomic pseudo-corpora in encoding taxonomic information. Indeed, this work serves to further emphasise the importance of the norm, showing that the taxonomic embeddings use the norm to supplement their encoding of taxonomic information. In other words, random walk corpora can improve taxonomic information in word representations, which is not always the case for natural language corpora.

Acknowledgements

This research was conducted with the financial support of Science Foundation Ireland under Grant Agreements No. 13/RC/2106 and 13/RC/2106_P2 at the ADAPT SFI Research Centre at Technological University Dublin. ADAPT, the SFI Research Centre for AI-Driven Digital Content Technology, is funded by Science Foundation Ireland through the SFI Research Centres Programme, and is co-funded under the European Regional Development Fund.

References

Yossi Adi, Einat Kermany, Yonatan Belinkov, Ofer Lavi, and Yoav Goldberg. 2017. Fine-grained analysis of sentence embeddings using auxiliary prediction tasks. In *Proceedings of ICLR, 2017.*

Marco Baroni, Raffaella Bernardi, Ngoc-Quynh Do, and Chung-chieh Shan. 2012. Entailment above the word level in distributional semantics. In *Proceedings of the 13th Conference of the European Chapter of the Association for Computational Linguistics*, pages 23–32, Avignon, France. Association for Computational Linguistics.

Marco Baroni and Alessandro Lenci. 2011. How we BLESSed distributional semantic evaluation. In *Proceedings of the GEMS 2011 Workshop on GEometrical Models of Natural Language Semantics*, pages 1–10, Edinburgh, UK. Association for Computational Linguistics.

Yonatan Belinkov and James Glass. 2019. Analysis methods in neural language processing: A survey. *Transactions of the Association for Computational Linguistics*, 7:49–72.

Gabriel Bernier-Colborne and Caroline Barrière. 2018. CRIM at SemEval-2018 task 9: A hybrid approach to hypernym discovery. In *Proceedings of The 12th International Workshop on Semantic Evaluation*, pages 725–731, New Orleans, Louisiana. Association for Computational Linguistics.

Guido Boella and Luigi Di Caro. 2013. Extracting definitions and hypernym relations relying on syntactic dependencies and support vector machines. In *Proceedings of the 51st Annual Meeting of the Association for Computational Linguistics (Volume 2: Short Papers)*, pages 532–537, Sofia, Bulgaria. Association for Computational Linguistics.

Gemma Boleda, Abhijeet Gupta, and Sebastian Padó. 2017. Instances and concepts in distributional space. In *Proceedings of the 15th Conference of the European Chapter of the Association for Computational Linguistics: Volume 2, Short Papers*, pages 79–85, Valencia, Spain. Association for Computational Linguistics.

Jose Camacho-Collados, Claudio Delli Bovi, Luis Espinosa-Anke, Sergio Oramas, Tommaso Pasini, Enrico Santus, Vered Shwartz, Roberto Navigli, and Horacio Saggion. 2018. SemEval-2018 task 9: Hypernym discovery. In *Proceedings of The 12th International Workshop on Semantic Evaluation*, pages 712–724, New Orleans, Louisiana. Association for Computational Linguistics.

Yejin Cho, Juan Diego Rodriguez, Yifan Gao, and Katrin Erk. 2020. Leveraging wordnet paths for neural hypernym prediction. In *Proceedings of the 28th International Conference on Computational Linguistics*, pages 3007–3018.

Daoud Clarke. 2009. Context-theoretic semantics for natural language: an overview. In *Proceedings of the Workshop on Geometrical Models of Natural Language Semantics*, pages 112–119, Athens, Greece. Association for Computational Linguistics.

Alexis Conneau, German Kruszewski, Guillaume Lample, Loïc Barrault, and Marco Baroni. 2018. What you can cram into a single $&!#* vector: Probing sentence embeddings for linguistic properties. In *Proceedings of the 56th Annual Meeting of the Association for Computational Linguistics (Volume 1: Long Papers)*, pages 2126–2136, Melbourne, Australia. Association for Computational Linguistics.

Nadir Durrani, Fahim Dalvi, and Hassan Sajjad. 2022. Linguistic correlation analysis: Discovering salient neurons in deepnlp models. *arXiv preprint arXiv:2206.13288*.

Nadir Durrani, Hassan Sajjad, Fahim Dalvi, and Yonatan Belinkov. 2020. Analyzing individual neurons in pre-trained language models. In *Proceedings of the 2020 Conference on Empirical Methods in Natural Language Processing (EMNLP)*, pages 4865–4880, Online. Association for Computational Linguistics.

Luis Espinosa-Anke, Jose Camacho-Collados, Claudio Delli Bovi, and Horacio Saggion. 2016. Supervised distributional hypernym discovery via domain adaptation. In *Proceedings of the 2016 Conference on Empirical Methods in Natural Language Processing*, pages 424–435, Austin, Texas. Association for Computational Linguistics.

Allyson Ettinger. 2020. What BERT is not: Lessons from a new suite of psycholinguistic diagnostics for language models. *Transactions of the Association for Computational Linguistics*, 8:34–48.

Allyson Ettinger, Ahmed Elgohary, and Philip Resnik. 2016. Probing for semantic evidence of composition by means of simple classification tasks. In *Proceedings of the 1st Workshop on Evaluating Vector-Space Representations for NLP*, pages 134–139, Berlin, Germany. Association for Computational Linguistics.

Christiane Fellbaum. 1998. *WordNet: An Electronic Lexical Database*. MIT Press, Cambridge, MA.

Tiziano Flati, Daniele Vannella, Tommaso Pasini, and Roberto Navigli. 2014. Two is bigger (and better) than one: the Wikipedia bitaxonomy project. In *Proceedings of the 52nd Annual Meeting of the Association for Computational Linguistics (Volume 1: Long Papers)*, pages 945–955, Baltimore, Maryland. Association for Computational Linguistics.

Tiziano Flati, Daniele Vannella, Tommaso Pasini, and Roberto Navigli. 2016. Multiwibi: The multilingual wikipedia bitaxonomy project. *Artificial Intelligence*, 241:66–102.

Ruiji Fu, Jiang Guo, Bing Qin, Wanxiang Che, Haifeng Wang, and Ting Liu. 2014. Learning semantic hierarchies via word embeddings. In *Proceedings of the 52nd Annual Meeting of the Association for Computational Linguistics (Volume 1: Long Papers)*, pages 1199–1209, Baltimore, Maryland. Association for Computational Linguistics.

Maayan Geffet and Ido Dagan. 2005. The distributional inclusion hypotheses and lexical entailment. In *Proceedings of the 43rd Annual Meeting of the*

Association for Computational Linguistics (ACL'05), pages 107–114, Ann Arbor, Michigan. Association for Computational Linguistics.

Josu Goikoetxea, Aitor Soroa, and Eneko Agirre. 2015. Random Walks and Neural Network Language Models on Knowledge Bases. In *Human Language Technologies: The 2015 Conference of the North American Chapter of the Association for Computational Linguistics*, pages 1434–1439, Denver, CO.

Yoav Goldberg. 2017. Neural network methods for natural language processing. *Synthesis Lectures on Human Language Technologies*, 10(1):117.

Amit Gupta, Francesco Piccinno, Mikhail Kozhevnikov, Marius Paşca, and Daniele Pighin. 2016. Revisiting taxonomy induction over Wikipedia. In *Proceedings of COLING 2016, the 26th International Conference on Computational Linguistics: Technical Papers*, pages 2300–2309, Osaka, Japan. The COLING 2016 Organizing Committee.

Marti A. Hearst. 1992. Automatic acquisition of hyponyms from large text corpora. In *Proceedings of the 14th conference on Computational linguistics-Volume 2*, pages 539–545. Association for Computational Linguistics.

John Hewitt and Christopher D. Manning. 2019. A structural probe for finding syntax in word representations. In *Proceedings of the 2019 Conference of the North American Chapter of the Association for Computational Linguistics: Human Language Technologies, Volume 1 (Long and Short Papers)*, pages 4129–4138, Minneapolis, Minnesota. Association for Computational Linguistics.

V. Ivan Sanchez Carmona and Sebastian Riedel. 2017. How well can we predict hypernyms from word embeddings? a dataset-centric analysis. In *15th Conference of the European Chapter of the Association for Computational Linguistics, EACL 2017-Proceedings of Conference*, volume 2, pages 401–407. Association for Computational Linguistics.

Magdalena Kacmajor and John D. Kelleher. 2019. Capturing and Measuring Thematic Relatedness. *Language Resources and Evaluation*, pages 1–38.

Filip Klubička. 2022. *Probing with Noise: Unpicking the Warp and Weft of Taxonomic and Thematic Meaning Representations in Static and Contextual Embeddings*. Ph.D. thesis, Technological University Dublin.

Filip Klubička, Alfredo Maldonado, and John D. Kelleher. 2019. Synthetic, yet natural: Properties of wordnet random walk corpora and the impact of rare words on embedding performance. In *Proceedings of GWC2019: 10th Global WordNet Conference*.

Filip Klubička and John D. Kelleher. 2022. Probing with noise: Unpicking the warp and weft of embeddings. In *Proceedings of the Fifth BlackboxNLP Workshop on Analyzing and Interpreting Neural Networks for NLP*, Abu Dhabi, UAE. Association for Computational Linguistics.

Filip Klubička, Alfredo Maldonado, Abhijit Mahalunkar, and John D. Kelleher. 2020. English wordnet random walk pseudo-corpora. In *Proceedings of The 12th Language Resources and Evaluation Conference*, pages 4893–4902, Marseille, France. European Language Resources Association.

Alessandro Lenci and Giulia Benotto. 2012. Identifying hypernyms in distributional semantic spaces. In **SEM 2012: The First Joint Conference on Lexical and Computational Semantics – Volume 1: Proceedings of the main conference and the shared task, and Volume 2: Proceedings of the Sixth International Workshop on Semantic Evaluation (SemEval 2012)*, pages 75–79, Montréal, Canada. Association for Computational Linguistics.

Omer Levy, Steffen Remus, Chris Biemann, and Ido Dagan. 2015. Do supervised distributional methods really learn lexical inference relations? In *Proceedings of the 2015 Conference of the North American Chapter of the Association for Computational Linguistics: Human Language Technologies*, pages 970–976, Denver, Colorado. Association for Computational Linguistics.

Alfredo Maldonado and Filip Klubička. 2018. ADAPT at SemEval-2018 task 9: Skip-gram word embeddings for unsupervised hypernym discovery in specialised corpora. In *Proceedings of The 12th International Workshop on Semantic Evaluation*, pages 924–927, New Orleans, Louisiana. Association for Computational Linguistics.

Alfredo Maldonado, Filip Klubička, and John D. Kelleher. 2019. Size matters: The impact of training size in taxonomically-enriched word embeddings. *Open Computer Science*.

Youness Mansar, Juyeon Kang, and Ismail El Maarouf. 2021. The finsim-2 2021 shared task: Learning semantic similarities for the financial domain. In *Companion Proceedings of the Web Conference 2021*, WWW '21, page 288–292, New York, NY, USA. Association for Computing Machinery.

Roberto Navigli and Paola Velardi. 2010. Learning word-class lattices for definition and hypernym extraction. In *Proceedings of the 48th Annual Meeting of the Association for Computational Linguistics*, pages 1318–1327, Uppsala, Sweden. Association for Computational Linguistics.

Kim Anh Nguyen, Maximilian Köper, Sabine Schulte im Walde, and Ngoc Thang Vu. 2017. Hierarchical embeddings for hypernymy detection and directionality. In *Proceedings of the 2017 Conference on Empirical Methods in Natural Language Processing*, pages 233–243, Copenhagen, Denmark. Association for Computational Linguistics.

Maximillian Nickel and Douwe Kiela. 2018. Learning continuous hierarchies in the lorentz model of hyperbolic geometry. In *International Conference on Machine Learning*, pages 3779–3788. PMLR.

Ellie Pavlick and Marius Paşca. 2017. Identifying 1950s American jazz musicians: Fine-grained IsA extraction via modifier composition. In *Proceedings of the 55th Annual Meeting of the Association for Computational Linguistics (Volume 1: Long Papers)*, pages 2099–2109, Vancouver, Canada. Association for Computational Linguistics.

Fabian Pedregosa, Gaël Varoquaux, Alexandre Gramfort, Vincent Michel, Bertrand Thirion, Olivier Grisel, Mathieu Blondel, Peter Prettenhofer, Ron Weiss, Vincent Dubourg, Jake Vanderplas, Alexandre Passos, David Cournapeau, Matthieu Brucher, Matthieu Perrot, and Édouard Duchesnay. 2011. Scikit-learn: Machine learning in Python. *Journal of Machine Learning Research*, 12:2825–2830.

Yuval Pinter and Jacob Eisenstein. 2018. Predicting semantic relations using global graph properties. In *Proceedings of the 2018 Conference on Empirical Methods in Natural Language Processing*, pages 1741–1751, Brussels, Belgium. Association for Computational Linguistics.

Abhilasha Ravichander, Eduard Hovy, Kaheer Suleman, Adam Trischler, and Jackie Chi Kit Cheung. 2020. On the systematicity of probing contextualized word representations: The case of hypernymy in bert. In *Proceedings of the Ninth Joint Conference on Lexical and Computational Semantics*, pages 88–102.

Marek Rei and Ted Briscoe. 2013. Parser lexicalisation through self-learning. In *Proceedings of the 2013 Conference of the North American Chapter of the Association for Computational Linguistics: Human Language Technologies*, pages 391–400, Atlanta, Georgia. Association for Computational Linguistics.

Stephen Roller, Douwe Kiela, and Maximilian Nickel. 2018. Hearst patterns revisited: Automatic hypernym detection from large text corpora. In *Proceedings of the 56th Annual Meeting of the Association for Computational Linguistics (Volume 2: Short Papers)*, pages 358–363, Melbourne, Australia. Association for Computational Linguistics.

Enrico Santus, Alessandro Lenci, Tin-Shing Chiu, Qin Lu, and Chu-Ren Huang. 2016. Nine features in a random forest to learn taxonomical semantic relations. In *Proceedings of the Tenth International Conference on Language Resources and Evaluation (LREC'16)*, pages 4557–4564, Portorož, Slovenia. European Language Resources Association (ELRA).

Enrico Santus, Alessandro Lenci, Qin Lu, and Sabine Schulte im Walde. 2014. Chasing hypernyms in vector spaces with entropy. In *Proceedings of the 14th Conference of the European Chapter of the Association for Computational Linguistics, volume 2: Short Papers*, pages 38–42, Gothenburg, Sweden. Association for Computational Linguistics.

Xing Shi, Inkit Padhi, and Kevin Knight. 2016. Does string-based neural MT learn source syntax? In *Proceedings of the 2016 Conference on Empirical Methods in Natural Language Processing*, pages 1526–1534, Austin, Texas. Association for Computational Linguistics.

Vered Shwartz, Yoav Goldberg, and Ido Dagan. 2016. Improving hypernymy detection with an integrated path-based and distributional method. In *Proceedings of the 54th Annual Meeting of the Association for Computational Linguistics (Volume 1: Long Papers)*, pages 2389–2398, Berlin, Germany. Association for Computational Linguistics.

Vered Shwartz, Enrico Santus, and Dominik Schlechtweg. 2017. Hypernyms under siege: Linguistically-motivated artillery for hypernymy detection. In *Proceedings of the 15th Conference of the European Chapter of the Association for Computational Linguistics: Volume 1, Long Papers*, pages 65–75, Valencia, Spain. Association for Computational Linguistics.

Rion Snow, Daniel Jurafsky, and Andrew Y Ng. 2005. Learning syntactic patterns for automatic hypernym discovery. In *Advances in neural information processing systems*, pages 1297–1304.

Peter D. Turney and Patrick Pantel. 2010. From Frequency to Meaning: Vector Space Models of Semantics. *Journal of Artificial Intelligence Research*, 37:141–188.

Sara Veldhoen, Dieuwke Hupkes, and Willem H Zuidema. 2016. Diagnostic classifiers revealing how neural networks process hierarchical structure. In *Workshop on Cognitive Computation: Integrating Neural and Symbolic Approaches (at NIPS)*.

Ivan Vulić, Daniela Gerz, Douwe Kiela, Felix Hill, and Anna Korhonen. 2017. HyperLex: A large-scale evaluation of graded lexical entailment. *Computational Linguistics*, 43(4):781–835.

Yogarshi Vyas and Marine Carpuat. 2017. Detecting asymmetric semantic relations in context: A case-study on hypernymy detection. In *Proceedings of the 6th Joint Conference on Lexical and Computational Semantics (*SEM 2017)*, pages 33–43, Vancouver, Canada. Association for Computational Linguistics.

Julie Weeds, Daoud Clarke, Jeremy Reffin, David Weir, and Bill Keller. 2014. Learning to distinguish hypernyms and co-hyponyms. In *Proceedings of COLING 2014, the 25th International Conference on Computational Linguistics: Technical Papers*, pages 2249–2259, Dublin, Ireland. Dublin City University and Association for Computational Linguistics.

Julie Weeds, David Weir, and Diana McCarthy. 2004. Characterising measures of lexical distributional similarity. In *COLING 2004: Proceedings of the 20th*

International Conference on Computational Linguistics, pages 1015–1021, Geneva, Switzerland. COLING.

Henry M. Wellman and Susan A. Gelman. 1992. Cognitive development: Foundational theories of core domains. *Annual review of psychology*, 43(1):337–375.

Laura Wendlandt, Jonathan K. Kummerfeld, and Rada Mihalcea. 2018. Factors influencing the surprising instability of word embeddings. In *Proceedings of the 2018 Conference of the North American Chapter of the Association for Computational Linguistics: Human Language Technologies, Volume 1 (Long Papers)*, pages 2092–2102, New Orleans, Louisiana. Association for Computational Linguistics.

Zheng Yu, Haixun Wang, Xuemin Lin, and Min Wang. 2015. Learning term embeddings for hypernymy identification. In *Twenty-Fourth International Joint Conference on Artificial Intelligence*.

Kelly Zhang and Samuel Bowman. 2018. Language modeling teaches you more than translation does: Lessons learned through auxiliary syntactic task analysis. In *Proceedings of the 2018 EMNLP Workshop BlackboxNLP: Analyzing and Interpreting Neural Networks for NLP*, pages 359–361, Brussels, Belgium. Association for Computational Linguistics.

A WordNet View on Crosslingual Contextualized Language Models

Wondimagegnhue Tufa
CLTL Lab, VU Amsterdam
w.t.tufa@vu.nl

Lisa Beinborn
CLTL Lab, VU Amsterdam
l.beinborn@vu.nl

Piek Vossen
CLTL Lab, VU Amsterdam
p.t.j.m.vossen@vu.nl

Abstract

WordNet is a database that represents relations between words and concepts as an abstraction of the contexts in which words are used. Contextualized language models represent words in contexts but leave the underlying concepts implicit. In this paper, we investigate how different layers of a pre-trained language model shape the abstract lexical relationship toward the actual contextual concept. Can we define the amount of contextualized concept forming needed given the abstracted representation of a word? Specifically, we consider samples of words with different polysemy profiles shared across three languages, assuming that words with a different polysemy profile require a different degree of concept shaping by context. We conduct probing experiments to investigate the impact of prior polysemy profiles on the representation in different layers. We analyze how contextualized models can approximate meaning through context and examine cross-lingual interference effects.

1 Introduction

WordNet (Fellbaum, 1998) is a manually created database that relates the words of a language to concepts. Concepts are represented through synsets, based on a weak synonymy relation, whereas explicit semantic relations between synsets place these concepts in a semantic space. Words of a language can be positioned in that same space but this can become complex when they are ambiguous. A polysemous word such as "star" can be represented in several positions of this space depending on its meaning.

Word embeddings (Mikolov et al., 2013) place words in a semantic space as well based on the dimensions of the vector that was derived when learning to predict their context words. Static word embeddings can be interpreted as an average across contexts, even when words occur with different meanings. For our example, this means that "star" would be positioned somewhere in between *celebrity* and synonyms for the concept *celestial body* as a compromise across contexts.

More recent pre-trained Transformer-based Language Models (PTLM) such as BERT (Devlin et al., 2018) and RoBERTa (Liu et al., 2019b) capture a more nuanced relationship between words and concepts by not only representing the vocabulary through embeddings but also distinguishing contexts: the word "star" will be represented differently depending on the context in which it occurs. From an abstract point of view, these context-sensitive representations approximate a relation between words and concepts. Ethayarajh (2019) investigates this relationship by measuring the impact of contextualization on the representation of meaning through the layers of PTLMs, showing that representations of tokens in contextualized models deviate from their static initialization. The research by (Ethayarajh, 2019) is limited to monolingual models, which leaves open what relationship between tokens or words and concepts is captured in cross-lingual models where words and concepts are shared across languages.

In cross-lingual language models (XPTLMs) such as XLM-RoBERTa (Conneau and Lample, 2019), the challenge of contextualizing concepts is even more complex because of the additional cross-lingual ambiguity. The same word can be mapped to the same or to different concepts across languages. For example, the Dutch word "star" is an adjective meaning *inflexible* whereas the translation for the English "star" corresponds to "ster" in both meanings. The Dutch language, therefore, adds ambiguity to the word-concept relationship of "star". As most XPTLMs use a shared vocabulary for all languages, the variation in meaning across languages can simply be interpreted as different contexts for a word that needs to be encoded in the representations of the model.

In most multi-lingual wordnet databases, cross-lingual ambiguity is underrepresented because they are commonly build using the *expand*-method (Vossen, 1998). This means that the English representation of concepts is maintained and cross-lingual links are established by mapping the vocabulary of the new language onto the existing concept taxonomy. This approach hampers research to the universality of concepts in wordnet models (Vossen and Fellbaum, 2009) but it has been applied widely because of its clear practical advantages over the alternative *merge*-method that requires intense manual labor. XPTLMs can be constructed in different ways as well, which partially mimics the difference between the *expand* and the *merge* approach: 1) *expanding* a monolingual PTML with static lexical embeddings for target languages while freezing the other layers (Artetxe et al., 2019) or 2) training a model from texts from all languages (Conneau and Lample, 2019) so that all languages contribute conceptual representations as contexts (*a merged approach*).

In this paper, we argue that XPTLMs provide new opportunities to move beyond the conceptual limitations of multilingual wordnet databases built through the expand method. We provide empirical evidence for the impact of languages on a shared conceptual XPTLM for both the lexical and conceptual levels by measuring to what extent sharing tokens in XPTLMs has a positive or negative impact on representing concepts and to what extent the contexts in which these words occur compensate for any disturbances in the token representation. In other words: to what extent is the representation of "star" a compromise across all language meanings and to what extent is it defined by the cross-lingual contexts in which it occurs? XPTLMs use a shared vocabulary for all languages to exploit semantic commonalities across languages (cognate effects). However, cross-lingual differences caused by semantic drift (Beinborn and Choenni, 2020) can contribute to semantic interference (Lauscher et al., 2020).

More specifically, we will address the following questions in our experiments:

- How consistent is the relationship between words and concepts with and without the influence of context for polysemous words?
- What are the effects of sharing vocabulary and contexts across languages on the representation of cross-lingual ambiguity?

In order to investigate the above questions, ideally a large sense-tagged parallel corpus would be required to identify a representative set of concepts shared across languages. Existing corpora (Bond et al., 2013) are however small and have skewed sense distributions. Another problem is that it is hard to determine the best level of granularity for identifying concepts associated with a word in contexts and they may not be distinguishable empirically through existing models (Ethayarajh, 2019). Instead of multilingual corpora with WordNet senses or all contextualized contexts, we, therefore use a controlled set of semantic classes as the representation of concepts following the work of (Zhao et al., 2020). Entity types such as *PERSON*, *ORGANIZATION*, and *LOCATION* can be seen as coarse-grained concepts for which large datasets exist. We use the XLEnt dataset (El-Kishky et al., 2021) which contains 160 million aligned entity pairs in 120 languages paired with English. We investigate how well the entity in this data are distinguished by contextualized models in contextualized layers.

Our contributions are:

- A probing method for measuring the lexical (token) and contextual (model) effects of languages within various cross-lingual models.
- Pilot results on cross-lingual interference and support effects for the typologically related languages English, German and Dutch.
- Pilot results for cross-lingual zero-shot probing for German, Dutch, Arabic, and Amharic.

The paper is further structured as follows. In the next section 2, we describe related work, especially on semantic probing of distributional models. After that, we describe in Section 3 our methodology, which is based on (Zhao et al., 2020) but applied to multilingual models. The dataset that we use is described in Section 4 and our experimental results are described in Section 5. We discuss the results and conclude in Section 6.

2 Related work

Analyzing the representational structure of contextualized models has become an essential means towards developing more transparent and interpretable AI models, for example in the BlackboxNLP workshop which is reaching its 5th edition this year (Bastings et al., 2021). However, only a limited amount of research has been done to investigate the relationship between the vocabulary of such models and the degree of context dependency of the concepts that are associated with the words in the vocabulary. In Ethayarajh (2019), this relationship is investigated by measuring the impact of contextualization on the representation of meaning through the layers of language models. This study indicates that 1) contextualized models do enhance the meaning compared to the static initialization of the token and 2) there is no finite and discrete set of representations (thus concepts) for single tokens across concepts.

Artetxe et al. (2019) show that it is possible to transfer an English transformer to a new language by freezing all the inner parameters of the network and learning a new set of embeddings for the new language through masked language modeling. This works because the frozen transformer parameters constrain the resulting representations to become aligned with English. This approach does not adapt the concept representation established for the original language English. It only learns the token embedding using the English concept model and is thus comparable to the multilingual wordnet expand model (which uses a single English concept space and learns token mappings to another language). It is not possible to learn new concepts from another language nor adapt biases learned from the English data. Phenomena of semantic drift across languages (Beinborn and Choenni, 2020) can therefore not be captured and it remains unclear how the addition of languages affects the conceptual distribution beyond the performance on the downstream tasks.

For analyzing how a contextual language model captures the relationship between a word and a concept, we can use word sense disambiguation as a proxy task. The task evaluates model performance in associating an ambiguous word with the correct concept from the possible concept inventory. For example, the word "state" could represent a 'government' or the concept corresponding to the WordNet synset called "a way something is". One limitation of using such an approach is the granularity of the sense category. WSD categories are often too fine-grained and allow only limited abstraction (Izquierdo et al., 2009).

We opt for a task on a higher abstraction level and apply semantic class-based probing to quantify the contextualization capability of a language model using Wiki-PSE in line with Zhao et al. (2020). Wiki-PSE contains tokens used in contexts corresponding to different semantic classes. For example, the word 'apple' can refer to a technology company corresponding to the 'Organization' class or it can refer to a fruit belonging to the 'Food' class (Yaghoobzadeh et al., 2019). A concept-tagged dataset can be used to investigate relationships between a word form and a concept in a language model in a simplified setup: word forms are limited to entity names and their semantic classes define the concept inventory.

Probing has been established as a tool to test whether linguistics information is encoded in language model representations (Adi et al., 2016; Belinkov et al., 2017b; Tenney et al., 2019). Adi et al. (2016) train a classifier to predict sentence characteristics such as length, semantic information, and word order from sentence representation. Higher performance in the classification task indicates that information about the measured property is encoded in the embedding. Liu et al. (2019a) extend the probing tasks to a wider range of linguistic phenomena such as coreference, semantic relations, and entity information. Tenney et al. (2019) introduced edge probing and establish a standard format to quantify the availability of linguistic structure in pre-trained language models using various NLP benchmark tasks.

Our work follows Zhao et al. (2020) in that we use sentence probing to measure the relationship between a word, its context, and the corresponding concept. We extend this approach to various multilingual models instead of English BERT. We present pilot experiments to explore the utility of using semantic class probing with these multilingual models.

3 Methodology

To analyze how language models capture the relationship between words and concepts, we identify words that illustrate edge cases for the relation between concepts and contexts: 1) a monosemous (**mono**) relation between a word and a single concept, 2) **balanced** polysemous relations between a word and multiple concepts, and 3) **skewed** polysemous relations where one concept is dominant in language use. We expect that the patterns in concept distribution are reflected in the probing performance of the cross-lingual models.

Our approach represents only a rough approximation of the set of concepts related to a word as well as the distribution of concepts in language use. The actual range of concepts is unknown and is the result of the pretraining of the model. Our pilot experiments, therefore, explore whether the large-scale annotations of XLEnt can serve as a proxy for probing word-concept relationships in multilingual models. We assume that such data provide sufficient information on the relation between words and concepts to measure the degree of ambiguity and the capability of models to identify concept relations from contexts. We hypothesize that our observations for a selected set of words can be generalized to a larger sample, which should be tested in future research.

In the probing setup, the model representation built during pretraining is not changed and can be tested for its capacity to represent a concept in target contexts at different layers. We assume that the lexical initialization in the first layer will reflect the prior ambiguity of the word in the pretraining data and that the integration of context will adjust the representation toward the target concept in higher layers. We expect the following observations for the respective profiles:

1. mono: only minor differences between the lexical initialization level and higher contextual levels
2. skewed:
   (a) **matching** distribution for test cases: same as mono
   (b) **diverging** distribution for test cases: low probing accuracy on the lexical level, strong indications of concept sensitivity in higher levels
3. balanced: low probing accuracy at the lexical level, improved concept knowledge in higher levels in all cases but not as strong as for diverging

In our experiments below, we report on the results for skewed and balanced ambiguous words in English and across the language English, Dutch, and German. Our code is publicly available at `https://github.com/cltl/probing-cross-linqual-model`.

4 Data set and Experiment

For our experiments, we use entities and their respective semantic class as a proxy for a more general notion of words and concepts due to data available for many languages with a controlled number of concepts in the form of entity types as semantic classes. Specifically, we select a sample from XLEnt which contains 160 million entity mentions annotated with 10 classes in 120 languages (El-Kishky et al., 2021). We describe the selection procedure in the following subsections.

4.1 Pre-processing and Sampling

We include English, German, and Dutch in our analysis.[1] Table 1 shows the statistical summary of the total available data.

	EN	NL	DE
Sentences	17,942,551	12,429,622	5,512,929
Entities	4,219,046	6,737,100	2,917,688
Unique Entities	59,054	60,777	38,930
LOC	512,219	744,024	329,030
ORG	1,690,244	3,282,967	1,580,477
PER	2,016,583	2,710,109	1,008,181

Table 1: Statistics of entities distribution in XLEnt for English, Dutch, and German.

For each of these languages, we selected sentences from one of the three semantic classes: Location, Organization, or Person. We selected these semantic classes because they correspond to clearly-distinct classes which cannot easily be used interchangeably in the same sentence, as opposed to clear metonymically-related classes such as Organization and Product.

The distribution across language and semantic classes in XLEnt varies. To maintain similar distribution across our target languages, we, therefore, sampled an equal number of sentences for each semantic class.

From the total set of entity names, we selected a sample of clear cases with monosemous, balanced polysemous, and skewed polysemous relations. Furthermore, the selected names should occur as tokens in the English, Dutch, and German data set. This results in a subset of 21 names related to the concepts of Person, Organisation, and Location. In the appendix B, the complete list of names

[1] The main reason for choosing these three languages is that we have native and up-to-native knowledge of these languages. In future research, we will also apply the same tests to other languages.

is given with the distributions and the division over the three polysemy profiles: mono, skewed and balanced. Table 2 shows a few examples of entities that are shared across languages. From these examples, *Tasman* and *Aquarias* are skewed towards a location interpretation, whereas *Chimera* is skewed towards an organization and *Prana* is balanced. *Sirius* is underrepresented towards Person.

To classify the distribution of an entity as balanced or skewed, we first normalized the frequency distribution between 0 and 1 using the total frequency across all types. We then applied a threshold value to categorize it into balanced and skewed. For a threshold value of 0.95 (95%) or higher, we classified an entity as skewed to a particular semantic class. If an entity occurs in more than one semantic class in a comparative way (at 0.35 or higher), we classify it as a balanced case.

Shared Entity	LOC	ORG	PER
Tasman	13	5	5
Prana	12	19	16
Sirius	391	481	42
Chimera	10	85	17
Aquarius	124	11	59

Table 2: Sample of names for entities with sufficient coverage and different polysemy profiles in English, Dutch, and German.

Using the same threshold, we further distinguish between cases where Dutch and German have similar distributions as English and cases with different distributions. We applied a similar approach to compare the distribution of entities across languages by comparing the normalized frequency distribution of entities. We assume that similar cross-lingual distributions result in better representation for a target language, whereas diverging distributions confuse the model and result in poorer representations. Note that the words are shared across these languages and get the same lexical initialization.

Our predictions should generalize over the sampled names per polysemy profile. Our probing framework can be used to test any language model that covers these words and the languages from the dataset. The results tell us to what extent pretraining resulted in a bias for the lexical initialization and to what extent the model can correct for this using the context. Below, we apply our probing methodology to XLM-RoBERTa and mBERT as a cross-lingual model to capture the relation between a word and concepts. We also apply the test to English BERT itself for comparison. We can easily extend the test to others models that include the probing words in the vocabulary.

4.2 Probing Experiment

For our probing experiment, we use a simple one-layer perceptron (MLP) similar to (Zhao et al., 2020). We designed a three-class classifier by taking each of the three distinct semantic classes. Figure 1 shows the architecture of our probing classifier.

For the experiments, we use the list of entities, a set of context sentences where these entities occur, and the semantic class associated with the entity for each context. In our probing, we first take the target sentence and pass it through a cross-lingual language model to generate the contextual representation associated with the target entity and the sentence which contains the entity word. From the language model output, we use the representation from the input layer (layer-0), the middle layer (layer-3), and the last layer(layer-12) as input for our classifier.[2] We use layer-0 as the baseline since it is initialized with the lexical token representation of the language model and should exhibit a prior ambiguity profile. In the middle and last layers, we get representations of our target words that are modified by the context. We train and test our probing model with these representations to detect the semantic class for the names in context.

4.3 Baseline

One of the core challenges of a probing method is how to interpret the results of a probing classifier. Previous works compare the result of the classifier with different approaches including majority baselines (Belinkov et al., 2017a; Conneau et al., 2018), static word embeddings (Belinkov, 2022; Tenney et al., 2019) and a random baseline by training the probing classifier on a randomized version of the input feature (Zhang and Bowman, 2018; Tenney et al., 2019). In our work, we include three baselines to compare and interpret the result of our probing model.

5 Results

We first examine our probing setup for resolving conceptual ambiguity in English entities and next

[2]We choose the third layer because it gave the best performance in most of our experiments

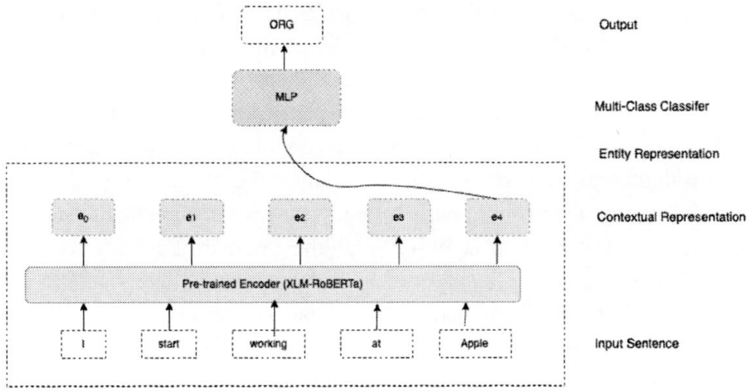

Figure 1: Architecture of our probing classifier

conduct additional analyses to examine the effect of shared tokens across multiple languages on conceptual ambiguity. Lastly, we conduct tests across typologically related and distant languages to check if a relationship learned between context and concept in one language is relevant for another language.

5.1 Probing Ambiguous Entities in English

In the first experiment, we focus on ambiguous entities in English and their representation in XML-RoBERTa. Entities are ambiguous if they have annotations for all three semantic classes in the data, either balanced or skewed towards one type as explained above. Table 3 shows the details of the distributions and the experimental results for the balanced and skewed cases respectively. Note that the train and test cases are randomly selected from the data and exhibit a similar distribution of balanced and skewed distribution. However, the test results are differentiated among them. For the balanced cases in Table 3, we see that layer-0 results are lowest, layer-3 are highest and layer-12 results are in between for all three concepts. Furthermore, location performs slightly better than organization and person. Looking at the skewed cases in Table 3, we see a similar pattern that results are lowest in layer-0, best in layer-3, and go down in layer-12. Overall, the results are better for skewed cases than for balanced cases at all levels, except for location. Remarkably, location performs lower than organization and person for the skewed cases.

The first conclusion we can draw here is that layers do correct for confusion at the lexical level by the context but some of this is lost in the higher levels. We can only partially confirm the prediction that balanced distributions are harder than skewed distributions. The prediction holds for organizations and persons, which perform lower for balanced than for skewed at all levels but not for location at layer-0 and layer-12. Apparently, the skewed cases are poorly represented for location at layer-0, which is correct in layer-3 (outperforming the balanced cases) but drops considerably in layer-12.

	LOC	ORG	PER
#Train	1506	1490	1504
#Test	494	510	496
#Single-Token Entity	252	779	1088
#Multi-Token Entity	1748	1221	912
Balanced			
#Test	417	334	314
Layer-0	0.65	0.58	0.52
Layer-3	0.81	0.78	0.79
Layer-12	0.78	0.75	0.75
Skewed			
#Test	77	176	182
Layer 0	0.61	0.75	0.76
Layer 3	0.86	0.87	0.9
Layer 12	0.78	0.82	0.86

Table 3: F1 scores for probing the different layers of XLM-RoBERTa on ambiguous entities. We run the experiment five times with seed from (0,1,2,3,4) Results are averaged over five runs. We observe a standard deviation between 0.003 and 0.009 For entities that are split into sub-tokens during tokenization, we took the mean of each of the vector embeddings

To investigate the impact of dominance on a concept at the lexical level, we differentiate the results for the skewed names into test cases that match the bias and cases that do not match. The results are shown in Table 4. We perform targeted analysis of the quantitative performance by explicitly distinguishing the dominant semantic classes. As can be expected, the probing performance for detecting the location concept for names that predominantly occur with this concept is already very high already at layer-0 and increases further at layer-3 and layer-12. We observe the same pattern for the other two classes. We also see that the layer-0 performances for the non-dominant concepts are very low (from 0 to max .38), while the probing performance increases slightly in layer-3 and layer-12. The integration of context in the higher layers thus balances out the bias towards the dominant concept during initialization but not completely. The fact that the final scores are significantly lower shows that the lexical layer initialization does matter for obtaining optimal results. This also implies that confusion in a cross-lingual model created by sharing tokens across languages could result in poorer initialization in layer-0 that needs more repairing in the context-sensitive layers. We investigate the impact of such token or vocabulary sharing in the next subsection.

	LOC	ORG	PER
Skewed to LOC			
Layer-0	0.82	0.38	0.25
Layer-3	0.9	0.63	0.73
Layer-12	0.9	0.53	0.67
Skewed to ORG			
Layer-0	0.24	0.81	0.34
Layer-3	0.85	0.93	0.75
Layer-12	0.59	0.85	0.5
Skewed to PER			
Layer-0	0	0	0.97
Layer-3	0.67	0.29	0.97
Layer-12	0.67	0.25	0.97

Table 4: Result of probing the different layers of XLM-RoBERTa on entities that are skewed toward a specific semantic class. Result evaluated on F1-Score averaged over five runs

5.2 Probing Shared Entities across English, Dutch, and German

In the second experiment, we specifically probe entity names that are shared across the English, Dutch, and German data. We first select names that occur in all three languages. In the second step, we filter entities that are ambiguous across the three target classes. From these shared ambiguous entities, we identify two subcategories: 1) entities that have a similar type distribution in all three languages, and 2) entities that clearly exhibit a deviating distribution in both Dutch and German compared to English. For the first category, we expect that the shared distribution should improve the probing accuracy for English, and in the second category, we expect cross-lingual interference. Table 5 shows the details of the distribution and the experimental results. We observe the same consistent pattern of lowest probing performance on the lexical layer, highest performance for layer-3, and intermediate performance on layer-12. Our analyses indicate an impact of sharing tokens across languages. When Dutch and German have similar type distributions the results are substantially higher than when they have a different distribution. This holds for most results except for the organization class in layer-3 and layer-12.

Table 5 also shows that we can apply the same probing to other models such as BERT and mBERT, in this case only testing on English target sentences. We observe exactly the same patterns as for XLM-RoBERTa and even the scores are very similar, even for the BERT which was pre-trained on English data only.

Our results confirm that the representation in contextualized language models varies across layers. Concepts can be identified less well at the lexical level (layer-0) unless they match the dominant meaning, while higher levels integrate contextual information for further disambiguation. This indicates that lexical biases get repaired and that we can measure the degree to which this happens in line with the findings by Ethayarajh (2019). Our pilot experiment provides a proof of concept for analyzing the effect of the shared vocabulary on conceptual representations in cross-lingual contextualized language models. In future work, we hope to use this insight to improve such models for languages that are most affected by sharing vocabulary.

5.3 Cross-Lingual Evaluation

In this part of the experiment, we evaluated a probing model trained on an English dataset with test data from German, Dutch, Amharic, and Arabic. We first select monosemous and polysemous words by using the frequency distribution of entities and their types. Based on these distributions, we classify a word as monosemous if it belongs to one semantic class frequently. We applied a threshold value in such a way that if a word occurs 90% of the time as a single semantic class, we consider it a monosemous word. If a word occurs in two or more classes, we consider it a polysemous word.

	LOC	ORG	PER						
#Train	589	600	611						
#Test	199	212	189						
	XLM-RoBERTa			BERT			mBERT		
Similar	LOC	ORG	PER	LOC	ORG	PER	LOC	ORG	PER
Layer-0	0.76	0.67	0.78	0.75	0.66	0.77	0.74	0.59	0.79
Layer-3	0.83	0.83	0.84	0.84	0.85	0.86	0.82	0.83	0.84
Layer-12	0.81	0.78	0.85	0.82	0.83	0.86	0.85	0.83	0.87
Diverging									
Layer-0	0.57	0.53	0.42	0.53	0.51	0.4	0.54	0.51	0.45
Layer-3	0.78	0.82	0.68	0.82	0.84	0.71	0.76	0.81	0.72
Layer-12	0.75	0.78	0.66	0.8	0.81	0.77	0.81	0.79	0.78

Table 5: Result of probing the different layers of XLM-RoBERTa, BERT, and mBERT on entities that are shared between English, Dutch, and German with similar/diverging distribution across types. Results are evaluated in F1-Score and are averaged over five runs.

We then applied three filtering criteria: (a) We focus on single-word entities instead of multi-word entities to control ambiguity that might be introduced by multi-word entities. (b) We only include sentences with a single target entity to control contextual information that might be associated with an additional entity. (c) We restrict our selection to entities that are labeled as one of the four semantic classes LOCATION, ORG, PERSON, and EVENT since these can barely be used interchangeably.

Zero-shot probing We train a multi-class probing classifier using the English dataset and the setting discussed in Section 4.2 and test it on randomly sampled sentences from each of the four semantic classes that adhere to the specified criteria. We distinguish two categories of target languages. In the first category, we sampled test sentences from Dutch and German which are typologically related to English and share the same script. In the second category, we sampled test data from Arabic and Amharic which are typologically distant from English and use a different script.

We distinguish between the following conditions: the model can be trained on English monosemous data or on English polysemous data. The test data is sampled from Dutch and German (category 1) and from Amharic and Arabic (category 2). For each language, we further distinguish between monosemous and polysemous test data. Figure 2 shows the result of evaluating the English probing model.

Results In the monosemous condition, we observe higher results for German and Dutch than for Arabic and Amharic. In a standard Zero-shot evaluation where a pre-trained language model is fine-tuned in a downstream task in a source language and evaluated on a target language, it has been widely reported that cross-lingual transfer yields better results for related languages (Pires et al., 2019; Wu and Dredze, 2019). As we probe the cross-lingual representation directly, we show that transfer occurs even before a pre-trained model is fine-tuned on a downstream task. Our results show that to a smaller extent transfer effects can even be observed for Arabic and Amharic although they are typologically different from English and use another script.

In the more difficult case of the polysemous condition, the performance of the classifier on correctly labeling the ambiguous semantic class is lower in comparison to the monosemous condition across all languages but outperforms a lexical baseline. With a closer look at the result per layer, we observe that the performance improves for representations extracted from higher layers. Remarkably, the differences across the related and unrelated languages got smaller in the polysemous condition. Apparently, there is a lower bound of performance at which the performances clutter together as a result of the complexity of the task and there are less differences for the languages.

6 Conclusions

In this paper, we investigated to what extent polysemous profiles play a role in establishing a relation between words and concepts. We focused on English but we also investigated words shared across languages in cross-lingual pre-trained language models. We selected representative cases for concept distributions from a large dataset of entity mentions as ambiguity profiles. Our prob-

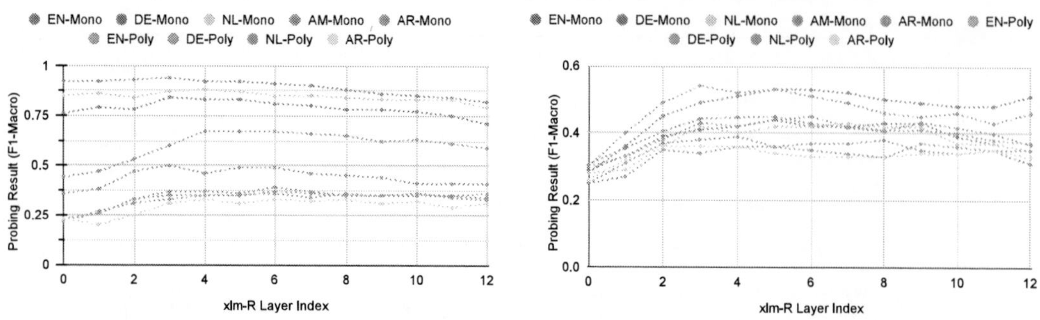

(a) Result for the English monosemous model

(b) Result for the English polysemous model

Figure 2: F1-scores for the different conditions macro-averaged across four classes. Mono refers to monosemous test data in the corresponding language. Poly refers to polysemous test data in the corresponding language. The result of the baseline experiment and detailed results per layer are presented in Appendix A.

ing experiments indicate that prior probabilities of polysemy profiles are reflected in the lexical initialization and that context is integrated for disambiguation in higher layers. Our cross-lingual results indicate that sharing of tokens and contexts across languages has an influence on probing accuracy.

Our experiments are restricted to five languages: English, Dutch, German, Arabic, and Amharic. In future work, we will extend our experiments to more languages. We plan to investigate the impact of optimizing the probing classifier with cross-lingual training data. Training on the data of other languages extends the fund of concepts in the classifier, which is comparable to an expand model for multilingual wordnets.

Our method is limited by the annotations in contexts. It is therefore difficult to extend it to other words and concepts than entity names. Nevertheless, the entity results can be seen as a proof of concept to develop more sophisticated methods for analyzing concept relations in multilingual models. When more sense-tagged data becomes available, this method can also be applied to other words and concepts.

Acknowledgements

We thank the anonymous reviewers for their insightful feedback and suggestions. W. Tufa's research was supported by Huawei Finland through the DreamsLab project. All content represented the opinions of the authors, which were not necessarily shared or endorsed by their respective employers and/ or sponsors. L. Beinborn's research was supported by the Dutch National Science Organisation (NWO) through the projects ClariahPlus (CP-W6-19-005) and VENI (VI.Veni.211C.039).

References

Yossi Adi, Einat Kermany, Yonatan Belinkov, Ofer Lavi, and Yoav Goldberg. 2016. Fine-grained analysis of sentence embeddings using auxiliary prediction tasks. *arXiv preprint arXiv:1608.04207*.

Mikel Artetxe, Sebastian Ruder, and Dani Yogatama. 2019. On the cross-lingual transferability of monolingual representations. *arXiv preprint arXiv:1910.11856*.

Jasmijn Bastings, Yonatan Belinkov, Emmanuel Dupoux, Mario Giulianelli, Dieuwke Hupkes, Yuval Pinter, and Hassan Sajjad, editors. 2021. *Proceedings of the Fourth BlackboxNLP Workshop on Analyzing and Interpreting Neural Networks for NLP*. Association for Computational Linguistics, Punta Cana, Dominican Republic.

Lisa Beinborn and Rochelle Choenni. 2020. Semantic Drift in Multilingual Representations. *Computational Linguistics*, 46(3):571–603.

Yonatan Belinkov. 2022. Probing classifiers: Promises, shortcomings, and advances. *Computational Linguistics*, 48(1):207–219.

Yonatan Belinkov, Nadir Durrani, Fahim Dalvi, Hassan Sajjad, and James Glass. 2017a. What do neural machine translation models learn about morphology? In *Proceedings of the 55th Annual Meeting of the Association for Computational Linguistics (Volume 1: Long Papers)*, pages 861–872, Vancouver, Canada. Association for Computational Linguistics.

Yonatan Belinkov, Lluís Màrquez, Hassan Sajjad, Nadir Durrani, Fahim Dalvi, and James Glass. 2017b. Evaluating layers of representation in neural machine translation on part-of-speech and semantic tagging tasks. In *Proceedings of the Eighth International Joint Conference on Natural Language*

Processing (Volume 1: Long Papers), pages 1–10, Taipei, Taiwan. Asian Federation of Natural Language Processing.

Francis Bond, Shan Wang, Eshley Huini Gao, Hazel Shuwen Mok, and Jeanette Yiwen Tan. 2013. Developing parallel sense-tagged corpora with wordnets. In *Proceedings of the 7th Linguistic Annotation Workshop and Interoperability with Discourse*, pages 149–158.

Alexis Conneau, German Kruszewski, Guillaume Lample, Loïc Barrault, and Marco Baroni. 2018. What you can cram into a single $&!#* vector: Probing sentence embeddings for linguistic properties. In *Proceedings of the 56th Annual Meeting of the Association for Computational Linguistics (Volume 1: Long Papers)*, pages 2126–2136, Melbourne, Australia. Association for Computational Linguistics.

Alexis Conneau and Guillaume Lample. 2019. Cross-lingual language model pretraining. *Advances in neural information processing systems*, 32.

Jacob Devlin, Ming-Wei Chang, Kenton Lee, and Kristina Toutanova. 2018. Bert: Pre-training of deep bidirectional transformers for language understanding. *arXiv preprint arXiv:1810.04805*.

Ahmed El-Kishky, Adi Renduchintala, James Cross, Francisco Guzmán, and Philipp Koehn. 2021. XLEnt: Mining cross-lingual entities with lexical-semantic-phonetic word alignment. In *Preprint*, Online.

Kawin Ethayarajh. 2019. How contextual are contextualized word representations? comparing the geometry of bert, elmo, and gpt-2 embeddings. *arXiv preprint arXiv:1909.00512*.

Christiane Fellbaum. 1998. Wordnet: An electronic lexical database and some of its applications.

Rubén Izquierdo, Armando Suárez, and German Rigau. 2009. An empirical study on class-based word sense disambiguation. In *Proceedings of the 12th Conference of the European Chapter of the ACL (EACL 2009)*, pages 389–397, Athens, Greece. Association for Computational Linguistics.

Anne Lauscher, Vinit Ravishankar, Ivan Vulić, and Goran Glavaš. 2020. From zero to hero: On the limitations of zero-shot language transfer with multilingual Transformers. In *Proceedings of the 2020 Conference on Empirical Methods in Natural Language Processing (EMNLP)*, pages 4483–4499, Online. Association for Computational Linguistics.

Nelson F Liu, Matt Gardner, Yonatan Belinkov, Matthew E Peters, and Noah A Smith. 2019a. Linguistic knowledge and transferability of contextual representations. *arXiv preprint arXiv:1903.08855*.

Yinhan Liu, Myle Ott, Naman Goyal, Jingfei Du, Mandar Joshi, Danqi Chen, Omer Levy, Mike Lewis, Luke Zettlemoyer, and Veselin Stoyanov. 2019b. Roberta: A robustly optimized bert pretraining approach. *arXiv preprint arXiv:1907.11692*.

Tomas Mikolov, Ilya Sutskever, Kai Chen, Greg S Corrado, and Jeff Dean. 2013. Distributed representations of words and phrases and their compositionality. *Advances in neural information processing systems*, 26.

Telmo Pires, Eva Schlinger, and Dan Garrette. 2019. How multilingual is multilingual BERT? In *Proceedings of the 57th Annual Meeting of the Association for Computational Linguistics*, pages 4996–5001, Florence, Italy. Association for Computational Linguistics.

Ian Tenney, Patrick Xia, Berlin Chen, Alex Wang, Adam Poliak, R Thomas McCoy, Najoung Kim, Benjamin Van Durme, Samuel R Bowman, Dipanjan Das, et al. 2019. What do you learn from context? probing for sentence structure in contextualized word representations. *arXiv preprint arXiv:1905.06316*.

Piek Vossen. 1998. A multilingual database with lexical semantic networks. *Dordrecht: Kluwer Academic Publishers. doi*, 10:978–94.

Piek Vossen and Christiane Fellbaum. 2009. Universals and idiosyncrasies in multilingual wordnets. *Multilingual FrameNets in Computational Lexicography: Methods and Applications*, 200:319–346.

Shijie Wu and Mark Dredze. 2019. Beto, bentz, becas: The surprising cross-lingual effectiveness of BERT. In *Proceedings of the 2019 Conference on Empirical Methods in Natural Language Processing and the 9th International Joint Conference on Natural Language Processing (EMNLP-IJCNLP)*, pages 833–844, Hong Kong, China. Association for Computational Linguistics.

Yadollah Yaghoobzadeh, Katharina Kann, T. J. Hazen, Eneko Agirre, and Hinrich Schütze. 2019. Probing for semantic classes: Diagnosing the meaning content of word embeddings. In *Proceedings of the 57th Annual Meeting of the Association for Computational Linguistics*, pages 5740–5753, Florence, Italy. Association for Computational Linguistics.

Kelly Zhang and Samuel Bowman. 2018. Language modeling teaches you more than translation does: Lessons learned through auxiliary syntactic task analysis. In *Proceedings of the 2018 EMNLP Workshop BlackboxNLP: Analyzing and Interpreting Neural Networks for NLP*, pages 359–361, Brussels, Belgium. Association for Computational Linguistics.

Mengjie Zhao, Philipp Dufter, Yadollah Yaghoobzadeh, and Hinrich Schütze. 2020. Quantifying the contextualization of word representations with semantic class probing. *arXiv preprint arXiv:2004.12198*.

A Result of English Monosemous and Polysemous Model With Baseline

	EN-Mono	DE-Mono	NL-Mono	AM-Mono	AR-Mono	EN-Poly	DE-Poly	NL-Poly	AR-Poly
Majority-Vote	0.13	0.12	0.11	0.16	0.12	0.15	0.15	0.15	0.15
Word Embeddings	0.87	0.13	0.10	NA	NA	0.30	0.19	0.21	NA
Tf-Idf	0.53	0.28	0.28	0.21	0.16	0.46	0.28	0.29	0.18
Layer-0	0.92	0.76	0.85	0.36	0.44	0.22	0.22	0.23	0.23
Layer-1	0.92	0.79	0.86	0.38	0.47	0.27	0.26	0.26	0.2
Layer-2	0.93	0.78	0.84	0.47	0.53	0.31	0.33	0.33	0.25
Layer-3	0.94	0.84	0.87	0.5	0.6	0.33	0.35	0.37	0.31
Layer-4	0.92	0.83	0.88	0.46	0.67	0.35	0.35	0.37	0.33
Layer-5	0.92	0.83	0.87	0.49	0.67	0.35	0.35	0.36	0.31
Layer-6	0.91	0.81	0.85	0.49	0.67	0.36	0.37	0.39	0.33
Layer-7	0.9	0.8	0.85	0.46	0.66	0.34	0.36	0.37	0.32
Layer-8	0.88	0.78	0.84	0.45	0.65	0.36	0.35	0.35	0.33
Layer-9	0.86	0.78	0.83	0.44	0.62	0.35	0.35	0.35	0.31
Layer-10	0.85	0.77	0.83	0.41	0.63	0.35	0.36	0.36	0.32
Layer-11	0.84	0.75	0.83	0.41	0.61	0.35	0.34	0.35	0.29
Layer-12	0.82	0.71	0.79	0.41	0.59	0.36	0.33	0.34	0.31
Majority-Vote	0.13	0.12	0.11	0.16	0.12	0.15	0.15	0.15	0.15
Word Embeddings	0.87	0.13	0.10	NA	NA	0.30	0.19	0.21	NA
Tf-Idf	0.53	0.28	0.28	0.21	0.16	0.46	0.28	0.29	0.18
Layer-0	0.92	0.76	0.85	0.36	0.44	0.22	0.22	0.23	0.23
Layer-1	0.92	0.79	0.86	0.38	0.47	0.27	0.26	0.26	0.2
Layer-2	0.93	0.78	0.84	0.47	0.53	0.31	0.33	0.33	0.25
Layer-3	0.94	0.84	0.87	0.5	0.6	0.33	0.35	0.37	0.31
Layer-4	0.92	0.83	0.88	0.46	0.67	0.35	0.35	0.37	0.33
Layer-5	0.92	0.83	0.87	0.49	0.67	0.35	0.35	0.36	0.31
Layer-6	0.91	0.81	0.85	0.49	0.67	0.36	0.37	0.39	0.33
Layer-7	0.9	0.8	0.85	0.46	0.66	0.34	0.36	0.37	0.32
Layer-8	0.88	0.78	0.84	0.45	0.65	0.36	0.35	0.35	0.33
Layer-9	0.86	0.78	0.83	0.44	0.62	0.35	0.35	0.35	0.31
Layer-10	0.85	0.77	0.83	0.41	0.63	0.35	0.36	0.36	0.32
Layer-11	0.84	0.75	0.83	0.41	0.61	0.35	0.34	0.35	0.29
Layer-12	0.82	0.71	0.79	0.41	0.59	0.36	0.33	0.34	0.31

B Distribution of Selected Ambiguous Entities

Entity	**LOC**	**ORG**	**PER**
Mercury	562	215	26
Sirius	391	481	42
Olympus	177	3	11
Uranus	385	7	169
Reich	12	16	266
Cloud	22	63	
Ceres	191	49	21
Aquarius	124	11	59
Chimera		85	17
Vesta	75	9	29
Quartz	12	73	7
Regulus	8	23	67
Terra	42	21	66
Sol	26	64	56
Lab	16	58	7
Triton	16	51	12
Solaris	9		24
Tyre	7		28
Electra	9	28	17
Beguinage	23	7	8
Prana	12	19	16

What to Make of *make*? Sense Distinctions for Light Verbs

Julie Kallini and **Christiane Fellbaum**
Department of Computer Science
Princeton University
jkallini@alumni.princeton.edu,
fellbaum@princeton.edu

Abstract

Verbs like *make*, *have* and *get* present challenges for applications requiring automatic word sense discrimination. These verbs are both highly frequent and polysemous, with semantically "full" readings, as in *make dinner*, and "light" readings, as in *make a request*. Lexical resources like WordNet encode dozens of senses, making discrimination difficult and inviting proposals for reducing the number of entries or grouping them into coarser-grained supersenses. We propose a data-driven, linguistically-based approach to establishing a motivated sense inventory, focusing on *make* to establish a proof of concept.

From several large, syntactically annotated corpora, we extract nouns that are complements of the verb *make*, and group them into clusters based on their Word2Vec semantic vectors. We manually inspect, for each cluster, the words with vectors closest to the centroid as well as a random sample of words within the cluster. The results show that the clusters reflect an intuitively plausible sense discrimination of *make*. As an evaluation, we test whether words within a given cluster cooccur in coordination phrases, such as *apples and oranges*, as prior work has shown that such conjoined nouns are semantically related. Conversely, noun complements from different clusters are less likely to be conjoined. Thus, coordination provides a similarity metric independent of the contextual embeddings used for clustering. Our results pave the way for a WordNet sense inventory that, while not inconsistent with the present one, would reduce it significantly and hold promise for improved automatic word sense discrimination.

1 Background and Related Work

Jespersen coined the term *light verb* to denote verbs like *have*, *take* and *make* that carry little (but not zero) semantic information and that select for a noun, verb, or adjective complement to form a complex predicate. In their light verb use, these verbs are semantically bleached versions of main verbs as in (1a) and (1b), respectively:

(1) a. She made an attempt to prove the theorem.
    b. She made a birthday party for her best friend.

English light verbs usually have a corresponding simple full verb (e.g., *attempt*), but there are a number of subtle semantic distinctions between the light verb construction and the full verb (for a discussion see Kearns (2002)).

Automatic word sense disambiguation often relies on look-up in lexical resources like WordNet, where one confronts the challenge of dozens of different senses. WordNet includes 49 senses for *make*, an inventory that is often criticized by its users, but that is in fact comparable to the number of sense distinctions found in other lexical resources. For example, Merriam-Webster lists 25 main senses of the transitive verb, most of them with multiple subsenses. Even more vexing is the fact that light and full verb uses of *make* are not distinguished. Different proposals for grouping senses into semantically underspecified clusters have been made (Hughes and Prakash, 2006; Wei et al., 2015), but different automatic or manual efforts have resulted in multiple sense inventories that overlap only partially.

We propose a data-driven method to suggest a reduced sense inventory for *make* based on clusters of its nominal complements. We also introduce a novel evaluation plan that is motivated by our previous study of coordination structures. In such structures, two constituents are conjoined by a coordinating conjunction, such as *and* or *or*. Prior work has shown that conjoined nouns are semantically related as measured via various

WordNet relations like synonymy, antonymy, and co-hyponymy (Kallini and Fellbaum, 2022). This makes anomalous utterances, such as *apples and/or texting gloves*, or instances of zeugma, as in *she made a salad and a mess in the kitchen*, unlikely or humorous. To our knowledge, previous attempts at sense distinctions via argument selection have considered only single noun complements of a verb, a difficult task given that light verbs combine with a large number of nouns. Our focus in this paper is on *make*, but we expect our analysis to extend straightforwardly to other light verbs.

2 Approach

We distinguish different senses of *make* by examining its nominal complements, or nouns that it selects as a direct object. We reason that these noun complements must be sufficiently semantically similar for the verb phrases headed by *make* to be well formed, and that grouping these nouns can reveal distinct uses of *make* that point to different senses. To achieve this aim, we extract complements from dependency corpora and find groupings by clustering their word embeddings.[1]

2.1 Universal Dependencies Corpora

We extract complements of *make* from corpora annotated within the Universal Dependencies (UD) project, which aims to provide a consistent dependency treebank annotation across many languages (Nivre et al., 2020). We use several English UD corpora to identify complements, and these corpora are listed and detailed in Table 1.

UD annotates direct objects of verbs with the OBJ dependency relation. An example sentence showing the dependency relation between a form of *make* and its direct object is shown in Figure 1. Our complement extraction script requires input files in the CoNLL-U format, the typical format in which UD corpora are provided. In the CoNLL-U format, sentences are represented using one or more lines, where each line corresponds to a single token or word. Several fields are used to describe each token or word, but we mainly use the `HEAD` field, which is a pointer to the word token's head in the sentence, and the `DEPREL` field, which represents the basic universal dependency relation to the head. If the `HEAD` of a word token is a form of the verb *make*, and its `DEPREL` relation is OBJ, then it is a direct

[1]Our code is available online at `https://github.com/jkallini/LightVerbAnalysis`.

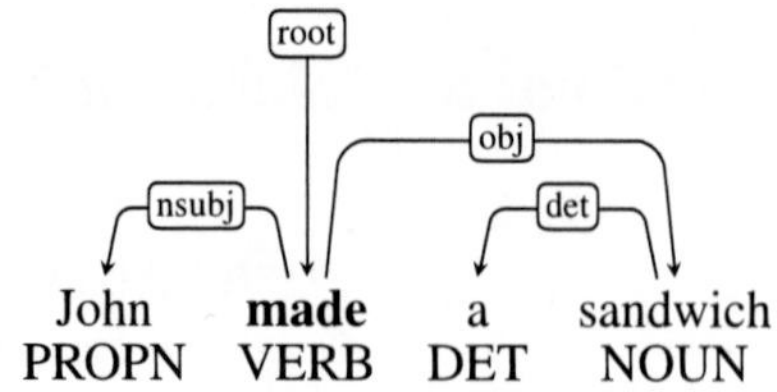

Figure 1: A sentence that uses the OBJ relation in UD to link *make* to its direct object.

object and thus a complement of *make*. We use a CoNLL-U parser to process corpus files into nested Python dictionaries (Stenström, 2021) and perform this check for each token in the corpora to extract complements.

2.2 Complement Clustering

To find groupings of complements, we perform k-means clustering on the complements' word embeddings. We use Google's Word2Vec word embeddings, which are 300-dimensional vectors pretrained on the Google News dataset (Mikolov et al., 2013a,b). We present two clustering analyses in this paper. As a first simple method, we run k-means clustering with $k = 30$ clusters on the unaltered 300-dimensional word vectors corresponding to the complements of *make*. In the second method, we also use principal component analysis (PCA) to reduce the embedding dimensionality for the complements' vectors and extract features that are relevant to the cluster structure, and we measure inertia to find an optimal value of k for clustering. PCA constructs a set of uncorrelated directions, or "components," that are ordered by their variance. Previous work has shown that removing features with low variance using PCA provides a filter that results in a more robust clustering, i.e. clusters with clearer structure that are less sensitive to noise (Ben-Hur and Guyon, 2003).

Figure 2 plots cumulative explained variance as well as individual explained variance as a function of the PCA index. Based on the cumulative explained variance plot, we determined that there is important information to be gained from the first 150 principal components, so we use the first 150 PCA features for the second clustering analysis. Along with PCA, we additionally performed an analysis of inertia, which measures how well the data is captured by clustering for different values of k, as shown in Figure 3. After trying values of $k \in [1, 30]$, we chose $k = 15$ clusters based on the

Corpus	Words	Sentences	Complements	Example media/sources
EWT	254,825	16,621	197	weblogs, newsgroups, emails, reviews, etc.
GUM	135,886	7,397	145	interviews, news stories, academic writings, etc.
GUMReddit	16,356	895	25	Reddit posts
LinES	94,217	5,243	109	fiction, nonfiction, spoken media
Atis	61,879	5,432	39	airline travel information
ParTUT	49,633	2,090	53	legal documents, news stories, webpages, etc.
PUD	21,176	1,000	21	news, wikipedia

Table 1: Word counts, sentence counts, *make* complement counts, and example sources for each corpus we use (Silveira et al., 2014; Zeldes, 2017; Behzad and Zeldes, 2020; Zeman et al., 2017)

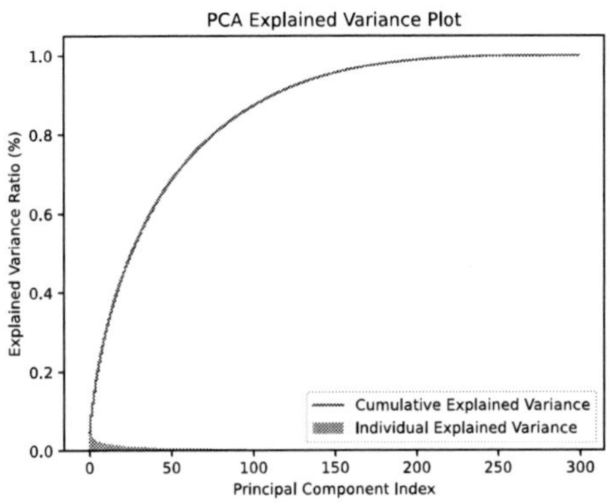

Figure 2: Explained variance plot derived from PCA on Word2Vec word embeddings.

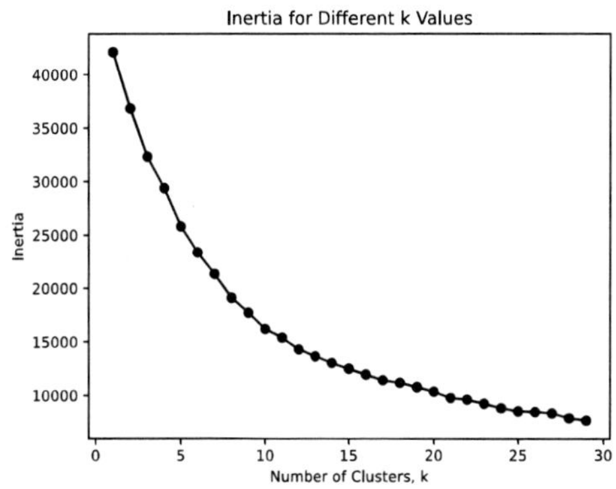

Figure 3: Inertia for different values of k.

elbow in the graph. For both clustering approaches, we used quantile outlier detection to filter out clusters that had too many or too few members. This removed clusters corresponding to senses that were either too generic or very specific.

2.3 Evaluation Using Coordination

Our evaluation is motivated by our previous work showing that pairs of nouns conjoined in coordination phrases are semantically similar; if the complements within a single cluster are sufficiently semantically similar in their functions as well as their contextual embedding representations, then we expect these complements to co-occur in coordination structures. To derive coordination data, we analyzed both automatically and manually parsed constituency corpora with Penn Treebank-style annotations collected for our previous study on coordination (Kallini and Fellbaum, 2021). We obtained constituency annotations of raw sentences from the Corpus of Contemporary American English (COCA) (Davies, 2015) using the Berkeley Neural Parser, a state-of-the-art constituency parser

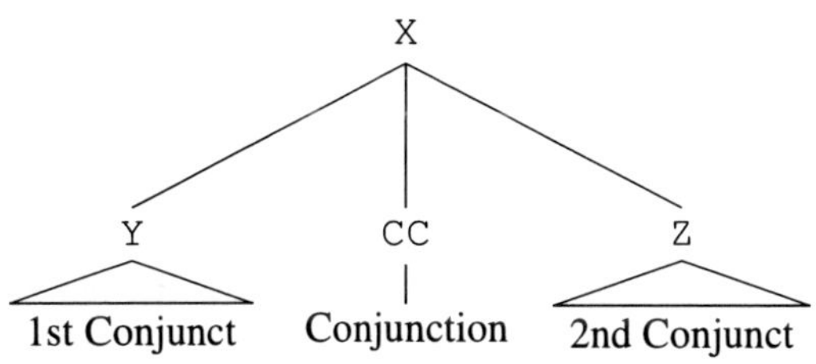

Figure 4: Simple ternary-branching coordination with Penn Treebank-style constituency annotations.

(Kitaev and Klein, 2018). As a second data source, we used a version of the Penn Treebank with an improved coordination annotation (Ficler and Goldberg, 2016). Figure 4 shows an example of a simple instance of coordination in a constituency tree.

We performed this coordination analysis for two lexically-rich clusters, and we indeed found it to be the case that complements from the same cluster would more often co-occur in coordination structures. This result is detailed in the next section.

For less lexically-rich clusters, we devise an additional evaluation plan inspired by coordination. We use an independent similarity metric to compare complements within clusters as well as complements between clusters. First, we generate complement pairs. For instance, take A and B to be distinct clusters. We can measure the similarity of the complements within these two clusters by generating a list of complement pairs, $A \times B$. The average similarity of complement pairs in $A \times B$ should be less than the average similarity of complement pairs in $A \times A$ or $B \times B$.[2] We use Wu-Palmer similarity as the metric for comparison, and to derive senses for each complement, we use the Lesk algorithm for word sense disambiguation, where the provided context is the sentence in the UD corpus in which the complement appeared.

3 Results and Discussion

In total, we found 493 noun complements of *make* in the corpora after removing stopwords and tokens that are not present in the Word2Vec dictionary. The clusters found using simple k-means clustering with $k = 30$ clusters are summarized in Table 2. Outlier clusters have been removed from this table, so we present a reduced set of 26 clusters. The clusters found using k-means clustering with $k = 15$ clusters using PCA are summarized in Table 3. Figure 5 presents a visualization of complement clusters from this second analysis using the first two PCA components.

The second clustering analysis motivates a significantly reduced sense inventory while aligning with senses of *make* currently present in WordNet. For instance, there is a clear cluster for cases where *make* corresponds to cooking or preparing food (cluster #7 in Table 3). The cluster including complements like *impact, donation, and contribution* roughly correspond to its "give" meaning. The cluster with noun complements related to "mistakes" relates to the sense of "causing" or giving rise to an event.

However, our first analysis with a larger number of clusters captures some meaningful distinctions that are lost with a smaller value of k. For instance, this analysis provides a cluster of complements like *statue* and *sculpture* that correspond to the sense of "building" or "creating." The cluster containing *money* presents the sense of "gaining," and the cluster with complements such as *progress* and *improvement* presents the sense of "reaching for a goal."

Cluster #	Size	Centroid Words	Sample Words
0	3	coup, coup_d'_etat, coup_d'_état	coup
1	5	entry, metastasis, breast	metastasis, breast, entry
2	16	word, phrase, language	word, reference, lyric
3	12	noise, ambient_noise, noises	noise, sound
4	25	sense, impression, feel	sense, assumption, representation
5	25	change, adjustment, alter	alteration, revision, change
6	20	decision, recommendation, announcement	conclusion, agreement, request
7	3	statue, bronze_statue, sculpture	statue, sculpture
8	13	friend, mother, daughter	child, love, mother
9	4	comment, leave	comment
10	3	cat, pet, bird	pet, cat, bird
11	19	effort, attempt, endeavor	project, plan, amendment
12	7	vodka, bottle, brandy	wine, bottle, vodka
13	7	contribution, donation, contributions	contribution, donation
14	4	reservation, reservations	reservation
15	11	money, funds, dollars	money, profit, buck
16	11	mistake, blunder, error	blunder, mistake, error
17	19	dessert, sandwich, soup	lunch, cheeseburger, food
18	10	debut, appearance, debuts	cameo, debut, appearance
19	14	joke, laugh, chuckle	chatter, mischief, joke
20	9	difference, disparity, discrepancy	distinction, gap, impact
21	5	appointment, appointments	appointment
22	7	progress, strides, improvement	recovery, improvement, progress
23	11	statement, remarks, press_release	statement, speech, filling
24	6	adaptation, adaption, film	adaptation, film
25	33	deal, agreement, offer	sale, package, transfer

Table 2: Size, word vectors close to the centroid, and a sample of cluster member words for 26 clusters created from basic k-means clustering.

Cluster #	Size	Sample Words
0	22	friend, life, love, girl, cat
1*	144	spot, stay, wave, west, nightlife
2	24	modification, alteration, change, adjustment, revision
3	114	comparison, sculpture, statue, cover, distinction
4*	4	comment
5	25	tour, travel, visit, pilgrimage, trip
6	9	noise
7	30	vodka, soup, wine, potato, food
8	21	objection, conclusion, proposal, submission, decision
9	11	blunder, error, mistake
10	33	deal, negotiation, effort, offer, attempt
11	12	debut, landfall, appearance, cameo
12	13	statement, announcement, speech
13	11	sense
14	20	impact, donation, difference, contribution, improvement

* Cluster identified as an outlier based on size.

Table 3: Size and sample words for each of the 15 clusters created from k-means clustering with PCA.

3.1 Evaluation Results and Discussion

For the evaluation using coordination structures, we picked two clusters and tested whether complements within those clusters tended to co-occur in coordination phrases pulled from separate, independent corpus data. We chose clusters 3 and 7 since these were lexically-rich compared to some others that were large but contained repeated entries. The results show, generally, that complements from within the same cluster tend to coordinate more often than complements paired from different clusters. We found 26 instances of coordinations where both conjuncts were members of cluster #3, such as "meaning and reference" and "writing and language." We found even more for cluster #7, since

[2] When computing pairs between distinct clusters A and B, we use the cross product. When computing in-cluster pairs for a single cluster A, we compute the combinations of elements in A. This avoids duplicate pairs or pairs in which both elements correspond to the same complement instance.

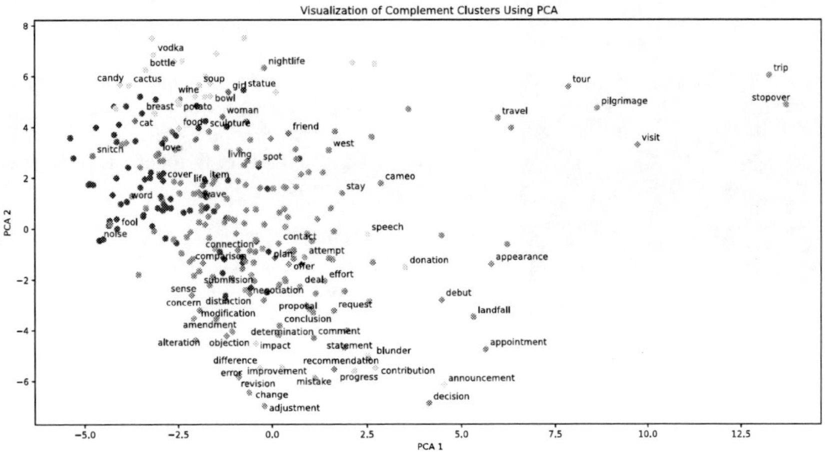

Figure 5: Visualization of complement clusters using the first two PCA components.

this cluster contains many types of food; there were 93 instances of coordination where both conjuncts were from cluster #7, such as "lunch or dinner," and "wine or cocktails." There were fewer (21) coordinations where conjuncts came from different clusters, such as "money and food."

We extended this initial analysis to cover the other clusters by generating complement pairs and measuring their Wu-Palmer similarity. Figure 6 shows that complement pairs where both complements are within the same cluster have a higher average Wu-Palmer similarity than pairs where the complements are members of different clusters, as shown by the brightness of the diagonal in the heatmap. The average similarity of complements within the same cluster was about 0.60, while the average similarity of complements between different clusters was 0.27. These two evaluation steps generally show that the clusters represent nouns that are not only semantically similar based on contextual embeddings but also on their functional similarity.

4 Limitations

A limitation of our coordination evaluation approach is that the clusters to be compared must have a large number of unique members. We found two such lexically-rich clusters, but most clusters did not contain many members that were also attested in coordination phrases. We expect that with more complement data (beyond the 493 nouns from this study), we can obtain larger clusters that will be better suited for this coordination evaluation. The senses captured by these clusters also require a manual evaluation in order to reach the optimal sense distinctions, but we expect that the methodology provided in this paper can aid the process through the use of real-world data.

5 Conclusion

In this paper, we presented a clustering analysis of complements of the light verb *make* using annotated UD corpora that can pave the way toward a reduced WordNet sense inventory for this verb. Furthermore, we proposed and tested a novel method using coordination structures to evaluate the robustness of the complement clustering. Future directions may apply this approach straightforwardly to other light verbs whose large sense inventories in WordNet have stymied word sense disambiguation efforts.

References

Shabnam Behzad and Amir Zeldes. 2020. A cross-genre ensemble approach to robust Reddit part of speech tagging. In *Proceedings of the 12th Web as Corpus Workshop (WAC-XII)*, pages 50–56.

Asa Ben-Hur and Isabelle Guyon. 2003. Detecting stable clusters using principal component analysis. *Methods in molecular biology*, 224:159–82.

Mark Davies. 2015. Corpus of Contemporary American English (COCA).

Jessica Ficler and Yoav Goldberg. 2016. Coordination annotation extension in the Penn Tree Bank. In *Pro-*

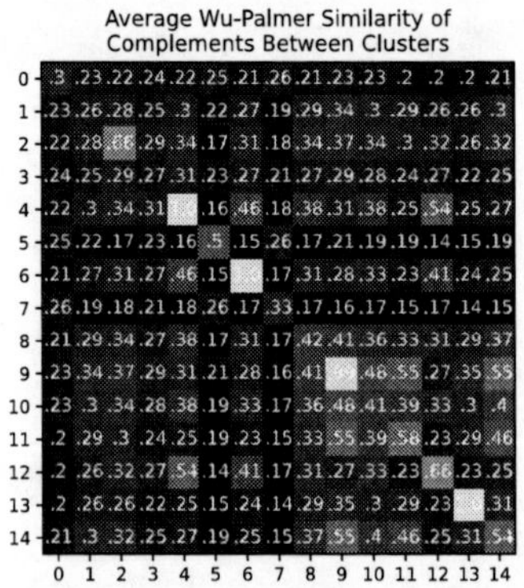

Figure 6: Average Wu-Palmer similarity for complement pairs between clusters from k-means clustering with PCA.

ceedings of the 54th Annual Meeting of the Association for Computational Linguistics (Volume 1: Long Papers), pages 834–842, Berlin, Germany. Association for Computational Linguistics.

Christopher Thad Hughes and Sushant Prakash. 2006. Clustering wordnet senses utilizing modified and novel similarity metrics.

Otto Jespersen. 1965. *A Modern English Grammar on Historical Principles: Syntax/Completed by Niels Hailslund.* Allen & Unwin.

Julie Kallini and Christiane Fellbaum. 2021. A corpus-based syntactic analysis of two-termed unlike coordination. In *Findings of the Association for Computational Linguistics: EMNLP 2021,*, pages 3998–4008, Punta Cana, Dominican Republic. Association for Computational Linguistics.

Julie Kallini and Christiane Fellbaum. 2022. Computational approaches for understanding semantic constraints on two-termed coordination structures. In *Proceedings of the 25th International Conference on Text, Speech and Dialogue,*, pages 64–76, Cham. Springer International Publishing.

Kate Kearns. 2002. Light verbs in english.

Nikita Kitaev and Dan Klein. 2018. Constituency parsing with a self-attentive encoder. In *Proceedings of the 56th Annual Meeting of the Association for Computational Linguistics (Volume 1: Long Papers)*, pages 2676–2686, Melbourne, Australia. Association for Computational Linguistics.

Tomas Mikolov, Kai Chen, Greg S. Corrado, and Jeffrey Dean. 2013a. Efficient estimation of word representations in vector space.

Tomas Mikolov, Ilya Sutskever, Kai Chen, Greg Corrado, and Jeffrey Dean. 2013b. Distributed representations of words and phrases and their compositionality. In *Neural Information Processing Systems (NeurIPS)*.

Joakim Nivre, Marie-Catherine de Marneffe, Filip Ginter, Jan Hajič, Christopher D. Manning, Sampo Pyysalo, Sebastian Schuster, Francis Tyers, and Daniel Zeman. 2020. Universal Dependencies v2: An evergrowing multilingual treebank collection. In *Proceedings of the Twelfth Language Resources and Evaluation Conference*, pages 4034–4043, Marseille, France. European Language Resources Association.

Natalia Silveira, Timothy Dozat, Marie-Catherine de Marneffe, Samuel Bowman, Miriam Connor, John Bauer, and Chris Manning. 2014. A gold standard dependency corpus for English. In *Proceedings of the Ninth International Conference on Language Resources and Evaluation (LREC'14)*, pages 2897–2904, Reykjavik, Iceland. European Language Resources Association (ELRA).

Emil Stenström. 2021. CoNLL-U parser. `https://github.com/EmilStenstrom/conllu/`.

Tingting Wei, Yonghe Lu, Huiyou Chang, Qiang Zhou, and Xianyu Bao. 2015. A semantic approach for text clustering using wordnet and lexical chains. *Expert Systems with Applications*, 42(4):2264–2275.

Amir Zeldes. 2017. The GUM corpus: Creating multilayer resources in the classroom. *Language Resources and Evaluation*, 51(3):581–612.

Daniel Zeman et al. 2017. CoNLL 2017 shared task: Multilingual parsing from raw text to Universal Dependencies. In *Proceedings of the CoNLL 2017 Shared Task: Multilingual Parsing from Raw Text to Universal Dependencies*, pages 1–19, Vancouver, Canada. Association for Computational Linguistics.

Towards Effective Correction Methods Using WordNet Meronymy Relations

Javier Álvez
Lorea Group

Itziar Gonzalez-Dios
Ixa Group, HiTZ Center

German Rigau
Ixa Group, HiTZ Center

University of the Basque Country (UPV/EHU)
{javier.alvez,itziar.gonzalezd,german.rigau}@ehu.eus

Abstract

In this paper, we analyse and compare several correction methods of knowledge resources with the purpose of improving the abilities of systems that require commonsense reasoning with the least possible human-effort. To this end, we cross-check the WordNet meronymy relation *member* against the knowledge encoded in a SUMO-based first-order logic ontology on the basis of the mapping between WordNet and SUMO. In particular, we focus on the knowledge in WordNet regarding the taxonomy of animals and plants. Despite being created manually, these knowledge resources —WordNet, SUMO and their mapping— are not free of errors and discrepancies. Thus, we propose three correction methods by semi-automatically improving the alignment between WordNet and SUMO, by performing some few corrections in SUMO and by combining the above two strategies. The evaluation of each method includes the required human-effort and the achieved improvement on unseen data from the WebChild project, that is tested using first-order logic automated theorem provers.

1 Introduction

The areas of commonsense knowledge representation and commonsense reasoning are of great interest for their application in many tasks related to Natural Language Processing (NLP) e.g. Recognizing Textual Entailment (RTE) (Bos and Markert, 2006; Dagan et al., 2013; Abzianidze, 2017), Natural Language Inference (NLI) (Bowman et al., 2015) or Interpretable Semantic Textual Similarity (ISTS) (Lopez-Gazpio et al., 2017). In the literature, among the knowledge resources, WordNet (Fellbaum, 1998) is one of the most frequently used semantic resources that is applied to NLP tasks. Furthermore, WordNet interlinks many other semantic resources e.g. the EuroWordNet Top Ontology (Rodríguez et al., 1998), or SUMO[1] (Niles and Pease, 2001).

When linking lexical resources such as WordNet (Fellbaum, 1998) and ontologies such as SUMO (Niles and Pease, 2001), DOLCE (Gangemi et al., 2002) or OpenCYC (Reed and Lenat, 2002), Prevot et al. (2005) generalised these three methodological options: restructuring, populating and aligning. But, moreover, ontologies and lexical resources can also be used to cross-check them and validate the knowledge content encoded.

In order to automatically cross-check the knowledge in WordNet and SUMO, Álvez et al. (2015, 2019) introduced a general framework that enables evaluating the competency of SUMO-based ontologies like Adimen-SUMO (Álvez et al., 2012) and proposed a method for the automatic creation of *competency questions* (CQs) (Grüninger and Fox, 1995). Their proposal is based on several predefined question patterns (QPs) that are instantiated using information from WordNet and its mapping into SUMO (Niles and Pease, 2003). In addition, the authors described an application of first-order logic (FOL) automated theorem provers (ATPs) for the automatic evaluation of the proposed CQs. However, a low percentage of the meronymy pairs from WordNet can be validated against SUMO using the proposed framework, as reported by Álvez and Rigau (2018); Álvez et al. (2018). Overall, three possible causes for this low validation ratio have been identified:

- Incorrect mappings between WordNet and SUMO: two cases are presented in Table 1. The first one is valid because the knowledge from WordNet, SUMO and its mapping is correctly aligned: individuals (*$parent^1_n$*) with an instance of *BiologicalAttribute* as property can be members of instances of *FamilyGroup* (*$family^2_n$*). However, the second case is invalid:

[1] http://www.ontologyportal.org

	Part		Whole	
Valid	$parent_n^1$: a father or mother; (...)	Subsumed by **BiologicalAttribute**	$family_n^2$: primary social group; (...)	Subsumed by **FamilyGroup**
Invalid	$hyaena_n^1$: doglike nocturnal mammal (...)	Subsumed by **Canine**	$family\_Hyaenidae_n^1$: hyenas	Subsumed by **Canine**

Table 1: Valid and invalid examples of the relation *member*

Canine (whole) is characterised as an individual (i.e. not a group); therefore, it cannot have members. In order to be able to validate the pair, $family\_Hyaenidae_n^1$ should be corrected to be subsumed by *GroupOfAnimals*.

- Discrepancies in the knowledge encoded in WordNet and SUMO: the groups (species, genus, family, order, ...) in the taxonomy of animals and plants are connected by the relation *member* of WordNet, while the relation *member* of SUMO connects individuals (which cannot be groups) to their groups.

- Limitations of ATPs.

In this paper, our aim is shedding light on the sources of difficulty when correcting knowledge resources, which is a mainly manual and never ending task. Exactly, we want to discover which correction methods and strategies lead to maximising the improvement with the least possible human-effort. To this end, we consider three correction approaches: i) the correction of the mapping between WordNet and SUMO on the basis of the WordNet hierarchy and our manual error analysis of the results reported in Álvez et al. (2018); ii) the correction of the knowledge in SUMO in order to its alignment to WordNet; iii) the combination of the previous two approaches. We report on a practical evaluation of the impact of each correction method on unseen data provided by the WebChild project (Tandon et al., 2014, 2017), which is a large collection of commonsense knowledge that has been automatically extracted and disambiguated from Web contents. To the best of our knowledge, this is the first work dealing with the problem of correcting FOL commonsense resources.

Outline. First, we present the related work in the next section and review the knowledge resources and evaluation framework in Section 3. Then, we describe the proposed correction methods in Section 4 and provide the evaluation results in Section 5. Finally, we conclude and outline the future work in Section 6.

2 Related Work

In this section, we present the works related to meronymy knowledge and its acquisition, cross-checking resources, mapping error detection and ontology debugging and repairing.

Meronymy is a semantic relation that *connects* the parts and the whole. This connection can be functional, homeomeric/homeomerous (consisting of similar parts), separable or simultaneous (Campenhoudt, 1996). In the typology of meronymy relations, the most important subrelations are constituent-object, member-collection and material-object. The importance of meronymy is pointed out by vor der Brück and Helbig (2010), which extract meronymy relations from Wikipedia by means of a logic-oriented approach. According to them, meronymy is necessary for many NLP tasks such as question answering. Following their example, if someone asks about the earthquakes in Europe, then the question could be answered thanks to the meronymy relation if we had the data of each European country.

Both manual and automated attempts have been made to acquire meronymy knowledge. Among the first ones, there are more than 22,000 meronymic pairs in WordNet (Fellbaum, 1998), that have been manually constructed and reviewed. WordNet is a large lexical database of English where nouns, verbs, adjectives and adverbs are grouped into sets of synonyms called *synsets*,[2] each one denoting a distinct concept. Moreover, synsets are interlinked

[2]In this paper, we will refer to the synsets using the format $word_p^s$, where s is the sense number and p is the part-of-speech: n for nouns and v for verbs e.g. $plant_n^2$ means that the word *plant* is a noun and that we are referring to its second sense in WordNet.

by means of lexical-semantic relations. WordNet encodes three main meronymy relations that relate noun synsets: i) *part*, the general meronymy relation; ii) *member*, which relates particulars and groups; and iii) *substance*, which relates physical matters and things. In total, WordNet v3.0 includes 22,187 (ordered) meronymy relations (around 10 % of the relations between synset pairs in WordNet): 9,097 pairs using *part*, 12,293 pairs using *member* and 797 pairs using *substance*. For example, the synsets $tongue_n^1$ and $mouth_n^1$ are related by *part*, $lamb_n^1$ and $genus\_Ovis_n^1$ are related by *member*, and $neuroglia_n^1$ and $glioma_n^1$ are related by *substance*.

Furthermore, additional relations were manually added to WordNet in Lebani and Pianta (2012) on the basis of featural descriptions. However, the coverage of the collected meronymy knowledge is quite restricted. This limitation is also present in some automated proposals like ConceptNet (Speer et al., 2017), which has been obtained by crowdsourcing and contains around 20,000 meronymy relation pairs between non-disambiguated words.

The coverage of the automatically acquired meronymy knowledge is larger in other works. For example, PWKB (the part-whole KB) (Tandon et al., 2016), which has been integrated into WebChild v2.0 (Tandon et al., 2017), consists of almost 6 millions of disambiguated meronymy pairs that have been obtained from Web contents and image tags by combining pattern-based information extraction methods and logical reasoning. However, this KB suffers from low salience since more pairs were obtained by expanding a small set of relations. A complementary resource is hasPartKB (Bhakthavatsalam et al., 2020), which contains more salient and accurate hasPart relations (around 50,000) extracted from a large corpus of generic statements. Finally, Quasimodo (Romero et al., 2019) and Aristo Tuple KB (Mishra et al., 2017) contain several thousands of non-disambiguated meronymy pairs, but their coverage is rather limited.

The knowledge in all the above cited resources is restricted to relation pairs. Regarding general knowledge, SUMO (Niles and Pease, 2001) contains both facts and axioms that encode more abstract information and properties about meronymy.

In relation with cross-checking knowledge resources, Álvez et al. (2008) exploit the EuroWordNet Top Ontology (Rodríguez et al., 1998) and its mapping to WordNet for detecting many ontological conflicts and inconsistencies in the WordNet nominal hierarchy.

Most of the works presented for error correction both in the mapping and in the ontologies have been proposed for OWL ontologies. Relating mapping error detection and correction, many methods have been proposed to detect mapping errors or invalid mappings between ontologies, knowledge resources, dictionaries and thesauri (Reis et al., 2015). Similar to us, Pathak and Chute (2009) reasoning strategies for the biomedical domain. Exactly, they use description logics to detect inconsistencies since they consider that ontologies are consistent, and therefore, errors come from the mappings. Wang and Xu (2012) divided the mapping errors in four categories (from now on, Wang&Xu classification): redundant, imprecise, inconsistent and abnormal mappings. Correction strategies are presented in Abacha et al. (2016) for the biomedical domain, where questions are proposed to experts in order to validate the mapping and the ontology. Surveys on mapping maintenance and ontology matching are respectively presented in Reis et al. (2015) and Ochieng and S. Kyanda (2018). Relating ontology error detection, recent work on ontology debugging involves detecting hidden modelling errors: Teymourlouie et al. (2018) use DBpedia during the ontology debugging process to detect contradictions in ontologies that seem coherent. Unfortunately, as far as we know, no correction approach has been proposed.

3 Knowledge Resources and Evaluation Framework for WordNet Meronymy

In this section, we describe the knowledge resources and framework that enable the automatic evaluation of the meronymy relation *member* of WordNet by using Automated Theorem Provers (ATPs).

Adimen-SUMO (Álvez et al., 2012) is a first-order logic (FOL) ontology obtained by means of a suitable transformation of most of the knowledge (around 88 % of the axioms) in the *top* and *middle* levels of SUMO (Niles and Pease, 2001). Adimen-SUMO enables the application of state-of-the-art FOL ATPs such as Vampire (Kovács and Voronkov, 2013) and E (Schulz, 2002) in order to automatically reason on the basis of the knowledge in SUMO (Niles and Pease, 2001). SUMO is organised around the notions of *particulars* (also called *instances* or *objects*) and *classes* by means of the meta-predicates *instance* and *subclass*. Amongst them, SUMO also differentiates *relations* and *attributes*, and provides specific predicates for their use that are inherited by Adimen-SUMO e.g. *subrelation* and *attribute*. We denote the nature of SUMO concepts by adding as subscript the following symbols: o for SUMO objects, c for SUMO classes, r for SUMO relations, a for SUMO attributes and A for classes of SUMO attributes. For example: $Waist_o$, $GroupOfAnimals_c$, $material_r$, $Solid_a$ and $BiologicalAttribute_A$.

WordNet and SUMO are linked by means of a semantic mapping that connects WordNet synsets to SUMO concepts using three relations: *equivalence*, *subsumption* and *instance* (Niles and Pease, 2003). The mapping relation *equivalence* connects WordNet synsets and SUMO concepts that are semantically equivalent. *Subsumption* (or *instance*) is used when the semantics of the WordNet synsets is less general than (or instance of) the semantics of the SUMO concepts to which the synsets are connected. For example, the synset $lamb_n^1$ is connected to $Lamb_c$ by *equivalence* and $neuroglia_n^1$ is connected to $Tissue_c$ by *subsumption*. From now on, we denote the semantic mapping relations by concatenating the symbols '$=$ ' (*equivalence*), '$+$' (*subsumption*) and '@' (*instance*) to the corresponding SUMO concept e.g. $lamb_n^1$ is connected to $Lamb_c{=}$ and $neuroglia_n^1$ is connected to $Tissue_c{+}$.

For the automatic evaluation of the WordNet meronymy relations, we apply the framework introduced in Álvez et al. (2019), which is an adaptation of the method proposed in Grüninger and Fox (1995) for the formal design and evaluation of ontologies on the basis of *Competency Questions* (CQs). This framework enables the use of ATPs in order to automatically classify CQs as follows: CQs are decided to be *passing* (if proved to be entailed by the ontology), *non-passing* (their negations are proved to be entailed by the ontology) and *unresolved* (neither the CQs nor their negations are proved to be entailed by the ontology).

Furthermore, we adapt the *Question Patterns* (QPs) for the meronymy relation *member* introduced in Álvez and Rigau (2018); Álvez et al. (2018), which enable the translation of its semantics into a suitable CQ or yield a semantically incorrect conjecture according to the restrictions for relations provided by SUMO. Those QPs employs the translation of the mapping information of synsets into Adimen-SUMO statements that is described in Álvez et al. (2019), which characterises the semantics of WordNet synsets in terms of SUMO instances and requires the use of a new variable for each synset. There is a different QP for each possible combination of mapping relations, which states the quantification of the introduced variables and the logical connectives that enable the construction of the final CQ. For example, the synsets $sheep_n^1$ and $flock_n^5$ are respectively connected to $Sheep_c{=}$ and $Group_c{+}$. Thus, we use the second QP proposed in Álvez and Rigau (2018) because of the use of the mapping relations *equivalence* and *subsumption*, and obtain the following conjecture:

```
(forall (?X)
    (=>
        ($instance ?X Sheep)
        (exists (?Y)
            (and
                ($instance ?Y Group)
                (member ?X ?Y) ) ) ) )
```

Finally, the WordNet meronymy pairs on *member* can be classified according to the following categories depending of: a) if the *member* pair is translated into a CQ, then it is decided to be *validated*, *unvalidated* or *unknown* if the CQ is passing, non-passing or unresolved respectively; b) the *member* pairs that yield to semantically incorrect conjectures are classified as *unvalidated*.

By using the above described framework and regarding the original versions of SUMO and its mapping from WordNet, from the 12,293 *member* pairs provided by WordNet only 19 are validated, while 11,963 pairs are unvalidated and 311 remains unknown. Moreover, from the 11,963 unvalidated pairs, only 24 yield a correct CQ. That is, the direct application of the introduced evaluation framework just allows to validate a mere 1.5% of the member pairs encoded in WordNet and, apparently, most of the unvalidated pairs yield semantically incorrect SUMO conjectures. This may be an indication of both misalignment in the knowledge encoded in WordNet and SUMO and the existence of a large number of discrepancies in their mapping.

4 Knowledge Correction Methods

In this section, we introduce the proposed correction strategies for knowledge resources. For our analysis and interventions, we have used the information contained in the Multilingual Central Repository (Gonzalez-Agirre et al., 2012). Exactly, we have consulted: the Basic Level Concepts (BLCs) (Izquierdo et al., 2007), which are frequent and salient concepts in WordNet that try to represent as many concepts as possible (abstract concepts) and as many distinctive features as possible (concrete concepts); the Top Concept Ontology (TCO) (Rodríguez et al., 1998); the Semantic Files (SF) from WordNet and the WordNet Domains (WND) (Bentivogli et al., 2004). Moreover, we have also consulted SUMO and its documentation.

4.1 Correction of the mapping

We have performed two kinds of interventions in order to realign the mapping between WordNet and SUMO: 1) structural corrections in the BLCs; 2) opportunistic corrections based on an error analysis. In both phases, we have performed a manual analysis that has served as the basis for proposing some criteria in order to automatically propagate or expand the corrections.

For performing structural corrections, from the 800 BLCs in WordNet we have manually inspected the topmost 200 ones. To that end, we have used information from WordNet, TCO and SUMO and for each BLC, we have decided whether the mapping was correct or not. If we have not considered it as correct, we have proposed a new mapping for it. During this intervention we have tried to make as few changes as possible; so, if the original mapping was acceptable, then it has not been changed. It is important to note that at this correction phase we have considered all the synsets from WordNet without restricting to those that are related to meronymy, that is, what we correct can appear or not in our benchmark.

This way, we have manually corrected the mapping of 50 BLCs (25 %). This manual correction can be classified in two types: a) groups that are characterised as individual classes (38 synsets), most of them related to plants and animals; b) punctual mapping errors (12 synsets). Following Wang&Xu classification, these errors are imprecise or inconsistent mappings: exactly, 10 are imprecise mappings and 40 are inconsistent. For example:

- *dicot_genus*$_n^1$ ("*genus of flowering plants having two cotyledons (embryonic leaves) in the seed which usually appear at germination*") and *fish_genus*$_n^1$ ("*any of various genus of fish*") belong to the first type of corrections because they were incorrectly connected to *FloweringPlant*$_c$+ and *Fish*$_c$+ and have now been linked to *Group*$_c$+ and *GroupOfAnimals*$_c$+ respectively.
- *agency*$_n^1$ ("*an administrative unit of government:*") and *substance*$_n^1$ ("*the real physical matter of which a person or thing consists:*") belong to the second type of corrections because *agency*$_n^1$ was imprecisely connected to *PoliticalOrganization*$_c$= (updated to *GovernmentOrganization*$_c$+) and *substance*$_n^1$ was incorrectly connected to *Object*$_c$= (corrected to *Substance*$_c$=).

During this intervention, we have been able to revise and correct when necessary around 20 BLCs per hour and, in total, we have spent 10 hours.

After the manual correction of the BLCs, we have automatically propagated the corrected BLC mappings to their hyponyms based on the following criterion:

> Propagate the corrected as long as the hyponym and its BLC are equally mapped in the original mapping.

By proceeding in this way, we have corrected a total of 3,883 mappings.

For the opportunistic correction of the mapping based on an error analysis, we have inspected the unclassified pairs in the experimentation introduced at the end of Section 3. More concretely, we have grouped the synset pairs according to their mapping to SUMO and ordered them by frequency. Apparently, most of the detected errors are due to the fact that species, genera, families, orders, etc. (taxonomic biological classification) and galaxies, constellations, etc. (collections of planets, stars, asteroids, etc.) are connected to SUMO classes representing individuals and not groups (group errors as presented before and inconsistent according to Wang&Xu classification). In order to correct this type of errors, we have designed four very simple heuristics:

1. If the synset is an hyponym of *group*$_n^1$ in WordNet, is connected to both *Animal*+ and *Group*+ in the TCO, is connected to a subclass of *Animal*$_c$ in SUMO and some of the words *family*, *genus*, *order*, *suborder*, *class*, *phylum*, *subphylum*, *kingdom*, *subkingdom*, *division*, *subdivision*, *algae*, *superfamily*, *subfamily*, *superorder*, *group*, *subclass* or *superclass* occurs in its gloss, then map the synset to *GroupOfAnimals*$_c$+.

2. If the synset is a hyponym of $group^1_n$ in WordNet, is connected to both *Plant*+ and *Group*+ in the TCO, is connected to a subclass of $Plant_c$ in SUMO and some of the words *family, genus, order, suborder, class, phylum, subphylum, kingdom, subkingdom, division, subdivision, algae, superfamily, subfamily, superorder, group* occurs in its gloss, then map the synset to $Group_c$+.

3. If the synset is a hyponym of $group^1_n$ in WordNet, is connected to *Group*+ in the TCO, is connected to a subclass of either $Microorganism_c$, $Virus_c$, $Bacterium_c$ or $Fungus_c$ in SUMO and some of the words *family, genus, order, suborder, class, phylum, subphylum, kingdom, subkingdom, division, subdivision, algae, superfamily, subfamily, superorder, group* occurs in its gloss, then map the synset to $Group_c$+.

4. If the synset is connected to a subclass of $AstronomicalBody_c$ in SUMO and the word *constellation* occurs in its gloss, then map the synset to $Group_c$+.

It is worth noting that there is no concept for representing groups of either plants, microorganisms, viruses, bacteria, fungi or astronomical bodies in SUMO. For example, the synset $animal\_kingdom^1_n$ ("*taxonomic kingdom comprising all living or extinct animals*") was incorrectly connected to $Animal_c$= and its mapping has been corrected to $GroupOfAnimals_c$+.

Furthermore, corrections have been also propagated as described for structural corrections. This way, the mapping of 1,961 synsets has been corrected with an human-effort of 2 hours.

4.2 Matching Knowledge Discrepancies

The objective of this intervention is detecting and solving the knowledge discrepancies between WordNet and SUMO that prevent the validation of many pairs where the mapping information is correct. For this purpose, we have augmented the manual error analysis described in the above subsection by also considering unvalidated pairs.

Overall, most of the detected conflicts are related to organisms. With respect to unvalidated pairs, the main problem is that the relation between taxonomic groups cannot be expressed in terms of SUMO due to the domain restrictions of the SUMO predicate $member_r$. In particular, the first argument of $member_r$ is restricted to be an instance of $SelfConnectedObject_c$, which is disjoint with the SUMO class $Collection_c$ and hence disjoint with the SUMO class $Group_c$. Consequently, we cannot construct a SUMO statement that expresses that an instance of $Group_c$ is a member of another instance of $Group_c$, as required for the validation of the examples in Table 1. In order to overcome this problem, we have proposed to replace the domain restriction of the first argument of the SUMO predicate $member_r$: instead of being instance of $SelfConnectedObject_c$, our proposal is restricting the first argument of $member_r$ to be instance of $Object_c$, which is superclass of $Group_c$ (1 axiom corrected). In addition, the characterization of $GroupOfPeople_c$ and $GroupOfAnimals_c$ has to be accordingly updated: in the new proposed axiomatization, the members of $GroupOfPeople_c$ can be instances of either $Human_c$ or $GroupOfPeople_c$, and the members of an instance of $GroupOfAnimals_c$ can be either instances $Animal_c$ that are not instance of $Human_c$ or instances of $GroupOfAnimals_c$ (2 axioms corrected).

Regarding unclassified *member* pairs, by a manual inspection of SUMO we have detected that the characterization of concepts representing groups is too weak. More concretely, there is no concept for the representation of groups of plants and the existing concepts for the representation of groups —$Group_c$ for general groups; $GroupOfPeople_c$, $AgeGroup_c$, $FamilyGroup_c$, $SocialUnit_c$, $EthnicGroup_c$ and $BeliefGroup_c$ for groups of people; GroupOfAnimals and $Brood_c$ for groups of animals— are only partially characterised. More concretely, the nature of the members of each kind of group is properly restricted, but individuals (including the instances of $Agent_c$) are not restricted to belong to some groups. In order to solve these issues, we have created and characterised a new concept for groups of plants ($GroupOfPlants_c$, 3 new axioms) and introduced another 9 new axioms for the characterization of groups).

In total, our interventions have required a human-effort of 2 hours.

4.3 Joining Mapping and Ontology Corrections

In order to integrate both interventions, we have made some changes in the mapping.

On one hand, we have updated the mapping of

9 synsets from the top 200 BLCs from *Group*$_c$+ to *GroupOfPlants*$_c$+, and this change has been propagated to 1,961 synsets. On the other hand, we have redefined the second heuristic presented in Subsection 4.1 in order to map the synset to *GroupOfPlants*$_c$+. The updated heuristic is the following:

- If the synset is an hyponym of the synset *group*^1_n in WordNet and is connected to a subclass of *Plant*$_c$ in SUMO, then map the synset to *GroupOfPlants*$_c$+

This heuristic is directly applied to 356 synsets and propagated to another 85 synsets. In total, we have updated 2,411 mappings that were previously mapped to *Group*$_c$+.

All these interventions have been performed with almost no human-effort.

5 Evaluation

In this section, we evaluate the proposed knowledge correction methods on both seen and unseen data, which is extracted from the WebChild project. In Table 2, we report on the results obtained by applying the evaluation framework described in Section 3 for the different intervention phases in WordNet (initial, correction of the mapping, matching knowledge discrepancies and joint intervention) and in WebChild data (initial and joint intervention). For each phase, we provide the number of pairs that are validated/unvalidated/unknown (Validated, Unvalidated and Unknown columns respectively) and three metrics that measure the performance of the evaluation: recall (calculated as the ratio between validated pairs and total pairs); precision (calculated as the ratio between validated pairs and validated+unvalidated pairs); and $F1$ (calculated as the harmonic mean of precision and recall) values. In the case of unvalidated pairs, we provide both the total number of pairs (T column) and the number of pairs which yield a correct CQ (C column).

Regarding seen data, it is easy to see that matching knowledge discrepancies outperforms mapping correction, although the improvement is low in both cases: correcting the mapping turns almost a half of the previously unvalidated pairs into unknown while matching knowledge discrepancies increases a bit the number of validated pairs. However, by combining both interventions the improvement is much higher: the amount of validated pairs is 500 times bigger and the amount of unvalidated pairs is almost 15 times smaller.

With respect to the data extracted from the WebChild project, the combined intervention heavily improves the results again, although the impact is a bit lower: many pairs still remain unknown and the ratio between validated and unvalidated pairs is lower than in the case of WordNet. For a better understanding of these results, we have manually analysed a sample of WebChild pairs consisting of five randomly selected cases from each output (validated, unvalidated and unknown).

Considering the validated pairs, 4/5 have been classified as validated for good reasons, e.g. *Acrocomia*^1_n is member of *Palmae*^1_n. The only error is a wrong pair in the knowledge base: the synset *genus*^2_n ("*(biology) taxonomic group containing one or more species*") is incorrectly asserted to be member of *Carapidae*^1_n ("*pearlfishes: related to the Brotulidae*").

From the unvalidated pairs, 2/5 pairs are wrong so they have been correctly classified as unvalidated e.g. *superphylum*^1_n is not a member of *locative_role*^1_n. However, 3/5 pairs are correct and should have been validated, but there are mapping errors e.g. *Auriculariaceae*^1_n is member of *Tremellales*^1_n, although the pair is classified as unvalidated because *Tremellales*^1_n is still mapped to *Fungus*$_c$.

Finally, in relation to unknown pairs, one pair is correct —*rice_weevil*^1_n is member of *Sitophylus*^1_n— and 4/5 pairs are wrong, e.g. *relative*^1_n is not a member of *Ming_dynasty*^1_n. However, these pairs cannot be resolved by ATPs because the required information is missed in the ontology or, as in the case of the correct pair, due to resource (specially time) restrictions.

6 Conclusions and Future Work

In this paper we have reported on several correction methods for the knowledge about meronymy in WordNet, SUMO and their mapping with the aim of improving the abilities of systems that require commonsense reasoning. To this end, we have applied FOL ATPs on a large set of CQs automatically constructed on the basis of several predefined QPs and the knowledge of the involved resources. Since finding and correcting errors in knowledge resources has always been time-consuming and required quite a lot of manual work, we have focused on the human-effort required for each cor-

Data	Phase	Validated	Unvalidated T	Unvalidated C	Unknown	Recall	Precision	$F1$
WordNet	Initial	19	11,963	24	311	0.002	0.002	0.002
	Mapping	29	6,561	5,811	5,703	0.002	0.004	0.003
	Knowledge	132	11,603	30	558	0.011	0.011	0.011
	Joint	10,071	808	58	1,414	0.819	0.926	0.869
WebChild	Initial	82	35,377	102	3,368	0.002	0.002	0.002
	Joint	18,569	3,526	136	17,032	0.475	0.840	0.607

Table 2: Evaluation of the knowledge correction methods

rection strategy. As a result, we have been able to increase the number of WordNet pairs that can be validated against the knowledge in SUMO with a total human-effort of 14 hours. All the resources —the corrected mapping, the augmented ontology and the experimental reports— are available at the Adimen-SUMO webpage.[3]

By analysing our evaluation results on WordNet, it seems at first glance to be worth investing effort correcting and matching the knowledge of the involved resources, since the improvement is slightly higher (see Table 2) and has required less human-effort (2 hours against 12 hours), although the combined strategy leads to the better results with almost no additional human-effort. More concretely, at the initial stage only a 0.15 % of the *member* pairs in WordNet could be validated and our interventions have enabled the validation of almost 82 % of the pairs.

Regarding the evaluation on unseen data, we have confirmed that our interventions are correct, although there is still a lot of work to do. Furthermore, our detailed analysis revealed some aspects for future work. For example, the capture of metonymy, solving additional misalignments (e.g. classifying humans as animals) and the need of analysing the inheritance of relations.

Moreover, we plan to test if the improved knowledge resources also obtain better results in other benchmarks based on antonymy and semantic roles (Álvez et al., 2017), and we would like to carry out similar experiments in other datasets e.g. BLESS[4] (Baroni and Lenci, 2010). Additionally, we also plan to consider additional WordNet relations: for example, the remaining relations about meronymy *part* and *substance*, cause or the semantic roles described in the Morphosemantic links (Fellbaum et al., 2009).

Longer term research includes a new mapping between WordNet and SUMO on the basis of formulae instead of labels, with the aim of providing a more precise definition of the semantics of synsets in terms of the SUMO language.

[3]http://adimen.si.ehu.es/web/AdimenSUMO

[4]https://sites.google.com/site/geometricalmodels/shared-evaluation

Acknowledgements

This work has been partly supported by: (i) the project DeepKnowledge (PID2021-127777OB-C21), funded by MCIN/AEI/10.13039/501100011033 and FEDER *Una manera de hacer Europa*; (ii) the European Union (ERDF funds) under grant PID2020-112581GB-C22; (iii) the project AWARE (TED2021-131617B-I00), funded by MCIN/AEI/10.13039/501100011033 and the European Union (NextGenerationEU/PRTR); (iv) the Basque Government (IXA excellence research group IT1570-22); (v) the University of the Basque Country (UPV/EHU) under project LoRea (GIU21/044).

References

A. B. Abacha, J. C. Dos Reis, Y. Mrabet, C. Pruski, and M. Da Silveira. 2016. Towards natural language question generation for the validation of ontologies and mappings. *Journal of Biomedical Semantics*, 7(1):48.

L. Abzianidze. 2017. LangPro: Natural language theorem prover. In *Proc. of the 2017 Conference on Empirical Methods in Natural Language Processing: System Demonstrations (EMNLP 2017)*, pages 115–120. Association for Computational Linguistics.

J. Álvez, J. Atserias, J. Carrera, S. Climent, E. Laparra, A. Oliver, and G. Rigau. 2008. Complete and consistent annotation of WordNet using the Top Concept Ontology. In *Proc. of the 6th Int. Conf. on Language Resources and Evaluation (LREC 2008)*, pages 1529–1534. European Language Resources Association (ELRA).

J. Álvez, I. Gonzalez-Dios, and G. Rigau. 2018. Cross-checking WordNet and SUMO using meronymy. In *Proc. of the 11th Int. Conf. on Language Resources and Evaluation (LREC 2018)*, pages 4570–4577. European Language Resources Association (ELRA).

J. Álvez, P. Lucio, and G. Rigau. 2012. Adimen-SUMO: Reengineering an ontology for first-order reasoning. *Int. J. Semantic Web Inf. Syst.*, 8(4):80–116.

J. Álvez, P. Lucio, and G. Rigau. 2015. Improving the competency of first-order ontologies. In *Proc. of the 8th Int. Conf. on Knowledge Capture (K-CAP 2015)*, pages 15:1–15:8. ACM.

J. Álvez, P. Lucio, and G. Rigau. 2017. Black-box testing of first-order logic ontologies using WordNet. *CoRR*, abs/1705.10217.

J. Álvez, P. Lucio, and G. Rigau. 2019. A framework for the evaluation of SUMO-based ontologies using WordNet. *IEEE Access*, 7:36075–36093.

J. Álvez and G. Rigau. 2018. Towards cross-checking WordNet and SUMO using meronymy. In *Proc. of the 9th Global WordNet Conference (GWC 2018)*, pages 25–33.

M. Baroni and A. Lenci. 2010. Distributional memory: A general framework for corpus-based semantics. *Computational Linguistics*, 36(4):673–721.

L. Bentivogli, P. Forner, B. Magnini, and E. Pianta. 2004. Revising the Wordnet domains hierarchy: semantics, coverage and balancing. In *Proc. of the Workshop on Multilingual Linguistic Ressources*, pages 101–108. Association for Computational Linguistics, COLING.

S. Bhakthavatsalam, K. Richardson, N. Tandon, and P. Clark. 2020. Do dogs have whiskers? A new knowledge base of haspart relations. *CoRR*, abs/2006.07510.

J. Bos and K. Markert. 2006. Recognising textual entailment with robust logical inference. In *Machine Learning Challenges. Evaluating Predictive Uncertainty, Visual Object Classification, and Recognising Tectual Entailment*, pages 404–426, Berlin, Heidelberg. Springer.

S. R. Bowman, G. Angeli, C. Potts, and C. D. Manning. 2015. A large annotated corpus for learning natural language inference. In *Proc. of the Conf. on Empirical Methods in Natural Language Processing (EMNLP 2015)*, pages 632–642. Association for Computational Linguistics.

M. Van Campenhoudt. 1996. Recherche d'équivalences et structuration des réseaux notionnels: le cas des relations méronymiques. *Terminology. International Journal of Theoretical and Applied Issues in Specialized Communication*, 3(1):53–83.

I. Dagan, D. Roth, M. Sammons, and F. M. Zanzotto. 2013. Recognizing textual entailment: Models and applications. *Synthesis Lectures on Human Language Technologies*, 6(4):1–220.

C. Fellbaum, editor. 1998. *WordNet: An Electronic Lexical Database*. MIT Press.

C. Fellbaum, A. Osherson, and P. E. Clark. 2009. Putting semantics into WordNet's "morphosemantic" links. In *Human Language Technology. Challenges of the Information Society*, pages 350–358, Berlin, Heidelberg. Springer.

A. Gangemi, N. Guarino, C. Masolo, A. Oltramari, and L. Schneider. 2002. Sweetening ontologies with DOLCE. In A. Gómez-Pérez et al., editor, *Knowledge Engin. and Knowledge Manag.: Ontologies and the Semantic Web*, LNCS 2473, pages 166–181. Springer.

A. Gonzalez-Agirre, E. Laparra, and G. Rigau. 2012. Multilingual Central Repository version 3.0. In *Proc. of the 8th Int. Conf. on Language Resources and Evaluation (LREC 2012)*, pages 2525–2529. European Language Resources Association (ELRA).

M. Grüninger and M. S. Fox. 1995. Methodology for the design and evaluation of ontologies. In *Proc. of the Workshop on Basic Ontological Issues in Knowledge Sharing (IJCAI 1995)*.

R. Izquierdo, A. Suárez, and G. Rigau. 2007. Exploring the automatic selection of basic level concepts. In *Proc. of the Int. Conf. on Recent Advances on Natural Language Processing (RANLP'07)*, volume 7.

L. Kovács and A. Voronkov. 2013. First-order theorem proving and Vampire. In N. Sharygina and H. Veith, editors, *Computer Aided Verification*, LNCS 8044, pages 1–35. Springer.

G. Lebani and E. Pianta. 2012. Encoding commonsense lexical knowledge into WordNet. In *Proc. of the 6th Global WordNet Conference (GWC 2012)*, pages 159–166.

I. Lopez-Gazpio, M. Maritxalar, A. Gonzalez-Agirre, G. Rigau, L. Uria, and E. Agirre. 2017. Interpretable semantic textual similarity: Finding and explaining differences between sentences. *Knowledge-Based Systems*, 119:186 – 199.

B. D. Mishra, N. Tandon, and P. Clark. 2017. Domain-targeted, high precision knowledge extraction. *Transactions of the Association for Computational Linguistics*, 5(0):233–246.

I. Niles and A. Pease. 2001. Towards a standard upper ontology. In *Proc. of the 2nd Int. Conf. on Formal Ontology in Information Systems (FOIS 2001)*, pages 2–9. ACM.

I. Niles and A. Pease. 2003. Linking lexicons and ontologies: Mapping WordNet to the Suggested Upper Merged Ontology. In *Proc. of the IEEE Int. Conf.*

on Inf. and Knowledge Engin. (IKE 2003), volume 2, pages 412–416. CSREA Press.

P. Ochieng and Swaib S. Kyanda. 2018. Large-scale ontology matching: State-of-the-art analysis. *ACM Comput. Surv.*, 51(4):75:1–75:35.

J. Pathak and C. Chute. 2009. Debugging mappings between biomedical ontologies: Preliminary results from the NCBO bioportal mapping repository. *Nature Proceedings*, 2009:95–98.

L. Prevot, S. Borgo, and A.Oltramari. 2005. Interfacing ontologies and lexical resources. In *Proc. of OntoLex 2005 - Ontologies and Lexical Resources*, pages 91–102.

S. L. Reed and D. B. Lenat. 2002. Mapping ontologies into Cyc. In *Papers from Workshop on Ontologies For The Semantic Web (AAAI 2002)*, pages 1–6. AAAI Press.

J. C.r Dos Reis, C. Pruski, and C. Reynaud-Delaître. 2015. State-of-the-art on mapping maintenance and challenges towards a fully automatic approach. *Expert Systems with Applications*, 42(3):1465 – 1478.

H. Rodríguez, S. Climent, P. Vossen, L. Bloksma, W. Peters, A. Alonge, F. Bertagna, and A. Roventini. 1998. The top-down strategy for building EuroWordNet: Vocabulary coverage, base concepts and top ontology. In *EuroWordNet: A multilingual database with lexical semantic networks*, pages 45–80. Springer.

J. Romero, S. Razniewski, K. Pal, J. Z. Pan, A. Sakhadeo, and G. Weikum. 2019. Commonsense properties from query logs and question answering forums. In *Proc. of the 28th ACM International Conference on Information and Knowledge Management (CIKM '19)*, pages 1411—1420, New York, NY, USA. ACM.

S. Schulz. 2002. E - A brainiac theorem prover. *AI Communications*, 15(2-3):111–126.

R. Speer, J. Chin, and C. Havasi. 2017. ConceptNet 5.5: An open multilingual graph of general knowledge. In *Proc. of the 31st AAAI Conference on Artificial Intelligence (AAAI'17)*, pages 4444—4451. AAAI Press.

N. Tandon, G. de Melo, F. Suchanek, and G. Weikum. 2014. WebChild: Harvesting and organizing commonsense knowledge from the Web. In *Proc. of the 7th ACM Int. Conference on Web Search and Data Mining (WSDM '14)*, pages 523–532. Association for Computing Machinery.

N. Tandon, G. de Melo, and G. Weikum. 2017. WebChild 2.0 : Fine-grained commonsense knowledge distillation. In *Proc. of the 55th Annual Meeting of the Association for Computational Linguistics (ACL 2017)*, pages 115–120.

N. Tandon, C. Hariman, J. Urbani, A. Rohrbach, M. Rohrbach, and G. Weikum. 2016. Commonsense in parts: Mining part-whole relations from the web and image tags. In *Proc. of the 30th AAAI Conf. on Artif. Intell. (AAAI 2016)*, pages 243–250. AAAI Press.

M. Teymourlouie, A. Zaeri, M. Nematbakhsh, M. Thimm, and S. Staab. 2018. Detecting hidden errors in an ontology using contextual knowledge. *Expert Systems with Applications*, 95:312–323.

T. vor der Brück and H. Helbig. 2010. Meronymy extraction using an automated theorem prover. *Journal for Language Technology and Computational Linguistics*, 25(1):57–81.

Peng Wang and Baowen Xu. 2012. Debugging ontology mappings: a static approach. *Computing and Informatics*, 27(1):21–36.

On the Acquisition of WordNet Relations in Portuguese from Pretrained Masked Language Models

Hugo Gonçalo Oliveira
CISUC, Department of Informatics Engineering
University of Coimbra, Portugal,
hroliv@dei.uc.pt

Abstract

This paper studies the application of pretrained BERT in the acquisition of synonyms, antonyms, hypernyms and hyponyms in Portuguese. Masked patterns indicating those relations were compiled with the help of a service for validating semantic relations, and then used for prompting three pretrained BERT models, one multilingual and two for Portuguese (base and large). Predictions for the masks were evaluated in two different test sets. Results achieved by the monolingual models are interesting enough for considering these models as a source for enriching wordnets, especially when predicting hypernyms of nouns. Previously reported performances on prediction were improved with new patterns and with the large model. When it comes to selecting the related word from a set of four options, performance is even better, but not enough for outperforming the selection of the most similar word, as computed with static word embeddings.

1 Introduction

As it happens for many other tasks in the domain of Natural Language Processing (NLP), transformer-based language models have been explored in the acquisition of semantic relations, towards their application in the creation or enrichment of knowledge bases, or on their direct usage as knowledge bases (AlKhamissi et al., 2022). More precisely, having in mind that a typical application of language models is text completion, transformer-based models have been used for completing lexical patterns, in what can be seen as a shortcut to earlier research on the acquisition of relations from textual corpora (e.g., Hearst (1992)). If the focus are lexico-semantic relations, such an approach can be useful for enriching wordnets (Fellbaum, 1998).

In this study, we build on previous efforts, specifically those targeting the Portuguese language (Gonçalo Oliveira, 2022), and evaluate the acquisition of synonymy, antonymy, and hypernymy-hyponymy from BERT models, namely the base and large versions of BERT pretrained exclusively for Portuguese (Souza et al., 2020), and the multilingual BERT. Evaluation is made on two test sets, both covering different variations of the target relations, and starting with source words, but with different goals: in B^2SG (Wilkens et al., 2016), a related word has to be selected from four options; in TALES (Gonçalo Oliveira et al., 2020), one related word has to be predicted. Since the approach is not just dependent on the models, several patterns were handcrafted for each target relation, building on previous work, but also on the adaptation of patterns used in the scope of VARRA (Freitas et al., 2015), a service for searching for and validating instances of lexico-semantic relations by resorting to Portuguese corpora.

After fixing the first argument of each instance as the source word, patterns were used to prompt the BERT models, results were evaluated in the test sets, and conclusions were drawn. Performance with the multilingual model was poor, and the large model is generally the best option. When selecting the correct candidate in B^2SG, results are positive, but end up being outperformed by simply selecting the option that maximises similarity, computed in a model fine-tuned for computing semantic similarity or in static word embeddings. Predicting the related words is more challenging. Nevertheless, top performances are achieved when predicting hypernyms and results can still be useful for suggesting new relation instances to wordnets. Moreover, using the large version of the model and including the VARRA patterns contributed to improvements in previously reported performance in TALES.

In the remainder of the paper, Section 2 overviews related work on the automatic acquisition of semantic relations from text and language models; Section 3 describes the adopted approach in more detail, focusing on the patterns, the test sets and the models; Section 4 reports on the best patterns for each relation and test set, together with their performance; Section 5 summarises the main conclusions and future directions of this work.

2 Related Work

The enrichment of wordnets with relations extracted automatically from corpora has a long tradition, following the work of Hearst (1992), where a set of lexico-syntactic patterns denoting hyponymy was presented and applied to the acquisition of relation instances. To minimise human intervention, hyponymy patterns were learned automatically with distant supervision (Snow et al., 2005), and patterns for other relations were learned and ranked with weak (Pantel and Pennacchiotti, 2006), in both cases using seed examples from Princeton WordNet (Fellbaum, 1998). On relation extraction from Portuguese text (de Abreu et al., 2013), only a minority is focused on lexico-semantic relations. These include rule-based approaches for acquiring hyponymy (de Freitas and Quental, 2007) and part-of (Markov et al., 2014) relations from corpora; as well as other relations from dictionary definitions (Gonçalo Oliveira et al., 2008).

A more recent alternative is to acquire relations from distributional models, such as word embeddings. Even if relations are not explicit, analogies (Mikolov et al., 2013) have been computed for a broad range of syntactic and semantic relations. Besides the unsupervised discovery of hypernymy instances (Chang et al., 2018), the performance of simple analogy was improved by learning to compute related words from multiple examples (Drozd et al., 2016), more specifically, from the BATS test set, which covers synonymy, antonymy and hypernymy, among other syntactic and encyclopaedic relations. The previous were also applied to Portuguese word embeddings, when used to solve lexico-semantic analogies in TALES (Gonçalo Oliveira et al., 2020), a test of with the same format as BATS (Drozd et al., 2016). Despite the low accuracy, among the predictions there are useful suggestions that may be manually added to wordnets, as it happened with OpenWordNet-PT (Gonçalo Oliveira et al., 2021).

But the current paradigm in NLP are transformer-based models, like BERT (Devlin et al., 2019) or GPT (Radford et al., 2019), and there has also been work on using them as knowledge bases (AlKhamissi et al., 2022). Even if they are not ready for explicitly retrieving semantic relations, using the right prompts can result in the acquisition of related words, in what can be seen as a shortcut for earlier corpora-based approaches, i.e., these models are pre-trained in large collections of text and are good at filling blanks (Petroni et al., 2019; Ettinger, 2020), completing sentences (Radford et al., 2019), or computing their likelihood (Goldberg, 2019; Paes, 2021).

Among other efforts, pretrained BERT has been assessed for the presence of relational knowledge using discrete prompts (Petroni et al., 2019); for relation induction (Bouraoui et al., 2020), starting with a small number of patterns and seeds; or for classifying semantic relations based on attention weights (Chizhikova et al., 2022). Some researchers conclude that the prompting approach suits better some relations (e.g., hypernymy) than others (Ettinger, 2020), while others have shown that BERT is not very good at predicting hyponymy relations inherited through transitivity (Lin and Ng, 2022). For Portuguese, recent work exploited BERT for detecting hyponymy pairs (Paes, 2021), ranking automatically extracted relation instances (Gonçalo Oliveira, 2022), or acquiring new instances (Gonçalo Oliveira, 2022).

3 Approach

Gonçalo Oliveira (2022) proposed the acquisition of lexico-semantic relations from BERTimbau (Souza et al., 2020), a BERT model pre-trained for Portuguese, using prompts that indicated the target relations. Since BERT is pretrained on masked language modelling in a large corpus, the pre-trained version should be enough for acquiring lexico-semantic relations. Some considerations were made on setting the prompts and results were evaluated in the TALES (Gonçalo Oliveira et al., 2020) test of lexico-semantic analogies. However, results were limited to using BERTimbau-base and to an initial set of handcrafted patterns. Here, we augment the previous work by considering a second dataset, B^{2}SG, other BERT models, and additional patterns adapted from VARRA (Freitas et al., 2015), which lead to improvements on performance. Moreover, we discuss synonymy in more detail.

3.1 Prompts

Our approach consists of acquiring triples $\langle x_1, r, x_2 \rangle$, where r is a relation predicate and x_1 and x_2 are the relation arguments. This is performed by prompting masked language models (MLMs) with cloze-style patterns indicating the target relation (r), where one of the arguments (x_1) is fixed and the other (x_2) is masked. For instance, the lexical pattern "a x_2 is a type of x_1" typically indicates hypernym(x_1, x_2). Thus, to acquire hypernyms of *dog*, x_1 and x_2 are respectively replaced by the word `dog` and by the `[MASK]` token, resulting in the prompt "`a dog is a type of [MASK]`". Expected predictions for the `[MASK]` would be *animal* or *mammal*.

Useful patterns for acquiring the relations of interest were compiled and made available by Gonçalo Oliveira (2022). However, they did not cover several patterns handcrafted for VARRA (Freitas et al., 2015), a service for searching for and validating instances of semantic relations in Portuguese, through the corpora of the AC/DC project (Santos and Bick, 2000). So, we decided to review the original list and include adaptations of the VARRA patterns. Table 1 illustrates this adaptation with some patterns and the resulting masked prompts. Since VARRA patterns include regular expressions, with some optional and alternative tokens, some adaptations resulted in more than one masked pattern.

3.2 Test Sets

Two different datasets were used for assessing to what extent BERT could predict correctly-related words for the masks. B^{2}SG (Wilkens et al., 2016) is similar to the WordNet-Based Synonymy Test (Freitag et al., 2005), but based on the Portuguese part of BabelNet (Navigli and Ponzetto, 2012) and partially evaluated by humans[1]. It contains frequent Portuguese nouns and verbs (source words) followed by four candidates, out of which only one is related, and is organised in six relations: synonymy (1,171 entries for nouns, 435 for verbs), antonymy (145 nouns, 167 verbs), and hypernymy (758 nouns, 198 verbs), all of them used in this study. The following are examples for noun-synonymy and verb-hypernymy:

- `cataclismo desastre_noun talha_noun obesidade_noun alusão_noun`
  (cataclysm disaster carving obesity allusion)

- `danificar lesar_verb rastrear_verb divertir_verb embaraçar_verb`
  (damage harm track amuse embarrass)

When using source words as the fixed argument, B^{2}SG can be used for assessing whether BERT ranks the related candidate as the best fit for the mask.

TALES (Gonçalo Oliveira et al., 2020) is a test of lexico-semantic analogies, created from the contents of ten Portuguese lexical resources[2]. It covers 14 relation types, but we focus on ten: synonymy (nouns, verbs, and adjectives); antonymy (adjectives); hypernymy and hyponymy (each between abstract nouns, concrete nouns, and verbs). TALES format is similar to BATS (Drozd et al., 2016). For each relation, it includes 50 entries with two columns: a source word and a list of related words (target). The following are examples for antonymy and concrete-hyponymy:

- `novo velho/idoso/entradote`
  (young old/aged/oldish);

- `edifício construção/estrutura/artefato`
  (building construction/structured/artefact)

When using source words as the fixed argument, TALES can be used for assessing whether the predictions for the mask correspond to target words.

Since the adopted naming of the files can be confusing, we note that in the hypernymy files of B^{2}SG, the source word is a hyponym of the correct option, whereas in the hypernymy files of TALES, the source word is a hypernym of the target words.

3.3 Masked Language Models

Three BERT models were used in this study, namely, two versions of BERTimbau (Souza et al., 2020), for Portuguese, and the multilingual version of BERT. All of them are available from the HuggingFace hub and were used with the `transformers`[3] Python library. Specifically, for answering TALES, the `fill-mask` pipeline of this library was used. For B^{2}SG, we resorted to the FitBERT[4] tool, also based on the `transformers` library.

BERTimbau was pretrained in a large corpus of Brazilian Portuguese and has two versions: BERTimbau-base[5], hereafter BERT-base, with 12

[1] B^{2}SG is available from `http://www.inf.ufrgs.br/pln/resource/B2SG.zip`

[2] TALES is available from `https://github.com/NLP-CISUC/PT-LexicalSemantics/tree/master/TALESv1.1`

[3] `https://huggingface.co/transformers/`

[4] `https://github.com/Qordobacode/fitbert`

[5] `neuralmind/bert-base-portuguese-cased`

<table>
<tr><th>Relation</th><th>VARRA</th><th>Masked</th></tr>
<tr><td>Synonym-of</td><td>[lema="PALAVRA1"] "," "isto" "é" "," [lema="PALAVRA2"]</td><td>X_1, isto é, [MASK]</td></tr>
<tr><td>Antonym-of</td><td>[word="nem|seja|quer"] [lema="PALAVRA1"] [lema=","]*
[word="nem|seja|quer"] [lema="PALAVRA2"]</td><td>nem X_1, nem [MASK]
seja X_1, seja [MASK]
quer X_1, quer [MASK]</td></tr>
<tr><td>Hypernym-of</td><td>[lema="PALAVRA1"] [pos="ADJ.*"]* [lema=","]* [lema="tal"]*
"como" [pos="DET.*"]* [pos="ADJ.*"]* [lema="PALAVRA2"]</td><td>X_1, tal como [MASK]</td></tr>
<tr><td>Hypernym-of</td><td>[lema="PALAVRA2" & pos="N.*"] "e" [lema="outro"]
[lema="PALAVRA1" & pos="N.*"]</td><td>X_1 e outro [MASK]</td></tr>
</table>

Table 1: VARRA patterns and their adaptation to masked patterns.

layers and 110M parameters; and BERTimbau-large[6], hereafter BERT-base, with 24 layers and 335M parameters. The multilingual BERT, hereafter BERT-ML[7], was pretrained on Wikipedia for 104 languages, has 12 layers and 110M parameters.

The multilingual model XLM-RoBERTA-large[8] was also explored, but it performed around the random chance in B^{2}SG (25% accuracy), so its results are omitted.

4 Results

This section reports on the best patterns for each test and relation, and discusses the achieved evaluation scores. For each test, scores are also compared with alternative approaches.

4.1 Performance in B^{2}SG

After fixing the source words for the prompt (X_1), BERT models were assessed in the selection of the related word for each entry in B^{2}SG, out of the four options. FitBERT was used for this – given a masked sentence and a list of options, this tool ranks the options according to their suitability for the mask, based on pre-softmax logit scores, as performed by Goldberg (2019).

From the resulting ranks, we compute two metrics: accuracy, i.e., the proportion of entries for which the related word was ranked first; and the average rank of the related word, a continuous value between 1 (top) and 4 (bottom). Table 2 summarises the achieved results. For each relation, it shows the most accurate pattern for each model, followed by its accuracy (Acc) and average rank (Rank) for the three models. When the best pattern was the same for multiple models, the table includes the best patterns overall. Patterns are translated to English, and those adapted from VARRA are marked with a V. The full list of patterns is available from a GitHub repository[9].

The first conclusion is that BERT-large is the best option for every relation but verb-antonymy, where the highest rank is achieved with this model, but not the highest accuracy, which is by BERT-base. This is not surprising because BERT-large has more layers and more parameters, used for better representations that should result in better predictions, even if this is not always the case. On the other hand, performance with BERT-ML is generally above random chance (25%), but consistently lower than for the other models. This only confirms that monolingual models are a better option for this monolingual task.

Performance is better for relations between nouns than for relations between verbs. The best performance is for noun-antonymy, followed by noun-hypernymy, and the worse is for verb-synonymy and verb-antonymy. This suggests either that relations between verbs are more difficult to capture by lexical patterns, or that the best patterns for verb relations are harder to think of.

Since the entries of B^{2}SG are limited to four options, a suitable approach for answering this test would be to simply select the candidate that maximises similarity with the source word. To analyse how the adopted pattern-based approach compares to the previous approach in this test, we resorted to embeddings for selecting the candidate word that was the most similar to the source. Different BERT models and models of static word embeddings were tested, namely: (i) `CLS` token of BERT-base and of BERT-large; (ii) mean pooling of BERT-base and BERT-large tokens; (iii) BERTimbau-large fine-tuned for Semantic Textual Similarity in Portuguese[10]; (iv) 300-sized word2vec (CBOW and Skip-gram) and GloVe embeddings, pretrained for Portuguese (Hartmann et al., 2017). Table 3 puts the accuracies of the previous side-by-side with the best accuracies of the pattern-based approach.

With BERT-large, the best performance for synonymy was slightly improved, but this was not

[6] neuralmind/bert-large-portuguese-cased
[7] bert-base-multilingual-cased
[8] xlm-roberta-large
[9] https://github.com/NLP-CISUC/PT-LexicalSemantics/tree/master/Patterns
[10] rufimelo/bert-large-portuguese-cased-sts

Relation	PoS	Pattern		BERT-ML		BERT-base		BERT-large	
				Acc	Rank	Acc	Rank	Acc	Rank
Synonym-of	N	X_1 é o mesmo que [MASK] (X_1 is the same as [MASK])		0.35	2.22	0.57	1.71	**0.64**	**1.58**
Synonym-of	N	X_1, isto é, [MASK] (X_1, this is, [MASK])	V	0.33	2.23	0.58	1.71	0.62	1.60
Synonym-of	N	X_1 é sinónimo de X_2 (X_1 is a synonym of [MASK])		0.37	2.20	0.50	1.88	0.52	1.82
Synonym-of	V	X_1, isto é, [MASK] (X_1, this is, [MASK])	V	0.32	2.28	0.50	1.80	**0.56**	**1.67**
Synonym-of	V	X_1, ou seja, [MASK] (X_1, i.e., [MASK])	V	0.49	1.85	0.54	1.73	0.37	2.17
Synonym-of	V	querer X_1 é o mesmo que querer [MASK] (willing to X_1 is the same as willing to [MASK])		0.38	2.14	0.47	1.86	0.44	1.86
Antonym-of	N	nem [MASK], nem X_1 (not X_1, nor [MASK])	V	0.44	2.03	0.76	1.64	**0.77**	**1.36**
Antonym-of	N	X_1 é o contrário de [MASK] (X_1 is the opposite of [MASK])		0.46	1.92	0.72	1.44	0.77	1.37
Antonym-of	N	X_1 é diferente de X_2 (X_1 is different than [MASK])		0.40	2.06	0.68	1.51	0.72	1.43
Antonym-of	V	se está a X_1 não está a [MASK] (if it is X_1, it is not [MASK])		0.46	1.95	0.60	1.69	0.62	**1.61**
Antonym-of	V	nem [MASK], nem X_1 (not X_1, nor [MASK])	V	0.29	2.31	**0.63**	1.64	0.61	**1.61**
Antonym-of	V	quer X_1, quer [MASK] (whether X_1 or [MASK])	V	0.30	2.26	0.60	1.71	0.61	1.69
Hypernym-of	N	X_1, isto é, um tipo de [MASK] (X_1, this is, a type of [MASK])	V	0.44	2.02	0.68	1.50	**0.71**	**1.43**
Hypernym-of	N	X_1, isto é, uma espécie de [MASK] (X_1, this is, a kind of [MASK])	V	0.41	2.06	0.63	1.57	0.70	1.44
Hypernym-of	N	X_1 é um tipo de [MASK] (X_1 is a type of [MASK])		0.42	2.04	0.65	1.58	0.67	1.54
Hypernym-of	V	a X_1 ou outras formas de [MASK] (X_1 or other forms of [MASK])	V	0.36	2.20	0.61	1.60	**0.66**	**1.54**
Hypernym-of	V	a X_1 ou outros modos de [MASK] (X_1 or other modes of [MASK])		0.37	2.13	0.57	1.65	0.61	1.56
Hypernym-of	V	[MASK] é hiperónimo de X_1 ([MASK] is a hypernym of X_1)		0.19	2.59	0.47	1.79	0.62	1.60

Table 2: Best performing patterns in B^{2}SG and their performance.

Relation	PoS	BERT-b (patterns)	BERT-l (patterns)	BERT-b (CLS)	BERT-l (CLS)	BERT-b (tokens)	BERT-l (tokens)	BERT-STS	CBOW	Skip	GloVe
Synonym-of	N	0.58	0.64	0.60	0.67	0.59	0.66	0.80	0.71	**0.83**	0.81
Synonym-of	V	0.54	0.56	0.55	0.51	0.54	0.54	**0.75**	0.66	0.68	0.70
Antonym-of	N	0.76	0.77	0.72	0.63	0.69	0.64	0.78	0.70	0.81	**0.83**
Antonym-of	V	0.63	0.62	0.51	0.51	0.49	0.57	0.68	0.67	0.69	**0.71**
Hypernym-of	N	0.68	0.71	0.59	0.61	0.59	0.62	0.76	0.65	0.76	**0.80**
Hypernym-of	V	0.61	0.66	0.52	0.51	0.54	0.54	**0.71**	0.64	0.66	0.70

Table 3: Accuracy of similarity methods in B^{2}SG.

the case for the other relations, suggesting that synonymy is better captured by approaches for computing semantic similarity, even if trained in longer sequences, than with fixed patterns. With BERT-STS, performance was improved for all relations. Despite being fine-tuned for computing the similarity between sentences, the model showed to adapt well-enough to single words, as in B^{2}SG, also confirming the benefits of fine-tuning. But this is was still not enough for outperforming the best static word embeddings, GloVe, in all relations. In fact, BERT-STS only achieved the best performance in two relations, both between verbs (synonymy and hypernymy). This might be related to the higher number of inflections of verbs and how each model handles them, i.e., a different entry for each inflection in static word embeddings *vs* word piece tokenization and contextual embeddings in BERT. Nevertheless, the fact that all target relations are connected to similarity, plus the constrain of only four candidates, make GloVe embeddings the best option overall for B^{2}SG, with the top performance in half of the relations.

4.2 Performance in TALES

With TALES, we wanted to assess how well the pattern-based approach could be used for actually predicting the related words, not restricted to a set of options. For each prompt, again, we fix the source word and use the models for predicting words for the mask. Based on the predictions, two metrics are computed, namely: accuracy, i.e., the proportion of entries for which the first prediction was correct; accuracy@10, i.e., the proportion of entries for which a correct prediction was among the top-10 predictions.

Table 4 summarises the achieved results. For

each relation, it shows the most accurate pattern for each BERTimbau model, followed by its accuracy (Acc) and accuracy@10 (Acc@10) for the three models. When the best pattern is the same for both, the table includes the two best patterns. Patterns are translated to English, and those adapted from VARRA are followed by a V.

As expected, when predictions are not constrained to four options, performance is much lower. BERT-large tends to perform better than BERT-base, except for hyponymy relations. i.e., when predicting hypernyms. Curiously, top performances are achieved for these relations, between abstract and concrete nouns, which is in line with previous work for English (Ettinger, 2020). A probable cause is the smaller number of hypernyms when compared to hyponyms. On the other hand, the lowest performances are in the prediction of synonym adjectives, concrete hyponyms, and verb hypernyms.

We note that some of the top performances were achieved by VARRA patterns, including for hypernymy and hyponymy. A particularly productive pattern was "`um(a)` X_1`, isto é, um tipo de [MASK]`", which achieved the best performance in abstract and concrete hyponymy. In addition to the new patterns, BERT-large also contributed to an overall improvement of the performances reported in previous work (Gonçalo Oliveira, 2022). We highlight the improvements on the relations between abstract nouns, specifically, an increase of 0.26 points in the accuracy of abstract hyponymy and of 0.14 in abstract hypernymy.

As in previous work, we compared the performances achieved by this approach with those of analogy-solving methods in static word embeddings. Table 5 puts the best accuracies with the pattern-based approach side-by-side the best accuracies with the four analogy-solving methods used by Drozd et al. (2016) – Similarity, 3CosAdd, 3CosAvg, LRCos – in the same three models of static word embeddings used in the B^2SG.

There are three relations for which performance is better with static word embeddings. Two of them are noun-synonymy and adjective-synonymy, which confirms the anticipated challenge of capturing synonymy with a single lexical pattern. The third relation is verb-hypernymy, for which there were no patterns in VARRA, and we could not add many more to the used list. Using BERT-large made it possible to improve the performance for concrete-hypernymy.

5 Conclusion

This paper reports on the experimentation of BERT models for Portuguese for answering relation tests, by prompting them with patterns that indicate synonymy, antonymy, hypernymy and hyponymy relations. Our first conclusion was that monolingual models perform substantially better than a multilingual model. Second, when it comes to selecting the related word from a limited set of options, the proposed approach performs ok, even if better for relations between nouns than between verbs. However, this turns out not being so useful, because it is outperformed by simply selecting the most similar word, as computed in a fine-tuned BERT or in static word embeddings. Third, this approach can be used for predicting related words, in this case, better for noun hypernyms, as in previous work for English (Ettinger, 2020). We also note the positive impact of using BERT-large and of including the patterns of a relation validation service, which enabled the improvement of previously reported results in the same dataset.

At the same time, there is still much room for improvement, and performances achieved suggest that it might be risky to create or enrich a knowledge base in a completely automatic fashion. Yet, given that the reported evaluation ends up being limited by the contents of the test sets, in the future, it could be interesting to test how far one could go by adopting this approach for the creation of a knowledge base completely from scratch. Additional conclusions could be taken from manually evaluating a sample of extracted instances. We should, nevertheless, look at BERT as an alternative source of knowledge, capable of providing suggestions for enriching knowledge bases, even if they need to be manually-validated before actual inclusion. This would be similar to what happened in the enrichment of OpenWordNet-PT (Gonçalo Oliveira et al., 2021), with suggestions computed from static word embeddings.

Finally, given that the prompts play a key role on this approach, it is always on our mind to test more and more patterns. So far, performance could be improved with the inclusion of patterns from a relation validation service, but additional patterns, potentially better, could be discovered by processing large corpora, as others did (Jiang et al., 2020;

Relation	PoS	Pattern	BERT-ML Acc	BERT-ML Acc@10	BERT-base Acc	BERT-base Acc@10	BERT-large Acc	BERT-large Acc@10
Synonym-of	N	X_1 é sinónimo de [MASK] (X_1 is a synonym of [MASK])	0.02	0.20	**0.28**	0.64	0.20	**0.70**
Synonym-of	N	X_1 é o mesmo que [MASK] (X_1 is the same as [MASK])	0.04	0.08	0.20	0.58	0.20	0.66
Synonym-of	V	X_1 é o mesmo que [MASK] (X_1 is the same as[MASK])	0.12	0.24	0.12	0.80	**0.34**	**0.90**
Synonym-of	V	estar a X_1 é o mesmo que estar a [MASK] (to be X_1 is the same to be [MASK])	0.18	0.44	0.20	0.68	0.26	0.82
Synonym-of	ADJ	estar X_1 é o mesmo que estar [MASK]. (being X_1 is the same as being [MASK])	0.14	0.42	0.06	0.46	**0.24**	0.54
Synonym-of	ADJ	ser X_1 é o mesmo que ser [MASK]. (being X_1 is the same as being [MASK])	0.06	0.24	0.14	0.54	0.22	**0.64**
Antonym-of	ADJ	ser [MASK] é o contrário de ser X_1 (being X_1 is the opposite of being [MASK])	0.08	0.22	0.26	0.40	**0.38**	**0.48**
Antonym-of	ADJ	nem X_1, nem [MASK] (not X_1, nor [MASK]) *V*	0.02	0.06	0.34	0.40	0.34	0.46
Hypernym-of	Abstract	a [MASK] é um tipo de X_1 (the [MASK] is a type of X_1)	0.08	0.24	0.22	0.60	**0.38**	0.66
Hypernym-of	Abstract	uma [MASK], isto é, um tipo de X_1 (a [MASK], this is, a type of X_1) *V*	0.04	0.32	0.32	**0.70**	0.26	0.62
Hypernym-of	Concrete	o [MASK], que é um tipo de X_1 (the [MASK], which is a type of X_1) *V*	0.08	0.20	0.20	0.54	**0.24**	**0.56**
Hypernym-of	Concrete	a [MASK] é um tipo de X_1 (the [MASK] is a type of X_1)	0.04	0.12	0.14	0.38	0.22	0.36
Hypernym-of	V	como [MASK] e outros modos de X_1 (like [MASK] and other modes of X_1)	0.00	0.04	0.08	0.54	**0.20**	**0.58**
Hypernym-of	V	como [MASK] ou outras maneiras de <r> (like [MASK] and other manners of X_1)	0.00	0.02	0.12	0.42	0.08	0.24
Hyponym-of	Abstract	um X_1, isto é, um tipo de [MASK] (a X_1, this is, a type of [MASK]) *V*	0.02	0.46	0.24	0.60	**0.40**	0.62
Hyponym-of	Abstract	uma X_1, isto é, uma espécie de [MASK] (a X_1, this is, a kind of [MASK]) *V*	0.06	0.38	0.12	**0.66**	0.28	0.64
Hyponym-of	Concrete	uma X_1, isto é, um tipo de [MASK] (a X_1, this is, a type of [MASK]) *V*	0.10	0.40	**0.60**	**0.88**	0.56	0.80
Hyponym-of	Concrete	um X_1, isto é, um tipo de [MASK] (a X_1, this is, a type of [MASK]) *V*	0.06	0.32	0.58	**0.88**	0.58	**0.88**
Hyponym-of	V	como X_1 ou outras maneiras de [MASK] (like X_1 and other manners of [MASK])	0.18	0.54	**0.24**	0.64	0.18	**0.70**
Hyponym-of	V	X_1 é como [MASK], mas (X_1 is like [MASK], but)	0.08	0.10	0.08	0.24	0.12	0.50

Table 4: Best performing patterns in TALES and their performance.

Relation	PoS	BERT-base	BERT-large	Sim	3CosAdd	3CosAvg	LRCos
Synonym-of	N	0.28	0.20	0.28^{*}	0.18^{*}	$0.32^{\times}$	$\mathbf{0.38}^{+}$
Synonym-of	V	0.12	**0.34**	0.20^{+}	0.12^{+}	0.24^{+}	0.30^{+}
Synonym-of	ADJ	0.06	0.24	0.26^{*}	0.10^{*}	$\mathbf{0.28}^{+}$	0.26^{+}
Antonym-of	ADJ	0.26	**0.38**	0.20^{*}	0.14^{*}	0.24^{+}	0.28^{*}
Hypernym-of	Abstract	0.22	**0.38**	0.20^{+}	$0.06^{\times +}$	0.20^{+}	0.16^{*+}
Hypernym-of	Concrete	0.20	**0.24**	0.18^{+}	$0.10^{\times}$	0.20^{*}	0.20^{+}
Hypernym-of	V	0.08	0.20	0.14^{*}	$0.08^{\times}$	0.12^{+}	$\mathbf{0.22}^{*}$
Hyponym-of	Abstract	0.24	**0.40**	0.08^{*}	0.08^{*}	0.10^{*}	0.12^{*}
Hyponym-of	Concrete	**0.60**	0.56	0.10^{+}	$0.04^{\times *+}$	0.14^{+}	$0.28^{\times}$
Hyponym-of	V	**0.24**	0.18	0.14^{+}	0.16^{*}	$0.16^{\times +}$	0.22^{+}

Table 5: Accuracy of analogy-solving methods in TALES. $^{\times}$GloVe; *word2vec-skip; $^{+}$word2vec-cbow.

Bouraoui et al., 2020). In any case, having in mind reproducibility and future improvements, the list of patterns was made available for anyone willing to use it.

Acknowledgements

This work was funded by national funds through FCT, within the scope of the project CISUC (UID/CEC/00326/2020) and by European Social Fund, through the Regional Operational Program Centro 2020. It is also based upon work from COST Action CA18209 Nexus Linguarum, supported by COST (European Cooperation in Science and Technology). `http://www.cost.eu/`.

References

Badr AlKhamissi, Millicent Li, Asli Celikyilmaz, Mona Diab, and Marjan Ghazvininejad. 2022. A review on language models as knowledge bases. `https://arxiv.org/abs/2204.06031`.

Zied Bouraoui, Jose Camacho-Collados, and Steven Schockaert. 2020. Inducing relational knowledge from BERT. In *Proc of AAAI Conference on Artificial Intelligence*, pages 7456–7463. AAAI Press.

Haw-Shiuan Chang, Ziyun Wang, Luke Vilnis, and Andrew McCallum. 2018. Distributional inclusion vector embedding for unsupervised hypernymy detection. In *Proceedings of the 2018 Conference of the North American Chapter of the Association for Com-*

putational Linguistics: Human Language Technologies, Volume 1 (Long Papers), pages 485–495.

Anastasia Chizhikova, Sanzhar Murzakhmetov, Oleg Serikov, Tatiana Shavrina, and Mikhail Burtsev. 2022. Attention understands semantic relations. In *Proceedings of the Language Resources and Evaluation Conference*, pages 4040–4050, Marseille, France. European Language Resources Association.

Sandra Collovini de Abreu, Tiago Luis Bonamigo, and Renata Vieira. 2013. A review on relation extraction with an eye on Portuguese. *Journal of the Brazilian Computer Society*, 19(4):553–571.

Maria Cláudia de Freitas and Violeta Quental. 2007. Subsídios para a elaboração automática de taxonomias. In *Anais do XXVII Congresso da SBC*, pages 1585–1594.

Jacob Devlin, Ming-Wei Chang, Kenton Lee, and Kristina Toutanova. 2019. BERT: Pre-training of deep bidirectional transformers for language understanding. In *Proc 2019 Conf of North American Chapter of the Association for Computational Linguistics: Human Language Technologies*, pages 4171–4186. ACL.

Aleksandr Drozd, Anna Gladkova, and Satoshi Matsuoka. 2016. Word embeddings, analogies, and machine learning: Beyond king - man + woman = queen. In *Proc 26th International Conference on Computational Linguistics: Technical papers COLING 2016*, COLING 2016, pages 3519–3530.

Allyson Ettinger. 2020. What BERT is not: Lessons from a new suite of psycholinguistic diagnostics for language models. *Transactions of the ACL*, 8:34–48.

Christiane Fellbaum, editor. 1998. *WordNet: An Electronic Lexical Database (Language, Speech, and Communication)*. The MIT Press.

Dayne Freitag, Matthias Blume, John Byrnes, Edmond Chow, Sadik Kapadia, Richard Rohwer, and Zhiqiang Wang. 2005. New experiments in distributional representations of synonymy. In *Procs 9th Conference on Computational Natural Language Learning (CoNLL-2005)*, pages 25–32, Ann Arbor, Michigan. ACL.

Cláudia Freitas, Diana Santos, Hugo Gonçalo Oliveira, and Violeta Quental. 2015. VARRA: Validação, Avaliação e Revisão de Relações semânticas no AC/DC. In *Pesquisas e perspetivas em linguistica de corpus (Livro do IX Encontro de Linguística de Corpus, 2010)*, ELC 2010, pages 199–232. Mercado de Letras, Rio Grande do Sul, Brasil.

Yoav Goldberg. 2019. Assessing BERT's syntactic abilities. `https://arxiv.org/abs/1901.05287`.

Hugo Gonçalo Oliveira. 2022. Drilling lexico-semantic knowledge in Portuguese from BERT. In *Computational Processing of the Portuguese Language – 14th International Conf, PROPOR 2022*, volume 12037 of *LNCS*, pages 387—397. Springer.

Hugo Gonçalo Oliveira, Diana Santos, Paulo Gomes, and Nuno Seco. 2008. PAPEL: A dictionary-based lexical ontology for Portuguese. In *Proceedings of Computational Processing of the Portuguese Language - 8th International Conference (PROPOR 2008)*, volume 5190 of *LNCS/LNAI*, pages 31–40, Aveiro, Portugal. Springer.

Hugo Gonçalo Oliveira, Tiago Sousa, and Ana Alves. 2020. TALES: Test set of Portuguese lexical-semantic relations for assessing word embeddings. In *Procs of ECAI 2020 Workshop on Hybrid Intelligence for Natural Language Processing Tasks (HI4NLP 2020)*, volume 2693 of *CEUR Workshop Proceedings*, pages 41–47. CEUR-WS.org.

Hugo Gonçalo Oliveira. 2022. Exploring transformers for ranking Portuguese semantic relations. In *Proceedings of the 13th Language Resources and Evaluation Conference*, LREC 2022, pages 2573–2582, Marseille, France. ELRA.

Hugo Gonçalo Oliveira, Fredson Silva de Souza Aguiar, and Alexandre Rademaker. 2021. On the Utility of Word Embeddings for Enriching OpenWordNet-PT. In *Proceedings of 3rd Conference on Language, Data and Knowledge (LDK 2021)*, volume 93 of *OASIcs*, pages 21:1–21:13, Dagstuhl, Germany. Schloss Dagstuhl – Leibniz-Zentrum für Informatik.

Nathan S. Hartmann, Erick R. Fonseca, Christopher D. Shulby, Marcos V. Treviso, Jéssica S. Rodrigues, and Sandra M. Aluísio. 2017. Portuguese word embeddings: Evaluating on word analogies and natural language tasks. In *Proc of 11th Brazilian Symposium in Information and Human Language Technology (STIL 2017)*.

Marti A. Hearst. 1992. Automatic acquisition of hyponyms from large text corpora. In *Proc 14th Conference on Computational Linguistics*, COLING 92, pages 539–545. ACL.

Zhengbao Jiang, Frank F Xu, Jun Araki, and Graham Neubig. 2020. How can we know what language models know? *Transactions of the Association for Computational Linguistics*, 8:423–438.

Ruixi Lin and Hwee Tou Ng. 2022. Does bert know that the is-a relation is transitive? In *Proceedings of the 60th Annual Meeting of the Association for Computational Linguistics (Volume 2: Short Papers)*, pages 94–99.

Ilia Markov, Nuno Mamede, and Jorge Baptista. 2014. Automatic Identification of Whole-Part Relations in Portuguese. In *Proceedings of 3rd Symposium on Languages, Applications and Technologies*, volume 38 of *OASICS*, pages 225–232. Schloss Dagstuhl–Leibniz-Zentrum fuer Informatik.

Tomas Mikolov, Kai Chen, Greg Corrado, and Jeffrey Dean. 2013. Efficient estimation of word representations in vector space. In *Proc of Workshop track of ICLR*.

Roberto Navigli and Simone Paolo Ponzetto. 2012. BabelNet: The automatic construction, evaluation and application of a wide-coverage multilingual semantic network. *Artificial Intelligence*, 193:217–250.

Gabriel Escobar Paes. 2021. Detecção de hiperônimos com bert e padrões de hearst. Master's thesis, Universidade Federal de Mato Grosso do Sul.

Patrick Pantel and Marco Pennacchiotti. 2006. Espresso: Leveraging generic patterns for automatically harvesting semantic relations. In *Procs of 21st International Conference on Computational Linguistics and 44th annual meeting of the Association for Computational Linguistics*, pages 113–120, Sydney, Australia. ACL Press.

Fabio Petroni, Tim Rocktäschel, Sebastian Riedel, Patrick Lewis, Anton Bakhtin, Yuxiang Wu, and Alexander Miller. 2019. Language models as knowledge bases? In *Proc 2019 Conf on Empirical Methods in Natural Language Processing and 9th Intl Joint Conf on Natural Language Processing (EMNLP-IJCNLP)*, pages 2463–2473. ACL.

Alec Radford, Jeffrey Wu, Rewon Child, David Luan, Dario Amodei, and Ilya Sutskever. 2019. Language models are unsupervised multitask learners. *OpenAI Blog*, 1(8):9.

Diana Santos and Eckhard Bick. 2000. Providing Internet access to Portuguese corpora: the AC/DC project. In *Proceedings of 2nd International Conference on Language Resources and Evaluation*, LREC 2000, pages 205–210.

Rion Snow, Daniel Jurafsky, and Andrew Ng. 2005. Learning syntactic patterns for automatic hypernym discovery. *Advances in neural information processing systems*, 17:1297–1304.

Fábio Souza, Rodrigo Nogueira, and Roberto Lotufo. 2020. BERTimbau: Pretrained BERT models for Brazilian Portuguese. In *Proc of Brazilian Conf on Intelligent Systems (BRACIS 2020)*, volume 12319 of *LNCS*, pages 403–417. Springer.

Rodrigo Wilkens, Leonardo Zilio, Eduardo Ferreira, and Aline Villavicencio. 2016. B2SG: a TOEFL-like task for Portuguese. In *Procs 10th International Conference on Language Resources and Evaluation (LREC 2016)*. ELRA.

Wordnet for Definition Augmentation with Encoder-Decoder Architecture

Konrad Wojtasik, Arkadiusz Janz, Bartłomiej Alberski, Maciej Piasecki
Wrocław University of Science and Technology
{konrad.wojtasik|arkadiusz.janz}@pwr.edu.pl

Abstract

Data augmentation is a difficult task in Natural Language Processing. Simple methods that can be relatively easily applied in other domains like insertion, deletion or substitution, mostly result in changing the sentence meaning significantly and obtaining an incorrect example. Wordnets are potentially a perfect source of rich and high quality data that when integrated with the powerful capacity of generative models can help to solve this complex task. In this work, we use plWordNet, which is a wordnet of the Polish language, to explore the capability of encoder-decoder architectures in data augmentation of sense glosses. We discuss the limitations of generative methods and perform qualitative review of generated data samples.

1 Introduction

Transformer models have appeared to be very successful in solving a large variety of Natural Language Processing tasks and applications. The research on neural language modeling has been intensified in recent years and has yielded many new developments, such as pre-trained autoregressive language models for text generation. Text generation models such as BART (Lewis et al., 2020), GPT (Brown et al., 2020) or T5 (Raffel et al., 2020) have increased the performance even further, due to their few-shot abilities (Radford et al., 2019).

The knowledge resources such as wordnets (Miller et al., 1990) are often incomplete and still require constant development, especially for low-resourced languages. In Słowosieć (Dziob et al., 2019) (also called plWordNet) – a wordnet of the Polish language, one of the largest wordnets in the world – over 40% senses still lack a definition, and over 60% of senses do not have any sense use example. This area might be addressed by utilising large language models pre-trained on text generation tasks. Adding missing definitions and sense use examples is a crucial task for further wordnet development.

The definition generation problem is tightly interconnected with Word Sense Disambiguation (WSD) problem, as the words have different meanings in different contexts. The modern language models have significantly improved WSD performance in recent years. Transformer-based models such as BERT (Devlin et al., 2019) have proved to be very effective in contextual word sense recognition (Bevilacqua et al., 2021). While very effective, large language models require at least a small data sample to effectively fine-tune them for the WSD task. Nevertheless, large pre-trained language models with billions of parameters have been shown to require less training data to effectively tune them for downstream tasks (Chowdhery et al., 2022).

In this paper, we investigate generation abilities of large pre-trained language models in the task of wordnet gloss generation for the Polish language. We treat this problem as a data augmentation problem, as some senses in under-resourced wordnets are missing their definitions. We evaluate gloss generation performance on the example of Polish wordnet – Słowosieć (Dziob et al., 2019) – in the version 4.2.[1]

2 Related Work

The acquisition and completion of missing sense glosses has been addressed in the literature in many different ways. Enrichment of synset glosses in wordnets can be partially achieved by utilising machine translation models (Chakravarthi et al., 2019). However, these approaches do not take into account the discrepancy between sense inventories in different languages, as some senses do not exist in the source or target languages. Thus, an automated translation of Princeton WordNet glosses (Miller et al., 1990) to other language might not be able

[1]The code and the training data, as well as the generated sense definitions, are available at https://gitlab.clarin-pl.eu/knowledge-extraction/prototypes/gwc-t5-wordnet.

to completely solve the task of gloss completion. The other approaches rely on interlinking the wordnets with external resources and semantic networks such as multilingual thesauri in linked open data, Wikipedia[2], Wikidata[3], BabelNet (Navigli et al., 2021), or with Open Multilingual WordNet grid (Bond and Foster, 2013). Some solutions solve the problem as a joint task in which translations and potential glosses available in large semantic networks are analysed with WSD algorithms to increase the accuracy of gloss acquisition (Camacho-Collados et al., 2019). Still, an overall coverage of senses is strongly dependent on the target domain of application, and for specific domains the WSD models are biased towards more frequent senses. The closest to our work are generative approaches in which the encoder–decoder architectures are used to generate definitions in an autoregressive manner and treating the language models as knowledge bases (Huang et al., 2021; Mickus et al., 2021; Bevilacqua et al., 2020; Zhang et al., 2022). The approaches such as (Huang et al., 2021) utilise large pre-trained transformers, mainly T5 (Raffel et al., 2020) and BART (Lewis et al., 2020) models, to generate definitions. The solution proposed in (Huang et al., 2021) is the closest to our work since it's based on the same pre-trained T5 transformer architecture, but the authors have added reranking models to control the specificity of generated sense definitions. In our work we expand the research on generative definition acquisition and investigate the performance of raw generative language models for the Polish language. The Japanese corpus for definition generation (Huang et al., 2022) also provides words with usage and definition, but it was generated via linking Wikidata items with sentences in Wikipedia articles.

3 Methods

3.1 Text Generation Models

Text generation task is formally defined as conditional sequence generation $\mathcal{Y} = (y_1, y_2, \ldots, y_M)$, where a model should predict sequence $\mathcal{Y}$ conditioned on the sequential input data $\mathcal{X} = (x_1, x_2, \ldots, x_P)$, with $p(\mathcal{Y}|\mathcal{X}) = p(y1, y2, \ldots, y_M|\mathcal{X})$. The models for text generation task usually descend from *sequence-to-sequence* architectures with sequential *encoders* and sequential *decoders*. Modern text generators such as BART (Lewis et al., 2020), T5 (Raffel et al., 2020), or GPT (Radford et al., 2018, 2019; Brown et al., 2020) utilise transformer networks and autoregressive decoders. In this work, we investigate text generation abilities of pre-trained T5 language models for Polish language, more specifically the `plT5` language models (Chrabrowa et al., 2022) pre-trained on Polish corpora.

[2]https://www.wikipedia.org/

[3]https://www.wikidata.org

3.2 Sense Definitions and Sense Examples

Following (Huang et al., 2021), we prepared a dataset of sense definitions and sense use examples for target words selected for the task of definition generation. Princeton WordNet has a great collection of glosses and sense examples, which have been frequently used in various natural language processing tasks, including word sense disambiguation (Huang et al., 2019; Bevilacqua and Navigli, 2020). Polish sense inventories, such as plWordNet, do not provide complete description of senses in terms of their glosses and sense use examples. Thus, we decided to incorporate sense annotated corpora from (Janz et al., 2022) and (Hajnicz and Bartosiak, 2019) to obtain a larger and diversified collection of sense definitions and their usage examples.

3.3 T5 for Definition Generation

Let $\mathcal{D} = \{(w, D, E)\}_{i=1}^{N}$ will be a dataset with instances representing a sense use example E and sense definitions D of a target word w and its sense $s \in \mathcal{S}_w$. Glosses D and a sense use examples E are defined as sequences of tokens $D = (d_1, d_2, \ldots, d_T)$ and $E = (e_1, e_2, \ldots, e_M)$. The senses and their textual descriptions are obtained from the sense inventory $s \in \mathcal{S}$. We use the data from plWordNet and additional sense-annotated corpora (see Section 3.2).

To fine-tune a model to the definition generation task for target words and their sense use contexts, we prepare the training data according to the methodology presented in (Raffel et al., 2020; Zhang et al., 2022) for the T5 model. A single training example consists of a word and its sense use example concatenated with a colon, e.g. „*cat: the cat was jumping on the bed in the middle of the night*". The target for T5 model represents the definition of the sense expressed by the given sense use example („*feline mammal usually having thick soft fur and no ability to roar, domestic cats*").

We split the dataset into two parts $(\mathcal{D}_L, \mathcal{D}_T)$, where $\mathcal{D}_L$ is a labeled training corpus for text generation model, and $\mathcal{D}_T$ is the held-out testing sample with lemmas outside the training set – lexical data split. The generation task is defined as follows.

$$p(D|E, w) = \prod_{t=1}^{T} p(D_t|w, D_{t-1}, \dots, D_1, E)$$

4 Evaluation

Output of generative models was a definition for a given word in relation to the particular context and the evaluation of such an output is a nontrivial task. In language generation different evaluation metrics are used. We chose BLEU (Papineni et al., 2002) and ROUGE (Lin, 2004) metrics which are widely applied in many benchmarks. This automatic evaluation gave us information, if a model is overfitting to provided data or not. We could also estimate the difference between basic and large models performance on the test set. But to evaluate definitions properly, syntactic-level metrics are not sufficient. That is why we also performed manual validation of the generated definitions together with doing error analysis of the model's predictions. The manual validation was performed by professional lexicographers specialising in wordnets. We used a subset of error tags from (Huang et al., 2021) as a basis for our manual evaluation, namely:

- `self-reference` – error is assigned when a word being defined is described by using the word itself,
- `completely-wrong` – the word being defined has been assigned a definition representing as wrong sense,
- `partially-wrong` – some part of the generated definition is incorrect or refers to a different sense,
- `incoherent` – the definition contains contradictory parts.

To decrease memorisation impact on our evaluation, we evaluated the predictions by ensuring both the lemmas and the definitions in our test data were not included in the training dataset. We also provide the results with respect to part-of-speech of analysed lemmas.

Hard evaluation In this setting, a lexicographer accepts a generated definition if and only if any of the defined errors has not occurred in it.

Soft evaluation A generated definition is considered to be correct, even if the `self-reference` or `partially-wrong` errors have been spotted, but other errors are not observed.

4.1 Experimental Setting

We fine-tuned a pre-trained plT5 (Chrabrowa et al., 2022) generative language model for the task of definition generation. We trained `plT5-base` and `plT5-large` models available on HuggingFace[4] model repository. They have correspondingly 220 millions a parameters and 770 millions parameters. We trained them on single Nvidia RTX3090 GPU. The batch size for `plT5-base` was set to 16 and the model was trained for 40 epochs. In case of `plT5-large`, the batch size was set to 4 and the model was trained for 15 epochs, due to increased computational complexity of the model. We applied batch gradient accumulation steps for every 8 the batches and set a learning rate to 1e-4. The prompts of pre-selected T5 language models were set to `'[generate definition]'`.

4.2 Datasets

Training Data To train the models we used the following sense annotated corpora. The main dataset used for training was created from plWordNet's sense definitions and sense use examples.

- Verb's Valency Dictionary – Składnica (SK) is a sense-annotated treebank (Hajnicz, 2014) used as a benchmark dataset for knowledge-based WSD solutions for Polish language (Kędzia et al., 2015). The dataset was updated at *PolEval's WSD competition Task 3* (Janz et al.).
- The Corpus of Wroclaw University of Science and Technology (KPWr) (Broda et al., 2012) – contains the documents from various sources and represents different genres and domains. The manual sense annotation was based on a lexical sampling approach – the occurrences of words pre-selected by experts were manually annotated with senses in relation to their contexts (Broda et al., 2012; Kędzia et al., 2015). In (Janz et al.) the corpus

[4] `https://huggingface.co`

was extended with full-text sense annotation – 100 documents were manually tagged with plWordNet senses.

- Sherlock Holmes: The Adventure of The Speckled Band (SPEC) by Sir Arthur Conan Doyle, translated to Polish by a team of experts as a part of The NTU Multilingual Corpus (Tan and Bond, 2011). The corpus was manually tagged both with morphological information and sense tags (Janz et al.).

All of the aforementioned datasets are fully compatible with sense inventory of plWordNet 4.2, as they were described in (Janz et al., 2022). To improve the coverage of senses, we incorporated additional silver dataset built upon plWordNet Corpus 10.0 (Kocoń and Gawor, 2019), in short KGR10.

- Data Sample for Monosemous Lemmas – the KGR10 corpus is a corpus built from web-based data sources, covering a broad range of styles, genres and topics. It contains over 4 billion tokens with over 18 million distinct words. We synthesized a collection of additional sense use examples by extracting context windows from KGR10 corpus for senses representing potentially monosemous lemmas. To select monosemous lemmas we used plWordNet's sense inventory, mainly its multi-word expressions and lemmas with single sense and lower occurrence frequency in the corpus.

Test Data We prepared two distinct test sets for the evaluation. The first test set was prepared for manual evaluation, and the second test set was created to perform automated evaluation using BLEU and Rouge-L scores.

To create the test set for automated evaluation, we have split the data from plWordNet and sense-annotated corpora into training part and test part. We acquired almost 237k examples with words, usage examples and definitions. From those examples around 213k were acquired from plWordNet, 6.2k from The Corpus of Wroclaw University of Science and Technology (KPWr), 16k from Verb's Valency Dictionary, and 1.5k Sherlock Holmes. To create the test set, we randomly sampled 10k examples.

The test set for manual evaluation contained 146 examples with words and representative usage examples. We sampled these examples from the test set prepared for automated evaluation. All usage examples were new and were not seen by the model before. We split the data by words according to the following criteria. There were 102 instances that were already provided with expected sense definition in plWordNet. We denoted this subset as *WordNet+*. The subset of 44 words that had no definition in plWordNet was denoted as *WordNet-*. The examples were given to experts to measure defining capabilities of language models.

5 Results and Discussion

The results indicate that there is a significant difference between *base* and *large* model sizes. Our automatic evaluation results on 10k test set containing definitions from plWordNet, showed that BLEU score (see figure 1) and Rouge-L score (see figure 2) were getting better over time at higher pace for the *large* model than for the *base* model. The highest scores achieved after 13k iterations were (*0.31*, *0.44*) and (*0.44*, *0.54*) for BLEU score and Rouge-L score, respectively. The final difference in scores was greater than *0.1* for both metrics.

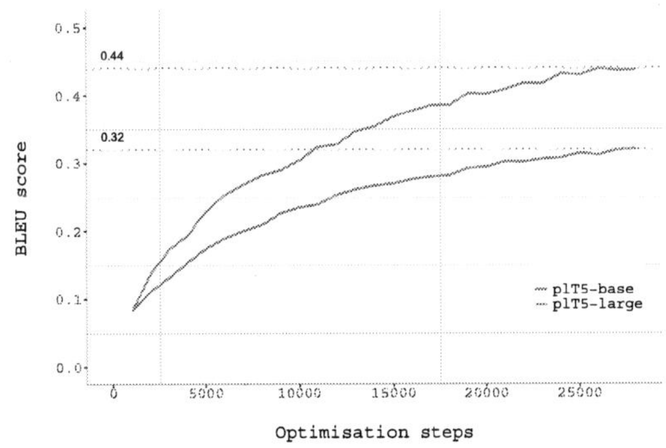

Figure 1: Evaluation of text generation models in the task of definition generation. We plot the performance of fine-tuned language models measured by BLEU score with respect to optimisation steps during fine-tuning. One iteration is equal to 256 shown examples.

The examples of generated definitions for provided contexts (see Table 1) showed different definition patterns. The first example represents the word *to devastate*. The model generated a correct definition explaining the meaning of analysed word. The second example, the word *to solve*, was explained using the word itself and passed the soft evaluation. However, the generated definition did not pass the hard evaluation test (*definiendum* case). The third example, the word *covered by*, had its meaning correctly explained by the generated definition in

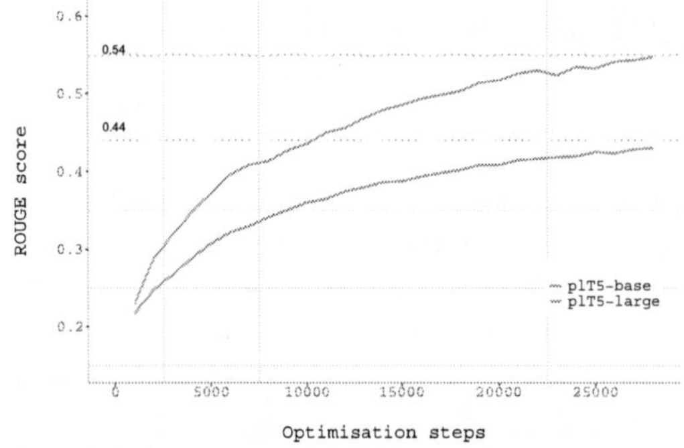

Figure 2: Evaluation of text generation models in the task of definition generation. We plot the performance of fine-tuned language models measured by ROUGE score with respect to optimisation steps during fine-tuning. One iteration is equal to 256 shown examples.

the given context, and the model did not repeat the existing definition from plWordNet. The fourth example, the word *tapir*, shows that the model was able to use previously acquired knowledge from Wikipedia pages or other knowledge bases (available at pre-training time) and created a new definition for that word, even though it was not present in plWordNet.

We also provided some examples of errors in the generated definitions (see Table 2). For the word *anesthetized*, the model resolved the first part of the definition correctly, but the second part was contradictory, because a person who is under anesthesia is out of touch with reality. The second example, the word *to guide*, was defined using the word itself, and was classified by the expert as incorrect. The third example represents the word *get involved*. It was defined in an unspecific way, and semantically the definition is only partially correct. In the fourth example, the word *snarky* not only defines itself, but the definition is wrong and the word is used in an incorrect sense.

The overall results are presented in Table 4. We measured the average accuracy of the model's predictions according to experts. There was a substantial difference between plT5-base and plT5-large models, where the larger model was better by more than 10 percent points in the overall evaluation. The words that existed already in plWordNet were easier to be defined and the unseen words seemed to be more challenging for the model. The main reason for that is that the model was able to memorize well seen texts and generated definitions accordingly, but for the unseen examples, we expected the model to generate definitions for meanings that have not been seen before.gw There were cases, where the model was able to access knowledge from pre-training corpora and use it to generate definition for new words. The accuracy difference between word examples that were not defined in plWordNet for hard evaluation and soft evaluation is almost doubled for both models. This may be the result of the model's understanding of the main concept of the word it defines, but at the same time hallucinating the definition, resulting in a formally incorrect definition. Another reason why the model performs poorly on unseen examples is that the sense-annotated resources for Polish language may be insufficient for learning to define senses completely unrelated to the training data and existing in completely different areas of plWordNet's lexico-semantic structure. This issue will be investigated in our future work.

6 Conclusion

The plWordNet definitions and usage examples are perfect data source for fine-tuning T5 generative models. Fine-tuned models are able to understand the new task and partially to generate definitions of unseen word senses. There is a significant difference in performance for seen and unseen words. Models are able to memorize definitions for examples in training set and modify them. Large model performs better than base, not only in automatic evaluation but also when evaluated by trained linguist. It is able to generalize better and recall more from it's memory.

As our results are promising, we believe that further research in this area will lead to models that are able to generalize better and define polysemic words properly in different contexts. Those models can be applied to WSD, Entity Linking and other knowledge intensive tasks.

Acknowledgements

The work was partially supported by (1) the Polish Ministry of Education and Science, CLARIN-PL; (2) the European Regional Development Fund as a part of the 2014-2020 Smart Growth Operational Programme, CLARIN – Common Language Resources and Technology Infrastructure, (3) project CLARIN-Q (agreement no. 2022/WK/09), and (4) the Department of Artificial Intelligence at Wroclaw University of Science and Technology.

Word	Context	Generated Definition
wyniszczać, verb	*„Wreszcie świadczenia na rzecz gospodarki okazały się* ***wyniszczające****. Stopa akumulacji kapitału osiągnęła bezprecedensowy poziom."*	powodować, że coś nie nadaje się do użytku albo straciło jakieś swoje funkcje;
(to devastate)	*(Finally, the benefits to the economy have proved* ***devastating*** *in the economic field: the rate of capital accumulation has reached unprecedented levels)*	cause something to become unusable or lose some of its functions;
rozwiązywać, verb	*„ Ich zdaniem obiekt tego rodzaju zostanie zrealizowany dopiero wówczas, gdy maszyna będzie w stanie* ***rozwiązywać*** *zadania, których dotąd nie udało się rozwiązać człowiekowi, i to nie na skutek braku szybkości i dokładność"*	zapoznawać się z jakimś problemem, rozwiązywać go, odgadywać na podstawie jakichś przesłanek
(to solve)	*(In their opinion, an object of this kind will be realized only when the machine will be able to solve tasks that humans have so far failed* ***to solve****, and not due to a lack of speed and accuracy.)*	get acquainted with some problem, solve it, make a guess based on some premises
opieka, noun	*„Klient Rekuperatory od pierwszego dnia funkcjonowania systemu objęty jest* ***opieką*** *Działu Serwisowego, który jest do dyspozycji od poniedziałku do piątku"*	czynność, zabezpieczenie kogoś lub czegoś przed czymś, strzeżenie czegoś, chronienie przed zagrożeniami
(covered by)	*(The customer of Rekuperatory from the first day of operation of the system is* ***covered by*** *the Service Department, which is available from Monday to Friday)*	action, protecting someone or something from something, guarding something, protecting from threats
tapirek, noun	*„****Tapirek*** *podszedł i otarł pysk o nogę Hala. Wielki wąż wpatrywał się w niego głodnym wzrokiem, a potem cofnął głowę i z potworną siłą uderzył nią o drzwi klatki."*	tapir górski, Tapirus pinchaque - ssak z rodziny tapirowatych, najmniejszy spośród czterech gatunków i jedyny, który może żyć na wolności poza regionem lasów tropikalnych;
(Tapir)	*(****Tapir*** *approached and rubbed his snout against Hal's leg. The big snake stared at him with hungry eyes.)*	mountain tapir, Tapirus pinchaque - a mammal of the tapir family, the smallest of the four species and the only one that can live in the wild outside the rainforest region;

Table 1: A sample of correctly predicted definitions for test words and their contexts. The T5 model was provided with words and their sense use examples as an input for definition generation.

Word	Context	Generated Definition	Error Tag
znieczulony, adj	*„Nic nie czułem! — Był pan **znieczulony**, sir. Zresztą podobno to nie boli.”*	o człowieku: taki, który jest pod wpływem znieczulenia, ma kontakt z rzeczywistością;	**incoherent**
(anesthetized)	(*I didn't feel anything! - You were **anesthetized**, sir. Anyway, supposedly it doesn't hurt.*)	about a person: one who is under anesthesia, is in touch with reality;	
przyświecać, verb	*„W rzeczywistości zapewne **przyświecała** mi zupełnie bezsensowna myśl, żeby spróbować ułożyć z kamieni coś w rodzaju muru.”*	przyświecać, przyświecać komuś;	**definiendum**
(to guide)	(*In fact, I was probably **guided** by a completely nonsensical thought to try to arrange something like a wall out of the stones.*)	to guide, to guide someone;	
wikłać, verb	*„Niestety, dziewczyna pada ofiarą zakazanej miłości i **wikła się** w niebezpieczny romans.”*	przenośnie: pakować się w coś, dawać się wciągnąć czemuś lub komuś;	**partially-wrong**
(get involved)	(*Unfortunately, the girl falls prey to forbidden love and **get involved** in a dangerous affair.*)	metaphorically: get sucked into something or someone;	
warkliwy, adj	*„Gdy spytałem go o tego człowieka, przyznał **warkliwym** tonem, że jest najlepszy z całej zgrai.”*	taki, który jest pełen warczenia, warczący;	**completely-wrong**
(snarky)	(*When I asked him about the man, he admitted in a **snarky** tone that he was the best of the bunch.*)	One that is full of growling, growling	

Table 2: A sample of incorrectly predicted definitions for test words and their contexts. The predictions were tagged with error tags explaining possible error types in definition generation.

Polysemic Word	Context	Generated Definition
`zamek, noun`	*„Na górze widniał wielki, piękny* ***zamek*** *otoczony fosą.*"	`budowla mieszkalna, rezydencja pana, króla, księcia lub magnata.`
(castle)	(*On the mountain was a large, beautiful* ***castle*** *surrounded by a moat.*)	`A residential building, the residence of a lord, king, prince or magnate.`
`zamek, noun`	*„ Masz rozpięty* ***zamek*** *w spodniach.*"	`wyrób tekstylny, który ma zamek, jest skonstruowany w taki sposób, że można go zamknąć.`
(zipper)	(*You have the* ***zipper*** *of your pants undone.*)	`a textile product that has a lock is constructed in such a way that it can be closed.`
`zamek, noun`	*„Dorobił sobie klucz do* ***zamka.***"	`urządzenie do zamykania np. drzwi, szuflad, walizek.`
(lock)	(*He made up a key for the* ***lock.***)	`A device for locking, for example, doors, drawers, suitcases.`
`zamek, noun`	*„Po raz któryś z kolei odciągnął* ***zamek*** *i zajrzał do komory nabojowej swego kałasznikowa.*"	`mechanizm broni palnej, wyposażony w ruchomy zamek.`
(bolt)	(*For the umpteenth time, he pulled back the* ***bolt*** *and looked into the cartridge chamber of his kalashnikov.*)	`firearms mechanism, equipped with a movable bolt.`

Table 3: A sample of predicted definitions for polysemic word in polish language *zamek*.

Model	All samples		WordNet$^+$		WordNet$^-$	
	hard eval.	*soft eval.*	*hard eval.*	*soft eval.*	*hard eval.*	*soft eval.*
`plT5-base`	0.43	0.62	0.82	0.95	0.27	0.54
`plT5-large`	0.59	0.74	0.95	0.99	0.37	0.64

Table 4: Manual evaluation of T5-based definition generation models on test data sample of 200 words with examples. We provide the accuracy of text generation model for *hard evaluation* and *soft evaluation* settings. We split the evaluation into three distinct settings: i) WordNet$^+$ – testing on senses with a proper definition in plWordNet, ii) WordNet$^-$ – testing on senses which definitions are missing in plWordNet, iii) testing on all test samples.

References

Michele Bevilacqua, Marco Maru, and Roberto Navigli. 2020. Generationary or "how we went beyond word sense inventories and learned to gloss". In *Proceedings of the 2020 Conference on Empirical Methods in Natural Language Processing (EMNLP)*, pages 7207–7221, Online. Association for Computational Linguistics.

Michele Bevilacqua and Roberto Navigli. 2020. Breaking through the 80% glass ceiling: Raising the state of the art in word sense disambiguation by incorporating knowledge graph information. In *Proceedings of the 58th Annual Meeting of the Association for Computational Linguistics*, pages 2854–2864.

Michele Bevilacqua, Tommaso Pasini, Alessandro Raganato, Roberto Navigli, et al. 2021. Recent trends in word sense disambiguation: A survey. In *Proceedings of the Thirtieth International Joint Conference on Artificial Intelligence, IJCAI-21*. International Joint Conference on Artificial Intelligence, Inc.

Francis Bond and Ryan Foster. 2013. Linking and extending an open multilingual wordnet. In *Proceedings of the 51st Annual Meeting of the Association for Computational Linguistics (Volume 1: Long Papers)*, pages 1352–1362.

Bartosz Broda, Michał Marcińczuk, Marek Maziarz, Adam Radziszewski, and Adam Wardyński. 2012. KPWr: Towards a free corpus of Polish. In *Proc. of the 8th International Conference on Language Resources and Evaluation*, pages 3218–3222, Istanbul, Turkey.

Tom Brown, Benjamin Mann, Nick Ryder, Melanie Subbiah, Jared D Kaplan, Prafulla Dhariwal, Arvind Neelakantan, Pranav Shyam, Girish Sastry, Amanda Askell, et al. 2020. Language models are few-shot learners. *Advances in neural information processing systems*, 33:1877–1901.

Jose Camacho-Collados, Claudio Delli Bovi, Alessandro Raganato, and Roberto Navigli. 2019. Sensedefs: a multilingual corpus of semantically annotated textual definitions. *Language Resources and Evaluation*, 53(2):251–278.

Bharathi Raja Chakravarthi, Mihael Arcan, and John Philip McCrae. 2019. Wordnet gloss translation for under-resourced languages using multilingual neural machine translation. In *Proceedings of the second workshop on multilingualism at the intersection of knowledge bases and machine translation*, pages 1–7.

Aakanksha Chowdhery, Sharan Narang, Jacob Devlin, Maarten Bosma, Gaurav Mishra, Adam Roberts, Paul Barham, Hyung Won Chung, Charles Sutton, Sebastian Gehrmann, Parker Schuh, Kensen Shi, Sasha Tsvyashchenko, Joshua Maynez, Abhishek B Rao, Parker Barnes, Yi Tay, Noam M. Shazeer, Vinodkumar Prabhakaran, Emily Reif, Nan Du, Benton C. Hutchinson, Reiner Pope, James Bradbury, Jacob Austin, Michael Isard, Guy Gur-Ari, Pengcheng Yin, Toju Duke, Anselm Levskaya, Sanjay Ghemawat, Sunipa Dev, Henryk Michalewski, Xavier García, Vedant Misra, Kevin Robinson, Liam Fedus, Denny Zhou, Daphne Ippolito, David Luan, Hyeontaek Lim, Barret Zoph, Alexander Spiridonov, Ryan Sepassi, David Dohan, Shivani Agrawal, Mark Omernick, Andrew M. Dai, Thanumalayan Sankaranarayana Pillai, Marie Pellat, Aitor Lewkowycz, Erica Moreira, Rewon Child, Oleksandr Polozov, Katherine Lee, Zongwei Zhou, Xuezhi Wang, Brennan Saeta, Mark Díaz, Orhan Firat, Michele Catasta, Jason Wei, Kathleen S. Meier-Hellstern, Douglas Eck, Jeff Dean, Slav Petrov, and Noah Fiedel. 2022. Palm: Scaling language modeling with pathways. *ArXiv*, abs/2204.02311.

Aleksandra Chrabrowa, Łukasz Dragan, Karol Grzegorczyk, Dariusz Kajtoch, Mikołaj Koszowski, Robert Mroczkowski, and Piotr Rybak. 2022. Evaluation of transfer learning for polish with a text-to-text model. *arXiv preprint arXiv:2205.08808*.

Jacob Devlin, Ming-Wei Chang, Kenton Lee, and Kristina Toutanova. 2019. BERT: Pre-training of deep bidirectional transformers for language understanding. In *Proceedings of the 2019 Conference of the North American Chapter of the Association for Computational Linguistics: Human Language Technologies, Volume 1 (Long and Short Papers)*, pages 4171–4186, Minneapolis, Minnesota. Association for Computational Linguistics.

Agnieszka Dziob, Maciej Piasecki, and Ewa Rudnicka. 2019. plWordNet 4.1 – a linguistically motivated, corpus-based bilingual resource. In *Proceedings of the 10th Global Wordnet Conference*, pages 353–362.

Elżbieta Hajnicz. 2014. Lexico-semantic annotation of składnica treebank by means of PLWN lexical units. In *Proc. of the 7th Global Wordnet Conference*, pages 23–31, Tartu, Estonia.

Elżbieta Hajnicz and Tomasz Bartosiak. 2019. Connections between the semantic layer of walenty valency dictionary and plwordnet. In *Proceedings of the 10th Global Wordnet Conference*, pages 99–107.

Han Huang, Tomoyuki Kajiwara, and Yuki Arase. 2021. Definition modelling for appropriate specificity. In *Proceedings of the 2021 Conference on Empirical Methods in Natural Language Processing*, pages 2499–2509, Online and Punta Cana, Dominican Republic. Association for Computational Linguistics.

Han Huang, Tomoyuki Kajiwara, and Yuki Arase. 2022. JADE: Corpus for Japanese definition modelling. In *Proceedings of the Thirteenth Language Resources and Evaluation Conference*, pages 6884–6888, Marseille, France. European Language Resources Association.

Luyao Huang, Chi Sun, Xipeng Qiu, and Xuanjing Huang. 2019. GlossBERT: BERT for word sense disambiguation with gloss knowledge. *arXiv preprint arXiv:1908.07245*.

Arkadiusz Janz, Joanna Baran, Agnieszka Dziob, and Marcin Oleksy. 2022. A unified sense inventory for word sense disambiguation in polish. In *Proceedings of the International Conference on Computational Science: ICCS 2022)*, London, United Kingdom.

Arkadiusz Janz, Joanna Chlebus, Agnieszka Dziob, and Maciej Piasecki. Results of the poleval 2020 shared task 3: Word sense disambiguation. *Proc. of the PolEval 2020 Workshop*, page 65.

Paweł Kędzia, Maciej Piasecki, and Marlena Orlińska. 2015. Word sense disambiguation based on large scale polish clarin heterogeneous lexical resources. *Cognitive Studies*, (15).

Jan Kocoń and Michal Gawor. 2019. Evaluating kgr10 polish word embeddings in the recognition of temporal expressions using bilstm-crf. *ArXiv*, abs/1904.04055.

Mike Lewis, Yinhan Liu, Naman Goyal, Marjan Ghazvininejad, Abdelrahman Mohamed, Omer Levy, Veselin Stoyanov, and Luke Zettlemoyer. 2020. BART: Denoising sequence-to-sequence pre-training for natural language generation, translation, and comprehension. In *Proceedings of the 58th Annual Meeting of the Association for Computational Linguistics*, pages 7871–7880, Online. Association for Computational Linguistics.

Chin-Yew Lin. 2004. Rouge: A package for automatic evaluation of summaries. In *Text summarization branches out*, pages 74–81.

Timothee Mickus, Mathieu Constant, and Denis Paperno. 2021. About neural networks and writing definitions. *Dictionaries: Journal of the Dictionary Society of North America*, 42(2):95–117.

George A Miller, Richard Beckwith, Christiane Fellbaum, Derek Gross, and Katherine J Miller. 1990. Introduction to wordnet: An on-line lexical database. *International journal of lexicography*, 3(4):235–244.

Roberto Navigli, Michele Bevilacqua, Simone Conia, Dario Montagnini, and Francesco Cecconi. 2021. Ten years of babelnet: A survey. In *Proceedings of the Thirtieth International Joint Conference on Artificial Intelligence, IJCAI-21*, pages 4559–4567.

Kishore Papineni, Salim Roukos, Todd Ward, and Wei-Jing Zhu. 2002. Bleu: a method for automatic evaluation of machine translation. In *Proceedings of the 40th annual meeting of the Association for Computational Linguistics*, pages 311–318.

Alec Radford, Karthik Narasimhan, Tim Salimans, Ilya Sutskever, et al. 2018. Improving language understanding by generative pre-training.

Alec Radford, Jeffrey Wu, Rewon Child, David Luan, Dario Amodei, Ilya Sutskever, et al. 2019. Language models are unsupervised multitask learners. *OpenAI blog*, 1(8):9.

Colin Raffel, Noam Shazeer, Adam Roberts, Katherine Lee, Sharan Narang, Michael Matena, Yanqi Zhou, Wei Li, and Peter J. Liu. 2020. Exploring the limits of transfer learning with a unified text-to-text transformer. *Journal of Machine Learning Research*, 21(140):1–67.

Liling Tan and Francis Bond. 2011. Building and annotating the linguistically diverse NTU-MC (NTU-multilingual corpus). In *Proc. of the 25th Pacific Asia Conference on Language, Information and Computation*, pages 362–371, Singapore.

Hengyuan Zhang, Dawei Li, Shiping Yang, and Yanran Li. 2022. Fine-grained contrastive learning for definition generation. *arXiv preprint arXiv:2210.00543*.

WordNet-based Data Augmentation for Hybrid WSD Models

Arkadiusz Janz and Marek Maziarz
Wrocław University of Science and Technology
{arkadiusz.janz|marek.maziarz}@pwr.edu.pl

Abstract

Recent advances in Word Sense Disambiguation suggest neural language models can be successfully improved by incorporating knowledge base structure. Such class of models are called hybrid solutions. We propose a method of improving hybrid WSD models by harnessing data augmentation techniques and bilingual training. The data augmentation consist of structure augmentation using interlingual connections between wordnets and text data augmentation based on multilingual glosses and usage examples. We utilise language-agnostic neural model trained both with SemCor and Princeton WordNet gloss and example corpora, as well as with Polish WordNet glosses and usage examples. This augmentation technique proves to make well-known hybrid WSD architecture to be competitive, when compared to current State-of-the-Art models, even more complex.

1 Introduction

Word Sense Disambiguation is well recognised issue in Natural Language Processing. Due to word ambiguity it is impossible to give *a priori* a proper semantic interpretation of a text, so senses ought to be disamiguated. In recent years a great improvement has been achieved in the field with the use of deep neural networks (DNN). For low-resourced languages, however, WSD is still an open problem because of the lack of large-scale sense annotated corpora required by modern neural models.

Large number of categories (which are senses themselves) makes the task very hard for DNN classifiers, because of the bottleneck of sense annotation sparseness. Constructing a large sense annotated corpus is a very laborious task, so this problem affects NLP for most world languages (the estimated number of which exceeds 6,000). On the other hand, even NLP for languages that possess vast WSD corpora (i.e. SemCors and extensive wordnet-based corpora) has to cope with a huge number of senses that are rarely occurring in texts (for such senses the available DNN representation might not be sufficient).

Two main solutions have been proposed to these problems: first, the usage of knowledge bases facilitates WSD algorithm through propagating information within a semantic network. Second, the use of pre-trained language models, especially multilingual (or language agnostic) allows to train a model on existing resources (especially English ones) and apply it to a new language context.

We present a slight but successful modification of the EWISER model (Bevilacqua and Navigli, 2020a) in which we merge both approaches. The novelty lies in special data augmentation technique focused on structural properties of knowledge bases in other than English language, namely Polish. Starting from EWISER language-agnostic architecture pre-trained on English and Polish sense annotated datasets, we then propagate DNN vector representations through combined structures of Princeton WordNet and Polish Wordnet, two largest nowadays wordnets in the world. This modification boost the WSD multilingual performance above current State-of-the-Art solutions based on multilingual language models e.g. XL-WSD framework (Pasini et al., 2021), and gives comparable behaviour to earlier SOTA model of CONSEC, despite the fact that EWISER architecture - even with our modifications - is much simpler.

2 Related Work

The supervised approaches have proved to be the most effective solution to WSD when a representative training sample is available. With recent progress in neural language modeling the supervised solutions have been improved even more and outperformed earlier models on almost every single benchmark. However, the existing WSD data yet has its flaws, including a non-representative training sample for verb, adverb and adjective senses, most frequent sense bias, and limited sense coverage. Although very successful, the supervised models are overfitting easily to training samples which harms their generalisation abilities and reduces sense coverage when non-representative samples are used for training (Kumar et al., 2019; Bevilacqua and Navigli, 2020a). The knowledge-based solutions were designed to increase the coverage of underrepresented word senses when a limited training sample is available. However, the performance gap between supervised and knowledge-based solutions encouraged the researchers to focus more on former approaches. The prior work on supervised models considered WSD task as token classification problem where the model learns to generate discrete labels representing predicted meanings (Iacobacci et al., 2016; Raganato et al., 2017; Popov, 2018). A typical architecture consisted of neural context encoder and sense discrimination layer e.g. LSTM with attention and softmax layer trained on SemCor data to disambiguate tokens in a fully supervised manner.

Recent studies in the area of Word Sense Disambiguation show that the most successful solutions are based on hybrid architectures with a strong emphasis on zero-shot supervision. A zero-shot component was introduced to replace full supervision and improve the ability of generalising to unseen senses (Kumar et al., 2019). Subsequent approaches utilised the benefits of transformer architectures (Huang et al., 2019; Du et al., 2019) and representation learning using external knowledge sources, such as sense definitions (Luo et al., 2018; Huang et al., 2019; Blevins and Zettlemoyer, 2020) and sense usage examples. On the other hand, structural properties of lexico-semantic networks used to be ignored in neural architectures. Recent studies show that hybrid solutions utilising textual descriptions of senses together with their structural properties can also improve WSD performance.

Most related to our work is XL-WSD framework with a crosslingual benchmark built on the basis of Open Multilingual WordNet data and BabelNet resources. The benchmark has been introduced as a platform to evaluate zero-shot WSD methods and crosslingual transfer with multilingual language models. Other multilingual solutions include MULAN (Barba et al., 2021a), EWISER (Bevilacqua and Navigli, 2020a), CONSEC (Barba et al., 2021b). However, only few of them were actually evaluated against all of datasets available in XL-WSD framework. The usual crosslingual evaluation setting consists of English, Spanish, French, German and Italian datasets proposed at SemEval competition. XL-WSD was a step towards preparing a crosslingual evaluation at scale including more languages. As far as we know, none of the previous solutions evaluated within XL-WSD framework were hybrid models joining neural text encoders with structural knowledge base features.

Regarding the Negative Transfer phenomenon, several studies were focused on identification of troublesome NLP tasks where simultaneous fine-tuning of multilingual language models to downstream tasks has a harmful impact on model performance (Wang et al., 2020). However, none of them were focused strictly on WSD task. It is an open issue whether Negative Transfer occurs when fine tuning multilingual language models to WSD task.

3 Resources

3.1 XL-WSD Framework

Pasini et al. (Pasini et al., 2021) prepared a framework of gold-standard resources for testing WSD models for 17 languages and English. They started from a sense inventories created on the basis of a version of Open Multilingual Wordnet (OMW) (Bond and Paik, 2012), and the extended version of OMW (based on Wiktionary data sets) (Bond and Foster, 2013). OMW identifiers are simply PWN synset IDs, so a new sense is announced each time a lemma is ascribed a new PWN synset. The sense inventories are obtainable online.[1] Princeton WordNet synset IDs were translated to BabelNet internal identifiers for authors' convenience. The authors pre-trained multilingual language model based on XLM-RoBERTa architecture (Conneau et al., 2020) to assess cross-lingual transfer capabilities of these models in a word sense disambiguation task. We made use of XL-WSD inventories of 14 languages (excluding Italian, Japanese and Korean due to sense inventory issues and missing senses discovered in XL-WSD framework).

Our models were trained on Princeton WordNet glosses and usage examples, as well as on SemCor and tested on SemEval tasks and texts (glosses and usage examples) from several wordnets. Table 1 describes the data sets in terms of annotated text origin (as either wordnet-based or SemEval-based).

[1] https://sapienzanlp.github.io/xl-wsd/

Language	Type	#Instances
en	SemEval	8 062
bg	WN-based	9 968
ca	WN-based	1 947
da	WN-based	4 400
de	SemEval	862
es	SemEval	1 851
et	WN-based	1 999
eu	WN-based	1 580
fr	SemEval	1 160
gl	WN-based	2 561
hr	WN-based	6 333
hu	WN-based	4 428
nl	WN-based	4 400
sl	WN-based	2 032
zh	WN-based	9 568

Table 1: Language-specific test sets, their type and size as reported in (Pasini et al., 2021) publication. SemEval datasets usually are easier to disambiguate when compared against WN-based datasets.

Link type	Count
i-hyponyms	181 029
i-hypernyms	181 032
i-synonyms	93 654
Total	455 715

Table 2: Number of interlingual connections between plWordNet-3.2 and Princeton WordNet by category.

3.2 Polish Data

Polish WordNet (plWN) was heavily inter-linked with Princeton WordNet (Rudnicka et al., 2012). More than two hundred thousand relation instances were used linking Polish-English counterpart synsets, among which inter-lingual synonymy, inter-lingual hyponymy and inter-lingual hypernymy were the most prominent. In Table 2 we present newest statistics concerning the manual mapping (Dziob et al., 2019). We used the mapping in the process of augmenting the structure of PWN with new links (see Sec. 4.1 below for details).

4 Models

As a baseline architecture we decided to use EWISER (Bevilacqua and Navigli, 2020b) as its codebase is extensible and freely available. EWISER is a supervised hybrid architecture utilising sense annotated corpora and knowledge base structure simultaneously. The model is based on transformer architecture with additional sense discrimination layer and structured logit mechanism injecting structural information into model during training. The key idea is to utilise existing wordnet links between senses to reinforce training procedure and incorporate logit scores of neighboring senses into scoring function of word's candidate meanings.

4.1 Augmenting the Structure

We augmented Princeton WordNet, PWN (Fellbaum, 1998), structure with semantic relations obtained from Polish WordNet, plWN (Maziarz et al., 2016) in the following manner:

Consider two pairs of counterpart synsets from plWN and PWN $s_1^{plWN} \overset{I-rel}{\longleftrightarrow} s_1^{PWN}$ and $s_2^{plWN} \overset{I-rel}{\longleftrightarrow} s_2^{PWN}$, where "*I*-rel" signifies an inter-lingual relationship. Each time when there exists a short path between the two Polish synsets in plWN, we add a new link: $s_1^{PWN} \leftrightarrow s_2^{PWN}$ to PWN. We assumed that for synonymous counterparts the distance should not exceed 2, while for homonymous counterparts the maximum path length was set to 1.

The above assumptions were fulfilled with simple matrix algebra. Let's talk about separate sets: (i) I^{hyp} of all plWN synsets that have their *I*-hypernyms or *I*-hyponyms on the PWN side and (ii) I^{syn} of all plWN synsets that have their *I*-synonyms in PWN.

(i) For the I-hyponymy/I-hypernymy case the procedure is straightforward. We simply took the original adjacency plWN matrix A and filter it leaving only synsets from the set I^{hyp}, i.e. $H = \{a_{ij}\}_{i,j \in I^{hyp}}$.

(ii) For the I-synonymy case we started from the plWN adjacency matrix A and took its square $S = A^2$ (i.e. the matrix product of 2 copies of A). Its elements $\{s_{ij}\}$ are indexed by synset identifiers i, j and represent the number of random walks of length 2 on the plWN graph (Kranda, 2011). Calculating $S' = \{\text{sign}\, s_{ij}\}$, i.e. setting non-zero elements of the matrix to 1, and adding $A + (S' - \mathbb{I}) = M = \{m_{ij}\}$, we get a matrix with new adjacency links (representing the distance of 2 or less steps in the original graph A). Out of the matrix M we construct the new matrix E with picking up only those synsets that are in the set

I^{syn}, i.e. $E = \{m_{ij}\}_{i,j \in I^{syn}}$.

Taking into account all relationships obtainable from matrices H and E we finally land with the set of new links to be added to PWN.

4.2 Augmenting the Data

Nearly 146,000 Polish synsets are described by a gloss and/or by (a) usage example(s). These samples were used to extend EWISER's training data. To obtain their textual descriptions we used interlingual links from plWordNet 3.2 including interlingual synonymy, hyponymy and hypernymy.

In (Pasini et al., 2021) authors used machine translated PWN glosses and usage examples and found no significant improvement over other models. In contrast to their approach, we used Polish glosses and native natural language examples avoiding translation disadvantages (see Sec. 4.3 below for details).

4.3 Bilingual Training

To investigate the impact of bilingual training on WSD performance we built a mixed sense inventory consisting of Polish and English lemmas with their candidate meanings. To create this inventory we used interlingual mapping between Polish and English wordnet meanings, mainly synonymy, hypernymy and hyponymy links. We believe multilingual downstream task fine-tuning might be beneficial for tasks such as WSD, since it is strongly interconnected with training procedure of multilingual language models (usually on parallel corpora), e.g. multilingual MLM in XLM-R. However, for tasks such as POS tagging or NER recognition issues such as Negative Transfer (also called Negative Interference) model performance is decreased during multilingual training (Wang et al., 2020). Thus our work is one of the first attempts to investigate Negative Transfer phenomenon in WSD task.

5 Experiments

In this section we present the results of our experimental part. We decided to split evaluation into two different settings. First, we would like to investigate the impact of underlying language model on WSD performance. The second setting is focused on data augmentation using plWordNet data (the network structure, as well as glosses and examples).

5.1 Settings

The authors of EWISER in their original work integrated their architecture with mBERT language model (Devlin et al., 2019). However, recent progress on multilingual language modeling brought new and more effective language models such as XLM-RoBERTa (Conneau et al., 2020), T5 (Raffel et al., 2020), mBART (Liu et al., 2020). The XLM architecture is oftenly choosed as a main language model for various downstream tasks. It was also the basis for crosslingual evaluation of zero-shot solutions within XL-WSD framework. However, as far as we know, the XLM architecture has never been evaluated within hybrid WSD approaches. Thus, in our first setting we evaluate the EWISER architecture with XLM-RoBERTa-Large model as underlying context encoder.

In second setting we focused mainly on the proposed data augmentation methods – structure expansion and corpora expansion. We investigate the impact of Polish data on WSD performance in English as well as in multilingual setting with multiple languages. The first baseline solution utilises a zero-shot architecture proposed in XL-WSD framework with XLMR-Large model. Contrary to EWISER, this architecture is not a hybrid solution and does not utilise structural properties of knowledge bases. We split this experiment into two parts. The first part is focused on structure augmentation using interlingual synonymy and relation propagation over wordnet. The second part of this setting evaluates a joint model where the structure augmentation technique is combined with additional sense data including glosses and sense utterances. A bilingual dataset and bilingual sense inventory are used to train the joint model.

5.2 Hyperparameter Tuning

The hyperparameters were finetuned using a preselected validation set. We chose SemEval 2015 data set as our development data following the way it was used in the literature. We applied early stopping procedure to prevent the models from overfitting to training data, as it was proposed in (Bevilacqua and Navigli, 2020b). The experiments were repeated at least 5 times for each model.

6 Results and Discussion

In tests on 15 languages our technique turned out to be successful in beating the XL-WSD and the EWISER model and comparable to some extent

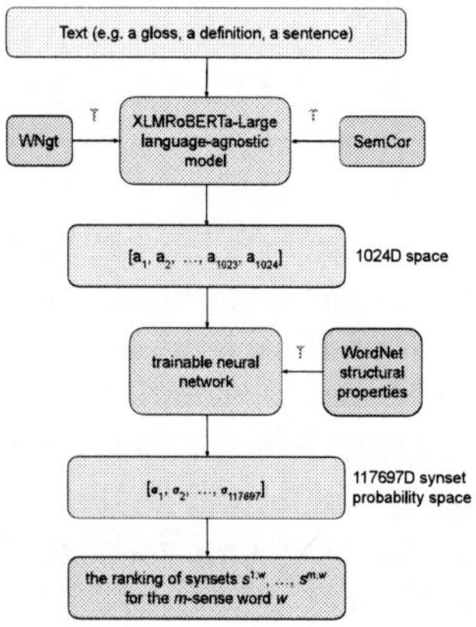

Figure 1: The DNN architecture of EWISER. We provided Polish language data both for XLM-RoBERTa language model (plWordNet glosses and usage examples) and for the output neural network layer (new relation instances for Princeton WordNet derived from plWordNet).

with the CONSEC model. Table 3 illustrates multilingual performance of all models, as compared with baselines - EWISER, CONSEC[2] and XLM-RoBERTa from XL-WSD framework.

Since testing data sets were constructed independently, we decided to compare average model F1 performances. U-Mann-Whitney paired test was applied to the task, separately for CONSEC and for XL-WSD with EWISER) and p-values were corrected for false discovery ratio through Benjamini-Hochberg procedure (Benjamini and Hochberg, 1995). Our two models performed better *on average* than XL-WSD (XLMR-L) and EWISER baseline models (for 15 languages) and not worse than CONSEC model (for 6 languages).

Presented in this paper experiments proved that augmenting English training data sets with glosses and examples from other than English wordnet can lead to the improvement of a multilingual WSD algorithm. The proposed novel technique of augmenting Princeton WordNet structure also resulted in better than or equal to SOTA scores. Surprisingly, used here EWISER architecture is simpler than current SOTA DNN models. This suggests the validity of training data enlargement and curation techniques. The step that could not be fully superseded by constructing new, even more sophisticated DNN architectures.

In the future we plan to investigate new ways of enriching Princeton WordNet structure with relation instances derivable from Polish WordNet network. Since we utilised only separate sets of I-synonyms and I-hyponyms/I-hypernyms, it is obvious that these two types of bilingual counterparts could be treated jointly. For instance, we may link in PWN an English I-synonym with an English I-hyponym, if a path is not too long. This enrichment will provide us with new, high quality relations. Also testing different path lengths via plWordNet is planned.

[2]The evaluation of CONSEC model was limited to the results provided by the authors in (Barba et al., 2021b). At the time of publication, the training procedure was not fully reproducible and the codebase was incompatible with XL-WSD sense indices.

Acknowledgments

This research was financed by the National Science Centre, Poland, grant number 2018/29/B/HS2/02919, and supported by the Polish Ministry of Education and Science, Project CLARIN-PL.

References

Edoardo Barba, Luigi Procopio, Niccolo Campolungo, Tommaso Pasini, and Roberto Navigli. 2021a. Mulan: Multilingual label propagation for word sense disambiguation. In *Proceedings of the Twenty-Ninth International Conference on International Joint Conferences on Artificial Intelligence*, pages 3837–3844.

Edoardo Barba, Luigi Procopio, and Roberto Navigli. 2021b. Consec: Word sense disambiguation as continuous sense comprehension. In *Proceedings of the 2021 Conference on Empirical Methods in Natural Language Processing*, pages 1492–1503.

Yoav Benjamini and Yosef Hochberg. 1995. Controlling the false discovery rate: a practical and powerful approach to multiple testing. *Journal of the Royal statistical society: series B (Methodological)*, 57(1):289–300.

Michele Bevilacqua and Roberto Navigli. 2020a. Breaking through the 80% glass ceiling: Raising the state of the art in word sense disambiguation by incorporating knowledge graph information. In *Proceedings of the 58th Annual Meeting of the Association for Computational Linguistics*, pages 2854–2864.

Michele Bevilacqua and Roberto Navigli. 2020b. Breaking through the 80% glass ceiling: Raising the state of the art in word sense disambiguation by incorporating knowledge graph information. In *Proceedings of the 58th Annual Meeting of the Association for Computational Linguistics*, pages 2854–2864.

Terra Blevins and Luke Zettlemoyer. 2020. Moving down the long tail of word sense disambiguation with gloss-informed biencoders. *arXiv preprint arXiv:2005.02590*.

Language ISO 639-1	Baselines EWISER [e]	CONSEC [c]	XLM-R [x]	EWISER-augmented +PLWN (Es)	+PLWN (Es+Ts)
en+	78,9	**83.4**	76.3	79.9	79.6
bg	74,2	—	72.0	74.7	**75.4**
ca	53,6	—	50.0	54.2	**55.2**
da	82,6	—	80.6	82.8	**83.3**
de+	83,1	**84.2**	83.2	83.1	82.9
es+	77,0	77.4	75.8	77.4	**78.2**
et+	71,1	69.8	66.1	70.9	**71.5**
eu	50,2	—	47.2	50.5	**50.8**
fr+	83,8	84.4	83.9	83.9	**84.7**
gl	**67,7**	—	66.3	66.4	67.4
hr	74,1	—	72.3	74.2	**74.3**
hu	**73,7**	—	67.6	73.6	**73.7**
nl+	63,2	63.3	59.2	63.5	**64.1**
sl	66,6	—	68.4	**68.0**	67.5
zh	56,1	—	51.6	56.3	**56.5**
mean+	76.1	**77.0**	74.1	76.5	76.8
mean	70.3	—	68.0	70.6	**71.0**
median+	77.9	**80.4**	76.1	**78.5** [c] (=)	**78.6** [c] (=)
median	73.6	—	68.4	**73.6** [e] * (↑) [x] ** (↑)	**73.7** [e] ** (↑) [x] *** (↑)

Table 3: Multilingual performance of different models in terms of F1 scores. Symbols: "+PLWN" – Polish data used as training sets, "Es" – Polish WordNet edges transferred to PWN, "Ts" – Polish texts of glosses and usage examples, languages are listed with ISO 639-1 codes. Medians and means are calculated either for 15 languages or for 6 languages (the plus sign). Statistical significance shows U-Mann-Whitney paired rank-sum test for differences between multilingual performance measures of models (in terms of F1 medians): *) $p \leq 0.05$, **) $p \leq 0.01$, ***) $p \leq 0.002$; baselines are marked with [*e*], [*c*] and [*x*] signs, respectively. We use arrows to mark that a tested model performs better (↑) or worse (↓) than a particular baseline, and the equal sign (=) when models are indistinguishable from baselines. The significance was corrected for false discovery ratio.

Francis Bond and Ryan Foster. 2013. Linking and extending an open multilingual wordnet. In *Proceedings of the 51st Annual Meeting of the Association for Computational Linguistics (Volume 1: Long Papers)*, pages 1352–1362.

Francis Bond and Kyonghee Paik. 2012. A survey of wordnets and their licenses. *Small*, 8(4):5.

Alexis Conneau, Kartikay Khandelwal, Naman Goyal, Vishrav Chaudhary, Guillaume Wenzek, Francisco Guzmán, Edouard Grave, Myle Ott, Luke Zettlemoyer, and Veselin Stoyanov. 2020. Unsupervised cross-lingual representation learning at scale. In *Proceedings of the 58th Annual Meeting of the Association for Computational Linguistics*, pages 8440–8451, Online. Association for Computational Linguistics.

Jacob Devlin, Ming-Wei Chang, Kenton Lee, and Kristina Toutanova. 2019. BERT: Pre-training of deep bidirectional transformers for language understanding. In *Proceedings of the 2019 Conference of the North American Chapter of the Association for Computational Linguistics: Human Language Technologies, Volume 1 (Long and Short Papers)*, pages 4171–4186, Minneapolis, Minnesota. Association for Computational Linguistics.

Jiaju Du, Fanchao Qi, and Maosong Sun. 2019. Using bert for word sense disambiguation. *arXiv preprint arXiv:1909.08358*.

Agnieszka Dziob, Maciej Piasecki, and Ewa Rudnicka. 2019. plWordNet 4.1 - a linguistically motivated, corpus-based bilingual resource. In *Proceedings of the 10th Global Wordnet Conference*, pages 353–362, Wroclaw, Poland. Global Wordnet Association.

Christiane Fellbaum, editor. 1998. *WordNet: An Electronic Lexical Database (Language, Speech, and Communication)*. The MIT Press.

Luyao Huang, Chi Sun, Xipeng Qiu, and Xuanjing Huang. 2019. GlossBERT: BERT for word sense disambiguation with gloss knowledge. *arXiv preprint arXiv:1908.07245*.

Ignacio Iacobacci, Mohammad Taher Pilehvar, and Roberto Navigli. 2016. Embeddings for word sense disambiguation: An evaluation study. In *Proceedings of the 54th Annual Meeting of the Association for Computational Linguistics (Volume 1: Long Papers)*, pages 897–907.

D. J. Kranda. 2011. The square of adjacency matrices.

Sawan Kumar, Sharmistha Jat, Karan Saxena, and Partha Talukdar. 2019. Zero-shot word sense disambiguation using sense definition embeddings. In *Proceedings of the 57th Annual Meeting of the Association for Computational Linguistics*, pages 5670–5681.

Yinhan Liu, Jiatao Gu, Naman Goyal, Xian Li, Sergey Edunov, Marjan Ghazvininejad, Mike Lewis, and Luke Zettlemoyer. 2020. Multilingual denoising pre-training for neural machine translation. *Transactions of the Association for Computational Linguistics*, 8:726–742.

Fuli Luo, Tianyu Liu, Zexue He, Qiaolin Xia, Zhifang Sui, and Baobao Chang. 2018. Leveraging gloss knowledge in neural word sense disambiguation by hierarchical co-attention. In *Proceedings of the 2018 Conference on Empirical Methods in Natural Language Processing*, pages 1402–1411, Brussels, Belgium. Association for Computational Linguistics.

Marek Maziarz, Maciej Piasecki, Ewa Rudnicka, Stan Szpakowicz, and Paweł Kędzia. 2016. plWordNet 3.0 – a comprehensive lexical-semantic resource. In *Proceedings of COLING 2016, the 26th International Conference on Computational Linguistics: Technical Papers*, pages 2259–2268, Osaka, Japan. The COLING 2016 Organizing Committee.

Tommaso Pasini, Alessandro Raganato, and Roberto Navigli. 2021. Xl-wsd: An extra-large and cross-lingual evaluation framework for word sense disambiguation. In *Proceedings of the AAAI Conference on Artificial Intelligence*. AAAI Press.

Alexander Popov. 2018. Neural network models for word sense disambiguation: an overview. *Cybernetics and information technologies*, 18(1):139–151.

Colin Raffel, Noam Shazeer, Adam Roberts, Katherine Lee, Sharan Narang, Michael Matena, Yanqi Zhou, Wei Li, and Peter J. Liu. 2020. Exploring the limits of transfer learning with a unified text-to-text transformer. *Journal of Machine Learning Research*, 21(140):1–67.

Alessandro Raganato, Claudio Delli Bovi, and Roberto Navigli. 2017. Neural sequence learning models for word sense disambiguation. In *Proceedings of the 2017 Conference on Empirical Methods in Natural Language Processing*, pages 1156–1167.

Ewa Rudnicka, Marek Maziarz, Maciej Piasecki, and Stan Szpakowicz. 2012. A strategy of mapping polish wordnet onto princeton wordnet. In *Proceedings of COLING 2012: Posters*, pages 1039–1048.

Zirui Wang, Zachary C Lipton, and Yulia Tsvetkov. 2020. On negative interference in multilingual models: Findings and a meta-learning treatment. *arXiv preprint arXiv:2010.03017*.

Mapping Wordnets on the Fly with Permanent Sense Keys

Eric Kafe
MegaDoc
Charlottenlund, Denmark
kafe@megadoc.net

Abstract

Most of the major databases on the semantic web have links to Princeton WordNet (PWN) synonym set (synset) identifiers, which differ for each PWN release, and are thus incompatible between versions. On the other hand, both PWN and the more recent Open English Wordnet (OEWN) provide permanent word sense identifiers (the sense keys), which can solve this interoperability problem.

We present an algorithm that runs in linear time, to automatically derive a synset mapping between any pair of Wordnet versions that use PWN sense keys. This allows to update old WordNet links, and seamlessly interoperate with newer English Wordnet versions for which no prior mapping exists.

By applying the proposed algorithm on the fly, at load time, we combine the Open Multilingual Wordnet (OMW 1.4, which uses old PWN 3.0 identifiers) with OEWN Edition 2021, and obtain almost perfect precision and recall. We compare the results of our approach using respectively synset offsets, versus the Collaborative InterLingual Index (CILI version 1.0) as synset identifiers, and find that the synset offsets perform better than CILI 1.0 in all cases, except a few ties.

1 Introduction

All the available multilingual wordnets (Bond et al., 2014) and important knowledge bases on the semantic web (Navigli and Ponzetto, 2010; Niles and Pease, 2003; Suchanek et al., 2008; Nielsen, 2018) were originally linked to different versions of *Princeton WordNet* (PWN) (Fellbaum, 1998), using version-specific *synset offsets* (WordNet-team, 2010, Wndb), which differ between releases, so mappings are necessary for interoperation, and for updating to a later English Wordnet versions.

Many of these resources have been remapped to Wordnet 3.0 or Wordnet 3.1, using *offset to offset* mappings obtained by relaxation labelling (Daudé et al., 2000), *offset to ILI* (InterLingual Index) mappings (Vossen, 2002; Vossen et al., 2016; Bond et al., 2016), *sensekey to sensekey* mappings (WordNet-team, 2010, Sensemap), and *offset to offset* mappings relying on sense key persistence (Kafe, 2018). Contrary to synset offsets, the sensekeys persist across database versions (WordNet-team, 2010, Senseidx), and can thus support the derivation of mappings with high precision and recall.

PWN *sensekeys* (WordNet-team, 2010, Senseidx) are composite database keys representing one particular word sense. They consist in the concatenation of the identifiers for the corresponding *lemma* and its *lexfile*, *lex_id*, and eventually *head adjective* (see examples in sections 2.1, 3.2 and 4.2). Each PWN version includes an *index.sense* file, linking the sense keys to their corresponding synset offsets.

However, the necessary mappings between synsets linked to different PWN versions are not always available, either because a resource is too new, or has too few users to justify the production of a mapping. This causes potentially long delays for interoperability, which may remain impossible as long as no relevant mapping exists. For example, *Edition 2022* of the *Open English Wordnet* (OEWN[1]) (McCrae et al., 2020) was released recently, and the *wndb*[2] project has also published the same data in a PWN-compatible format (including the relevant *index.sense*). These two variants of the OEWN 2022 Edition use different, mutually incompatible synset offsets; no mapping exists for neither yet, and no known project currently aims to produce such mappings.

On the other hand, OEWN has adopted PWN sensekeys as its main sense identifier, so it is easy to

[1] https://github.com/globalwordnet/english-wordnet

[2] https://github.com/x-englishwordnet/wndb

extract a sense index from the database, and almost instantly produce a sensekey-based mapping, since this only requires joining the *index.sense* of the relevant wordnet versions. Therefore, we propose to carry out the mapping process on the fly, whenever loading wordnets that are linked to different English Wordnet (PWN or OEWN) versions.

2 Methods

2.1 Mapping Strategy

Between two Wordnet versions, word senses can be either *added* or *removed*, and the same applies to synonym sets, in the case where all their elements are respectively completely new or entirely deleted. In addition to that, synonym sets can also be *split* and/or *merged*, when one or more of their elements are moved to another (existing or new) synset.

For example, between versions 3.0 and 3.1 of PWN, *Pluto* was moved from the *god of the underworld* in Greek mythology, to the synset with the names of the corresponding Roman "god of the underworld":

Sense Key	**PWN$_{3.0}$**	**CILI$_{3.0}$**	**CILI$_{3.1}$**	**PWN$_{3.1}$**
aides%1:18:00::	09570298-n	i86957	i86957	09593427-n
aidoneus%1:18:00::	09570298-n	i86957	i86957	09593427-n
hades%1:18:00::	09570298-n	i86957	i86957	09593427-n
pluto%1:18:00::	09570298-n	i86957	i86958	09593643-n
dis%1:18:00::	09570522-n	i86958	i86958	09593643-n
orcus%1:18:00::	09570522-n	i86958	i86958	09593643-n
dis_pater%1:18:00::	∄	∄	i86958	09593643-n

The problem is that foreign language translations of the involved synsets cannot deal with this change by simply applying a *concept to offset* mapping like the Collaborative Interlingual index (CILI[3]). In the French Wordnet, for example, *Pluton* is a synonym of *Hadès* and *Aides*, and thus a member of the Greek gods, and remains so, even after applying the CILI mapping. Unlike the English *Pluto*, the French *Pluton* keeps the CILI *i86957* identifier, and still translates to *Hades* in later English Wordnet versions. Conversely, the French translation of the PWN 3.1 synset with CILI *i86958* does not include *Pluton*. To adequately deal with this situation, the French *Pluton* would need a link to the corresponding English sense key, instead of being linked at the synset level.

Here, where both gods are the same and the name *Plouton* actually exists in the Greek mythology, it would make sense to apply the *map-to-all* strategy, and insert *Pluto* in both target synsets, as in the mappings from the Sense Key Index (SKI)[4]. But mapping to all possible targets is not guaranteed to be adequate in all cases, so it is always preferable to review all the synset splits manually.

We aim to support wordnet interoperability in the general-purpose natural language toolkit NLTK[5] (Bird et al., 2009), which is increasingly used in very diverse Machine Learning projects, without specialized lexicographic knowledge. So a *one-to-many* synset mapping strategy would not be an adequate default, because users would not know how to choose the most adequate target synset from a list of mapping candidates. In such cases, it is more convenient that the system only picks one target synset for each source synset.

Mapping the wordnets on the fly, at load time, requires an algorithm that performs as close to instantly as possible, so we prefer a simple frequency-based approach, rather than a more complex analysis of relation links. Therefore, we map each source synset to the target that retains most of the source lemmas and, in the case of equality, to the synset with the highest offset. In most cases, though, the choice is limited to one single target synset, since choosing between synsets is only relevant in the cases where a source synset is split into two (or eventually three) synsets. These cases are rare (Kafe, 2018), so candidates with an equal number of lemmas are even rarer.

So we apply a *many-to-one* mapping strategy, where potentially many (though most often only one) source synsets are merged into a single target synset. This is the only difference between this work and the *many-to-many* mappings from the Sense Key Index (SKI), resulting in slightly different numbers of False Positives (fp) and False Negatives (fn), and only tiny differences in overall performance.

2.2 Linear Time Algorithm

Algorithm 1 constructs a mapping between two English Wordnet (PWN or OEWN) versions (respectively *source* and *target*), using intermediate mappings, implemented here as Python dictionaries (see the NLTK listing in Appendix A).

First, we construct a mapping from the sensekeys to the corresponding synset identifier (*synset_id*) for each of the *source* and *target* Wordnet versions. For this, we use either the *index.sense* file

[3]https://github.com/globalwordnet/cili

[4]https://github.com/ekaf/ski

[5]https://www.nltk.org

Algorithm 1 Map synsets from *source* to *target* Wordnet version using sense keys

$\text{SENSE\_INDEX}_{source} \leftarrow \{\forall \text{ sense} \in source : \text{sense}_{key} \rightarrow \text{synset\_id}_{source}\}$
$\text{SENSE\_INDEX}_{target} \leftarrow \{\forall \text{ sense} \in target : \text{sense}_{key} \rightarrow \text{synset\_id}_{target}\}$
$\text{MAP\_TO\_MANY} \leftarrow \{\forall \text{ synset\_id}_{source} \in \text{values}(\text{SENSE\_INDEX}_{source}) : \text{synset\_id}_{source} \rightarrow \emptyset\}$
for $\text{sense}_{key} \in \text{SENSE\_INDEX}_{source} \cap \text{SENSE\_INDEX}_{target}$ **do**
  $\text{MAP\_TO\_MANY}[\text{synset\_id}_{source}].\text{append}(\text{synset\_id}_{target})$
end for
$\text{MAP\_TO\_ONE} \leftarrow \{\forall \text{ synset\_id}_{source} \in \text{MAP\_TO\_MANY} : \text{synset\_id}_{source} \rightarrow \text{argmax}(\text{count}(\text{synset\_id}_{target}))\}$
return MAP_TO_ONE

included in each PWN release, or the *sense id* attribute of the OEWN senses, since OEWN now uses sensekeys directly as its main sense identifier. NLTK does not yet support ILI identifiers, so the current NLTK implementation can only use *offset-part_of_speech* synset identifiers, but it is straightforward to replace these by ILI concept identifiers. Each sensekey is linked to at most one synset in each version, but may be absent from either the source or target version (in the cases where a sense was added or removed). This step does one pass over the *index.sense*, which consists in one record per sensekey, so its complexity is obviously linear.

Then the MAP_TO_MANY step joins the two INDEX_SENSE maps in order to produce a *synset_to_many* mapping from the *source* synset identifiers to lists of corresponding synset identifiers in *target*. Python sets are implemented as hash tables, with $O(1)$ lookup, so the intersection of both versions' sense keys is computed in $O(n)$ time. Then we do one pass over the sources' offsets, to initialize empty candidate bags, and one pass over the common sense keys, to populate the MAP_TO_MANY mapping, which is identical to the corresponding SKI mapping (Kafe, 2018).

Finally, a MAP_TO_ONE step chooses the most adequate target synset for each source synset, among a bag of candidates provided by the MAP_TO_MANY mapping. This step is optional for use cases where we want to retain all the candidate targets. Here, we use the max[6] function to pick the target synset that retains most lemmas from the source synset, but we also discuss using $sort$ as an alternative in section 4.3. We do one pass over each of the candidate bags, where we use the $O(n)$ max function to pick the target synset, so this step also runs in linear time.

2.3 Complexity

Since each of its steps runs in linear time, the total complexity of this mapping algorithm is also $O(n)$, where n corresponds to the numbers of sense keys and synset offsets in the involved wordnets. To our knowledge, this is the simplest mapping algorithm yet proposed for wordnets, and considerably less complex than the deep relation analysis in Daudé et al. (2000) and Daudé et al. (2001), although both approaches have similar performance, but also complementary strengths and weaknesses (Kafe, 2018).

2.4 Implementation

We first integrated this mapping process in the *wordnet* library of NLTK version 3.6.6, and used it to map the multilingual wordnets from OMW 1.4 (Bond et al., 2020) at load time, converting their PWN 3.0 synset identifiers to those used in any of the more recent English Wordnets, in order to support the seamless interoperation of the involved databases.

NLTK is developed on an open software development platform[7], which provides free access for all, to not only the software code, but also its various incarnations, and the corresponding discussions before and after its release. Everyone is free to modify the source code, and welcome to contribute improvements back to the community.

When using synset offsets, the implementation differs from algorithm 1 by adding a supplementary mapping link from adjectives, when the source synset is an adjective satellite. This is necessary for handling OMW data, where most languages ignore the $satellite$ category. But this step does not apply to ILI identifiers, since these don't include any part-of-speech reference.

We rewrote the implementation for NLTK version 3.8, in order to closely follow algorithm 1. In the initial implementation, the source wordnet was hard-coded to PWN version 3.0, for handling the

[6]Thanks to Steven Bird, who reviewed the initial implementation, and pointed out that max is quicker than $sort$.

[7]`https://github.com/nltk/nltk`

OMW data. An optional *version* parameter has been added in the forthcoming NLTK 3.8.2, which allows to produce mappings for any pair of English Wordnet versions. Appendix A includes the listing of this slightly more elaborated implementation, which additionally collects the *split* or *lost* synsets in structures called respectively $splits$ and $nomap$, which should be useful for further improving the mappings. We also adapted the functions in the appendix for the Wn[8] library (Goodman and Bond, 2021), in order to compare the performance of algorithm 1 using respectively synset offsets versus ILIs as synset identifiers. We thus used *Wn* to produce the Map_{CILI} results in table 1, while we computed the Map_{Offset} results in table 1 using both NLTK and *Wn*, and verified that both libraries yield identical outputs.

3 Results

3.1 Multilingual Coverage

Table 1 displays the number of synsets and lemmas in NLTK's data package for OMW 1.4, when loaded with respectively the default PWN 3.0, and OEWN Edition 2021. The languages are listed by their number of synsets in decreasing order, and we report the number of synsets lost, as well as percentages, when mapping between the two English Wordnet versions, using either synset offsets or the CILI 1.0 synset identifiers currently included in the *Wn* library.

All the multilingual wordnets suffer a loss in the mapping, but this loss is almost negligible with either type of synset identifier: at most 0.19% (corresponding to 99.81% recall) for Standard Arabic with synset offsets, and 0.21% using CILI with Lithuanian. Except a small number of ties with the smallest wordnets, the synset offset mappings perform better than the CILI 1.0 mappings in all cases. This is surprising since the CILI mappings were partially curated manually, so we expected them to provide an advantage over the completely automatic offset mappings. However, the difference is small, and might be attributed to known issues [9] with the CILI 1.0 mappings, which could be remedied in a future version.

With PWN 3.0, some numbers are identical to those reported by Bond et al. (2014). These concern wordnets that have not been updated since OMW 1.0. On the other hand, some wordnets in OMW 1.4 are not current, as for ex. the Basque, Catalan, Galician and Spanish wordnets date back to the 2012 edition of the Multilingual Core Repository (MCR) described by Gonzalez-Agirre et al. (2012), although the coverage of these wordnets was greatly expanded in the 2016 edition of MCR.

NLTK also has a PWN 3.1 data package, where the mapping loss is usually less than half, compared to OEWN 2021, and for ex. only 0.09% for Standard Arabic, corresponding to 99.91% recall. We also mapped two variants of OEWN Edition 2022: the official release [10], and an alternative version provided by the XEWN[11] project. Their databases have different sizes, and hence different synset offsets, but both yielded identical mapping losses, which were slightly better than OEWN 2021 in all cases, for ex. 0.17% synset lost with Standard Arabic. Standard mappings are not likely to become available for different variants of the same Wordnet version, so an advantage of our method is that it nevertheless allows a downstream comparison of these variants, which would not be possible otherwise.

3.2 Splits and Merges

As a consequence of our mapping strategy, where we only pick one target for each source synset, the synsets are never split. On the contrary, all lemmas belonging to a source synset, that would be split according to a many-to-many strategy, are mapped to the same target synset, and synonymy persists.

With the example from section 2.1, since *Pluto* is not split out of its *source* synset, it is not *merged* into its *target* synset, but remains a synonym of the other Greek gods:

Sense Key	$PWN_{3.0}$	$CILI_{3.0}$	$CILI_{3.1}$	$PWN_{3.1}$
aides%1:18:00::	09570298-n	i86957	i86957	09593427-n
aidoneus%1:18:00::	09570298-n	i86957	i86957	09593427-n
hades%1:18:00::	09570298-n	i86957	i86957	09593427-n
pluto%1:18:00::	09570298-n	i86957	i86957	09593427-n
dis%1:18:00::	09570522-n	i86958	i86958	09593643-n
orcus%1:18:00::	09570522-n	i86958	i86958	09593643-n
dis_pater%1:18:00::	$\nexists$	$\nexists$	i86958	09593643-n

The result is mostly a one-to-one mapping, with only 44 many-to-one cases occurring, when different source synsets are merged into the same target synset. Our method maps all the merged foreign language synsets to their correct target, as for ex. with the *baseball* example below. This contrasts

[8] https://github.com/goodmami/wn

[9] CILI issue #16, https://github.com/globalwordnet/cili/issues/16

[10] https://en-word.net/static/english-wordnet-2022.zip

[11] https://github.com/x-englishwordnet

Table 1: Multilingual synsets in OMW 1.4 mapped to OEWN 2021 using synset offsets vs. CILI 1.0

	Synsets	**Map$_{Offset}$**			**Map$_{CILI}$**		
Language	*PWN 3.0*	*OEWN 2021*	*Lost*	*%*	*OEWN 2021*	*Lost*	*%*
English	117659	117454	**205**	0.17	117427	232	0.20
Finnish	116763	116562	**201**	0.17	116535	228	0.20
Thai	73350	73240	**110**	0.15	73223	127	0.17
French	59091	59015	**76**	0.13	59005	86	0.15
Japanese	57184	57086	**98**	0.17	57080	104	0.18
Romanian	56026	55941	**85**	0.15	55931	95	0.17
Catalan	45826	45773	**53**	0.12	45769	57	0.12
Portuguese	43895	43844	**51**	0.12	43840	55	0.13
Slovenian	42583	42520	**63**	0.15	42513	70	0.16
Mandarin Chinese	42300	42249	**51**	0.12	42240	60	0.14
Spanish	38512	38431	**81**	0.21	38418	94	0.24
Indonesian	38085	38018	**67**	0.18	38011	74	0.19
Standard Malay	36911	36843	**68**	0.18	36836	75	0.20
Italian	35001	34964	**37**	0.11	34960	41	0.12
Polish	33826	33798	**28**	0.08	33794	32	0.09
Dutch	30177	30154	**23**	0.08	30151	26	0.09
Basque	29413	29387	**26**	0.09	29386	27	0.09
Croatian	23115	23081	**34**	0.15	23077	38	0.16
Galician	19311	19290	**21**	0.11	19283	28	0.14
Slovak	18507	18478	**29**	0.16	18472	35	0.19
Modern Greek (1453-)	18049	18025	**24**	0.13	18023	26	0.14
Italian (iwn)	15563	15553	**10**	0.06	15553	**10**	0.06
Standard Arabic	9916	9897	**19**	0.19	9896	20	0.20
Lithuanian	9462	9446	**16**	0.17	9442	20	0.21
Swedish	6796	6784	**12**	0.18	6784	**12**	0.18
Hebrew	5448	5441	**7**	0.13	5439	9	0.17
Bulgarian	4959	4950	**9**	0.18	4950	**9**	0.18
Icelandic	4951	4942	**9**	0.18	4942	**9**	0.18
Albanian	4675	4668	**7**	0.15	4668	**7**	0.15
Danish	4476	4468	**8**	0.18	4468	**8**	0.18
Norwegian Bokmål	4455	4447	**8**	0.18	4447	**8**	0.18
Norwegian Nynorsk	3671	3666	**5**	0.14	3666	**5**	0.14
Average	32811.12	32762.97	**48.16**	0.15	32757.16	53.97	0.16

We computed the Map$_{Offset}$ results using both the NLTK and *Wn* software libraries, and the Map$_{CILI}$ results with only *Wn*, since NLTK does not yet support ILI identifiers.

with the current implementation of the *Wn* library's standard *translate* function, which finds no translation for the first $PWN_{3.0}$ synset (*i37881*) in $PWN_{3.1}$. Conversely, translating *i37882* back from $PWN_{3.1}$ to $PWN_{3.0}$, *Wn* does not find the *i37881* lemmas.

Sense Key	$PWN_{3.0}$	$CILI_{3.0}$	$CILI_{3.1}$	$PWN_{3.1}$
baseball%1:04:00::	00471613-n:	i37881	i37882	00472688-n
baseball_game%1:04:00::	00471613-n:	i37881	i37882	00472688-n
ball%1:04:01::	00474568-n	i37882	i37882	00472688-n

The problem is that *Wn* only knows the correspondence between ILIs and offsets *within* each involved Wordnet version, but has no mapping *between* these versions. Merged synsets disappear in translation[12], because only one of the merged CILI identifiers is available in the target, so the synsets with the other ILIs are no longer reachable. This problem with merged ILIs in *Wn* only concerns a small number of synsets, since each foreign language wordnet covers only a fraction of the 44 merged English synsets. It does not affect the Map_{CILI} results in Table 1, since we computed these using our mapping algorithm, instead of *Wn*'s standard *translate* function.

3.3 Performance

We found that our method could not map 205 English synset offsets from PWN 3.0 to an OEWN 2021 target. The small mapping losses in table 1 correspond to the subset of these 205 synsets included in each multilingual wordnet. These losses represent all the *negatives* in a confusion matrix, amounting to the addition of the *True Negatives* (*tn*), which were truly removed in the target Wordnet, and the *False Negatives* (*fn*), which we ideally should be able to map. So among the mapping losses, only the *fn* are fallacies.

The minority lemmas in the split English synsets, which are induly mapped to the same synset as in the source, constitute the *False Positives* (*fp*). These only amount to the 44 splits between PWN 3.0 and OEWN 2021, so their number is small, compared to the True Positives (117454 minus eventual sense key violations).

Synsets	**Mapped**	**Not Mapped**
True	$PWN_{3.0} \cap OEWN_{2021}$ $tp = 117454$	$\emptyset$ $tn = 0$
False	$Splits$ $fp = 44$	$\complement^{PWN_{3.0}}_{OEWN_{2021}}$ $fn = 205$

[12] `https://github.com/goodmami/wn/issues/179`

We evaluate the performance of our algorithm using the values above, and obtain almost perfect performance results:

$$precision = \frac{tp}{tp + fp} = 0.9996 \quad (1)$$

$$recall = \frac{tp}{tp + fn} = 0.9983 \quad (2)$$

$$f1 = \frac{2 * precision * recall}{precision + recall} = 0.9989 \quad (3)$$

Thus, the overall performance of the English mapping is 99.89%, which compares favorably with more complex mapping strategies like Daudé et al. (2000).

Comparing the lost English synsets between the two types of synset identifiers (offsets vs. ILIs), we found that 143 were lost using both types, while 62 were only lost with offsets (always due to satellite adjectives becoming standard adjectives), and 89 were only lost with CILI 1.0. The respective additions of these losses yield the total loss reported for English in table 1 (205 with offsets vs. 232 with the ILI).

4 Discussion

We have shown that mapping between different English Wordnet versions is feasible in linear time, by relying on the stability of PWN sense keys. Our method allows to transparently update the database links on-the-fly, to another English Wordnet version, even though no prior mapping exists yet. This can benefit any database linked with an English Wordnet, and enhance any downstream task that uses such a database.

4.1 Coverage and Integrity

Our results show that almost all the vocabulary of the multilingual wordnets in OMW 1.4 persisted after the mapping.

Some doubts remain necessarily, though, concerning the referential integrity of the sensekeys, on which the mappings rely. Sensekeys are meant to always refer to the same wordsense across wordnet versions, but Kafe (2018) reported a few violations of sensekeys' referential integrity. The number of these violations seems negligible in PWN, but their impact has not yet been studied in OEWN. However, the fact that OEWN now uses the PWN sensekeys as principal wordsense identifier, is a reason for considering that the sensekeys are indeed persistent in OEWN, and that we can rely on their referential integrity in theory. Still, it would be helpful to investigate in practice, whether the addition of a new wordsense in OEWN could entail a modification of the sensekeys for other existing senses of the same word.

4.2 Challenges and Opportunities

In the mapping between PWN 3.0 and OEWN 2021, which we investigated here, our method displayed two shortcomings: 205 English synsets were completely lost in the mapping, and 44 split synsets were somewhat arbitrarily mapped to one single target. It is questionable, to which extent any automatic mapping can provide linguistically satisfying targets for each of these cases. Fortunately, their number is sufficiently small to allow a manual review, of which we can already attempt to sketch some outlines.

It is possible, for ex., to identify genuinely lost synsets, which do not have any plausible target. This happens when all the words included in the source synset are completely absent from the target Wordnet version. Here, it occurred in particular with a number of racially tainted expressions, like the synset $\{darky, darkie, darkey\}$, defined as "(ethnic slur) offensive term for Black people". In these cases, relaxing the equivalence criteria, and mapping the synset to for ex. a superordinate, would entail losing an essential nuance, and might often not be adequate. So these losses may be unavoidable, unless choosing to retain the synset with its original meaning.

On the other hand, many losses are relatively easy to avoid. For example, out of the 205 English synsets that our algorithm doesn't map, 62 concern adjective satellites which were changed to plain adjectives. These have an obvious mapping through the ILI, where both Wordnet versions share the same concept identifier.

In other cases, we can identify changes in a part of the sense key, for words that keep identical definitions. This reveals that unfortunate changes can occur in any sense key part between two wordnet versions. For example, Table 2 shows how the *lex_id* of a sense of "sequoia" changed from *00* to *01* between PWN 3.0 and OEWN 2021, while the *lexfile* of a sense of "stub out" changed from *30* to *35*, the adjective category of "obtrusive" changed from *3* to *5*, and the satellites' head adjective of "newfangled" changed from *original* to *new*.

Table 2: Changed Sense Key Parts (Examples)

Sense Key	PWN 3.0	OEWN 2021
sequoia%1:20:00::	*either of two huge coniferous California trees that reach a height of 300 feet; sometimes placed in the Taxodiaceae*	∄
sequoia%1:20:01::	∄	*either of two huge coniferous California trees that reach a height of 300 feet; sometimes placed in the Taxodiaceae*
stub_out%2:30:00::	*extinguish by crushing*	∄
stub_out%2:35:01::	∄	*extinguish by crushing*
obtrusive%3:00:00::	*undesirably noticeable*	∄
obtrusive%5:00:00-:noticeable:00	∄	*undesirably noticeable*
newfangled%5:00:00-:original:00	*(of a new kind or fashion) gratuitously new*	∄
newfangled%5:00:00-:new:00	∄	*(of a new kind or fashion) gratuitously new*

In all these cases, we see different sense keys pointing to the same word sense, and this is different from *key violations* (one sense key pointing to different word senses). In some cases, the English lexicographers could prevent this problem, but it can also be remedied downstream, by an additional mapping link between the few changed sense keys, which would allow even higher quality mappings. Our implementation (see Appendix A) supports eventual further improvements of the mappings through the *map_to_many* function, and by providing the *splits* and *nomap* lists of problematic cases to study in greater depth.

4.3 Variants of the mapping algorithm

Applying our mapping algorithm to other synset identifiers than the offsets only requires a simple modification of the initial $IndexSense$ function, while our two other functions remain unchanged. So we extended our approach, to also map ILI concept identifiers instead of synset offsets. This is not always practical yet though, because of inherent delays in the current attribution process for new ILI identifiers[13].

We applied max to a list of candidate

[13]CILI issue #9, https://github.com/globalwordnet/cili/issues/9

$(count, offset)$ pairs, in order to pick the target synset that retains most lemmas from the source synset. As a consequence, in the case of equal counts, the max function picks the target synset with the highest offset. But instead of the highest offset, it would be possible to use the min function, and pick the lowest offset instead when the counts are equal. Alternatively, this strategy can be implemented by taking the first pair in a sorted list, eventually sorting the counts in decreasing order and the offsets in increasing order. Generally, the lowest offset corresponds to a synset that was included in the PWN databases before those with higher offsets, so the choice between using min or max often induces a preference for older versus newer synsets. More research could be useful, in order to assess which difference this choice makes in practice.

Concerning the complexity of *max*, which is $O(n)$ versus *sort*, which is $O(n.logn)$, their difference is not substantial here, where n represents the number of target $(count, offset)$ pairs, which is normally one, and only two or three in the rare cases where the source synset is split.

5 Conclusion

We presented an algorithm for mapping wordnets, that runs in linear time, thus moving the frontier of wordnet interoperability by allowing to almost instantly combine different database versions, for which no prior mapping exists. We illustrated this capability by combining the OMW with OEWN. Other potential uses include seamlessly updating existing PWN links in any Wordnet-linked semantic web database, to newer OEWN versions.

We saw how our mappings only lose tiny amounts of data when mapping multilingual wordnets, which indicates that the performance of this approach is comparable to the best results obtained with alternative strategies.

Now that OEWN has adopted the original PWN sensekeys as main wordense identifier, we may expect that the proposed algorithm remains relevant with future OEWN versions. However, if more wordnet resources start to use a common set of persistent identifiers like the PWN sensekeys, mappings could become unnecesary between these resources, as they would be natively interoperable.

Acknowledgments

Thanks to Tom Aarsen and Steven Bird for their useful review of the NLTK implementation, and to the anonymous GWC 2023 reviewers for their many detailed and accurate suggestions. The final version of this article also benefited from helpful comments by participants at the GWC 2023 presentation, in particular Francis Bond and Piek Vossen.

References

Steven Bird, Ewan Klein, and Edward Loper. 2009. *Natural language processing with Python: analyzing text with the natural language toolkit.* O'Reilly Media, Inc.

Francis Bond, Christiane Fellbaum, Shu-Kai Hsieh, Chu-Ren Huang, Adam Pease, and Piek Vossen. 2014. A multilingual lexico-semantic database and ontology. In *Towards the Multilingual Semantic Web*, pages 243–258. Springer.

Francis Bond, Luis Morgado da Costa, Michael Wayne Goodman, John Philip McCrae, and Ahti Lohk. 2020. Some issues with building a multilingual Wordnet. In *Proceedings of the 12th Language Resources and Evaluation Conference*, pages 3189–3197, Marseille, France. European Language Resources Association.

Francis Bond, Piek Vossen, John McCrae, and Christiane Fellbaum. 2016. CILI: the collaborative interlingual index. In *Proceedings of the 8th Global WordNet Conference (GWC)*, pages 50–57, Bucharest, Romania. Global Wordnet Association.

J. Daudé, L. Padró, and G. Rigau. 2000. Mapping WordNets using structural information. In *Proceedings of the 38th Annual Meeting of the Association for Computational Linguistics*, pages 504–511, Hong Kong. Association for Computational Linguistics.

J. Daudé, L. Padró, and G. Rigau. 2001. A complete wn1.5 to wn1.6 mapping. In *Proceedings of the NAACL Workshop 'WordNet and Other Lexical Resources: Applications, Extensions and Customizations' (NAACL'2001)., Pittsburg, PA, USA.*

Christiane Fellbaum. 1998. *WordNet, An Electronic Lexical Database.* MIT Press, Cambridge.

A. Gonzalez-Agirre, E. Laparra, and G. Rigau. 2012. Multilingual central repository version 3.0: upgrading a very large lexical knowledge base. In *Proceedings of the Sixth International Global WordNet Conference (GWC2012). Matsue, Japan.*

Michael Wayne Goodman and Francis Bond. 2021. Intrinsically interlingual: The wn python library for wordnets. In *Proceedings of the 11th Global Wordnet Conference*, pages 100–107, University of South Africa (UNISA). Global Wordnet Association.

Eric Kafe. 2018. Persistent semantic identity in wordnet. *Cognitive Studies | Études cognitives*, 18.

John Philip McCrae, Alexandre Rademaker, Ewa Rudnicka, and Francis Bond. 2020. English WordNet 2020: Improving and extending a WordNet for English using an open-source methodology. In *Proceedings of the LREC 2020 Workshop on Multimodal Wordnets (MMW2020)*, pages 14–19, Marseille, France. The European Language Resources Association (ELRA).

Roberto Navigli and Simone Paolo Ponzetto. 2010. Babelnet: Building a very large multilingual semantic network. In *Proceedings of the 48th Annual Meeting of the Association for Computational Linguistics, Uppsala, Sweden, 11-16 July 2010*, pages 216–225.

Finn Årup Nielsen. 2018. Linking imagenet wordnet synsets with wikidata. In *Proceedings of The 2018 Web Conference Companion (WWW'18 Companion)*. ACM, New York, USA.

Ian Niles and Adam Pease. 2003. Linking lexicons and ontologies: Mapping wordnet to the suggested upper merged ontology. In *Ike*, pages 412–416.

Fabian M Suchanek, Gjergji Kasneci, and Gerhard Weikum. 2008. Yago: A large ontology from wikipedia and wordnet. *Web Semantics: Science, Services and Agents on the World Wide Web*, 6(3):203–217.

Piek Vossen. 2002. *EuroWordnet General Document*. EWN.

Piek Vossen, Francis Bond, and John McCrae. 2016. Toward a truly multilingual GlobalWordnet grid. In *Proceedings of the 8th Global WordNet Conference (GWC)*, pages 424–431, Bucharest, Romania. Global Wordnet Association.

WordNet-team. 2010. Wordnet 3.0 reference manual. In *WordNet Documentation*. Princeton University, `https://wordnet.princeton.edu/documentation`.

A Appendix: Implementation in NLTK (Python)

```
def index_sense(self, version=None):
    """Read sense key to synset id mapping from index.sense file in corpus directory"""
    fn = "index.sense"
    if version:
        from nltk.corpus import CorpusReader, LazyCorpusLoader

        ixreader = LazyCorpusLoader(version, CorpusReader, r".*/" + fn)
    else:
        ixreader = self
    with ixreader.open(fn) as fp:
        sensekey_map = {}
        for line in fp:
            fields = line.strip().split()
            sensekey = fields[0]
            pos = self._pos_names[int(sensekey.split("%")[1].split(":")[0])]
            sensekey_map[sensekey] = f"{fields[1]}-{pos}"
    return sensekey_map

def map_to_many(self, version="wordnet"):
    sensekey_map1 = self.index_sense(version)
    sensekey_map2 = self.index_sense()
    synset_to_many = {}
    for synsetid in set(sensekey_map1.values()):
        synset_to_many[synsetid] = []
    for sensekey in set(sensekey_map1.keys()).intersection(
        set(sensekey_map2.keys())
    ):
        source = sensekey_map1[sensekey]
        target = sensekey_map2[sensekey]
        synset_to_many[source].append(target)
    return synset_to_many

def map_to_one(self, version="wordnet"):
    self.nomap[version] = set()
    self.splits[version] = {}
    synset_to_many = self.map_to_many(version)
    synset_to_one = {}
    for source in synset_to_many:
        candidates_bag = synset_to_many[source]
        if candidates_bag:
            candidates_set = set(candidates_bag)
            if len(candidates_set) == 1:
                target = candidates_bag[0]
            else:
                counts = []
                for candidate in candidates_set:
                    counts.append((candidates_bag.count(candidate), candidate))
                self.splits[version][source] = counts
                target = max(counts)[1]
            synset_to_one[source] = target
            if source[-1] == "s":
                # Add a mapping from "a" to target for applications like omw,
                # where only Lithuanian and Slovak use the "s" ss_type.
                synset_to_one[f"{source[:-1]}a"] = target
        else:
            self.nomap[version].add(source)
    return synset_to_one

def map_wn(self, version="wordnet"):
    """Mapping from Wordnet 'version' to currently loaded Wordnet version"""
    if self.get_version() == version:
        return None
    else:
        return self.map_to_one(version)
```

Linking the Sanskrit WordNet to the Vedic Dependency Treebank: a pilot study

Erica Biagetti, Chiara Zanchi, Silvia Luraghi
University of Pavia
erica.biagetti@unipv.it, chiara.zanchi01@unipv.it, luraghi@unipv.it

Abstract

The Sanskrit WordNet is a resource currently under development, whose core was induced from a Vedic text sample semantically annotated by means of an ontology mapped on the Princeton WordNet synsets. Building on a previous case study on Ancient Greek (Zanchi et al. 2021), we show how sentence frames can be extracted from morphosyntactically parsed corpora by linking an existing dependency treebank of Vedic Sanskrit to verbal synsets in the Sanskrit WordNet. Our case study focuses on two verbs of asking, *yāc-* and *prach-*, featuring a high degree of variability in sentence frames. Treebanks enhanced with WordNet-based semantic information revealed to be of crucial help in motivating sentence frame alternations.

1 Introduction

WordNets (WNs) are lexical databases storing meaning in a relational way; they usually include little or no morphosyntactic information (sentence frames, SFs) for verb senses (Fellbaum, 1998; 2012). Instead, morphosyntactically annotated corpora (treebanks) store parsed sentences in the form of trees and allow automatically extracting all SFs available for each verb.

Building on previous work on Ancient Greek (Zanchi et al., 2021), we present a pilot study in which the Sanskrit WordNet (SWN) is linked to the Vedic Treebank (VTB). By discussing the SFs of two Sanskrit ditransitive verbs of asking, *yāc-* 'beg for' and *prach-* 'ask, ask for, seek', we show how treebanks enhanced with WN-based semantic information (and, vice versa, WNs enhanced with treebank-based syntactic information) can motivate SF alternations. Other ditransitive verbs denote physical ('give', 'lend', 'hand', 'sell') or mental ('tell', 'show') transfer. Generalizations on SF alternations featured by verbs of asking can thus be partially extended and compared with those on other ditransitive verbs.

The paper is organized as follows. Sec. 2 describes the features of the SWN and of the family of WNs to which it belongs. Sec. 3 introduces the VTB and shows how we link the data. Sec. 4 reviews the morphosyntactic information contained in some WNs. Sec. 5 discusses the sentence frames of *yāc-* and *prach-*. Sec. 6 concludes the paper.

2 The Sanskrit WordNet in the family of WordNets for ancient IE languages

The SWN is part of a family of WNs developed by an international team at the Universities of Pavia, Exeter, and Düsseldorf, the Catholic University of Milan, and the Center for Hellenic Studies at Harvard University (Biagetti et al. 2021a).[1] The family also comprises WNs for Ancient Greek and Latin. To enable crosslinguistic comparison of meanings and structures, WNs of the family are designed to be interoperable with each other and facilitate the integration with other linguistic resources, such as treebanks. This is possible thanks to a standardized set of lemma based URIs that ensure identification and allow linking external resources.

The SWN is based on, and extends, original work by Oliver Hellwig at the *Digital Corpus of Sanskrit* (DCS).[2] The core of the SWN was built by manually annotating selected texts in the DCS for lexical semantics using the OpenCyc ontology (Lenat, 1995), a knowledge base containing concepts with English glosses and relations

[1] https://sanskritwordnet.unipv.it.

[2] http://www.sanskrit-linguistics.org/dcs/index.php.

among them. About 600,000 tokens and 32,200 lemmas were semantically tagged, resulting in a semantic network of over 124,000 concepts and 194,000 relations. If OpenCyc lacked concepts for specific words, the ontology was enhanced with Sanskrit-specific concepts and glosses (ca. 24,400), whereas anachronistic concepts were partly dropped from the inventory. Synonymic sets were populated by the Sanskrit words annotated with the same OpenCyc concept, and a large subset of OpenCyc was automatically mapped onto the synsets of the PWN 2.1 and onto WN 45 lexicographic files using OpenCyc concept glosses (Hellwig, 2017). This yielded 50,595 mappings onto PWN 2.1 and 78,198 onto the lexicographer files (out of a total of 124,040 annotated concepts). Lexical relations in SWN were automatically imported from the .xml version of the Sanskrit-English dictionary Monier-Williams, which lists lemmas under their root and specifies the morphological relation deriving lemmas from the root.[3]

Currently, annotators are working on manually validating the imported annotation and framing it in a cognitive linguistic view of polysemy: all non-literal senses of a lemma can be organized in a network and linked to the literal ones through cognitive metonymies and metaphors (Tyler and Evans, 2003; see Biagetti et al., 2021a and Zanchi et al., 2021). To allow investigating semantic change and variation, annotators are adding etymological, morphological, stylistic and diachronic metadata to each synset gloss associated to a lemma, including etymology, principal parts, prosodic information, irregular and/or alternative forms, periodization(s), literary genre(s), author(s) and work(s) (examples are in Biagetti et al. 2021 and Zanchi et al. 2021).

3 Enhancing the Sanskrit WordNet with sentence frames

3.1 The Vedic Treebank

Vedic is the oldest attested sub-branch of Indo-Aryan, handed down to us by a massive corpus of religious and ritual texts. Despite its historical and linguistic importance, scholars only recently undertook the endeavor of building large-scale digital resources for Vedic. Among the outcomes, the VTB is a syntactically annotated corpus of Vedic literature based on the Universal Dependencies standards (UD; Nivre et al., 2016; Hellwig et al., 2020).

Three versions of the VTB have been released (Hellwig and Sellmer, 2021), accompanied by annotation guidelines that fully account for cases in which the VTB annotation diverges from UD.[4] The third release, still under development within the ChronBMM project,[5] currently contains ca. 18,958 sentences and 140,442 tokens, covering the whole diachrony of the Vedic corpus (Hellwig and Sellmer, 2022).

3.2 A pilot study

In this section, we present a pilot study in which the VTB is enriched with WN-based semantic information on the verbs *yāc-* and *prach-*. As the VTB contains selected passages from the whole of Vedic literature, we selected the entire *R̥gveda*, its oldest representative, as a sub-corpus for our study. We then extracted all occurrences of *yāc-* (9x) and *prach-* (49x) in this text and performed a manual syntactic annotation of the sentences in which they occur.

Like other ditransitive verbs, verbs of asking such as *yāc-* and *prach-* take an agent-like argument (A), a recipient-like argument (R), and a theme-like argument (T) (Malchukov et al., 2010). In case a verb requires more than two core arguments, the UD annotation scheme[6] assigns the role of 'object' (label `obj`) to the noun phrase that is most 'directly affected' by the state of affairs brought about by the verb; the additional argument is labeled as 'indirect object' (`obj`). The UD guidelines further specify that, in languages distinguishing morphological cases, the object is often marked by the accusative, whereas the indirect object takes most commonly the dative.

Determining the SF of verbs such as *yāc-* and *prach-* was a reason for disagreement for the developers of the VTB as both R and T arguments can take the accusative case and it was not clear which of the two arguments should be annotated as the direct object (Biagetti et al., 2021b). Since both R and T can be passivized with the verb

[3] https://www.sanskrit-lexicon.uni-koeln.de/scans/MWScan/2020/web/webtc/indexcaller.php.
[4] Only the first release of the VTB is available at the UD repository. The subsequent two versions can be found at https://raw.githubusercontent.com/OliverHellwig/sanskrit/master/papers/2020lrec/treebank/sanskrit.conllu.
[5] https://chronbmm.phil.hhu.de.
[6] https://universaldependencies.org/u/dep/index.html.

prach- (Hettrich, 1994), and since *yāc-* is only attested in the active, deciding which argument to label as the direct object based on its similarity to the prototypical patient did not seem the best solution. Instead, since R is always encoded by a nominal in the accusative, whereas T can be encoded in different ways (noun/pronoun in the accusative, infinitival dative, complement clause, direct speech), we decided to label R as `obj` and T as `iobj` when they are both realized as nominals in a sentence. When only one of the two arguments is expressed, it takes the relation `obj`. Finally, when T is encoded by a subordinate clause or by direct speech, it takes the relation `ccomp` (complement clause). Cf. example (1).

(1) R̥V 1.164.34

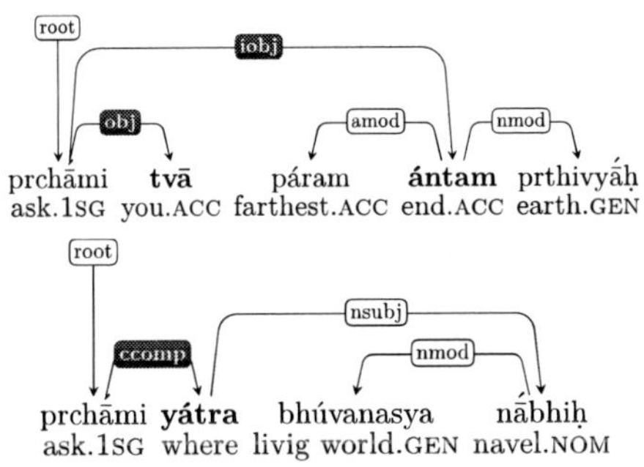

'I ask you about the farthest end of the earth. I ask where (is) the navel of the living world.'

As a second step, exploiting the MISC field of the CoNLLU format, [7] we manually added the appropriate synset to each occurrence of the two verbs in the treebank. For instance, the verb *pr̥cchā́mi* in (1) was assigned the synset v#00608227 "address a question to and expect an answer from". As we will see in Sec. 5, adding sematic information to all forms of a verb in the VTB allows automatically extracting all SFs available for such verb along with information concerning their frequency (see Sec. 5).

4 Sentence frames in WordNets

The verb *request* in the Princeton WN (PWN) is associated to three synsets, including v#00510998 "express the need or desire for". In this sense, *request* features two SFs:

(i) *Somebody ---s something*;
(ii) *Somebody ---s somebody.*

Such SFs provide limited semantic information about animacy of verbal arguments, by distinguishing *somebody* vs. *something*, and aspectual information concerning the verb, in the form of the simple present third singular ending ---*s*. Overall, the PWN contains 35 SFs, which indicate "the number of noun arguments that the verb subcategorizes for" (Fellbaum, 1998). [8] In contrast, no information is given on the semantic roles of the noun slots in the frame, and a direct linking between the PWN and other resources richer in this respect (e.g., those in the Unified Verb Index) [9] has not been implemented yet. Finally, SFs of the PWN are intuition-based, and no corpus-based examples accompany SFs.

As pointed out in Zanchi et al. (2021), as SFs are language-specific, they cannot be automatically ported from the PWN to other WNs. Furthermore, the relevant information in SFs is language-specific too, depending, e.g., on how grammatical relations are encoded or on whether verbal aspect is grammaticalized in a specific language. For this reason, WNs greatly vary as to the type of information provided along with SFs. In GermaNet, the German WN, [10] the verb *bitten* 'request', glossed as "jemanden in höflicher Form nach etwas fragen", features two SFs (examples are from GermaNet):

(2) NN.An.AZ – *Er bat mich, ihm zu helfen.*
(3) NN.An.PP – *Meine Eltern haben mich um Hilfe gebeten.*

In (2)-(3), the abbreviations are as follows:

- NN: grammatical subject that is realized as a noun phrase in the nominative case;
- An: optional accusative complement;
- AZ: obligatory accusative plus infinitive clause introduced by *zu*;
- PP: obligatory prepositional phrase.

Thus, GermaNet provides information about case marking and distinguishes between complements and adverbials, which can be either obligatory or optional. In contrast, GermaNet lacks information on verbal aspect, which is not grammaticalized in German, and on animacy. The examples provided by GermaNet are partly corpus-based.

[7] https://universaldependencies.org/format.html.
[8] Instead, the Open English WN (https://en-word.net/lemma/request) does not contain SFs.
[9] https://uvi.colorado.edu.
[10] (https://weblicht.sfs.uni-tuebingen.de/rover/

In the case study on Ancient Greek in Zanchi et al. (2021: 734 ff.), the SFs were modelled on those of GermaNet and integrated with animacy information on nominals and aspectual information on verbs, as verbal aspect is grammaticalized in Ancient Greek and interacts with tense and voice. The Ancient Greek verb *aggéllō*, in the synset v#00659537 "make known", features four SFs (and five additional sub-frames, see Zanchi et al. 2021: 735 f.), represented as follows:

1. NN(+a) ...ptcp.fut/aor Nd(+a);
2. NN(+a) ...impf/aor Na(-a) Nd(+a);
3. NN(+a) ...aor ND(+a) INFINITIVE;
4. NN(+a) ...impf/aor COMPL CLAUSE.

The abbreviations indicate the following:

- NN: as in GermaNet;
- Nd: optional dative complement;
- ND: obligatory dative complement;
- (+a): animate noun;
- (-a): inanimate noun;
- aor, fut, impf, ptcp: usual glosses for tenses and moods (aorist, future, imperfect, participle), which are related to aspectual information.

5 A case study with two verbs of asking: *yāc-* and *prach-*

We now discuss the SFs we extracted for the verbs *yāc-* and *prach-*. Note that Vedic is a null subject language, but we still indicate subject NPs as NN (nominative NP), as it triggers verbal agreement (there are no impersonal forms among the occurrences analyzed). The verb shows a complex aspectual system, with the present stem indicating imperfective, the aorist stem perfective and the perfect resultative aspect. It is not clear to what extent this system, that Vedic inherited for Proto-Indo-European and that is reflected in verbal morphology, was still relevant at the time of the Vedic texts; the VTB allows retrieving only partial information about verbal aspect, as the aorist and the perfect are not kept distinct. The SFs we found in our corpus are discussed in sections 5.1-5.2 and summarized in Table 1. For each SF, the table lists the synset(s) it occurs with as well as the example(s) provided in Sections 5.1 and 5.2.

N	Sentence Frame – Synset(s)	Ex.
1	NN(+a) ...pres/past NA(+a) Na(-a): - v#00515892 "call upon in supplication; entreat" - v#00608227 "address a question to and expect an answer from" NN(+a) ...pres/past pass NA(+a) Na(-a) - v#00511577 "ask (a person) to do something" (passive)	(4), (5)
2	NN(+a) ...pres NA(-a) - v#00510727 "make a request or demand for something to somebody" - v#00608227 "address a question to and expect an answer from" - v#00532796 "inquire about" - v#00494502 "have a wish or desire to know something"	(6)
2_i	NN(+a) ...pres/past NA(±a) - v#01533628 "try to get or reach"	
3	NN(+a) ...pres NA(+a) - v#00608227 "address a question to and expect an answer from" - v#01727931 "make amorous advances"	(7), (11)
4	NN(+a) ...pres NA(+a) Ques - v#00608227 "address a question to and expect an answer from"	(8)
5	NN(+a) ...pres NA(+a) NG(-a) - v#00608227 "address a question to and expect an answer from"	(9)
6	NN(+a) ...pres Ques - v#00532796 "inquire about" - v#00494502 "have a wish or desire to know something"	(10)

Table 1. Sentence frames found in our corpus.

5.1 *yāc-*

The verb *yāc-* occurs nine times in our corpus and comprises two synsets: v#00515892 "call upon in supplication; entreat" and v#00510727 "make a request or demand for something to somebody". The first synset is more frequent and shows SF 1 (NA indicates an obligatory accusative complement). The linear order reflects our assumption that the R argument functions as second argument of the verb (see Sec. 3.2).

1. NN(+a) ...pres/past NA(+a) Na(-a)

(4) *sómam* *ín* *mā* *sunvánto*
soma.ACC PTC 1SG.ACC press.PTCP.NOM
yācatā *vásu*
beg.IMPV.2PL good(N).ACC

'Just when you are pressing soma, beg me for good things.' (RV 10.48.5)[11]

(5) *mā́ tvā ... sádā yā́cann*
NEG 2SG.ACC always beg.PTCP.N
ahám girā́ ... cukrudham
1SG.NOM song(F).INST anger.INJ.AOR.1SG
'Always begging you with my song [...] let me not anger you.' (RV 8.1.20)

The second synset, v#00510727 "make a request or demand for something to somebody", is instantiated in a single occurrence with the SF 2, in which the T argument functions as second argument of the verb.

2. NN(+a) ...pres NA(-a)

(6) *śukrā́ ā́śiram yācante*
clear.NOM.PL mixture(F).ACC beg.IND.MID.3PL
'The clear ones beg for the milk mixture.' (RV 8.2.10)

5.2 *prach-*

The verb *prach-* is not only more frequent than *yāc-* as it occurs 49 times, but also shows a more nuanced semantics, comprising six synsets (in order of decreasing frequency):[12]

- v#00608227 "address a question to and expect an answer from" (27x)
- v#00532796 "inquire about" (9x)
- v#01533628 "try to get or reach" (8)
- v#00494502 "have a wish or desire to know something" (2x);
- v#00511577 "ask (a person) to do something" (2x);
- v#01727931 "make amorous advances towards" (1x)

The meaning v#00608227 "address a question to and expect an answer from" features SFs 1 and 2 discussed in Sec. 5.1; further SFs are 3, as in (7), 4, as in (8) and 5, as in (9) (the latter only attested once). All SFs occur with verb forms based on the present stem (present and imperfect); only SF 2 occurs once with a past verb form. In SF 4, "Ques" indicates a direct or indirect question.

3. NN(+a) ...pres NA(+a)

(7) *tám pṛchatā ... sá veda*
3SG.ACC ask.IMPV.2PL 3SG.NOM know.PF.3SG
'Ask him: [...] he knows.' (RV 1.145.1)

4. NN(+a) ...pres NA(+a) Ques

(8) *kavī́n pṛchāmi ajásya*
poet.ACC.PL ask.1SG unborn.GEN
rūpé kím ... ékam
form.LOC what(N).NOM one(N).NOM
'I ask the perceptive poets [...]: What is the One in the form of the Unborn [=the Sun]?' (RV 1.164.6)

5. NN(+a) ...pres NA(+a) NG(-a)

(9) *ví pṛchāmi pākyā̀*
PV ask.2SG ignorance.INST
ná devā́n ... adbhutásya
NEG god.ACC.PL unerring.GEN
'In my naïveté I ask (you), not (other) gods, about the unerring (soma).' (RV 1.120.4)

The meaning v#00532796 "inquire about" selects SFs that do not involve a R argument. The T argument can be an accusative NP, instantiating SF 2, or a direct question. In this case the SF is 6, as in (10).

6. NN(+a) ...pres Ques

(10) *yám smā pṛchánti kúha*
REL.ACC PTC ask.3PL where
sá íti ghorám
3SG.NOM QUOT terrifying.ACC
'The terrifying one about whom they always ask: Where is he?' (RV 2.12.5)

Verbal tense is always present, except for an occurrence of a passive past participle, in which the T argument is passivized (RV 3.20.3).

The meaning v#01533628 "try to get or reach" features a T argument which can be animate or inanimate, hence a variant of SF 2:

2ᵢ NN(+a) ...pres/past NA(±a)

In our corpus we also found some passive occurrences that contain a passive past participle, in which the T argument is passivized. Synset v#00494502 "have a wish or desire to know something" occurs twice without a R argument because both occurrences feature the reflexive middle: hence the R is also the subject. The SFs are 2 and 6. We tagged as instantiating synset v#00511577 "ask (a person) to do something" two occurrences, both featuring passive forms with the R argument functioning as subject and no T argument. These occurrences are passive versions of SF 1, in which the non-obligatory T argument does not occur. Finally, the meaning "make amorous advances" features an animate R argument and the SF is 3; note that the only

[11] Abbreviations in glosses follow the *Leipzig Glossing Rules* (https://www.eva.mpg.de/lingua/pdf/Glossing-Rules.pdf).

[12] Two occurrences of the compound verb *sám prach-* feature the synset v#00517734 "discuss the terms of an arrangement" (e.g. *They negotiated the terms*). We have not included them in our discussion.

occurrence we found in the corpus, shown in (11), has a referential null object as R.

(11) *yád aśvinā pṛchámānāv* ***Ø**ᵢ*
when A.voc ask.PTCP.MID.NOM.DU
áyātaṁ ... vahatúṁ sūryā́yāḥᵢ
drive.IMPF.2DU wedding.acc S.GEN
'When, o Aśvins, you two drove [...] to the wedding of Sūryā to ask for her.' (RV 10.85.14)

Summing up, the most frequent SFs with *prach-* are 1 and 2, which are also the only two SFs that occur with *yāc-*. They both involve the occurrence of a referential T argument, coherently with the meaning of *yāc-* 'beg (for)'; SF 2 is the only one we found that does not involve a R argument. In addition, *prach-* which most often indicates the activity of asking questions, also frequently occurs in SFs 4 and 6 that contain questions as T argument; the latter does not appear in SF 3 while SF 5 constitutes a sporadic variant in our corpus.

Concerning verbal voice, while both verbs are ditransitive, *yāc-* does not occur in the passive in our corpus. In its turn *prach-* can passivize when it features SFs 1 and 2. In the first case, it is the R argument that becomes the passive subject, while with SF 2, which does not contain the R, the T is the passive subject. SFs 2 and 6, with no R as second argument (synset v#00494502 "wish to know something") may contain middle verb forms, in which case the R is also the subject, as the verb has reflexive meaning. Notably, middle voice is not annotated in VTB, and these occurrences have been considered as instantiation of SF 2 and 6, similar to occurrences in which the R does not occur in any syntactic position. However, they are semantically different. A further improvement would be enriching the VTB with information concerning verbal voice, as we discuss in Sec. 6.

6 Future work

We plan to add semantic information to all verbs in the VTB and to extract SFs attested for each verb as well as information on their frequency. While in some cases it will be necessary to manually add synsets to each occurrence of a verb, the process can be partly automated when the relationship between the SF and a verb's sense is stable. Cf. the different synsets associated to active and middle forms of the verb *duh-*:

a. Active 'milk', 'extract', 'benefit from':
- Intransitive/transitive + cognate object: v#00133336 "take milk from female mammals"
- Transitive: v#00925055 "obtain from a substance, as by mechanical action"
- Metaphoric: v#01565865 "benefit from"

b. Middle 'give milk':
- Intransitive/transitive + cognate object: v#00806715 "give suck to"
- Transitive: v#01119839 "give or supply"

As alternations in a verb's SFs often co-occur with voice alternations, automatic annotation will be possible once the VTB has been enriched with information on verbal voice. We also plan to enhance the annotation interface of the SWN to include syntactic information. Since the SWN is enriched with chronological information on the attestation of every single sense of a word, enhancing the annotation interface in such a way will allow studying changes in valency over time.

Acknowledgments

This article results from the joint work of the authors. For academic purposes, Chiara Zanchi is responsible of sections 1, 2 and 3, Erica Biagetti of sections 4 and 6, and Silvia Luraghi of section 5. Furthermore, Erica Biagetti is responsible of data extraction and annotation.

References

Erica Biagetti, Chiara Zanchi and William M. Short. 2021a. Toward the creation of WordNets for ancient Indo-European languages. In *Proceeding of the 11th Global WordNet Conference*. University of South Africa (UNISA): Global Wordnet Association, pages 258–266. https://aclanthology.org/2021.gwc-1.30

Erica Biagetti, Oliver Hellwig, Salvatore Scarlata, Elia Ackermann and Paul Widmer. 2021b. Evaluating Syntactic Annotation of Ancient Languages: Lessons from the Vedic Treebank. *Old World: Journal of Ancient Africa and Eurasia*, 1(1), 1–32.

Christiane Fellbaum (ed.). 1998. *WordNet: An electronic lexical database*. MIT Press, Cambridge, MA.

Christiane Fellbaum. 2012. WordNet. In *The Encyclopedia of Applied Linguistics*, Wiley Online Library. https://doi.org/10.1002/9781405198431.wbeal1285

Heinrich Hettrich. 1994. Semantische und syntaktische Betrachtungen zum doppelten Akkusativ. In *Früh-, Mittel-, Spätindogermanisch: Akten der IX.*

Fachtagung der Indogermanischen Gesellschaft, pages 111–134.

Oliver Hellwig. 2017. Coarse semantic classification of rare nouns using cross-lingual data and recurrent neural networks. In *IWCS 2017-12th International Conference on Computational Semantics-Long papers*, Montpellier, France.

Oliver Hellwig, Salvatore Scarlata, Elia Ackermann, and Paul Widmer. 2020. The Treebank of Vedic Sanskrit. In *Proceedings of The 12th Language Resources and Evaluation Conference* (LREC 2020), pages 5137–5146.

Oliver Hellwig and Sven Sellmer. 2021. The Vedic Treebank. In Erica Biagetti, Chiara Zanchi and Silvia Luraghi (eds.), *Building New Resources for Historical Linguistics*. Pavia, Pavia University Press, pages 31–40.

Oliver Hellwig and Sven Sellmer. 2022. Detecting Diachronic Syntactic Developments in Presence of Bias Terms. In *Proceedings of the Second Workshop on Language Technologies for Historical and Ancient Languages*, pages 10–19.

Douglas B. Lenat. 1995. CYC: A large-scale investment in knowledge infrastructure. *Communications of the ACM*, 38(11), pages 33–38.

Andrej Malchukov, Martin Haspelmath and Bernard Comrie. 2010. Ditransitive constructions: a typological overview. In Andrej Malchukov, Martin Haspelmath and Bernard Comrie (eds.), *Studies in Ditransitive Constructions. A Comparative Handbook*. Berlin, New York: Mouton De Gruyter, pages 1–64.

Joakim Nivre, Marie-Catherine de Marneffe, Filip Ginter et al. 2016. Universal Dependencies V1: A Multilingual Treebank Collection. In *Proceedings of the Tenth International Conference on Language Resources and Evaluation (LREC'16)*, Portorož, Slovenia. European Language Resources Association (ELRA), pages 1659–1666.

Andrea Tyler and Vyvyan Evans. 2003. *The semantics of English prepositions: Spatial scenes, embodied meaning, and cognition.* Cambridge, Cambridge University Press.

Chiara, Zanchi, Erica Biagetti and Silvia Luraghi. 2021. Linking the Ancient Greek WordNet to the Homeric Dependency Lexicon. In *Computational Linguistics and Intelligent Technologies. Papers from the Annual International Conference "Dialogue"*, No. 20, pages 729–737.

StarNet: A WordNet Editor Interface

Ezgi Sanıyar, Oğuzhan Kuyrukçu
Starlang Yazılım Danışmanlık
ezgi.saniyar@gmail.com, kuyrukcuoguz@gmail.com

Olcay Taner Yıldız
Özyeğin University
olcay.yildiz@ozyegin.edu.tr

Abstract

In this paper, we introduce StarNet WordNet Editor, an open-source annotation tool designed for natural language processing. It's mainly used for creating and maintaining machine-readable dictionaries like WordNet (Miller, 1995) or domain-specific dictionaries. WordNet editor provides a user friendly interface and since it is open-source, it is easy to use and develop. Besides English and Turkish WordNet (KeNet) (Bakay et al., 2020), it is also applicable to several languages and their domain specific dictionaries.

1 Introduction

Wordnets are natural language processing resources used in tasks like information retrieval or categorization. As a broad definition, a WordNet is a machine-readable dictionary with the lexicographic information of words including synsets and separate senses of those synsets. Mainly, synsets are the single units that the semantic relations or mappings are built on. Senses, on the other hand, are the definitions given for each synset. Based on the idea that words can be explained by their relations to other words, WordNets offer basic semantic relations such as hypernymy, meronymy, or antonymy between synsets.

After the Princeton WordNet (PWN) (Miller, 1995) several WordNets in different languages have been created. Finnish WordNet FinnWord- Net (Lindén and Carlson, 2010), Polish Word-Net (Derwojedowa et al., 2008) , and French WordNet WOLF (Sagot and Fiser, 2008) are some of the pioneering WordNets in the world. The multilingual WordNet EuroWordNet (EWN) (Vossen, 1997) is another significant WordNet comprising seven European languages, namely English, Dutch, Italian, Spanish, German, French, Czech, and Estonian. Turkish, on the other hand, has mainly two WordNets; BalkaNet (TR-WordNet) (Bilgin et al., 2004) and KeNet (Bakay et al., 2020). TR-Wordnet of BalkaNet is the first WordNet of Turkish and has 14,626 synsets, while KeNet is currently the largest Turkish WordNet with 76,757 synsets.

Wordnets can be presented or edited by software (editors) designed for this purpose. These editors are used to edit WordNets and they have a crucial role in correcting or updating items, matching synsets with their synonyms and composing semantic relations like hypernyms.

StarNet WordNet Editor is one such software. It is designed to perform multipurpose functions in order to build, edit and group synsets and senses in WordNets. It has been primarily used for Turkish and English. However, it is suitable to be used for any target language, regardless of the morphological complexity of the language across the analytic-synthetic spectrum. In this paper, we present our multi-functional WordNet editor StarNet and discuss each of its functions and process applied to it. We present a literature review on editors in section 2, describe and discuss the functions of each component of our editor in sections 3 and 4, and present a conclusion in section 5.

2 Literature Review

Originally intended to be manually consulted, the purpose of Wordnets turned more towards automatic processing, and a need for interfaces to connect this resource onto different applications was born (Tufis et al., 2004). Visdic, developed by the team of Czech WordNet (Horák and Smrž, 2004) and Polaris (Louw, 1997) and Periscope (Cuypers and Adriaens, 1997), employed by EuroWordNet are examples of softwares designed for this purpose. Visdic is used for presenting and editing dictionaries stored in XML format and it's configurable with regards to program behaviour and dictionary design. Polaris is used to create and edit WordNets, while Periscope is used to view said WordNets. Both are in addition used to export WordNets. However, when it comes to building

WordNets from scratch, these softwares are not very convenient options. Polaris is a licensed and rather expensive software that is no longer being developed and Visdic is not optimized for building but rather presenting & editing WordNets. Here we present a new, easy to use and open source alternative that can be used effectively to build new WordNets as well and view and edit existing ones.

In creating and mapping WordNets, two main approaches are being used; the expand approach and the merge approach. The expand approach takes PWN as the base and translates it to the target language (Vossen, 1996). Once the relations are transferred from English, they are checked manually. French (Sagot and Fiser, 2008) and Finnish (Lindén and Carlson, 2010) WordNets are examples of the expand approach. On the other hand, in the merge approach, PWN/English WordNet is not taken as the base. WordNets are created independently with intra-lingual relations and these are then linked to English. Our approach is based on the merge approach like Polish WordNet (Derwojedowa et al., 2008), Russian WordNet (Balkova et al., 2004), Norwegian WordNet NorNet (Fjeld and Nygaard, 2009) and Danish WordNet DanNet (Pedersen et al., 2009). The expand approach is assumed to be a practical way for building a new WordNet in target languages, but it may be biased towards the imitated WordNet. Merge approach, on the other hand, results in more concrete and accurate structures for languages that differ from English in their semantic patterns and potentially allows us to maintain language-specific properties (Bakay et al., 2020), (Vossen et al., 1998).

We used five different editors for different components of a WordNet. This allows the user to modify these components independently of each other. Our program works with XML format. It works as a desktop application and employs Java for back end structure. It can thus be used with all major operating systems. In the following, we will explain how our program works component by component.

3 Editors

3.1 Literal Matcher

The construction of the synsets presented and edited in our interface is derived from the latest Contemporary Dictionary of Turkish (CDT) (Ehsani et al., 2018) published by the Turkish Language Institute (TLI). In the dictionary, it is stated that the synonym literals are mainly used in the definitions of senses, which are given in one line separated with commas. For example, the definition of word *kırmızı* (red), is 'Kırmızı renkte olan, kızıl, al' (Something in red color); and possible synonym literals of word *kırmızı* are *kızıl* and *al*. After extracting possible synonym literals from the definitions, they are annotated by human annotators. In this part of the process, the Literal Matcher is a great help in viewing the literals that are possible synonyms in a synset.

The Literal Matcher is a tool enabling synonym literal matching in the target languages. This interface offers many facilities such as presenting every sense definition of a unique literal, convenient editing and a quick tag-save mode, which saves processes as soon as literals are matched, without further operation (Figure 1). Synonym candidates will appear in two groups in this component. The interface enables us to annotate and match approximately 250 synset literals in an hour. While the tool is easy to use and practical in many ways, checking multiple meanings and synonyms in every step can decrease the speed of the matching process.

The Literal Matcher is a practical option for matching intralingual synonym literals. However, transitivity may cause problems as a result of multi-matching. Even if the first literal and the second literal sense definitions are completely synonymous, when these literal matches are prolonged, the first literal definition and the fourth/fifth literal definitions may not be exactly synonymous. As a solution to this problem, StarNet presents the editor Synset Matcher. Such overgrown synsets with weak or absent synonym relations between its literals can be viewed and edited in the Synset Matcher by using split/merge processes.

3.2 Synset Matcher

As mentioned above, creating synsets with synonym literals can be challenging especially when the mapping is overgrown, the transitivity decreases. This process poses a problem in creating meaningful and accurate synsets. Here, the Synset Matcher plays a crucial role as it enables us to view all the literals in synsets and merge/split the synsets when necessary.

The Synset Matcher receives data from the Literal Matcher and acts as a supportive editor. It provides editing options for synonym literals in languages and provides an easy and practical interface

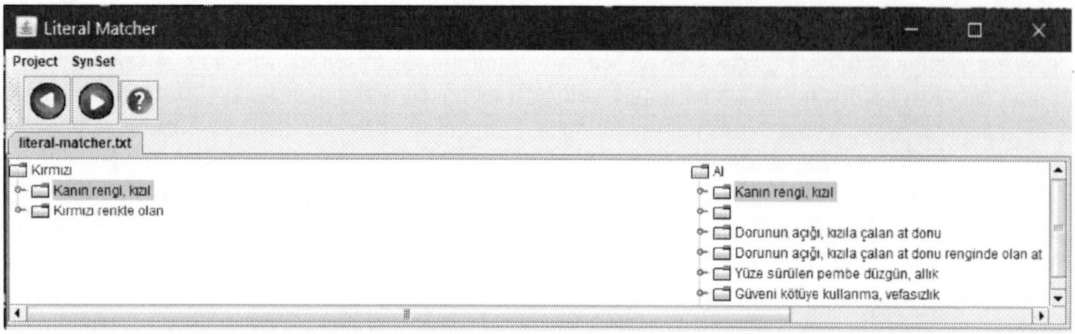

Figure 1: Interface of Literal Matcher with the synonyms of *red* in Turkish

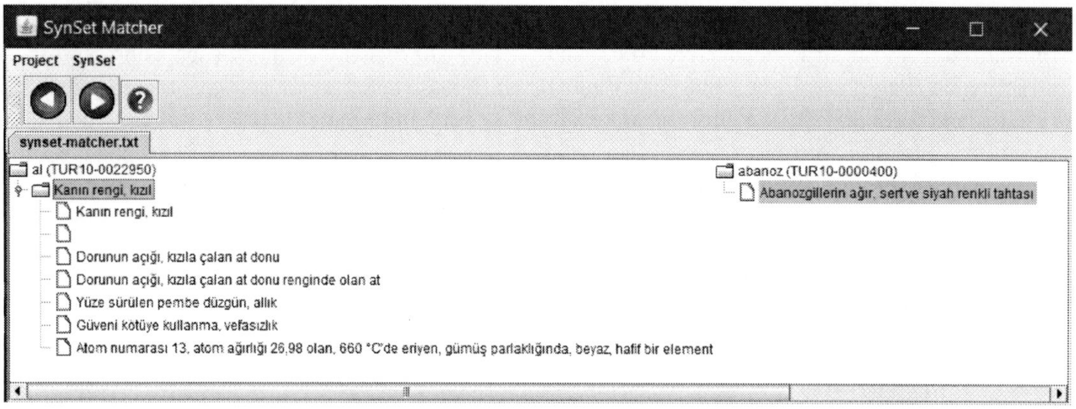

Figure 2: Interface of Synset Matcher; the first and final match example of red

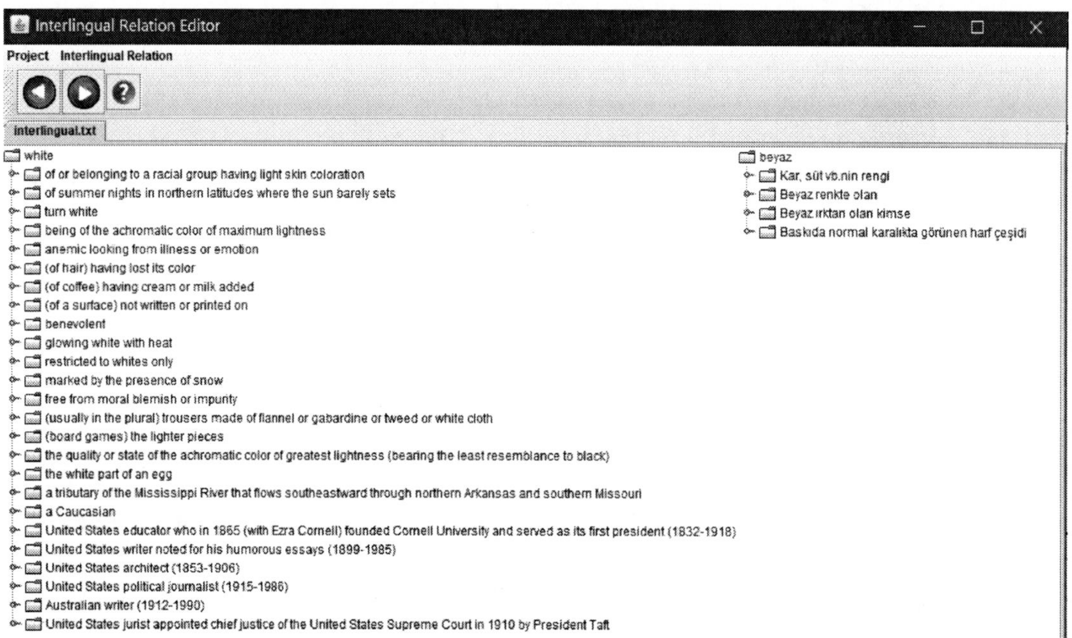

Figure 3: Interface of Interlingual Matcher with the English-Turkish synsets of white

to check the synsets built in the Literal Matcher. It allows us to identify the different synsets that should be grouped together because of their meanings and enables us to merge them. Similarly, any synsets whose literals should be separated because of their unrelated definitions that are grouped together as a result of transitivity problems or any other mistakes during the previous processes can be split via the Synset Matcher. The Synset Matcher makes it possible to see the whole picture of a synset by showing us the final matching maps of all of its literals and to prune the synset if need be. As a result of this mapping and editing process in the Synset Matcher, we obtain the final version of synsets (Figure 2).

3.3 Interlingual Matcher

Interlingual relations and matching have great importance in the development of WordNets since creating these relations and linking the WordNets of different relations provide us with an important resource in many areas like machine translation. Therefore, an editor that works interlingually is a crucial tool in creating internationally applicable and useful resources and connecting the created WordNets to each other.

StarNet WordNet editor has an interface that enables inter-lingual matching. In creating KeNet, a merge approach is used and synsets in KeNet and PWN are matched as a result of this merging process. Both the synset matches and possible multilingual relations are checked by human annotators. The synset groups created in this process are transferred to the Interlingual Matcher to view and edit the matches.

The Interlingual Matcher is used by English PWN and Turkish KeNet data and matched synsets one-to-one between the languages by human annotators. As a result of this process, the existing matches can be checked and confirmed, and new matches can be created when needed. This process is potentially applicable to all languages via the Interlingual Matcher.

The Interlingual Matcher interface is quite similar to the Literal Matcher's interface and is easy to understand. The tag-save mode is active for the Interlingual Matcher as well. Unlike the Literal Matcher, however, only one-to-one matching is offered in the Interlingual Matcher: For each English word, suggested synonyms from the other language can be chosen and tagged (Figure 3).

3.4 WordNet Hypernym Editor

The WordNet Hypernym Editor provides an interface to build semantic hierarchies between synsets. With this component, we can annotate synsets in separate categories through semantic relations. This interface has enabled us to create our hypernym relations, and has been providing great convenience in other ongoing projects (Figure 4) like Turkish Estate WordNet and Turkish Tourism WordNet. Figure 4 shows us the interface of the hypernym editor and synsets derived from domain-specific Turkish WordNets.

The WordNet Hypernym Editor toolbar provides us with the opportunity to quickly and practically execute all the operations we might need to perform in the dictionary. It has options such as "quick save", "edit", "insert child", "remove child" (see below for *child*), "merge" or "change font size" (which may prove important for the well-being of the annotators' eyes). In addition, it includes the options "add to WordNet from dictionary" and "add to dictionary from WordNet" that enables editing via WordNet and matching the dictionary with the WordNet of the language. Senses are at the forefront in this component and fast access to them is of great importance. For this reason, all synsets can be reached easily with all their senses. When we type literals in the search bar, we can see all the senses of that literal and organize hypernym relations according to the senses (Figure 5). The WordNet Hypernym Editor provides two operations, merge and split: During or after the editing phase, synsets that should be grouped with the same unique sense can be merged, or incorrectly combined synsets (such as those originating from meaning-related drifts or POS-related drifts (Bakay et al., 2019)) can be split.

Taking the PWN editing style (Miller et al., 1990) as an example, the WordNet Hypernym Editor allows us to organize words in four categories: noun, verb, adjective and adverb. This allows obtaining a synset tree similar to the English WordNet (Miller, 1995).

It should be noted that there would be too many items in a natural language dictionary to organize into a sensible semantic hierarchy on-the-go for the annotators. At least the upper levels of the intended hierarchy would need to be specified outside the program and serve as a guide for the annotators. Of course, the more comprehensive this guide hierarchy, the better; but majority of lexical items in a language would still need to be put in its proper place in the hierarchy by the annotators. Principles for placing individual senses into the hierarchy should be specified. However, since annotators will

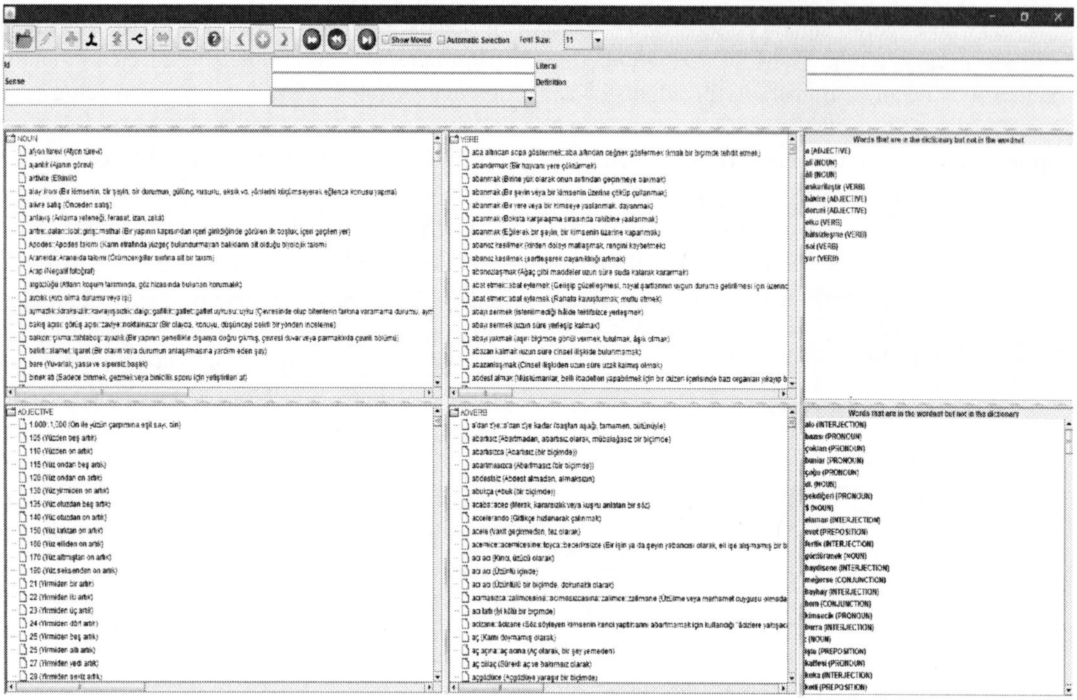

Figure 4: Interface of Hypernym Editor

have different understanding of some senses, there will inescapably be some subjectivity in the hierarchy that results, even if the annotators follow the same principles.

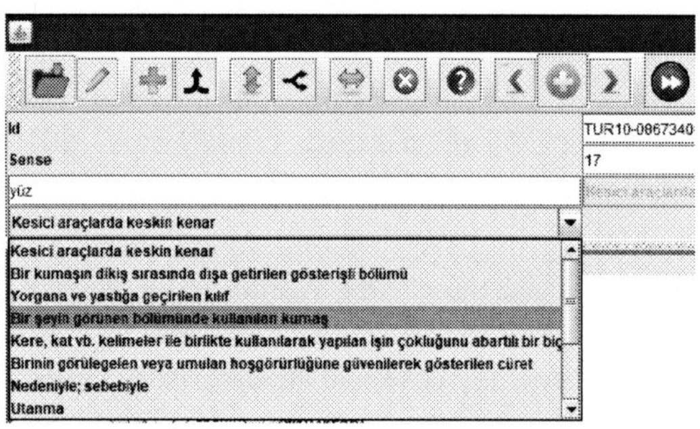

Figure 5: Synset Sense search of yüz which has different senses such as face, side, or part of something

Within the semantic hierarchy, we refer to a synset that is placed under another as a "child", and a synset with another synset placed below it is referred to as a "parent". In a completed hierarchy, every noun synset, except for the one designated at the top of the hierarchy (for example, in our WordNet, KeNet, this was *varlık* (being/entity), will have a parent. This is not necessitated by the editor, so if desired, items can be left out of the hierarchy or the dictionary could contain multiple independent hierarchies. Except for the end nodes, every synset will also have a child or children. Importantly, some synsets could have multiple parents. This is a rarer occurrence but natural languages might exhibit such semantic relations. *Su* (water) for example, is a child of both *sıvı* (liquid) and *ikili bileşik* (binary compound) in our WordNet. Of course, a synset could be assigned multiple parents by mistake too. When a synset has multiple parents, our editor will show it in red colors to distinguish it, so that it is easy to find them and correct their hypernym relations if necessary. Overall, since it has a practical interface, the WordNet Hypernym Editor allows an annotator to match approximately 70-80 synsets in one hour.

3.5 Dictionary Editor

The Dictionary Editor is distinct from the previous components in that it is an interface designed to create domain-specific dictionaries, whereas the former components are for building and maintaining natural language dictionaries. With the Dictionary Editor, synsets inside a WordNet can be added or removed and sense inputs of synsets can be edited in order to obtain a domain-specific dictionary. Whichever sense of a synset in the WordNet is used in that domain can be selected and

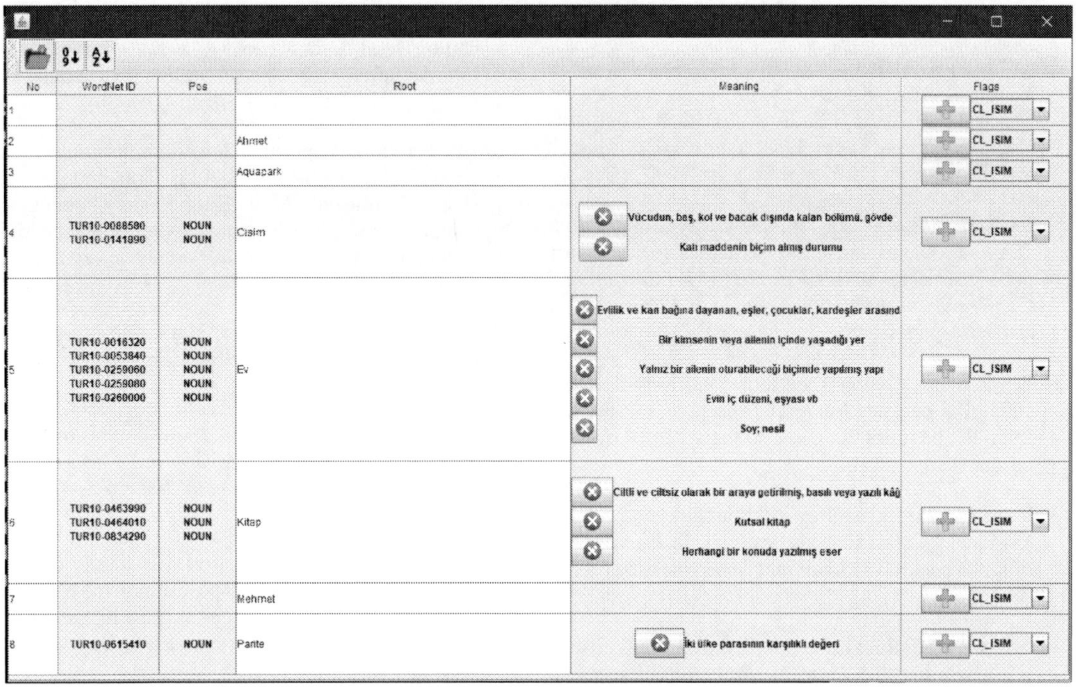

Figure 6: Interface of Dictionary Editor

transferred to the new dictionary or synsets can be transferred automatically from an existing WordNet to the domain-specific dictionary. Finally, if the sought sense is lacking, it can simply be added to the dictionary with this editor. This interface also makes sure that the dictionary and the WordNet are in accord: When an entry is added to the dictionary, it will be added to the WordNet too, and vice versa. The editor can also sort synsets numerically or alphabetically. The Dictionary Editor can be a practical tool for improving applications such as chat-bots or search engines. With the Dictionary editor, we have created several domain specific dictionaries including Turkish Estate WordNet and Turkish Tourism WordNet mentioned above. See (Figure 6) for the Dictionary Editor interface.

4 Discussion

StarNet WordNet Editor stands as a robust and open source alternative for people looking to develop a new WordNet. It can be used to view and build a domain-specific WordNet as well as a WordNet for a new target language. Being especially suitable for the merge approach, our editor will allow users to create new WordNets that preserve the language-specific features, which is especially important for agglutinative languages such as Turkish. Our editor also allows direct matching between WordNet and the morphological analyzer. Works on agglutinative languages such as Turkish or Hungarian, which may require exhaustive accuracy in morphological analysis for some expressions to be processed correctly in the WordNet, can particularly benefit from this feature. WordNet editor can be used on any operating system that supports Java, including Windows, Linux and Mac OS. It is in this regard unique among open source tools developed as a WordNet interface. In addition to being available and having advantages for various platforms and languages, WordNet Editor will present a user friendly interface for editing and maintaining a WordNet.

5 Conclusion

In this paper, we introduced a multipurpose editor. The editor we present has features that can be useful in establishing accurate synonym/hypernym relations and building domain-specific dictionaries. For future work, we intend to use it in other target language WordNets and incorporate Turkish FrameNet (Baker et al., 1998) (Marsan et al., 2021) into this editor and make it able to create and edit frame relations of languages.

References

Ozge Bakay, Ozlem Ergelen, Elif Sarmis, Selin Yıldırım, Atilla Kocabalcioglu, Bilge Nas Arican, Merve Ozcelik, Ezgi Saniyar, Oguzhan Kuyrukcu, Begüm Avar, and Olcay Taner Yıldız. 2020. Turkish WordNet KeNet. In *Proceedings of GWC 2021*.

Ozge Bakay, Ozlem Ergelen, and Olcay Taner Yildiz. 2019. Problems caused by semantic drift in wordnet synset construction. In *2019 4th International Conference on Computer Science and Engineering (UBMK)*, pages 1–5.

Collin F. Baker, Charles J. Fillmore, and John B. Lowe. 1998. The berkeley framenet project. ACL '98/COLING '98, page 86–90, USA. Association for Computational Linguistics.

Valentina Balkova, Andrey Sukhonogov, and Sergey Yablonsky. 2004. Russian wordnet. In *Proceedings of the Second Global Wordnet Conference*, pages 31–38.

O. Bilgin, O. Cetinoglu, and K. Oflazer. 2004. Building a wordnet for Turkish. *Romanian Journal of Information Science*, 7:163–172.

I Cuypers and G Adriaens. 1997. Periscope: the ewn viewer. *EuroWordNet Project LE4003, Deliverable D008d012. University of Amsterdam.*

M. Derwojedowa, M. Piasecki, S. Szpakowicz, M. Zawisławska, and B. Broda. 2008. Words, Concepts and Relations in the Construction of Polish WordNet. In *Proceedings of GWC 2008*, pages 162–177.

R. Ehsani, E. Solak, and O.T. Yildiz. 2018. Constructing a WordNet for Turkish Using Manual and Automatic Annotation. *ACM Transactions on Asian and Low-Resource Language Information Processing (TALLIP)*, 17(3).

Ruth Vatvedt Fjeld and Lars Nygaard. 2009. Nornet—a monolingual wordnet of modern norwegian.

Ales Horák and Pavel Smrž. 2004. Visdic–wordnet browsing and editing tool. In *Proceedings of the Second International WordNet Conference–GWC*, pages 136–141.

Krister Lindén and Lauri Carlson. 2010. Finnwordnet–finnish wordnet by translation. *LexicoNordica–Nordic Journal of Lexicography*, 17:119–140.

M Louw. 1997. The polaris user manual. Technical report, Internal Report, Lermout & Hauspie.

B. Marsan, N. Kara, M. Ozcelik, B. N. Arican, N. Cesur, A. Kuzgun, E. Saniyar, O. Kuyrukcu, and O. T. Yıldız. 2021. Building the Turkish FrameNet. In *Proceedings of GWC 2021*.

George A. Miller. 1995. Wordnet: a lexical database for english. *Communications of the ACM*, 38:39–41.

George A Miller, Richard Beckwith, Christiane Fellbaum, Derek Gross, and Katherine J Miller. 1990. Introduction to wordnet: An on-line lexical database. *International journal of lexicography*, 3(4):235–244.

Bolette Sandford Pedersen, Sanni Nimb, Jørg Asmussen, Nicolai Hartvig Sørensen, Lars Trap-Jensen, and Henrik Lorentzen. 2009. Dannet: the challenge of compiling a wordnet for danish by reusing a monolingual dictionary. *Language resources and evaluation*, 43(3):269–299.

Benoît Sagot and Darja Fiser. 2008. Building a free french wordnet from multilingual resources.

Dan Tufis, D Cristeau, and Sofia Stamou. 2004. Balkanet: Aims, methods, results and perspectives – a general overview. *Romanian Journal of Information Science and Technology Special Issue*, 7:9–43.

Piek Vossen, Laura Bloksma, Paul Boersma, M. Verdejo, Julio Gonzalo, Horacio Madrid, German Rodriquez, Politecnica Rigau, Barcelona Catalunya, Nicoletta Calzolari, Carol Peters, Eugenio Picchi, Simonetta Montemagni, and Wim Peters. 1998. Eurowordnet tools and resources report.

PJTM Vossen. 1996. Right or wrong: combing lexical resources in the eurowordnet project. In *M. Gellerstam, J. Jarborg, S. Malmgren, K. Noren, L. Rogstrom, CR Papmehl, Proceedings of Euralex-96, Goetheborg, 1996*, pages 715–728. Vrije Universiteit.

P.J.T.M. Vossen. 1997. Eurowordnet: a multilingual database for information retrieval. In *Proceedings of the DELOS workshop on Cross-language Information Retrieval, March 5-7, 1997 Zurich*. Vrije Universiteit. Proceedings of the DELOS workshop on Cross-language Information Retrieval, March 5-7, 1997, Zurich.

Identifying FrameNet Lexical Semantic Structures for Knowledge Graph Extraction from Financial Customer Interactions

Cécile Robin[1] and **Atharva Kulkarni** and **Paul Buitelaar**[1]
[1]Insight SFI Research Centre for Data Analytics,
Data Science Institute, University of Galway
cecile.robin@insight-centre.org,
atharvaak66@gmail.com,
paul.buitelaar@universityofgalway.ie

Abstract

We explore the use of the well established lexical resource and theory of the Berkeley FrameNet project to support the creation of a domain-specific knowledge graph in the financial domain, more precisely from financial customer interactions. We introduce a domain independent and unsupervised method that can be used across multiple applications, and test our experiments on the financial domain. We use an existing tool for term extraction and taxonomy generation in combination with information taken from FrameNet. By using principles from frame semantic theory, we show that we can connect domain-specific terms with their semantic concepts (semantic frames) and their properties (frame elements) to enrich knowledge about these terms, in order to improve the customer experience in customer-agent dialogue settings.

1 Introduction

Improving customers experience is a desirable task for companies. This can be tackled at different levels: improving the accuracy of the information given to solve a query or a problem, improving the speed of the information given, improving the response time to solve the problem, and, going further into the experience, recommending a relevant service or product to a customer. Extensive understanding of the domain and the customer needs is required for improving customer satisfaction.

With this motivation in mind, Pereira et al. (2019) explored the use of a domain-specific taxonomy of terms built from customer-agent dialogues without manual input. The resource was built to be used as an intermediate and complementary resource, with the aim to contribute towards improving the efficiency of customer service agents, leveraging the issue of prior domain knowledge necessary in digital conversational agents (DCAs), and bridging the gap between the experts knowledge and the customer needs.

In this paper, we propose to go a step further by integrating semantic knowledge into the taxonomy and moving towards a Knowledge Graph (KG). More specifically, we use semantic knowledge from the well established resources from the Berkeley FrameNet project[1] and the frame semantic theory it follows (Fillmore and Baker, 2009).

FrameNet provides a database of concepts following lexical semantic structures, as well as a dataset of sentences annotated following these structures. Semantic Frames, referred to as Frames in this paper, make up the core of FrameNet. They represent situations, objects or events, and are given a label to represent them. Each Frame depends on one or more core (ie. essential to the meaning of a frame) and non-core (ie. non-essential to the meaning of a frame) arguments, the Frame Elements (FEs). While Frames and FEs are at the conceptual level, the Lexical Unit (LU) is the realisation of these concepts as words: the LU is said to evoke a Frame or FE. For example, the *REQUEST* frame describes a common situation involving a *Speaker*, an *Addressee* and a *Message* (the content of the request), and is evoked by words such as "demand". For example, this Frame is evoked in the sentence "The customer demanded a refund.". The frame semantic theory is useful to understand the deeper meaning of terms and what they depend on, and this is why, for this work, we decided to integrate Frames and FEs into a KG, with the aim of further improving the customer-agent dialogue experience.

Our approach is data-driven and domain independent, therefore flexible and adaptable to new data, and relies on a rich resource widely recognised and used over the years. These characteristics of our method allow for a wide range of applications in a variety of domains. A typical example of use is in question-answering systems, eg. *who did what and to whom?* (identified through FEs).

[1]https:\/\/framenet.icsi.berkeley.edu\/FrameNetdrupal\/

Furthermore, KGs in general are beneficial to many applications, from text classification (Zhong et al., 2021) to recommender systems(Guo et al., 2020) or chatbot development (Varitimiadis et al., 2020). In this paper we test our approach in the context of a financial customer-agent interaction setting.

After exploring the related work on the use of FrameNet in information extraction tasks and KG construction (Section 2), we describe the data used in our experiments (Section 3). We then detail our approach to extract the FrameNet concepts (Frames and FEs) from our dataset of financial customer-agent interactions, integrate them in a KG, and describe the RDF model design to generate the final KG (Section 4). In Section 5, we present the results of the KG creation as well as the evaluation, and discuss the results and challenges faced. Finally, we present some directions for future work in Section 6.

2 Related Work

The use of FrameNet in natural language processing tasks has been widely explored, specifically in the context of Information Extraction (IE), Semantic Role Labelling (SRL), and Frame Semantic Parsing (FSP) (ie. extracting frame-semantic structures from textual data).

In terms of FSP systems, Das et al. (Das et al., 2014) presented the first computational and statistical model for frame-semantic parsing. In the SemEval-2007 Task 19 (Baker et al., 2007), the goals of the frame semantic structure extraction task were to recognise words and phrases that evoke semantic frames, label them, identify and label their arguments, and integrate them into an overall semantic dependency graph. Three groups submitted results, with only one submitting full results, while the others submitted only the frames identification step. Several systems have then followed, including one of the latest, OpenSesame (Swayamdipta et al., 2017). The authors use a softmax-margin segmental RNN, i.e. a combination of bidirectional RNNs with a semi-markov Conditional Random Field (CRF), to segment and label the sentence relative to each frame (Kong et al., 2016).

FrameNet has also been used for relation extraction and KG construction tasks. Gabryszak et al. (2016) describe their approach using Linked Open Data and combining FrameNet and sar-graphs, knowledge resources that connect semantic relations from factual knowledge graphs to a linguistic phrases. Mandya et al. (2017) explore relation extraction through exploiting frame element and frame annotations, and TakeFive (Alam et al., 2021) uses also VerbNet for the semantic role labeling. FRED (Gangemi et al., 2017) generates an RDF graph representations out of the data extracted from text (for each sentence of the input text) using deep semantic parsing, verbal event detection, semantic role labeling with VerbNet and FrameNet roles. Spikes (Corcoglioniti et al., 2016a) is another similar tool of the state-of-the-art from 2016, extracting RDF triples of sentences using FrameBase, a Semantic Web ontology derived from FrameNet. It is based on a two step process: first the linguistic feature extraction to build a linguistic-oriented structured representation of the text (graph), and second the knowledge distillation, which combines structured information to build a knowledge graph made of instances of events and entities. All these systems either extract relations only, or they construct a full KG out of each sentence, while our aim is to represent a full domain and lexical semantic structures associated to it, not each individual piece of text. We are therefore not interested in the semantic representation of individual sentences.

Additionally, FrameNet has been used in domain-specific tasks. With the SpiNet system, Ferreira and Pinheiro (2020) describe how they use the principles of FrameNet coupled with the specific domain knowledge of the MeSH thesaurus[2] to extract information and classify sentences about spine and its disease to their semantic types. They identified 4 Frames (*Condition Symptom Relation*, *Medical Intervention*, *Cure* and *Medical Conditions*) and FEs such as *Disease*, *Treatment*, *Organism Function* relevant to this domain and their dataset.

In the area of customer-agent interaction in the financial domain, Pereira et al. (2019) made a first step towards a data-driven system for knowledge graph extraction, by using the tool Saffron[3] for the creation of a domain-specific taxonomy of terms, without the need for a domain-specific lexical resource. In this paper, we extend this approach by using the lexical semantic structures from FrameNet and automatically extracting and adding domain-relevant relations and concepts to the taxonomy, in the aim to create a KG.

[2]https://www.nlm.nih.gov/mesh/meshhome.html

[3]https://saffron.insight-centre.org/

3 Data

In our experiments, we use three resources: a proprietary dataset of chatlogs, the open source FrameNet annotated dataset, and a taxonomy of terms extracted from the chatlog dataset using the Saffron tool.

3.1 Chatlog dataset

The chatlog dataset is a proprietary collection of textual data from 2019 of interactions between agents and customers discussing financial matters in English provided by our industry partner in the financial domain. It contains 300,000 conversations of customer service chatlog and 5,655,660 sentences. It is anonymised using tokens representing the category of the information hidden to replace any personal information referring to the agent or the customer (e.g. *[PHONE_NUMBER]*). It includes customer query specific information, as well as general conversation language, greetings, etc.

3.2 FrameNet annotated dataset

The FrameNet annotated dataset is an open source dataset of texts provided by FrameNet, where LUs within the text are identified and manually annotated with their corresponding Frame or FE concepts. At the time of writing, there were 203,000 sentences annotated with 1,224 Frames, 10,478 FEs and over 13,500 LUs identified. The data from the English FrameNet covers a wide range of text types[4], from broadcast conversations, newswires, fiction, web text, transcripts of phone conversations to contemporary written and spoken American English from the American National Corpus[5].

3.3 Taxonomy of terms

A taxonomy of terms from financial customer interactions was created using the approach for taxonomy generation provided in the Saffron tool and described in (Pereira et al., 2019), in the same domain.

4 Methodology

We describe in this section our approach to create a KG by enriching a domain-specific taxonomy with FrameNet-based information. New links and nodes are added to the taxonomy, that contain information about Frames and FEs corresponding to the terms in the taxonomy and the content of the input dataset. The whole pipeline can be visualized in Figure 3.

4.1 Taxonomy creation

We first generate the taxonomy from the chatlog dataset. We adopt the best settings for the Saffron tool identified in (Pereira et al., 2019) which are as follows: terms to be extracted are between one and four words length, the ComboBasic scoring function is used to rank candidate terms, and the Bhattacharyya-Poisson likelihood scoring function together with the greedy search strategy for the taxonomy construction. Using these settings and the chatlog dataset, a taxonomy of 100 terms was created and used as a base for the KG construction. 100 was chosen to cover a wide range of topics, while being generic enough to represent the domain at a higher level. Table 1 shows a sample of 20 extracted terms from the taxonomy. This step corresponds to the processes 1 and 2 in Figure 3.

Extracted Terms	
401k account	bank wire
401k loan	bill pay
401k plan	brokerage account
account balance	business day
account information	buying power
account number	cash account
active trader	cash management
automatic investment	cash management account
automatic withdrawal	check deposit
bank account	checking account

Table 1: Sample of 20 extracted terms from the chatlog dataset

4.2 FrameNet semantic frame extraction using OpenSesame

We then perform Frame Semantic Parsing (FSP) on the chatlog dataset, ie. we identify all LUs in the dataset that evoke a concept in FrameNet and identify their evoked Frame or FEs. In our approach, only LUs that correspond to a term in the taxonomy are relevant. We note that LUs in FrameNet are always single words, while terms in our extracted taxonomy can be multi-words. To alleviate this, we manually identified the head word of each term and used it for comparison with the LUs. For example, in the term "index fund", we

[4]https://framenet.icsi.berkeley.edu/fndrupal/fulltextIndex

[5]https://anc.org/data/anc-second-release/

select the head of the term "fund"). In future work, we plan to achieve this using dependency parsing and a rule-based system to automatically select the head of the noun phrase and avoid manual intervention. This Frame and FE identification step is represented in an example in Figure 1. The LU *transfer.v* (verb) is identified in the text as evoking a Frame, *TRANSFER*, and is also a term in the taxonomy. In FrameNet, *TRANSFER* has core FEs (*Donor*, *Recipient*, *Theme*), and non-core FEs (*Explanation*, *Manner*, *Means*, *Place*, *Purpose*, *Time*). In this sentence, three LUs are identified (*how long*, *electronic*, *funds*) that evoke three of the FEs of *TRANSFER* (respectively *Theme*, *Means*, *Time*).

In order to perform the FSP described above, we use the state-of-the-art tool OpenSesame. OpenSesame[6] is available under an Apache-2.0 license, and is a FSP system, which identifies LUs within sentences, and map them to their relevant Frame or FE. Its performance was reported at 70% precision on the SemEval 2007 dataset (Baker et al., 2007) (see Section 2 for more details). OpenSesame is composed of three tasks: the target identification (identification of LUs in the text), the frame identification (which Frame is evoked by the LU) and the argument identification (recognition of FEs in the text and the LUs that evoke these elements for the identified Frame). Once we have gathered all the information about the Frames, the FEs and their associated term in the taxonomy, the next and final step is the KG creation. This step corresponds to the processes 3 in Figure 3.

4.3 Knowledge graph creation

The KG creation step corresponds to the enrichment of the taxonomy with Frames and FEs. We integrate the information from FrameNet to the taxonomy through additional links and create the KG described using the Resource Description Framework (RDF) [7] standard, which provides a data model for metadata. We represent these new links using semantic web established vocabularies, as presented in the following subsections.

4.3.1 The OntoLex-Lemon model

We choose the ontological resources OntoLex-Lemon[8] (McCrae et al., 2017) from the W3C Ontology Lexicon Community Group[9] to represent the individual terms in the taxonomy. The OntoLex-Lemon model was developed as a way to describe the lexicalisation of elements in the vocabulary of the ontology (individuals, classes, properties) in a given natural language. It is split into different modules tackling different linguistics and lexical aspects. The Ontology-lexicon interface (*ontolex*) (namespace *http://www.w3.org/ns/lemon/ontolex#*) module is the core module of the model, in which we identified the class *ontolex:lexicalEntry* to represent the terms of the taxonomy. It is described as "a word, multi-word expression or affix with a single part-of-speech, morphological pattern, etymology and set of senses".

4.3.2 PreMOn - Predicate Model for Ontologies

To represent the rest of the concepts and relations in the KG, we used the Predicate Model for Ontologies (PreMOn) (Corcoglioniti et al., 2016b). It is based on OntoLex-Lemon but further refined to represent predicate models such as the one by FrameNet. The namespace is *http://premon.fbk.eu/ontology/core#* with prefix *pmo*. It includes a class *pmo:SemanticClass* which represents a semantic class, or a Frame in the case of FrameNet. *pmo:SemanticClass* is defined as a subclass of the more generic *ontolex:LexicalConcept*, and therefore inherits its link to lexical entries (*ontolex:lexicalEntry*). An instance of *pmo:SemanticClass* has a number of semantic roles, represented by the class compare*pmo:SemanticRole*. SemanticRoles represent the roles that the arguments of a SemanticClass can play (corresponding to the FEs from FrameNet). SemanticClass links to SemanticRole via the property *pmo:semRole*.

4.3.3 Knowledge graph design

The whole RDF design is displayed in Figure 2. In this representation, each term is given the type *ontolex:LexicalEntry*. For each term that is also recognised as an LU in the dataset, a connector link *ontolex:evokes* is created directed towards the node that represents the corresponding Frame label. This node in the graph belongs to the class *pmo:SemanticClass* and links to new nodes through *pmo:semRole* connectors. Each of these node represent an FE identified from the text for the particular Frame, and attributed the class *pmo:SemanticRole*. The step of adding FrameNet information to the taxonomy to create the KG corresponds to the process

[6] https://github.com/swabhs/open-sesame

[7] https://www.w3.org/RDF/

[8] https://www.w3.org/2016/05/ontolex/

[9] https://www.w3.org/community/ontolex/

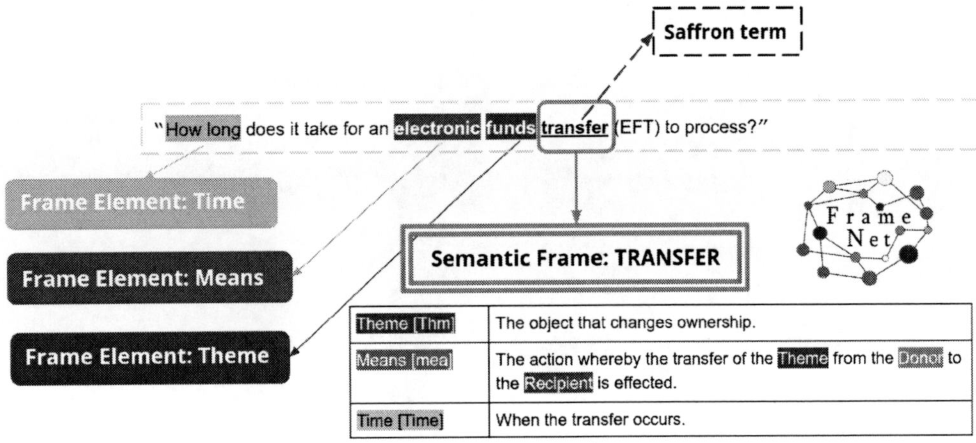

Figure 1: Example of a FrameNet analysis on a sentence where the LU, *transfer*, is also a term in the taxonomy

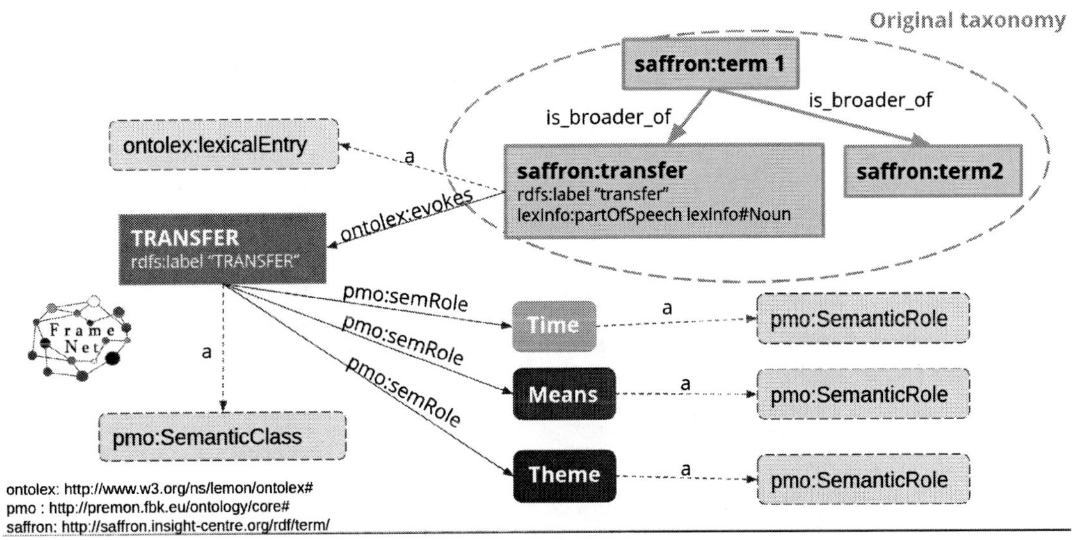

Figure 2: RDF representation of the KG, using the OntoLex-Lemon and PreMOn vocabularies

4 in Figure 3.

By using this semantic approach and this representation, we open the possibility for different terms of the taxonomy to evoke the same Frame. This allows to connect semantically related areas of the taxonomy and to bring together similar semantic information for different terms. In our use case, this has the potential to help identify related intents of customers, and therefore related requirements or needs of their enquiry, through direct and indirect links within the KG.

4.4 Evaluation

We perform a manual evaluation of the results to identify the precision of our implemented approach. The evaluation protocol includes three evaluators, experienced in KG and natural language processing, who evaluated the terms which were matched to the LUs identified by OpenSesame, and their mapped Frame. For each pair {Term, Frame}, the evaluators are given the task to determine whether the Frame extracted represents a semantic class relevant to the extracted term or not, in the context of the domain of the dataset and the application. The sentences where these pairs originated from are also presented to the evaluators for context. Since the dataset and the terms are domain-specific, the terms bear the same meaning across the sentences. Table 2 shows an excerpt of the evaluation sheet. After they all performed their evaluation separately, they conferred together to make a decision on the ones they disagreed on. The final list was con-

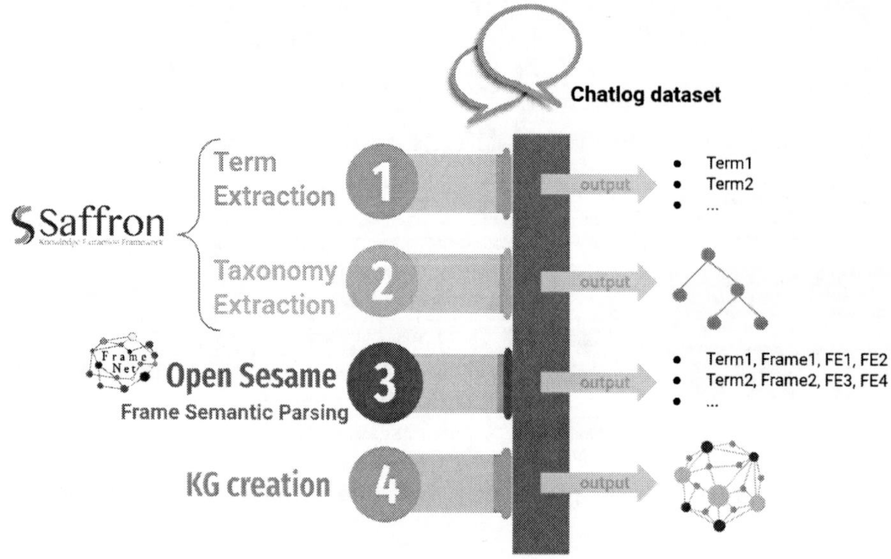

Figure 3: Pipeline of the KG creation

sidered our base to calculate the precision of the {Term, Frame} pairs.

5 Results and Discussion

42 unique Frames were identified by OpenSesame out of the chatlog dataset, and 84 {Term, Frame} pairs. Some Frames applied to several terms. The Frame that occurred the most in the dataset is *Text*, and corresponds to the LU "account" which appears in several terms ("retirement account", "brokerage account", etc.). This Frame is described in FrameNet as "an entity that contains linguistic, symbolic information on a Topic, created by an Author at the Time_of_creation", which is incorrect for our context (and was not retained by the evaluators). The FrameNet dataset, used to train the OpenSesame system, contains multiple occurrences of "account" in non-financial contexts such as: "Lurid semi-fictional *accounts* by James Greenwood", or "An *account* of my recent visit to Dubai will be in my next diary.", which do have the meaning of *Text*. This LU is therefore lacking an appropriate semantic concept in FrameNet. 0.55 of the Frames were identified as correct by the evaluators, which corresponds to 23 Frames, 38 unique terms, and 40 {Term, Frame} pairs (some extracted terms matched two Frames). Table 3 gives the final list of all the Frames extracted using the terms, how many times they occur in the dataset, the LUs that evoke them, the terms to which they are matched, and their corresponding FEs extracted from the dataset. We observe that most of the Frames identified from the dataset are directly related to the financial domain, such as *Funding*, *Money*, *Expensiveness*, *Commerce_pay*, even though we also retrieved more generic ones, for example *Calendric_unit*, *Information*. This is explained by the fact that our dataset covers conversations between agents and customers, which contain terms related to communication, and others more specific to financial topics. This echoes in our Frame extraction results. The FEs provide interesting relevant elements in the context of a customer-agent conversation. For example, the Frame *Expensiveness* calls for arguments *Origin*, *Goods*, *Asset*, *Degree*, *Intended event*, *Rate*, according to what was extracted from the dataset.

The inter-annotator agreement Fleiss Kappa (Fleiss, 1971) is 0.60, which is a moderate agreement for the evaluation task. Despite a clear description of each Frame in FrameNet, it is not always clear whether or not a term can be represented by a particular Frame based on its definition. 48% {Term, Frame} unique pairs (40 pairs) were identified as correct, and 52% (44 pairs) as incorrect. The precision was calculated by taking into account the number of occurrence of the Frames in the dataset (some terms, and therefore Frames, are repeated more than others). 544,065 Frame instances were extracted from the dataset by OpenSesame, among which 199,441 correct ones (based on the 40 correct {Term, Frame} pairs identified in our base),

{Term, Frame} pairs	Occurrences	Eval 1	Eval 2	Eval 3
{Mutual fund, Funding}	36,632	yes	no	yes
{Bank account, Text}	28,936	no	no	no
{Cash management, Being_in_control}	6,279	yes	yes	yes
{Mutual fund, Money}	6,020	yes	yes	yes
{Retirement plan, Purpose}	5,133	yes	yes	no
{Brokerage account, Text}	27,299	no	no	no

Table 2: Sample of evaluation sheet of the {Term, Frame} pairs by the three evaluators

Semantic Frame	# of Occ.	Lexical Units	Terms	Frame Elements
Calendric_unit	39,504	year.n, night.n, day.n, week.n	next year, last year, next week, last week, business day, last night	Relative_time, Salient_event, Name, Unit, Trajector_event, Whole, Count
Funding	39,011	fund.n	mutual fund, index fund	Money, Period_of_iterations, Manner, Recipient, Source, Time, Supplier, Imposed_purpose
Purpose	32,968	plan.n, purpose.n	pension plan, savings plan, stock plan, retirement plan, 401k plan, tax purpose	Value, Goal, Attribute, Domain, Time, Agent
Information	14478	information.n	account information, contact information	Means_of_gathering, Source, Information, Topic, Cognizer
Money	8,399	fund.n	mutual fund, index fund	Money
Removing	8,131	withdrawal.n	automatic withdrawal, hardship withdrawal	Means_of_motion, Cause, Theme, Degree, Agent
Expensiveness	7,290	cost.n	cost basis	Origin, Goods, Asset, Degree, Intended_event, Rate
Being_in_control	6,279	management.n	cash management	Dependent_entity, Manner, Degree, Time, Controlling_entity
Transfer	5,040	transfer.n	wire transfer	Donor, Theme, Recipient
Alternatives	4,679	option.n	investment option, stock option	Situation, Agent
Questioning	4,356	inquiry.n	inquiry today	Medium, Message, Speaker
Aggregate	4,302	group.n	service group	Name, Aggregate, Individuals, Aggregate_property
Commerce_pay	4,280	payment.n	loan payment	Place, Money, Manner, Goods, Time, Buyer, Purpose, Seller
People_by_vocation	3,730	trader.n	trader pro, active trader	Employer, Place_of_employment, Descriptor, Person
Lending	3,040	loan.n	401k loan	Theme, Borrower
Request	2,616	request.n	transfer request	Medium, Manner, Message, Speaker
Rate_quantification	2,604	rate.n	interest rate	Event, Attribute, Degree, Descriptor, Type, Rate
Trust	2,568	faith.n	good faith	Information_source, Information, Cognizer
Being_at_risk	2,039	security.n	social security	Situation, Asset
Earnings_and_losses	1,430	income.n	fixed income	Earner, Explanation, Unit, Buyer, Time, Earnings
Businesses	1,344	business.n	small business	Place, Business_name, Descriptor,Service_provider, Proprietor, Business
Temporal_subregion	1,322	end.n	year end	Subpart, Time_period, Time
Chatting	31	chat.n	via chat	Interlocutors, Interlocutor_2, Language, Interlocutor_1

Table 3: Frames correctly extracted from the dataset, along with their occurrence, the Lexical Unit which evoked them, the corresponding term(s), and the Frame Elements identified

therefore a precision of 36.7%.

To our knowledge, there is no other system directly comparable in relation to the task performed and the domain of the experiment. FRED (see Section 2) is a related system, but it extracts Semantic Web compliant RDF graphs from texts, per sentence. It reports 75% precision in the frame detection task, however the benchmark used for evaluation is based on sentences taken from the FrameNet dataset itself, the latter which was used to create the Frames in FrameNet. Gangemi et al. (2017) also provide the performance of systems that are using FRED as part of their solution. The precision rates go as high as 84% with the Legalo system (Presutti et al., 2016) on the task of providing alignment to Semantic Web vocabularies, and as low as 34.8% for CiTalO (Di Iorio et al., 2013), on the task of identifying the nature of citations. There is therefore a great variability depending on the end task and the domain.

In terms of FEs extracted, Table 4 shows the percentage of FEs that were extracted by OpenSesame from the dataset, compared to the total of FEs present in FrameNet for each Frame. For example, for the Frame *Purpose*, the FEs *Goal, Attribute, Domain, Agent* are extracted (see Table3), while *Time, Value, Means* and *Restrictor* are in FrameNet but not identified in our dataset. On average, per Frame, 54% of FEs were extracted. Restricting the extraction to FEs that only belong to our dataset (instead of taking all the FEs of a Frame) allows us to select properties more specific to the domain to show in the KG, and therefore avoids to represent information that is not needed in our use case.

Semantic Frame	# of FEs in FrameNet	% of FEs extracted
Aggregate	6	67
Alternatives	5	40
Being_at_risk	12	17
Being_in_control	9	56
Businesses	7	86
Calendric_unit	8	88
Chatting	13	31
Commerce_pay	14	57
Earnings_and_losses	13	46
Expensiveness	8	75
Information	5	100
Lending	8	25
Money	10	10
Funding	10	80
People_by_vocation	13	31
Purpose	8	75
Questioning	9	33
Rate_quantification	7	86
Removing	23	22
Request	12	33
Temporal_subregion	5	60
Transfer	10	30
Trust	8	38

Table 4: Percentage of all FEs extracted by OpenSesame

Several reasons can explain the results from the evaluation. First of all, the terms which are originally multi-words loose their specificity when we select the head noun to match them to the LUs. Extracting multi-word terms is an important capability of the Saffron tool, as it allows to cover broader concepts as well as domain-specific ones.

Moreover, despite the training data from FrameNet covering a wide range of conversational data and the reported precision of OpenSesame on the SemEval 2007 dataset, the latter fails to identify some domain-specific concepts of our data. In particular, the results from the Saffron tool contained a large amount of terms composed with *account*. Since *account* was the head of these terms, the same Frame was identified for all of them, which was, as we saw earlier, the Frame *Text*. Other errors are related to Frames not being from the correct domain (e.g. *customer_service* identified as *Public services*) or other ambiguity issues (*buying power* identified as *Electricity*). For some of these errors, there exists a relevant Frame in FrameNet (e.g. *lump sum* originally identified as *Commutative_statement* could be instead identified as the Frame *Money*), however for some others, like *account*, we have not identified an appropriate Frame in FrameNet. Despite this, a number of Frames and their FEs were correctly extracted, and allowed us to enrich the taxonomy with semantic information relevant for 37 of the 100 extracted terms. SpiNet reports the precision rate for each of the four Frames identified as relevant for their domain (see Section 2) and used to annotate sentences of their dataset. The Frame showing the best precision is *Condition Symptom Relation* with 0.77, and the lowest precision was recorded for the Frame *Cure* with 0.45. The inter-annotator agreement of the evaluators was not reported. We show that our system for domain-specific KG creation is domain independent in its design, in that it does not require additional domain-specific resources, and uses the richness of FrameNet to add information about domain-relevant lexical semantic structures.

6 Conclusion and Future Work

In this work, we combine the strength of the term extraction and domain taxonomy generation capabilities of the Saffron tool, with lexical semantic structures from FrameNet and the OpenSesame tool to create a KG from financial customer interactions in an unsupervised manner and without the need of a domain specific lexical resource. We have observed challenges to overcome, such as the ambiguity and incorrect Frames identification increased by the single word limitation, as well as the lack of some relevant semantic concepts. We have contributed towards constructing a data-driven fully unsupervised and domain-independent system for KG extraction in domain-specific settings. We have identified a number of semantic concepts from FrameNet with their arguments related to the financial domain, and enriched a taxonomy, in the aim of improving the customer-agent interaction. There is no other system, to our knowledge, that creates a domain KG from terms, includes taxonomic relations and lexical semantic structures, all based on a dataset of unstructured textual data.

In future work, we want to optimise the application and accuracy of OpenSesame in our approach, as well as building a fully automated method where human intervention is not required anymore. The processing time has proven to be significantly long on our dataset, due to the output format chosen by the tool not optimal for processing large datasets. FrameNet being a collaborative project, we also intend to contribute with the proposal of new Frames to cover the missing concepts, as well as to provide new annotations of texts from our domain of interest. Also, our system does not currently deal with negation in the text, which would be an important feature to take into account. Finally, we would like to work further on the issue of single word LU and the ambiguity it entails.

7 Acknowledgements

This project has received funding from the SFI/12/RC/2289_P2 (Insight), co-funded by the European Regional Development Fund.

References

Mehwish Alam, Aldo Gangemi, Valentina Presutti, and Diego Reforgiato Recupero. 2021. Semantic role labeling for knowledge graph extraction from text. *Progress in Artificial Intelligence*, 10(3):309–320.

Collin Baker, Michael Ellsworth, and Katrin Erk. 2007. SemEval-2007 task 19: Frame semantic structure extraction. In *Proceedings of the Fourth International Workshop on Semantic Evaluations (SemEval-2007)*, pages 99–104, Prague, Czech Republic. Association for Computational Linguistics.

Francesco Corcoglioniti, Marco Rospocher, and Alessio Palmero Aprosio. 2016a. Frame-based ontology population with pikes. *IEEE Transactions on Knowledge and Data Engineering*, 28(12):3261–3275.

Francesco Corcoglioniti, Marco Rospocher, Alessio Palmero Aprosio, and Sara Tonelli. 2016b. PreMOn: a lemon extension for exposing predicate models as linked data. In *Proceedings of the Tenth International Conference on Language Resources and Evaluation (LREC'16)*, pages 877–884, Portorož, Slovenia. European Language Resources Association (ELRA).

Dipanjan Das, Desai Chen, André F. T. Martins, Nathan Schneider, and Noah A. Smith. 2014. Frame-semantic parsing. *Computational Linguistics*, 40(1):9–56.

Angelo Di Iorio, Andrea Nuzzolese, and Silvio Peroni. 2013. Towards the automatic identification of the nature of citations. In *Proceedings of 3rd Workshop on Semantic Publishing (SePublica 2013)*, volume 994, Montpellier, France.

Vanessa C. Ferreira and Vládia C. Pinheiro. 2020. Spinet - A framenet-like schema for automatic information extraction about spine from scientific papers. In *AMIA 2020, American Medical Informatics Association Annual Symposium, Virtual Event, USA, November 14-18, 2020*. AMIA.

Charles J Fillmore and Collin Baker. 2009. A frames approach to semantic analysis. In B. Heine and H. Narrog, editors, *The Oxford handbook of linguistic analysis*. Oxford University Press, Oxford, UK/New York, New York.

Joseph L. Fleiss. 1971. Measuring nominal scale agreement among many raters. *Psychological Bulletin*, 76:378–382.

Aleksandra Gabryszak, Sebastian Krause, Leonhard Hennig, Feiyu Xu, and Hans Uszkoreit. 2016. Relation- and phrase-level linking of FrameNet with sar-graphs. In *Proceedings of the Tenth International Conference on Language Resources and Evaluation (LREC'16)*, pages 2419–2424, Portorož, Slovenia. European Language Resources Association (ELRA).

Aldo Gangemi, Valentina Presutti, Diego Reforgiato Recupero, Andrea Giovanni Nuzzolese, Francesco Draicchio, and Misael Mongiovì. 2017. Semantic web machine reading with fred. *Semantic Web*, 8:873–893.

Qingyu Guo, Fuzhen Zhuang, Chuan Qin, Hengshu Zhu, Xing Xie, Hui Xiong, and Qing He. 2020. A survey on knowledge graph-based recommender systems. *IEEE Transactions on Knowledge and Data Engineering*, PP:1–1.

Lingpeng Kong, Chris Dyer, and Noah A. Smith. 2016. Segmental recurrent neural networks. *CoRR*, abs/1511.06018.

Angrosh Mandya, Danushka Bollegala, Frans Coenen, and Katie Atkinson. 2017. Frame-based semantic patterns for relation extraction. In *Computational Linguistics - 15th International Conference of the Pacific Association for Computational Linguistics, PACLING 2017, Yangon, Myanmar, August 16-18, 2017, Revised Selected Papers*, volume 781 of *Communications in Computer and Information Science*, pages 51–62. Springer.

John P. McCrae, Julia Bosque Gil, Jordi Gràcia, Paul Buitelaar, and Philipp Cimiano. 2017. The ontolex-lemon model: Development and applications. In *Proceedings of eLex 2017*, pages 587–597, Leiden, The Netherlands.

Bianca Pereira, Cécile Robin, Tobias Daudert, John P. McCrae, Pranab Mohanty, and Paul Buitelaar. 2019. Taxonomy extraction for customer service knowledge base construction. In *Semantic Systems. The Power of AI and Knowledge Graphs*, pages 175–190, Cham. Springer International Publishing.

Valentina Presutti, Andrea Nuzzolese, Sergio Consoli, Aldo Gangemi, and Diego Reforgiato Recupero. 2016. From hyperlinks to semantic web properties using open knowledge extraction. 7:351–378.

Swabha Swayamdipta, Sam Thomson, Chris Dyer, and Noah A. Smith. 2017. Frame-semantic parsing with softmax-margin segmental rnns and a syntactic scaffold. *CoRR*, abs/1706.09528.

Savvas Varitimiadis, Konstantinos Kotis, Dimitris Spiliotopoulos, Costas Vassilakis, and Dionisis Margaris. 2020. "talking" triples to museum chatbots. In *Culture and Computing: 8th International Conference, C&C 2020, Held as Part of the 22nd HCI International Conference, HCII 2020, Copenhagen, Denmark, July 19–24, 2020, Proceedings*, page 281–299, Berlin, Heidelberg. Springer-Verlag.

Yuyanzhen Zhong, Zhiyang Zhang, Weiqi Zhang, and Juyi Zhu. 2021. Bert-kg: A short text classification model based on knowledge graph and deep semantics. In *Natural Language Processing and Chinese Computing: 10th CCF International Conference, NLPCC 2021, Qingdao, China, October 13–17, 2021, Proceedings, Part I*, page 721–733, Berlin, Heidelberg. Springer-Verlag.

Some Considerations in the Construction of a Historical Language WordNet

Anas Fahad Khan
Istituto di Linguistica Computazionale "A. Zampolli"
Pisa, Italy
fahad.khan@ilc.cnr.it

John P. McCrae
University of Galway
Galway, Ireland
john.mccrae@insight-centre.org

Francisco Javier Minaya Gómez and **Rafael Cruz González** and **Javier E. Díaz-Vera**
University of Castilla-La Mancha
Ciudad Real, Spain
{Francisco.Minaya, Rafael.Cruz, JavierEnrique.Diaz}@uclm.es

Abstract

This article describes the manual construction of a part of the Old English WordNet (OldEWN) covering the semantic field of emotion terms. This manually constructed part of the wordnet is to be eventually integrated with the automatically generated/manually checked part covering the whole of the rest of the Old English lexicon (currently under construction). We present the workflow for the definition of these emotion synsets on the basis of a dataset produced by a specialist in this area. We also look at the enrichment of the original Global WordNet Association Lexical Markup Framework (GWA LMF) schema to include the extra information which this part of the OldEWN requires. In the final part of the article we discuss how the wordnet style of lexicon organisation can be used to share and disseminate research findings/datasets in lexical semantics.

1 Introduction

In this article, we look at the manual construction of that part of the Old English WordNet (OldEWN) dealing with the semantic field of emotion terms and which is based on previous scholarship on the emotion vocabulary for Old English (OE). This completely manual compilation process contrasts with the rest of the OldEWN which will be (primarily) the result of an initial phase of automated synset assignment followed by a subsequent post-correction phase; in this latter phase, scholars and specialists in OE will check generated synsets for correctness using a specialised platform developed for this task; more details on the full resource can be found in (Khan et al., 2022). Like the whole OldEWN, the emotion sub-wordnet is based on the second edition of Clark-Hall's *A Concise Anglo-Saxon Dictionary*[1] (Clark Hall, 1916) (CH).

We have several different aims in this article one of which is to describe some of the most recent developments in the construction of the OldEWN as a historical wordnet resource (following on from (Khan et al., 2022)). More generally, however, we wish to take a closer look into how to use legacy lexicographic resources such as the CH to create wordnets for historical languages (we present our workflow in detail in Section 2). In addition, we will present an extension of the Global WordNet Association (GWA) schema, in Section 3, that includes diachronic and etymological information and which we have developed for our emotion sub-wordnet; this may be useful for other similar wordnet projects. Finally, in Section 4, we discuss how the wordnet style of lexicon organisation can be used to share and disseminate research data in lexical semantics and how, even in cases where the coverage of a wordnet resource is low, such *sub*-wordnets can still be highly useful if they cover whole semantic fields.

2 Manually Creating an Emotion Lexicon in the Old English WordNet

Note that as the current article concentrates on the manually compiled part of the OldEWN dealing with emotions, and which we refer to as the *emotion lexicon* in what follows, we will not go into details as to the origins of the entire resource, its construction, or its scope[2]. The origin of the emotion lexicon lies in a dataset analysing emotion terms in OE which was compiled by Díaz-Vera and which

[1] We chose this edition because it has already been OCR'ed and is freely available online.

[2] These and other details of a more general nature can, however, be found in our previous article, (Khan et al., 2022).

is the result of a research program described in publications such as (Díaz-Vera, 2014). In this dataset, which is organised in a series of spreadsheets, OE words with emotion related meanings are classified on the basis of the emotion terms listed in the Geneva Emotion Wheel (GEV) (Scherer, 2005), with each word being listed in a separate spreadsheet under the appropriate GEV emotion term. Individual spreadsheets contain the following information for each of the lexical entries listed under that heading:

- The **lemma** for the entry, its **part of speech**, along with the different **orthographic** and **morphological variants** of the entry and their **distribution** in the corpus of surviving Old English texts, as well as **etymological information** on roots,
- A **gloss** of the literal sense of the entry – if the emotion term is literal or its emotion sense is primary; in cases of polysemic or derived terms where the emotion sense is secondary, both primary and secondary senses are described, as well as the **kind of figurative (metonymic/metaphoric) sense shift** (if any) which is hypothesised to have taken place between the two.

For instance, in the spreadsheet listing *shame* related terms in OE, we currently have 77 entries. These include the noun *scand* which literally means 'shame', but also include the polysemic verb *ablysian* which means both 'to blush' and 'to be ashamed'. The lexical information in these spreadsheets is derived from several different sources but crucially, lemma and sense information is based on that given in the Dictionary of Old English (DOE)[3]. Having become aware of this dataset our feeling was that it would lend itself very well to being incorporated within the OldEWN, especially since the lexical entries in the spreadsheets were already grouped together (provisionally) into synsets based on emotion terms. On the other hand, we were also eager to begin integrating the kind of information on figurative sense shifts included in the original Díaz-Vera dataset into OldEWN and extending the basic wordnet framework in order to do so; indeed data on figurative sense shifts is already being added to the Latin WordNet[4]. Once we made the decision to build the emotion lexicon part of the OldEWN on the basis of the Díaz-Vera dataset, we had to reconcile this with our previous choice to use the CH as the basis of the whole OldEWN; this is further discussed in Section 4. In what follows we give a description of our workflow for constructing the emotion lexicon[5]. In what follows we give a description of our workflow for the creation of the emotion lexicon.

For each of the emotion words in a spreadsheet, we look for the corresponding entry in the CH; we then use the information contained in the latter as the basis of the OldEWN lexical entry in the emotion lexicon[6]. In case either the entry or one or more of the senses does not exist in the CH we use another OE dictionary, the Bosworth-Toller *An Anglo-Saxon dictionary* (Bosworth, 1882) (BT) as the basis of a new lexical entry and/or senses. As regards the creation of OE synsets in the emotion lexicon, we use the synset which is the closest modern day English equivalent to the word sense in question in the Open English WordNet[7] (OEWN)[8] as a reference. For instance, in the case of OE words in the *shame* spreadsheet we look for synsets in OEWN containing the verb *to shame*, the noun *shame*, the adjective *ashamed*, etc. This gives us a set of relevant (modern) English synsets which we use as pivots to define new Old English synsets: using the definitions in the CH (or the BT in case of missing definitions) to decide which synset to link to (this is a purely manual process for now). We then map our new Old English synsets to their corresponding Open English synsets using the latter's Collaborative Interlingual Index ID (described below in Section 3). Finally, we add information on figurative sense shifts between the entries at the level of the sense (rather than at the synset level) using a modified version of the GWA LMF format; see the next section for more details.

3 Extending the Global WordNet LMF format

The Global WordNet Association (GWA) formats were introduced by Bond et al. (2016) and Mc-

[3]The electronic version of the latest draft can be found here `https://doe.artsci.utoronto.ca/`

[4]See `https://latinwordnet.exeter.ac.uk/lexicon`

[5]Note that although the emotion lexicon takes the Díaz-Vera dataset as a starting point, we do not necessarily keep to the synset assignation proposed therein.

[6]In particular we take the lemma and the sense definitions from CH. Although, these defintions may also sometimes be modified in case they do not accord with latter scholarship.

[7]`https://en-word.net/`

[8]Although their acronyms are similar, the OEWN is not to be confused with OldEWN.

Crae et al. (2021) to serve as a common set of schemata for the representation of wordnets and to enable their integration in the Open Multilingual Wordnet[9] through the Collaborative Interlingual Index (CILI). The formats describe three fully convertible serializations: an XML format based on Kyoto-LMF (Soria et al., 2009), a JSON serialization, and a RDF serialization that is a subset of the OntoLex-Lemon (McCrae et al., 2012) model. The three formats have been adopted by a number of projects and initiatives in the wordnet community including the OEWN mentioned above. Since all of the formats are fully interoperable and have the same underlying conceptual model, we focus on the XML based LMF format (GWA LMF) in what follows. These formats, which are closely based on the original Princeton WordNet (Miller, 1995) data model, model wordnets as containing **lexical entries** which have a number of **senses** that are linked to **synsets**[10]. As the formats are designed for the interchange of wordnets, they were developed with the goal of providing only a minimal number of common features. As such, the intention was for users to extend the set of elements in these schemas to represent their own data. And in fact, this is the strategy we pursued in order to be able to encode the OldEWN, and in particular the emotion lexicon, as we describe next.

An Extension of the GWA LMF Format for Diachronic Lexical Data

To start with, our resource is closely aligned to a pre-existing dictionary but with various new additions to the original content, including new lemmas and senses (and therefore sense definitions). We therefore felt it would be desirable to add definitions for individual senses along with metadata for specifying when entries/senses/definitions have been added or modified[11] to our wordnet. None of these features is available in the current GWA formats, and neither are a number of others that are important for historical languages such as OE (although these features can also be important for contemporary languages). For instance, we would like to include markers of rarity/uniqueness such as are found in the CH, as well as, more generally, information regarding dating, variations in forms along with information about word etymologies and specifically sense shifts. Finally, the GWA formats do not permit for the inclusion of salient (to OE) morpho-syntactic features like grammatical gender which we would also like to include in our resource[12]. Consequently, we made the following modifications to the GWA LMF format:

- The introduction of an **Etymology** element to be associated with both **LexicalEntry** and **Sense** elements from the original schema; this element consists of a series of one or more **EtyLink**s, where the latter represent an etymological link between two elements.

- This new **EtyLink** element carries attributes for specifying the source and target of an etymological link as well as for type of link; this allows us to indicate the kind of figurative conceptual shift which has taken place between two senses.

- The addition of a @grammaticalGender attribute to the **LexicalEntry** element.

- The addition of a **SenseDefinition** element related to the Sense element (with relevant Dublin Core metadata attributes for provenance information).

Our intention is for this extended schema to be reusable across a more general family of diachronic wordnet use cases. Indeed, in order to enhance this re-usability, we based the etymological part our expanded schema on a pre-existing ISO standard, namely, the latest multi-part version of LMF (Romary et al., 2019). We have made our new extended version of the GWA LMF format with these new features available as a DTD[13]. We have also defined an XSLT transformation from our extended version of the GWA LMF format to the original GWA LMF format[14].

In the listing below, we use our new extended schema to represent the OE noun *āblysung* which means both 'blushing' and 'shame' and where there is a resultative metonymy relation between the two senses of the word which we have listed:

[9]https://omwn.org/

[10]Further documentation can be found at https://globalwordnet.github.io/schemas/.

[11]Adding definitions for individual senses would help users to see what we based our decisions on when assigning synsets to individual senses.

[12]One way of circumventing these restrictions would be to include this information in another resource to be linked to the OldEWN, perhaps a digital edition of the CH dictionary in a format like TEI-XML. However our intention is to make OldEWN as self contained a resource as possible.

[13]https://github.com/anasfkhan81/OldEnglish/blob/main/WN-IELMF-0.DTD

[14]https://github.com/anasfkhan81/OldEnglish/blob/main/IELMF2GWALMF.xsl

```
<LexicalEntry id = "ABLYSUNG_N">
   <Lemma writtenForm="āblysung" partOfSpeech="n"
        grammaticalGender = "f"/>
   <Sense id ="oew5_s1" synset = "example-ang-
        XXXXXX2-n">
      <Definition gloss = "blushing"/>
   </Sense>
   <Sense id ="oew5_s2" synset = "example-ang-
        XXXXXX1-n">
      <Definition gloss = "shame"/>
   </Sense>
   <etymology>
      <etyLink type = "resultative-metonymy" source=
           "oew5_s1" target="oew5_s2"/>
   </etymology>
</LexicalEntry>
```

In our resource, shifts don't directly apply to synsets themselves but to individual senses; the networks of synsets and their relations, then, help us to 'locate' such changes in meaning within the wider lexicon. In the next section, we look in more detail at some of the issues behind the use of pre-existing, legacy resources in the creation of the OldEWN and the use of the wordnet format for disseminating and sharing research data.

4 Discussion: the use of Pre-Existing Dictionaries and focusing on semantic fields in creating a wordnet

As previously reported in (Khan et al., 2022), we made the decision to use a dictionary as the basis of our wordnet for OE quite early on in its development, in part as an experiment in how to create such a resource for a historical language using freely available, legacy lexicographic resources. The idea being to use dictionary definitions, along with collocation information from the corpus of existing Old English texts, to help bootstrap a first provisional round of synsets. For reasons of convenience, the dictionary we chose was the CH[15] since its definitions are shorter and generally simpler than the BT's (e.g., without the latter's nested sense structure) and the CH generally follows a consistent and straight-forward separation of terms into different senses, all of which make entries easier to process. On the other hand, the BT includes far more semantic information and indeed more senses than the CH and is generally much more comprehensive than the latter (which was targeted specifically towards students). This became abundantly clear during the process of putting together our emotion lexicon: indeed, we very quickly came up against cases where Díaz-Vera's original dataset – which takes the even more comprehensive DOE as its reference – described senses which were present neither in the CH or the BT. In many cases, these senses occurred just once in the corpus of Old English texts and in several cases only as translation glosses, i.e., these were senses which wouldn't necessarily be seen as good candidates for inclusion in a general purpose wordnet.

However, as we mentioned above, one of our central aims in this project is to show the usefulness of publishing specialised datasets using the wordnet model: even if we subsequently end up with a wordnet or subwordnet where the coverage of various different parts of the lexicon of the language in question is very uneven or perhaps non-existent[16]. Such resources be valuable for what they tell us about single semantic fields or thematic parts of the lexicon. Therefore, in our opinion, the wordnet format should be promoted as a shared semantic framework for disseminating and sharing research in lexical semantics and related fields, with a view to making such research data as interoperable as possible.

It is worth pointing out here that the original inspiration behind the creation of the Old English Wordnet was to enable the comparison of concepts (and their interrelationships) across different ancient Indo-European language lexicons. Our work is based on previous efforts on the creation of Latin, Ancient Greek and Sanksrit WordNets and the effort to harmonise their structure using a shared schema (Biagetti et al., 2021); with the inclusion of semantic shift information, we facilitate even richer kinds of comparison between languages.

5 Conclusion

In this article we have reported on some recent experiences of the authors' in the development of an emotion lexicon as an (enriched) part of a wordnet for Old English. We are currently only part way through the encoding of the original Díaz-Vera dataset. When completed it will be made available in all three GWA formats as a separate wordnet

[15]The are three main dictionaries for Old English, two of which (CH and BT) date from the late 19th century and are both in the public domain. The third, the *Dictionary of Old English* (DOE), is still very much under copyright – indeed, users require a paid subscription in order to access it – and we could not therefore use it as the basis of our resource, which we intend to be published with a Creative Commons licence. The DOE is the most authoritative of the three and includes an extensive if not exhaustive list of citations for each entry. It is however currently unfinished and covers the letters A to I.

[16]This entails, however, that the kind of metadata which we referred to above, dealing with e.g., provenance, distribution, etc in Section 3 becomes especially important for the usability of the OldEWN.

based motion lexicon as well as being integrated into the main OldEWN resource.

References

Erica Biagetti, Chiara Zanchi, and William Michael Short. 2021. Toward the creation of Wordnets for ancient Indo-european languages. In *Proceedings of the 11th Global Wordnet Conference*, pages 258–266.

Francis Bond, Piek Vossen, John P. McCrae, and Christiane Fellbaum. 2016. CILI: the Collaborative Interlingual Index. In *Proceedings of the Global WordNet Conference 2016*.

Joseph Bosworth. 1882. *An Anglo-Saxon Dictionary: Based on the Manuscript Collections of the Late Joseph Bosworth...*, volume 1. Clarendon Press.

John R Clark Hall. 1916. *A concise Anglo-Saxon dictionary: for the use of students*, second edition. Swan Sonnenschein & Company.

Javier E Díaz-Vera. 2014. From cognitive linguistics to historical sociolinguistics: The evolution of old english expressions of shame and guilt. *Cognitive Linguistic Studies*, 1(1):55–83.

Fahad Khan, Francisco J Minaya Gómez, Rafael Cruz González, Harry Diakoff, Javier E Diaz Vera, John Philip McCrae, Ciara O'Loughlin, William Michael Short, and Sander Stolk. 2022. Towards the construction of a wordnet for old english. In *Proceedings of the Thirteenth Language Resources and Evaluation Conference*, pages 3934–3941.

John McCrae, Guadalupe Aguado de Cea, Paul Buitelaar, Philipp Cimiano, Thierry Declerck, Asunción Gómez-Pérez, Jorge Gracia, Laura Hollink, Elena Montiel-Ponsoda, Dennis Spohr, and Tobias Wunner. 2012. Interchanging lexical resources on the Semantic Web. *Language Resources and Evaluation*, 46(6):701–709.

John P. McCrae, Michael Wayne Goodman, Francis Bond, Alexandre Rademaker, Ewa Rudnicka, and Luis Morgado Da Costa. 2021. The GlobalWordNet Formats: Updates for 2020. In *Proceedings of the 11th Global Wordnet Conference*, pages 91–99.

George A Miller. 1995. Wordnet: a lexical database for english. *Communications of the ACM*, 38(11):39–41.

Laurent Romary, Mohamed Khemakhem, Fahad Khan, Jack Bowers, Nicoletta Calzolari, Monte George, Mandy Pet, and Piotr Bański. 2019. Lmf reloaded. *arXiv preprint arXiv:1906.02136*.

Klaus R Scherer. 2005. What are emotions? and how can they be measured? *Social science information*, 44(4):695–729.

Claudia Soria, Monica Monachini, and Piek Vossen. 2009. Wordnet-LMF: fleshing out a standardized format for wordnet interoperability. In *Proceedings of the 2009 International Workshop on Intercultural Collaboration*, pages 139–146.

Hidden in Plain Sight: Can German Wiktionary and Wordnets Facilitate the Detection of Antithesis?

Ramona Kühn
Innstraße 43
94032 Passau
Germany

Jelena Mitrović
Innstraße 43
94032 Passau
Germany

Michael Granitzer
Innstraße 43
94032 Passau
Germany

{ramona.kuehn, jelena.mitrovic, michael.granitzer}@uni-passau.de

Abstract

Existing wordnets mainly focus on synonyms, while antonyms have often been neglected, especially in wordnets in languages other than English. In this paper, we show how regular expressions are used to generate an antonym resource for German by using Wiktionary as a source. This resource contains antonyms for 45499 words. The antonyms can be used to extend existing wordnets. We show that this is important by comparing our antonym resource to the antonyms in OdeNet, the only freely available German wordnet that contains antonyms for 3059 words. We demonstrate that antonyms are relevant for the detection of the rhetorical figure antithesis. This figure has been known to influence the audience by creating contradiction and using a parallel sentence structure combined with antonyms. We first detect parallelism with part-of-speech tags and then apply our rule-based antithesis detection algorithm to a dataset of the messenger service Telegram. We evaluate our approach and achieve a precision of 57 % and a recall of 45 % thus overcoming the existing approaches.

1 Introduction

The goal of Natural Language Processing (NLP) is to enable computers to automatically analyze text and to understand its (sometimes subtle) underlying meaning. While this is a relatively easy task for most humans, it is difficult for computers, as good results depend on available language resources. Examples of such resources are lexicons, dictionaries, or databases. One of the most well-known lexical-semantic databases, or knowledge bases, is the Princeton WordNet (Fellbaum, 2010) for the English language.

For text understanding of non-English texts, wordnets in other languages have been developed. However, two problems are often encountered. The first problem is common in NLP: Good resources are only available in "popular" languages with many speakers (e.g., English), while less- or low-resourced languages are often neglected. The second problem is that some wordnets are not freely accessible or have poor quality (Nhut Lam et al., 2022).

In this paper, we want to focus on antonyms in the German language: While synonyms are easier to obtain from existing wordnets, antonyms only get marginal attention. So far, freely available German antonyms can only be found in the open German OdeNet (Siegel and Bond, 2021) and BabelNet, a multilingual encyclopedic dictionary and semantic network that combines different sources like WordNet, Wikipedia, Wiktionary, etc. (Navigli and Ponzetto, 2012; Navigli et al., 2021).

We aim to use a different antonym resource for the task of antithesis detection – a rhetorical figure that is constructed by using parallel phrases that contain a pair of antonyms. As rhetorical figures always have a function (Givón, 1985), this figure is used to express tension, to make a comparison, or to reveal contradicting behavior, ideas, or statements. For example, the biblical antithesis **"The spirit is willing, but the flesh is weak"** (Matthew 26:41) expresses the contrast between mind and body. Green (2021) presents a study on how antitheses are used in arguments in environmental science policy journal articles to show the contrast between the view of environmentalists and engineers. In politics, its usage can influence the audience and increase the scepticism towards the authorities by showing that their actions are contradictory, raising a feeling that they are unable to govern people successfully. By detecting antitheses in politically related texts, people's opinions can be better evaluated by understanding the hidden notions expressed by this figure: By using it for contrasting comparisons ("they are allowed to do this" vs. "we are not allowed to do that"), people are made jealous and incited to riot. It is important to prevent this by understanding the role of antithesis, especially in crisis situations, e.g., a pandemic, war, or in energy crises.

We consider antithesis detection as a binary classification problem and tackle it with a rule-based approach. As a dataset, we use posts by a German journalist on the messenger service Telegram in which he criticizes the German government during the COVID-19 pandemic. The parallel structure of those posts is identified by using part-of-speech (POS) tags. For the antonym detection, we rely on a word-based comparison. However, we realized that both OdeNet and Babelnet cannot satisfy our requirements for this task: We expect the antonym resource to be as complete as possible, i.e., containing antonyms for as many words as possible. Furthermore, we are interested in achieving a high recall to find most of the antitheses. In addition, we want the resource to be freely available. For Babelnet, it was difficult to retrieve all words with their respective antonyms, as we could not locate a list of all words contained in Babelnet. Furthermore, the extraction is limited by so-called Babelcoins where one coin represents one query: To retrieve one antonym, at least three different queries are necessary. In addition, by manually checking Babelnet, we realized that only few words contain antonyms which are often not German. OdeNet offers more antonyms and it provides a file of every word. With this file, we were able to extract all antonyms from OdeNet. However, we were still not able to identify most of the relevant antitheses (see Section 5 for a detailed comparison, especially Table 2). To meet all of those requirements, we built our own dictionary for German antonyms. With regular expressions, we extracted antonyms using the semi-structured data from the German Wiktionary.[1]

Our contributions are as follows:

- We show how Wiktionary can be used for creating a language resource for German, which can be used for the extension of existing wordnets.
- Our resource covers more German antonyms than OdeNet, resulting in a better performance in the task of antithesis detection.
- We present an algorithm based on the antonym dictionary that not only detects parallelism but also antitheses.
- We create the first annotated German dataset of antitheses.

The remainder of this paper is structured as follows: In Section 2, we describe related work on wordnets, Wiktionary as data source, and antithesis detection. Section 3 gives insights into the process of building the antonym dictionary. The antithesis detection process is described in Section 4. The evaluation in Section 5 compares our antonym resource with the antonyms in OdeNet. We also evaluate the performance of the rule-based antithesis detection approach. The following discussion includes a critical review of our methods and results. The paper concludes in Section 6. The code and data relevant for this paper are available online.[2]

2 Related Work

We will first give an overview of different wordnets for the German language and the sources that can be used to construct a language resource. The second part briefly defines antithesis and presents approaches for its detection.

2.1 Wordnets and Language Resources

Some advances have already been made to develop a German wordnet: GermaNet (Hamp and Feldweg, 1997) tries to be the German counterpart of WordNet. However, it is not freely available, and its functionality is limited. The Leipzig corpora (Biemann et al., 2007) and OpenThesaurus (Naber, 2005), a dictionary for German, contain only synonyms. BabelNet (Navigli and Ponzetto, 2010) includes some German antonyms but is far from being complete. Only OdeNet (Siegel and Bond, 2021), which is based on WordNet, contains more antonyms.

To extend the list of antonyms, we rely on Wiktionary as a source: Wikipedia and Wiktionary have already proved to be useful for different tasks, such as building an n-gram corpus (Cacho et al., 2021) or extending the GermaNet with definitions (Henrich et al., 2011). As Wiktionary consists of semi-structured text, effective scrapers and parsers are required. Scrapers or parsers for Wikipedia and Wiktionary are mostly used to create English resources: wiktextract (Ylonen, 2022) is a great tool to parse the English Wiktionary as it even includes

[1] https://de.wiktionary.org/wiki/Wiktionary:Hauptseite

[2] GitHub repository:
Wiktionary Parser: https://github.com/kuehnram/Wiktionary_Parser_German_Antonyms
Antithesis Detection: https://github.com/kuehnram/Antithesis_Detection

English dictionaries. Unfortunately, this resource does not work for other languages yet. For the German language, the wiktionary-de-parser[3] extracts different elements of a Wiktionary page, but it does not parse the text that contains the actual antonyms. This is actually the difficult part, as the content of a Wiktionary page is just "ordinary text" (Krizhanovsky, 2010). We developed a parser that can not only be used to extract antonyms but also to extract other elements of a Wiktionary page, e.g., synonyms, idiomatic expressions, examples, etc. in a similar way.

2.2 Antithesis

We want to show the relevance of antonyms for the detection of the rhetorical figure antithesis. Fahnestock (2002) describes this figure as "pleasing" and "persuasive" and defines it as "a verbal structure that places contrasted or opposed terms in parallel or balanced [...] phrases". Both a parallel structure and predictable antonyms are required, e.g., "the night is long, the day is short". A taxonomy of antithesis and examples from the environmental domain is presented by Green (2021).

Despite the relevance of rhetorical figures nowadays, e.g., in argument mining (Mitrović et al., 2017), there is no common definition, making it even more important to formalize their properties. Mladenović and Mitrović (2013) formally described rhetorical figures by creating RetFig, a formal domain ontology for almost 100 figures in the Serbian language. GRhOOT (Kühn et al., 2022) is the adaption and extension of the Serbian RetFig for the German language. In the GRhOOT ontology, an antithesis is described by the properties (in bold) that it is a **semantic figure of thought** which appears over a **whole sentence** and affects a **word** or a **phrase**. An element of the **opposite meaning** is **added**, expressing the use of an antonymous pair. However, this formal description cannot be used for detection yet.

A detection algorithm was developed by Lawrence et al. (2017) who split a text into "constitutive dialogue units" and "associated propositional units". They use the Princeton WordNet to find antonyms that appear in the other part of the unit. However, polarity shifters and negation cues are problematic.

Green and Crotts (2020) also try to detect antitheses: They use the antimetabole dataset of Dubremetz and Nivre (2018), as Harris et al. (2018) state that antitheses often occur with antimetabole - a repetition of words in reverse order. Green and Crotts found 120 antitheses in this dataset. For the detection, they rely on the algorithm by Lawrence et al. (2017) but use a broader definition of antonyms: They do not only look for antonyms in WordNet and ConceptNet (Speer et al., 2017) but also consider synonyms of the antonyms. They criticize that the publicly available resources are limited, as the used wordnets are not complete and contain "wrong" antonyms.

As the language resources prove to be insufficient for the English language, it is even more challenging in other languages: For German, we will show that our antonym dictionary outperforms the antonyms from OdeNet. We also advance the detection of antitheses by identifying not only antonyms but also parallelism.

3 Antonym Resource Creation

The data on Wiktionary pages are only semi-structured and the structure even differs between languages (Krizhanovsky, 2010). Typically, a German Wiktionary page of a certain word contains subsections describing its pronunciation, meanings, synonyms, antonyms, idiomatic expressions, etc.[4] Below the section of the German entry are properties often displayed in other languages, e.g., English, Swedish, etc.

The German Wiktionary dumps (here: from 2021-11-21 17:50:44) that are created regularly and are available online[5] are used to create the antonym resource. The structure of such a file is shown in Appendix A.1. We parse the XML dump file with ElementTree[6] from the Python Standard Library, and search for the string "Gegenwörter" (*antonyms*). Antonyms are extracted by using regular expressions. We ensure that only German antonyms are extracted and not words from other languages that are also present on some pages.

So far, we have identified five different variants of antonym representations on the Wiktionary page. There is no guarantee that this list is complete, and the different examples can also appear combined

[3] `https://pypi.org/project/wiktionary-de-parser/`

[4] Example for the word "gut" (*good*): `https://de.wiktionary.org/wiki/gut`

[5] `https://dumps.wikimedia.org/dewiktionary/latest/`

[6] `https://docs.python.org/3/library/xml.etree.elementtree.html`

on a single page:

1. :[1] [[antonym1]], [[antonym2]]/[[antonym3]]
2. :[1] [[antonym(plural s/n)]]
3. :[1] [[multi]] [[word]]
4. :[1] Explanatory text sometimes with [[link]]: [[antonym]]
5. :[1] [[Text: Antonym]] (e.g., [[*Substantive*: Antonym]]

Obviously, the first case is the easiest to extract, whereas the other cases induce more complexity to the parsing process. In the second case where the plural word is given within brackets, e.g., "Wolke(n)" *(cloud(s))*, we consider both the singular "Wolke" *(cloud)* and the plural "Wolken" *(clouds)* separately. If there are multiwords like in the third case, we concatenate them: e.g., [[darüber]] [[halten]] (literally: *over hold*) is concatenated to "darüber halten". The problem with the German language is that the position changes with inflexion, e.g., "ich halte darüber" (*I hold over*). Even lemmatization cannot resolve this conflict. In the fourth and fifth cases, additional free text is added as an explanation or further specification of the antonyms. In the fourth case, we are able to extract the antonym as it is normally provided within two square brackets. The fifth case, however, requires semantic understanding. Therefore, those few cases are ignored completely. We also ensure that the antonyms are implications: For example, the antonym of the German word "mother" is father, but "father" does not have any antonyms in the German Wiktionary. In our dictionary, the antonym relation is bidirectional: If x is an antonym of y, then y is also an antonym of x: A(x)=y → A(y)=x.

The approach of using regular expressions is simple yet effective: The final data structure is a Python key-value Dictionary consisting of 45,499 keys, where the key is the actual word/page title in lowercase, and the values are the set of antonyms, e.g., the antonyms of "woman" are "man, mister, exwife, husband", whereas for "freedom" it is "dependency, heteronomy":

```
{...
`frau`: {`mann`, `herr`, `exfrau`,
      `ehemann`},
`freiheit` :
      {`abhängigkeit`, `fremdbestimmung`}
...}
```

4 Antithesis Detection

To highlight the relevance of antonyms in NLP in general and especially in the context of rhetorical figure detection, we focus on the figure antithesis, a figure combining parallel phrases with antonyms. As definitions for rhetorical figures have never been precise or uniform, the detection of antitheses poses the following challenges:

1. How to define a relevant phrase?
2. How to define if phrases have a parallel structure?
3. How strict does the parallelism have to be to maintain the effect of an antithesis?
4. When is a word considered as an antonym of another word?

Those issues are tackled in the following way:

Challenge 1 - Phrases: We define relevant phrases by the occurrence of specific markers such as punctuation marks, the word "als" (*as/when*), or "und" (*and*). Considering quotation marks as such markers or removing them can also yield a parallel structure. A sentence is split at the occurrence of such markers into individual phrases. Only phrases that consist of more than one word are considered.

Challenge 2 & 3 - Parallelism: Parallel phrases do not have to be necessarily within one sentence, only within one post. We define parallelism by repeating POS tags, e.g.,

```
the/DET night/NOUN is/AUX long/ADV,
the/DET day/NOUN is/AUX short/ADV ./
   PUNCT
```

The spaCy POS tagger[7] also supports the German language. We use the trained pipeline `de_dep_news_trf` with the highest accuracy for POS tags (99%).[8] Despite the high accuracy, false labelled POS tags can occur, causing the algorithm not to recognize the parallel structure. Furthermore, we replace the POS tag "PROPN" for proper nouns with the tag "NOUN", as proper nouns are just a further specification of general nouns (e.g., (company) names, brands, etc.).

We do not use a strict definition of parallelism but accept some deviations: If a phrase consists of 3 or fewer words, perfect parallelism is required, i.e., perfectly repeating POS tags. If a phrase consists of

[7] https://spacy.io/models/de

[8] https://spacy.io/models/de#de_dep_news_trf

more than three words, we defined a Levenshtein distance: In our case, the number of POS tags between two phrases has to match at least to 75 %. To investigate parallelism further to find the optimal threshold for parallelism is considered future work.

Challenge 4 - Antonyms: With adequate language resources, finding antonyms should not be a challenge. However, as already mentioned, the functionality of existing resources is limited. With our generated dictionary from Wiktionary, we hope to cover most of the existing antonyms. Dependent on how strictly Fahnestock's definition is interpreted, it would be necessary to define for each antonym pair a distance function to determine the appropriateness of an antonym pair. Green and Crotts (2020) consider synonyms of antonyms in their antithesis detection. We will not include synonyms, not only because of the lack of resources but also because the function of the antithesis is weakened if the predictability of antonyms decreases. Another problem that both Green and Crotts (2020) and Lawrence et al. (2017) face are polarity shifters and negation cues: For example, "unethical" is considered to be the opposite of "ethical". However, "unethical" is semantically very close to "not ethical". As we are looking for antonyms on a word basis, we are not able to capture those negations. Another problem that was also identified by Green and Crotts (2020) is that opposing concepts cannot be recognized. A further challenge in the German language is the so-called tmesis with separable verbs: a particle is split from its core, or prefixes are inserted in the process of inflection, changing their position in a sentence. Even lemmatizers are not able to transform those words into their original lemma.

4.1 Dataset

We use two different sources for the dataset: First, we reuse the annotated antithesis dataset of Green and Crotts (2020). In this dataset, both parallelism and antonyms are loosely defined, as synonyms of antonyms are allowed.We translated it from English into German with Deepl[9] and manually checked the output. Some entries lost their parallel structure in the translation process, resulting in 106 out of 120 entries that can be considered as an antithesis in German.

As second source, we use 3433 posts from a German channel on the messenger service Telegram. The data was collected by Peter et al. (2022). We choose the channel of `reitschusterde`, which is operated by a German journalist criticizing the COVID-19 strategy of the German government. His posts are polarizing, so he is sometimes referred to as a right-wing populist (Bednarz, 2020). Populists are persons that "pit the pure, innocent, always hardworking people against a corrupt elite

[9] `deepl.com`

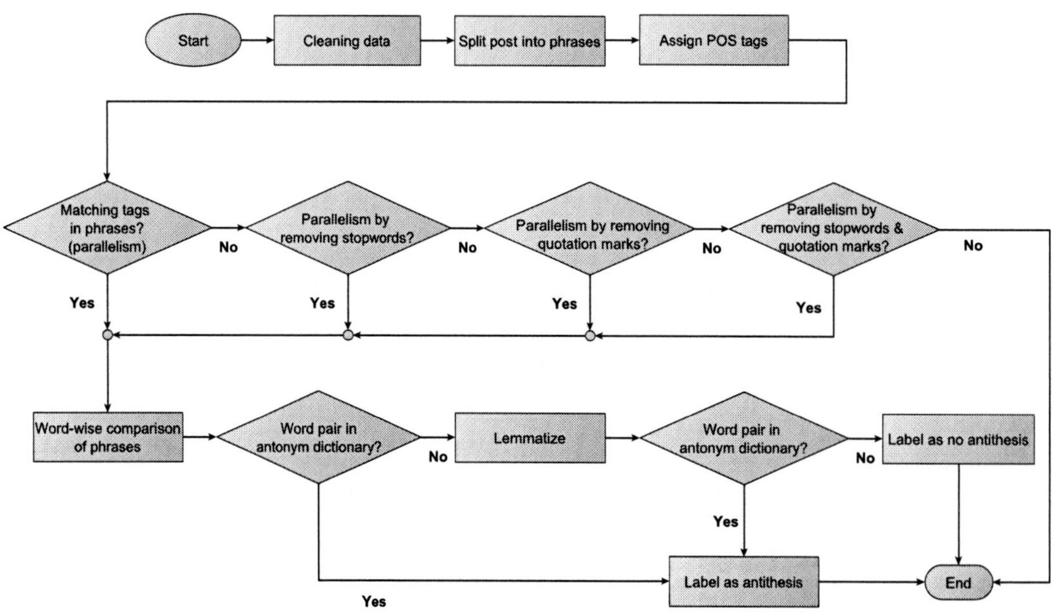

Figure 1: Steps of the parallelism and antonym detection algorithms.

who do not really work" (Müller, 2016), opposing normal people to the elites (Wodak, 2015). Simply said, they often display the world in binary schemes like "good" vs. "evil", "citizens" vs. "elites", which resembles the structure of antithesis. Furthermore, the political actions of the German government during the COVID-19 pandemic were actually contradictory, as even neutral newspapers reported (Suchy, 2021; Hierholzer, 2021; Gerd Antes, 2021). We therefore hope to find good examples of the figure antithesis in this data. In the following, we will refer to each post from Telegram and each instance of Green's dataset as "entry".

4.2 Annotation

It is widely known that annotation is a tedious task. Only one annotator was available who was introduced to the characteristics of detecting antithesis. To reduce the workload, the data was pre-filtered by only selecting entries where the parallelism algorithm based on POS tags could identify at least one pair of parallel phrases. This results in a reduction of the dataset. Overall, it consists of 954 distinct entries.

The structure of the overall annotated dataset is shown in Table 1. For readability, the entries are translated from German to English and the opposing words are highlighted in bold. For each entry, the parallelism algorithm first identifies all combinations of parallel phrases (column *Phrase 1/Phrase 2*. In the next step, the antithesis algorithm looks for opposing words in each phrase (column *Algorithm*; the steps of the algorithms are described in Subsection 4.3). The human annotator decides if the phrases are parallel and contain an antithesis (column *Human* is 1 if yes, 0 otherwise). There can be multiple parallel phrases for each post (cf. Table 1). This means that if a post contains an antithesis in general, it is possible that there may be parallel pairs of phrases that do not contain antonyms. This resulted in 1251 different annotated phrase pairs originating from the 954 initial entries.

4.3 Antithesis Detection Algorithm

Fig. 1 shows the flowchart of the parallelism and antithesis detection algorithms. After cleaning the data, the post is split at specific markers into phrases. POS tags are assigned to each word while repeating POS tags in two phrases mean parallelism. If no parallelism is detected, common German stopwords are removed. If there is still no parallelism, we first remove quotation marks, which leads to another split of the phrases, and then try removing stopwords and quotation marks.

If parallelism was detected, we search for opposing words in the two phrases with the help of the created antonym dictionary, which we described in Section 3. If no antonym pair is found, we try lemmatizing each word.

5 Evaluation

We evaluate two aspects: (1) We want to quantitatively compare the created antonym resource with OdeNet's antonyms, which is so far the best wordnet for German antonyms. (2) We want to give

Entry	Phrase 1	Phrase 2	Algorithm	Human
'Many media focus on escalation and [...]. The police are focusing on de-escalation."	['Many','media', 'focus', 'on', **'escalation'**]"	['the', 'police', 'are', 'focusing', 'on', **'de-escalation'**]	1	1
"Who is a fascist here? "Antifa old" against "Antifa new": [...]. His thesis: The counter-protest is controlled. A search."	['antifa', **'old'**]	['antifa', **'new'**]	1	1
"Who is a fascist here? "Antifa old" against "Antifa new": [...]. His thesis: The counter-protest is controlled. A search."	['his', 'thesis']	['a', 'search']	0	0

Table 1: Three example entries in the dataset.

	Precision	Recall	Accuracy	F1-Score
OdeNet Antonyms	50.00 %	8.80 %	90.00 %	14.97 %
Wiktionary Antonym Dict	57.00 %	45.24 %	91.05 %	50.44 %

Table 2: Performance metrics for rule-based antithesis detection.

insights into how good the rule-based approach for antithesis detection performs both with OdeNet and our created antonym resource.

5.1 Comparison of Antonym Resources

We compare the antonyms from OdeNet and our created antonym resource. From OdeNet's lexical entries[10] we extracted all antonyms to build a dictionary that has the same structure as our antonyms dictionary. On average, OdeNet has more antonyms per word (16.43 vs. 2.45 in our resource), but it has antonyms for only 3,059 words, whereas our antonym resource contains antonyms for 45,499 words.

Another feature of OdeNet is that it contains several multiwords, idiomatic expressions, or tmeses. Due to the specialty of the German language, the word order is changed by inflection. As we perform a word-by-word comparison in our case, those multiwords cannot be detected, as lemmatizers are not yet able to respect those constructions.

5.2 Evaluation of Antithesis Detection

We evaluate the performance of OdeNet and our antonym resource in the task of detecting the rhetorical figure antithesis: We apply both resources to our annotated dataset and compare the results with those of the human annotator. In this step, we compare phrase-wise.

In those 1251 phrase pairs, 126 antitheses were identified by the human annotator. We are aware that the dataset is highly imbalanced, which can lead to problems regarding the evaluation metrics. The imbalance is often inherent in datasets with rhetorical figures. Our work is a step towards the creation of more datasets and enlarging existing ones. The confusion matrix in Fig. 2a shows that 57 antitheses are correctly identified (`Predicted label`=1 and `True label`=1). As the dataset is unbalanced, Subfig. 2b on the right shows the normalized confusion matrix.

As orientation for our evaluation serves the result of Green and Crotts (2020): They achieved a precision of 41.1 % and a recall of 38.4 %. However, their approach was different and is therefore difficult to compare. Moreover, their dataset consists solely of antithesis, so they focused on detecting only antonyms and not on identifying parallelism in addition. Table 2 shows the metrics of the antithesis detection with OdeNet and our antonym dict. OdeNet is only able to find 8.8 % of relevant antithesis. This was too low for our requirements. With our antonym resource from Wiktionary, we achieve a precision of 57 % and a recall of 45.24 %. However, the accuracy has to be taken with a grain of salt due to the imbalanced dataset.

There is no antithesis that OdeNet finds that our antonym resource did not find. This means a combination of both resources would not improve the results here, but can be useful for other datasets. We also took a closer look when the antonym dictionary fails (see Table 3): Most cases were no "typical" or "proper" antonyms (see Appendix A.2 for details).

Not in antonym resource	40
Wrong lemmatization	15
Negation	4
Opposed concepts/ideas	10

Table 3: Reasons for false negatives.

As already mentioned, an antithesis can evoke emotions of doubt by opposed comparison: We want to illustrate this by showing two examples the algorithm found. For readability, they are translated into English, and antonyms are in bold.

Example 1: **In former times**, the CSU (*German party*) used to stand for Bavarian lifestyle and culture. **Nowadays**, the CSU leader is destroying centuries-old traditions, [...].

Example 2: Good and bad demonstrators - well framed on ARD (*news channel*). Christopher Street Day **allowed** in Berlin, Corona Demo **banned** in Kassel.

[10] `https://github.com/hdaSprachtechnologie/odenet`

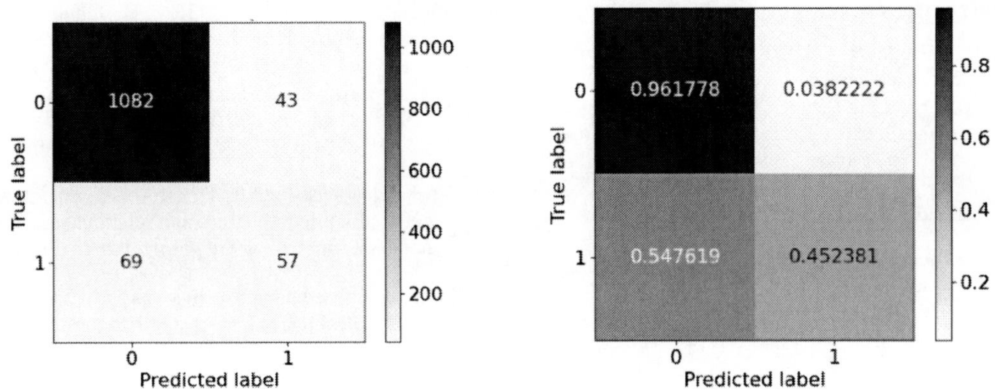

(a) Confusion Matrix.

(b) Normalized Confusion Matrix.

Figure 2: Confusion Matrices.

Example 3: Monday **morning**: Markus Söder (*German politician*) proposes to vaccinate politicians specifically with AstraZeneca's vaccine. Monday **afternoon**: Germany suspends Corona vaccinations with AstraZeneca as a precautionary measure on the recommendation of the Paul Ehrlich Institute.

5.3 Discussion

We want critically assess our approaches and discuss aspects that need improvement in the future. The detection of parallelism –another rhetorical figure– needs more attention in the future. The defined Levenshtein threshold needs more evaluation to discover at what distance the effect of parallelism is achieved. We also unveiled the property of lemmatizers that their precision increases with the number of words provided. As we performed lemmatization on single words, we obtained false lemmas of words, leading the algorithm to not find the antonym pair in the dictionary.

Although we cover more antonyms in our dictionary than OdeNet, we are only able to find opposing words, not separable words, multiword expressions, or contrasting concepts. Although OdeNet contains multiword expressions, it is not possible to reflect concepts based on a word-level comparison. This problem was already faced by Green and Crotts (2020) for English antonyms: "The current [...] resources [...] are incomplete in their coverage of opposite lexical concepts".

6 Conclusion

As wordnets mainly focus on synonyms, we constructed a resource for antonyms from the German Wiktionary. We highlighted the relevance of antonyms by using the created resource to detect the rhetorical figure antithesis, a persuasive figure that is often used in arguments.

Antithesis detection can enable the identification of bias and persuasion, which is helpful in a political context as our dataset demonstrated. With our rule-based approach, we were able to identify parallel phrases and achieved a recall of 45 %, whereas OdeNet was only able to identify 8.8 % of the antitheses. The limited availability of language resources, their functionality, and the need of datasets are still challenges that must be addressed.

In the future, we want to improve the detection of antithesis. With language models and deep learning, we assume to achieve higher precision and recall. Data augmentation techniques need to be considered to tackle the imbalance of the dataset. Wordnets can help here by replacing words with their synonyms.

Acknowledgment

The project on which this report is based was funded by the German Federal Ministry of Education and Research (BMBF) under the funding code 01IS20049. The author is responsible for the content of this publication.

We would like to thank Nancy L. Green very much for sharing her annotated dataset with us. We also thank the anonymous reviewers for their helpful comments.

References

Liane Bednarz. 2020. Lebensgefährliche "Lebensschützer". https://www.spiegel.de/politik/deutschland/christliche-corona-verharmloser-lebensgefaehrliche-lebensschuetzer-a-8c5ac68a-c030-414d-bb89-ed81cd992cf7. Accessed: 2022-07-29.

Chris Biemann, Gerhard Heyer, Uwe Quasthoff, and Matthias Richter. 2007. The leipzig corpora collection-monolingual corpora of standard size. *Proceedings of Corpus Linguistic*, 2007.

Jorge Ramón Fonseca Cacho, Ben Cisneros, and Kazem Taghva. 2021. Building a wikipedia n-gram corpus. In *Intelligent Systems and Applications: Proceedings of the 2020 Intelligent Systems Conference (IntelliSys) Volume 2*, pages 277–294. Springer.

Marie Dubremetz and Joakim Nivre. 2018. Rhetorical figure detection: chiasmus, epanaphora, epiphora. *Frontiers in Digital Humanities*, 5:10.

Jeanne Fahnestock. 2002. *Rhetorical figures in science*. Oxford University Press on Demand.

Christiane Fellbaum. 2010. Wordnet. In *Theory and applications of ontology: computer applications*, pages 231–243. Springer.

Jürgen Zurheide Gerd Antes. 2021. Medizinstatistiker: Bevölkerung wird mit widersprüchlichen Aussagen konfrontiert. https://www.deutschlandfunk.de/corona-massnahmen-medizinstatistiker-bevoelkerung-wird-mit-100.html. Accessed: 2022-07-09.

Talmy Givón. 1985. Iconicity, isomorphism and non-arbitrary coding in syntax. *Iconicity in syntax*, pages 187–219.

Nancy L Green. 2021. Some argumentative uses of the rhetorical figure of antithesis in environmental science policy articles. *Computational Models of Natural.*

Nancy L Green and L Joshua Crotts. 2020. Towards automatic detection of antithesis. In *CMNA@ COMMA*, pages 69–73.

Birgit Hamp and Helmut Feldweg. 1997. Germanet-a lexical-semantic net for german. In *Automatic information extraction and building of lexical semantic resources for NLP applications*.

Randy Allen Harris, Chrysanne Di Marco, Sebastian Ruan, and Cliff O'Reilly. 2018. An annotation scheme for rhetorical figures. *Argument & Computation*, 9(2):155–175.

Verena Henrich, Erhard Hinrichs, and Tatiana Vodolazova. 2011. Semi-automatic extension of germanet with sense definitions from wiktionary. In *Proceedings of the 5th Language and Technology Conference (LTC 2011)*, pages 126–130.

Michael Hierholzer. 2021. Ohne Kompass durch die Krise. https://www.faz.net/aktuell/rhein-main/kultur/widerspruechliche-corona-politik-ohne-kompass-durch-die-krise-17261870.html. Accessed: 2022-07-09.

AA Krizhanovsky. 2010. Transformation of Wiktionary entry structure into tables and relations in a relational database schema. *arXiv preprint arXiv:1011.1368*.

Ramona Kühn, Jelena Mitrovic, and Michael Granitzer. 2022. GRhOOT: Ontology of Rhetorical Figures in German. *LREC. Marseille, France*.

John Lawrence, Jacky Visser, and Chris Reed. 2017. Harnessing rhetorical figures for argument mining. *Argument & Computation*, 8(3):289–310.

Jelena Mitrović, Cliff O'Reilly, Miljana Mladenović, and Siegfried Handschuh. 2017. Ontological representations of rhetorical figures for argument mining. *Argument & Computation*, 8(3):267–287.

Miljana Mladenović and Jelena Mitrović. 2013. Ontology of rhetorical figures for serbian. In *Text, Speech, and Dialogue: 16th International Conference, TSD 2013, Pilsen, Czech Republic, September 1-5, 2013. Proceedings 16*, pages 386–393. Springer.

Jan-Werner Müller. 2016. *What is populism?* University of Pennsylvania Press.

Daniel Naber. 2005. OpenThesaurus: ein offenes deutsches Wortnetz. *Sprachtechnologie, mobile Kommunikation und linguistische Ressourcen: Beiträge zur GLDV-Tagung, Bonn, Germany*, pages 422–433.

Roberto Navigli, Michele Bevilacqua, Simone Conia, Dario Montagnini, and Francesco Cecconi. 2021. Ten years of babelnet: A survey. In *IJCAI*, pages 4559–4567.

Roberto Navigli and Simone Paolo Ponzetto. 2010. Babelnet: Building a very large multilingual semantic network. In *Proceedings of the 48th annual meeting of the association for computational linguistics*, pages 216–225.

Roberto Navigli and Simone Paolo Ponzetto. 2012. Babelnet: The automatic construction, evaluation and application of a wide-coverage multilingual semantic network. *Artificial intelligence*, 193:217–250.

Khang Nhut Lam, Feras Al Tarouti, and Jugal Kalita. 2022. Automatically constructing Wordnet synsets. *arXiv e-prints*, page arXiv:2208.03870.

Valentin Peter, Ramona Kühn, Jelena Mitrović, Michael Granitzer, and Hannah Schmid-Petri. 2022. Network analysis of german covid-19 related discussions on telegram. In *Natural Language Processing and Information Systems: 27th International Conference on Applications of Natural Language to Information Systems, NLDB 2022, Valencia, Spain, June 15–17, 2022, Proceedings*, pages 25–32. Springer.

Melanie Siegel and Francis Bond. 2021. OdeNet: Compiling a GermanWordNet from other Resources. In *Proceedings of the 11th Global Wordnet Conference*, pages 192–198.

Robyn Speer, Joshua Chin, and Catherine Havasi. 2017. Conceptnet 5.5: An open multilingual graph of general knowledge. In *Thirty-first AAAI conference on artificial intelligence*.

Clara Suchy. 2021. Herr Spahn, was ist Ihr Plan? `https://www.n-tv.de/politik/politik_kommentare/Herr-Spahn-was-ist-Ihr-Plan-article22896673.html`. Accessed: 2022-07-09.

Ruth Wodak. 2015. The politics of fear: What right-wing populist discourses mean. *The Politics of Fear*, pages 1–256.

Tatu Ylonen. 2022. Wiktextract: Wiktionary as machine-readable structured data. *LREC. Marseille, France*.

A Appendix

A.1 Structure of Wiktionary

Fig. 3 shows the structure (xml tags) of the dump file of the German Wiktionary. We are interested in the "'text" part, as it contains both the visible text of the Wiktionary website and the antonyms. Unfortunately, it is a semi-structured text string, making it more difficult to parse.

For example, for the word "gut" (*"good"*), an excerpt of the text tag's content is shown in Fig. 4.

```
└─mediawiki
   ├─siteinfo
   │  ├─sitename
   │  ├─dbname
   │  ├─base
   │  ├─generator
   │  ├─case
   │  └─namespaces
   │     └─namespace {...}
   ├─page
   │  ├─title
   │  ├─ns
   │  ├─id
   │  └─revision
   │     ├─id
   │     ├─parentid
   │     ├─timestamp
   │     ├─contributor
   │     │  ├─username
   │     │  └─id
   │     ├─comment
   │     ├─model
   │     ├─format
   │     ├─text
   │     └─sha1
   └─page {...}
```

Figure 3: XML structure of German Wiktionary.

A.2 Details on False Negatives

We want to show some example sentence where the antithesis detection algorithm fails.

Not in antonym resource: Most cases fail because their antonym pairs are not in the antonym dictionary. Surprisingly, the antonym pair "mehr – weniger" (*"more – less"*) is not in the dictionary. Another example from the dataset is "**Föderalimus** ade - **Zentralstaat** hurra" (*"**federalism** goodbye - **centralstate** hooray"*. The antonym of federalism is centralism in the antonym resource, but not centralstate. Another example is "**Aufregung** über Rassismus, **Wegsehen** bei Islamismus" (*"**agitation** over racism, **look away** from islamism"*): Agitation is contrasting to look away but more in a transferred sense. A further example uses numbers as antonym pairs to express the contrast that left-wing demonstations are more dangerous than Covid-19 demonstrations that are often considered to be led by right-wing activists: "**43** Verletzte bei der linksextremen demo, **7** bei der Corona Demo" (*"**43** injured at the extreme left demo, **7** at the Corona demo"*).

Wrong lemmatization: In the sentence "**Deeskalierende** Polizei, **eskalierende** Presse. (*"**de-escalating** police, **escalating** press."*, the words are not correctly lemmatized by spaCy, leading to the non-detection of the pair escalate – de-escalate. In Table 1, the words are in their basic form and are therefore correctly detected.

Negation: "Erfolg **ist nicht der Schlüssel** zum Glück, Glücklichsein **ist der Schlüssel** zum Erfolg." (*"Success **is not the key** to happiness, happiness **is the key** to success."*): The negation cannot be detected yet by the algorithm.

Opposed concepts and ideas: The following sentence shows the contrast between restrictions in two states. It is however not expressed by an antonym pair, therefore the algorithm fails to detect this antithesis. Please note that "north" and "south" is not a German antonym pair as they are no German words: "In South Dakota gab es **fast keine Einschränkungen**, Schulen und Restaurants blieben offen. North Dakota setzte auf **Maskenpflicht und Restriktionen**." (*South Dakota had **almost no restrictions**, schools and restaurants remained open. North Dakota relied on **mandatory masks and restrictions**.*)

```
{{Siehe auch|[[Gut]], [[güt]]}}
{{Wort der Woche|30|2008}}
== gut ({{Sprache|Deutsch}}) ==
=== {{Wortart|Adjektiv|Deutsch}} ===

{{Deutsch Adjektiv Übersicht
|Positiv=gut
|Komparativ=besser
|Superlativ=besten
}}

{{Worttrennung}}
:gut, {{Komp.}} bes·ser, {{Sup.}} am bes·ten

{{Aussprache}}
:{{IPA}} {{Lautschrift|gu:t}}
:{{Hörbeispiele}} {{Audio|De-gut.ogg}}, {{Audio|De-gut2.ogg}}, {{Audio|De-at-gut.ogg|spr=at}}
:{{Reime}} {{Reim|u:t|Deutsch}}

{{Bedeutungen}}
:[1] vom Menschen her [[positiv]] [[bewerten|bewertet]], [[empfinden|empfunden]], [[fühlen|gefühlt]] und dergleichen
::[a] ''prädikativ oder attributiv gebraucht''
::[b] ''adverbiell gebraucht''
:[2] eine Schulnote
::[a] ''(Deutschland und Österreich<ref>In Österreich großgeschrieben: „Mit „Gut“ sind Leistungen zu beurteilen, mit denen der Schüler …“
([https://www.ris.bka.gv.at/Dokumente/Bundesnormen/NOR12119641/NOR12119641.pdf Leistungsbeurteilungsverordnung, § 14. (3))]</ref>)''
entspricht der Note 2
::[b] ''(Schweiz)'' entspricht der Note 5
:[3] mit Zahl- oder Maßangaben: reichlich bemessen, etwas mehr als angegeben
:[4] jemandem [[freundlich]] gesinnt, jemandem zugetan
:[5] für besonders [[feierlich]]e Anlässe gedacht
:[6] ohne größere Mühen zu erledigen, leicht machbar

{{Herkunft}}
:[[mittelhochdeutsch]] und [[althochdeutsch]] ''guot'', ursprünglich „[[passend]]“<ref>{{Ref-Duden|gut}}</ref><ref>{{Ref-DWDS|gut}}</ref>

{{Synonyme}}
:[1] [[schön]], [[fein]], [[O. K.]], [[okay]]
:[1b] [[wohl]]
:[2] (österreichisch) [[Gut]]

{{Gegenwörter}}
:[1] [[schlecht]], [[negativ]], [[böse]], [[übel]]
:[3] [[knapp]]

{{Beispiele}}
:[1] Es geht mir ''gut.''
```

Figure 4: Semi-structured content of the Wiktionary text-tag. The heading {{Gegenwörter}} contains the antonyms.

How do We Treat Systematic Polysemy in Wordnets and Similar Resources? – Using Human Intuition and Contextualized Embeddings as Guidance

Nathalie Sørensen[1], Sanni Nimb[2] & Bolette S. Pedersen[1]

Centre for Language Technology, NorS, University of Copenhagen[1], Society for Danish Language and Literature [2]
Emil Holms Kanal 2, 2300 Copenhagen S[1], Christian Brygge 1, 1219 Copenhagen K [2]
nmp828@hum.ku.dk, sn@dsl.dk, bspedersen@hum.ku.dk

Abstract

Systematic polysemy is a well-known linguistic phenomenon where a group of lemmas follow the same polysemy pattern. However, when compiling a lexical resource like a wordnet, a problem arises regarding when to underspecify the two (or more) meanings by one (complex) sense and when to systematically split into separate senses. In this work, we present an extensive analysis of the systematic polysemy patterns in Danish, and in our preliminary study, we examine a subset of these with experiments on human intuition and contextual embeddings. The aim of this preparatory work is to enable future guidelines for each polysemy type. In the future, we hope to expand this approach and thereby hopefully obtain a sense inventory which is distributionally verified and thereby more suitable for NLP.

1 Introduction

Systematic polysemy, also called regular polysemy, is a well-known linguistic phenomenon where a group of lemmas follow the same polysemy pattern (Apresjan 1974, Malmgren, 1988, Pustejovsky 1995, Nimb 2016 and several others). For instance, the lemmas *chicken* and *school* belong to the patterns ANIMAL/FOOD and LOCATION/INSTITUTION due to their inherently dual meanings with different ontological types.

The phenomenon is challenging to describe in theoretical linguistics as well as in practical lexicography where decisions need to be made regarding whether to split regular polysemous lemmas into several senses, or whether to see the meaning of these lemmas as inherently complex, with the individual context simply highlighting one or the other meaning. At times, a context does not specify any of the meanings and may highlight both equally. This kind of *underspecification* (Cruse, 1986) thus invokes two ontological types simultaneously, as seen in sentence a), where *taste* highlights a FOOD reading of *salmon*, while *lived a good life* draw attention to the ANIMAL reading:

a) You can taste if the **salmon** has lived a good life.

In lexicons, systematic polysemy can be dealt with in two ways (Vicente and Falkum, 2017, Ruhl, 1989). First, a *sense enumeration lexicon* can be established where different readings of a lexical item are listed under a single dictionary entry. In the case of *salmon*, such an approach would list both the ANIMAL and FOOD sense. This method is typically used in traditional dictionaries. Alternatively, it can be treated with a *one-representation approach* motivated by the fact that it is impossible in praxis to list all existing meanings of a lexical item. Instead, the lexicon describes regular patterns of sense alternations which also predict senses in a systematic way. A well-known example of the one-representation approach is provided in *The Generative Lexicon* (Pustejovsky, 1995). According to this approach, the *salmon* would be considered a *complex type* that denotes both the living animal and its corresponding meat.

This paper describes the challenges of achieving a homogenous approach to represent systematic polysemy in lexical resources and discusses when to rely on *a sense enumeration* approach and when to underspecify. We perform our studies within the framework of the COR [1] lexicon, which is based on previous lexical

[1] The Danish abbreviation of 'the central word register'.

resources that were not consistent in their treatment of systematic polysemy. Overall, COR aims towards a restricted sense inventory where only distributionally 'verified' senses are maintained.

The new lexicon is primarily based on the corpus-based monolingual Danish dictionary: *Den Danske Ordbog* (DDO). Even though the dictionary mostly follows a sense enumeration approach, it occasionally uses a joint sense description for instances of systematic polysemy, typically in the case of less frequent lemmas in the corpus. In the COR lexicon, we rely heavily on our experience from compiling two other resources based on the DDO dictionary. First, in the Danish WordNet project *DanNet* (Pedersen et al., 2009), in which we took steps towards expanding the representations for specific systematic polysemy patterns, see Pedersen et al. (2010). Later, we compiled a Danish thesaurus based on senses in DDO and DanNet (Nimb et al., 2014, 2016). We also take inspiration from Alonso (2013), who examines expert and laymen annotations of the underspecified sense, however only on selected number of patterns.

In the COR project we aim at a homogenous treatment of similar polysemy patterns throughout the whole vocabulary, and with specific information on the type of pattern as part of the lexical semantic information. We adopt a similar idea to Nimb (2016) who suggests a method for systematic polysemy detection through lexical resources. The strategy is based on the initial hand annotations of a set of polysemous lemmas in DDO, which are again informed with information from DanNet. Thereby, we examine the vocabulary both bottom-up and top-down to establish a typology of Danish systematic polysemy patterns. The registered patterns lead to a set of rules stating whether the senses of a certain pattern must be reflected as either one or two COR lexicon senses. A subset of these rules is supplemented by two additional investigations, namely i) surveys on the human intuition, and ii) distributional investigations using a large, contextualised embedding model (BERT).

The idea of evaluating systematic polysemy by use of multiple information sources originates from the work of McCrae et al., (2022), who investigate an integrative method for distinguishing senses. They treat the sense distinction problem by including four perspectives: formal, cognitive, distributional, and multilingual. In our case, the combination of a formal semantic resource (DanNet), a study of the human intuition, and a distributional analysis, allows us to analyse systematic polysemy from different angles, including how the patterns are perceived by humans and used in texts. For instance, we investigate whether cases of systematic polysemy are conceptualised by humans as one or multiple senses by asking informants whether context pairs invoke the same or different senses. By using a distributional approach, we examine whether the ontological types in a pattern are represented in texts. This is particularly relevant in the application of NLP, as texts do not necessarily reveal the metonymic relationship between the senses in systematic polysemy, and distributional models may not be able to distinguish such senses.

The representation of systematic polysemy in lexical resources has been explored and discussed before (Peters & Kilgariff, 2000, Barque & Chaumartin, 2009). Although, to our knowledge, this is the first study to use both language models and informants to analyse systematic polysemy to compile valid encoding guidelines for a practical resource, in our case the COR lexicon. The study also gives valuable feedback to the treatment of systematic polysemy in DanNet and the DDO dictionary.

The structure of the paper is as follows. Section 2 introduces a typology of Danish systematic polysemy patterns. In Section 3 and 4, we present a preliminary study that analyses a selection of patterns in two ways, first using a survey of human intuition, then using a distributional model (BERT). In section 5, we discuss the interaction of the different approaches, and discuss how the treatment of systematic polysemy in lexical resources can benefit from the results.

2 A Typology of Danish Systematic Polysemy Patterns

In our annotation work, we have identified 28 Danish systematic polysemy patterns based on the compilation of the central vocabulary in the COR lexicon (Pedersen et al., 2022). The project is initiated by the annotation of ~3,300 polysemous lemmas in the DDO dictionary. We consider this a core vocabulary of Danish since they all have at least one sense which is linked to a core concept in the Princeton WordNet (PWN) (Fellbaum, 1998). In total, more than 15,000 senses are annotated.

In the dataset, all patterns of systematic polysemy are identified based on information in the sense definitions in DDO and the taxonomies in DanNet. The different patterns are analysed and discussed, resulting in a list of the most prominent systematic polysemy patterns in Danish.

As briefly mentioned above, an overall goal of the COR-project is not to reflect the fine-grained DDO sense inventory 1:1, but to compile a more coarse-grained sense inventory for Danish which is suitable for AI purposes and computational applications. By identifying the patterns, we can apply a homogenous analysis across multiple lemmas with the same patterns.

The starting point is the patterns registered in the projects DanNet (Pedersen et al., 2010) and the Danish thesaurus (Nimb, 2016), e.g., PROCESS/RESULT, PLANT/ FOOD, and ANIMAL/ FOOD. However in contrast to these projects, we consider the entire lemma information including all senses, and not just concepts represented as standalone DDO senses. This allows us to detect patterns of polysemy in a systematic way, lemma by lemma. For instance, it is typical for the lemmas that hold the pattern LOCATION/INSTITUTION to have 'building/ location' senses with similar definitions, which are typically listed under the same main sense as the 'institution' senses. By looking into DanNet, we can also compare the ontological types and thereby detect the patterns top-down.

During the discussion of the initially identified patterns, we questioned whether some patterns were actually cases of systematic polysemy or rather a case of the annotators being too eager to register patterns. Therefore, we include a pattern in the typology only if it fulfils the following three criteria:

a) At least five instances of the pattern can be found in the COR-dataset of ~3300 polysemous core lemmas.
b) The Danish Dictionary (DDO) or DanNet must distinguish between both senses of the pattern for most of the identified lemmas.
c) Each sense in a pattern must have distinct ontological types.

The criteria a) and b) ensure that a pattern is prominent in Danish by taking frequency and previous sense descriptions into account. If the pattern is systematic in Danish, we assume that it would be reflected in the core polysemous part of the Danish vocabulary. In the case of b), we must consider that the DDO in some cases prefers a single sense description. This is partly due to space limitations in the originally printed dictionary. The DDO typically uses sense enumeration when the lemma is frequent and a central simplex lemma, e.g., *bog* ('book'), while for compound nouns (e.g., *kogebog* ('cooking book')) as well as more rare

Pattern	Examples
Group 1	1stOrder
ANIMAL / FOOD	*laks* 'salmon'
PLANT / FOOD	*tomat* 'tomato'
PLANT / MATERIAL	*eg* 'oak'
ARTIFACT / MATERIAL	*sølv* 'silver'
SHOP / PERSON	*bager* 'bakery, baker'
ANIMAL (body part) / FOOD	*vinge* 'wing'
BODY PART / GARMENT (part)	*ærme* 'sleeve'
Group 2	2ndOrder (/1stOrder)
PROCESS / RESULT (concrete)	*bygning* 'building'
ARTIFACT / ACTIVITY	*fodbold* 'football'
ARTIFACT / PROPERTY	*sølv* 'silver'
ACT / EVENT	*bøje* 'bend'
Group 3	1stOrder / 3rdOrder
CONTAINER / CONTENTS	*glas* 'glass'
LOCATION / INSTITUTION	*skole* 'school'
ARTIFACT / FORM	*klokke* 'bell'
ARTIFACT / CONTENT	*bog* 'book'
ARTIFACT(s) / INSTITUTION	*arkiv* 'archive'
OBJECT / SYMBOL	*hjerte* 'heart'
COUNTABLE / UNCOUNTABLE	*øl* '(a bottle of) beer, (the liquid) beer'
Group 4	2ndorder / 3rdorder
PROCESS / RESULT (abstract)	*forandring* 'change'
ACT / THOUGHT	*metode* 'method'
ACTIVITY / INSTITUTION	*cykelløb* 'bicycle race'
ACT / INSTITUTION (acting)	*administration*
ACT / COMMUNICATE	*pive* 'whine'
EVENT / POINT IN TIME	slutning 'ending'
ACT / SOUND	*klask* 'smack'
Group 5	3rdOrder / 3rdOrder
DANCE / MUSIC STYLE	*disko* 'disco'
TASK / INSTITUTION	*autoritet* 'authority'
AREA OF KNOWLEDGE / SCHOOL SUBJECT	*matematik* 'mathematics'

Table 1: Overview of the systematic polysemy typology. We group the 28 patterns based on Lyons' semantic divisions (Lyons, 1977).

lemmas it includes both senses in only one definition (often indirectly, for example by referring to the genus proximum), e.g., *bog* ('book') which has two senses for *kogebog*.

Criterion c) excludes patterns found for adjectives describing people vs. objects or acts as in 'an ambitious student' vs. 'an ambitious jump'. In these cases, one could argue that the contrast lies within the described ('student' and 'jump') rather than the descriptor ('ambitious'). Another excluded pattern regards acts with or without a realized cognate object, e.g. at *svømme* ('to swim') and at *svømme crawl* ('to swim crawl').

For each pattern, we decide whether the sense descriptions should be enumerated or combined. A combined sense gets the ontological type of the most prominent sense, unless both senses are evaluated as being equally important. In that case, the merged sense will be assigned two ontological types. In all cases, the pattern is labelled explicitly in the lexicon The decisions are based on the available information from DanNet and DDO and supplemented by introspection and searches in corpora.

We further partition the 28 patterns into five groups based on Lyons' semantic divisions (Lyons, 1977). Thus, patterns that only include semantically concrete types fall into one group, while patterns that include a mix of concrete and abstract types fall into another. The groups are shown in Table 1[2].

3 Humans' intuition on systematic polysemy – an experiment

To support our set of polysemy rules, we first, examine the phenomenon by including investigations on the *human intuition.*

3.1 A systematic polysemy dataset

We limit this preliminary study to four patterns. First, we analyse ANIMAL/FOOD, and PLANT/FOOD as they have been considered during the compilation of DanNet (Pedersen et al., 2010). In addition, the ontological types in the patterns are all concrete (group 1) characterized by the contrast between the botanical/zoological world and the function as food. We examine two patterns that have an abstract INSTITUTION sense in common, i.e., the patterns ACTIVITY/ INSTITUTION (group 4) and LOCATION/INSTITUTION (group 3). These patterns are challenging since the meaning is quite often underspecified.

We compile a small dataset with contexts for eight target lemmas: *laks* ('salmon'), *jomfruhummer* ('langoustine'), *kål* ('cabbage'), *forårsløg* ('spring onion'), *badminton, ishockey* ('ice hockey'), *parlament* ('parliament'), and *hospital*. Each context is hand labelled with a broad ontological type (e.g., PLANT, FOOD, LOCATION). To facilitate this task, we restrict the target lemmas to those who have no more than two senses in the DDO dictionary, as well as no homonyms.

As previously mentioned, DDO is inconsistent in the treatment of systematic polysemy as it varies between a sense enumeration approach and a one-representation approach. Generally, a one-representation approach is used for low frequent lemmas, although it is not always the case. For instance, the high frequency lemma *hospital* is described as only having a LOCATION sense in DDO, even though it can be understood as both a LOCATION and/or an INSTITUTION. This might be an illustration of the duality of the systematic polysemy patterns – it is difficult to separate the senses as they co-exist. For this reason, we select two lemmas for each pattern: one with exactly two senses in DDO that corresponds to the senses in the pattern, and a DDO monosemous example.

We retrieve the contexts from *KorpusDK* – a Danish text corpus of 110 million words collection from the period 1985-2010. We randomly select 100-200 contexts for each target lemma. We hand-label approx. 60 with ontological types. The reduced number of annotated contexts is caused by three factors. First, we aim at having the same number of contexts for each target lemma. Secondly, we balance the labels to ensure a fair representation of each sense of a pattern, although this might not reflect the actual frequency distribution of the senses in use. For instance, it was challenging to find LOCATION examples of *parlament* 'parliament' in the 200 contexts. Lastly, we exclude contexts containing named entities with the target. In particular, the INSTITUTION patterns included several named entities (e.g., *Dansk Ishockey Union* and *Herlev Hospital*).

[2] The typology with additional examples and our strategy is available at https://github.com/kuhumcst/pycor/

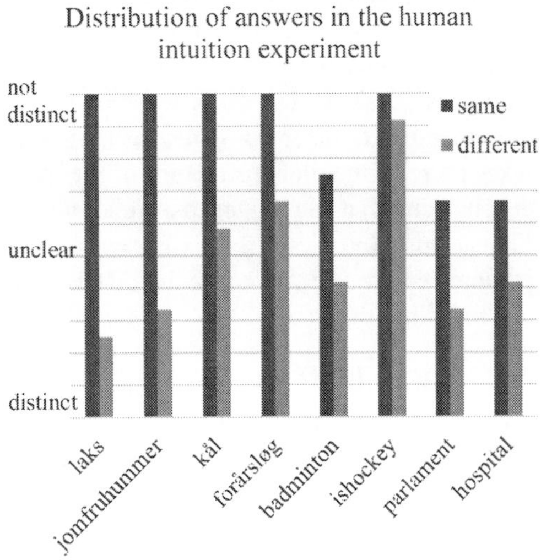

Figure 1: Distribution of answers across instances with either the same (blue) or two different (orange) ontological labels.

3.2 Experimental setup

The purpose of the experiment is to test the human intuition isolated from the task of creating a semantic lexicon. The question is whether the informants can distinguish senses of systematic polysemy given only minimal information. The experimental setup is inspired by the Word-in-Context task (Pilehvar & Camacho-Collados, 2018). The idea is that the participants are shown a target lemma and two contexts. The task is to answer whether the target lemma has the same sense in the two contexts.

The experiment is done through an online survey that consists of 24 context pairs and a few additional questions to ensure that the informants understand the task. Even if this is a low number of pairs, it resembles how intuitive the sense distinctions in patterns are. We frame the task as input to an automatic method for dictionary quote selection. Therefore, we ask the informants whether the two contexts would fit as quotes for the same sense entry.

Figure 1 shows the distribution of survey answers. The answers are divided by context pairs with the same ontological label (blue) or different labels (orange). A low column indicates intuitively distinct senses, while a tall column suggests no distinction of senses. Mid-range columns show cases without consensus among the informants.

We calculate a moderate agreement score of 0.49 using fleiss kappa (Fleiss, 1971). We see a large difference in the agreement depending on whether the contexts pairs have the same ontological label or not. In the pairs with the same label, we find a high agreement (0.72), while the agreement is drastically lower for pairs with different types (0.11). This means that the informants are close to guessing when the pairs differ in ontological type, and that it is indeed difficult to intuitively separate the senses of the patterns. This falls in line with the comments from some of the informants who comment that they are not consistent in their answers.

Some informants notice that the survey is related to systematic polysemy, and they report that the distinction in the concrete patterns (related to FOOD) is clearer than the more abstract patterns (related to INSTITUTION). This adds up with the actual results, where the most distinct pattern is ANIMAL/FOOD. The PLANT/FOOD is overall perceived as the same sense, although this is less clear as some participants still make the distinction. Generally, the INSTITUTION patterns are the least clear; they show lower agreement scores on instances where the ontological type is INSTITUTION for both contexts. We hypothesise that this can be caused by the patterns being even more complex due the relation between INSTITUTION and another ontological type, HUMAN_GROUP. We discuss this further in Section 6.

4 A distributional analysis with BERT

According to the distributional hypothesis, we can estimate the senses of a lemma from its distribution in language (Harris, 1954, Firth, 1957).. We investigate the distribution by performing a clustering experiment using the dataset described in section 0. The idea is to cluster the representations of a contextualised embedding model that has been pretrained on a large amount of textual data. If a systematic polysemy pattern is distinguishable in text, then the result will show separate clusters for each sense.

4.1 Model

We represent each occurrence of the target lemma with the base Danish BERT model which is

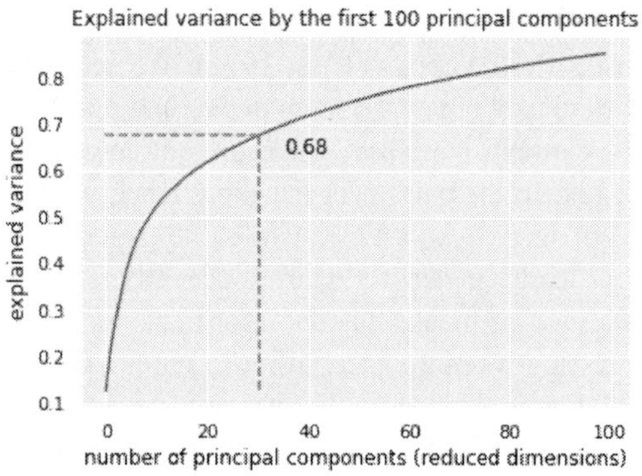

Figure 2: Explained Variance on the first 100 principal components from PCA experiment. The orange lines show the explained variance at 30 dimensions.

pretrained by Certainly[3]. The pretraining material included 1.6 billion words from different text sources (Common Crawl, Danish Wikipedia, web scraped forums, OpenSubtitles (Lison & Tiedemann, 2016)). To compute the contextualised target embedding, we first embed each context and then retrieve the token embedding corresponding to the target lemma. The token embedding is an average of the output of the last four layers.

4.2 Dimensionality reduction

Since our dataset contains a low number of samples (492) compared to the high dimensionality of the embeddings (768), it may be beneficial to reduce the dimensions in the embeddings[4]. The goal is to arrive at a level that retrains the most relevant information, but still reduces the complexity of the embedding space. We choose to reduce to 30 dimensions. We analyse this choice by an experiment with Principal Component Analysis (PCA). The purpose of PCA is to transform correlated dimensions into uncorrelated principal components that explain the most variance in the initial dimensions. Figure 2 shows how much variance each principal component can account for. We see that the first 30 principal components explain 68% of the variance in the 492 embeddings. Although, 32% of the variance is yet to be captured, any increase in the dimensionality does not give us drastic improvements. Instead, we attempt to retain more of the information by using a non-linear reduction technique: Uniform Manifold Approximation and Projection (UMAP) (McInnes et al., 2018). This technique has two advantages over other non-linear techniques: a) it takes more of the global structure of the data into account, and b) it can reduce to a higher number of dimensions (30 vs. 2-3). For the UMAP parameters, we use *cosine as* the distance metric and set min_dist to *0.0*.

4.3 Sense Clustering

We use a density-based clustering method: HDBSCAN[5] (Campello et al., 2013). The method is useful when we do not have any assumption about the shape, size, and number of clusters. We use the following parameter settings: *min_samples* =10 and *min_cluster_size*=15.

We apply the clustering method on the entire dataset and arrive at total of 11 clusters. The clusters are visualised in Figure 3 (FOOD related) and Figure 4 (INSTITUTION related) after further dimensionality reduction with UMAP. Of the eight lemmas, three have contexts distributed to multiple clusters: *laks* ('salmon'), *parlament* ('parliament'), and *hospital*. The remainder have a single cluster representation. To evaluate the clusters, we calculate an average silhouette score of 0.82 across all clusters. From this, we conclude that the clusters are distinct with a minimal to no overlap.

5 Discussion

In this section, we discuss how the formal, the intuition-based, and the distributional approaches, respectively, contribute to our understanding of the different cases of systematic polysemy. We start by analysing the how each pattern is formally represented in the lexical resource, DanNet.

ANIMAL/FOOD: All three approaches support that we separate our sense descriptions into an ANIMAL and FOOD sense. In DanNet, the pattern is consistently distinguished when both senses occur in DDO. Each sense has its own synset with non-overlapping taxonomic structures. In the survey, the participants are also able to recognize the contrast between the living animal and its meat.

[3] More information about the model is available here: https://github.com/certainlyio/nordic_bert

[4] This is to avoid the curse of dimensionality, where the high number of dimensions hinder the optimisation of algorithms.

[5] The python implementation is available here: https://hdbscan.readthedocs.io/en/latest/index.html

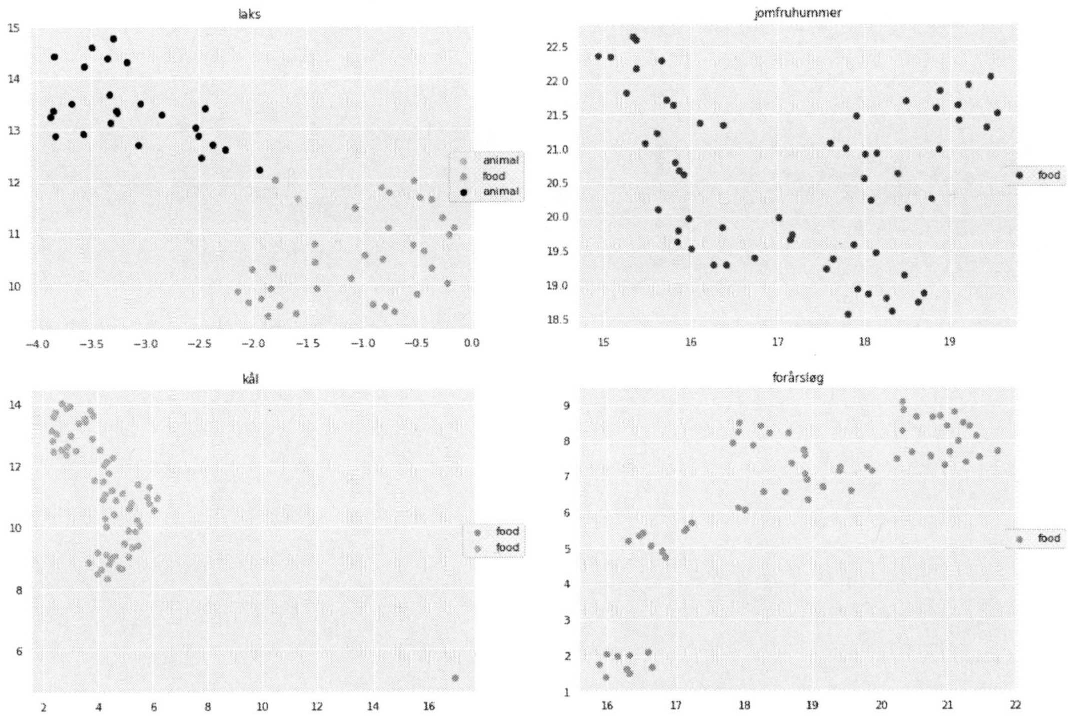

Figure 3: Sense clusters for lemmas with a FOOD sense and either one (right column) or two senses (left column) in DDO. The labels indicate the most common label in that cluster.

The distributional approach separates the senses of the pattern for the frequent target *laks* ('salmon') but does not separate the less frequent target *jomfruhummer* ('langoustine'). We can explain the difference with the frequency of the FOOD sense of *jomfruhummer.* Since the BERT model is trained on mostly web crawled texts, we expect a high number of recipes and food reviews in the text collection. Therefore, the model might not have seen enough clear ANIMAL examples to create distinct representations. Unfortunately, we do not have access to the exact training data and cannot confirm this hypothesis. However, we do know that our lexical resources contain this missing real-world knowledge, although for the infrequent lemmas, we see a mismatch between the sense descriptions and the language use. In DanNet, the DDO genus proximum *dyr* 'animal' has led to only one sense, the ANIMAL sense, and the FOOD sense has not been included even though the example is food.

PLANT / FOOD: The approaches mostly support combined representation of the pattern. In DanNet, the specialist and folk taxonomies of plants are treated differently from animals. Here, the specialist and folk perspectives are merged in a single synset by using two hypernyms, related to PLANT and FOOD respectively. The dual taxonomies indicate that we can merge the pattern into a single representation that incorporates both ontological types depending on the situation.

The distributional analysis also supports a one-representation approach, although we see an error in the clustering. A single instance of *kål* 'cabbage' has been wrongly added to the same cluster of *forårsløg* 'spring onion'. The confusion arises from the morphological similarity of the use of *kål* in that specific context and a typical use of *forårsløg*: the definite plural form (e.g., *kål -ene* and *forårsløg -ene*). This is one of the flaws of using a "black box" distributional model – we cannot guarantee that the BERT embeddings only include the semantic information and are not sensitive to other variation in the input. Still, a promising observation is the small sub-cluster on the bottom left of the blue cluster ('spring onion') on Figure 3. Here, we find an extra sense that we did not consider during the creation of the dataset. The PLANT sense can arguably be split into two: 'the edible plant' and 'flower bulbs' that are planted during the spring. With the current clustering parameters, this sub-cluster is too small to be represented as a separate

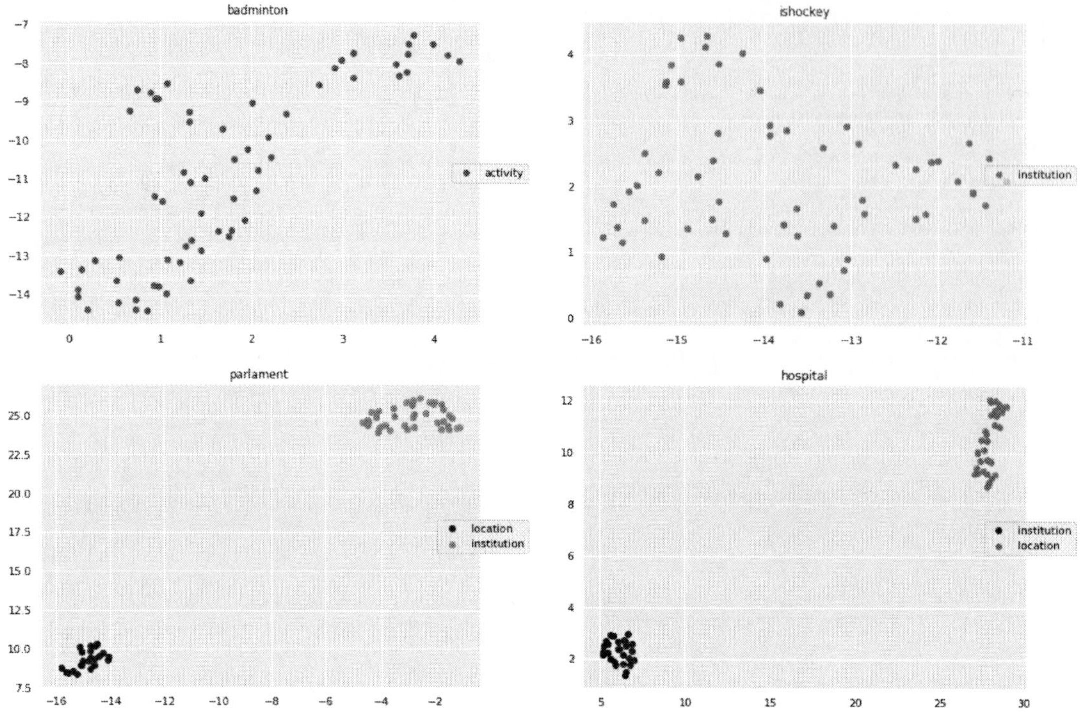

Figure 4: Sense clusters for lemmas with an INSTITUTION sense and either one (right column) or two senses (left column) in DDO. The labels indicate the most common label in that cluster.

cluster. The fact that they are still grouped together is a sign that BERT embeddings can detect this sense to some degree.

The human intuition survey gives a mixed result on this pattern. On the one hand, most of the informants do not distinguish between PLANT and FOOD. Yet, a few informants still detect the difference, and some even mention the pattern in their comments. The survey includes a low number of examples, and it is possible that the distinction is not expressed clearly enough in those examples. A further study with more contexts and target lemmas is needed for us to determine the human intuition on this pattern.

ACTIVITY / INSTITUTION: This pattern is not clearly distinguishable in neither DanNet, nor in the distributional analyses. Although DanNet includes both the ACTIVITY and INSTITUTION senses from DDO, we cannot find a contrast between these synsets as they are close to being structurally identical. Additionally, the hypernyms and ontological types only express the ACTIVITY sense. This questions why both synsets are maintained as they do not reflect the systematic polysemy patterns. In the survey, we see that *ishockey* 'ice hockey' is the only lemma where the informants almost all agree that there is no difference between the senses. In the case of *badminton*, about half of the informants distinguish between ACTIVITY and INSTITUTION. This can be related to *badminton* being a more widely known and played sport in Denmark and therefore more likely to be institutionalised. Along with the previously mentioned case of *jomfruhummer*, this shows the difficulty of making a top-down approach to polysemy. We must consider the story of each lemma and its presence in the language.

LOCATION / INSTITUTION: The possible third HUMAN_GROUP interpretation complicates the analysis of this pattern as is evident from the survey results. The complexity is also visible in DanNet, where three senses are sometimes included [6]. However, most often only the LOCATION/INSTITUTION contrast is maintained by a 'concrete building' synset and an 'abstract institution' synset, respectively.

[6] In some cases the dictionary that DanNet is based did not include all three senses, which means a manual effort has been put into DanNet to express this three-way pattern.

Surprisingly, *hospital* only has a LOCATION sense in DanNet. For cases like this, the distributional analysis tells us where we can improve our lexical resources, as the contrast between LOCATION and INSTITUTION is clearly reflected in the clusters. However, we note that there is no guarantee that the clusters can be directly mapped to distinct LOCATION and INSTITUTION senses. Being at the hospital is expressed by the preposition *på* 'on/at'. However, a strictly LOCATION reading could mean that one is physically on top of the building, whereas we usually mean that we are in a building. Thus, the LOCATION cluster may be a clustering of underspecified senses that superficially appears to highlight a concrete LOCATION. Likewise, if a politician is *in the parliament*, the context may highlight HUMAN_GROUP and/or INSTITUTION more than a LOCATION. To understand how we should interpret the clusters, we need to investigate which semantic information they contain and whether this corresponds to the sense descriptions in the lexical resources.

6 Future work

The approach described in this paper provides new insights into how to treat four frequent systematic polysemy patterns in the COR lexicon. A noticeable finding is that, as in the case of many other lexical phenomena, the patterns, and to some degree also lemmas within a pattern, tend to dispose quite individual properties. We would like to carry out similar investigations on the remaining part of the patterns in the typology we have presented, both in order to examine the prototypical behaviour for each pattern, and how this should correspondingly be represented in COR, but also to reveal the deviant cases. We think that by including information from both a survey among informants and statistical methods, we will be able to treat the many cases of systematic polysemy across the Danish vocabulary in a more appropriate manner.

References

Apresjan, J. D. (1974). Regular Polysemy. *Linguistics*, *142*(142), 5–32.

Barque, L., & Chaumartin, F. R. (2009). Regular polysemy in WordNet. *Journal for language technology and computational linguistics*, *24*(2), 5-18.

Campello, R. J., Moulavi, D., & Sander, J. (2013, April). Density-based clustering based on hierarchical density estimates. In *Pacific-Asia conference on knowledge discovery and data mining* (pp. 160-172). Springer, Berlin, Heidelberg.

Cruse, D. A., Cruse, D. A., & Cruse, D. A. (1986). *Lexical semantics*. Cambridge university press.

Devlin, J., Chang, M-W., Lee, K. & Toutanova, K. (2019). BERT: Pre-training of deep bidirectional transformers for language understanding. In: *Proceedings of the 2019 Conference of the North American Chapter of the Association for Computational Linguistics: Human Language Technologies*, Volume 1 (Long and Short Papers), pages 4171–4186, Minneapolis, Minnesota. Association for Computational Linguistics.

Fellbaum, C. (ed.). (1998). *WordNet: An Electronic Lexical Database*. MIT press.

Firth, J. R. (1957). A Synopsis of Linguistic Theory, 1930-1955. *Studies in Linguistic Analysis.*

Fleiss, J. L. (1971). Measuring nominal scale agreement among many raters. *Psychological bulletin*, *76*(5), 378.

Harris, Z. S. (1954). Distributional structure. *Word*, *10*(2-3), 146-162.

Lyons, J. (1977). *Semantics. Volumes 1-2*. Cambridge University Press.

Malmgren, S. G. (1988). On regular polysemy in Swedish. *Studies in computer-aided lexicology*, 179-200.

Martínez A., H. (2013). *Annotation of regular polysemy: an empirical assessment of the underspecified sense* (Doctoral dissertation, Universitat Pompeu Fabra).

McCrae, J. P., Fransen, T., Ahmadi, S., Buitelaar, P., & Goswami, K. (2022). Towards an Integrative Approach for Making Sense Distinctions. *Frontiers in Artificial Intelligence*, 3.

McInnes, Healy, J., & Melville, J. (2018). *UMAP: Uniform Manifold Approximation and Projection for Dimension Reduction.*

Nimb, S., Trap-Jensen, L., & Lorentzen, H. (2014). The Danish thesaurus: Problems and perspectives. In *Proceedings of the XVI EURALEX International Congress: The User in Focus* (pp. 15-19).

Nimb, Sanni (2016) Der er ikke langt fra tanke til handling. Simon Skovgaard Boeck & Henrik Blicher (eds.): *Danske Studier 2016*, København, Universitets-Jubilæets danske Samfund, pp. 25-59Pedersen, B. S., Nimb, S., Asmussen, J., Sørensen, N. H., Trap-Jensen, L., & Lorentzen, H.

(2009). DanNet: the challenge of compiling a wordnet for Danish by reusing a monolingual dictionary. *Language resources and evaluation, 43*(3), 269-299.

Pedersen, B. S., Nimb, S., & Braasch, A. (2010). Merging specialist taxonomies and folk taxonomies in wordnets-a case study of plants, animals and foods in the Danish wordnet. In *Proceedings of the Seventh International Conference on Language Resources and Evaluation (LREC'10).*

Pedersen, B. S., Sørensen, N. C. H., Nimb, S., Flørke, I., Olsen, S., & Troelsgård, T. (2022). Compiling a Suitable Level of Sense Granularity in a Lexicon for AI Purposes: The Open Source COR Lexicon. In *Proceedings of the Thirteenth Language Resources and Evaluation Conference* (pp. 51-60).

Peters, W., & Kilgarriff, A. (2000). Discovering semantic regularity in lexical resources. *International Journal of Lexicography, 13*(4), 287-312.

Pilehvar, M. T., & Camacho-Collados, J. (2018). WiC: the word-in-context dataset for evaluating context-sensitive meaning representations. *arXiv preprint arXiv:1808.09121.*

Pustejovsky, J. (1995). *The Generative Lexicon.* MIT Press. Cambridge, Massachusetts.

Ruhl, C. (1989). *On monosemy: A study in linguistic semantics.* Albany: State University of New York Press.

Vicente, A., & Falkum, I. L. (2017). Polysemy. In *Oxford research encyclopedia of linguistics.*

Language Resource References

Danish Systematic Polysemy Typology and dataset: https://github.com/kuhumcst/pycor/tree/master/data/systematic_polysemy

DanNet: wordnet.dk; https://andreord.nors.ku.dk.

Den Danske Ordbog (DDO): Hjorth, E. & K. Kristensen red. (2003-2005). *Den Danske Ordbog*, volume 1-6, Det danske Sprog- og Litteraturselskab/Gyldendal, Copenhagen. Online: https://ordnet.dk/ddo

Den Danske Begrebsordbog (DDB): Nimb, Sanni, Henrik Lorentzen, Thomas Troelsgård, Liisa Theilgaard, Lars Trap-Jensen (2014). *Den Danske Begrebsordbog*, Det Danske Sprog- og Litteraturselskab. Copenhagen.

KorpusDK. Det Danske Sprog- og Litteraturselskab. Copenhagen. korpus.dsl.dk/resources/details/korpusdk.html

The Romanian Wordnet in Linked Open Data Format

Elena Irimia and **Verginica Barbu Mititelu**
Romanian Academy Research Institute for Artificial Intelligence
Bucharest, Romania
{elena,vergi}@racai.ro

Abstract

In this paper we present the standardization of the Romanian Wordnet by means of conversion to the Linked Open Data format. We describe the vocabularies used to encode data and metadata of this resource. The decisions made are in accordance with the characteristics of the Romanian Wordnet, which are the outcome of the development method, enrichment strategies and resources used for its creations. By interlinking with other resources, words in the Romanian Wordnet have now the pronunciation associated, as well as syntagmatic information, in the form of contexts of occurrences.

1 Introduction

The Romanian Wordnet (RoWN) as available today has been created starting with the BalkaNet project (Tufiș et al., 2004). The working methodology (Tufiş et al., 2004) followed mainly (see below) the expand approach (Vossen, 1996): synsets from the Princeton WordNet (Miller, 1995; Fellbaum, 1998) (PWN) were translated into Romanian and the relations between implemented synsets were transferred from corresponding PWN synsets. Using a bilingual electronic dictionary, the literals in the selected PWN synsets were first automatically translated and the Romanian equivalents were suggested to lexicographers as literals to be included in the Romanian synsets. For each selected word, its sense was chosen from the parsed electronic version of the Explanatory Dictionary of Romanian (DEX) (Coteanu and Mareș, 1996).

The selection[1] of the synsets to be implemented during BalkaNet was done so as to cover words with high frequency (according to corpora available at that moment), polysemy (according to the number of senses in DEX), as well as avoidance of dangling nodes in the RoWN structure (which meant that choosing a synset to implement in Romanian implied choosing all its unimplemented synsets in PWN up to the unique beginners of the hierarchies, in the case of nouns and verbs, which have a hierarchical structure). The synsets IDs were also transferred from PWN.

The BalkaNet team also aimed at reflecting some of the specificities of this geographic and cultural region in the wordnets under development. Consequently, a various number of such synsets were included in the wordnets: for Romanian, there were 541 synsets. They were included in the hierarchies mostly as hyponyms of existing synsets. Their IDs were generated so as to keep them distinct from those of the translated synsets. One such synset contains the literal *tobă* with the gloss "a type of cold cooked meat, containing pieces of chopped meat, fat, offal, all stuffed in a pig's stomach and suspended din aspic". It is a Romanian traditional cold dish, specific to Christmas season and looking like a wide sausage. For this reason it is a hyponym of the noun *cârnat*, which translates the English *sausage*.

Besides the automatic transfer of the semantic relations holding between equivalent English synsets, the Romanian team also transferred the lexical relations from PWN: these are relations marked at the literal (not synset) level in PWN. Examples include antonymy and derivation relations. In the case of the former, it was considered that this lexical relation has a conceptual counterpart: the semantic opposition between the concepts lexicalized by the words in antonymy relations (Miller, 1995). Consider the synsets {*sterile, unfertile, infertile*} (gloss: "incapable of reproducing") and the synset {*fertile*} (gloss: "capable of reproducing"). Antonymy is marked between *sterile* and *fertile* in PWN. However, speakers understand a semantic opposition between *fertile* and *infertile*, as well as between *fertile* and *unfertile*[2]. Given that there is no literal

[1] Further selections, in other projects in which the RoWN was enriched, were made so as to ensure the lexical coverage required by the respective projects.

[2] See this example: "By contrast, fertility is the ac-

```
<SYNSET>
  <ID>ENG30-09448090-n</ID>
  <POS>n</POS>
  <SYNONYM>
    <LITERAL>stratosferă
      <SENSE>1</SENSE>
    </LITERAL>
  </SYNONYM>
  <DEF>Stratul superior al atmosferei
  (situat deasupra troposferei),care
  începe la o înălțime de aproximativ 11 km
  de la suprafața Pământului. </DEF>
  <ILR>ENG30-08591680-n
    <TYPE>hypernym</TYPE>
  </ILR>
  <ILR>ENG30-09210604-n
    <TYPE>part_holonym</TYPE>
  </ILR>
</SYNSET>
```

Table 1: One synset associated to the literal "stratosferă" (en. "stratosphere")

correspondence between PWN and RoWN, which could have allowed for the transfer of antonymy at literal level, this assumption allowed for its transfer at the synset level. Thus, the RoWN equivalents of such synsets establish between them an antonymy relation. Table 1 shows an example of a RoWN synset in the original XML format.

2 Conversion of RoWN to LOD format

Linked Data (LD) refers to a set of best practices in publishing structured data on the Web (Chiarcos et al., 2013). When an open type of license, namely Creative Commons (CC), is associated with a resource, then we talk about *linked open data* (LOD). The conversion of Romanian language resources to the LOD format is an internal project[3] of the Romanian Academy Research Institute for Artificial Intelligence, running in parallel with the NexusLinguarum COST Action[4]. We have already made several resources available in this format and, more important, this way some of them are made open to the community for the first time: this is also the case with RoWN, of which only a core has been freely available throughout time.

Original format	LOD format
domain_member_TOPIC	domain_topic
cause	causes
entailment	entails
domain_member_REGION	has_domain_region
domain_member_TOPIC	has_domain_topic
member_holonym	holo_member
part_holonym	holo_part
substance_holonym	holo_substance
member_meronym	mero_member
part_meronym	mero_part
substance_meronym	mero_substance
similar_to	similar
near_antonym	antonym

Table 2: Renaming of synset relations to comply to the LOD standards

The LOD format for RoWN was automatically generated using a conversion tool developed in C#. Preliminary actions that had to be taken were: (1) mapping RoWN to the CILI[5] IDs (through the PWN mapping) to enable its linking to the international network of wordnets[6] mapped to CILI, and (2) renaming some lexical and semantic relations to correspond to the LOD guidelines (see Table 2 for the renamed relations; the following relations kept their original name: attribute, hypernym, hyponym, instance_hypernym, instance_hyponym).

In accordance with the recommended standard for representing wordnets, our Turtle RDF LOD representation model is mainly based on the *OntoLex-Lemon* vocabulary (Cimiano et al., 2016) developed by the Ontology-Lexica community group (OntoLex), but is also supported by other useful vocabularies like the OWL Web Ontology Language[7], the wordnet specific ontology *wn*[8] and the variation and translation lemon module *vartrans*[9] to represent the various encoded properties. The serialisations in LMF-XML and JSON format are also available, but the linking with external resources was implemented only in the Turtle RDF format, which will, therefore, be the focus of this section.

tual production of live offspring and is the antonym of infertility", https://academic.oup.com/humrep/article/19/7/1497/2356621, accessed 19th Dec, 2022.

[3]https://www.racai.ro/p/llod/index_en.html

[4]https://nexuslinguarum.eu/

[5]https://github.com/globalwordnet/cili

[6]Open Multilingual Wordnet (Bond and Foster, 2013)

[7]https://www.w3.org/TR/owl-guide/

[8]http://globalwordnet.github.io/schemas/wn

[9]http://www.w3.org/ns/lemon/vartrans

As can be seen in Figure 1, the main level entry in the original XML format of RoWN was the synset, comprising an ID, the part-of-speech label (POS), a definition, the synonym set and a list of relations specified by their target synset (ILR1 and ILR2 objects) and their relation type (type1, type2). The synonym set was a list of different literals together with their associated senses, unique to the synset they belong to.

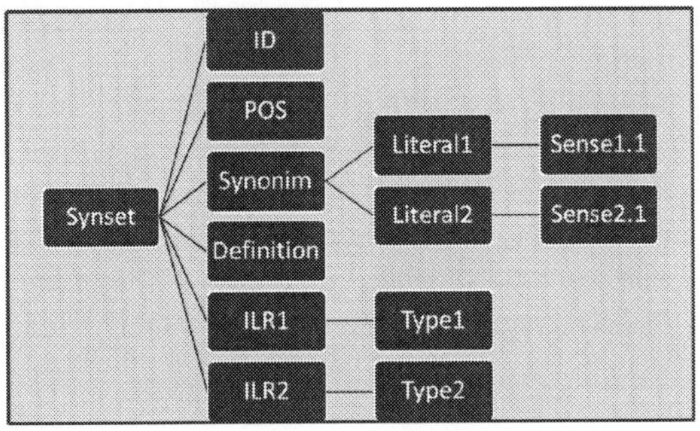

Figure 1: Diagram of the objects in the original XML format of RoWN

To comply with the OntoLex-Lemon model[10], the information in RoWN had to be restructured as shown in Figure 2. The color code for the nodes in the diagram is the following: *blue* stands for objects, *yellow* for properties and the correspondence between the new classes and properties and the ones in the original format (see Figure 1) are marked in *red*: e.g., each LexicalEntry in RoWN has an associated canonicalForm object and the ontolex:writtenRep property of this object has as value one of the literals in the synonym set of one of the original format synsets.

Basically, the information in the original file was organised around synonym sets (with specific meaning), accompanied by their associated lexical representations (literal1, literal2, etc.), while in the LOD format the data is organised around literals, accompanied by their possible meanings (represented as a list of senses: sense1, sense2, etc.).

The new format has four types of main entries:

- *ontolex:LexicalEntry.* Each LexicalEntry, representing a specific literal, has an associated ontolex:CanonicalForm object with an ontolex:writtenRep property and a list of declarations for ontolex:Sense objects that specify possible senses of the literal.

[10]see the guidelines at https://www.w3.org/2016/05/ontolex/

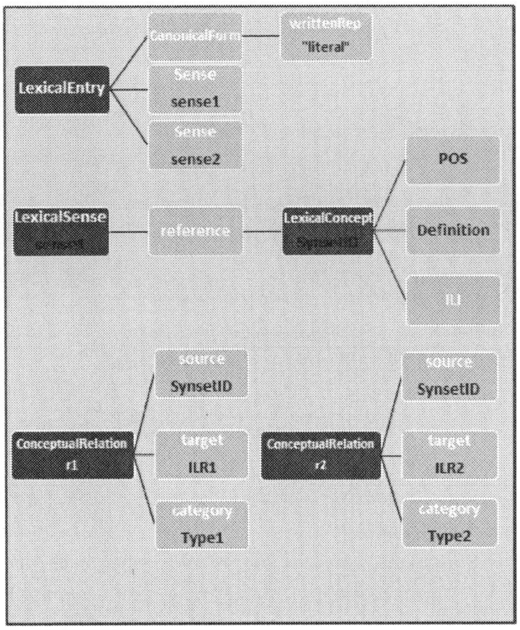

Figure 2: Diagram of the objects and properties used to represent information in the LOD format of RoWN, with correspondences with the original XML object labels (see Figure 1) marked in red.

- *ontolex:LexicalSense.* Each ontolex:Sense object is then described as a separate entry through an ontolex:reference to an ontolex:LexicalConcept whose value is a synset ID (previously copied in RoWN from PWN).

- *ontolex:LexicalConcept.* The LexicalConcept has, in turn, an associated part-of-speech (POS) description and a definition, encoded through wn:partOfSpeech and wn:definition, respectively. The recent ILI mapping is specified through the wn:ili property.

- a list of *vartrans:ConceptualRelation* objects associated to a specific LexicalConcept, encoding all the relations with other lexical concepts (synsets) in RoWN; the vartrans:target and vartrans:category properties are used to describe the relation's target synset and the relation type.

Table 3 shows the information in Table 1 (i.e., the XML representation of the concept *stratosferă* (EN. 'stratosphere')) converted to the LOD specifications.

```
<#stratosferă-n> a ontolex:LexicalEntry;
  ontolex: canonicalForm [
    ontolex:writtenRep "stratosferă"];
  wn: partOfSpeech wn:n;
  ontolex:Sense <#stratosferă-n-09448090-1>.

<#stratosferă-n-09448090-1> a
                ontolex:LexicalSense;
  ontolex:reference <#09448090-n>.

<#09448090-n> a ontolex:LexicalConcept;
  wn:partOfSpeech wn:n ;
  owl:sameAs ili:i86260 ;
  wn:definition [
  rdf:value "Stratul superior al atmosferei (si-
    tuat deasupra troposferei), care începe la
    o înălțime de aproximativ 11 km de la su-
    prafața Pământului."@ro ].

<#09448090-n-r1> a vartrans:ConceptualRe-
lation
vartrans:source <#09448090-n> ;
vartrans:category wn:hypernym ;
vartrans:target <#08591680-n> .

<#09448090-n-r2> a vartrans:ConceptualRe-
lation
vartrans:source <#09448090-n> ;
vartrans:category wn:holo_part ;
vartrans:target <#09210604-n> .
```

Table 3: The information associated to "stratosferă" in the LOD format

Object type	No. of objects
Lexical Entry	52,802
LexicalSense	85,277
LexicalConcept	59,348
Semantic Relation	138,592
CILI link	59,348
RoLEX sameAs link	16,196

Table 4: Statistics of objects and links in LOD RoWN

3 Interlinking

One of the important advantages LOD comes with is the possibility of putting language resources in a broader context, by means of interlinking them, which further ensures their FAIR characteristics (Wilkinson et al., 2016).

3.1 Other wordnets

As already mentioned, a mapping of each synset in RoWN to CILI IDs was done by exploiting the mapping of RoWN to PWN 3.0 and the public availability of a PWN3.0-CILI mapping[11]. A total of 59,348 concepts from RoWN are, at the moment, linked to the corresponding concepts in any wordnet linked to CILI. The property *owl:sameAs* has also recently been used to directly link synsets in the LOD reprtesentation of RoWN and PWN 3.0.

3.2 RoLEX

RoLEX (Lőrincz et al., 2022) is a Romanian lexicon of 330,000 word forms having associated information about their lemma, morphosyntactic description (MSD[12]), syllabification, lexical stress and phonemic transcription with an extended version of Speech Assessment Methods Phonetic Alphabet[13] (SAMPA) for Romanian. An entry in the tabular format of RoLEX is presented in Table 5.

The original 6-column tabular format of RoLEX was also converted to LOD using the same OntoLex-Lemon model. Lemmas in the tabular format became ontolex:LexicalEntries that have a list of associated ontolex:lexicalForms. In turn, each lexicalForm has the MSD encoded using the POS property in the conll vocabulary and the remaining information described by the ontolex:writtenRep[14] and the ontolex:phoneticRep[15] properties.

In the Turtle RDF LOD version of RoLEX, a linking to ROWN was implemented by associating possible corresponding CILI IDs to each LexicalEntry. LexicalEntry labels in RoLEX were automatically matched with LexicalEntry labels in RoWN, and via all the associated LexicalSenses and respective LexicalConcepts, the corresponding CILI IDs were retrieved and encoded in RoLEX.

[11]https://github.com/globalwordnet/cili/blob/master/ili-map-pwn30.tab

[12]https://github.com/clarinsi/mte-msd/blob/master/tables/msd-canon-ro.tbl

[13]https://www.phon.ucl.ac.uk/home/sampa/

[14]"stratosfera"@ro, "stra.to.sfe.ra"@syl, "stratosf'era"@stress

[15]"s t r a t o s f e r a"@ro-RO-sampa

Column type	Value
word-form	stratosfera
lemma	stratosferă
MSD	Ncsfry
syllabification	stra.to.sfe.ra
stress marking	stratosf'era
phonetic transcription	s t r a t o s f e r a

Table 5: The tabular entry associated to the wordform "stratosfera", the singular nominative-accusative definite form of the lemma "stratosferă".

Recently, a direct linking of RoWN and RoLEX was also implemented, through LexicalEntry matching and using the owl:sameAs property. The matching was done by ignoring clitic pronouns (*o*, *i*, *se*, *-și*) existing in the labels associated to verbal entries in RoWN but being absent from RoLEX: 872 verbal reflexive and pronominal lemmas have been linked to their transitive forms. A number of 16,492 compound lexical entries in RoWN were not matched at all and therefore not linked to entries in RoLEX.

By linking these two resources, 16,196 literals in RoWN have a great deal of new linguistic information associated: their full inflected paradigms are now accessible, altogether with the respective morphosyntactic description, the pronunciation of each form, its syllabification, and the position of lexical stress in each form. Table 4 shows number of objects and links in the LOD RoWN format.

4 Use case scenarios

LD provides mechanisms for exploiting the resources' content, by means of their common elements; these are either identifiers (see ILI) or words co-occurring in several resources. The resources we have converted to LOD format are made available for querying as SPARQL endpoints[16]. This allows for federated queries[17] to be created and, thus, exploit the content of all these resources or only some of them. Such an example would be a conceptual search in a speech corpus, as described by Barbu Mititelu et al. (2022). The following steps are taken: (i) the input word (i.e., a possible lexicalization of a concept of interest) is looked up in RoWN and conceptually identical words (i.e., literals in the same synset, or synonyms) are retrieved; (ii) for each literal, its RoLEX entries are found by means of the ILI identifiers, and thus its inflectional paradigm is retrieved; (iii) these forms are then located in the files of a speech corpus.

The interlinked RoWN and RoLEX prove their usefulness in a Question Answering scenario related to COVID-19 (Ion et al., 2022). An important element for the system being able to find an answer in a set of documents was for it to be able to recognize all the various ways in which a question can be formulated. After the manual creation of several such possible formulations, two steps were taken for expanding them: (i) content words were associated to other semantically related words (synonyms, hypernyms) in RoWN by exploiting the semantic relations therein, and (ii) these newly found words were associated with their inflected forms from RoLEX, also taking advantage of the fact that the interlinking between these two resources was made with manual assignment in the case of homographs. The POS-tagging of the question and the morphosyntactic descriptions in RoLEX helped to find the inflected form necessary in each context.

5 Access to LOD RoWN

The LOD format of RoWN is available for download on the website of the internal LOD project (see Section 4). This is the first time the whole Romanian Wordnet is made freely available for download. Previously (Pianta et al., 2002), only a core of it was accessible. Only by means of the dedicated API (Dumitrescu et al., 2018) could any kind of information therein be exploited. A SPARQL endpoint is also made available for it on the SPARQL Apache Jena Fuseki server installed on one of our servers. The resource's metadata has already been registered in the LOD Cloud[18], as well as in the European Language Grid catalogue[19].

6 Conclusions and future work

Although not currently under development, RoWN is still considered a valuable resource for the Romanian language, as shown by its recent use in a query expansion task (Ion et al., 2022) and its evaluation in a word similarity task (Barbu and Barbu Mititelu, 2022).

We have presented here its conversion to LOD specifications, a new format that can help RoWN

[16]https://relate.racai.ro/datasets/

[17]https://www.w3.org/TR/sparql11-federated-query/

[18]https://lod-cloud.net/#

[19]https://live.european-language-grid.eu/catalogue/search/Romanian%20wordnet

become a more FAIR resource. In the future, we are going to add the Balkan-specific concepts and derivational relations to the LOD RoWN and then reuse the resource in its interlinked format in various scenarios.

References

Eduard Barbu and Verginica Barbu Mititelu. 2022. Evaluating computational models of similarity against a human rated dataset. *Baltic Journal of Modern Computing*, 10(3):295–306.

Verginica Barbu Mititelu, Elena Irimia, Vasile Pais, Andrei-Marius Avram, and Maria Mitrofan. 2022. Use case: Romanian language resources in the LOD paradigm. In *Proceedings of the 8th Workshop on Linked Data in Linguistics within the 13th Language Resources and Evaluation Conference*, pages 35–44, Marseille, France. European Language Resources Association.

Francis Bond and Ryan Foster. 2013. Linking and extending an open multilingual wordnet. In *Proceedings of the 51st Annual Meeting of the Association for Computational Linguistics (Volume 1: Long Papers)*, pages 1352–1362.

Christian Chiarcos, John McCrae, Philipp Cimiano, and Christiane Fellbaum. 2013. *Towards Open Data for Linguistics: Linguistic Linked Data*, pages 7–25. Springer Berlin Heidelberg, Berlin, Heidelberg.

Philipp Cimiano, John P McCrae, and Paul Buitelaar. 2016. Lexicon model for ontologies: Community report. *W3C Ontology-Lexicon Community Group.*

Ion Coteanu and Lucreția Mareș, editors. 1996. *Dicționarul explicativ al limbii române, ediția a II-a.* Editura Univers Enciclopedic, Bucharest.

Stefan Daniel Dumitrescu, Andrei Marius Avram, Luciana Morogan, and Stefan-Adrian Toma. 2018. Rowordnet–a python api for the romanian wordnet. In *2018 10th International Conference on Electronics, Computers and Artificial Intelligence (ECAI)*, pages 1–6. IEEE.

Christiane Fellbaum. 1998. *WordNet: An Electronic Lexical Database*. MIT Press, Cambridge, MA.

Radu Ion, Andrei-Marius Avram, Vasile Păiș, Maria Mitrofan, Verginica Barbu Mititelu, Elena Irimia, and Valentin Badea. 2022. An open-domain QA system for e-governance. In *Proceedings of the Fifth International Conference Computational Linguistics in Bulgaria (CLiB)*, pages 105–112.

Beáta Lőrincz, Elena Irimia, Adriana Stan, and Verginica Barbu Mititelu. 2022. RoLEX: The development of an extended Romanian lexical dataset and its evaluation at predicting concurrent lexical information. *Natural Language Engineering*, page 1–26.

George A. Miller. 1995. Wordnet: A lexical database for english. *Communications of the ACM*, 38(11):39–41.

Emanuele Pianta, Luisa Bentivogli, and Christian Girardi. 2002. MultiWordNet: developing an aligned multilingual database. In *Proceedings of the First International Conference on Global WordNet.*

Dan Tufiş, Eduard Barbu, Verginica Barbu Mititelu, Radu Ion, and Luigi Bozianu. 2004. The romanian wordnet. *Romanian Journal of Information Science and Technology Special Issue*, 7(1–2):107–124.

Dan Tufiș, Dan Cristea, and Sofia Stamou. 2004. Balkanet: Aims, methods, results and perspectives. a general overview. *Romanian Journal of Information Science and Technology Special Issue*, 7(1–2):9–43.

Piek Vossen. 1996. Right or wrong: Combining lexical resources in the eurowordnet project. In *Proceedings of the 7th EURALEX International Congress*, pages 715–728, Göteborg, Sweden. Novum Grafiska AB.

Mark D. Wilkinson, Michel Dumontier, IJsbrand Jan Aalbersberg, Gabrielle Appleton, Myles Axton, Arie Baak, Niklas Blomberg, Jan-Willem Boiten, Luiz Bonino da Silva Santos, Philip E. Bourne, Jildau Bouwman, Anthony J. Brookes, Tim Clark, Mercè Crosas, Ingrid Dillo, Olivier Dumon, Scott Edmunds, Chris T. Evelo, Richard Finkers, Alejandra Gonzalez-Beltran, Alasdair J.G. Gray, Paul Groth, Carole Goble, Jeffrey S. Grethe, Jaap Heringa, Peter A.C 't Hoen, Rob Hooft, Tobias Kuhn, Ruben Kok, Joost Kok, Scott J. Lusher, Maryann E. Martone, Albert Mons, Abel L. Packer, Bengt Persson, Philippe Rocca-Serra, Marco Roos, Rene van Schaik, Susanna-Assunta Sansone, Erik Schultes, Thierry Sengstag, Ted Slater, George Strawn, Morris A. Swertz, Mark Thompson, Johan van der Lei, Erik van Mulligen, Jan Velterop, Andra Waagmeester, Peter Wittenburg, Katherine Wolstencroft, Jun Zhao, and Barend Mons. 2016. The FAIR Guiding Principles for scientific data management and stewardship. *Scientific data*, 3:1–9.

Combining WordNets with Treebanks to study idiomatic language: A pilot study on Rigvedic formulas through the lenses of the Sanskrit WordNet and the Vedic Treebank

Luca Brigada Villa,° Erica Biagetti,* Riccardo Ginevra,+ Chiara Zanchi*

°University of Pavia/Bergamo, *University of Pavia, +Università Cattolica del Sacro Cuore (Milan)

Abstract

This paper shows how WordNets can be employed in tandem with morpho-syntactically annotated corpora to study poetic formulas. Pairing the lexico-semantic information of the *Sanskrit WordNet* with morpho-syntactic annotation from the *Vedic Treebank*, we perform a pilot study of formulas including SPEECH verbs in the *RigVeda*, the most ancient text of the. Sanskrit literature.

1 Introduction

The *Sanskrit WordNet* (SWN; Hellwig 2017)[1] is currently under construction in the framework of an international project carried on by the University of Pavia, the UCSC of Milan, the University of Exeter, and the Center for Hellenic Studies at Harvard University, which aims to build a family of WordNets (WNs) for ancient Indo-European (IE) languages. The family additionally comprises WNs for Ancient Greek[2] and Latin (Biagetti et al. 2021). These WNs are designed to be interoperable with each other and with other WNs for modern languages, as well as linkable to external resources (see also Zanchi et al. 2021). Furthermore, these WNs bring together WN relational semantics with semantic theories of Cognitive Linguistics, while introducing a number of innovations to the WN architecture to account for the specificities of ancient IE languages (Biagetti et al. 2021).

By means of a case study employing the SWN, this paper shows how WNs can be employed in tandem with morpho-syntactically annotated corpora to study poetic formulas, and more generally idiomatic expressions of ordinary language. Building on the methodology by Zanchi et al. (2022), we develop a pilot study on the *RigVeda* (RV), the most ancient text of Sanskrit literature, composed in the so-called Vedic variety. [3] To extract formulas with different degrees of schematicity, we pair the lexico-semantic information of the SWN with the morpho-syntactic annotation of the *Vedic Treebank*. The Vedic Treebank (VTB, Hellwig et al. 2020) is a morpho-syntactically annotated corpus of Vedic literature, tagged according to the Universal Dependencies formalism (Nivre et al. 2016).

The paper is structured as follows. Sec. 2 introduces the background. Sec. 3 explains our methodology. In Sec. 4, we show and discuss our results. Sec. 5 concludes the paper and draws future lines of research.

2 Formulas as constructions

2.1 The path toward a constructionist approach to formularity

By investigating South Slavic oral epic poetry, M. Parry (1971[1928]) and A. B. Lord (1960) demonstrated that the *Iliad* and the *Odyssey* are examples of oral poetry: these poems result from online composition during bards' performances, and their written versions are secondary. Within this research, Parry gave a first definition of *formulas* in oral poetry as "traditional fixed expressions regularly employed in fixed metrical

[1] https://sanskritwordnet.unipv.it.

[2] https://greekwordnet.chs.harvard.edu.

[3] See https://glottolog.org/resource/languoid/id/sans1269 for the position of Vedic among Indo-Aryan and IE languages as well as for grammars of this language.

conditions to express a given essential idea". As later stressed by Lord, formulas are organized in larger scenes and narrative themes to be productively manipulated by mature bards to continuously re-build poetry in their performances.

Since Parry and Lord's seminal work, research on formularity has flourished. Different investigations have granted major emphasis to the semantic aspects or the formal constrains of formulas (see, among many others, Nagy 1974, Nagler 1976, Watkins 1976, 1995, Russo 1963, 1966, Hainsworth 1968). Notably, all the studies mentioned so far look at formulas as a phenomenon *sui generis*. Kiparsky (1976) first proposed a unified account for formulas and idioms of ordinary language. He distinguished flexible/deep-structure formulas (1)a vs. bound phrases (1)b (or idioms/ready-made surface formulas):

(1) a. *The X-er, the Y-er*
    b. *It takes one to know one*

Admittedly, Kiparsky did not prove that flexible formulas and bound phrases belong to two discrete categories, but meanwhile, from his generative perspective, it was not possible to settle these types along a *continuum*.

Bozzone (2014) and Pagán Cánovas and Antović (2016; see also Antović and Pagán Cánovas 2016) found a solution to this issue, by identifying usage-based linguistics, and Construction Grammar in particular, as a theoretical framework that allows providing a definition of formulas that accounts for their functional and formal components and handles their gradience. In Construction Grammar (e.g., Fillmore and Kay 1993, Goldberg 1995), constructions are understood as learned pairings of form and function, just as formulas. In this view, lexicon and syntax arrange along a *continuum*, varying for their degree of abstractedness and complexity. Lexically filled formulas, partially filled formulas, lexically empty formulas, and fully schematic syntactic structures (such as the transitive construction) are all constructions, which can be arranged along the lexicon-syntax *continuum*.

This definition of formulas, accounting for their semantic and formal flexibility, suits well the Rigvedic formulaic style: the form of the hymns relies on the tradition of preceding poets, but at the same time Vedic poets stress the novelty of their poems. As Biagetti (forthc.) puts it, "this tension between tradition and innovation is mirrored in continuous and conscious variations in expressing traditional themes" (see Sec. 4.1).

2.2 A case study on Ancient Greek

Zanchi et al. (2022) adopted this approach to perform a case study on the Iliadic KILL and SPEECH formulas. They enhanced F. Mambrini's *Universal Dependency* conversion of the *Ancient Greek Dependency Treebank,* [4] containing the Homeric poems, with the *Ancient Greek WordNet* [5] synsets for KILL and SPEECH. Specifically, they automatically annotated the relevant verbal lemmas with the synsets v#00903723 "cause to die; put to death", v#00652168 "use language", v#00554194 "reply or respond to", v#00608227 "address a question to and expect an answer from", and v#00696790 "greet by a prescribed form". Then, by means of a Python script employing the Udapi package,[6] they extracted the relevant pattern from the enhanced treebank: a transitive construction with some additional restrictions concerning the relative position of its elements and their occurrence within a single Homeric verse: $\text{obj}_{\text{accusative}}$ ptc X $\text{verb}_{\text{finite}}$ $\text{atr}_{\text{nominative}}$ $\text{subj}_{\text{nominative}}$.[7] The analysis of the extracted occurrences confirmed that this syntactic and metrical configuration is frequently – but not exclusively – employed to express two basic ideas, that is, KILL and SPEECH. The output verses make up a family of formulas, whose members share some – but not necessarily all – functional and/or formal features with the other members of the family, as exemplified by (2). The verses in (2)a-b share their basic idea, SPEECH, but their formal realization is different: the verb in (2)a occupies the 4th position in the verse, whereas the verb in (2)b occurs in the third place. Instead, (2)a and (2)c convey two distinct basic ideas, SPEECH and KILL, but are formally more similar: the initial accusative is followed by a particle and a connective; then a third person singular aorist

[4] https://github.com/francescomambrini/katholou/tree/main/ud_treebanks/agdt/data.
[5] https://greekwordnet.chs.harvard.edu.

[6] https://github.com/unipv-larl/formulHomer.
[7] Abbreviations stand for: obj = object, ptc = particle, atr = attribute, subj = subject.

form occurs; the nominative subject modified by two attributes concludes the verse. Finally, the verse in (2)d is formally closer to (2)a and (2)c than to (2)b (the verb occurs in exactly the same position as in (2)a and (2)c, but is preceded by a participle and not by a connective), but conveys a further basic idea: THINK. Traditionally, the verses in (2)a-d are not treated as belonging to a single family of formulas, despite their evident similarities.

(2) Il.24.668, 1.121, 22.376, 11.599

	obj	ptc	X	verb	atr	subj
a.	*tòn*	*d'*	*aûte*	*proséeipe*	*podárkēs dîos*	*Akhilleús*
b.	*tòn*	*d'*	--	*ēmeíbet'*	*podárkēs dîos*	*Akhilleús*
c.	*tòn*	*d'*	*epeì*	*exenárixe*	*podárkēs dîos*	*Akhilleús*
d.	*tòn*	*dè*	*idȭn*	*enóēse*	*podárkēs dîos*	*Akhilleús*

3 Data and methods[8]

3.1 The Vedic Treebank

Our initial data comes from the Rigvedic section of the VTB, [9] which is currently only partially annotated for syntax. Since elements of the formulas are linked to each other by syntactic relations, we needed a fully annotated treebank to extract the relevant patterns. Thus, we matched the syntactically annotated portion of the treebank with silver annotation produced by an automatic parser for Vedic, and obtained a fully annotated version of the RV.[10]

3.2 Enhancing the VTB with synsets

To check whether it is possible to extract formulas as pairings of form and function/basic idea, we further annotated the treebank with synsets. Similarly to Zanchi et al. (2022), we chose three synsets for SPEECH (CALL, ASK, SAY) and automatically assigned one of them to each relevant verbal lemma occurring in the treebank.[11] Furthermore, since Rigvedic hymns are mainly devoted to praising the gods of the Vedic pantheon, we automatically added the synset DEITY to proper names of all such gods, to check whether they constitute the main addressees of the SPEECH verbs under investigation (see the Appendix for the list of synsets and associated lemmas).

3.3 Extraction of the formulas

The extraction consisted of two phases: initially, we focused on trigrams involving at least a SPEECH verb. We noticed that most trigrams involved an obj, an adverbial clause modifier in the dative case (advcl), and optionally a subj, in addition to the SPEECH verb. We thus focused on patterns involving these four elements: verb, obj, advcl, and optionally subj.

We further enriched the treebank with metric information of all the sentences in which an advcl modifier in the dative case occurred. To do so, we added a feature "PositionInVerse" to the MISC field of the conllu file, which can take one of two values: Initial or Final.[12] To extract the patterns, we used UDeasy (Brigada Villa 2022), a tool for querying treebanks.

Nodes	verb	upos=VERB
	obj	deprel=`obj`
	subj (optional)	deprel=`nsubj`
	advcl (optional)	deprel=`advcl` | `advcl:fin`
Relations	verb governs all the other nodes in the query	

Table 1: Query employed for data extraction

As shown in Table 1, we extracted patterns consisting of four nodes, in which subj and advcl were optional elements and, together with obj, had to depend syntactically on the verb. In addition, we restricted the results to those patterns involving a verb whose synset was CALL, ASK or SAY.

[8] Data employed for this study are available at the following GitHub repository: https://github.com/unipv-larl/rv-formulas.

[9] https://github.com/OliverHellwig/sanskrit/tree/master/papers/2020lrec/treebank.

[10] The automatic parsing of the RV was performed by Oliver Hellwig and can be found at the following GitHub repository: https://github.com/OliverHellwig/sanskrit/tree/master/dcs/data/conllu/files/Rgveda. In order to recognize sentences annotated by the parser, we added a feature SyntaxAnnotation=silver to the MISC field of the conllu file.

[11] Since formulas convey a "given essential idea", in this case study we were not interested in capturing all the different senses of each verb, but rather in detecting all formulas conveying the basic idea of SPEECH. Therefore, we assigned one single synset to each verb based on its first meaning in the Monier-Williams Sanskrit Dictionary.

[12] Rigvedic verses (*ślokas*) are divided into text lines (*pādas*); different verses can be distinguished based on the number of *pādas* they contain and on the number of syllables of each *pāda*. When taking metric information into account, in this phase we did not focus on the number of syllables nor on syllable lengths, but simply on the position of verb, obj, advcl and subj in each *pāda*.

4 Results

4.1 Rigvedic constructions

Composed and transmitted orally for centuries, the RV did not follow the same principles of oral composition as we know it from Homeric epic: its compositional technique makes little use of the metrically defined and invariant formulas (ready-made surface formulas; Kiparsky 1976:83) that are common in Homeric poetry. As our results confirm, the RV rather consists of a texture of schematic (deep-structure) formulas, which are variously instantiated in the text due to, e.g., lexical or grammatical substitution and metrical variation (Jamison and Brereton 2014:14, cf. Jamison 1998).

As noted by Nagy (1974: 196), metrical patterns seem to result from the crystallization of phraseology, i.e., idiomatic expressions, which are known to display restricted syntax (Croft and Cruse 2004:290). We thus started our inquiry by looking at the most common orders for the elements obj, verb and advcl, and then analyzed each pattern with respect to the position of its elements in the verse. We found three patterns to be the most frequent ones:

1. obj, verb, advcl (25x)
2. obj, advcl, verb (24x)
3. verb, obj, advcl (16x)

For reasons of space, we exclusively discuss pattern 1. We arrange constructions along a *continuum* from more schematic morpho-syntactic structures to metrically- and lexically-fixed formulas, with the latter inheriting formal and semantic properties from the former (on inheritance, see Goldberg, 1995: 70-81).

4.2 Formulas with different degrees of schematicity: obj, verb, advcl constructions

We found the syntactic order obj, verb, advcl to occur 25x with verbs for CALL/SAY, always with an animate object referring to the addressee, as in (3)a. Most of these occurrences (21x) are instances of a metrically-fixed construction, in which advcl is always found in verse-final position, as in (3)b. This construction may be further analyzed according to two lexico-semantically specified subtypes: a more frequent pattern (19x) with a DEITY as obj (addressee) and forms of *hvā-/brū-*[13] as verb, as in (3)b1, and a less common pattern (2x) with a 1.Sg/Pl pronoun referring to POETS as obj and forms of *vac-/ah-* as verb, as in (3)b2. The former construction deserves further attention.

(3)	obj	verb	advcl
a	ANIMATE	CALL/SAY	Dat
b	ANIMATE	CALL/SAY	Dat, verse-final
b1	DEITY	*hvā-/brū-*	Dat, verse-final
b2	1Sg/Pl.POET	*vac-/ah-*	Dat, verse-final

For the construction b1 with a DEITY as obj and a verse-final advcl, we observed three more metrically- and lexically-fixed patterns, as displayed in (4); in all three, the obj may be both preceded and followed by an optional slot (X) of *n* syllables (σ).

(4) Constructions inheriting from b1

	X	obj	X	verb	X	advcl
b1.1	n_σ	INDRA/ DEITY	n_σ	*hvā-* /*brū-* ($2/3_\sigma$)	--	*ūtaye*(3_σ), verse-final
b1.2	n_σ	DEITY	n_σ	*hvā-*, verse-final	n_σ	*ūtaye*/ *somapītaye*/ *svastaye*, verse-final
b1.3	n_σ	INDRA	n_σ	*hvā-* ($2/3_\sigma$), verse-initial	n_σ	ACQUISITION(3_σ), verse-final

In construction b1.1, which occurs 9x in lines such as (5), the obj may have INDRA or another DEITY as referent. The construction is characterized by a bi- or tri-syllabic form of the verb *hvā-* or *brū-* directly preceding the advcl *ūtaye* 'for help', which occupies the last 3 syllables of the verse.

(5) Instances of the b1.1 construction

a. ***táṁ tvā***$_{\mathbf{obj}}$ *havíṣmatīr víśa*
úpa ***bruvata***$_{\mathbf{verb}}$ ***ūtáye***$_{\mathbf{advcl}}$
'Upon you the clans, offering oblations, call for help.' (RV 8.6.27ab)

b. ***indravāyū́***$_{\mathbf{obj}}$ *manojúvā*
víprā ***havanta***$_{\mathbf{verb}}$ ***ūtáye***$_{\mathbf{advcl}}$
'Indra and Vāyu, mind-swift, do the inspired poets call for help.' (RV 1.23.3ab)

Construction b1.2 and b1.3 both occur in sequences composed of two verses. Construction b1.2 occurs 5x in examples like (6). The former verse has any DEITY as the obj and ends with a form of the verb *hvā-*, whereas the latter verse always ends with one of the three advcl *ūtaye* 'for

[13] The citation form for Vedic verbs is the root followed by a hyphen (cf. the root *hvā-* 'call' and the 3Pl form *havanta* 'they call'). The citation form for nouns is the stem followed by a hyphen (cf. *ūtí-* 'help' with the dative form *ūtáye* 'for help').

help', *somapītaye* 'for the drinking of soma', and *svastaye* 'for well-being'.

(6) Instances of the b1.2 construction

a. ***víśvān devā́n***$_{obj}$ ***havāmahe***$_{verb}$
marútaḥ ***sómapītaye***$_{advcl}$
'The All Gods we call, the Maruts, for soma-drinking.' (RV 8.23.10ab)

b. *ihá_**indrāṇī́m***$_{obj}$ *úpa* ***hvaye***$_{verb}$
varuṇānī́ṁ ***suastáye***$_{advcl}$
'Here I call upon Indrāṇī, Varuṇānī for well-being.' (RV 1.22.12a)

Construction b1.3 occurs 3x in two-verse sequences like (7). In the former verse the obj always has INDRA as one of its referents (lexically realized either by a pronoun, as in (7)a, or by a specialized epithet, as in (7)b), whereas the latter verse starts with a bi- or tri-syllabic form of the verb *hvā-* and ends with a trisyllabic word for ACQUISITION as advcl.

(7) b1.3

a. *índrāvaruṇa* ***vām***$_{obj}$ *ahám*
huvé$_{verb}$ ***citrā́ya rā́dhase***$_{advcl}$
'Indra and Varuṇa, I invoke you two for brilliant bounty. (RV 1.17.7ab)

b. ***ugrám***$_{obj}$ *pūrvī́ṣu pūrvyám*
hávante$_{verb}$ ***vā́jasātaye***$_{advcl}$
'They call on (you) the strong, foremost among the many (peoples), for the winning of prizes.' (RV 5.35.6cd)

LEMMA	SYNSET	N
ūtí- (22), *ávas-* (8), *adhivākā́-* (1), *gopīthá* (1)	PROTECTION n#00522858	32
vā́jasāti- (6), *sātí-* (3), *dhánasāti-* (1), *rā́dhas-* (1), *gṛbh* (1)	ACQUISITION n#00045827	13
sakhyá- (10)	FRIENDSHIP n#10038317	10
svastí- (6), *saúbhaga-* (1)	WELL-BEING n#10366086	7
sómapīti- (3), *pītí-* (2)	DRINKING n#00540820	5
rayí- (2)	WEALTH N#9614312	2
mṛḍīká- (1), *sumná-* (1)	FAVOUR n#05575676	2
sadhástuti- (1)	PRAISE n#05018478	1
śvetanā́- (1)	WHITENING n#00176075	1
nirṇíj- (1)	RAIMENT n#02212047	1

Table 2: Synsets of lemmas exployed as advcl.

4.3 Many expressions, same basic ideas

We analyzed all lemmas employed as advcl and observed that most are synonyms sharing the same synset (see Table 2). The most frequent synset is PROTECTION (n#00522858 "the activity of protecting someone or something"), mostly instantiated by the lemma *ūtí-* 'help, protection' (22x), followed by *ávas-* 'assistance, protection' (8x). Expressions with either term may thus be considered the core of this construction, whereas expressions with *adhivākā́-* 'advocacy, protection' and *gopīthá-* 'protection', both occurring only once, seem to belong to its periphery.

Further frequently recurring synsets are ACQUISITION, FRIENDSHIP, WELL-BEING and RITUAL, with ACQUISITION attesting to a high degree of lexical variation: *sātí-* and its compounds *vā́ja-sāti-* and *dhána-sāti-* belong to the core, whereas *rā́dhas-* and *gṛbhá-* are more peripheral.

Notably, *pītí-* 'drink' and its compound *sóma-pīti-* 'soma drinking', together with *sadhá-stuti-* 'joint praise' and *śvetanā́-* 'whitening (of dawn)' instantiate WN's well-known "tennis problem", that is, the impossibility to capture semantic solidarity between lemmas sharing membership in the same topic of discourse (Fellbaum, 1998: 10-11). In this specific case, the ritual drinking of soma and the joint praise were part of a Vedic ritual taking place at dawn. Thus, in the constructions under investigation, the four lemmas employed as advcl all have the function of calling the gods to take part in the ritual.

5 Conclusion and future work

With this case study, we showed the potential of employing WNs in tandem with other language resources to study idiomatic expressions. Pairing the lexico-semantic information of the SWN with morpho-syntactic annotation contained in the VTB, we were able to extract poetic formulas involving a SPEECH verb in the RV, and to detect recurring pairings of form and meaning at various levels of schematicity. In the future, as the SWN grows, we intend to add semantic annotation to the entire VTB. Furthermore, the same approach may be applied to the study of idiomatic expressions in everyday language by combining information contained in WNs and treebanks of modern languages.

Acknowledgements

This article results from the joint work of the authors. For academic purposes, Luca Brigada Villa is responsible of sections 1 and 3, Erica Biagetti of sections 4.1, 4.3 and 5, Riccardo Ginevra of section 4.2, and Chiara Zanchi of section 2. Furthermore, Luca Brigada Villa is responsible for data extraction.

References

Mihailo Antović and Cristóbal Pagán Cánovas (eds.). 2016. *Oral Poetics and Cognitive Science*. Berlin/Boston, de Gruyter.

Erica Biagetti, Chiara Zanchi and William M. Short. 2021. Toward the creation of WordNets for ancient Indo-European languages. In *Proceeding of the 11th Global WordNet Conference*. University of South Africa (UNISA): Global Wordnet Association, pages 258–266. https://aclanthology.org/2021.gwc-1.30

Erica Biagetti. Forthc. Integrare Sanskrit WordNet e Vedic TreeBank: uno studio pilota sulla formularità del Rigveda tra semantica e sintassi. In Isabella Bossolino and Chiara Zanchi, *Prospettive sull'antico. Decennalia dei Cantieri d'Autunno*. Pavia, Pavia University Press.

Chiara Bozzone. 2014. *Homeric Constructions*. PhD thesis, University of California, Los Angeles.

Luca Brigada Villa. 2022. UDeasy: a Tool for Querying Treebanks in CoNLL-U Format. In *Proceedings of the Workshop on Challenges in the Management of Large Corpora* (CMLC-10), pages 16–19.

William Croft and D. Alan Cruse. 2004. *Cognitive Linguistics*. Cambridge, Cambridge University Press.

Christiane Fellbaum (ed.). 1998. *WordNet: An electronic lexical database*. MIT Press, Cambridge, MA.

Charles J. Fillmore and Paul Kay. 1993. *Construction grammar coursebook*. Berkeley, University of California.

Adele E. Goldberg. 1995. *Constructions: a Construction Grammar Approach to Argument Structure*. Chicago, Chicago University Press.

John B. Hainsworth. 1968. *The Flexibility of the Homeric Formula*. Oxford, Clarendon.

Oliver Hellwig. 2017. Coarse semantic classification of rare nouns using cross-lingual data and recurrent neural networks. In *IWCS 2017-12th International Conference on Computational Semantics-Long papers*, Montpellier, France.

Oliver Hellwig, Salvatore Scarlata, Elia Ackermann, and Paul Widmer. 2020. The Treebank of Vedic Sanskrit. In *Proceedings of The 12th Language Resources and Evaluation Conference* (LREC 2020), pages 5137–5146.

Stephanie W. Jamison 1998. Rigvedic *viśvátaḥ sīm*, or, Why syntax needs poetics. In Jay Jasanoff, H. Craig Melchert and Lisi Oliver, *Mir curad: Studies in honor of Calvert Watkins*, Innsbruck, Innsbrucker Beiträge zur Sprachwissenschaft, pages 291–299.

Stephanie W. Jamison and Joel P. Brereton. 2014. *The Rigveda. The Earliest Religious Poetry of India*. Oxford, Oxford University Press.

Paul Kiparsky. 1976. Oral Poetry: Some Linguistic and Typological Considerations. In Benjamin A. Stolz and Richard Stoll Shannon (eds.), *Oral Literature and the Formula*. Ann Arbor, Center for Coordination of Ancient and Modern Studies, pages 73-106.

Albert B. Lord. 1960. *The Singer of Tales*. Cambridge, MA, Harvard University Press.

Michael N. Nagler. 1967. Towards a Generative View of the Homeric Formula. *Transactions of the American Philological Association* 98:269–311.

Gregory Nagy. 1974. *Comparative Studies in Greek and Indic Meter*. Cambridge, MA, Harvard University Press.

Joakim Nivre, Marie-Catherine de Marneffe, Filip Ginter et al. 2016. Universal Dependencies V1: A Multilingual Treebank Collection. In *Proceedings of the Tenth International Conference on Language Resources and Evaluation (LREC'16)*, Portorož, Slovenia. European Language Resources Association (ELRA), pages 1659–1666.

Cristóbal Pagán Cánovas and Mihailo Antović. 2016. Formulaic creativity: Oral poetics and cognitive grammar. *Language & Communication* 47:66–74.

Parry, Milman. 1971 [1928]. The Traditional Epithet in Homer. In Adam Parry (ed.), *The Making of Homeric Verse: The Collected Papers of Milman Parry*. Oxford, Oxford University Press, pages 1–190.

Joseph Russo. 1963. A Closer Look at Homeric Formulas. *Transactions of the American Philological Association* 94:235–247.

Joseph Russo. 1966. The Structural Formula in the Homeric Verse. *Yale Classical Studies* 20: 217-240.

Calvert Watkins. 1976. Answer to P. Kiparsky's Paper: Oral Poetry: Some Linguistic and Typological Considerations. In Benjamin A. Stolz and Richard S. Shannon (eds.), *Oral Literature and the Formula*. Ann Arbor, Center for Coordination of Ancient and Modern Studies, pages 107–111.

Calvert Watkins. 1995. *How to Kill a Dragon: Aspects of Indo-European Poetics*. New York and Oxford, Oxford University Press.

Chiara Zanchi, Silvia Luraghi and Erica Biagetti. 2021. Linking the Ancient Greek WordNet to the Homeric Dependency Lexicon. In *Computational Linguistics and Intellectual Technologies. Papers from the Annual International Conference "Dialogue"*, Vol. 20:729-737.

Chiara Zanchi, Luca Brigada Villa, and Andrea Farina. 2022. *Toward combining Ancient Greek WordNet and AGDT2 for linguistic research: A pilot study on formulas of Iliad.* Paper presented at the 3rd International Colloquium on Ancient Greek Linguistics, Universidad Autónoma de Madrid, Spain, 16-18 June 2022.

Appendix

Table 3 contains synsets and their respective lemmas as they were added to the VTB.

SYNSET	LEMMAS
v#00501506 "utter in a loud voice or announce"	*hvā-*, *vac-*, *brū-*
v#00608227 "address a question to and expect an answer from"	*yāc-*, *pracch-*
v#00652168 "use language"	*vad-*, *ah-*
n#06861622 "any supernatural being worshipped as controlling some part of the world or some aspect of life or who is the personification of a force"	*deva-*, *indra-*, *agni-*, *varuṇa*, *aśvin-*, *vāyu-*, *marut-*, *mitra-*, *savitṛ-*, *sūrya-*, *uṣas-*, *aditi-*, *rudra-*, *viṣṇu-*

Table 3: Synsets and their associated lemmas.

Word Sense Disambiguation Based on Iterative Activation Spreading with Contextual Embeddings for Sense Matching

Arkadiusz Janz and Maciej Piasecki
Wrocław University of Science and Technology
{arkadiusz.janz|maciej.piasecki}@pwr.edu.pl

Abstract

Many knowledge-based solutions were proposed to solve Word Sense Disambiguation (WSD) problem with limited annotated resources. Such WSD algorithms are able to cover very large sense repositories, but still being outperformed by supervised ones on benchmark data. In this paper, we start with analysis identifying key properties and issues in application of spreading activation algorithms in knowledge-based WSD, e.g. influence of the network local structures, interaction with context information and sense frequency. Taking our observations as a point of departure, we introduce a novel solution with new context-to-sense matching using BERT embeddings, iterative parallel spreading activation function and selective sense alignment using contextual BERT embeddings. The proposed solution obtains performance beyond the state-of-the-art for the contemporary knowledge-based WSD approaches for both English and Polish data.

1 Introduction

Contextual neural embeddings have strongly influenced Word Sense Disambiguation (henceforth WSD), and resulted in extraordinary improvement on benchmark WSD datasets. However, the vast majority of such approaches follow the supervised learning scheme. Thus, they suffer from the lack of annotated data, especially sparse for WSD, and their coverage, i.e. practical applicability, is limited only to a subset of word senses. Moreover, they express bias towards most frequent senses.

Many knowledge-based solutions (i.e. weakly supervised) were proposed to solve the problem of limited sense annotated corpora. They are able to cover very large sense repositories, but still being outperformed by supervised ones on benchmark data. Knowledge-based WSD algorithms were initially based on spreading activation scheme, most on Personalised PageRank algorithm (PPR) (Agirre and Soroa, 2009). PageRank (Brin and Page, 1998) was originally proposed for modelling the Web, a highly connected network with many hubs and loops.As we show in Figure 1, PPR scores are often strangely biased by some local wordnet structures. Knowledge-based WSD approaches interact with the contextual information in a rather shallow way and also are biased by sense frequencies. That is why, we wanted to develop a version spreading activation for WSD which better reflects wordnet structures and more deeply explores context representation by using contextual text embeddings. Our goal was to develop a novel knowledge-based WSD algorithm which combines context-to-sense matching informed by BERT embeddings (Devlin et al., 2019) with a new iterative parallel spreading activation to process the wordnet.

The main contributions of our paper are:

1. a novel iterative parallel spreading activation algorithm for knowledge-based WSD,
2. enhancing spreading activation with context-to-sense matching using BERT embeddings,
3. and promotion of activations that are more central or salient for the given context.

The proposed solution expressed performance beyond the state-of-the-art of the knowledge-based WSD approaches in the all-words tasks for English. In addition, we performed also tests on WSD test data for Polish, a language that is significantly different from English, equiped with a very large wordnet – *plWordNet* (Dziob et al., 2019). Our solution showed superior performance in comparison to the previous approaches on the Polish data.

2 Related Work

Lesk-like (Lesk, 1986) methods use information about wordnet graph structures to a very little extent, e.g. (Banerjee and Pedersen, 2003; Navigli and Ponzetto, 2012), while local subgraphs are the primary tool for sense description, distinguishing senses in a wordnet, cf (Maziarz et al., 2013). The idea of better exploration of wordnet graphs for WSD appeared in several works, e.g. in (Mihalcea et al., 2004). (Agirre and Soroa, 2009) proposed Personalised PageRank (PPR) algorithm which uses the Princeton WordNet graph (Fellbaum, 1998) with the initial activation limited to nodes (synsets) correspond to the words from a textual context. The initial activation depends on contextual word frequencies. PPR became the core part of the UKB WSD system (Agirre et al., 2014) with WordNet enhanced by several semantic resources, including sense links derived from Princeton WordNet Gloss Corpus (Wor, 2021). UKB refers to sense frequency twice: in initial activation values (normalised together with the word frequency in the context) and finally as a kind of weights to the synset scores. UKB is freely available, but is sensitive to proper setting and selection of knowledge resources. (Agirre et al., 2018) showed that UKB if properly used is still a state-of-the-art knowledge-based WSD system. UKB achieves the best results in a mode called "W2W" (word-to-word), in which the WSD is restarted for each text word separately. This results in several times slower processing, than the standard mode in which all words in the context are disambiguated in one go.

Babelfy (Moro et al., 2014) utilised spreading activation in a indirect way. It was entirely based on BabelNet (Navigli and Ponzetto, 2012) – a complex semantic resource originating from the automated merging WordNet and Wikipedia[1]. Due to the BabelNet content, Babelfy was able to disambiguate words and perform Entity Linking at the same time. Semantic signatures introduce some generalisation, and the extraction of a "dense subgraph" results in a kind of topic related clustering.

(Scozzafava et al., 2020) applied PPR on WordNet structure, but significantly expanded it with SyntagNet (Maru et al., 2019) – a large, manually constructed resource of semantic sense collocations. The main limitation of WordNet-based spreading activation is the lack of topical relations between senses. Adding SemCor-derived sense links and connections from wordnet glosses partially resolves this issue. On the other hand the structure of the network becomes more complex. Some solutions solve approach the problem by joining *topic modelling* with knowledge-based techniques. For instance, (Wang et al., 2020) collected a corpus related to words from the WSD test data sets and obtained Latent Dirichlet Allocation (LDA) topic model (Blei et al., 2003). The graph was expanded with eXtended WordNet. Finally PPR was applied to the graph, where the initialisation was informed by the similarity of a node to the context. This complex approach requires construction of semantic resources focused on the datasets to be disambiguated.

(Chaplot and Salakhutdinov) adapted LDA topic modelling to represent a text document as derived from synsets (modelled by synset probabilities) and synsets as corresponding to word probability distributions. Prior synset distribution was constrained by wordnet-based synset similarity. This approach depends on the knowledge base to a minimal extent, but it is not clear how it can be expanded to more complex and richer knowledge bases.

The idea of restricting disambiguation context to sense semantically related to the disambiguated words is also central for (O et al., 2018). The authors proposed a distributional representation of senses based on generating pseudo-documents from BabelNet. For each sense, other sense nodes in short distance are retrieved and paths linking senses of the same lemma are searched for and used as pseudo-sentences of pseudo-documents for lemmas, next transformed by Doc2vec (Le and Mikolov, 2014) into a distributional space. Local disambiguation graphs are built sequentially from related sense nodes and next processed by PPR.

Local disambiguation graphs of related senses indirectly address topical homogeneity of word senses in a broader context. (Tripodi and Pelillo, 2017) perceived the WSD problem as a constraint satisfaction problem and model it on the basis of evolutionary game theory. Influence of words on senses by other words is weighted by distributional information. Semantic similarity information is used to calculate the amount of compatibility among the selected senses. Sense frequency from SemCor is indirectly used during disambiguation.

Concerning Polish language, the early work was built upon PageRank-based solutions such as UKB and its variations focused on wordnet expansions (Piasecki et al., 2016; Janz and Piasecki, 2019a,b). However, the frequency distribution of senses was unrepresentative as the large-scale sense-annotated corpora were not available.

[1] `https://en.wikipedia.org/`

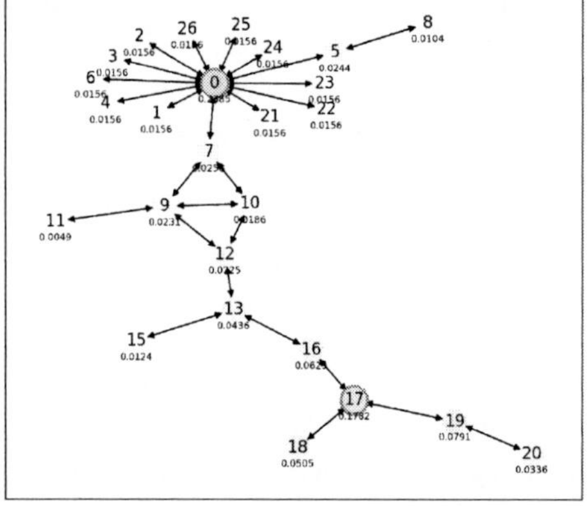

Figure 1: PPR scores computed for artificial data. The graph has been initialized with two seed nodes (v_0, v_{17}). The local structures have a great impact on score distribution.

3 PageRank in Knowledge-based WSD

A wordnet is a mixture of synset and sense relations: some of them directed, other not. Many directed relations exist in one way, but other are in symmetric pairs. Density of a wordnet graph is very diversified – it is not a densely connected graph in general, and many regions may be very sparse. For WSD, a wordnet is typically transformed into a graph with all relations being directed and symmetric and defined on the synset level, e.g. in UKB.

A wordnet has generally a tree-like shape. Its sparseness and shape change after adding links from external resources, e.g. sense links from the gloss corpus. Nevertheless, the final expanded graph for WSD still is not as recursively connected as the Web for which PageRank was designed.

In the case of WSD we assume that from sense nodes activated for a given context activation should evenly spread along the links to senses that are likely to co-occur with them. Activation amount passed to the next nodes should depend mainly on their semantic distance correlated with the number and types of links to be traversed. However, PageRank, modelling of a random walker, seems to work according to a different philosophy. In Fig.1 we have visualised activation scores (below the nodes) obtained with PPR in a simple graph resembling some local wordnet subgraph. The two initial nodes end with the very different final scores. Moreover, we can observe increased activations of nodes located in the same distance from both seeds. This is in contradiction to our above assumptions and results from the recursive character of PPR, e.g. the v_0 high degree and its star-shape local subgraph influence the scoring. In wordnet-based networks such specific local subgraphs, e.g. hub nodes, result from hierarchical categorisation or network editing practices, and do not express node importance due to being 'cited'.

Some of post-processing PPR scoring may decrease such negative bias. However, we decided to completely change the way in which spreading activation is performed. In the following section we propose a non-recursive spreading scheme in which every source node independently broadcast activation that is gradually transmitted along the network paths. It is the path characteristic that matters for activation strength. The final activation of the nodes is the result of overlapping of independent waves crossing the network.

4 Fast Spreading Activation and Contextual Matching

Learning from the PPR analysis, but also literature, two aspects seem especially important for knowledge-based WSD. First, spreading activation should transmit support from contextually related senses to the senses of a disambiguated word. Second, not all context words are equally informative for WSD – a good measure for contextual informativeness is needed. Thus, we proposed a redesigned WSD process based on three main components:

1. Use of contextual embeddings (a neural language model) to express similarity of senses and the context.
2. Iterative, parallel spreading of sense support across the network.
3. Identification of contextually salient senses as markers of context semantic dimensions.

A knowledge-base is a graph $G = (V, E)$, where the vertices V are senses, and the edges E – semantic links encoded in an adjacency matrix $\boldsymbol{A}^{N \times N}$: $\boldsymbol{A}_{s_n, s_{n'}} = 1$ if $(s_n, s_{s'}) \in E$, otherwise 0.

A typical WSD knowledge graph is quite sparse. Several fast graph traversal algorithms (Yang et al., 2015) were proposed for sparse adjacency matrices. A simple sparse–matrix dense–vector or even sparse–matrix sparse–vector multiplications can be interpreted as a single traversal step over graph. This property was used in parallel versions of well known graph algorithms e.g. Breadth First Search (BFS) and quick graph traversal algorithms using

GPUs (Gilbert et al., 2006). More specifically, to design a parallel BFS with multiple independent searches one can use sparse–matrix sparse–matrix multiplication (SpMSpM) where the second matrix represents an initial seed of starting nodes. In this work we adapt SpMSpM to design a fast spreading activation algorithm for WSD.

4.1 Parallel Spreading Activation with Contextual Sense Matching

We define spreading activation as a sequence of SpMSpM steps. The process starts from a set of initial seed nodes $T : (t_1, t_2, ..., t_M)$ with sense specific activation weights $\mathbf{w} = (w_1, w_2, ..., w_M)$. The decay factor d dampens the impact of initial nodes on their neighborhood in propagation procedure. In SpMSpM graph traversal framework the seed nodes are encoded as sparse matrix $P^{N\times M}$ using one-hot encoding where $\boldsymbol{P}_{n,m} = 1, n \in [1, N]$, $m \in [1, M]$ if $s_n \in T$ and $s_n = t_m$. SpMSpM allows us to quickly compute consecutive steps of graph traversal process starting independently from different seed nodes.

$$\boldsymbol{P}' = \boldsymbol{AP} \tag{1}$$

As we will show in the next section, with a single multiplication we can generate the output $Q^{N\times M}$ and select M columns from the adjacency matrix A in the first step. Each column $Q_{\star,m}$ represents in fact a set of visited nodes reached from the initial node t_m. Thus, we obtain independent outputs for every single seed node separately.

Parallel Spreading Activation defined in this way is an iterative process. We can easily reuse the outputs of the first multiplication step to generate the K new traversals starting from them.

$$\begin{aligned} \boldsymbol{P}^{(0)}_{n,m} &= \begin{cases} 1, & \text{if } s_n \in T \wedge s_n = t_m \\ 0, & \text{otherwise} \end{cases} \\ \boldsymbol{P}^{(k)} &= \boldsymbol{AP}^{(k-1)},\ k = 0, 1, \ldots, K \end{aligned} \tag{2}$$

To enforce that the consecutive P matrices encode only 0 and 1 where 1 represent visited nodes in k-th traversal step, we apply a simple clipping step using sign function, if non-negative values are greater than one. The clipping should counteract the results of multiple matrix multiplications. Since the multiplication steps accumulate visited nodes in the P matrices we also add subtraction step to ensure that the k-th output matrix contains only newly visited nodes. The final traversal matrix Q for the k-th step with only newly visited nodes is:

$$\begin{aligned} \widetilde{\boldsymbol{P}}^{(k)} &= \text{sign}(\boldsymbol{P}^{(k)}) \\ \boldsymbol{Q}^{(0)} &= \widetilde{\boldsymbol{P}}^{(0)} \\ \boldsymbol{Q}^{(1)} &= \max\{0, \widetilde{\boldsymbol{P}}^{(1)} - \widetilde{\boldsymbol{P}}^{(0)}\} \\ \boldsymbol{Q}^{(k)} &= \max\{0, \widetilde{\boldsymbol{P}}^{(k)} - \widetilde{\boldsymbol{P}}^{(k-1)} - \widetilde{\boldsymbol{P}}^{(k-2)}\} \end{aligned} \tag{3}$$

The values of $\boldsymbol{P}$ matrices are manipulated in a way that allows us to prevent backward traversals since $\boldsymbol{AP}$ multiplication does not prevent it. Only two-step subtractions are necessary to completely exclude them from the traversal procedure. The matrix $\boldsymbol{Q}^{(k)}_{n,m} = \max\{0, \widetilde{\boldsymbol{P}}^{(k)}_{n,m} - \widetilde{\boldsymbol{P}}^{(k-1)}_{n,m} - \widetilde{\boldsymbol{P}}^{(k-2)}_{n,m}\}$ contains 1 if a node s_n has been discovered starting from node t_m, otherwise 0.

By repeating this process we obtain a sequence of $(\boldsymbol{Q}^{(1)}, \boldsymbol{Q}^{(2)}, ..., \boldsymbol{Q}^{(K)})$ matrices where K is the total number of traversal steps. The final matrix $\boldsymbol{R}^{N\times M}$ represents accumulated activations computed M times for all nodes in the graph starting from each initial seed node $t_m \in T$ independently.

$$\boldsymbol{R} = \Big(\sum_{k=0}^{K} d^k \boldsymbol{Q}^{(k)}\Big) \tag{4}$$

Contextual Sense Matching The activation scores resulting from the parallel spreading represent support coming from different input nodes. We could immediately combine different activations coming to a node into one scoring value, but signals coming from different input senses may be of different informativeness for the context and a word to be disambiguated. To effectively disambiguate words in the context we need to incorporate only the most relevant signals. To do this, we introduce below a context-sensitive weighting $\mathbf{w}$ for activations coming from different seed nodes.

Two strategies can be applied to compute a contextually sensitive scoring from raw activations. The first one mixes all coming in activations with a dot product of the $\boldsymbol{R}$ rows and weight factors. The second is focused only on the most informative activations by applying maximum function.

$$\boldsymbol{z}_{s_n} = \boldsymbol{R}_{n,\star} \cdot \mathbf{w} \tag{5}$$

$$\widetilde{\boldsymbol{z}}_{s_n} = \max\{\boldsymbol{R}_{n,\star} \odot \mathbf{w}\} \tag{6}$$

(7)

To implement *Word-to-Word*-like mode of WSD (W2W), known from UKB, we can use a binary masking matrix $\boldsymbol{U}^{N\times M}$ excluding all senses of the same lemma from weight factors w and traversal-based scoring function z_{s_n}. The output of masking $\boldsymbol{R}'$ can be obtained by applying Hadamard product of the $\boldsymbol{R}$ matrix entries with $\boldsymbol{U}$:

$$\boldsymbol{R}' = \boldsymbol{R} \odot \boldsymbol{U}$$
$$\boldsymbol{z}'_{s_n} = \boldsymbol{R}'_{n,\star} \cdot \mathbf{w}$$
$$\widetilde{\boldsymbol{z}}'_{s_n} = \max\{\boldsymbol{R}'_{n,\star} \odot \mathbf{w}\}$$

On-path logit tracking Knowledge-bases are noisy, just like the text data. The lexico-semantic structure of wordnet and its extensions is non-uniform which implies one can find some areas that might be semantically incoherent. On the other hand, lexico-semantic structure usually extends beyond statistical disambiguation context. Additional supervision might be disastrous to model's generalisation ability and decrease its performance on unseen senses. However, by measuring semantic coherence of traversal paths one can reduce underlying noise and *filter* out unnecessary signals reaching target nodes representing disambiguated senses. For this reason, we propose an *on-path-logit-tracking* mechanism such that it uses sense embeddings (see section 4.3) of the intermediate nodes on traversal paths by utilising traversal matrices $(\boldsymbol{Q}^{(1)}, \boldsymbol{Q}^{(2)}, ..., \boldsymbol{Q}^{(K)})$ context-dependent scores. For a given seed node t_m, we analyse the nodes visited on its paths encoded by a sequence $(\boldsymbol{Q}^{(1)}_{*,m}, \boldsymbol{Q}^{(2)}_{*,m}, \dots \boldsymbol{Q}^{(K)}_{*,m})$ of columns in traversal matrices $\boldsymbol{Q}$. Let $(H^{(1)}_m, H^{(2)}_m, \dots, H^{(K)}_m)$ represent the sets of visited nodes discovered in each traversal step, starting from the node t_m. We compute a score representing a degree of contextual matching between the seed node t_m and the disambiguated word w_c, by measuring the contextual match of the embeddings of nodes visited during the traversal and contextual embedding of disambiguated word.

$$\mathcal{G}\left(H^{(k)}_m\right) = \max_{v \in H^{(k)}_m} \mathcal{G}'(v)$$
$$\mathcal{G}'(v) = \max\left\{e(v) \cdot e(w_c|C),\, e(v) \cdot e(w_{c'}|C)\right\}$$

where w_c and $w_{c'}$ represent, respectively, the disambiguated word itself and another content word in the given disambiguation context. This allows us to incorporate out-of-context senses existing in a wordnet into the final score. The procedure is computed for every seed node from the disambiguation context. We use the scores $\mathcal{G}\left(H^{(k)}_m\right)$ as a replacement for plain reduction model from Equation 4 and plug them into Equation 5. Before we will finally describe the disambiguation model in Sec. 4.4, we introduce the contextual embedding models used for generating weight factors and similarities in contextual sense matching and on-path logit tracking procedures.

4.2 Sense Encoder

To encode wordnet senses for contextual sense selection we use pre-trained BERT model in a similar way to (Du et al., 2019). We modified this architecture by dropping additional MLP layers as our approach is not supervised, see Fig. 2. Sense vector space is generated as follows: for each synset $s_n \in V$ its definition and examples are obtained from Princeton WordNet Gloss Corpus and BERT embeddings are generated for all their tokens. As BERT uses its own tokenizer based on WordPiece (Wu et al., 2016) words are segmented into subtokens and from the sequence of subtoken embeddings we generate a synset embedding by averaging only the embeddings of subtokens being a part of the synset's lemmas in its context (definition or example, see Figure 2). If a synset s_n has both a definition and an example, we generate separate contextual embeddings $e_d(s_n)$ and $e_s(s_n)$ and average them into a single synset embedding $e(s_n)$.

4.3 Context Encoder

Context size is a significant factor in WSD. To verify the impact of this factor on WSD performance we decided to test two context generation methods. First, the context generation heuristic from the UKB implementation (Agirre et al., 2018) takes 30 distinct content words around a target word to be disambiguated. It assumes that the location of target words is known in advance and a specific number of content words can be pre-selected to form the disambiguation context. As we rely on BERT embeddings in our method, not a bag of content words as, e.g. in UKB, we take a sequence of sentences the words belong to as a context. To convert the context to its vector space representation we apply BERT model on concatenation of input sentences and we store output token embeddings for further usage during disambiguation process.

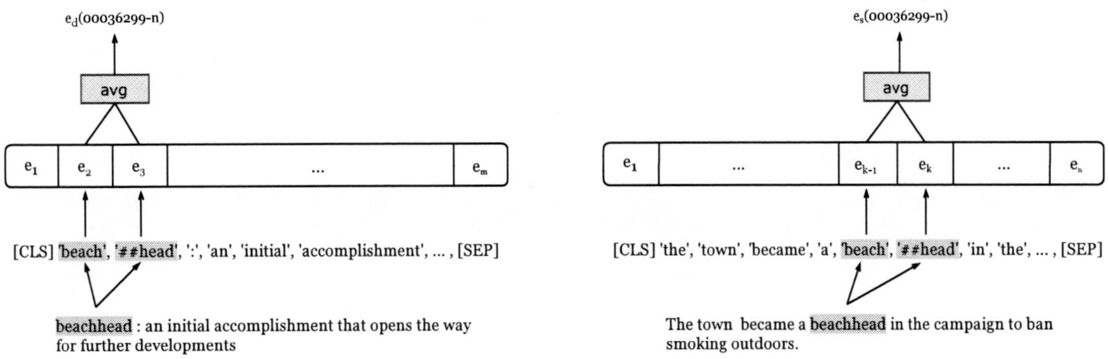

Figure 2: Transformer-based sense encoder used to encode wordnet senses. We modified the architecture proposed by (Du et al., 2019) and adapted it to our setting by dropping MLP layers originally being used to tune the model for supervised setting.

The second method uses a sliding window of three sentences and disambiguating content words in the middle one. In this case, we use BERT to obtain contextual embeddings of all content words. As both context and sense encoders work in the same vector space the fit between sense candidates and context words corresponds to vector similarity. With the context embedding model we generate contextual word embeddings $e(w_c|C)$ for each content word $w_c \in C$ being a part of input context C using the same sub-token embedding averaging model, see Fig. 2).

4.4 Sense Selection

Spreading activation scores are an input to the word sense selection. For the seed senses T extracted from the context C we initialise weight factors $\mathbf{w}$ for weighting the outputs of spreading activation function. Sense-specific activations in $\mathbf{w}$, cf Sec. 4.1, are based on cosine similarity $\mathrm{sim}(e(w_c|C), e(t_m))$ between the embeddings of the input seed senses $t_m \in T$ (Sec. 4.2) and the contextual embedding of the disambiguated word w_c (Sec. 4.3), where $t_m \notin S(w_c)$.

Word-to-word masking The nodes $t_m \in S(w_c)$ representing the senses of the lemma w_c are excluded. Technically, the obtained $\mathbf{w}$ factors are directly plugged into scoring function $z'_{s_n} = \max\{\boldsymbol{R}'_{n,\star} \odot \mathbf{w}\}$ where we take the maximum and the masking matrix U simulates W2W behaviour (see Sec. 4.1). The z'_{s_n} values are used as the first factor in our disambiguation function.

Disambiguation The disambiguation model merges two aforementioned factors. The first factor z_s is based on spreading activation with contextual sense matching and on-path logit tracking. The second factor g_s is computed simply as a dot product between a candidate sense embedding and the contextual embedding of a disambiguated word. For a set of sense candidates $s \in S(w_c)$ of the disambiguated word w_c, the final score is:

$$score(s) = \frac{z'_s + g_s}{2}$$

$$\hat{s} = \underset{s \in S(w_c)}{\mathrm{argmax}}\{score(s)\} \quad (8)$$

This model does not use word or sense frequencies yet. However, we can easily include them by changing the weight factors $\mathbf{w}$ or by multiplying the output scoring o_{s_n} with the frequency factor of a specific sense. We have chosen the latter.

5 Experiments

In this section we report the setup and the results of our experimental part.

5.1 Setting

We focused on comparison with several other knowledge-based solutions (see Sec.2) as well as analysis of the impact of sense frequency and an underlying knowledge graph on the performance of the proposed method. We tested two knowledge graphs: a graph based on Princeton WordNet expanded with eXtended WordNet (WN), and next it further expanded with syntagmatic links (SGN) as in (Maru et al., 2019; Scozzafava et al., 2020). We also evaluated the proposed model with two different context generation heuristics (see Sec. 4.3).

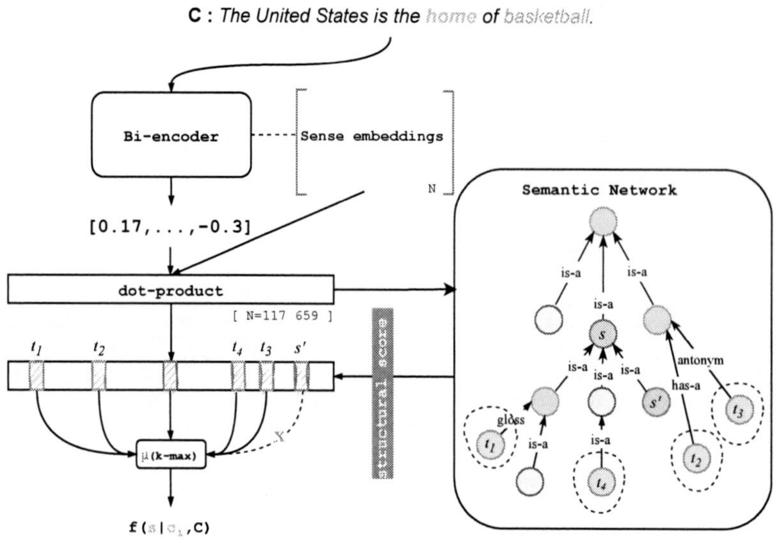

Figure 3: A general view on the proposed WSD model. The spreading activation model is provided with *sense-to-context* similarity scores computed with contextual embeddings. The scores from spreading activation model are combined with candidate sense score, excluding the incoming activations from the nodes representing disambiguated word (UKB's *word-to-word* heuristic). To avoid biasing towards frequent senses, we use *k-max* selection ($k = 3$) of incoming activation scores.

As a text encoder we used a pre-trained BERT_{BASE} (Devlin et al., 2019) uncased model with hidden 12 layers, 12 attention heads and the hidden layer size of 768. For the Polish dataset we used PolBERT uncased model which is pre-trained on Polish corpora and has the same BERT_{BASE}[2] architecture. For Polish data we present only the results of the model without sense frequency factor since a large sense-annotated corpora do not exist for the Polish language, so we could not compute frequency scores for senses.

5.2 Evaluation Corpora

The performance of our method was measured using English all-words WSD framework (Raganato et al., 2017) built upon Senseval-2 (Palmer et al., 2001), Senseval-3 (Snyder and Palmer, 2004), SemEval-2007 (Pradhan et al., 2007), SemEval-2013 (Navigli et al., 2013) and SemEval-2015 (Moro and Navigli, 2015) datasets. To compute performance metrics we used a standard scorer provided with this framework. We also conducted the evaluation on the Polish annotated corpora prepared for PolEval'2020 competition (Ogrodniczuk and Łukasz Kobyliński, 2020) in a similar way.

[2] `https://github.com/kldarek/polbert`

5.3 Parameter Tuning

To tune the parameters of the activation spreading algorithm and the sense selection function we decided to utilise available wordnet data and glosses from Princeton WordNet Gloss Corpus.

5.4 Results and Discussion

Sense frequency We compare the results from literature with the performance of our method measuring the impact of SemCor-based sense frequencies. The WSD models without prior information of sense frequencies showed lower performance on almost every dataset. Still, our model performed quite well in comparison with PageRank-based model implemented in UKB and WoSeDon, even if we compare the model without prior sense frequency information with the models using this prior during the disambiguation (see Table 1).

Knowledge graph We can also notice that the knowledge graph itself has a great impact on WSD performance. The methods proposed in the literature usually utilise eXtended WordNet (e.g. UKB) which introduces additional semantic links extracted from Princeton WordNet Gloss Corpus as a basis for disambiguation process. However, the resources like BabelNet or SyntagNet have been showed to increase the performance even more.

Table 1: F1-scores computed for different evaluation datasets in all–words WSD competition. The methods using sense frequencies from SemCor (SF) were marked with ✓ symbol. We also mentioned the knowledge bases used in cited methods (KB column). The (Wang et al., 2020) approach has used a knowledge base augmented with additional documents retrieved from external corpora (WN†).

Method	KB	SF	Test set					
			S2	S3	S7	S13	S15	All
(Agirre et al., 2018)	WN	✓	68.8	66.1	53.0	68.6	70.3	67.3
(Moro et al., 2014)	BN	?	67.0	63.5	51.6	66.4	70.3	65.5
(Maru et al., 2019)	SGN	✓	71.2	71.6	59.6	72.4	75.6	69.3
(Janz and Piasecki, 2019a)	WN	✓	69.6	66.5	52.8	68.6	70.2	67.7
(Chaplot and Salakhutdinov)	WN	?	69.0	66.9	55.6	65.3	69.6	66.9
(Tripodi and Pelillo, 2017)	BN	?	61.2	59.1	43.3	70.8	–	–
(Scozzafava et al., 2020)	SGN	✓	71.6	72.0	59.3	72.2	75.8	71.7
(Wang et al., 2020)	WN†	?	72.7	71.5	61.5	**76.4**	79.5	73.5
(Wang et al., 2020)*	WN†	?	71.9	69,9	60,5	75,7	79,0	72,5
The proposed model								
Parallel Spreading Activation	WN	✓	72.9	71.0	61.8	74.9	78.9	73.1
Parallel Spreading Activation	X-WN	✓	**75.3**	**72.2**	**63.9**	76.2	**81.0**	**74.8**

Table 2: F1-scores computed for different models on test in Polish language. We used the test data prepared for PolEval's Task 3: All-words WSD competition (Janz et al., 2020).

Method	Test set	
	SPEC	KPWr-100
(Kłeczek, 2020)	58.40	59.40
(Janz et al., 2020)	62.28	64.65
Parallel Spreading Activation	**65.79**	**66.12**

In this work we analysed the performance of our model working with SyntagNet knowledge-graph as it appeared to be very effective for WSD. We noticed that the model has obtained the best results among other knowledge-based solutions. We did not test BabelNet, as it is not open and we could not get access to this resource. When we compare the methods based on WordNet+eXtended WordNet, our model has obtained better results than PageRank solutions which suggests that selective approach is indeed more effective.

6 Conclusions

We propose the Parallel Spreading Activation with Contextual Sense Matching (PSA) method for knowledge-based, weakly supervised WSD. Its core is a novel spreading activation algorithm that is based on the idea of iterative spreading of support from the context seed senses across the network. The activation comes to the candidate senses from different directions and can be combined into the final score according to a selected scheme. This spreading scheme seems to fit better to the character of the wordnet-based semantic networks. Moreover, it allows for efficient implementation based on the multiplication of sparse matrices. The contextual sense matching function uses contextual embeddings for more accurate and selective information processing to avoid unnecessary mixing of all input signals from disambiguation context and reduce the impact of knowledge-base imperfections. We showed that two kinds of contextual information, namely informativeness of seed senses for the disambiguated word and association of the seed senses with the semantic dimensions of the context can be introduced into our spreading activation model on the basis of contextual embeddings, in our case we used BERT for this purpose. It is worth to notice that our approach uses versatile, general neural language models, and does not require construction of any further WSD-specific text models. We provide the code and the data at `https://gitlab.clarin-pl.eu/knowledge-extraction/prototypes/wsd-psa`.

Acknowledgments

The work was partially supported by (1) the Polish Ministry of Education and Science, the CLARIN-PL project (agreement no. 2022/WK/09); (2) the European Regional Development Fund as a part of the 2014-2020 Smart Growth Operational Programme, CLARIN – Common Language Resources and Technology Infrastructure.

References

[online]. 2021. [link].

Eneko Agirre, Oier Lopez de Lacalle, and Aitor Soroa. 2014. Random Walks for Knowledge-Based Word Sense Disambiguation. *Computational Linguistics*, 40(1):57–84.

Eneko Agirre, Oier López de Lacalle, and Aitor Soroa. 2018. The risk of sub-optimal use of Open Source NLP software: UKB is inadvertently state-of-the-art in knowledge-based WSD. In *Proceedings of Workshop for NLP Open Source Software (NLP-OSS)*, pages 29–33, Melbourne, Australia. Association for Computational Linguistics.

Eneko Agirre and Aitor Soroa. 2009. Personalizing PageRank for Word Sense Disambiguation. In *Proceedings of the 12th Conference of the European Chapter of the Association for Computational Linguistics*, EACL '09, pages 33–41, Stroudsburg, PA, USA. Association for Computational Linguistics.

Satanjeev Banerjee and Ted Pedersen. 2003. Extended Gloss Overlaps as a Measure of Semantic Relatedness. In *Proceedings of the 18th International Joint Conference on Artificial Intelligence*, IJCAI'03, page 805–810, San Francisco, CA, USA. Morgan Kaufmann Publishers Inc.

David M. Blei, Andrew Y. Ng, and Michael I. Jordan. 2003. Latent dirichlet allocation. *Journal of Machine Learning Research*, 3(null):993–1022.

Sergey Brin and Lawrence Page. 1998. The anatomy of a large-scale hypertextual Web search engine. *Computer Networks and ISDN Systems*, 30(1-7):107–117.

Devendra Singh Chaplot and Ruslan Salakhutdinov. Knowledge-based Word Sense Disambiguation using Topic Models. In *32nd AAAI Conference on Artificial Intelligence (AAAI-18), New Orleans, USA*.

Jacob Devlin, Ming-Wei Chang, Kenton Lee, and Kristina Toutanova. 2019. BERT: Pre-training of Deep Bidirectional Transformers for Language Understanding.

Jiaju Du, Fanchao Qi, and Maosong Sun. 2019. Using BERT for word sense disambiguation. *arXiv preprint arXiv:1909.08358*.

Agnieszka Dziob, Maciej Piasecki, and Ewa K. Rudnicka. 2019. plWordNet 4.1 – a linguistically motivated, corpus-based bilingual resource. In *Proceedings of the Tenth Global Wordnet Conference : July 23-27, 2019, Wrocław (Poland)*, pages 353–362.

Christiane Fellbaum, editor. 1998. *WordNet: An Electronic Lexical Database (Language, Speech, and Communication)*. The MIT Press.

John R Gilbert, Steve Reinhardt, and Viral B Shah. 2006. High-performance graph algorithms from parallel sparse matrices. In *International Workshop on Applied Parallel Computing*, pages 260–269. Springer.

Arkadiusz Janz, Joanna Chlebus, Agnieszka Dziob, and Maciej Piasecki. 2020. Results of the poleval 2020 shared task 3: Word sense disambiguation. *Proceedings of the PolEval 2020 Workshop*, pages 65–77.

Arkadiusz Janz and Maciej Piasecki. 2019a. A Weakly supervised word sense disambiguation for Polish using rich lexical resources. *Poznan Studies in Contemporary Linguistics*, 55(2):339 – 365.

Arkadiusz Janz and Maciej Piasecki. 2019b. Word Sense Disambiguation based on Constrained Random Walks in Linked Semantic Networks. In *Proceedings of the International Conference on Recent Advances in Natural Language Processing (RANLP 2019)*, pages 516–525, Varna, Bulgaria. INCOMA Ltd.

Dariusz Kłeczek. 2020. Polbert: Attacking polish nlp tasks with transformers. In *Proceedings of the PolEval 2020 Workshop*. Institute of Computer Science, Polish Academy of Sciences.

Quoc Le and Tomas Mikolov. 2014. Distributed Representations of Sentences and Documents. In *Proceedings of the 31st International Conference on International Conference on Machine Learning - Volume 32*, ICML'14, page II–1188–II–1196. JMLR.org.

Michael Lesk. 1986. Automatic sense disambiguation using machine readable dictionaries: how to tell a pine cone from an ice cream cone. In *Proceeding SIGDOC '86 Proceedings of the 5th annual international conference on Systems documentation*, pages 24–26. ACM Press.

Marco Maru, Federico Scozzafava, Federico Martelli, and Roberto Navigli. 2019. SyntagNet: Challenging supervised word sense disambiguation with lexical-semantic combinations. In *Proceedings of the 2019 Conference on Empirical Methods in Natural Language Processing and the 9th International Joint Conference on Natural Language Processing (EMNLP-IJCNLP)*, pages 3525–3531.

Marek Maziarz, Maciej Piasecki, and Stanisław Szpakowicz. 2013. The chicken-and-egg problem in wordnet design: synonymy, synsets and constitutive relations. *Langauge Resources and Evaluation*, 47(3):769–796.

Rada Mihalcea, Paul Tarau, and Elizabeth Figa. 2004. PageRank on semantic networks, with application to Word Sense Disambiguation. In *Proceedings of the 20th International Conference on Computational Linguistics*, COLING '04, Stroudsburg, PA, USA. Association for Computational Linguistics.

Andrea Moro and Roberto Navigli. 2015. SemEval-2015 task 13: Multilingual all-words sense disambiguation and entity linking. In *Proceedings of the 9th International Workshop on Semantic Evaluation (SemEval 2015)*, pages 288–297, Denver, Colorado. Association for Computational Linguistics.

Andrea Moro, Alessandro Raganato, and Roberto Navigli. 2014. Entity Linking meets Word Sense Disambiguation: a Unified Approach. *Transactions of the Association for Computational Linguistics*, 2:231–244.

Roberto Navigli, David Jurgens, and Daniele Vannella. 2013. SemEval-2013 task 12: Multilingual word sense disambiguation. In *Second Joint Conference on Lexical and Computational Semantics (*SEM), Volume 2: Proceedings of the Seventh International Workshop on Semantic Evaluation (SemEval 2013)*, pages 222–231, Atlanta, Georgia, USA. Association for Computational Linguistics.

Roberto Navigli and Simone Paolo Ponzetto. 2012. BabelNet: The automatic construction, evaluation and application of a wide-coverage multilingual semantic network. *Artificial Intelligence*, 193:217–250.

Dongsuk O, Sunjae Kwon, Kyungsun Kim, and Youngjoong Ko. 2018. Word Sense Disambiguation Based on Word Similarity Calculation Using Word Vector Representation from a Knowledge-based Graph. In *Proceedings of the 27th International Conference on Computational Linguistics*, pages 2704–2714, Santa Fe, New Mexico, USA. Association for Computational Linguistics.

Maciej Ogrodniczuk and Łukasz Kobyliński, editors. 2020. *Proceedings of the PolEval 2020 Workshop*. Institute of Computer Science, Polish Academy of Sciences, Warsaw, Poland.

Martha Palmer, Christiane Fellbaum, Scott Cotton, Lauren Delfs, and Hoa Trang Dang. 2001. English tasks: All-words and verb lexical sample. In *Proceedings of SENSEVAL-2 Second International Workshop on Evaluating Word Sense Disambiguation Systems*, pages 21–24, Toulouse, France. Association for Computational Linguistics.

Maciej Piasecki, Paweł Kędzia, and Marlena Orlińska. 2016. plWordNet in word sense disambiguation task. In *Proceedings of the 8th Global Wordnet Conference, Bucharest, 27-30 January 2016*, pages 280–289. Global Wordnet Association.

Sameer Pradhan, Edward Loper, Dmitriy Dligach, and Martha Palmer. 2007. SemEval-2007 task-17: English lexical sample, SRL and all words. In *Proceedings of the Fourth International Workshop on Semantic Evaluations (SemEval-2007)*, pages 87–92, Prague, Czech Republic. Association for Computational Linguistics.

Alessandro Raganato, Jose Camacho-Collados, and Roberto Navigli. 2017. Word sense disambiguation: A unified evaluation framework and empirical comparison. In *Proceedings of the 15th Conference of the European Chapter of the Association for Computational Linguistics: Volume 1, Long Papers*, pages 99–110.

Federico Scozzafava, Marco Maru, Fabrizio Brignone, Giovanni Torrisi, and Roberto Navigli. 2020. Personalized PageRank with syntagmatic information for multilingual word sense disambiguation. In *Proceedings of the 58th Annual Meeting of the Association for Computational Linguistics: System Demonstrations*, pages 37–46.

Benjamin Snyder and Martha Palmer. 2004. The English all-words task. In *Proceedings of SENSEVAL-3, the Third International Workshop on the Evaluation of Systems for the Semantic Analysis of Text*, pages 41–43, Barcelona, Spain. Association for Computational Linguistics.

Rocco Tripodi and Marcello Pelillo. 2017. A game-theoretic approach to word sense disambiguation. *Computational Linguistics*, 43(1):31–70.

Yinglin Wang, Ming Wang, and Hamido Fujita. 2020. Word sense disambiguation: A comprehensive knowledge exploitation framework. *Knowledge-Based Systems*, 190:105030.

Yonghui Wu, Mike Schuster, Zhifeng Chen, Quoc V Le, Mohammad Norouzi, Wolfgang Macherey, Maxim Krikun, Yuan Cao, Qin Gao, Klaus Macherey, et al. 2016. Google's neural machine translation system: Bridging the gap between human and machine translation. *arXiv preprint arXiv:1609.08144*.

C. Yang, Y. Wang, and J. D. Owens. 2015. Fast Sparse Matrix and Sparse Vector Multiplication Algorithm on the GPU. In *2015 IEEE International Parallel and Distributed Processing Symposium Workshop*, pages 841–847.

Documenting the Open Multilingual Wordnet

Francis Bond
Palacký University
bond@ieee.org

Michael Wayne Goodman
LivePerson, Inc.
goodmami@uw.edu

Ewa Rudnicka
Wrocław University of Science and Technology
ewa.rudnicka@pwr.edu.pl

Luis Morgado da Costa
Vrije Universiteit Amsterdam
lmorgado.dacosta@gmail.com

Alexandre Rademaker
Fundação Getulio Vargas & IBM Research
arademaker@gmail.com

John P. McCrae
National University of Ireland, Galway
john@mccr.ae

Abstract

In this project note we describe our work to make better documentation for the Open Multilingual Wordnet (OMW), a platform integrating many open wordnets. This includes the documentation of the OMW website itself as well as of semantic relations used by the component wordnets. Some of this documentation work was done with the support of the Google Season of Docs. The OMW project page, which links both to the actual OMW server and the documentation has been moved to a new location: `https://omwn.org`.

1 Introduction

In this paper we present an ongoing effort to document the Open Multilingual Wordnet (Bond and Foster, 2013), a multilingual platform that currently brings together 33 open, human-curated wordnets.[1] This is possible due to shared links to the Princeton WordNet of English (PWN) (Fellbaum, 1998), which serves as an interlingual interface. OMW's main contributions consist of (i) creating a common format, (ii) building software that allows the display data from a multitude of wordnets, (iii) and encouraging people to choose open licenses. The aligned wordnet data can be searched through the OMW webpage.[2] We also offer an extended version of the OMW enriched with the data for 150 languages extracted from Wiktionary[3] and the Unicode Common Locale Data Repository[4] (Bond and Foster, 2013).

The ultimate goal of the OMW is to produce a resource covering as many languages as possible, with as much useful information as possible. Structurally, it is a collection of linked lexicons with a common format and interfaces. From an engineering point of view, we want to proceed in an incremental fashion, at each stage making the resource more useful. Generally, language resources, to be useful, must be both **accessible** (legally usable) and **usable** (of sufficient quality, size and with a documented interface) (Ishida, 2006). These ideas have become widespread through the FAIR data principles (Wilkinson et al., 2016): Findable, Accessible, Interoperable and Reusable. From the start, we have followed these principles: Linking to Open Multilingual Wordnet makes wordnets easy to find. This became even easier when we added the data to the widely used NLTK[5] package. Having a web interface and Python library makes the data accessible. A shared, well-documented format makes the data inter-operable, and versioned releases on a stable platform (GitHub[6]) along with a variety of libraries to access it makes it easily reusable.

Our focus in this paper is the process and progress of creating the OMW documentation (along with the software). Wordnet projects have a long history of excellent documentation, either as MAN pages[7], as on the Princeton WordNet

[1]OMW v1.4 had 33 wordnets: English (Fellbaum, 1998); Albanian (Ruci, 2008); Arabic (Sabri et al., 2006); Chinese (Huang et al., 2010; Wang and Bond, 2013); Danish (Pedersen et al., 2009); Dutch (Postma et al., 2016); Finnish (Lindén and Carlson., 2010); French (Sagot and Fišer, 2008); Hebrew (Ordan and Wintner, 2007); Icelandic (Sigmundsson, 1985); Indonesian and Malaysian (Nurril Hirfana et al., 2011); Italian (Pianta et al., 2002); Japanese (Isahara et al., 2008); Norwegian (Bokmål and Nynorsk: Lars Nygaard 2012, p.c.); Persian (Montazery and Faili, 2010); Portuguese (de Paiva and Rademaker, 2012); Polish (Piasecki et al., 2009); Romanian (Tufiş et al., 2008); Swedish (Borin et al., 2013); Thai (Thoongsup et al., 2009) Slovak and Lithuanian (Garabík and Pileckytė, 2013); and Basque, Catalan, Galician and Spanish from the Multilingual Common Repository (Gonzalez-Agirre et al., 2012). OMW v2 adds German (Siegel and Bond, 2021), Kurdish (Aliabadi et al., 2014), Kristang (Morgado da Costa, 2020), Abui (Kratochvil and Morgado da Costa, 2022) and Cantonese (Sio and Morgado Da Costa, 2019).

[2]`https://compling.upol.cz/ntumc/cgi-bin/wn-gridx.cgi?gridmode=grid`

[3]`https://www.wiktionary.org/`

[4]`https://compling.upol.cz/ntumc/cgi-bin/wn-gridx.cgi?gridmode=gridx`

[5]`https://www.nltk.org/`

[6]`https://github.com`

[7]A software documentation format originally found on

webpage[8], or through technical reports (Vosssen, 2002) and books (Fellbaum, 1998; Vossen, 1998; Piasecki et al., 2009; Dash et al., 2017). However, once a project has finished, the documentation typically does not get updated, even though the actual wordnets are maintained.

Despite the high quality of some of the wordnet documentation, there are still some major problems. Specifically, the documentation is: (i) inconsistent across projects; (ii) not always up-to-date; (iii) hard to access online and (iv) not integrated with the wordnets or their interfaces. In answer to these challenges, the Global WordNet Association (GWA)[9] set up a Working Group on Documentation, which includes the first five authors of this paper.[10] In Section 2 we discuss these issues, and then in Section 3 we outline our solutions. We link to the online documentation and interface at `https://omwn.org`.

2 Problems

In the next section we discuss the problems in more detail, giving examples.

2.1 Inconsistency Across Projects

Often projects call the same relation by different names. The Princeton WordNet labels the relation between a word and its supertype as **`hypernym`** for nouns and **`troponym`** for verbs. However, if we consider two synsets A and B linked by **`hypernym`** (A **`hypernym`** B) it is not clear which is which. Should this be read as "A is the hypernym of B" or "A has hypernym B"? EuroWordnet makes this clear by calling the equivalent relationship **`has_hyponym`**: A **`has_hyponym`** B is not ambiguous. But if we want to use data from different projects, we must be able to determine that **`hypernym`** and **`has_hyponym`** are the same.

Another example is in the abbreviations for parts of speech (POS). Princeton WordNet uses **n** for **n**oun, **v** for **v**erb, **a** for **a**djective and **r** for adve**r**b. The Slovenian wordnet (Fišer et al., 2012) uses a different POS for adverb: **b** (adver**b**), as this is the default for the tool they use (DEBVisDic: Horák et al., 2006). If you just download the individual wordnets, it is not immediately clear that **r** and **b** refer to the same thing.

2.2 Outdated Content

Another big issue with documentation is that, as projects progress, new information is added (and sometimes removed) and the documentation does not always reflect this. Online documentation has its own issues, with linkrot being a real problem: in academic literature the half life of a link is typically not much longer than four years (Lawrence et al., 2001). A related problem for wordnets is that it is not always clear where the newest version of a wordnet can be found, especially if the new version is being prepared by a new group. The *Wordnets in the World* page[11] is a page listing wordnet projects, maintained by the GWA. This goes some way toward improving this, but it is only sporadically updated. It currently lacks, for example, any mention of the Open English Wordnet (McCrae et al., 2019).

Even outdated documentation is better than no documentation (Lethbridge et al., 2003), but it is, of course, better to keep documentation up-to-date.

2.3 Inaccessible Online

Print books have many advantages: many people find them less fatiguing to read, and reading a print book versus an e-book appears to boost reading comprehension, although improved screen quality may alleviate this (Jeong, 2012). However, they can be expensive and hard to access. Further, they are not searchable or hyperlinkable. For documentation, accessibility is extremely important.

Documentation updates are often informally given in academic papers, the recent archiving of Global WordNet Conference papers on the ACL Anthology (Gildea et al., 2018) has made wordnet papers much more accessible, which is a great boon.

2.4 Stand alone

Finally, one potential advantage of having documentation online is linking it directly to the wordnets themselves for examples. Another potential advantage is linking specialist terms in the wordnet interfaces to the documentation.

Linking to wordnets allows examples to be given in different languages, makes sure the examples are up-to-date, and allows browsing. The disadvantage

Unix systems.

[8] `https://wordnet.princeton.edu/documentation`

[9] `http://globalwordnet.org/`

[10] `http://globalwordnet.org/resources/working-groups/`, `https://globalwordnet.github.io/gwadoc/group.html`

[11] `http://globalwordnet.org/resources/wordnets-in-the-world/`

is that if the wordnet used for the example goes offline for some reason, then the examples will not be available.

Linking the wordnet interfaces to the documentation improves usability both for casual users, who may not know specialist terms, and expert users, who may want to see links to more detailed documentation and further references.

3 Shared Documentation

Our solution to the above problems relies on two new initiatives. Both are hosted on GitHub, a well-funded site with a good open source track record. GitHub hosts code and other projects using the version control system Git, and it also serves static webpages for these projects. GitHub is backed up by the internet archive, as well as having snapshots stored in the Arctic Code Vault,[12] so the data is well-preserved. The URLs should also last for the foreseeable future, thus guarding against linkrot.

The general documentation is supported by the Global Wordnet Association Documentation Working Group: having a group responsible rather than an individual project makes it more likely to be kept up-to-date, and having contributors from multiple projects makes sure attention is paid to consistency across different projects. Further, the GitHub infrastructure for raising issues and discussing them lowers the cost to keeping the documentation up-to-date. The actual task of writing the documentation requires considerable investment of time, and so for 2020 we applied for and received support from the Google Season of Docs.[13] Three technical writers helped contribute documentation for the wordnet structure, primarily semantic relations, and the Open Multilingual Wordnet interface.

3.1 Documenting the Semantic Relations: GWADOC

To document semantic relations, we made a Python package that can be used to provide (i) user-facing documentation of things like relations and parts of speech used by wordnets and (ii) a Python API for querying this documentation, such as for retrieving the localized name or definition for specific relations. This is available at `https://globalwordnet.github.io/gwadoc/`.

We give screenshots of the user facing documentation in Figures 1 and 2. The documentation starts with a non-specialist friendly definition followed by a summary of properties and a short example. It then gives a longer definition, some examples, tests, comments, shows how the relation would be defined in the Global Wordnet Association LMF format (McCrae et al., 2021) and links to names in other projects.

The interface is reactive, changing to fit different screen sizes and hyperlinks to examples and documentation.

We give an example of using the Python API in Figure 3. You can set the language to one of the languages for which we have documentation (currently English, Japanese and Polish). Note that when information is missing in any particular language, it seamlessly backs off to giving the English documentation.

All semantic relations from the latest release (version 1.2) of the Global Wordnet Association LMF format[14] are documented. Our long-term goal is to keep this documentation in sync with the schemas.

3.2 Documenting the Open Multilingual Wordnet

The Open Multilingual Wordnet is available here: `https://omwn.org`. We give an example of the documentation of the OMW in Figure 4. It shows how the semantic documentation from Section 3.1 is used to provide a mouseover tooltip when semantic relations are shown in the interface. Clicking the relation name sends you to the full documentation of the relation as shown in Figure 1.

The documentation includes information about the wordnets' structure, the OMW interface, and the documentation itself.

- OMW Wordnet Structure
  - Semantic Relations (as described above)
  - Parts of Speech
  - Definitions and Examples
  - Orthographic Variants
  - Glossary of Terms
- OMW Interface Documentation
  - Searching for words or concepts
  - Get Involved! Contribute to OMW

[12] https://github.blog/2020-07-16-github-archive-program-the-journey-of-the-worlds-open-source-code-to-the-arctic/

[13] `https://developers.google.com/season-of-docs/docs/2020/participants/`

[14] `https://globalwordnet.github.io/schemas/`

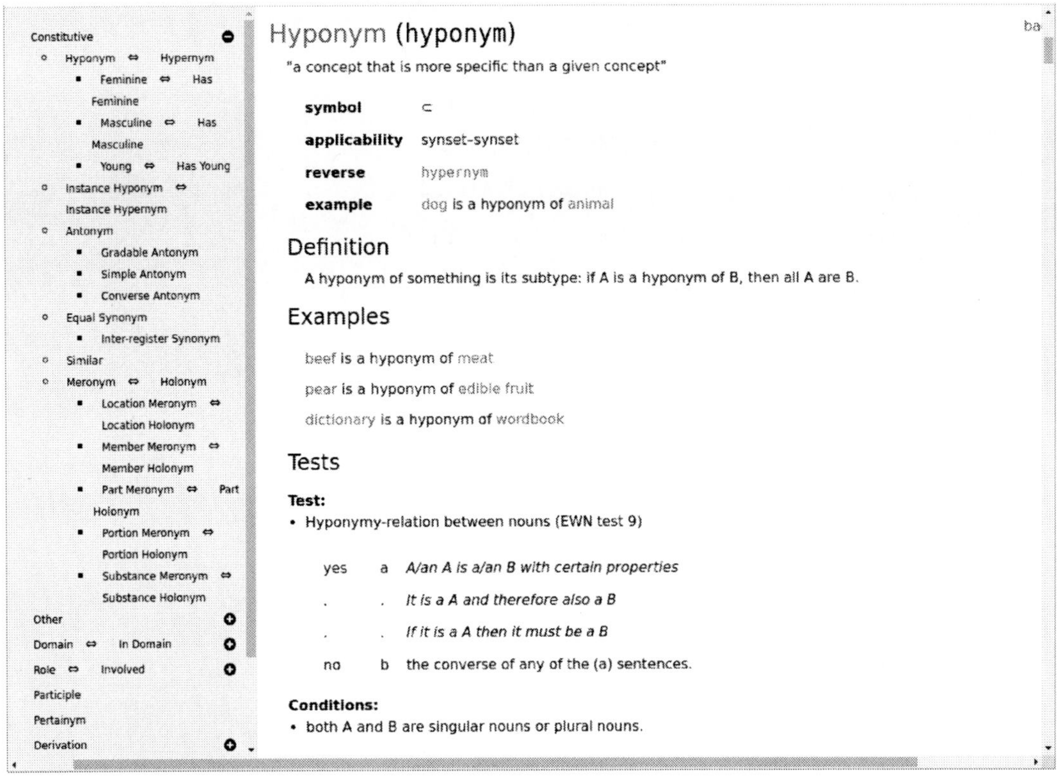

Figure 1: User Facing Documentation for Hyponym (1)

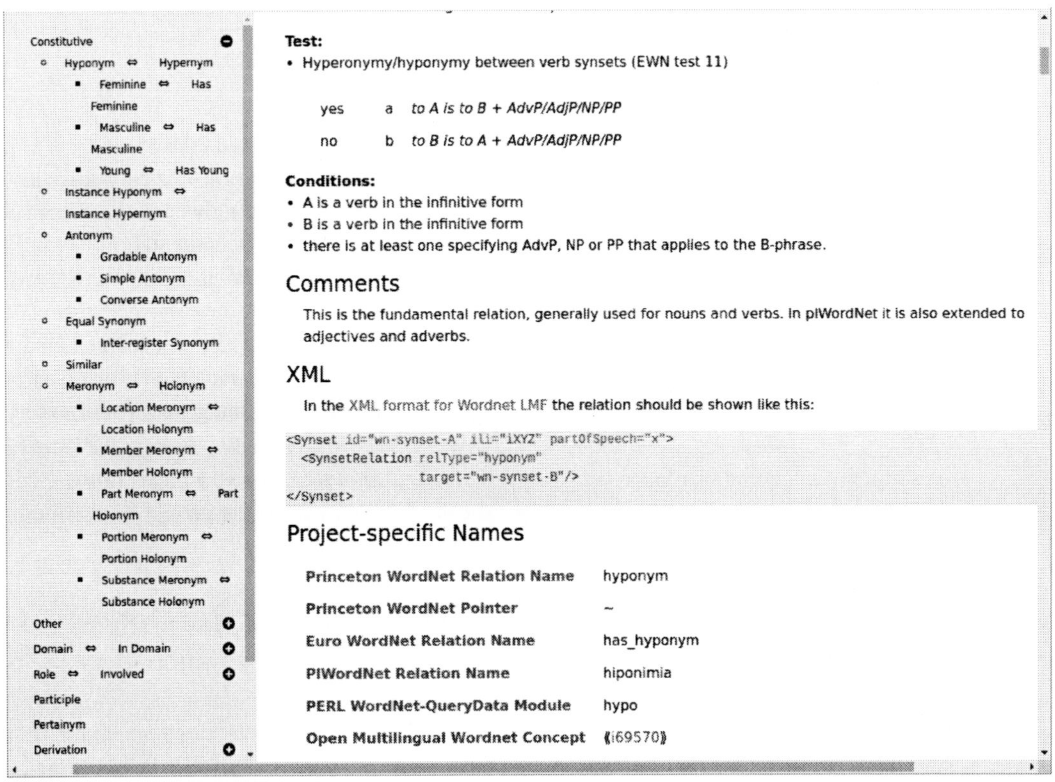

Figure 2: User Facing Documentation for Hyponym (2)

```
>>> import gwadoc
>>> for relname in gwadoc.RELATIONS[:5]:
...     print(relname, '\n    ', gwadoc.relations[relname].df.en)
...
constitutive
    Core semantic relations that define synsets
hyponym
    a word that is more specific than a given word
hypernym
    a word that is more general than a given word
instance_hyponym
    an occurrence of something
instance_hypernym
    the type of an instance

### Change default language
>>> gwadoc.set_preferred_language('ja')
>>>
>>> for relname in gwadoc.RELATIONS[:5]:
...     print(f"""{relname} ({gwadoc.relations[relname].name})
    {gwadoc.relations[relname].df}""")
...
constitutive (Constitutive)
   Core semantic relations that define synsets
hyponym (下位語)
   当該synsetが相手synsetを包含する
hypernym (上位語)
   a word that is more general than a given word
instance_hyponym (事例)
   当該synsetは相手synsetの事例である
instance_hypernym (事例あり)
   当該synsetは相手synsetを事例として持つ
```

Figure 3: GWADOC Python Example

  - Uploading a wordnet (an LMF-formatted file)
  - The structure of the LMF file
  - A script for converting the simple tab-separated format used in OMW 1.0 to WN-LMF (external tool)
  - Interconverter for desired formats (external tool)
  - More information about the LMF metadata
  - A script for uploading wordnets from the command line
  - Documentation on the feedback after uploading a wordnet
  - A summary of the wordnets in OMW
  - Information about reporting an issue and giving feedback

- OMW documentation on documentation style guides, useful macros and more

4 Future Work

In future work, we would like to add more languages to the documentation, and encourage its use in more projects. We strongly encourage more people to contribute to the documentation.

At least some of the documentation of wordnet structure should probably be moved to the GWA documentation project, rather than being tied to the OMW. For example, the documentation on parts of speech, sense relations, the glossary and so forth.

We will also move the *Wordnets in the World* and *WordNet Annotated Corpora* pages to the GitHub site to make it easier for people to add new resources.

5 Conclusions

In this project note we described an ongoing push to make better documentation for wordnets available online, through the documentation of the Open Multilingual Wordnet (OMW). This includes the documentation of the OMW website itself and the semantic relations. Some of this was done as

Figure 4: OMW Search Documentation

part of the Google Season of Docs. We sketched some ways we want to improve this even further in the future.

Acknowledgments

Thanks to the Google Season of Docs for their support and to the technical writers who contributed: Glory Agatevure, Rohitesh Jain, and Yoyo Wu. Luis Morgado da Costa was supported by EU's Horizon 2020 Marie Skłodowska-Curie grant H2020-MSCA-IF-2020 CHILL – No.101028782. Thanks also to Maciej Piasecki and German Rigau for their fruitful discussions and Arthur Bond for his help.

References

Purya Aliabadi, Sina Ahmadi, Shahin Salavati, and Kyumars Sheykh Esmaili. 2014. Towards building KurdNet, the Kurdish wordnet. In *Proceedings of the Seventh Global Wordnet Conference*, pages 1–6, Tartu, Estonia.

Francis Bond and Ryan Foster. 2013. Linking and extending an open multilingual wordnet. In *51st Annual Meeting of the Association for Computational Linguistics*, pages 1352–1362, Sofia.

Lars Borin, Markus Forsberg, and Lennart Lönngren. 2013. Saldo: a touch of yin to wordnet's yang. *Language Resources and Evaluation*, 47(4):1191–1211.

Niladri Sekhar Dash, Pushpak Bhattacharyya, and Jyoti D. Pawar, editors. 2017. *The WordNet in Indian Languages*. Springer.

Valeria de Paiva and Alexandre Rademaker. 2012. Revisiting a Brazilian wordnet. In *Proceedings of the 6th Global WordNet Conference (GWC 2012)*, Matsue.

Christine Fellbaum, editor. 1998. *WordNet: An Electronic Lexical Database*. MIT Press.

Darja Fišer, Jernej Novak, and Tomaž Erjavec. 2012. sloWNet 3.0: development, extension and cleaning. In *Proceedings of 6th International Global Wordnet Conference (GWC 2012)*, pages 113–117. The Global WordNet Association.

Radovan Garabík and Indrė Pileckytė. 2013. From multilingual dictionary to Lithuanian wordnet. In *Natural Language Processing, Corpus Linguistics, E-Learning*, pages 74–80. Lüdenscheid: RAM-Verlag.

Daniel Gildea, Min-Yen Kan, Nitin Madnani, Christoph Teichmann, and Martín Villalba. 2018. The ACL Anthology: Current state and future directions. In *Proceedings of Workshop for NLP Open Source Software (NLP-OSS)*, pages 23–28, Melbourne, Australia. Association for Computational Linguistics.

Aitor Gonzalez-Agirre, Egoitz Laparra, and German Rigau. 2012. Multilingual central repository version 3.0: upgrading a very large lexical knowledge base. In *Proceedings of the 6th Global WordNet Conference (GWC 2012)*, Matsue.

Aleš Horák, Karel Pala, Adam Rambousek, and Martin Povolny. 2006. Debvisdic - first version of new client-server wordnet browsing and editing tool. In *Proceedings of the Third International WordNet Conference (GWC 2006)*, pages 325–328.

Chu-Ren Huang, Shu-Kai Hsieh, Jia-Fei Hong, Yun-Zhu Chen, I-Li Su, Yong-Xiang Chen, and Sheng-Wei Huang. 2010. Chinese wordnet: Design and implementation of a cross-lingual knowledge processing infrastructure. *Journal of Chinese Information Processing*, 24(2):14–23. (in Chinese).

Hitoshi Isahara, Francis Bond, Kiyotaka Uchimoto, Masao Utiyama, and Kyoko Kanzaki. 2008. Development of the Japanese WordNet. In *Sixth International conference on Language Resources and Evaluation (LREC 2008)*, Marrakech.

Toru Ishida. 2006. Language grid: An infrastructure for intercultural collaboration. In *IEEE/IPSJ Symposium on Applications and the Internet (SAINT-06)*, pages 96–100. (keynote address).

Hanho Jeong. 2012. A comparison of the influence of electronic books and paper books on reading comprehension, eye fatigue, and perception. *The Electronic Library*, 30(3):390–408.

Frantisek Kratochvil and Luis Morgado da Costa. 2022. Abui Wordnet: Using a toolbox dictionary to develop a wordnet for a low-resource language. In *Proceedings of the first workshop on NLP applications to field linguistics*, pages 54–63, Gyeongju, Republic of Korea. International Conference on Computational Linguistics.

S. Lawrence, D.M. Pennock, G.W. Flake, R. Krovetz, F.M. Coetzee, E. Glover, F.A. Nielsen, A. Kruger, and C.L. Giles. 2001. Persistence of web references in scientific research. *Computer*, 34(2):26–31.

T.C. Lethbridge, J. Singer, and A. Forward. 2003. How software engineers use documentation: the state of the practice. *IEEE Software*, 20(6):35–39.

Krister Lindén and Lauri Carlson. 2010. Finnwordnet — wordnet påfinska via översättning. *LexicoNordica — Nordic Journal of Lexicography*, 17:119–140. In Swedish with an English abstract.

John P. McCrae, Michael Wayne Goodman, Francis Bond, Alexandre Rademaker, Ewa Rudnicka, and Luís Morgado da Costa. 2021. The global wordnet formats: Updates for 2020. In *11th International Global Wordnet Conference (GWC2021)*.

John P. McCrae, Alexandre Rademaker, Francis Bond, Ewa Rudnicka, and Christiane Fellbaum. 2019. English WordNet 2019 —an open-source wordnet for English. In *Proceedings of the 11th Global Wordnet Conference (GWC 2019)*.

Nurril Hirfana Mohamed Noor, Suerya Sapuan, and Francis Bond. 2011. Creating the open Wordnet Bahasa. In *Proceedings of the 25th Pacific Asia Conference on Language, Information and Computation (PACLIC 25)*, pages 258–267, Singapore.

Mortaza Montazery and Heshaam Faili. 2010. Automatic Persian wordnet construction. In *23rd International conference on computational linguistics*, pages 846–850.

Luis Morgado da Costa. 2020. Pinchah kristang: A dictionary of kristang. In *Proceedings of the Globalex2020 at the 12th Edition of the Language Resources and Evaluation Conference*, Marseille, France. European Language Resources Association (ELRA).

Noam Ordan and Shuly Wintner. 2007. Hebrew wordnet: a test case of aligning lexical databases across languages. *International Journal of Translation*, 19(1):39–58.

BoletteSandford Pedersen, Sanni Nimb, Jørg Asmussen, NicolaiHartvig Sørensen, Lars Trap-Jensen, and Henrik Lorentzen. 2009. DanNet — the challenge of compiling a wordnet for Danish by reusing a monolingual dictionary. *Language Resources and Evaluation*, 43(3):269–299.

Emanuele Pianta, Luisa Bentivogli, and Christian Girardi. 2002. Multiwordnet: Developing an aligned multilingual database. In *In Proceedings of the First International Conference on Global WordNet*, pages 293–302, Mysore, India.

Maciej Piasecki, Stan Szpakowicz, and Bartosz Broda. 2009. *A Wordnet from the Ground Up*. Wroclaw University of Technology Press. (ISBN 978-83-7493-476-3).

Marten Postma, Emiel van Miltenburg, Roxane Segers, Anneleen Schoen, and Piek Vossen. 2016. Open Dutch WordNet. In *Proceedings of the Eight Global Wordnet Conference*, Bucharest, Romania.

Ervin Ruci. 2008. On the current state of Albanet and related applications. Technical report, University of Vlora. (`http://fjalnet.com/technicalreportalbanet.pdf`).

Elkateb Sabri, William Black, Horacio Rodríguez, Musa Alkhalifa, Piek Vossen, Adam Pease, and Christiane Fellbaum. 2006. Building a wordnet for Arabic. In *In Proceedings of The fifth international conference on Language Resources and Evaluation (LREC 2006)*.

Benoît Sagot and Darja Fišer. 2008. Building a free French wordnet from multilingual resources. In *Proceedings of the Sixth International Language Resources and Evaluation (LREC'08)*, Marrakech, Morocco.

Melanie Siegel and Francis Bond. 2021. OdeNet: Compiling a German wordnet from other resources. In *Proceedings of the 11th Global Wordnet Conference (GWC 2021)*, pages 192–198.

Svavar Sigmundsson, editor. 1985. *Íslensk samheitaorðabók*. Styrktarsjóður Þórbergs Þórðarsonar og Margrétar Jónsdóttur, Háskóli Íslands, Reykjavík.

Joanna Ut-Seong Sio and Luis Morgado Da Costa. 2019. Building the Cantonese wordnet. In *Proceedings of the 10th Global WordNet Conference (GWC 2019)*, Wroclaw, Poland.

Sareewan Thoongsup, Thatsanee Charoenporn, Kergrit Robkop, Tan Sinthurahat, Chumpol Mokarat, Virach Sornlertlamvanich, and Hitoshi Isahara. 2009. Thai wordnet construction. In *Proceedings of The 7th Workshop on Asian Language Resources (ALR7), Joint conference of the 47th Annual Meeting of the Association for Computational Linguistics (ACL) and the 4th International Joint Conference on Natural Language Processing (IJCNLP),*, Suntec, Singapore.

Dan Tufiş, Radu Ion, Luigi Bozianu, Alexandru Ceauşu, and Dan Ştefănescu. 2008. Romanian wordnet: Current state, new applications and prospects. In *Proceedings of the 4th Global WordNet Association Conference*, pages 441–452, Szeged.

Piek Vossen, editor. 1998. *Euro WordNet*. Kluwer.

Piek Vosssen. 2002. Eurowordnet general document. Technical report, University of Amsterdam. Version 3.

Shan Wang and Francis Bond. 2013. Building the Chinese open wordnet (COW): Starting from core synsets. In *Sixth International Joint Conference on Natural Language Processing*, pages 10–18.

Mark D Wilkinson, Michel Dumontier, IJsbrand Jan Aalbersberg, Gabrielle Appleton, Myles Axton, Arie Baak, Niklas Blomberg, Jan-Willem Boiten, Luiz Bonino da Silva Santos, Philip E Bourne, et al. 2016. The FAIR guiding principles for scientific data management and stewardship. *Scientific data*, 3.

Adapting GermaNet for the Semantic Web using OntoLex-Lemon

Claus Zinn
Department of Linguistics
University of Tuebingen
Germany
claus.zinn
@uni-tuebingen.de

Marie Hinrichs
Department of Linguistics
University of Tuebingen
Germany
marie.hinrichs
@uni-tuebingen.de

Erhard Hinrichs
Department of Linguistics
University of Tuebingen
Germany
erhard.hinrichs
@uni-tuebingen.de

Abstract

GermaNet is a large lexical-semantic net that relates German nouns, verbs, and adjectives semantically. The word net has been manually constructed over the last 25 years and hence presents a high-quality, valuable resource for German. While GermaNet is maintained in a Postgres database, all its content can be exported as an XML-based serialisation. Recently, this XML representation has been converted into RDF, largely by staying close to GermaNet's principle of arrangement where *lexunits* that share the same meaning are grouped together into so-called *synsets*. With each lexical unit and synset now globally addressable via a unique resource identifier, it has become much easier to link together GermaNet entries with other lexical and semantic resources. In terms of semantic interoperability, however, the RDF variant of GermaNet leaves much to be desired. In this paper, we describe yet another conversion from GermaNet's XML representation to RDF. The new conversion makes use of the OntoLex-Lemon ontology, and therefore, presents a decisive step toward a GermaNet representation with a much higher level of semantic interoperability, and which makes it possible to use GermaNet with other wordnets that already support this conceptualisation of lexica.

1 Introduction

GermaNet was conceived in the mid-nineties (Hamp and Feldweg, 1997) and soon became the largest lexical-semantic wordnet for German. While it is still maintained as a relational database, it profited from quite a few format conversions in the meantime. With the wide adoption of the data interchange format XML, GermaNet's internal data representation – it is represented as a collection of relational database tables – was reformalized in terms of DTD-based document types. Four DTDs were defined: for synsets and their lexical unit children, for lexical and conceptual relations between them, for mapping GermaNet via the interlingual index to the Princeton Wordnet (Miller, 1995; Fellbaum, 1998), and for enriching GermaNet entries with Wiktionary paraphrases.[1] The current distribution of GermaNet provides both the database dump as well as an XML serialisation with XML documents that adhere to the DTD, and hence are syntactically valid. In total, the distribution encompasses 54 files (23 files for nouns, 15 files for verbs, and 16 files for adjectives). Each file name encodes the word category and the semantic class of the synsets they contain.[2] For each of the three word classes, there is also an XML file which encodes Wiktionary entries, and there is a single file for the XML encoding of the interlingual index and another file to encode the conceptual and lexical relations.

The single source of truth for GermaNet, however, is the Postgres-based database. A special-purpose tool called *GernEdit* is used to edit and extend the German wordnet (Henrich and Hinrichs, 2010a). Programming APIs in Java and Python are available to access all GermaNet information programmatically.[3] Users without a usage licence for GermaNet can use the web-based *Rover* application to explore GermaNet content. With Rover, users can also calculate and visualize the semantic relatedness between any two given synsets.

The latest version of GermaNet (release 17.0, April 2022) has about 205,000 lexical units and 159,514 synsets. There are 1,29 lexical units per

[1] In the EuroWordNet framework (Vossen, 1998) (see `https://archive.illc.uva.nl/EuroWordNet`), about 28,500 concepts from GermaNet have been linked to Princeton WordNet(R) 2.0. We have used mappings from WordNet(R) 2.0 to WordNet(R) 3.0 provided by the NLP group of the Universitat Politècnica de Catalunya to link GermaNet synsets to WordNet(R) 3.0. The mapping to WordNet(R) 3.0 was created automatically thus 100% accuracy of those mappings cannot be guaranteed.

[2] For instance, all nouns related to humans are given in the XML file nomen.Mensch.xml.

[3] `https://uni-tuebingen.de/en/142806` (Applications & Tools).

```xml
<synset id="s25806" category="nomen" class="Tier">
  <lexUnit id="l35305" sense="3" source="core" namedEntity="no" artificial="no" styleMarking="no">
    <orthForm>Ei</orthForm>
  </lexUnit>
</synset>
<synset id="s39427" category="nomen" class="Nahrung">
  <lexUnit id="l57850" sense="4" source="core" namedEntity="no" artificial="no" styleMarking="no">
    <orthForm>Ei</orthForm>
  </lexUnit>
  <lexUnit id="l57851" sense="1" source="core" namedEntity="no" artificial="no" styleMarking="no">
    <orthForm>Hühnerei</orthForm>
    <compound>
      <modifier category="Nomen">Huhn</modifier>
      <head>Ei</head>
    </compound>
  </lexUnit>
</synset>
<synset id="s73239" category="nomen" class="Form">
  <lexUnit id="l100105" sense="1" source="core" namedEntity="no" artificial="no" styleMarking="no">
    <orthForm>Ei</orthForm>
  </lexUnit>
</synset>
<synset id="s25813" category="nomen" class="Koerper">
  <lexUnit id="l35317" sense="1" source="core" namedEntity="no" artificial="no" styleMarking="no">
    <orthForm>Eizelle</orthForm>
    <compound>
      <modifier category="Nomen">Ei</modifier>
      <head>Zelle</head>
    </compound>
  </lexUnit>
  <lexUnit id="l35318" sense="1" source="core" namedEntity="no" artificial="no" styleMarking="no"> [2 lines]
  <lexUnit id="l90270" sense="1" source="core" namedEntity="no" artificial="no" styleMarking="yes"> [2 lines]
  <lexUnit id="l103438" sense="2" source="core" namedEntity="no" artificial="no" styleMarking="no">
    <orthForm>Ei</orthForm>
  </lexUnit>
</synset>
```

Figure 1: Four different entries for *Ei*.

synset. Moreover, GermaNet defines 173,742 conceptual relations between synsets, and 12,204 lexical relations between lexical units (excluding synonymy). In addition to conceptual relations known from Princeton WordNet, GermaNet also features a good number of lexical relations that have no correspondance in the Princeton Wordnet. The German language makes good use of compounds, and this is also reflected in the high number of compounds and their proper segmentation in subterms (115,366 compounds are represented).

GermaNet already has some substantial linking to external data sources such as 28,564 pointers to the interlingual index and 29,546 links to Wiktionary. Note that any linking to external data sources is established through "local" identifiers only so that contextual information (say, this is an identifier in Princeton Wordnet 2.0) is required to resolve or look-up such linkages.

It is worth pointing out that GermaNet has also been converted to the lexical markup framework (LMF, see (Vossen et al., 2013)), which is discussed in (Henrich and Hinrichs, 2010b).

Recently, we have converted GermaNet's XML serialisation of its database into RDF (Zinn et al., 2022). The conversion stayed close to GermaNet's conceptualisation of organising lexical-semantic nets (see Sect. 2). While our conversion of GermaNet into RDF comes with no information loss, it ignores the work of others that aim at defining a standard for the description of wordnets. One such standard for representing wordnets is the OntoLex-Lemon conceptualisation[4], which we briefly describe in Sect. 3. In Sect. 4, we show how we converted GermaNet's XML serialisation to the OntoLex-Lemon format and that most but not all of GermaNet content can be expressed in terms of this ontology. The conclusion and future work is discussed in Sect. 5.

2 Background

2.1 GermaNet Overview

In GermaNet, the meaning of a word, its word sense, is represented as a *lexical unit*. Word senses that express the same semantic concept are grouped together into *synsets*, a short form of synonym

[4]https://www.w3.org/2016/05/ontolex/

```
<relations>
  <con_rel name="has_hypernym" from="s68168" to="s25806" dir="revert" inv="has_hyponym"/> <!--- Vogelei -->
  <con_rel name="has_hypernym" from="s25806" to="s25809" dir="revert" inv="has_hyponym"/> <!--- Keim -->
  <lex_rel name="is_container_for" from="l115250" to="l57850" dir="one" />   <!--- Eierbecher -->
  <lex_rel name="has_ingredient" from="l58624" to="l57850" dir="one" />      <!--- Eierkuchen -->
</relations>

<interLingualIndex>
  <iliRecord lexUnitId="l103438" ewnRelation="synonym" pwnWord="egg cell" pwn20Id="ENG20-05144345-n"
    pwn30Id="ENG30-05457973-n" pwn20paraphrase="the female reproductive cell; the female gamete"
    source="initial"/>
  <iliRecord lexUnitId="l35305" ewnRelation="synonym" pwnWord="egg" pwn20Id="ENG20-01383930-n" [4 lines]
  <iliRecord lexUnitId="l57850" ewnRelation="synonym" pwnWord="egg" pwn20Id="ENG20-07367088-n"
    pwn30Id="ENG30-07840804-n"
    pwn20paraphrase="oval reproductive body of a fowl (especially a hen) used as food"
    source="initial"/>
</interLingualIndex>

<wiktionaryParaphrases>
    <wiktionaryParaphrase lexUnitId="l100105" wiktionaryId="w18622" wiktionarySenseId="3"
        wiktionarySense="ein ovales, dreidimensionales und entlang einer Achse symmetrisches Gebilde"
        edited="no"/>
    <wiktionaryParaphrase lexUnitId="l103438" wiktionaryId="w18622" wiktionarySenseId="0"
        wiktionarySense="eine Keimzelle" edited="no"/>
    <wiktionaryParaphrase lexUnitId="l35305" wiktionaryId="w18622" wiktionarySenseId="1" [2 lines]
    <wiktionaryParaphrase lexUnitId="l57850" wiktionaryId="w18622" wiktionarySenseId="2" [2 lines]
</wiktionaryParaphrases>
```

Figure 2: ILI and Wiktionary entries for *Ei*.

sets. To a large extent, GermaNet follows the design rationale of the Princeton WordNet for English, but there are, however, subtle differences that reflect the specifics of the German language. GermaNet's verbal frames, for instance, capture more detail than those represented in WordNet: reflexives, grammatical case, expletive subjects, and to-infinitives are explicitly encoded in GermaNet. With the German language making extensive use of compound constructions, GermaNet has rich descriptive means to describe them (see below).

2.2 GermaNet Example

GermaNet has four different lexical units with an orthographic form *Ei* (egg), which are distributed over the thematic domains *Form* (form), *Körper* (body), *Nahrung* (food), and *Tier* (animal), and therefore, distributed over four different files. Fig. 1 depicts the four lexical units, each of which is part of a different synset. Each synset comes with an identifier unique to GermaNet, a category encoding the part of speech of its lexUnits, and a class that marks their thematic domain. In GermaNet's XML representation, a lexical unit is always a child element of a synset. Each lexical unit also comes with a unique identifier, a sense identifier, and four other attributes: *namedEntity* specifies whether the lexical unit denotes a named entity or not; *styleMarking* is true if the lexical unit represents a stylistic variant; *artificial* is true if the lexical unit is used to represent an artificial node in the graph.[5] The source attribute is for internal use only. All attributes are mandatory. Each lexical unit must have a child *orthForm*. If the lexical unit is a compound, its head and modifier are also given. Fig. 1 also depicts two lexical units whose orthographic form is a compound, for instance, *Eizelle* (egg cell). In this case, GermaNet specifies the head of the compound *Zelle* and its modifier *Ei*. Note that GermaNet encodes eight different properties for compound constituents and seven modifier classes.

Fig. 2 depicts the three ILI records and the four entries into Wiktionary that GermaNet knows about the lemma *Ei*. An ILI record links a lexical unit of GermaNet via some relation to an entry into the Princeton Wordnet. It is worth to note that the target of the relation is (also) not an URI but an identifier locally unique to the wordnet. Note that *ewnRelation* encompasses not only *synonym* relationships but also *hypernym*, *hyponym*, *is_caused_by*, *causes* relationships, among others. Usually, a paraphrase from Princeton WordNet 2.0 is given.

Fig. 2 also shows four entries into Wiktionary paraphrases (again, some lines omitted), a useful addition to GermaNet data. – Note that both linkages were established more than 10 years ago and need to be updated and extended, where possible.

[5]GermaNet is a completely connected graph hierarchy without any dangling subgraphs, whereas WordNet consists of several distinct hierarchies – one for each semantic field.

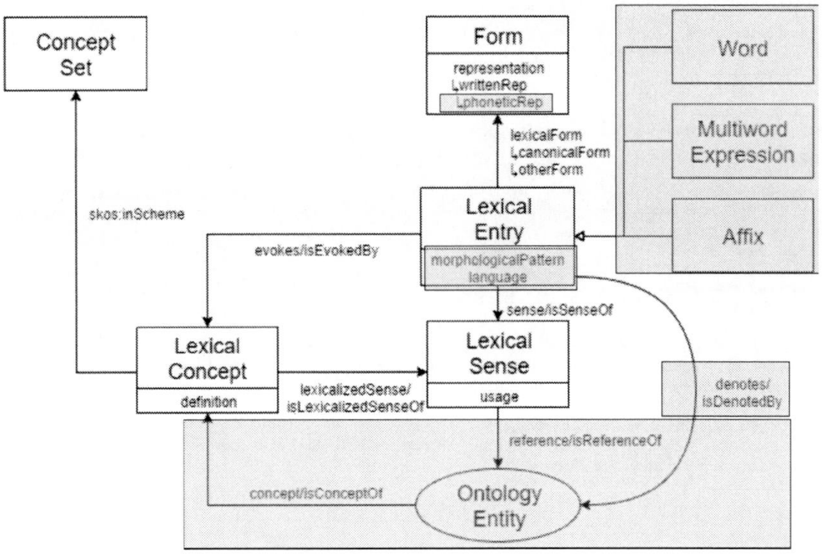

Figure 3: Core model of OntoLex.

3 OntoLex-Lemon's Design Principle

Fig. 3 depicts the core model of OntoLex, see also (McCrae et al., 2012).

In GermanNet's XML serialisation, a *synset* element contains one or more elements of type *lexUnit*, which in turn has a single obligatory child *orthForm* and optional children such as *compound*, or orthographic variants. Much information is encoded into XML attributes. The *category* attribute at the *synset* level encodes part-of-speech information whereas the *sense* attribute at the *lexUnit* level encodes a sense identifier marking a lemma (*orthForm*) as being part of several synsets.

In OntoLex, the structure of a lexical-semantic net is different with *Lexical Entry* encoding the entries of a lexicon. Each entry has a *Form* (the written representation, mirroring GermaNet's *orthForm* element), and a *Lexical Sense*, which in turn is the lexicalized sense of a *Lexical Concept*, the equivalent of a GermaNet *synset*.

4 Conversion and Extension

4.1 Conversion to OntoLex-Lemon

Our conversion makes use of all parts of OntoLex-Lemon apart from the items greyed out in Fig. 3.

Fig. 4 depicts a fragment of our conversion from GermaNet to the OntoLex-Lemon conceptualisation. Compared with the four occurrences shown in Fig. 1, there is now a single lexical entry having a *Form* with the written representation *Ei*.[6] In line with our example entries given in Fig. 1, this lexical entry has four different lexical senses, and hences evokes four different lexical concepts. Each sense inherits the *lexUnit* identifier of our XML representation, and each lexical concept inherits the respective *synset* identifier.

Note that our conversion failed to map information that in the GermaNet representation of *lexunit* is expressed in terms of attributes: *namedEntity*, *artificial*, and *styleMarking*. In these cases, we fall back to our initial conversion approach using our own *gn* vocabulary.

Fig. 4 also shows a number of conceptual relations between the lexical concept evoked by *Ei* and its super- and subclasses (hypernym and hyponym). Lexical relations are attached to the resources of type *LexicalSense*. At the time of writing, we still reuse our own vocabulary to express lexical relations.

Note that a lexical concept comes with two attributes that specify their semantic field: *skos:inScheme* carries the German name of the semantic field. and *dc:subject* carries its English translation.[7]

[6]For the sake of brevity, we have chosen to use a blank node to refer to something that has a written representation.

[7]As Henrich (2015) pointed out: "the semantic fields resemble the unique beginners in WordNet. However, mainly due to language specific differences of the two wordnets, the lists are not exactly identical: for instance, labels Verhalten and privativ are not available in WordNet, while act and process are not used in GermaNet".

```
gn:Ei-n
        a ontolex:LexicalEntry ;
        lexinfo:partOfSpeech lexinfo:noun ;
        ontolex:canonicalForm [ ontolex:writtenRep "Ei"
                              ] ;
        ontolex:evokes gn:s25806 , gn:s25813 , gn:s39427 , gn:s73239 ;
        ontolex:sense gn:l100105 , gn:l103438 , gn:l35305 , gn:l57850 .

gn:l35305
        a ontolex:LexicalSense ;
        ontolex:isLexicalizedSenseOf gn:s25806 ;
        ontolex:isSenseOf gn:Ei-n ;
        gn:pwn20Id "ENG20-01383930-n" ;
        gn:pwn30Id "ENG30-01460457-n" ;
        gn:pwn31Id pwn:01463098-n ;
        gn:pwnWord "egg" ;
        gn:ewnRelation "synonym" ;
        gn:pwn20paraphrase "animal reproductive body consisting of an ovum or embryo
             together with nutritive and protective envelopes, especially the thin-shelled
             reproductive body laid by e.g. female birds  " ;
        gn:source "extension2" ;
        gn:wiktionaryId deu:__ws_2_Ei__Substantiv__1 ;
        gn:wiktionaryParaphraseSense "ein Schalengebilde, in dem sich der Embryo oviparer
             Tierarten (zum Beispiel Vögel) bildet" .

gn:s25806
        a ontolex:LexicalConcept ;
        dc:subject "animal" ;
        lexinfo:hypernym gn:s25809 ;
        lexinfo:hyponym gn:s135770 , gn:s149751 , gn:s160160 , gn:s162329 , gn:s162330 ,
                        gn:s25807 , gn:s68168 , gn:s90915 ;
        skos:inScheme gn:Tier ;
        ontolex:isEvokedBy gn:Ei-n ;
        ontolex:lexicalizedSense gn:l35305 .

gn:l120904
        a ontolex:LexicalSense ;
        ontolex:isLexicalizedSenseOf gn:s90038 ;
        ontolex:isSenseOf gn:Eizahn-n ;
        gn:has_purpose_of_usage gn:l35305 .

gn:l115784
        a ontolex:LexicalSense ;
        ontolex:isLexicalizedSenseOf gn:s85952 ;
        ontolex:isSenseOf gn:Eischale-n ;
        gn:is_part_of gn:l35305 .

gn:l115785
        a ontolex:LexicalSense ;
        ontolex:isLexicalizedSenseOf gn:s85952 ;
        ontolex:isSenseOf gn:Eierschale-n ;
        gn:is_part_of gn:l35305 .

gn:s68168
        a ontolex:LexicalConcept ;
        dc:subject "animal" ;
        lexinfo:hypernym gn:s25806 ;
        skos:inScheme gn:Tier ;
        ontolex:isEvokedBy gn:Vogelei-n ;
        ontolex:lexicalizedSense gn:l94207 .
```

Figure 4: OntoLex example encoding of GermaNet.

German Compounds. GermaNet has information about over 115,000 nominal compounds, splits them into their constituent parts, and labels them with linguistic information. In GermaNet, the constituents of compounds can have one of the following eight properties, see Fig. 5, also see (Henrich, 2015, Chapt. 3.6) and (Henrich and Hinrichs, 2011). This kind of information makes particular sense for German, where compounds are almost always spelled as one word.

Consider, for instance, the GermaNet's lexical unit *l36389* with orthographic form *Tollwut* (rabies). The modifier of the compound is *toll* of class *adjective* and its head is *Wut*.[8]

In our representation in Ontolex, we have chosen the following representation:

```
gn:Tollwut-n
        a ontolex:LexicalEntry ;
        lexinfo:partOfSpeech lexinfo:noun ;
        decomp:subterm gn:Wut-n ,
                       gn:toll-adj ;
        ontolex:canonicalForm [ ontolex:writtenRep "Tollwut"
                              ] ;
        ontolex:evokes gn:s26628 ;
        ontolex:sense gn:l36389 .
```

It consists of two *subterm* triples pointing to the lexical entries *Wut-n* and *toll-adj*. In this case, both lexical entries are part of GermaNet so that both subterms properly resolve. There are many other examples, however, where this is not the case, in particular in cases where modifiers are adverbs, particles, prepositions, or pronouns. Those word classes are not (yet) represented in GermaNet. This is an issue we have yet to resolve.

It is also clear that the *decomp:subterm* property does not distinguish between heads and modifiers, and cannot represent the information given in Fig. 5, so more work is required here.

GermaNet has a rich representation of verbal frames. For the representation of syntactic frames, we consider using the lexinfo ontology[9] (verb frame), but this is not done yet.

4.2 Processing ILI and Wiktionary Information

Fig. 4 has a number of triples whose properties have the namespace *gn:*, and hence do not make use of vocabularies such as *ontolex* or *lexinfo*. Consider, for instance, the information stemming from the Interlingual Index, which are all associated with the lexical sense of the lexical entry *Ei*:

```
gn:l35305
   gn:pwn20Id "ENG20-01383930-n" ;
   gn:pwn30Id "ENG30-01460457-n" ;
```

[8]The other classes are *adverb*, *noun*, *particle*, *preposition*, *pronoun*, and *verb*, see (Henrich, 2015, Chapt. 3.6).

[9]http://www.lexinfo.net/ontology/3.0/lexinfo.

Property	Example (and explanation, if needed)
abbreviation*	*IP* 'IP' in *IP-Paket* 'IP packet'
affixoid*	affixoids have a special grammatical status between bound and free morphemes; e.g., *haupt* 'main' in *Hauptbahnhof* 'main station'
foreign word*	*Offset* 'offset' in *Offsetdruck* 'offset printing'
combining form*§ (German: *konfix*)	bound morphemes which are borrowed from a foreign language and whose meaning stems from that particular language, e.g., *bio-* 'organic' in *Biosiegel* 'organic seal'
opaque morpheme*	*Him-* in *Himbeere* 'rasperry'
proper name†	*Valentin* 'Valentine' in *Valentinstag* 'Valentine's Day'
virtual word form‡	*Zieher* nominalization for 'to pull' (word does not exist in isolation) in *Schraubenzieher* 'screwdriver'
word group†	*drei Zimmer* 'three-room' in *Dreizimmerwohnung* 'three-room flat'

Figure 5: Properties for compound constituents, see (Henrich, 2015, Chapt. 3.6)

```
gn:pwn31Id pwn:01463098-n ;
gn:hasILIid ili:i42980 ;
```

Note that the first two triples stem from the mapping between GermaNet and the Interlingual Index.[10] Their objects make use of Princeton Wordnet (PWN) identifiers that do not resolve automatically. As part of the conversion, we have used a mapping from PWN 3.0 to PWN 3.1 to update the identifiers to the latest version of PWN (Zendel, 2019). The predicate `pwn31Id` now points to a resolvable URI into the RDF version of the Princeton WordNet.[11] Moreover, using the mapping between PWN 3.0 to the CILI (Bond et al., 2016) supplied by Francis Bond[12], `gn:hasILIid` points to the `http://globalwordnet.org/ili/` (namespace prefix `ili`).

The linkage of GermaNet with Wiktionary dates back to 2011 and made use of a large Wiktionary dump in order to automatically harvest sense definitions from the German Wiktionary for GermaNet senses (Henrich et al., 2014b). The *wiktionaryId* on Fig. 2 was introduced for purely technical reasons and cannot be used to lookup Wiktionary content in the current release.

During the conversion process, we downloaded a recent RDF version of Wiktionary and established a local SPARQL endpoint. We then queried the endpoint for all subjects that have a *skos:definition* to a node whose value is string-identical to the passphrase of the 2011 data linkage. The *gn:wiktionaryId* now points to a new resolvable URI.

4.3 Linkage to Other Lexical Resources

With GermaNet now being available in RDF, it is tempting to link its content to other resources in the Linked Data world. As a start, we have established links to Wikidata and the authority files of the German National Library.

GermaNet has a wealth of information on nouns with the semantic field *Ort* (*location*). Entries range from *Tagungshotel* (conference hotel) to 25 entries centered around the concept of *Gefängnis* (prison) such as *Frauengefängnis* and *Gefängnisinsel*. A substantial part of the information, however, represents names for cities, rivers, and mountains, and other geographic places. For this kind of information, a valuable subset of the *Integrated Authority File* (GND)[13] of the German National Library is available, namely, the subset holding *Geographika* with approximately 4.5 million triples.

The query for the geographical dataset is rather simple, searching for all entities where the *preferredNameForThePlaceOrGeographicName* of an entity is the location name, say *Potsdam*. As a result, the synset *s43887* with its lexical unit *l63714* and its orthographic form *Potsdam* was automatically linked to the entity `https://d-nb.`

[10] `https://tinyurl.com/y9znkzjz`

[11] `http://wordnet-rdf.princeton.edu/id`

[12] `https://github.com/globalwordnet/cili.git`

[13] `https://gnd.network`

info/gnd/4046948-7 of the GND dataset. The semantic linkage gives users access to a variety of information such as alternative names or lexicalisations (*e.g.*, Bostanium, Potestampium, Pozdam), the geographical coordinates in terms of latitude and longitude, and other information (*Hauptstadt vom Bundesland Brandenburg, kreisfreie Stadt, 993 als Poztupimi urkundl. erwähnt, 1317 Stadt*), hence demonstrating the potential of linked data. In this initial work, 1778 GermaNet entries were linked to entities in the subset of the GND dataset.

We have also queried Wikidata for location names. Here, the situation is more complicated, in part due to the crowd-sourcing approach of the platform, and because no geographical subset of Wikidata is readily available. We hence had to guide our search to only take into account entities whose type indicate their geographic nature. In Wikidata, there are a large amount of location types such as *big city*, *capital*, *city*, *state of the USA*, *river*, *commune of France*, *town*, *geographic region*, *country*, *historical country*, *inferior planet*, *peninsula*, *sea*, *ocean etc.* so that the query to Wikidata becomes quite complex.

At the time of writing, we were able to establish 2,564 links to Wikidata entries of type location. For *Potsdam*, two Wikidata entries were found: the wikidata entity *Q1711*, found via the location type *big city* (Q1549591), and the wikidata entity *Q1022943*, identified via the location type *town of the United States* (Q15127012). For GermaNet, it can be argued that only the first hit should be linked, but we decided to include all associations.

4.4 Implementation Details

Our conversion takes GermaNet's XML-based serialisation of its database content as a starting point. The conversion has been implemented in Prolog using SWI-Prolog, its built-in library `sgml` for XML parsing and its semantic web library `semweb/rdf11`. The conversion processes all main input files for nouns, verbs, and adjectives, the XML file that defines conceptual and lexical relations, and the ILI and Wiktionary files. While those files are being parsed, RDF triples are being asserted. At the end of the process, the triple store is written into a file resulting in approximately 3.5 million triples.

5 Conclusion and Future Work

There have been two prominent translations of Princeton Wordnet into RDF (Graves and Gutierrez, 2006; van Assem et al., 2006), but there is only one that uses the *lemon* vocabulary (McCrae et al., 2014). In this paper, we have described our conversion of GermaNet's XML format to a RDF representation that makes use of the OntoLex-Lemon conceptualisation, hence mirroring the work of McCrae and colleagues for GermaNet. This makes it possible for GermaNet to be part of a linked data cloud that combines rich linguistic information from various, high-quality resources.

In the near future, we will complement our conversion to include a more detailed representation of nominal compounds, and we still have to tackle the issue of representing syntactic frame information using the *lexinfo* vocabulary. The aim is to replace, whenever possible, our local vocabulary (in the namespace *gn*) with well-known terminology well-defined elsewhere. In this regard, GermaNet is monitoring recent developments in the Global Wordnet Formats (McCrae et al., 2021). Hence, our RDF version of GermaNet should not be considered final (yet) but open to change in the future.

Future work includes linking GermaNet with other RDF-based resources. In part, this is already done, as we have seen with the introduction of the ILI link into the RDF-based Princeton WordNet. At the time of writing, our GermaNet resource identifiers are not yet web-resolvable. In the future, an HTTP request to, say, `https://uni-tuebingen.de/germanet/v17/Ei-n`, will return the top left part of Fig. 4.

Rover, a web-based user interface for the exploration and visualization of GermaNet data (Hinrichs et al., 2020) is currently using the XML representation and the Java API in the back-end. In the future, we would like to experiment with using a back-end that executes SPARQL queries on the triple store.

GermaNet is free for academic users with a signed license.[14] For licence holders, both the database and the XML export are included in the data download.[15] In the future, licence holders will also be able to obtain the RDF export of GermaNet.

[14] `https://uni-tuebingen.de/en/142806` (Licenses).

[15] The mapping from GermaNet to Wiktionary and the ILI can be downloaded separately from GermaNet.

For accessing RDF-data via the Web, we will follow our technical solution taken for our web-based Rover application: a sign-in via the CLARIN Service Provider Federation will allow users to authenticate as academic user, and subsequently, make use of the SPARQL endpoint to GermaNet.

The main reason for having an RDF-based representation of GermaNet, however, is to unleash its potential when properly linked to other high-quality lexical sources. In the context of the Text+ project, it is our aim to link GermaNet with the DWDS dictionary of the German language[16] and also with the Leipzig Corpora Collection[17]. There are plans to convert both resources into RDF, which would allow the creation of a linked data cloud for the German language. In addition, we plan to link GermaNet to the lexicographical data of Wikidata[18].

Mapping location entities of one dataset to the locations of another dataset is relatively straightforward. In general, the main task to properly link together nodes from different RDF graphs is – essentially – a word disambiguation task. Our work will build upon Henrich et al. (2014b), where GermaNet senses were linked to wiktionary senses, and Henrich et al. (2014a), where word senses in GermaNet were linked with those in the DWDS Dictionary of the German Language. The linking task will be supported by the WebCAGe corpus (Henrich et al., 2012).

[16]https://www.dwds.de

[17]https://corpora.uni-leipzig.de/

[18]https://wikidata.org

References

Francis Bond, Piek Vossen, John McCrae, and Christiane Fellbaum. 2016. CILI: the Collaborative Interlingual Index. In *Proceedings of the 8th Global WordNet Conference (GWC)*, pages 50–57, Bucharest, Romania. Global Wordnet Association.

Christiane Fellbaum. 1998. *WordNet: An Electronic Lexical Database*. The MIT Press.

Alvaro Graves and Claudio Gutierrez. 2006. Data representations for WordNet: A case for RDF. In *3rd International WordNet Conference, GWC 2006*. Masaryk University, Brno. South Jeju Island, Korea.

Birgit Hamp and Helmut Feldweg. 1997. GermaNet - a Lexical-Semantic Net for German. In *Proceedings of the ACL workshop Automatic Information Extraction and Building of Lexical Semantic Resources for NLP Applications*. Madrid, Spain.

Verena Henrich. 2015. *Word Sense Disambiguation with GermaNet*. Ph.D. thesis, Univerisity of Tuebingen. http://dx.doi.org/10.15496/publikation-4706.

Verena Henrich and Erhard Hinrichs. 2010a. GernEdiT: A graphical tool for GermaNet development. In *Proceedings of the ACL 2010 System Demonstrations*, pages 19–24, Uppsala, Sweden. Association for Computational Linguistics.

Verena Henrich and Erhard Hinrichs. 2010b. Standardizing wordnets in the ISO standard LMF: Wordnet-LMF for GermaNet. In *Proceedings of the 23rd International Conference on Computational Linguistics (Coling 2010)*, pages 456–464, Beijing, China. Coling 2010 Organizing Committee.

Verena Henrich and Erhard Hinrichs. 2011. Determining immediate constituents of compounds in GermaNet. In *Proceedings of the International Conference Recent Advances in Natural Language Processing 2011*, pages 420–426, Hissar, Bulgaria. Association for Computational Linguistics.

Verena Henrich, Erhard Hinrichs, and Reinhild Barkey. 2014a. Aligning Word Senses in GermaNet and the DWDS Dictionary of the German Language. In *Proceedings of the 7th Global WordNet Conference (GWC 2014)*, pages 63–70. Tartu, Estonia.

Verena Henrich, Erhard Hinrichs, and Tatiana Vodolazova. 2012. WebCAGe – a Web-Harvested Corpus Annotated with GermaNet Senses. In *Proceedings of the 13th Conference of the European Chapter of the Association for Computational Linguistics (EACL 2012)*, pages 387–396. Avignon, France.

Verena Henrich, Erhard Hinrichs, and Tatiana Vodolazova. 2014b. Aligning GermaNet Senses with Wiktionary Sense Definitions. In *Human Language Technology: Challenges for Computer Science and Linguistics*, pages 329–342.

Marie Hinrichs, Richard Lawrence, and Erhard Hinrichs. 2020. Exploring and Visualizing Wordnet Data with GermaNet Rover. In *Proceedings of the CLARIN Annual Conference*, pages 32–36.

John P. McCrae, Guadalupe Aguado de Cea, Paul Buitelaar, Philipp Cimiano, Thierry Declerck, Asunción Gómez-Pérez, Jorge Gracia, Laura Hollink, Elena Montiel-Ponsoda, Dennis Spohr, and Tobias Wunner. 2012. Interchanging lexical resources on the Semantic Web. *Lang. Resour. Evaluation*, 46(4):701–719.

John P. McCrae, Christiane D. Fellbaum, and Philipp Cimiano. 2014. Publishing and Linking WordNet using lemon and RDF. In *Proceedings of the 3rd Workshop on Linked Data in Linguistics*.

John P. McCrae, Michael Wayne Goodman, Francis Bond, Alexandre Rademaker, Ewa Rudnicka, and Luís Morgado da Costa. 2021. The Global Wordnet Formats: Updates for 2020. In *Proceedings of the 11th Global Wordnet Conference, GWC 2021, University of South Africa (UNISA), Potchefstroom, South Africa, January 18-21, 2021*, pages 91–99. Global Wordnet Association.

George A. Miller. 1995. Wordnet: A lexical database for english. *Commun. ACM*, 38(11):39–41.

Mark van Assem, Aldo Gangemi, and Guus Schreiber. 2006. Conversion of wordnet to a standard RDF/OWL representation. In *Proceedings of the Fifth International Conference on Language Resources and Evaluation, LREC 2006, Genoa, Italy, May 22-28, 2006*, pages 237–242. European Language Resources Association (ELRA).

Piek Vossen, editor. 1998. *EuroWordNet: A multilingual database with lexical semantic networks*. Springer Dordrecht.

Piek Vossen, Claudia Soria, and Monica Monachini. 2013. *Wordnet-LMF: A Standard Representation for Multilingual Wordnets*, pages 51–66. Wiley.

Oliver Zendel. 2019. Wordnet v3.0 vs. v3.1 mapping. `https://github.com/ozendelait/wordnet-to-json`.

Claus Zinn, Marie Hinrichs, and Erhard Hinrichs. 2022. Adapting GermaNet for the Semantic Web. In *Proceedings of the 18th Conference on Natural Language Processing (KONVENS 2022)*, pages 41–47, Potsdam, Germany.

Incorporating Prepositions in the BulTreeBank WordNet

Zara Kancheva
Institute of Information and Communication Technologies,
Bulgarian Academy of Sciences / Sofia, Bulgaria
zara@bultreebank.org

Abstract

A model for preposition incorporation in the BulTreeBank WordNet is presented which follows the model for presenting open class words in wordnets. An adapted semantic classification of prepositions is done on the base of Bulgarian grammars and the classes are used for synset categories. The good coverage of prepositions in the wordnet will be used for the aim of neural language models creation for Bulgarian. This extension of the wordnet improves its utility for semantic annotation.

1 Introduction

The paper aims at presenting a model for preposition incorporation in the BulTreeBank WordNet (BTB-WN) (Osenova and Simov, 2018). Prepositions are considered a beneficial extension of the part of speech coverage of BTB-WN, because they would improve its utility for semantic annotation, word sense disambiguation, machine translation, etc. Additionally, they would provide a better quality of neural language models for Bulgarian, which is the long term purpose of this task.

BTB-WN was created on the base of the Core WordNet subset[1] of Princeton WordNet (PWN) (Fellbaum, 1998) that contains the 5000 most frequent English senses. After that it was expanded with content words from the BulTreeBank and a Bulgarian frequency list, as well as with senses from the Bulgarian versions of Wikipedia and Wiktionary. Initially it was mapped to the PWN, but since 2020 it shifted to the Open English WordNet (McCrae et al., 2020), because it is being developed and updated, in contrast to the PWN. The current version of BTB-WN[2] – 4.0 – contains more than 33 000 synsets and could be browsed online[3]. BTB-WN will be soon freely available for downloading in the WordNet LMF format.

Prepositions like any other closed class words usually are not presented in wordnets, including BTB-WN, which contains the four most common parts of speech – nouns, verbs, adjectives and adverbs. Prepositions are one of the most frequent and at the same time ambiguous parts of speech and additionally the independence of their semantics is often argued (Baldwin et al., 2009). Here a semantic categorisation of Bulgarian prepositions is done and the model for presenting prepositions in BTB-WN follows the model for the open class words.

Prepositions serve to establish different relations between words: on one hand grammatical – they indicate the syntactic position of words in phrases (object, adverbial, modifier), and on the other hand semantic – they reveal their sense relations (local, temporal, causal, etc.). In this research only the semantic function of prepositions is considered. Section 2 gives an overview of different preposition research, Section 3 presents the semantic preposition classification that is used, Section 4 contains the synset model for prepositions in BTB-WN, and Section 5 concludes the paper.

2 Related Works

Bulgarian grammars classify prepositions by their origin, morphological composition and semantics. A detailed review of the history of preposition classifications is presented in Konstantinova (1982). For the aim of preposition incorporation in BTB-WN two classifications are considered and a new more compact categorization is compiled (Boyadzhiev et al. (1998), Stoyanov (1983)).

The role of prepositions in NLP and the variety of approaches towards their processing are thor-

[1] http://wordnetcode.princeton.edu/standoff-files/core-wordnet.txt

[2] https://clada-bg.eu/bg/centers-and-services/language-technologies/btb-wordnet.html

[3] https://concordance.webclark.org/

Semantic Class	Synset category	Prepositions
locative	prep.location	в, всред, върху, въз, връз, до, за, зад, из, низ, изпод, измежду, извън, край, към, между, на, над, насред, о, около, от, откъм, отвъд, отсам, оттам, оттатък, по, под, подир, подире, помежду, посред, пред, през, при, против, след, сред, срещу, спроти, у
temporal	prep.time	в, всред, до, за, между, край, към, на, насред, около, от, по, подир, подире, помежду, посред, пред, през, при, с, след, спроти, сред, срещу
manner and instrument of action	prep.manner	без, в, като, на, по, под, посредством, при, с (със), според, чрез
cause	prep.cause	за, заради, от, по, поради, пред
purpose	prep.purpose	върху, до, за, заради, към, по, поради
possession	prep.possession	на, от, с, у
origin and part of a whole	prep.origin	в, от
quantitative, degree and exceeding of a limit	prep.quantity	до, за, към, между, на, над, около, от, с (със), около, свръх
exchange	prep.obj.exchange	вместо, за, заради, наместо, срещу, спроти
exclusion	prep.obj.exclusion	без, освен
opinion	prep.obj.opinion	за, по, според, спрямо
thought	prep.obj.thought	върху, връз, въз, за, заради, около, по, спрямо
transition	prep.transition	в, на, от
comparison	prep.comparison	като
opposition	prep.opposition	въпреки, против, пряко, спроти, срещу

Table 1: Semantic classes and synset categories of prepositions

oughly presented in Baldwin et al. (2009) and here I will outline only some of the most relevant research on the topic. Schneider et al. (2015) introduce a taxonomy of preposition functions called supersenses for classification of prepositions. The work is directed towards automatic word sense disambiguation and the classification is aimed to be suitable for manual annotation. 73 preposition supersenses are determined and mapped to other resources such as VerbNet[4].

There are two resources particularly dedicated to prepositions: PrepNet (Saint-Dizier, 2008) and the Preposition Project (Litkowski and Hargraves, 2005). The Preposition Project is a semantic database for English prepositions which has been used for word sense disambiguation. It combines data for prepositions from a dictionary and from FrameNet[5], where English prepositions are functionally tagged. PrepNet was originally build for French, but later extended for several languages. The approach in PrepNet is inspired by thematic role classifications and it also uses data from FrameNet.

O'Hara and Wiebe (2009) approached preposition disambiguation using the semantic roles from Penn Treebank, the semantic network Factotum and FrameNet, and hypernyms from the Princeton WordNet[6].

Preposition classifications particularly directed towards wordnets are done by Amaro (2018) and Harabagiu (1996). Harabagiu (1996) shows an approach where by using information from Princeton WordNet and applying inferential heuristics two types of phrases are analysed – *noun+preposition+noun* and *verb+preposition+noun*. The phrases are organized in classes if there are *hyperonymy*, *hyponymy* or *synonymy* relations between the verbs and the nouns in the phrases or if they have common hypernym/hyponym.

Amaro (2018) presents a very interesting approach towards preposition integration in wordnet, including visual description by using typical wordnet relations for Portuguese prepositions. The integration is not large scale, only prepositions for movement are processed and the following relations are introduced: *synonymy*, *antonymy*, *hyponymy/hyperonymy* and *causes/is caused by*.

As far as I am concerned BulNet[7] is the only wordnet that has prepositions but the incorporation in it is not beneficial enough for many NLP tasks – they are presented with definitions, synonyms,

[4]https://verbs.colorado.edu/verbnet/

[5]https://framenet.icsi.berkeley.edu/fndrupal/

[6]https://wordnet.princeton.edu/

[7]http://dcl.bas.bg/en/resursi/wordnet/

examples and English translations, but they do not have any relations.

Another relevant work is the research of Da Costa and Bond (2016) on the incorporation of non referential words in wordnet. They expand the Open Multilingual Wordnet[8] with interjections and numeral classifiers motivated by the task of semantic annotation, similarly to the case of BTB-WN. For interjections two relations are used: *exemplifies* (with other parts of speech) and *see also* (with interjections). For the classifiers *exemplifies* is used, but also two new relations are introduced: *classifies* and *classified by*. The Penn Discourse Treebank also contains annotations of closed class words including some prepositions Prasad et al. (2019).

My approach is similar to that of Amaro (2018) and Harabagiu (1996), because the presentation of prepositions in BTB-WN is following the model for the open class words in wordnets.

3 Semantic Classification of Prepositions

For their integration in BTB-WN prepositions have been semantically classified in 15 groups: `location`, `time`, `transition`, `manner and instrument of action`, `possession`, `quantity`, `degree and exceeding of limit`, `purpose`, `origin and part of a whole`, `opposition`, `comparison`, `cause` and `object class`: `exchange`, `exclusion`, `opinion` and `thought`.

There are several differences from the grammars in the adapted classification mainly motivated by the aim of having a more compact and general-purpose system. For example, the classes `manner of action` (слушам с внимание 'listen with attention') and `instrument of action` (пиша с молив 'write with a pencil') here are united in one class, because they are very closely related. The same applies for the `origin` (тя е от града 'she is from the city') and `part of a whole` (яж от този хляб 'eat from this bread') classes. The `approximation of time` (към 9 часа 'around 9 o'clock') and `approximation of quantity` (около 3 килограма 'about 3 kilograms') classes from Stoyanov (1983) here are included respectively in the `time` and `quantity` classes. The `exceeding of limit` sense (това е свръх възможностите ми 'this is beyond my abilities') is included in the `quantity` category. An `object` superclass is outlined to unite the expression of relations for `exchange` (отиди вместо мен 'go instead of me'), `exclusion` (няма други гости освен семейството 'there are no other guests except the family'), `thought` (разкажи ми за пътешествието 'tell me about the journey') and `opinion` (според мен това е добра идея 'to me this is a good idea'). The *prep.obj.thought* class includes expression of object of thought, speech and writing. The metaphorical usages of a given class are considered part of it, not a separate class. For instance, usages like "Тия неща са врязани в паметта ми." ('These things are etched in my memory') are considered as examples of the `location` class.

4 Preposition Synset Model

Preposition synsets have synset category (based on their semantic class), detailed definition, examples, synonyms if available and as much as possible relations. The part of speech value for prepositions in BTB-WN is `p`, following the format of the Global WordNet Association[9]. An example is shown in Figure 1 with the synsets for preposition в ('in').

The main intention for the preposition relations is that they follow the relations model of any other part of speech in wordnets. Two types of relations are used: between preposition synsets and between a preposition synset and other parts of speech. Examples for the first type are: *synonymy* (the prepositions върху, във, връз, на 'over, on' all express position or motion over some surface, something or someone), *antonymy* (върху 'over' is antonym of под 'under'), *hyperonymy* and *hyponymy* (в 'in' in its most general meaning for 'position or action in the limits of something, somewhere' is hypernym of several prepositions which express more specific location relations, such as сред, всред, насред, посред 'in the middle', из, низ, по 'through', между 'between', през, пряко 'across'), *similar* (върху 'over' is similar with над 'above'). The second type is intended to link combinations of verbs and prepositions (and as a plan for future work – nouns and prepositions) which tend to express a particular meaning together (such as the combination of the verb превръщам се 'turn into' and the preposition в 'in, into' express `transition in new state`). The *sem-derived-from* relation can be

[8] compling.hss.ntu.edu.sg/omw/

[9] https://globalwordnet.github.io/schemas/

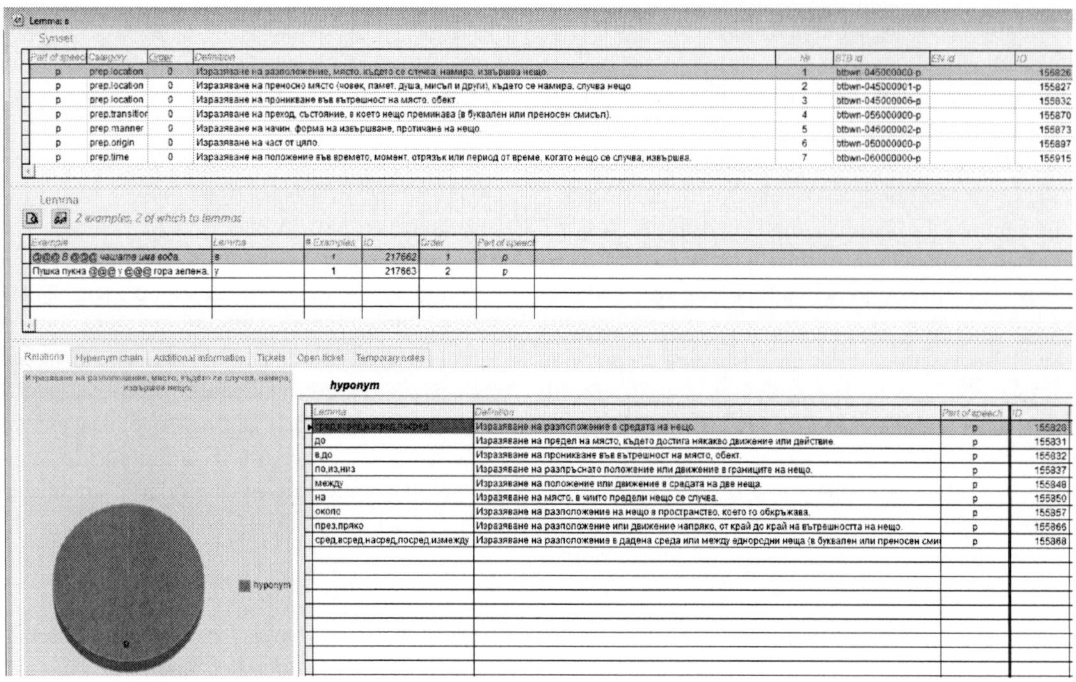

Figure 1: Preposition synsets in the CLaDA-BG Dict – the editing system for BTB-WN

used both between prepositions and between prepositions and other parts of speech (върху 'over' is derived from the noun връх 'top' and so does the preposition свръх 'above', so they are also linked with this relation). More relations applicable to prepositions are planned to be considered.

Currently 62 preposition lemmas are available in BTB-WN with 105 synsets. The most polysemous prepositions prove to be на (most frequently could be translated as 'on', 'of', 'in', etc.) with 12 synsets, followed by по ('over', 'in', 'on', etc.) with 11 synsets. The prepositions за ('for', 'to', 'about', etc.) and от ('from') are part of nine synsets each; с ('with') is in eight synsets and до ('to', 'until', etc.) and в ('in', 'at') are found in seven. As Table 1 shows the `locative` class has the most prepositions – 42, followed by `time` with 24 and `manner` and `quantity` with 11 prepositions.

5 Conclusion and Future Work

An attempt for preposition incorporation in the BTB-WN is presented. A semantic classification of prepositions is adapted on the base of Bulgarian grammars. The preposition synsets follow the structure and relations model of the nouns, verbs, adjectives and adverbs in wordnets and currently six semantic relations are introduced for prepositions: *synonymy*, *antonymy*, *hyperonymy*, *hyponymy*, *similarity* and *semantic derivation*. There are several directions in which this research would be elaborated: the hierarchy inheritance and categorization of the verbs and nouns in wordnet will be used and also features from a valency lexicon for Bulgarian – it will provide data about the types of prepositions which occur in the verbs' frames and about the semantic roles of their arguments. A classification based on semantic roles could be applied, given the good results that it provides for different languages.

Recent research (Amaro (2018), Da Costa and Bond (2016), etc.) show that closed class words have a place in wordnets and contribute for different NLP tasks if integrated. The good coverage of prepositions in BTB-WN will benefit its utility for semantic annotation and generation of pseudo corpora, which to be used for creation of neural language models in Bulgarian.

Acknowledgements

This work was supported by *the Bulgarian National Interdisciplinary Research e-Infrastructure for Resources and Technologies in favor of the Bulgarian Language and Cultural Heritage, part of the EU infrastructures CLARIN and DARIAH – CLaDA-BG*, Grant number DO01-377/18.12.2020. and the Grant No. BG05M2OP001-1.001-0003, financed by *the Science and Education for Smart Growth Operational Program (2014-2020)* and co-financed by *the European Union through the European structural and Investment funds*.

References

Raquel Amaro. 2018. Integrating prepositions in wordnets: Relations, glosses and visual description. In *Proceedings of the Eleventh International Conference on Language Resources and Evaluation (LREC 2018)*, Miyazaki, Japan. European Language Resources Association (ELRA).

Timothy Baldwin, Valia Kordoni, and Aline Villavicencio. 2009. Prepositions in applications: A survey and introduction to the special issue. *Computational Linguistics*, 35(2):119–149.

Todor Boyadzhiev, Ivan Kutsarov, and Yordan Penchev. 1998. *Contemporary Bulgarian language. Phonetics, lexicology, word formation, morphology, syntax.* Petar Beron, Sofia, Bulgaria.

Luis Morgado Da Costa and Francis Bond. 2016. Wow! what a useful extension! introducing non-referential concepts to Wordnet. In *Proceedings of the Tenth International Conference on Language Resources and Evaluation (LREC'16)*, pages 4323–4328, Portorož, Slovenia. European Language Resources Association (ELRA).

Christiane Fellbaum. 1998. *WordNet: An Electronic Lexical Database*. MIT Press.

Sanda M. Harabagiu. 1996. An application of wordnet to prepositional attachment. In *Proceedings of the 34th annual meeting on Association for Computational Linguistics (ACL 1996)*, page 360–362, Santa Cruz, USA. Association for Computational Linguistics.

Violeta Konstantinova. 1982. *Prepositions in Bulgarian grammar literature*. Publishing house of BAS, Sofia, Bulgaria.

Ken Litkowski and Orin Hargraves. 2005. The preposition project. In *ACL-SIGSEM Work- shop on "The Linguistic Dimensions of Prepositions and Their Use in Computational Linguistic Formalisms and Applications"*, pages 171–179.

John P. McCrae, Ewa Rudnicka, and Francis Bond. 2020. English WordNet: A new open-source WordNet for English. *K Lexical News*, (28):37–44.

Tom O'Hara and Janyce Wiebe. 2009. Exploiting semantic role resources for preposition disambiguation. *Computational Linguistics*, 35:151–184.

Petya Osenova and Kiril Simov. 2018. The data-driven Bulgarian Wordnet: BTBWN. *Cognitive Studies – Études cognitives", 2018(18)*.

Rashmi Prasad, Bonnie Webber, Alan Lee, and Aravind Joshi. 2019. The Penn Discourse Treebank 3.0 Annotation Manual.

Patrick Saint-Dizier. 2008. Syntactic and semantic frames in PrepNet. In *Proceedings of the Third International Joint Conference on Natural Language Processing: Volume-II*.

Nathan Schneider, Vivek Srikumar, Jena D. Hwang, and Martha Palmer. 2015. A hierarchy with, of, and for preposition supersenses. In *Proceedings of the 9th Linguistic Annotation Workshop*, pages 112–123, Denver, Colorado, USA. Association for Computational Linguistics.

Stoyan Stoyanov. 1983. *Grammar of contemporary Bulgarian standard language. Morphology.* Publishing house of BAS, Sofia, Bulgaria.

Are there just WordNets or also SignNets?

Ineke Schuurman
KU Leuven
Leuven, Belgium
ineke.schuurman@ccl.kuleuven.be

Thierry Declerck
DFKI GmbH, Saarland Informatics Campus
Saarbrücken, Germany
declerck@dfki.de

Caro Brosens and **Margot Janssens**
Vlaams GebarentaalCentrum
Antwerpen, Belgium
caro.brosens,margot.janssens@vgtc.be

Vincent Vandeghinste
Instituut voor de Nederlandse Taal
Leiden, The Netherlands
vincent.vandeghinste@idvnt.nl

Bram Vanroy
KU Leuven
Leuven, Belgium
bram.vanroy@kuleuven.be

Abstract

For Sign Languages (SLs), can we create a SignNet, like a WordNet for spoken languages: a network of semantic relations between constitutive elements of SLs? We first discuss approaches that link SL data to wordnets, or integrate such elements with some adaptations into the structure of WordNet. Then, we present requirements for a SignNet, which is built on SL data and then linked to WordNet.

1 Introduction

Wordnets are semantic networks for *in se* spoken natural languages, containing lexical semantics relations between the words (mainly for nouns, verbs, adjectives and adverbs) in these languages. Full wordnets are currently only available for spoken languages, encoded in written form. In many cases, there are links between distinct wordnets, often using Princeton WordNet (Fellbaum, 2005) as a pivot, using interlingual wordnet indices (Bond et al., 2016).

There is an increasing interest in offering automated translations between spoken and signed natural languages. This is demonstrated by two ongoing large European research projects: SignON[1] (Saggion et al., 2021; Shterionov et al., 2022) and EASIER[2] (McDonald et al., 2021). The topic of automated translations between Sign Languages (SLs) is also being addressed.

Research is also addressing the role that WordNet(s) can play. (Bigeard et al., 2022), for instance, shows how to include SL data in WordNet(s) and how the shared synset IDs in the Open Multilingual Wordnet (OMW, (Bond and Foster, 2013)) infrastructure can help in cross-linking and aligning signs used in both German and Greek Sign Languages. This extends related work on building ASLNet (Lualdi et al., 2019, 2021), which deals with Princeton WordNet (PWN) and American Sign Language (ASL), using the semantic structure offered by PWN to support the semantic organization of ASL signs.

Complementary to this, we investigate whether the development of a specific (lexical) semantic network for SL data is an option for establishing (cross-lingual) semantic relations between elements of SL data sets and whether it supports a better linking to wordnets related to spoken languages, instead of "merely" integrating SL data in WordNet(s). We call such networks SignNets. Constructing sign languages specific SignNet(s) may help to bridge between Sign Languages and spoken languages. (Lualdi et al., 2019) already express the need to encode SL specific phonological and lexical relations (going beyond purely PWN-based relations) between ASL signs. It may be worth considering extending this approach to a full SignNet.

A SignNet can help in the extended publication and visibility of (some) SL data, as we can consider all SLs as low resource languages, esp. when taking into account that the resources should be machine-readable to overcome some translation issues, esp. when using MT. So, for example, a significant part of the corpus for the Flemish Sign Language (Vlaamse Gebarentaal, VGT) is not yet machine-readable, cf (Wille et al., 2022). In

[1] https://signon-project.eu/
[2] https://www.project-easier.eu/

the VGT dictionary[3] each sign comes with a few keywords, but esp. when translating from spoken (Northern) Dutch to VGT, several words are missing. The availability of hypernyms etc may also be useful. Making use of signnets and wordnets, esp when translating from spoken language to sign language, it becomes easier to detect which words can be related to which signs. This is one of the possible uses in a project like SignON, dealing with low resource languages.

A last, but important issue: a wordnet should ideally be accessible to users having the language under consideration as their mother tongue, cf the app for PWN 3.1.[4] For a language like VGT it should be accessible in that SL (their mother tongue), not just in a 'foreign' spoken language.

2 Wordnets and Sign Languages

Currently, there are no wordnet-like resources publicly available for SLs, which rely on their visual-manual modality to express meaning. Some papers on this topic, however, are available, like (Ebling et al., 2012), (Shoaib et al., 2014), (Lualdi et al., 2019), (Lualdi et al., 2021), and (Bigeard et al., 2022).

Thus, work on resources for Greek and German, spoken and signed, are well under way, while currently work on ASLNet seems to be more or less at a standstill. However, it seems that in none of these cases a full 'wordnet' for an SL (a SignNet?) is being built.

As mentioned above, *in se*, a wordnet is a large semantic network stored in a database. We aim at including in such a semantic network all types of data available for a specific SL, also signs (and images/videos showing them), with their phonological elements, like hand shapes, position, orientation, as well as the glosses,[5] their phonetic transcriptions (like HamNoSys (Hanke, 2004), cf. Fig. 3), examples of use (in both the SL environment and the surrounding spoken language), definitions and identifiers of entries in corpora, where some attestations of the signs can be found, etc. This would make SignNets semantic networks on their own, applied to visual-gestural data, and containing links to wordnets, rather than being integrated in those.

We are framing SLs as natural languages in their own right, and not as an appendix to spoken language (spoken language with signs/gestures). The latter was more or less the case, although with pictographs, in (Vandeghinste and Schuurman, 2014) where pictographs were linked to Cornetto[6] synsets in order to enable people with intellectual disabilities to communicate with others using an app.

2.1 Semantic Networks for Sign languages (SignNets)

A wordnet containing words in a specific spoken language, expressing the semantic relations between these, comes in a written format.

This is rather important, as one of the characteristics of SLs is that there is no generally accepted written form. This means that the WordNet format as such is not directly applicable, although often glosses are used as a kind of written representation format. The same holds for some phonetic transcription formats, like HamNoSys, SiGML[7] and Sign_A (Murtagh, 2019).

In an ideal world, deaf people should be able to use a SignNet using 1) video (automatic sign language recognition), 2) written input, for example in Dutch when consulting VGTNet[8], 3) glosses and keywords, 4) picture-based parameters (handshape, location, movement, and orientation) whether or not enriched with info concerning region, topic/-category and 5) transcribed format (like SiGML or Sign_A). The same holds for dictionaries or other SL resources. As (Lualdi et al., 2021) points out for ASLNet: "The semantic relations encoded by a wordnet enable semantically-driven language acquisition, resulting in a powerful first-language (L1) and second-language (L2) pedagogical resource that will also contribute to ASL linguistics."

Our starting point while building a SignNet are the lexical resources available for the SL under consideration. These are likely to contain just signs (plus glosses) approved by the deaf community, plus some keywords in the relevant spoken language, Dutch for VGT. Another point is that, for

[3] https://woordenboek.vlaamsegebarentaal.be/

[4] https://wordnet-rdf.princeton.edu/

[5] Not to be confused with Wordnet glosses: glosses in the SL community are a simple way to name a sign, so that one can refer to it. The design and use of such glosses are subject to conventions by the community (Ormel et al., 2010). Nevertheless, not all communities are using exactly the same approach.

[6] An older wordnet for Dutch

[7] Machine-readable conversion of HamNoSys, cf https://vh.cmp.uea.ac.uk/index.php/SiGML_Tools

[8] Currently, often only words in spoken language explicitly mentioned as keywords (or translations) can be used in the SL SignNet

example for VGT, signed corpora are scarce, and not always machine-readable (Wille et al., 2022), so that starting with lexical resources is a valuable option. This means that we are using a *merge* approach, as SLs have other characteristics than a spoken language like English (reflected in PWN). We are dealing in this paper with VGT, but will also consider the SL of the Netherlands (Nederlandse Gebarentaal, NGT) in the near future.[9] In our approach, the glosses and esp. the keywords associated with them, play a central role.

2.2 Glosses

A rather important point when working with SLs: signs often have a somewhat broad meaning, expressing concepts linked to a series of words in spoken language, not just the meaning of one specific word. So the glosses are used to overcome the lack of a natural written format for signs and tend to have a broader meaning than the name suggests, i.e. it is a label for a concept, and does not represent the corresponding word in the spoken language at hand. In fact, a number could have been used instead.

Figure 1 shows the result when searching within the Dutch WordNet: the outcome is a series of homonyms. However, searching within the VGT dataset using a gloss results in a series of a) regional variants and/or b) full synonyms, i.e. a synset is shown. While searching for BANK, several signs will be shown, all with the keywords *bank, bankier, financiële instelling* (bank, banker, financial institution). They are marked as being used in various parts of Flanders. In the regional variants the phonetics differ, but the signs represented are the same.

Synonyms or dialectal variants may occur when older signs originated in schools in different parts of Flanders, while there was not that much contact between them.

The choice of the gloss for naming a sign is in some sense arbitrary. The gloss POOR referring to the concept 'poor' (Dutch 'arm') in VGT is ARMOEDE (a noun), in NGT it is BEHOEFTIG (an adjective), in both cases the gloss ARM is avoided, as in both languages it is used for the sign(s) referring to the limb. However, in the *Gebarenwoordenboek* for NGT, created by the Nederlands Gebarencentrum (and not by the Radboud University in Nijmegen, who also maintain such a dictionary), the gloss for the concept 'poor' is ARM and that for the limb 'ARM ledemaat'.[10] In VGT at least 4 signs come with the gloss ARMOEDE. The different origins of the signs are mentioned in the accompanying metadata. In NGT, there are 2 signs to be found in their signbank, with the glosses BEHOEFTIG-A and BEHOEFTIG-B, the latter having a broader coverage than the first.

ID	Written Form	Semantics
bank-n-1	bank	zitmeubel
bank-n-2	bank	geldverlenende instelling
bank-n-3	bank	zandbank
bank-n-4	bank	wolkenbank
bank-n-5	bank	bij het kaarten
bank-n-6	bank	bankgebouw
bank-n-7	bank	werkbank

Figure 1: *'bank'* in Dutch Wordnet (Cornetto demo)

Figure 2: Pictographic aids: 'arm' and 'red'

2.3 Transcriptions

While there are systems to transcribe signs, these formats are not readily accessible for the general audience because of several reasons. One reason: the lack of formal education in and about SLs means that not many people are familiar with transcription systems like HamNoSys. And as most deaf people are functionally bilingual, meaning that they can communicate through their second language in written form, this greatly reduced the need for a widely known transcription system. Besides, signers are now able to benefit from all sorts of technological advances (video calls, video messages, ...) further reducing the need for writing down sign language in one of these formats. However, for Natural Language Processing (NLP) purposes a machine-readable written format (SiGML or Sign_A) is still needed. But these formats will only be used by a limited group of (deaf) people. Most people will want to consult a SignNet using

[9]This because VGT and NGT differ quite a lot, for example in using glosses, and the keywords associated with related glosses.

[10]An additional feature sometimes presented in the Gebarencentrum version of the dictionary are pictographs depicting the meaning of a sign, cf Figure 2

recorded signs, spoken language in written format, handshape descriptions, just like they consult a sign language dictionary.
Examples in written form are shown in Figures 3, 4 and 5. Both SiGML and Sign_A are machine-readable.

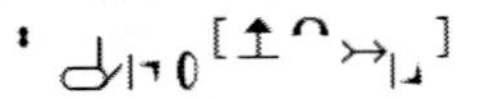

Figure 3: HamNoSys, 'going-to'

```
<?xml version="1.0" encoding="iso-8859-1"?>
<!DOCTYPE sigml SYSTEM .../sigml.dtd>
<sigml>
<hns_sign gloss="DGS_going-to">
  <hamnosys_manual>
    <hamsymmpar/>
    <hamfinger2/>
    <hamthumboutmod/>
    <hamextfingeruo/>
    <hampalml/>
    <hamparbegin/>
    <hammoveo/>
    <hamarcu/>
    <hamreplace/>
    <hamextfingerdo/>
    <hamparend/>
  </hamnosys_manual>
</hns_sign>
</sigml>
```

Figure 4: SiGML, 'going-to'

```
Sign_A Manual Feature Description <MF>
<HAND><dh>"right"</dh><ndh>"left"</ndh></HAND>
<HS><HMMode>unique</HMMode><HSID><value>24</value></HSID>
<AM><BHEAD><rightCheek_i><EDti></EDti><EDtn></EDtn></rightCheek_i>
             <rightCheek_n><EDti></EDti><EDtn></EDtn></rightCheek_n>
             <TLti></TLti><TLtn></TLtn>
</BHEAD></AM>
<PO>
 <dh>
 <p1><p1_i><EDti></EDti><EDtn></EDtn></p1_i>
     <p1_n><EDti></EDti><EDtn></EDtn></p1_n>
     <TLti></TLti><TLtn></TLtn>
 </p1>
 </dh>

 <ndh>
 <p_Def><pDef_i><EDti></EDti><EDtn></EDtn></p_Def_i>
        <pDef_n><EDti></EDti><EDtn></EDtn></pDef_n>
        <TLti></TLti><TLtn></TLtn>
 </p_Def>
 </ndh>
</PO>
Sign_A Non Manual Feature Description <NMF>
<MOUTHING><NOUN_ONE_TO_ONE><NOUNIPA>"/gɜ:(r)l/"</></NOUN_ONE_TO_ONE></MOUTHIN
G>
```

Figure 5: 'girl' in Sign_A

In a user survey, the possibility to search from VGT to Dutch was reported to be of importance, (Brosens et al., 2022). In the current version of the VGT dictionary, users can select handshape(s), location(s), region(s) and/or semantic category/categories to search for specific signs and their meanings. The meanings are currently only displayed through possible translations into Dutch, cf. Fig. 6. Each entry has a page detailing more information. At the bottom of this page, regional variants (based on the glosses) as well as similar signs (i.e. phonologically related signs, based on the handshape and location) are displayed.

The glosses involved in Fig. 6 are RIBBEN (rib)

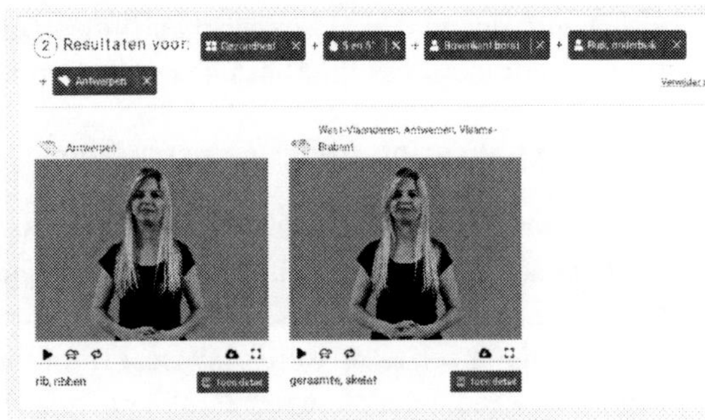

Figure 6: Using handshapes etc to find a sign

and SKELET (skeleton).[11] Neglecting the region, one more sign comes up, with gloss FYSIEK(-A) (physical), and not specifying the category results in a total of 11 signs. These are not all homophones. The current series of information on pictures available for VGT is not fine-grained enough to offer a more accurate subset of homophones, this would improve largely when for example pictures for 'movement' could be selected as well: is there a circular motion, a vertical or horizontal one, is it repeated, etc. In ASL, for example, some twenty movements are described (Stokoe et al., 1965).

The search function through handshape, location, movement, ... is not designed or meant to yield homonyms as results. It would be similar to looking for all words containing a schwa sound in English and expecting these to be homonyms. A far better way would be using signs as such (recorded by the user's camera, the recording being recognized as a specific sign in the SL by a sign language recognition tool).

But even though when using handshapes, location, etc., the user has to have a look at some (videos of) signs to find the one looked for, and find its meaning in spoken Dutch. An advantage is that this user does not need to be familiar with HamNoSys, Sign_A or the like, for example to use an interface in agreement with the one available for Princeton WordNet 3.1, cf https://wordnet-rdf.princeton.edu, but adapted for SLs.

Taking all of this into account, the best way to find SL *synonyms* and phonetic variants is to make use of the words in written language presented in the SL dictionary as keywords. For the time being, in most SLs *homonyms* are to be hard-coded (in VGT for example 'honger' and 'Hongarije',[12] or

[11] Rather RIBBEN-D and SKELET-B for these specific instantiations

[12] HONGER-A (hunger) and HONGARIJE-B (Hungary)

'geel' and 'donderdag'[13]) rather than (videos of) signs and/or transcriptions[14] can be used as input.

3 An Application under Construction

The glossing system described above is widely used by linguists. But there is this major difference between using words and glosses, the latter in fact representing a series of words (synset) from the beginning. And quite often representing a broader concept for gloss X than the one reflected in the synset resulting from the search for word X, sometimes also smaller!

A semantic network for SLs (SignNet) also presenting such data is to be set up more or less from scratch, taking advantage of the wordnet of a surrounding spoken language. For both VGT and NGT that would be ODWN.[15]

However, this might involve adaptations in the (spoken) wordnet, in our case ODWN, as well. In selecting the ODWN synsets to connect with a VGT gloss, the few words in spoken language (keywords) provided by the people behind the VGT dictionary[16] are really helpful.

We will also provide links with other Wordnets and Signnets. The central position of Princeton WordNet will be replaced by Open English WordNet (McCrae et al., 2019), derived from PWN, and updated regularly. We will also make use of Open Multilingual WordNet to connect with other wordnets (Bond and Foster, 2013).

3.1 Glosses representing a series of signs: consequences for wordnet/SignNet

Considering signs as the core of a SignNet does not at all mean that we will neglect the glosses. As mentioned above, they provide a very good link to resources available for surrounding spoken languages. Quite often, an SL synset is broader than that in the surrounding spoken language. The gloss HANGEN (hang) in VGT, corresponds to at least two synsets in ODWN. We found them making use of the keywords mentioned in the SL dictionaries. So the gloss HANGEN comes with four such keywords: *hangen, aanhangen, ophangen, aanhaken.* (hang, couple (on), hang (up), hook up/on).

These 4 verbs belong to at least 2 synsets: *aanhaken, haken, vasthaken* and *hangen, neerhangen, ophangen* which give the impression to be (semantically) closely related. In such cases we may have to adapt the current version of ODWN, for example by creating a new 'higher' synset, to which the other synsets are related (hyponyms). But ... before doing so, we will first present these to the people behind the SL dictionary at hand, and, when approved by them, in a later stage to representatives of the deaf community. Only when they approve the proposal, it will be made public.[17]

It would be interesting to see how NGT handles signs with more or less the same meaning. They may even use another gloss (cf BEHOEFTIG-A and -B mentioned above). In the case mentioned above, all words involved are verbs. But that is not necessary, it can even be a mixture of verbs, nouns, adjectives: Gloss: AFBREKEN (pull down), possible keywords *afbreken,* **afbraak**, *slopen* (pull down / demolish, **demolition**, demolish) i.e. two verbs, one noun.

In such a case we may have to create a 'derivational related form',[18] thus connecting the noun '*afbraak*' with the verb '*afbreken*'. In some wordnets, like PWN, such links are already available, but it is not yet a common characteristic. Other types of mixes are also possible, see (Vossen, 2002).[19]

For the time being, once we've handled the keywords (and these were accepted by VGTC), we will look for their hypernyms, hyponyms, antonyms, ... mentioned in the wordnet and try to link them with signs (or rather their glosses/keywords) in our SignNet. Once more, the people behind the dictionary and the representatives are asked for their approval. This way a full SignNet is being constructed. In short: a SignNet contains glosses, coming with

- a synset: series of subglosses or constituting glosses (SIGN-A, SIGN-B, SIGN-D, etc),
- example sentences (signed and spoken), pictographs (like ARASAAC)[20]are linked to wordnet (Schwab et al., 2020),

[13]GEEL-A (yellow) and DONDERDAG-B (Thursday)

[14]Not yet available for many SLs

[15]Replacing Cornetto, the older, not open version

[16]These keywords are approved by the deaf community

[17]For VGT and NGT, while accepting several elements out of the wordnet synset as new keywords, others may be rejected being considered as only usable in the Netherlands or Flanders (false friends)

[18]Terms in different syntactic categories that have the same root form and are semantically related

[19]"In WordNet, nouns, verbs and adjectives form separate sub-networks that are not interrelated. This strict separation between the parts of speech has been abandoned in EuroWordNet." (p. 32) when claiming that the Dutch adjective *aardig* often should be linked with the verb 'to like' in English

[20]`https://arasaac.org/)`

- series of keywords (using surrounding spoken language),
- links with glosses expressing hypernyms, hyponyms, antonyms, ... etc,
- wordnet link (interlingual identifiers), thus relations with wordnets and other signnets can be made traceable

Subglosses (SIGN-A etc.) come with

- video of the sign itself,
- transcription in SiGML, Sign_A, ...,
- homonyms,[21]
- description of handshapes, position, movement, location in picture-format,
- pictograph (like ARASAAC),
- category (family, nature, occupation, animal, education, etc ...),
- metadata like region, gender when available.[22]

4 Conclusion

Our pilot study made it clear to us that building real SignNets, comparable with wordnets for spoken languages, is possible, doing justice to the characteristics of the sign language under consideration. Mainly linking signs with surrounding wordnet synsets does so to a lesser extent. Another advantage is that, for example, an application comparable to that of Princeton WordNet 3.1, but for SLs, is accessible to a much larger set of users. So, we'll continue working on developing SignNets! Our signnets are in some respect an extension of the work done by (Lualdi et al., 2019), (Lualdi et al., 2021), and (Bigeard et al., 2022). Their results can *in se* be used as a first step towards a full signnet, and be extended with for example examples in the relevant SLs, recognition of video of a particular sign, etcetera.

[21]like HONGARIJE-B and HONGER-A; GEEL-A and DONDERDAG-B

[22]For Irish SL for example the gender of the persons using the specific variant of a sign

Acknowledgements

Work in this paper is part of the SignON project.[23] This project has received funding from the European Union's Horizon 2020 Research and Innovation Programme under Grant Agreement No. 101017255. A smaller part of the work proposed in this paper work is linked with the COST Action NexusLinguarum CA 18209, Taskgroup Multimodality.[24]

References

Sam Bigeard, Marc Schulder, Maria Kopf, Thomas Hanke, Kiki Vasilaki, Anna Vacalopoulou, Theodoros Goulas, Athanasia-Lida Dimou, Stavroula-Evita Fotinea, and Eleni Efthimiou. 2022. Introducing Sign Languages to a Multilingual Wordnet: Bootstrapping Corpora and Lexical Resources of Greek Sign Language and German Sign Language. In *Proceedings of the LREC2022 10th Workshop on the Representation and Processing of Sign Languages: Multilingual Sign Language Resources*, pages 9–15, Marseille, France. European Language Resources Association (ELRA).

Francis Bond and Ryan Foster. 2013. Linking and Extending an Open Multilingual Wordnet. In *Proceedings of the 51st Annual Meeting of the Association for Computational Linguistics (Volume 1: Long Papers)*, pages 1352–1362, Sofia, Bulgaria. Association for Computational Linguistics.

Francis Bond, Piek Vossen, John McCrae, and Christiane Fellbaum. 2016. CILI: the Collaborative Interlingual Index. In *Proceedings of the 8th Global WordNet Conference (GWC)*, pages 50–57, Bucharest, Romania. Global Wordnet Association.

Caro Brosens, Margot Janssens, Sam Verstraete, Thijs Vandamme, and Hannes De Durpel. 2022. Moving towards a Functional Approach in the Flemish Sign Language Dictionary Making Process. In *Proceedings of the LREC2022 10th Workshop on the Representation and Processing of Sign Languages: Multilingual Sign Language Resources*, pages 24–28, Marseille, France. European Language Resources Association (ELRA).

Sarah Ebling, Katja Tissi, and Martin Volk. 2012. Semi-Automatic Annotation of Semantic Relations in a Swiss German Sign Language Lexicon. In *Proceedings of the LREC2012 5th Workshop on the Representation and Processing of Sign Languages: Interactions between Corpus and Lexicon*, pages 31–36, Istanbul, Turkey. European Language Resources Association (ELRA).

[23]All authors but Thierry Declerck

[24]Thierry Declerck and Ineke Schuurman

Christiane Fellbaum. 2005. WordNet and wordnets. In *Encyclopedia of Language and Linguistics*, pages 665–670, Oxford. Elsevier.

Thomas Hanke. 2004. HamNoSys – Representing Sign Language Data in Language Resources and Language Processing Contexts. In *Proceedings of the LREC2004 Workshop on the Representation and Processing of Sign Languages: From SignWriting to Image Processing. Information techniques and their implications for teaching, documentation and communication*, pages 1–6, Lisbon, Portugal. European Language Resources Association (ELRA).

Colin Lualdi, Jack Hudson, Christiane Fellbaum, and Noah Buchholz. 2019. Building ASLNet, a Wordnet for American Sign Language. In *Proceedings of the 10th Global Wordnet Conference*, pages 315–322, Wroclaw, Poland. Global Wordnet Association.

Colin Lualdi, Elaine Wright, Jack Hudson, Naomi Caselli, and Christiane Fellbaum. 2021. Implementing ASLNet V1.0: Progress and Plans. In *Proceedings of the 11th Global Wordnet Conference, GWC 2021, University of South Africa (UNISA), Potchefstroom, South Africa, January 18-21, 2021*, pages 63–72. Global Wordnet Association.

John P. McCrae, Alexandre Rademaker, Francis Bond, Ewa Rudnicka, and Christiane Fellbaum. 2019. English WordNet 2019 – an open-source WordNet for English. In *Proceedings of the 10th Global Wordnet Conference*, pages 245–252, Wroclaw, Poland. Global Wordnet Association.

John C. McDonald, Rosalee Wolfe, Eleni Efthimiou, Evita Fontinea, Frankie Picron, Davy Van Landuyt, Tina Sioen, Annelies Braffort, Michael Filhol, Sarah Ebling, Thomas Hanke, and Verena Krausneker. 2021. The Myth of Signing Avatars. In *Proceedings 1st International Workshop on Automatic Translation for Signed and Spoken Languages (AT4SSL)*, pages 33–42. Association for Machine Translation in the Americas.

Irene E. Murtagh. 2019. *A Linguistically Motivated Computational Framework for Irish Sign Language*. PhD Thesis, Trinity College London, School of Linguistic Speech and Comm Sci.

Ellen Ormel, Onno Crasborn, Els van der Kooij, Lianne van Dijken, Ellen Yassine Nauta, Jens Forster, and Daniel Stein. 2010. Glossing a multi-purpose sign language corpus. In *Proceedings of the LREC2010 4th Workshop on the Representation and Processing of Sign Languages: Corpora and Sign Language Technologies*, pages 186–191, Valletta, Malta. European Language Resources Association (ELRA).

Horacio Saggion, Dimitar Shterionov, Gorka Labaka, Tim Van de Cruys, Vincent Vandeghinste, and Josep Blat. 2021. SignON: Bridging the gap between Sign and Spoken Languages. In *Proceedings of the Annual Conference of the Spanish Association for Natural Language Processing: Projects and Demonstrations (SEPLN-PD 2021) co-located with the Conference of the Spanish Society for Natural Language Processing (SEPLN 2021), Málaga, Spain, September, 2021*, volume 2968 of *CEUR Workshop Proceedings*, pages 21–24. CEUR-WS.org.

Didier Schwab, Pauline Trial, Céline Vaschalde, Loïc Vial, Emmanuelle Esperanca-Rodier, and Benjamin Lecouteux. 2020. Providing Semantic Knowledge to a Set of Pictograms for People with Disabilities: a Set of Links between WordNet and Arasaac: Arasaac-WN. In *Proceedings of the Twelfth Language Resources and Evaluation Conference*, pages 166–171, Marseille, France. European Language Resources Association.

U. Shoaib, N. Ahmad, P. Prinetto, and G. Tiotto. 2014. Integrating MultiWordNet with Italian Sign Language lexical resources. *Expert Systems with Applications*, 41(5):2300–2308.

Dimitar Shterionov, Mirella De Sisto, Vincent Vandeghinste, Aoife Brady, Mathieu De Coster, Lorraine Leeson, Josep Blat, Frankie Picron, Marcello Paolo Scipioni, Aditya Parikh, Louis ten Bosch, John O'Flaherty, Joni Dambre, and Jorn Rijckaert. 2022. Sign Language Translation: Ongoing Development, Challenges and Innovations in the SignON Project. In *Proceedings of the 23rd Annual Conference of the European Association for Machine Translation*, pages 325–326, Ghent, Belgium.

William C. Stokoe, Dorothy C. Casterline, and Carl G. Croneberg. 1965. *A dictionary of American sign language on linguistic principles*. Gallaudet research publication. Centennial series 1. Gallaudet Press, Washington, D.C.

Vincent Vandeghinste and Ineke Schuurman. 2014. Linking pictographs to synsets: Sclera2cornetto. In *Proceedings of the Ninth International Conference on Language Resources and Evaluation (LREC'14)*, Reykjavik, Iceland. European Language Resources Association (ELRA).

Piek Vossen. 2002. WordNet, EuroWordNet and Global WordNet. *Revue Française de Linguistique Appliquée*, VII:27.

Beatrijs Wille, Inez Beukeleers, Mieke Van Herreweghe, and Myriam Vermeerbergen. 2022. Big Things Often Have Small Beginnings: A Review on the Development, Use and Value of Small and Big Corpora for Flemish Sign Language Linguistic Research. *Frontiers in Psychology*, 12.

Japanese Wordnet 2.0

Francis Bond
Palacký University
bond@ieee.org

Takayuki Kuribayashi
takkur@gmail.com

Abstract

This paper describes a new release of the Japanese wordnet. It uses the new global wordnet formats (McCrae et al., 2021) to incorporate a range of new information: orthographic variants (including hiragana, katakana and Latin representations) first described in Kuroda et al. (2011), classifiers, pronouns and exclamatives (Morgado da Costa and Bond, 2016) and many new senses, motivated both from corpus annotation and linking to the TUFs basic vocabulary (Bond et al., 2020). The wordnet has been moved to github and is available at `https://bond-lab.github.io/wnja/`.

1 Introduction

This paper describes a new release of the Japanese wordnet, v2.0. This new version of the Japanese wordnet includes orthographic variants and transliterations (Kuroda et al., 2011), classifiers, exclamatives (Morgado da Costa and Bond, 2016) and pronouns (Seah and Bond, 2014), as well as words introduced during the annotation of the NTU Multilingual Corpus (Bond et al., 2013). This is the first release in almost 10 years, and has a numerous changes.

The Japanese Wordnet was started at the National Institute of Information and Communications Technology (NICT) based on the **expand** approach of adding Japanese lemmas to existing Princeton Wordnet 3.0 (PWN: Fellbaum, 1998) synsets, with plans to follow this up by annotating a corpus and adding missing words (**extend**). This allowed us to take advantage initially of the rich information in the Princeton Wordnet.

The progress of construction is shown in Table 1. The first release (v0.9: 2009-02) contained 48,190 synsets. These were created by linking to the structure of Princeton Wordnet (Fellbaum, 1998, 3.0) through four languages: English, French, Spanish and German (Bond et al., 2008).

The second release (v0.91: 2009-08) was a bug-fix release, with slightly more synsets (50,739) but fewer senses, as we checked more of the automatically built synsets. This release included links to images in the Open Clip Art Library (OCAL Phillips, 2005) and the Suggested Upper Merged Ontology (SUMO Niles and Pease, 2001; Pease, 2011). Finally, there was one more bug-fix release (v0.92: 2009-11) this time with fewer synsets as well as senses.

The next major release (v1.0: 2010-03) saw the addition of definitions and example sentences (Kuribayashi et al., 2010). These were automatically translated from English, using a specialized corpus of example sentences, and then hand corrected. As this was part of research to produce a large parallel corpus at NICT, all definitions and examples were translated, even if they did not have any Japanese lemmas associated with them.

We next decided to do some work on producing sense-tagged corpora in order to see how well the wordnet did on describing real world Japanese text. For our first attempt, we created the Japanese SemCor (JSemCor) a (partially) sense-tagged corpus of Japanese (Bond et al., 2012). The final corpus consists of 14,169 sentences with 150,555 content words of which 58,265 are sense tagged. It allowed us to provide sense frequency data for the Japanese Wordnet.

We next annotated over 7,000 sentences in the NTU Multilingual Corpus (Tan and Bond, 2012), including news text, tourism text, short stories and an essay. This has led us to identify many missing concepts as well as many missing senses. There are 20,386 sense tagged words (including multi-word expressions) annotated in the Japanese portion of the corpus, with 6,706 distinct senses.

In 2014 a python module was developed that allowed the wnja 1.1 data to be used in NLTK (Bird et al., 2009). Goodman and Bond (2021) made a module for the new wordnet structure, which can

Year-Mon	Ver	Concepts	Words	Senses	Misc
2009-02	0.90	49,190	75,966	156,684	initial release
2009-08	0.91	50,739	88,146	151,831	SUMO, OCAL
2009-11	0.92	49,655	87,133	146,811	
2010-03	1.00	56,741	92,241	157,398	+ def, ex
2010-10	1.10	57,238	93,834	158,058	
2012-01					Japanese Semcor
2014-02					NLTK module
2023-01	2.0	58,527	90,320	148,676	262,196 forms

Table 1: Japanese wordnet milestones

be used with this release.

This release has more concepts, slightly fewer senses and words (as we delete bad entries) and many more variant forms (described in the next section).

2 Richer Information

This release of the wordnet gathers together several improvements.

2.1 Orthographic variants

The Japanese writing system is particularly complex. It consists of three separate sets of characters: hiragana, katakana and kanji. Modern Japanese also makes frequent use of Arabic numbers, Latin script and increasingly emoji.

Hiragana and **katakana** are isomorphic syllabaries made up of 46 basic characters.

The third character system is **kanji**, derived historically from Chinese characters. 2,136 kanji are in common use, based on the set of Joyo Kanji stipulated by the Japanese Ministry of Education, Culture, Sports, Science and Technology which are taught in Japanese primary and middle schools. Thousands more are used in place names, person names and historical texts.

A single kanji character generally has at least one **on**-reading which is loosely derived from its Chinese pronunciation at the time of borrowing,[1] and at least one native Japanese **kun**-reading where a Japanese word which pre-existed the orthographic borrowing was mapped onto a kanji character based on rough semantic correspondence. For example, 動 has a unique on-reading of *dō*, and a unique kun-reading of *ugo(ku/kasu)*;[2] in both cases, its basic meaning is "motion, change".

Hiragana is typically used for inflections, function words and onomatopoeic expressions. Katakana is typically used for foreign words. Words normally written in Kanji can be written in hiragana (to ease reading) or katakana (for emphasis, similar to italics in English). A single word, such as *ugoita* (動いた) "moved (intrans.)" could thus be written as うごいた or ウゴイタ. Further, some kanji have variants (typically more complicated older forms and newer simpler ones). Typically, a dictionary for human users will just list the standard form and any character variants, with possibly the pronunciation in Katakana or Hiragana (see Backhouse (1993); Bond and Baldwin (2016) for more discussion).

We have decided to list all possible forms, with one chosen as the display form. There is no universal standard for what the display form should be. However the widely used morphological analyser **juman** (Kurohashi and Nagao, 1998) lists canonical forms for all words in its dictionary ((Okabe et al., 2007)) and we use them when available.

Overall we decide as follows:

1. If there is an entry in **jumandic** we use their canonical form
2. Prefer kanji to hiragana
3. Prefer new forms to old forms
   (we compiled our own table of new and old forms)
4. If there are multiple katakana variants, prefer the longest

[1] Indeed, many kanji still have corresponding hanzi in traditional Chinese, although there are also a few kanji which were devised in Japan and are unique to Japanese, such as *hatake* (畑) "field" and *tōge* (峠) "mountain pass".

[2] The reading of 動 itself is *ugo*, and it combines with a kana-based conjugational suffix (**okurigana**) derived from *ku* or *kasu* (corresponding to intransitive and transitive verb usages, respectively), e.g. *ugoita* (動いた) "moved (intrans.)" or *ugokashiteiru* (動かしている) "is moving (trans.)".

We give an example of variants for the synset meaning "form an arch or curve" in Table 2. The first katakana entry can be used to give the pronunciation and is also used to generate a variant in Latin script, so that the dictionary can be searched by users with no Japanese input system.

We have added up to two Latin transliterations, the standard Kunrei-siki romanization (preferred by the Japanese Ministry of Education), and where it differs, the commonly used Hepburn romanization (more similar to English orthography). In Figure 1 we show the different representations of *jisho* "dictionary". Conversion is done automatically from the katakana form using the python `romkan` library.[3]

Note that due to differences in use of old and new Chinese characters and the option of omitting hiragana, a word may have many different forms: *nomikomu* "swallow" can have at least the following 飲み込む, ノミコム, 飲込む, 呑込む, 呑み込む, のみ込む, のみこむ.

Unfortunately, the display form cannot simply be the canonical form, as it can be the case that the same display form has different pronunciations for different meanings (or the same meaning), and some variants are not possible for all senses. For example *kedamono* (獣) "beast" and *shishi* (獣) "boar" are used for all mammals, but only *shishi* (獣) "boar" has the variants 猪 and 鹿. *inoshishi* (猪) "wild boar" has no variant, whereas *i* (猪) "boar (in the Chinese Zodiac)" has variants 豕 and 豬. Because of such idiosyncrasies, all entries had to be hand-checked, which was a monumental task: this is why there was such a long gap between releases. We summarize the number of forms in Table 3.

Increasing the number of variants is necessary to increase the coverage of the lexicon on corpora. It also makes the dictionary more useful to language learners, who may not be able to read the kanji, but should be able to read kana or Latin versions.

2.2 Frequencies

We include sense frequencies based on the annotation in the NTU Multilingual Corpus (Tan and Bond, 2012) and the Japanese SemCor (Bond et al., 2012).

For example, in the synset `00174412-n` "any maneuver made as part of progress toward a goal" the Japanese senses have the following frequencies: 対策$_3$, 策$_3$, 措置$_2$, 方略, 方策, 術, 打つ手. The frequencies are used in the Open Multilingual Wordnet (OMW: Bond and Foster, 2013) to order the senses in the display, and to chose the most appropriate label for each synset. They can also be used for choosing the most frequent sense for word sense disambiguation.

2.3 Grammatical Notes

We also marked the major verb inflectional class of Sino-Japanese verbs, with a usage note (`note='sahen'`). These verbs typically appear with a support verb (such as *suru* "do" or *dekiru* "can"). On their own they look similar to nouns and typically link to a zero-derived noun. We show an example in Figure 2.

3 New Entries

We have expanded the vocabulary of the Japanese wordnet through a combination of corpus annotation and systematic expansion of lexical fields. We try to add not just individual words, but also complete semantic fields together, especially when there is a difference in conceptual structure with English. Here are some of the major additions in this release

1. Numeral classifiers (not used in English)
2. Pronouns (not in the Princeton Wordnet)
3. Exclamatives (not in the Princeton Wordnet)
4. Time/Date expressions (often split into different units than in English)
5. Japanese kinship terms (richer than English)

The semi-closed classes of pronouns, classifiers and exclamatives were added to the Chinese, English, Indonesian and Malay wordnets at the same time, as described in Seah and Bond (2014) and Morgado da Costa and Bond (2016). The numbers of new entries for the different classes are given in Table 4. We do not consider the coverage to be anywhere near complete, but we cover most common words from these classes.

Pronouns

Japanese pronouns differ on several dimensions from English — in particular there are different levels of formality for personal pronouns, and demonstrative pronouns distinguish between proximal *kono*, medial *sono* and distal *ano* as opposed

[3]`https://pypi.org/project/romkan/`

Display form	Pronunciation	Variants	Latin
湾曲	ワンキョク	彎曲, 弯曲, わん曲	wankyoku
反る	ソル	そる	soru
カーブ	カーブ	カーヴ	ka-bu …

Table 2: Variants of "form an arch or curve"

```
<LexicalEntry id="wnja-n-3023"> <!-- 辞書 0 n -->
  <Lemma writtenForm="辞書" partOfSpeech="n"/>
     <Form writtenForm="ジショ" script="kana"/>
     <Form writtenForm="じしょ" script="hira"/>
     <Form writtenForm="zisyo" script="latn"/>
     <Form writtenForm="jisho" script="latn-hepburn"/>
     ...
</LexicalEntry>
```

Figure 1: Different forms for *jisho*, showing scripts

Script	Number
Mixed	83,049
Katakana	89,542
Hiragana	89,605
Latin	89,542
Latin (Hepburn)	36,753
Total	388,491

Table 3: Numbers of forms by script

(2)

80002405-x (お疲れ様)	
lemmas:jpn	お疲れ様, ご苦労様
def:jpn	相手の苦労をねぎらう発話
def:eng	an expression that is uttered when you appreciate someone's work; typically used when someone leaves work
exemplifies	07109847-n (utterance)
see also	01805982-v (appreciate)
similar to	80000666-x (thank you)

to English's two-way distinction: *this* proximal and *that* medial/distal.

Exclamatives

We added exclamatives (including greetings, interjections and many more), following Morgado da Costa and Bond (2016, who only added English and Chinese), which is loosely based on the classification of Jovanović (2004). Some exclamatives are similar in many languages, such as the greetings *konnichiwa* "good day" or *sayonara* "good bye". We also added some purely Japanese expressions, such as *onegai-shimasu* (1) and *otsukaresama* (2).

(1)

80002404-x (お願いします)	
lemmas:jpn	お願いします, お願い
def:jpn	よくしてくれることを求める意味合いの発話
def:eng	an expression that is uttered when you ask for a favor
exemplifies	07109847-n (utterance)
see also	00903098-v (wish)
similar to	80001988-x (please)

Classifiers

Again we followed Morgado da Costa and Bond (2016) for the numeral classifiers. Because usage is significantly different across languages, we have no classifiers shared exactly across even such similar languages as Chinese and Japanese. We show an example of the idiosyncratic Japanese classifier for birds and rabbits in 3.

(3)

76100129-x (羽)	
lemmas:jpn	羽
def:jpn	ツバメやタカやペンギンなどの鳥、またウサギに対しても用いられる分類辞
exe:jpn	日本では、月で一羽のウサギが餅を搗いていると考えられています; 彼は４羽のオウムを飼っています
def:eng	a sortal classifier used for birds such as a swallow, a hawk or a penguin, and also specifically for rabbits
exe:eng	in Japan, people think a rabbit is making rice cake on the moon; he has 4 parrots
exemplifies	06308436-n (classifier)
classifies	01503061-n (bird)
classifies	02324045-n (rabbit)

```
<LexicalEntry id="wnja-v-74345" note="sahen"> <!-- 読書 0 v -->
      <Lemma writtenForm="読書" partOfSpeech="v"/>
        <Form writtenForm="ドクショ" script="kana"/>
        <Form writtenForm="どくしょ" script="hira"/>
        <Form writtenForm="dokusyo" script="latn"/>
        <Form writtenForm="dokusho" script="latn-hepburn"/>
       <Sense id="wnja-00625119-v-74345" synset="wnja-00625119-v" confidenceScore="1.0"/>
 </LexicalEntry>
```

Figure 2: Entry for *dokusho*, showing the usage note `sahen`

Class	Synsets	Lemmas	Examples
Classifier	47	47	人, 匹, 機
Exclamation	24	37	ああ, なるほど, さよなら
Pronoun	21	70	あちら, こちら
Personal Pronoun	19	29	私, あなた, 彼, 彼女
Reflexive Pronoun	2	6	自分, 己れ
Demonstrative Pronoun	22	25	これ, それ, あれ
Interrogative pronoun	10	13	どれ

Table 4: New Classes of Words

Time Expressions

Many time expressions which are phrases in English are single words in Japanese (such as 今週 *konshuu* "this week", or 今朝 *kesa* "this morning"). Historically, these were compounds in Chinese, but have been borrowed as single words. We added some 280 time senses, looking simultaneously at Japanese, Chinese and English. These included days of the month, compound dates and holidays. English was added for two reasons. The first was that it is useful for those that use the wordnets as bilingual lexicons. The second is that there is some lexicalization: we say *last year, this year, next year* but *yesterday morning, this morning, tomorrow morning* and *last night, tonight, tomorrow night.*[4] Chinese equivalents are arguably also lexicalized (and were typically segmented as two character expressions by the Penn Chinese Treebank (Xue et al., 2005)), adding them also made crosslingual linking easier. We give an example of an entry (including English and Chinese) in (4).

(4)

90000501-n (last year)	
lemmas:jpn	昨年, 去年
lemmas:eng	last year
lemmas:cmn	去年
def:jpn	現在の属する年の直前の年
exe:jpn	去年は盛りだくさんな年だった
def:eng	the year before this year
exe:eng	last year was an eventful one
def:cmn	今年的前一年
hypernym	15203791-n (year)

Kinship Terms

As well as distinguishing older and younger brothers and sisters, Japanese distinguishes aunts and uncles older and younger than the parent they are related to. For example, *oba* (伯母) "an aunt who is older than one's parent" vs *oba* (叔母) "an aunt who is younger than one's parent". Most kin terms have formal and informal variants, for the moment they are added to the same synset, in future work we wish to distinguish them using sense-based usage links.

Other new vocabulary

One other interesting difference between Japanese and English is in describing temperature. English uses the same words for temperature experienced by touching or as a general feeling (5). Japanese on the other hand distinguishes a general feeling (6) used for example when feeling cold, or

[4] Ross (1995) argues that English temporal nouns are **defective**: they are typically pronominalized by *then* and have idiosyncratic determiner use.

cold weather; and experiencing by touch (7) used for example for a cold soup or cold hands.

(5) ⟨*cold, cool, warm, hot*⟩

(6) feel: ⟨ 寒い, 涼しい, 暖かい, 暑い⟩

(7) touch: ⟨ 冷たい, 温かい, 熱い⟩

In fact, the words for warm and hot are pronounced the same whether for feeling or to-touch: *atatakai* and *atsui*, the difference is only written. These words were identified due to their presence in the TUFS basic vocabulary for teaching (Bond et al., 2020). We show their structure in 3.

Finally, we have added many new synsets that came up in the corpora being annotated: altogether 770 new synsets have been added. We give some examples below, some are from Japanese culture (8,9), some from Singapore (10: as we annotated Singapore tourist documents) and some from news and essays (11). Many of these should also be added to the Open English Wordnet (McCrae et al., 2020).

(8)

80001626-n (soba_noodle)	
lemmas:jpn	蕎麦
lemmas:eng	soba
def:jpn	そば粉で作られた細い麺
def:eng	narrow noodle made from buckwheat
hypernym	(noodle)

(9)

80000338-n (Shunto)	
lemmas:jpn	春闘
lemmas:eng	spring wage negotiation
def:jpn	毎年労働組合が、賃金引き上げなどの要求を掲げて行う全国的な闘争
def:eng	annual event by Japanese workers union when wages are renegotiated
hypernym	(protest)

(10)

80002377-n (castle construction)	
lemmas:jpn	築城
def:jpn	城の建設
def:eng	the construction of castles
hypernym	(construction)

(11)

90000315-n (hajjah)	
lemmas:jpn	ハジャ
lemmas:eng	hajjah
def:jpn	メッカへの巡礼を行った女性
def:eng	a woman who has made the pilgrimage to Mecca
hypernym	(haji)
category	(muslim)

(12)

80001731-n (exchange student)	
lemmas:jpn	留学生
lemmas:eng	exchange student
def:jpn	海外で勉強する学生
def:eng	a student who studies abroad
hypernym	(student)

4 More Accessible

Earlier versions of the Japanese wordnet were available at a university web site, with the data stored in sourceforge. For this release, data and documentation are stored in github, to make them more permenant. The wordnet is available online, both as plain xml, and as a released tarball with the license and canonical citation. This can be loaded directly from the Python WN module (Goodman and Bond, 2021), or the OMW interface. The Japanese wordnet can be found here: `https://bond-lab.github.io/wnja/`.

5 Conclusions

This paper presents the current state of the Japanese Wordnet: **wnja**. We hope that **wnja** will continue to be a useful resource not only for natural language processing, but also for language education/learning and linguistic research.

In future work, we want to look more at the description of formality and politeness, as well as to increase the coverage.

Acknowledgements

This research was supported in part by the JSPS/NUS Grant *Automatically determining meaning by comparing a text to its translation*, MOE Tier 2 grant *That's what you meant: a Rich Representation for Manipulation of Meaning* (MOE ARC41/13), the MOE Tier 1 grant on *Shifted in Translation: An Empirical Study of Meaning Change Across Languages (RG51/12)*, the Creative Commons grant on *Assessing the effect of license choice on the use of lexical resources* and joint research with Fuji-Xerox on *Multilingual Semantic Analysis*. Especial thanks to the other Japanese wordnet developers, Hitoshi Isahara, Kyoko Kanzaki, Kow Kuroda, Kiyotaka Uchimoto, Masao Utiyama, Darren Cook, Asuka Sumida and Kentaro Torisawa, as well as the many contributors who gave feedback. Some of this work was done while visiting the Humanities Center at Tokyo University, thanks to Tsuneko Nakazawa and Tsuneaki Kato.

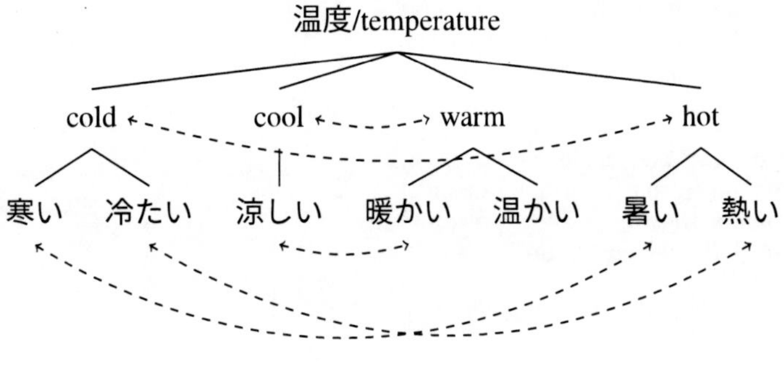

Figure 3: Structure for temperature words

Some nodes are not lexicalized in Japanese, but are still useful for the structure
temperature is linked by ATTRIBUTE (属性); tree is HYPONYM; dashed arrows are ANTONYM

References

Anthony E. Backhouse. 1993. *The Japanese Language: An Introduction.* Oxford University Press, Oxford.

Stephen Bird, Ewan Klein, and Edward Loper. 2009. *Natural Language Processing with Python.* O'Reilly. (`www.nltk.org/book`).

Francis Bond and Timothy Baldwin. 2016. Introduction to Japanese computational linguistics. In Francis Bond, Timothy Baldwin, Kentaro Inui, Shun Ishizaki, Hiroshi Nakagawa, and Akira Shimazu, editors, *Readings in Japanese Natural Language Processing*, chapter 1, pages 1–28. CSLI Publications.

Francis Bond, Timothy Baldwin, Richard Fothergill, and Kiyotaka Uchimoto. 2012. Japanese SemCor: A sense-tagged corpus of Japanese. In *Proceedings of the 6th Global WordNet Conference (GWC 2012)*, pages 56–63, Matsue.

Francis Bond and Ryan Foster. 2013. Linking and extending an open multilingual wordnet. In *51st Annual Meeting of the Association for Computational Linguistics: ACL-2013*, pages 1352–1362, Sofia.

Francis Bond, Hitoshi Isahara, Kyoko Kanzaki, and Kiyotaka Uchimoto. 2008. Boot-strapping a WordNet using multiple existing WordNets. In *Sixth International Conference on Language Resources and Evaluation (LREC 2008)*, Marrakech.

Francis Bond, Hiroki Nomoto, Luís Morgado da Costa, and Arthur Bond. 2020. Linking the TUFS basic vocabulary to the open multilingual wordnet. In *Twelth International Conference on Language Resources and Evaluation (LREC 2020)*, Marseilles.

Francis Bond, Shan Wang, Eshley Huini Gao, Hazel Shuwen Mok, and Jeanette Yiwen Tan. 2013. Developing parallel sense-tagged corpora with wordnets. In *Proceedings of the 7th Linguistic Annotation Workshop and Interoperability with Discourse (LAW 2013)*, pages 149–158, Sofia.

Christine Fellbaum, editor. 1998. *WordNet: An Electronic Lexical Database.* MIT Press.

Michael Wayne Goodman and Francis Bond. 2021. Intrinsically interlingual: The Wn Python library for wordnets. In *11th International Global Wordnet Conference (GWC2021).*

Vladimir Ž Jovanović. 2004. The form, position and meaning of interjections in English. *FACTA UNIVERSITATIS-Linguistics and Literature*, (Vol. 3/11):17–28.

Takayuki Kuribayashi, Francis Bond, Kow Kuroda, Kiyotaka Uchimoto, Hitoshi Isahara, Takayuki Kuribayashi, and Kyoko Kanzaki. 2010. Japanese WordNet 1.0. In *16th Annual Meeting of the Association for Natural Language Processing*, pages A5–3, Tokyo.

Kow Kuroda, Takayuki Kuribayashi, Francis Bond, Kyoko Kanzaki, and Hitoshi Isahara. 2011. Orthographic variants and multilingual sense tagging with the Japanese WordNet. In *17th Annual Meeting of the Association for Natural Language Processing*, pages A4–1, Toyohashi.

Sasao Kurohashi and Makoto Nagao. 1998. *Japanese morphological analysis system JUMAN version 3.6 manual.* Kyoto University.

John P. McCrae, Michael Wayne Goodman, Francis Bond, Alexandre Rademaker, Ewa Rudnicka, and Luís Morgado da Costa. 2021. The global wordnet formats: Updates for 2020. In *11th International Global Wordnet Conference (GWC2021).*

John P. McCrae, Alexandre Rademaker, Ewa Rudnicka, and Francis Bond. 2020. English wordnet 2020: Improving and extending a wordnet for English usingan open-source methodology. In *Workshop on Multimodal wordnets at LREC 2020.*

Luís Morgado da Costa and Francis Bond. 2016. Wow! what a useful extension to wordnet! In *10th International Conference on Language Resources and Evaluation (LREC 2016)*, Portorož.

Ian Niles and Adam Pease. 2001. Towards a standard upper ontology. In *Proceedings of the 2nd International Conference on Formal Ontology in Information Systems (FOIS-2001)*, Maine.

Kouji Okabe, Daisuke Kawahara, and Sadao Kurohasi. 2007. Improving nlp resources using canonical forms. In *13th Annual Meeting of The Association for Natural Language Processing*, Kyoto.

Adam Pease. 2011. *Ontology: A Practical Guide*. Articulate Software Press, Angwin, CA.

Jonathan Phillips. 2005. Introduction to the open clip art library. `http://rejon.org/media/writings/ocalintro/ocal_intro_phillips.html`. (accessed 2007-11-01).

John Robert Ross. 1995. Defective noun phrases. In *Papers from the Regional Meeting of the Chicago Linguistic Society*, volume 31, pages 398–440. University of Chicago.

Yu Jie Seah and Francis Bond. 2014. Annotation of pronouns in a multilingual corpus of Mandarin Chinese, English and Japanese. In *10th Joint ACL - ISO Workshop on Interoperable Semantic Annotation*, Reykjavik.

Liling Tan and Francis Bond. 2012. Building and annotating the linguistically diverse NTU-MC (NTU-multilingual corpus). *International Journal of Asian Language Processing*, 22(4):161–174.

Naiwen Xue, Fei Xia, Fu-Dong Chiou, and Martha Palmer. 2005. The Penn Chinese TreeBank: Phrase structure annotation of a large corpus. *Natural Language Engineering*, 11(2):207–238.

Latvian WordNet

Pēteris Paikens, Agute Klints, Ilze Lokmane,
Lauma Pretkalniņa, Laura Rituma, Madara Stāde, Laine Strankale
University of Latvia, Institute of Mathematics and Computer Science
Raina bulvaris 29, Riga, LV-1459, Latvia

Abstract

This paper describes the recently developed Latvian WordNet and the main linguistic principles used in its development. The inventory of words and senses is based on the Tēzaurs.lv online dictionary, restructuring the senses of the most frequently used words based on corpus evidence.

The semantic linking methodology adapts Princeton WordNet principles to fit the Latvian language usage and existing linguistic tradition. The semantic links include hyponymy, meronymy, antonymy, similarity, conceptual connection and gradation. We also measure inter-annotator agreement for different types of semantic links.

The dataset consists of 7609 words linked in 6515 synsets. 1266 of these words are considered fully completed as they have all the outgoing semantic links annotated, corpus examples assigned for each sense, as well as links to the English Princeton WordNet formed. The data is available to the public on Tēzaurs.lv as an addition to the general dictionary data, and is also published as a downloadable dataset.

1 Introduction

A wordnet (Fellbaum, 1998) is a lexico-semantic resource, which links an inventory of senses in synonym sets and other semantic relations, making it a valuable resource for NLP applications that can benefit from a formal structure of language semantics and relationships between specific word meanings.

Over the last three years we have been developing the first wordnet for Latvian, which is finally being formally released. We have chosen to form this resource based on corpus evidence and existing Latvian lexical resources, similar to the approach taken by plWordNet(Maziarz et al., 2016) and PolNet (Vetulani et al., 2010), instead of extending or translating word senses of some existing resource from other languages, such as the English Princeton WordNet.

The key tasks for forming Latvian WordNet were reviewing the sense inventory of the most frequently used Latvian words based on corpus evidence, annotating corpus examples to specific word senses, determining the members of synsets (synonym sets) and annotating outgoing semantic links, as well as later forming interlingual links to the English Princeton WordNet where applicable. The annotation work was performed with a custom lexicographic tool used for Tēzaurs.lv online dictionary, as described in (Paikens et al., 2022a).

The resulting manually curated resource consists of 7609 words linked in 6515 synsets. In addition we have an ongoing manual review of automatically obtained candidate links to Princeton WordNet (Strankale and Stāde, 2022). The consistency of semantic links was evaluated in an inter-annotator agreement experiment with three annotators on a limited subset of this data.

The following section describes the linguistic principles used in the development of Latvian WordNet, followed by a discussion of semantic links and an evaluation of their inter-annotator agreement in sections 3 and 4 respectively. After that, the article discusses the process of linking Latvian synsets to the Princeton WordNet in section 5 and the evaluation of these links in section 6. The concluding part consists of a discussion of the public availability of the resource in section 7 and conclusions and future work in section 8.

2 Linguistic Principles of Latvian WordNet

The decision was made to develop Latvian WordNet based on the inventory of Latvian word senses instead of adapting semantic hierarchy and relations from another language. It was also decided to build semantic relations between synsets from bottom up, allowing the hierarchy of word senses to grow and develop on its own. All word sense relations are made between synsets.

To choose the initial set of senses to work with, a list of 2000 most frequently used words was created based on The Balanced Corpus of Modern Latvian (Levane-Petrova, 2019). The list was then revised, leaving only words from four main word classes - nouns (except proper nouns), verbs, adjectives and adverbs. The resulting list of words and their senses are the core of Latvian WordNet. The senses of these words were taken from from the Explanatory Latvian Dictionary Tezaurs.lv (Spektors et al., 2016), after which an additional sense revision was carried out, as the first attempts of semantic linking showed many outdated word senses, as well as inconsistent sense granularity. We chose to look for corpus evidence if the senses are still currently relevant, whether any new senses have appeared or whether specific uses of a word demonstrate the validity of word sense distinction, in a manner similar to how sense distinctions and definitions were done in Estonian WordNet (Kerner et al., 2010).

The sense revision was primarily based on data from The Balanced Corpus of Modern Latvian, however, for rare meanings that are only used in colloquial language or other specific language genres we looked for additional corpus evidence from several different corpora from Latvian National Corpora Collection (Saulite et al., 2022). The specific principles of distinguishing word senses were developed for the convenience of both annotators and target users of the dictionary (Lokmane et al., 2021). Given that the most frequently used words are also often polysemous, the lexicographic work of processing them proved time-consuming, but also resulted in a thorough, high-quality inventory for the core wordnet.

Regarding other linguistic principles, the semantic relations of Latvian WordNet are usually annotated between synsets of the same word class, with only rare, well-argumented exceptions when such a link is allowed between the senses of different word classes. For example, participles are considered as verb forms but can also be related to synsets of adjectives. Additionally, some meanings of definite adjectives can be linked to synsets of nouns. Such cases are often characteristic of partial word conversion, when a separate form of a word begins to perform the function of another word class and therefore has a separate meaning while still belonging to the same word entry in a dictionary. Word class boundaries are a separate research issue that was not addressed within the scope of our task.

3 Semantic Links in Latvian WordNet

The most common and better studied semantic relations traditionally included in wordnets of various languages are synonymy, antonymy, hyponymy and meronymy (Jurafsky and Martin, 2022, Chapter 18, pp. 4-5)

In addition to these four major relations, Latvian WordNet is enriched with gradation relations which are not included in most wordnets, an exception being e.g. plWordNet (Maziarz et al., 2012, 2015).

The basic unit of a wordnet is a **synset**. The opinions of language users about the synonymy of certain senses may differ, so the following set of criteria is used to determine a set of synonyms. Firstly, dictionary definitions, namely, semantic features are compared: if most of them match, the senses are considered synonymous. Secondly, a substitution criterion is applied: if the words are interchangeable in most contexts, the senses are considered synonymous. It should be noted that a synset may include both neutral and expressive meanings. The fact that the subtler semantic distinctions among the elements of a synset are beyond the scope of description might be considered one of the most serious shortcomings of wordnets (Geeraerts, 2009, p. 160). In Latvian WordNet, this is compensated by the representation of data in Tezaurs.lv which includes the definitions and stylistic nuances of the specific sense for each word, not a single definition for the whole synset. One of the sources used in annotating synset relations was an existing Latvian synonym dictionary (Grīnberga and Kalnciems, 1998), however, its application was limited as it lists synonyms on a word (not sense) level and includes many words that are related but not strictly synonymous.

As the degree of synonymy between senses may be different, Latvian WordNet also includes a **similarity** link for senses which do not fall under the category of a full synonym. Firstly, the similarity link is established between senses if the semantic differences are too significant to be considered synonymous, e.g. the synset (*diskusija, pārrunas*) 'discussion, treatment, discourse' is considered as similar to the synset (*apspriede, sanāksme, sēde, sapulce, konference, saruna*) 'meeting, group meeting'. Secondly, the similarity link is estbalished between words which cannot be substituted for each other in the context due to grammatical peculiarities, e.g. the sense of the word *konteksts* 'circumstance, setting' is characteristic only to the locative case form and can not be substituted with the locative forms of seemingly synonymous (*apstākļis, situācija, stāvoklis*) 'situation, state of affairs'. Thirdly, verbs with distributional differences are also considered similar, e.g. the transitive *spēlēt* 'to play' can not be substituted with the intransitive *rotaļāties* 'to play' despite their semantic closeness.

Hyponymy is mainly observed in nouns and verbs. The hyponymy between verbs is widespread (Cruse, 2004, p. 148), and wordnets tend to include a special subtype of verb hyponymy, namely, troponymy (Fellbaum, 1998, p. 80), in which case the hypernym denotes a more general action or process whereas the hyponyms differ in the manner of how the action or process happens or is carried out. Since the concept of troponymy is not known in Latvian linguistics so far, the Latvian WordNet does not differentiate any subtypes of hyponymy. Hyponymic relations are not established between adjectives and adverbs.

Meronymy is characteristic mainly of nouns especially those having a concrete meaning. In some cases, meronymy borders on hyponymy. This type of semantic relation can be applied mainly to physical objects, as well as to other more abstract ones, such as institutional units, e. g. the meronyms of (*uzņēmums*) 'enterprise' are (*filiāle, nodaļa*) 'subsidiary company'.

Antonymy is a relationship between semantic opposites. However, there are several subtypes of opposition and not all of them are considered antonymic. A prototypical group of antonyms consists of words denoting gradable notions (Löbner, 2002, pp. 88-90), e.g. for the synset (*brangs, dižens, dižs, ievērojams, liels, pamatīgs, prāvs*) 'large, big, great' the antonym is (*mačs, mazs*) 'small, little'. In Latvian WordNet, a wide understanding of antonymy is adopted, including other types of opposites as well. They are, firstly, complementaries, e. g. (*klātbūtne, klātiene*) 'presence' vs. (*trūkums*) 'absence', secondly, reversives, e.g. (*ārā*) 'outside' vs. (*iekšā*) 'inside', thirdly, converses, e.g. (*pārdot*) 'to sell' vs. (*pirkt*) 'to buy'. Other words that are often contrasted in language use are also considered antonyms, e.g. (*praktisks*) 'practical' vs. (*teorētisks*) 'theoretical' and (*sekas*) 'effect' vs. (*cēlonis*) 'cause'.

Words and synsets in one **gradation set** express different values of the same attribute. The relation of gradation is mainly seen between adjectives, however, it also occasionally occurs in nouns and verbs. In gradation sets, other semantic links may exist as well, e.g., if the gradable values cover the whole scale, antonymic relations are also included. On the other hand, gradation sets of verbs and nouns may include hyponymy, e.g. the word *līt* 'to rain' has a series of semantically linked verbs denoting raining of various intensity, which can also be considered types of raining and, thus, hyponyms. In the future, it is planned to develop a system of simultaneous marking for gradation and hyponymy where necessary.

In addition to the semantic links mentioned above, we also annotate conceptual connections (as **"see also"**), as a category for words that are semantically related, but not by any of the mentioned semantic relations.

4 Evaluation of Semantic Linking

In order to assess how consistently the linking principles developed during the project are applied, a three-person inter-annotator agreement (IAA) evaluation was conducted on 15 words (5 nouns, 5 verbs and 5 adjectives) with 85 senses altogether. Adverbs were excluded from the experiment as they are poorly represented in the dictionary due to the lexicographic tradition. The words were chosen from the core list of the most frequently used words by selecting words with a moderate number of senses (2-6 superordinate senses and possible subsenses). Revision of the sense inventory was not included in the scope of this experiment, so it was ascertained beforehand that the words selected from the dictionary already had comparatively suitable senses for wordnet linking.

The experiment was carried out in three stages.

1. In the given list of words, each linguist offered possible semantic links (including synonymy to form a synset); they could pick any sense or synset in the dictionary to form the link with.

2. All linked synset pairs (324 in total; 96 pairs for initial 5 nouns; 105 - for verbs, 123 - for adjectives) that appeared in the first step of the experiment (even if only one linguist suggested it) were collected into a list, and each linguist repeatedly considered what kind of a

	R1 All	R1 N	R1 V	R1 ADJ	R2 All	R2 N	R2 V	R2 ADJ
Given synset pairs	∞	∞	∞	∞	324	96	105	123
Overall annotated links†	535	160	166	209	833	252	262	319
Any link: 3 people	75	23	22	30	221	70	68	83
Any link: 2 people	60	18	17	25	69	16	23	30
Any link: 1 person	190	55	66	69	32	10	12	10
No link	-	-	-	-	6	0	2	4
Matching linking: 3 people	47	15	17	15	129	43	49	37
Matching linking: 2 people	295	90	98	107	277	85	92	100
No matching links	30	6	7	17	51	11	13	27

Table 1: Results of the first two stages of the experiment (R1 and R2).
† The total number of links annotated in the IAA experiment, i.e., if three annotators provide the same link, it is counted in this sum thrice.

semantic link (if any) was necessary in each case.

3. In the third stage, the results of the second round were compared and discussed by all three linguists. In this stage, differing answers were discussed, as well as the possibility to agree on one answer (a specific relation or the absence of it between the senses); the linguists also had the option of leaving their decision unchanged.

We are using Fleiss' kappa measurement to judge inter-annotator agreement between multiple annotators. It is interesting to note that most evaluations of wordnet quality in literature only rarely (e.g Ehsani et al. (2018)) attempt to make such estimates for the semantic links within the wordnet,

The results of the first stage (see *R1* part of Table 1) showed that the endpoints of the selected links were sufficiently different; at this point, Fleiss' kappa measurement was 0.55 (CI95% 0.48 - 0.63), i.e., moderate agreement. Out of 324 different linkable synset pairs which were proposed by annotators, only 47 had exact matching links for all three annotators. This was partially due to each annotator choosing different potential senses to link or not thinking of other possibly corresponding senses at all. Thus, it was concluded that additional automatic solutions for offering potential candidates would prove useful in the future; the identification of such candidates could be based, for example, on similarity of sense definitions. It should also be noted that data from a synonym dictionary were also available during the experiment. However, the coverage of such data is incomplete, as only some words from the experiment have synonym dictionary suggestions, and such a resource does not provide recommendations for any of the other types of semantic relations. This stage also demonstrated the differences in each annotator's individual approach: as seen from the data, one annotator connects synsets comparatively cautiously and less often, another much more freely, which also affects the inter-annotator agreement. Given the low number of matches in the chosen sense pairs themselves, it would be difficult to distinguish an actual agreement on semantic link creation. For this reason, the second stage of experiment was organised, with a prepared list of potential sense pairs to be linked.

The results of the second round where annotators got a pre-made list of potential sense are given in *R2* part of Table 1. Surprisingly the inter-annotator agreement showed by Fleiss' kappa was lower but still in the range of moderate agreement – 0.46 (CI95% 0.40 - 0.46), however this might also be due to the relatively small size of this experiment. As it was suspected before the experiment, the overall amount of proposed links increased dramatically – from 535 to 833. It seems that when annotators are provided a large quantity of proposed candidates, more links are made but inter-annotator agreement decreases as annotators are forced to make a choice about words they did not consider themselves.

The level of agreement on adjective links is lower than the agreement on noun and verb links, which indicates that the methodology of marking adjectival links should be further expanded and clarified. When looking at separate link types, a precise agreement also appeared in antonyms and gradation sets, suggesting that when such candidates are presented, the semantic relation is recognized.

The results of the third round were also used for making the McNemar's test, resulting in a p-value of 2.51×10^{-23} indicating that consultations made statistically significant changes to the data. In 15% of the discussed cases disagreements still remained even after consultations. From this it can be concluded that the linguists' seminars organized regularly during the project to solve various labeling and annotation dilemmas for specific words are notably beneficial for the creation of a more consistent system. At the same time, it can be seen that even after a unified theoretical base, a developed methodology and regular discussions, there are cases when annotators have differing opinions.

Some of the cases of disagreement are as follows. Firstly, there were varying opinions as to whether the synset (*vebkamera*) 'webcam' is a hyponym of synset (*kamera*) 'photografic or video camera', considering that a webcam carries out an additional function of transmitting an image instantly, which a regular camera does not. This raised speculations about whether a webcam is a new type of camera or they both are types of some more general meaning of camera that is not represented in the dictionary. Secondly, there were discussions regarding the synsets (*inspekcija*) 'inspection' and (*apskate*) 'examination'. Opinions differed as to whether they are members of the same synset or whether the 'inspection' includes 'examination', but 'examination' can exist without 'inspection'. Both of the given examples show a different understanding of the importance of one seme to distinguish a new meaning or a new semantic relation. The difference of opinion also occurred in situations where the linguist feels a close semantic connection between the senses, but is unable to define it in the currently available relation set, or in moments, when each linguist indicated a different type of relation, although most likely none of the currently available relations fully corresponds to it in its general sense. The synset (*tonis*) 'tone - a quality of a given color that differs slightly from another color' and synset (*krāsa*) 'color' serves as an illustrative example for this. One linguist suggested that color consists of various tones and therefore a meronymy/holonymy link could be used; at the same time, another linguist believed that tone is an attribute of color and therefore the appropriate link type is "See also". It should also be noted that none of the linguists suggested a relation to a hierarchy in this case, although that is exactly the type of link used in Princeton WordNet between these synsets.

In order to obtain a gold standard, it may be necessary to assign an authoritative linguist who will determine the final opinion in such cases.

The qualitative analysis of the data gave sufficient grounds for the additional conclusion that link formation can successfully highlight cases, when sense revision is necessary during the process of annotation. There were cases when it was agreed that the reason for disagreement was the vague definition of certain word senses, which, in turn, complicated the possibility if agreement, as there was too much space for interpretation.

In short, the experiment has demonstrated the complexity of the given problem, but also provides an opportunity to evaluate the consistency of annotated data. A more detailed analysis of separate semantic link types is planned in future, to further improve our methodology.

5 Linking Latvian WordNet to Princeton WordNet

As a part of the project, Latvian WordNet to Princeton WordNet sense mapping is carried out to identify English equivalents for Latvian word meanings. Currently, only a manual mapping has been implemented for the 2000 most frequently used Latvian words. However, the manually generated data are being used to develop and train the algorithm for automated sense linking, which will be carried out for a significantly broader scope of word meanings. The version that the Latvian word meanings are presently being mapped to is Princeton WordNet 3.0.

Currently, the project implements wordnet to wordnet interlinking on the level of synsets, as opposed to linking individual word senses as seen, for example, in plWordNet (Rudnicka et al., 2019). Such choice of approach is motivated by the need to primarily secure a foundation of optimal interlingual equivalence based on meaning, that would later potentially serve as a basis for more intricate equivalence structures based on stylistic register, dialect, gender and other aspects, which can be linked sense to sense.

The project's main theoretical base for creating interlingual links and word sense equivalence is taken from translation theories that offer various perspectives on equivalence (e.g. natural vs. directional) (Pym, 2014; Venuti and Baker, 2000; Chesterman, 2016), to better understand the potential asymmetry between two or more languages. Thus, not only full or direct equivalence is taken into account, but also such types as functional, formal, stylistic, situational and semantic equivalence (Venuti and Baker, 2000; Chesterman, 2016). This provides additional context for each decision to minimise inconsistency or artificially rigid or symmetrical interlingual structures.

The current process of interlinking is facilitated by automatic suggestions of possible equivalents for each word, based on bilingual dictionaries and machine translation. This feature is integrated in the editing tool, but the linguist may also freely choose and select other English word meanings if the suggestions do not seem to fit the specific meaning in Latvian. Therefore, both automated and manual methods are already combined in this step of the process. So far, 3139 interlingual links of various types have been created between Latvian WordNet and Priceton WordNet.

However, during the early stages of wordnet to wordnet linking it was concluded that direct links alone cannot fully convey the various cases of interlingual hyponymy, namely, cases when a synset in the source language conveys a broader or narrower scope of meanings than its closest equivalent in the target language. Consequently, three types of interlingual links were created, enabling the editors to mark a Latvian synset as a full equivalent, as well as being broader or narrower than its English counterpart. If an equivalent synset can be identified, links of narrower or wider meanings are not allowed. If an equivalent synset can not be identified, multiple links of narrower and wider meanings are allowed.

Full equivalence may be seen in the Latvian synset (*jautājums, prasījums, vaicājums*) and the Princeton WordNet synset (question, interrogation, interrogative, interrogative sentence): the meanings describe a sufficiently similar concept with the same level of semantisation. This type of direct link is the most often used – it constitutes 1891 of all interlingual links. But, for example, considering the Latvian synset (*pārmest*), roughly translated as 'reprimand' or 'reprove', it can be concluded that there is no single equivalent for it in the Princeton WordNet; instead, several, broader synsets, such as (reproach, upbraid) and (admonish, reprove, reproof) are linked to it through interlingual hyponymy links, each denoting a part of its full, comparatively broader range of meanings. There are currently 545 such links.

Conversely, there are also certain cases, when Princeton WordNet synsets have a broader set of meanings than their Latvian counterparts. For example, the synset (sibling), which includes both brothers and sisters, does not have a direct equivalent in Latvian[1]. Therefore two separate hyponymy links need to be made with the more specific (*bāleliņš, bāliņš, brālis*) 'brother', and (*māsa*) 'sister' to convey the full meaning of the concept of a sibling. 703 such links have been created in Latvian WordNet so far. Interlingual hyponymy links not only help in the previously described cases, but also in linking cultural realia to more general meanings in the other language. Thus, the data that would otherwise be left unmarked can be involved in forming the interlingual hierarchies between Latvian WordNet and Princeton WordNet.

A notably problematic aspect in the formation of interlingual links are word meaning definitions, which in some cases have become outdated over the course of time or have been left unnecessary broad or narrow. For example, Princeton WordNet lists only the general meaning of 'dispute' (disagreement), without separating the meaning of a legal dispute, which exists in Latvian WordNet. Similar cases have been observed in Latvian WordNet, especially in instances when meaning definitions list two aspects separated by a semicolon. Such ambiguous cases automatically involve selective use of annotators' personal knowledge or additional research to discern the true level of meaning equivalence; such cases are discussed in greater detail during the weekly project linguist seminars to reach the most objective solution.

So far, distinguishing three types of interlingual links has proved useful to bridge the gaps and differences between Latvian and English. It is expected, that this approach will also facilitate the future aspirations of incorporating Latvian WordNet into Open Multilingual Wordnet (Bond and Foster, 2013), as a working mechanism will already be established to deal with any potential inconsistencies or language differences.

6 Evaluating Interlingual Links

To evaluate our process of automatic interlingual link creation, another IAA experiment was car-

[1]In Latvian, *brālis* 'brother' refers exclusively to males. There is an English calque 'sibs' used as a term in genetics, but it is not understood or used by non-specialists.

ried out. In the experiment, annotators evaluated the machine-translated suggestions, taking into account the opinions of three annotators. The proposed links were separated in the following four categories:

1. link corresponds perfectly;
2. the proposed link points to a semantically wider or narrower sense than the Latvian word sense;
3. more information is needed to make a decision, as it is clear that there is some semantic relation but not obvious what type of relation;
4. the proposed link does not correspond at all.

The IAA experiment was performed using words from common vocabulary with only one sense in Latvian (including homonyms), excluding regional words, slang etc. There are up to five possible candidates of English equivalents offered by the system which the annotators can choose from.

Three linguists annotated 684 instances in total. On 272 corresponding outputs all annotators agreed that the proposed interlingual link should be approved, and in 94 cases all annotators decided that the suggested links definitely do not match the Latvian meaning. In 57% cases annotators fully agree, and out of all the automatically provided candidate links 40% are undisputed interlingual matches.

In cases when all three annotators chose to select the "wider/narrower meaning" option, several links were proposed. For example, *apnikums* (a mental state when a person is bored and tired of everything) had four suggested links: (boredom, ennui, tedium), (depression), (fatigue, weariness, tiredness), (tediousness, tedium, tiresomeness). All of suggested links are somehow semantically connected to *apnikums*, but none of them corresponds completely. From this it can be concluded that the automated system has already noted the absence of complete equivalence in this case.

The main reason of annotators' disagreement with automatic suggestions was the occasional inability of MT to correctly interpret the meaning of derived words. For example, *apgaismniecība* 'Enlightenment' (derived from *gaisma* 'light') had the automatic MT suggestion of "lighting" (the craft of providing artificial light).

Another reason for disagreement was based on grammatical differences between Latvian and English, especially in the use of genitive case. In Latvian, a noun in genitive case is often used to name a quality, taking the place of adjective. For example, inflexible genitive noun *apļveida* (derived form *aplis* 'circle') is used only in this (genitive) case and implies quality (circular, round). Because it is a noun, MT suggests a link to the noun synset (circle, round).

Differences in word meaning definitions between wordnets may occur for seemingly similar concepts. In that case answers between annotators may vary. For instance, *apašs* 'apache' is defined in Latvian a "a French gangster", whereas Princeton WordNet suggests that it is "a Parisian gangster". Two annotators considered this as a direct link, one viewed this as wider/narrower case. Thus, the annotators had to look at each case individually and decide whether to base their decision on their knowledge of the subject or to stick to the given definitions, leading to the conclusion that the result in this case cannot be completely objective. It also brings to attention the difference which even a minimal manual control can make in automatically created data.

Disagreement based on annotators' personal opinion frequently appeared on words that name state, condition, sensation and other abstract concepts. These differences are mainly based on annotators' personal understanding of the concept in Latvian. Personal opinion also may vary on how we perceive translation quality and which semantic differences are essential when choosing between direct, wider/narrower or no link. For example the Latvian meaning *asthma* "a fit of loss of breath, shortness of breath" and the English synset (asthma, asthma attack, bronchial asthma) "respiratory disorder characterized by wheezing; usually of allergic origin" has a different answer from each annotator: 1 "corresponds", 1 "wider/narrower" and 1 "needs more information".

The IAA results for interlingual links not only have helped reinforce the importance of multiple link types, but also aided in the future the development of clearer strategies and criteria for annotating ambiguous, more complicated meanings.

7 Publishing Results

The main access point for this resource to the general public is through the Tēzaurs.lv (`https://`

tezaurs.lv) online dictionary, which is widely used in Latvia. However, for the purposes of the research community we also publish this data in various formats and in multiple repositories. Latvian WordNet is developed and maintained in the Tezaurs.lv lexicographic platform with a PostgreSQL database custom data structure, which then can be exported in multiple widely recognised data formats.

Currently we provide an Open Multilingual Wordnet compatible LMF XML[2] export for the wordnet data, and a more detailed TEI 5 (Text Encoding Initiative) Dictionary chapter XML[3] which contains both Tezaurs.lv dictionary data and Latvian WordNet synsets and links. The TEI format also contains information about gradation sets, which is not available in LMF due to format restrictions.

All the latest version data (including a full database dump) are available on the project homepage[4], where we also provide a list of Latvian Wordnet core words. The TEI XML dataset is also regularly published in the CLARIN-LV repository[5] (Skadina et al., 2020). Our intent is to publish LMF export both via CLARIN-LV and OMW infrastructure. We do quarterly releases for all our dictionary and wordnet data.

8 Conclusions and future work

To summarize, we are happy to present the first major release of Latvian WordNet, providing a manually curated resource of a reasonable size, based on Latvian corpus evidence and linguistic tradition that can be a solid basis for future research work.

The current Latvian WordNet consists of 7609 words linked in 6515 synsets, out of which 1266 synsets are considered completed as they have all the outgoing semantic links annotated, corpus examples assigned for at least one word in the synset, as well as links to the English Princeton WordNet formed, and the remainder being less frequently used words that have been joined by outgoing semantic links from the 'core' synsets. 70826 corpus examples were linked to specific word senses and subsenses. This information is available to public as an integrated part of the Tēzaurs.lv online dictionary and has received positive user feedback regarding its usefulness.

From the perspective of linguistic principles, we are satisfied with our choice to form a wordnet from scratch. Even if bootstrapping from English resources would have taken less effort, our experience with linking to the Princeton WordNet has indicated many interlingual differences, which through automatic means would have imposed an artificial, English-derived structure upon this resource.

It is interesting to note that sense granularity is still an issue open for debate among the annotators, with no clear consensus despite the fact that it was one of the primary drivers for restructuring the existing sense inventory and a key part of the methodology discussion over the last three years. Developing an adequate sense inventory takes a large amount of time and effort compared to forming synonym sets and other semantic links.

Our approach of word sense selection based on corpus evidence has also resulted in a large quantity of corpus examples aligned to the specific word senses, which forms a useful dataset for training word sense disambiguation systems (Paikens et al., 2022b). Ongoing future work in this direction is annotating a gold standard text - the first two chapters of The Little Prince - with specific word senses from Latvian WordNet.

The results of our inter-annotator agreement experiments for semantic links within Latvian WordNet indicate the difficulty and the subjective nature of semantic linking. A relevant observation is that providing automatically generated candidates improves the linking coverage, as annotators often agree that the link should be made if they are aware of the option, but might not come up with the related word on their own. It seems that when annotators are provided a large quantity of proposed candidates, more links are made but inter-annotator agreement decreases as annotators are forced to make a choice about words they did not consider themselves. It also indicates that annotator discussions improve consistency, so the differences apparently involve also a different understanding of methodology, not a fundamental disagreement about the discussed words.

In 57% cases annotators fully agree, and out of all the automatically provided candidate links 40% are undisputed interlingual matches.

[2]https://globalwordnet.github.io/schemas/#xml

[3]https://tei-c.org/release/doc/tei-p5-doc/en/html/DI.html

[4]https://wordnet.ailab.lv/data/

[5]https://repository.clarin.lv/repository/

For Latvian-English links we observe 57% exact match IAA between all three annotators, with some disagreement whether a certain sense is the same or broader in one of the languages. We observe less agreement over abstract concepts, as their perception seems to be more subjective, and it is difficult to decide on the most appropriate interlingual link. In general, the generation of automatically provided candidates were very helpful in rapidly creating links, as the 40% of candidates were clearly proper links, but they do need manual review.

For further improvement of Latvian WordNet the planned future tasks involve adding links for word derivation, extending the automatic link candidate derivation also for intra-language semantic links based on existing word definitions and language models from large corpora, and also continuing the manual review of proposed Latvian-English links which could then enable a transfer of semantic relations from Princeton WordNet to Latvian WordNet.

It would be interesting to apply this resource for cross-lingual research on semantic alignment and differences between Latvian and Lithuanian WordNet (Garabík and Pileckytė, 2013), as well as going beyond current semantic links to word derivation and etymology.

Continued extension of the manually developed Latvian WordNet is also an obvious direction of future work, but is highly contingent on funding opportunities. We are also considering a specific project to integrate idiomatic expressions and other multiword entities in the Latvian WordNet.

Acknowledgements

This work was supported by the Latvian Council of Science, project "Latvian WordNet and Word Sense Disambiguation", project No. LZP-2019/1-0464. We also thank the anonymous reviewers for their input in improving this paper.

References

Francis Bond and Ryan Foster. 2013. Linking and extending an open multilingual Wordnet. In *Proceedings of the 51st Annual Meeting of the Association for Computational Linguistics (Volume 1: Long Papers)*, pages 1352–1362, Sofia, Bulgaria. Association for Computational Linguistics.

Andrew Chesterman. 2016. *Memes of translation: The spread of ideas in translation theory*. John Benjamins Publishing Company.

Alan Cruse. 2004. *Meaning in Language: An Introduction to Semantics and Pragmatics*.

Razieh Ehsani, Ercan Solak, and Olcay Taner Yildiz. 2018. Constructing a wordnet for turkish using manual and automatic annotation. *ACM Trans. Asian Low-Resour. Lang. Inf. Process.*, 17(3).

Christiane Fellbaum, editor. 1998. *WordNet: An electronic lexical database*. MIT Press.

Radovan Garabík and Indrė Pileckytė. 2013. From multilingual dictionary to lithuanian wordnet. *Natural Language Processing, Corpus Linguistics, E-Learning*, pages 74–80.

Dirk Geeraerts. 2009. *Theories of lexical semantics*. OUP Oxford.

E. Grīnberga and O. Kalnciems, editors. 1998. *Latviešu valodas sinonīmu vārdnīca*. Avots, Rīga. 3. papildinātais un pārstrādātais izdevums.

Daniel Jurafsky and James H Martin. 2022. Speech and language processing (3rd edition draft). Available from: `https://web.stanford.edu/~jurafsky/slp3/` [cited 2022 Jan 13].

Kadri Kerner, Heili Orav, and Sirli Parm. 2010. Growth and revision of Estonian WordNet. *Principles, Construction and Application of Multilingual Wordnets*, pages 198–202.

Kristīne Levane-Petrova. 2019. Līdzsvarotais mūsdienu latviešu valodas tekstu korpuss, tā nozīme gramatikas pētījumos. *Language: Meaning and Form*, 10:131–146. The Balanced Corpus of Modern Latvian, its role in grammar studies.

Sebastian Löbner. 2002. *Understanding Semantics*. UK: Hodder Arnold.

Ilze Lokmane, Laura Rituma, Madara Stade, and Agute Klints. 2021. The Latvian WordNet and word sense disambiguation: Challenges and findings. In *Proceedings of the 7th Biennial Conference on Electronic Lexicography (eLex)*, pages 232–246.

Marek Maziarz, Maciej Piasecki, Ewa Rudnicka, Stan Szpakowicz, and Paweł Kędzia. 2016. plwordnet 3.0–a comprehensive lexical-semantic resource. In *Proceedings of COLING 2016, the 26th International Conference on Computational Linguistics: Technical Papers*, pages 2259–2268.

Marek Maziarz, Maciej Piasecki, Stanisław Szpakowicz, and Joanna Rabiega-Wiśniewska. 2015. Semantic relations among nouns in polish wordnet grounded in lexicographic and semantic tradition. *Cognitive Studies| Études cognitives*, (11):161–181.

Marek Maziarz, Stanisław Szpakowicz, and Maciej Piasecki. 2012. Semantic relations among adjectives in Polish WordNet 2.0: a new relation set, discussion and evaluation. *Cognitive Studies| Études cognitives*, (12):149–179.

Peteris Paikens, Mikus Grasmanis, Agute Klints, Ilze Lokmane, Lauma Pretkalniņa, Laura Rituma, Madara Stāde, and Laine Strankale. 2022a. Towards Latvian WordNet. In *Proceedings of the Thirteenth Language Resources and Evaluation Conference*, pages 2808–2815, Marseille, France. European Language Resources Association.

Pēteris Paikens, Laura Rituma, and Lauma Pretkalniņa. 2022b. Towards word sense disambiguation for latvian. *Baltic journal of modern computing*, 10(3):402–408.

Anthony Pym. 2014. *Exploring translation theories*. Routledge.

Ewa Rudnicka, Maciej Piasecki, Francis Bond, Łukasz Grabowski, and Tadeusz Piotrowski. 2019. Sense equivalence in plwordnet to princeton wordnet mapping. *International Journal of Lexicography*, 32(3):296–325.

B. Saulite, R. Dargis, N. Gruzitis, I. Auzina, K. Levane-Petrova, L. Pretkalnina, L. Rituma, P. Paikens, A. Znotins, L. Strankale, K. Pokratniece, I. Poikans, G. Barzdins, I. Skadina, A. Baklane, V. Saulespurens, and J. Ziedins. 2022. Latvian national corpora collection – korpuss.lv. In *Proceedings of the 13th Language Resources and Evaluation Conference (LREC)*, pages 5123–5129.

Inguna Skadina, Ilze Auzina, Normunds Gruzitis, and Arturs Znotins. 2020. Clarin in latvia: From the preparatory phase to the construction phase and operation. In *Proceedings of the 5th Conference on Digital Humanities in the Nordic Countries (DHN)*, pages 342–350.

Andrejs Spektors, Ilze Auzina, Roberts Dargis, Normunds Gruzitis, Peteris Paikens, Lauma Pretkalnina, Laura Rituma, and Baiba Saulite. 2016. Tēzaurs.lv: the largest open lexical database for Latvian. In *Proceedings of the Tenth International Conference on Language Resources and Evaluation (LREC'16)*, pages 2568–2571, Portorož, Slovenia. European Language Resources Association (ELRA).

Laine Strankale and Madara Stāde. 2022. Automatic word sense mapping from Princeton WordNet to Latvian WordNet. In *Proceedings of the 14th International Conference on Agents and Artificial Intelligence*, volume 1, pages 478–485.

Lawrence Venuti and Mona Baker, editors. 2000. *The translation studies reader*. Routledge London.

Zygmunt Vetulani, Marek Kubis, and Tomasz Obrębski. 2010. PolNet — Polish WordNet: Data and tools. In *Proceedings of the Seventh International Conference on Language Resources and Evaluation (LREC'10)*, Valletta, Malta. European Language Resources Association (ELRA).

Initial Experiments for Building a Guarani WordNet

Luis Chiruzzo[1] **Marvin M. Agüero-Torales**[2,3] **Aldo Alvarez**[4] **Yliana Rodríguez**[1]
[1]Universidad de la República, Montevideo, Uruguay
[2]University of Granada, Granada, Spain
[3]Global CoE of Data Intelligence, Fujitsu, Madrid, Spain
[4]Universidad Nacional de Itapúa, Encarnación, Paraguay
luischir@fing.edu.uy, maguero@correo.ugr.es, aldo.alvarez@fiuni.edu.py, yrodriguez@fhuce.edu.uy

Abstract

This paper presents a work in progress about creating a Guarani version of the WordNet database. Guarani is an indigenous South American language and is a low-resource language from the NLP perspective. Following the *expand* approach, we aim to find Guarani lemmas that correspond to the concepts defined in WordNet. We do this through three strategies that try to select the correct lemmas from Guarani-Spanish datasets. We ran them through three different bilingual dictionaries and had native speakers assess the results. This procedure found Guarani lemmas for about 6.5 thousand synsets, including 27% of the base WordNet concepts. However, more work on the quality of the selected words will be needed in order to create a final version of the dataset.

1 Introduction

Guarani is an indigenous South American language spoken by around 6.5 million native speakers, mainly in Paraguay and in parts of Bolivia, Argentina and Brazil. Despite being one of the most widely spoken languages in the region, it has received little attention from a computational linguistic perspective. In the latest years, interest in natural language processing (NLP) research for indigenous languages of the Americas has increased, and nowadays, a number of researchers are building tools and resources for many of these languages, such as multilingual corpora (Mager et al., 2021). However, the creation of lexical databases and ontologies, such as WordNets, is only very recently starting to gather attention.

WordNet (Miller, 1995) is a lexical database, originally created for English but later on for many other languages (e.g. Gonzalez-Agirre et al., 2012; Vossen, 1998), that organizes concepts in an ontology of inter-related terms. The basic unit of WordNet is the synset, defined as a set of words that could be used interchangeably, at least in some context, and is similar to the notion of a sense or meaning in a dictionary. Synsets are organized in an ontology with hyponymy as the central relation between concepts, but also including (depending on the POS) other relations such as meronymy, antonymy or implication. The concepts stored in WordNet belong to one of the four lexical categories: nouns, verbs, adjectives and adverbs.

Historically there have been two main approaches to building WordNets (Bosch and Griesel, 2017; Vossen, 1998), which are: manually creating a new set of concepts for each language and establishing links to the original Princeton WordNet (named the *merge* approach), or using the original structure of Princeton WordNet and translating the lemmas corresponding to the different concepts into the target language (named the *expand* approach). In this paper, we present a work in progress for building a WordNet database for the Guarani language using the *expand* approach. We collected different bilingual datasets (i.e. Guarani-Spanish dictionaries), and implemented some heuristics to select the correct Guarani lemmas that correspond to WordNet synsets. Then native speakers annotated a sample of the results obtained by the heuristics in order to assess the quality of the built resource.

2 Related Work

There have been very few attempts at creating WordNets for indigenous American languages. Two of them are about languages spoken mainly in Peru, Shipibo-Konibo (Maguiño-Valencia et al., 2018), and several varieties of Quechua (Melgarejo et al., 2022). Previous attempts for Quechua do not focus on building a WordNet ontology, but include using links to the Spanish WordNet in order to help word sense disambiguation (Rudnick, 2011) or morphological analysis (Gasser, 2010).

Bosch and Griesel (2017) describe an attempt to build WordNets in several indigenous African languages. These attempts, as well as the ones mentioned above, generally use the *expand* approach to building WordNets, as it is the easiest one to use when at least there are bilingual datasets available.

Our work is, as far as we know, the first attempt to build a WordNet for Guarani. We focus on the modern Paraguayan variety of Guarani. Similarly to Melgarejo et al. (2022), we use the Spanish version of WordNet to support the translation, because there are more Guarani-Spanish bilingual resources available. Guarani is a low-resource language (Joshi et al., 2020) and, like other languages in this category, it lacks large monolingual and parallel corpora to build even some relatively simple NLP applications. There are some small multilingual (Mager et al., 2021) and bilingual (Chiruzzo et al., 2022, 2020) corpora that include Guarani, and even the newest version of the Google Translate tool includes Guarani as one of its options[1], but so far, the size and performance of these resources is not enough to obtain accurate lexical information.

3 Guarani language

Modern Paraguayan Guarani belongs to the Tupi-Guarani family, part of a posited Tupian stock comprising between 60 and 70 different languages. The Tupi-Guarani family is the largest family within the Tupian stock, and within it, Guarani is the language with the most speakers. Tupian languages are spoken in Brazil, Argentina, Bolivia, French Guiana, Paraguay and Peru.

3.1 Historical perspective

Following the arrival of Europeans to South America, Franciscans and Jesuits documented and standardized Guarani (Meliá, 1992). The Jesuits reduced the indigenous language to writing, and cunningly used it as the language of evangelization until they were expelled in 1767 (see Rodríguez, 2019). Guarani was declared a national language by Paraguayan leader Stroessner in 1967 in article 5 of the first chapter of the new constitution. However, it was only in 1992 that it was given co-official status together with Spanish in the Ley de Lenguas (Law of Languages) and bilingual education began to be established in 1994 (see Penner, 2016 for an analysis of the law's practical implications and outreach). Analysis of recent census data confirms previous observations that Guarani-Spanish bilingualism is higher in urban and border areas (e.g. Rubin, 1963; Solé, 1991), while high rates of Guarani monolingualism at home are limited to rural areas (Gynan, 2001).

Five centuries after Guarani was given a written code by means of using the Latin alphabet, Guarani is still not frequently used in writing. When it comes to NLP, the challenge is taken even further, as there are not many digital resources and corpora that could be used for automatic processing. The contact between the two languages and their many varieties, and its repercussions, has been studied by numerous scholars, amongst which Dietrich (2001, 2004), Kallfell (2006), Thun (2006) and Zajícová (2010) stand out. Within the ample scope of the contact scenario and its outcomes, we will constrain to the matter of Jopara, the very commonly used code in Paraguay that resorts both to Guarani and Spanish (for a structural analysis of Jopara see Thun, 2005; Gómez Rendón, 2008 and Kallfell, 2011). Although scholars do not agree on whether Jopara is a variety of Spanish, a variety of Guarani, a new mixed language, the result of code-switching (as Estigarribia, 2015 states) or languages that keep mixing (the latter is argued by Thun, 2005, p. 311), the fact that there is a code in which two languages are being mixed is relevant for the purpose of our work. The features of a mixture of languages (that is what the word *Jopara* actually means in Guarani: mixture) can hinder our work in the manners presented in section 5.3. Interestingly, Guasch (1948) was the first to use the term to refer to the language mixing that had to be avoided (see Blestel, 2021). The sociological and attitudinal significance of such an idea has had repercussions until to date.

3.2 Language features

We now move on to present Guarani's trait characteristics following Estigarribia (2020). The overview is narrowed down to morphology given the aim of this paper. At the level of word formation, most meanings are built into a word as parts of it, as affixes or other particles (i.e. Guarani has an agglutinative morphology). There are remnants of an extensive polysynthetic behaviour, most words are composed of many parts, each with its own meaning to contribute to the whole. As a consequence, what would otherwise be a whole sentence in English is a single word in a polysynthetic language like Guarani. There are two first-person

[1]https://ai.googleblog.com/2022/05/24-new-languages-google-translate.html

plural pronouns, one that includes the addressees (*ñande*) and one that excludes them (*ore*).

Guarani has specific prefixes that simultaneously represent a first-person agent acting on a second-person patient, and there are two kinds of intransitive verbs whose subjects look different (split intransitivity). There is a class of words that take different prefixes when they are in the same phrase with other words and three ways to indicate events where a participant makes another participant do something (i.e. three different morphological causatives). Verbs and other predicates are also negated by a circumfix, that is, a negation that has two parts: a prefix that comes before the verb and a suffix that comes after. For example, the verb "ndaguatái" (I do not walk) can be analyzed as *nd-a-guata-i*: the first person singular affix *a-* and the base verb form *guata* (to walk) surrounded by the negation circumfix *nd-V-i*. We consider that the base form of a verb, without any of the affixes, is the appropriate way to represent Guarani verbal lemmas in WordNet.

When it comes to nouns, they take suffixes that indicate past or future, among other interpretations (nominal temporal-aspectual inflection). Guarani has an extensive system of postpositions that come at the end of a noun phrase to indicate its relation to a predicate. Guarani's lexicon has been influenced by Spanish, however, in Paraguayan Guarani most of the basic lexicon is still of Tupi-Guarani extraction.

Even though we have used traditional grammatical relations to describe Guarani, restraining from using units of observation from other languages as units of analysis could provide a wider hold of how Guarani works, i.e. analyzing Guarani data without relying on antecedently given formal or relational structure (see Otheguy, 2002 for an elaboration on this theoretical matter). For example, there is a class of nouns in Guarani called triform nouns or relational nouns (Estigarribia, 2020; Academia de la Lengua Guaraní (ALG), 2018) which are written with a different prefix depending on their use within a sentence or structure. They take forms prefixed by *t-*, *h-* or *r-* depending on whether they are referring to the generic form of the noun, or if they relate to another participant in the sentence. However, there is a discussion around whether these sets of nouns should be considered as a base form with a set of prefixes, or as sets of three distinct lemmas. As we will see, dictionaries and native speakers tend to consider them as different lemmas, and under this assumption, the three forms would be generally included in the same synsets.

4 Process

This section describes the heuristics we use to select Guarani lemmas for the synsets, and the datasets we obtain the information from.

4.1 Selectors

We follow the selector-based strategy similar to (Pradet et al., 2014; Herrera et al., 2016; Methol et al., 2018). In these works, they define a *selector* as a strategy that takes the set of lemmas in a synset for a source language, and the set of translation candidates for those lemmas in the target language, and chooses which target language lemmas should be assigned to the synset.

The main difference we have is that in those previous works, the source language was always English, which is the best possible scenario as English is the original and most complete language of WordNet. However, there are no bilingual Guarani-English dictionaries available, at least not with a considerable size that could be used for our purposes. Because of this, we resort to the Spanish version of WordNet, which has much fewer lemmas, and Guarani-Spanish dictionaries. The efficacy of the selectors will depend on the quality of the dictionaries, but also on the adequate coverage of the Spanish version of WordNet.

The three selectors we use in this work are the following:

Monosemy Given a lemma sl in the source language that belongs to only one synset s, we consider that the lemma is monosemic. In that situation, assign all the possible translations of sl in the target language $\{tl_1, ..., tl_n\}$, to the synset s. The intuition is that if sl only has one sense, its counterparts tl_i should have the same sense.

Single Translation Consider a lemma sl in the source language that belongs to one or more synsets $\{s_1, ..., s_n\}$, and according to the dictionary, the lemma has only one possible translation tl in the target source. In this case, assign tl to all synsets $\{s_1, ..., s_n\}$. The intuition is that if we had a perfect dictionary with all possible translations and there is only one way to translate sl, that translation should be valid for all senses of sl. Of course, this assumption does not happen in real life, so it will depend on the quality and coverage of the available dictionaries.

Factorization Given a synset s that has lemmas $\{sl_1, ..., sl_n\}$ in the source language. Each source lemma sl_i has a corresponding set of lemmas in the target language $\{tl_{i,1}, ..., tl_{i,k_i}\}$. This selector takes the intersection of all these sets and assigns all the lemmas in the intersection to s. In this case we also ask that s has at least two lemmas in the source language.

4.2 Dictionaries

As mentioned above, the success of these selectors will be significantly influenced by the quality of the translation resources we can find. Given that Guarani is a low-resource language from the point of view of NLP, and the existing machine translation (MT) systems for this language are still not accurate enough, we relied mainly on bilingual Guarani-Spanish dictionaries. These are the sources we collected:

Avalos The Ñe'ẽryruguasu bilingual dictionary (Ávalos, 2011) contains more than 17,000 entries of Guarani words with Spanish translations and examples in Guarani. It also contains the POS of each Guarani entry, which is very helpful for determining the appropriate synsets. The dictionary was compiled in PDF format, and there were many transcription issues when converting it to plain text format for processing. We used rules to detect full spans that were appropriately transcribed and contained entries with available translations, such as:

```
"guarani_lemmas [guarani_pos]
spanish_lemmas"
```

Not all entries and variants could be converted in this way, but we ended up with a set of 18,698 Guarani-Spanish lemma pairs.

DC Descubrir Corrientes[2] is a web portal that contains an online Guarani-Spanish bilingual dictionary. The entries in this dictionary also indicate the POS (in this case in Spanish) of the words. We processed this dictionary (as in Borges et al., 2021) and compiled a set of 14,164 Guarani-Spanish lemma pairs.

Wiktionary Wiktionary[3] is a project for creating open multilingual dictionaries, part of the Wikimedia foundation. The Guarani language still has very few resources inside the Wiki ecosystem, and Wikipedia and Wiktionary are no exception. In the latest dump of the Guarani Wiktionary (September 1, 2022), there were only 2,499 Guarani-Spanish pairs, 207 Guarani-English pairs, and 113 Guarani-Portuguese pairs. The words in the Guarani Wiktionary also lacked a clear way of determining their POS, so we used the Spanish lemmas lists categorized by POS from the FreeLing project (Padró and Stanilovsky, 2012). We assigned the POS of the Spanish lemma associated with a Guarani word, which is not perfect since a word could have multiple POS but only one of them could be appropriate in the other language, so this is a potential source of noise for these lemmas. After this process, we ended up with 2,276 Guarani-Spanish lemma pairs for this source.

Category		Unique Pairs	Unique Synsets	Unique Lemmas
POS	Noun	6,618	3,514	2,791
	Verb	3,977	2,110	1,364
	Adjective	1,182	802	391
	Adverb	190	93	146
Rule	Monosemy	3,589	1,716	2,837
	Single Tran.	8,412	5,322	2,182
	Factorization	952	615	592
Source	Avalos	4,082	2,403	1,800
	DC	6,757	4,583	2,678
	Wiktionary	2,088	1,754	653
Base concept	Yes	2,604	1,263	1,550
	No	9,363	5,256	3,837
Overall		11,967	6,519	4,298

Table 1: Number of <synset, lemma> pairs extracted for each POS, by each rule, from each source, and belonging to the base concepts. Notice that the number of pairs for rules and sources do not add up to the overall value because some pairs were found by more than one rule or belonged to more than one source.

5 Results and evaluation

Table 1 shows the number of <synset, lemma> pairs found using the described selectors and dictionaries. We show the number of unique pairs, unique synsets, and unique lemmas. The table also breaks down the information for each POS, each selector rule, and each dictionary source. Note that the selector that yielded the most results was the *Single Translation* selector, while the one with the fewest results is *Factorization*.

The rules also found possible lemmas for 1,263 (around 27%) out of 4,689 synsets considered base concepts of WordNet[4], defined to be high in the

[2]https://descubrircorrientes.com.ar/2012/index.php/diccionario-guarani/

[3]https://www.wiktionary.org/

[4]http://globalwordnet.org/resources/gwa-base-concepts/

semantic hierarchy and to have many connections to other concepts.

5.1 Precision of the selectors

In order to evaluate the quality of the lemmas chosen by the selectors, we sampled a set of <synset, lemma> pairs generated by our rules. Two native speakers (authors of this paper) annotated the samples to identify if the selected lemmas were suitable for the corresponding synsets. We then calculated the precision of the selector based on the number of pairs considered correct by the annotators, over the total number of extracted pairs. This can be calculated as an overall measure, but we can also break it down by POS, selector or dictionary source to have a more fine-grained analysis.

The annotators were given the ID of the synset, a Spanish translation of the synset's definition, the known Spanish lemmas, and all the Guarani lemmas found by the rules. They had to indicate, for each lemma, if it was appropriate for that synset, and optionally, they could also indicate other suitable Guarani lemmas and some comments.

For example, one of the synsets to annotate was `play.v.29`, which has the definition "make bets". The Spanish lemmas for this synset are "apostar" (to bet) and "jugar" (to play or to gamble). The rules selected the Guarani lemmas "ha'ã", "ra'ã" and "ñembosarái". In this case, both annotators agreed that "ha'ã", "ra'ã" are appropriate lemmas for `play.v.29`, while "ñembosarái" was not.

Each annotator had to label 106 synsets with approximately 300 lemmas in total, but 40 of these synsets were annotated by both, so we were able to calculate the inter-annotator agreement between them. We calculated the inter-annotator agreement using Cohen's Kappa, which was 0.561 for our sample, which indicates moderate agreement.

In total, they annotated 476 <synset, lemma> pairs, having 172 unique synsets and 412 unique lemmas, approximately 4% of the total number of extracted pairs. We sampled the pairs so that there were at least some samples of each POS, rule and source, and also samples from synsets that belong to the base concepts. We aimed to have at least 60 samples (<synset, lemma> pairs) for each category.

Table 2 shows the number of samples for each category and its precision according to the annotators, calculated as the number of pairs considered correct over the total number of pairs for that category. The overall category considers all sample pairs, which have a precision of 61.3%. From the point of view of rules, the *Factorization* rule seems to work much better than the other heuristics. One possible explanation for this is that it is the most restrictive of the selectors, as we ask that there are at least two Spanish lemmas before doing the factorization process. This means that the selector can only be applied to a reduced number of synsets (see Table 1), but at the same time it helps to achieve more precise results.

Category		Samples	Precision
POS	Noun	171	0.667
	Verb	141	0.638
	Adjective	93	0.484
	Adverb	71	0.606
Rule	Monosemy	213	0.610
	Single Tran.	233	0.579
	Factorization	95	0.758
Source	Avalos	217	0.520
	DC	267	0.708
	Wiktionary	108	0.683
Base concept	Yes	120	0.625
	No	356	0.610
Overall		476	0.613

Table 2: Number of <synset, lemma> sample pairs for each category and their precision based on the annotations. Notice that the number of samples for rules and sources do not add up to 476 because some lemmas were found by more than one rule or belonged to more than one source.

If we take into account the sources, the DC and Wiktionary dictionaries seem to be much more precise than Avalos, even if in the Wiktionary case we did not have the original POS, but we had to assign them automatically from a Spanish dictionary. Additionally, the performance for adjectives is also much lower than for any other POS.

5.2 Coverage of the sources

Given that the annotators were asked to include more Guarani lemmas that they considered suitable for the synsets, we could create a small set of manually curated synsets with lemmas. For each synset, we kept the lemmas selected by at least one annotator as correct, as well as all the lemmas included as extras by them. With this information, we created a collection of 164 synsets with 446 unique lemmas we consider our small *gold standard*. There were only eight synsets for which the annotators

	Noun	Verb	Adj.	Adv.
Avalos	0.494	0.562	0.126	0.155
DC	0.607	0.711	0.116	0.239
Wiktionary	0.274	0.248	0.179	0.141
Union	0.815	0.942	0.305	0.408

Table 3: Coverage of the gold standard created by the annotators in terms of Guarani lemmas for each source. The last line shows the coverage of the union of all the dictionaries.

considered no selected lemma was suitable, and no alternatives were given.

Table 3 shows the coverage of the Guarani lemmas considered in the gold standard for each source. We consider the Guarani lemma as covered if it exists on the source associated to a particular POS, even if it is not associated to a suitable Spanish lemma. So these numbers give us an idea of how good the different dictionaries are at representing the words expected by the annotators, and are consequently an upper bound to the performance we can get when designing selectors that use these dictionaries as sources, as the selectors cannot find lemmas that are not in the sources. When we take the union of dictionaries (last line of the Table 3) the coverage seems very good for nouns and verbs, but it is notably low for adjectives.

5.3 Issues

First of all, as mentioned in section 4.1, the selectors work under some assumptions. The *Single Translation* selector would work best if we had a perfect bilingual dictionary with all possible Guarani-Spanish translations. However, no dictionary is perfect, and this is probably one of the reasons the *Single Translation* selector had poor performance in this experiment.

Furthermore, unlike other works, we use WordNet's Spanish version as starting point instead of the English version. This is not ideal, because the Spanish WordNet has considerably fewer lemmas than the English WordNet. This could have different effects on the different selectors. For example, the *Monosemy* selector relies on finding Spanish lemmas that belong to only one synset, but as the Spanish WordNet is incomplete, it is likely that many possibly polysemous lemmas are erroneously only present on one synset. This hinders the efficacy of the selector.

Finally, the three selectors we chose are very simple, and they only capture certain configurations of synsets and lemmas. We still need to design more and better selectors that could extract more information from the datasets we have, as well as collect more datasets. One way of doing this is using the parallel corpora and MT systems that are being created lately. We could also make use of similarities in some written forms of Spanish loans, similar to the Levenshtein selector described in Pradet et al. (2014), or use gloss information and word vectors as in Maguiño-Valencia et al. (2018).

About the triform nouns mentioned in section 3.2, we noticed the annotators indicated that all forms of a noun should be included as lemmas of a synset. For example, the selectors chose ten possible lemmas for the synset `branch.n.02` with the definition "a division of a stem, or secondary stem arising from the main stem of a plant", and in particular there were two sets of triform nouns selected: {takã, hakã, rakã} and {takãmby, hakãmby, rakãmby}. Both annotators agreed that the first triplet of nouns was appropriate for the synset, but disagreed about the second one. However, it was always the case that the triplets were accepted or rejected together, e.g. {tete, hete, rete} were rejected for the synset `entity.n.01` because they are more suitable to a physical entity or body.

Inconsistencies in orthography are another source of problems for this process. The Wiktionary source was the one with the most problems in this respect. For example, these three words were associated with Spanish "rama" (branch) in Guarani: {taka, hakã, rakä}. This is a triplet of nouns written in three different orthographic conventions for marking a nasal vowel: with no diacritic, with the standard tilde diacritic, and with the diaeresis diacritic, which is not standard.

6 Conclusions

We presented a work in progress on building a version of the WordNet lexical database for Guarani, an indigenous South American language. Our process obtains data from three bilingual Guarani-Spanish dictionaries, and we implemented three simple selectors that decide which Guarani lemmas should be used as the translation of the lemmas present in the Spanish WordNet synsets. The selectors are *Monosemy*, *Single Translation* and *Factorization*.

We extracted lemmas for 6,519 synsets, but the quality of the selected lemmas is highly variable. The *Factorization* method is the one that has the highest precision according to the human annotators (around 76%), and the sources with the highest precisions are DC (71%) and Wiktionary (68%). However, there is still a lot of room for improvement. As future work, we plan to expand the manual evaluation in order to have a bigger set of curated synsets and lemmas, design new selectors that could extract better information from the sources, and collect or create more datasets, for example, using the existing bilingual corpora or MT systems.

References

Academia de la Lengua Guaraní (ALG). 2018. *Gramática Guaraní.*

Celso Ávalos. 2011. *Ñe'ẽryguasu (Gran Diccionario) Guaraní-Español, Español–Guaraní.*

Élodie Blestel. 2021. Entramados lingüísticos e ideológicos a prueba de las prácticas: español y guaraní en paraguay. *Sánchez Moreano, Santiago; Blestel, Élodie (éds). Prácticas lingüísticas heterogéneas: Nuevas perspectivas para el estudio del español en contacto con lenguas amerindias*, pages 69–86.

Yanina Borges, Florencia Mercant, and Luis Chiruzzo. 2021. Using guarani verbal morphology on guarani-spanish machine translation experiments. *Procesamiento del Lenguaje Natural*, 66:89–98.

Sonja E Bosch and Marissa Griesel. 2017. Strategies for building wordnets for under-resourced languages: The case of african languages. *Literator: Journal of Literary Criticism, Comparative Linguistics and Literary Studies*, 38(1):1–12.

Luis Chiruzzo, Pedro Amarilla, Adolfo Ríos, and Gustavo Giménez Lugo. 2020. Development of a Guarani - Spanish parallel corpus. In *Proceedings of the 12th Language Resources and Evaluation Conference*, pages 2629–2633. European Language Resources Association.

Luis Chiruzzo, Santiago Góngora, Aldo Alvarez, Gustavo Giménez-Lugo, Marvin Agüero-Torales, and Yliana Rodríguez. 2022. Jojajovai: A parallel guarani-spanish corpus for mt benchmarking. In *Proceedings of the Thirteenth Language Resources and Evaluation Conference*, pages 2098–2107.

Wolf Dietrich. 2001. Zum historischen Sprachkontakt in Paraguay: Spanische Einflüsse im Guaraní. *Sprachkontakt und Sprachvergleich. Münster: Nodus*, pages 53–73.

Wolf Dietrich. 2004. La influencia castellana en la sintaxis de la coordinación y subordinación de lenguas tupí-guaraníes. *Paper presented ar the conference Lenguas amerindias en contacto con el castellano: aspectos lingüísticos y sociolingüísticos, Amsterdam, June 24th-25th.*

Bruno Estigarribia. 2015. Guarani-spanish jopara mixing in a paraguayan novel: Does it reflect a third language, a language variety, or true codeswitching? *Journal of Language Contact*, 8(2):183–222.

Bruno Estigarribia. 2020. *A grammar of Paraguayan Guarani.* UCL Press.

Michael Gasser. 2010. Antimorfo 1.1 user's guide.

Jorge Gómez Rendón. 2008. *Typological and social constraints on language contact: Amerindian languages in contact with Spanish.* Netherlands Graduate School of Linguistics.

Aitor Gonzalez-Agirre, Egoitz Laparra, and German Rigau. 2012. Multilingual central repository version 3.0. In *LREC*, pages 2525–2529.

Antonio Guasch. 1948. *El idioma guaraní.* Asunción: Imprenta Nacional.

Shaw N Gynan. 2001. Language planning and policy in paraguay. *Current Issues in Language Planning*, 2(1):53–118.

Matías Herrera, Javier González, Luis Chiruzzo, and Dina Wonsever. 2016. Some strategies for the improvement of a spanish wordnet. In *Proceedings of the 8th Global WordNet Conference (GWC)*, pages 115–122.

Pratik Joshi, Sebastin Santy, Amar Budhiraja, Kalika Bali, and Monojit Choudhury. 2020. The state and fate of linguistic diversity and inclusion in the NLP world. In *Proceedings of the 58th Annual Meeting of the Association for Computational Linguistics*, pages 6282–6293, Online. Association for Computational Linguistics.

Guido Kallfell. 2006. Uso de las voces verbales del yopará, en comparación con las del guaraní. *Guaraní y "Mawetí-Tupí-Guaraní": Estudios Históricos y Descriptivos sobre una Familia Lingüística de América del Sur, Wolf Dietrich y Haralambos Symeonidis (eds.)*, pages 333–354.

Guido Kallfell. 2011. *Grammatik des Jopara: Gesprochenes Guaraní und Spanisch in Paraguay.* Frankfurt am Mein: Peter Lang.

Manuel Mager, Arturo Oncevay, Abteen Ebrahimi, John Ortega, Annette Rios Gonzales, Angela Fan, Ximena Gutierrez-Vasques, Luis Chiruzzo, Gustavo Giménez Lugo, Ricardo Ramos, et al. 2021. Findings of the americasnlp 2021 shared task on open machine translation for indigenous languages of the americas. In *Proceedings of the First Workshop on Natural Language Processing for Indigenous Languages of the Americas*, pages 202–217.

Diego Maguiño-Valencia, Arturo Oncevay-Marcos, and Marco A. Sobrevilla Cabezudo. 2018. WordNet-shp: Towards the building of a lexical database for a Peruvian minority language. In *Proceedings of the Eleventh International Conference on Language*

Resources and Evaluation (LREC 2018), Miyazaki, Japan. European Language Resources Association (ELRA).

Nelsi Melgarejo, Rodolfo Zevallos, Héctor Gómez, and John E Ortega. 2022. Wordnet-qu: Development of a lexical database for quechua varieties. In *Proceedings of the 29th International Conference on Computational Linguistics*, pages 4429–4433.

Bartomeu Meliá. 1992. La lengua guarani del paraguay, historia, sociedad, literatura.

Alfonso Methol, Guillermo López, Juan Álvarez, Luis Chiruzzo, and Dina Wonsever. 2018. Using context to improve the spanish wordnet translation. In *Proceedings of the 9th Global Wordnet Conference*, pages 17–24.

George A Miller. 1995. Wordnet: a lexical database for english. *Communications of the ACM*, 38(11):39–41.

Ricardo Otheguy. 2002. Saussurean anti-nomenclaturism in grammatical analysis: A comparative theoretical perspective. In *W. Reid, R. Otheguy and N. Stern (eds.) Signal, Meaning and Message. Perspectives on Sign Based Linguistics*. Amsterdam/Philadelphia: John Benjamins.

Lluís Padró and Evgeny Stanilovsky. 2012. Freeling 3.0: Towards wider multilinguality. In *LREC2012*.

Hedy Penner. 2016. La ley de lenguas en el paraguay: ¿un paso decisivo en la oficialización de facto del guaraní? *Signo y seña*, (30):108–136.

Quentin Pradet, Gaël De Chalendar, and Jeanne Baguenier Desormeaux. 2014. Wonef, an improved, expanded and evaluated automatic french translation of wordnet. In *Proceedings of the Seventh Global Wordnet Conference*, pages 32–39.

Yliana Rodríguez. 2019. Spanish-guarani diglossia in colonial paraguay: A language undertaking. *The Linguistic Heritage of Colonial Practice*, 13:153–168.

Joan Rubin. 1963. *National bilingualism in Paraguay*. The Hague: Mouton.

Alex Rudnick. 2011. Towards cross-language word sense disambiguation for quechua. In *Proceedings of the Second Student Research Workshop associated with RANLP 2011*, pages 133–138.

Yolanda R Solé. 1991. The Guarani-Spanish situation. *Georgetown Journal of Languages and Linguistics*, 2:297–348.

Harald Thun. 2005. 'code switching','code mixing','reproduction traditionnelle' et phénomènes apparentés dans le guarani paraguayen et dans le castillan du paraguay. *Italian Journal of Linguistics, 17-2*, pages 311–346.

Harald Thun. 2006. 'a dos mil la uva, a mil la limón'. historia, función y extensión de los artículos definidos del castellano en el guaraní jesuítico y paraguayo. *Guaraní y "Mawetí-Tupí-Guaraní": Estudios Históricos y Descriptivos sobre una Familia Lingüística de América del Sur, Wolf Dietrich y Haralambos Symeonidis (eds.)*, pages 357–414.

Piek Vossen. 1998. Eurowordnet: A multilingual database with lexical semantic networks. *Dordrecht: Kluwer Academic Publishers*, 10:978–94.

Lenka Zajícová. 2010. Differences in incorporation of spanish elements in guarani texts and guarani elements in spanish texts in paraguayan newspapers. *A new look at language contact in Amerindian Languages*, pages 185–203.

A CCGbank for Turkish: From Dependency to CCG

Aslı Kuzgun
Boğaziçi University
Starlang Yazılım Danışmanlık
asli.kuzgun@boun.edu.tr

Oğuz Kerem Yıldız
Starlang Yazılım Danışmanlık
oguz@starlangyazilim.com

Olcay Taner Yıldız
Ozyegin University
olcay.yildiz@ozyegin.edu.tr

Abstract

In this paper, we present the building of a CCG-bank for Turkish by using standardised dependency corpora. We automatically induce Combinatory Categorial Grammar (CCG) categories for each word token in the Turkish dependency corpora. The CCG induction algorithm we present here is based on the dependency relations that are defined in the latest release of the Universal Dependencies (UD) framework. We aim for an algorithm that can easily be used in all the Turkish treebanks that are annotated in this framework. Therefore, we employ a lexicalist approach in order to make full use of the dependency relations while creating a semantically transparent corpus. We present the treebanks we employed in this study as well as their annotation framework. We introduce the structure of the algorithm we used along with the specific issues that are different from previous studies. Lastly, we show how the results change with this lexical approach in CCGbank for Turkish compared to the previous CCGbank studies in Turkish.

1 Introduction

Semantic parsing is a vital tool for natural language processing (NLP) studies. Automated inquiry systems, chat-box tools, search engines, and all sorts of other NLP applications make use of semantic information. The semantic information, however, is not encoded in the dependency or phrase treebanks directly. The syntactic relations in these frameworks do not follow from the semantic types of tokens such as the argument structure of predicates. Therefore, there is a trend in converting these dependency annotated treebanks into a semantically transparent framework, which is CCG. CCG creates a categorical lexicon where each token is assigned a lexical category according to how it combines with the other tokens in a given sentence. This approach increases parsing scores compared to dependency parsing studies (Hockenmaier and Steedman, 2007; Bosco et al., 2000; Çakıcı, 2009; Ambati et al., 2018). However, the CCG approach requires a bigger corpus for the machines to learn each lexical type.

There are languages that have adequate dependency corpora such as English, Hindi, and Italian. Consequently, there are CCG induction studies over the dependency corpora of these languages (Hockenmaier and Steedman, 2007; Ambati et al., 2018; Bosco et al., 2000). Turkish, on the other hand, did not have a big dependency annotated corpus. There was only the METU-Sabancı Treebank (Oflazer et al., 2003; Atalay et al., 2003). The first CCGbank conversion studies in Turkish was conducted with a smaller corpus and therefore some rare categories were not repeated enough. Today, bigger dependency corpora are available in Turkish under the UD Framework. These corpora are not only valuable because they provide a bigger parsing tool, but also they are annotated according to a universal annotation scheme that can be used for parallel annotation studies. Today all the Turkish dependency corpora are standardized in order to be a part of the UD framework. In this study, we aimed to employ the UD annotation framework to induce a CCGbank for Turkish that can be used in all the Turkish annotated corpora in the UD that consists of 671K tokens. In contrast to the previous CCG studies in Turkish, we used a lexical approach in CCG instead of a morphemic approach. This is because the syntactic relations are defined based on lexemes and not morphemes in the UD framework for Turkish and employing this framework has several advantages explained above. However, the UD standards keep improving for all languages and it might become morphemic in the later releases. Then, the algorithm we provided here can be adapted to those changes in the UD framework and turn into a morphemic approach.

This paper consists of 6 sections. First section introduces the study and our motivations for this study and it continues with an introduction to the CCG. The second section provides information about the CCGbank studies in different approaches and languages. In Section 3, we introduce the dependency treebanks we used in this study. After this, we explain the algorithm we used to convert this treebank into a CCGbank in Section 4. The last two sections are devoted to present the statistics from the resulting CCGbank corpus and to conclude our study.

1.1 Combinatory Categorial Grammar

Combinatory Categorial Grammar is a lexical grammar formalism that offers a transparent interface between syntax and semantics. CCG approaches define all kinds of language properties in the lexicon. The lexicon consists of the syntactic categories of words and CCG combines these categorical tokens together to derive sentences. This kind of derivation follows from the same logic behind the type-driven semantics where words are associated with functions and the sentences are built by the application of these functions to each other.

The lexicon is built by considering the syntactic categories of words. For instance, an intransitive verb is labelled as category S \NP and a transitive verb is labelled as (S \NP) \NP in Turkish. The S corresponds to the root which is what is left from the sentence at the end of the derivation. The amount of NP's signifies the amount of arguments that a verb can take. The intransitive verb has only one NP because it has no object argument, the only NP this verb interacts with is the subject NP. A transitive verb has an object relation with an NP by definition, therefore, they are assigned an extra NP to their syntactic category.

Akkuş (2014) defines two types of CCG categories, namely, atomic and complex. The atomic categories consist of single units of parts of speech tokens such as NP, PP, S and so on. The complex categories, on the other hand, consist of the combination of other categories. For instance, S is an atomic category and it is the category of an intransitive verb that does not take any overt subject argument, which is a common instance in pro-drop languages like Turkish. S \NP, however, is a complex category which combines two atomic categories. (S \NP) \NP is also a complex category where the complex category S \NP is combined with the atomic category NP. The direction of the slashes in the complex categories label the direction of the argument in which that token will enter into a relationship. The S \NP tag provides the information that the verb has its subject on its left. Similarly, the category (S \NP) \NP shows that both the object and the subject are located on the left of the verb. Such a system also predicts that the object will be on the right of the subject. This is possible as a result of the derivation system of the CCG. For instance, an example of a category (S \NP) \NP verb is "to read". The semantic category of this verb in function terms would be as shown in (1). Here, the object x has to be defined before the subject y. Similarly, in (S \NP) \NP, the object is the NP on the right edge which will be closer to the verb and will be applied before the subject NP. Once the object NP enters into a relationship with the verb (S \NP) \NP, it drops the NP on the right edge and the verb becomes S \NP. This shows that there is only one argument left in the derivation for this verb to enter into a relation.

(1) λx. λy. y reads x

In addition to the composition operations defined above, there are also type raising operations. Type raising occurs when there is a case of ellipsis, movement, or a similar syntactic operation that causes a type mismatch between the two tokens in the derivation. Since CCG is completely transparent between syntax and semantics, these kinds of syntactic phenomena are covered by the type raising rules where the category of a word token is "raised" in order to continue the derivation.

The compositional and type raising rules used in the CCG can be formulated as follows:

Forward Application : X/Y applied to Y becomes X

Backward Application : Y applied to X\Y becomes X

Forward Composition : X/Y applied to Y/Z becomes X/Z

Backward Composition : Y\Z applied to X\Y becomes X\Z

Forward Type-raising : X becomes T/(T\X)

Backward Type-raising : X becomes T\(T/X)

2 Related Work

The first CCGbank was introduced by Hockenmaier and Steedman (2007) for English. This CCGbank was converted automatically from the first phrase structure corpus of English, the Penn Treebank (Marcus et al., 1993). In addition, Hocken-

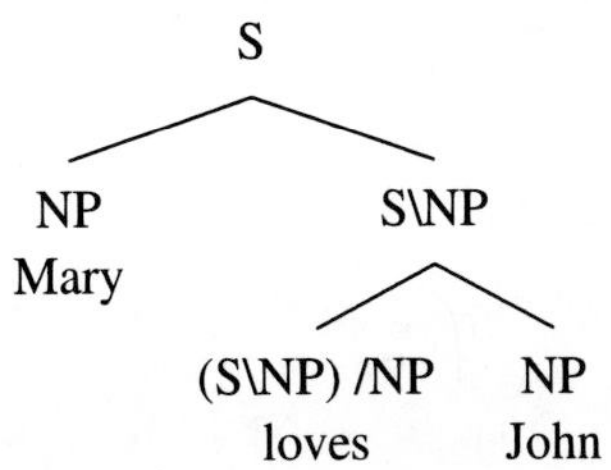

Figure 1: CCG labeled binary tree structure

maier (2006) converted the Tiger treebank (Brants et al., 2004) in German to a CCGbank. These conversion studies were held when the phrase treebanks were only recently being converted into dependency treebanks (De Marneffe et al., 2006). Therefore, several CCGbank studies in languages with already existing treebanks were also converted from phrase treebanks such as the Chinese Treebank developed by Tse and Curran (2010).

This type of conversion studies consist of four main stages. First, they preprocess the existing phrase treebank and correct any errors that could cause combination errors. Then, they determine the constituent types by considering the part-of-speech (POS) tag information and the mother node of each token. For instance, if an NP node branches from a VP node, then that NP is considered as an object constituent. Likewise, PP constituents in the phrase structure are considered as adjunct constituents. After this, they binarize the phrase structure. Binarization is a necessary step in CCG conversion since it is crucial to determine which word token is in the domain of the other to derive the correct compositions. Then, they assign CCG categories to each lexical token in the binarized structure according to the type of relationship between the two tokens. If there is a complement relationship between the two tokens, then the lexical category of the complement is added to the head token with a slash pointing its location to the head word. Figure 1 illustrates an example to this final structure.

Languages that did not already have a phrase treebank started to build dependency treebanks to begin with. Therefore, in the following years CCGbank studies started to be converted from the dependency treebanks. Johan et al. (2009) converted The Turin University Treebank (TUT) (Bosco et al., 2000) in Italian, Çakıcı (2009) converted the METU-Sabancı Treebank (Oflazer et al., 2003; Atalay et al., 2003) in Turkish, Ambati et al. (2018) created Hindi CCGbank from the Hindi Dependency Treebank (Bhatt et al., 2009).

Unlike the previous studies, Çakıcı (2009) and Çakıcı (2005) offer a morphemic CCGbank lexicon. That is, she assigns categories to the morphological units as well as the lexical units. She argues that lexical category assignment cannot cover all the syntactic phenomena in agglutinative languages like Turkish. Following the work of Çakıcı (2005) in Turkish, Ambati et al. (2018) also employed a morphemic lexicon in Hindi, which is another agglutinative language.

It should be noted that CCG approaches with morphemic lexicon do not assign CCG to each morpheme in a word but rather the derivational morphemes such as relativizers that derive adjectives from verbs. Çakıcı (2009) shows that assigning CCG categories to these morphemes decreases the amount of categories that each verb has and thus provides better parsing results by increasing the average frequency of the word roots. However, lexical rules can also account for the derivational changes with the combination of the case, POS tag, and dependency relation information.

3 The Input Corpora

The dependency treebanks that we induced a CCGbank corpus are Turkish version of The Penn Treebank (Marcus et al., 1993), FrameNet, KeNet, Atis, and Tourism. These treebanks employ the annotation framework provided by the Universal Dependencies (UD). All of our input corpora are manually annotated according to the UD annotation framework (de Marneffe et al., 2021) and they are in the CoNLL format. All of them are available online at UD[1], and free of license.

The dependency annotation employed in the treebanks we used is illustrated in Figure 2. The relations build constituents. The morpho-syntactic layer of the treebank consists of POS tag, and morphological information. The morphological features change according to the word category. For instance, definiteness is only defined for nouns, tense/aspect/modality are only defined for verbs, degree information is only defined for adjectives, and so on. As illustrated in figure 2, the relations used in this treebank differ from the previous treebanks used in the earlier works of the CCGbank studies in Turkish. Çakıcı (2005) employed The

[1] `https://universaldependencies.org`

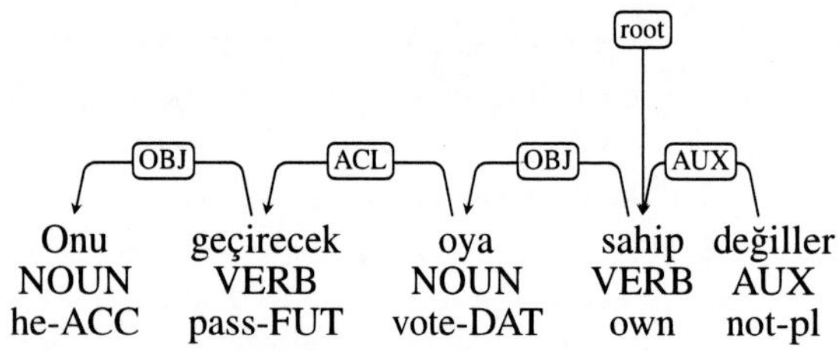

"They don't have the votes to pass it."

Figure 2: Surface dependency structure

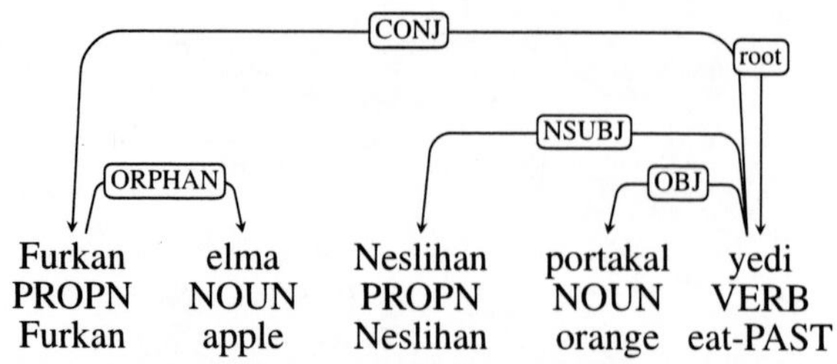

"Neslihan ate oranges, Furkan apples."

Figure 3: Ellipsis in The Turkish Penn Treebank

METU-Sabancı Treebank corpus (Atalay et al., 2003; Oflazer et al., 2003). For instance, in figure 2, the adjectival modifier with the verbal root is labelled as ACL, and this signifies that it is a clausal adjective, otherwise, an adjectival modifier of an NP would be labeled as an AMOD. The morphemes are encoded in the morpho-syntactic layer, however, they are not labelled as a separate token in the surface dependency structure[2].

The morphological analysis of these corpora is processed by a semi-automatic morphological analyzer Yıldız et al. (2019). This semi-automatic approach increased the accuracy of the analysis. The analyzer provides the possible analyses of a word token to the annotator and the annotator selects the correct one considering the context of the sentence. This way, a consistent and contextually accurate morphological analysis was achieved. Semantic and dependency annotation is performed manually.

3.1 The Universal Dependencies

The UD framework provides an inclusive annotation scheme that enables parallel annotations between languages. There are more than 100 languages represented in this framework. Turkish has 8 up-to-date dependency annotated corpora represented in the UD. The METU-Sabancı Treebank used in the previous CCGbank studies unfortunately cannot be updated to meet the latest UD standards. However, the 8 other treebanks provide corpora in a variety of genres such as reviews, articles, automated inquiry system inputs, and so on. All of these manually annotated dependency corpora make the UD databank of Turkish an invaluable source for NLP studies.

The UD annotation framework offers labels to account for the ellipsis cases. There is a combination of two relations, namely, ORPHAN and CONJ to account for ellipsis phenomenon. These two relations overcome the problem of the lack of traces in the dependency treebanks. Figure 3 illustrates how ellipsis is encoded in the treebank. Since there cannot be two subjects in a sentence, one of them is labelled with the CONJ relation to the root, and the object of that subject/verb pair is linked to its subject with the ORPHAN relation.

3.2 The Penn Treebank

The Turkish Penn Treebank consists of a total of 9560 sentences and 87,367 word tokens which are translated from the original Penn Treebank corpus. The corpus only includes sentences that are less than 15 words long. The sentences are from the written texts such as Wall Street Journal articles, exchange rate information and also some advertisement dialogues. This corpus was first annotated according to an earlier version of the UD (Kuzgun et al., 2020), however, it is updated to fulfill the latest UD annotation standards (de Marneffe et al., 2021).

3.3 The FrameNet

Turkish FrameNet is a manually annotated dependency corpus that is built from the sentences taken from the Turkish FrameNet Project. It consists of 2,700 manually annotated example sentences and 19,221 tokens. The treebank can be separated according to the semantic frames. For instance, "cognitive comprehension" is a frame, and the sentences that include a verb that means anything related to this semantic concept can be filtered. There are 139 semantic frames that the treebank can be filtered into.

The dependency annotation of thic corpus is fully manual and also it can be combined with the framenet annotation. Which means the tokens of this corpus are annotated with thematic roles. For example in the frame "cognitive comprehension"

[2]ACC=accusative, DAT=dative, AUX=auxiliary

the subject is not only marked as the subject, but it also carries the information that it is the "thinker".

3.4 The KeNet Treebank

The KeNet is the largest treebank of Turkish. The sentences are not domain specific, they are mostly the dictionary example sentences of the Turkish National Dictionary. There are 18,700 manually annotated sentences and 178,700 tokens in this corpus.

3.5 The Atis Treebank

The Atis Treebank in Turkish consists of the translated sentences of the original Atis Dataset in English (Ward, 1990). This is a domain specific dataset which is built from the audio recordings of people inquiring for flight information from automated systems. The sentences were first translated by an automated translator. Then, human translators fine grained the sentences before the annotation to create the final version of the Turkish Atis corpus. The dependency annotation is made by human annotators as the other treebanks used in this study. The annotated Atis corpus in Turkish contains 5432 sentences and 45875 tokens.

3.6 The Tourism Treebank

The Tourism Treebank consists of a domain specific corpus of Turkish. There are 19,750 manually annotated sentences and 92,200 tokens in this treebank. The sentences are taken from the customer reviews of a booking company. The reviews were written unlike the Atis data. They were not subjected to a transcription process. Therefore they contain orthographic mistakes. In order not to distort the features of a natural speech data, we used the "GOESWITH" tag of the UD where we combined the tokens that were supposed to be together. When the tokens were mistakenly written together, then we separated them manually.

4 The CCG Algorithm

The CCG label assignment is carried out by an algorithm that makes use of the POS information of the word tokens, the head/complement relationship between the tokens, and the dependency label between the tokens. The algorithm starts from the left edge of the sentence, sees the POS tag of the first token, and then finds where that token is connected. Together with these, the relationship between the two tokens defines the CCG label of the token.

```
CASE: "NMOD"
    IF headcat="NP[nom]"
        WHEN myrel="NMOD"
            SET NP [nom]/ NP [nom]
    ELSE
        IF headcat="NP"
            WHEN myrel= "NMOD"
                SET NP/ NP
```

Table 1: Algorithm for nominal modifiers

Once one token is defined, the algorithm continues to the next token. However, CCG assignment algorithm does not end in one iteration because of the complex CCG categories that contain X. If the token being processed, or the head word of a constituent has an X in its rule, then it means that token is not identified yet. Therefore, these tokens are left for the following iterations. This process repeats itself until all the categories are defined.

Table 1 illustrates an instance from the algorithm. According to this rule, an NP token that is connected to another NP with the NMOD relation will take the NP/NP CCG label. If the modified NP is the subject of the sentence, then it will be labeled as $NP_{[nom]}$, therefore, the modifier token will not be NP/NP but $NP_{[nom]}/NP_{[nom]}$ for the subjects.

The algorithm is not morphemic as the previous Turkish CCGbank studies (Çakıcı, 2009; Akkuş, 2014). One reason for that is the dependency annotation structure of the treebank we employed. The UD Turkish framework offers a detailed and consistent annotation scheme, however, it does not separate the morphemes as Çakıcı (2009) did in her dissertation. Therefore, the input corpus does not include separate tokens. However, as the annotation scheme that was used in The Turkish Penn Treebank accounts for cases like ellipsis which other dependency annotation frameworks fail to cover, we employed the lexical approach as the previous studies on The Penn Treebank induction did (Hockenmaier and Steedman, 2007). Even though they were phrase treebanks, the dependency annotation scheme we employed offers similar kind of information. Our motivation in applying lexical approach is to make use of the universal and standard annotation scheme in our algorithm.

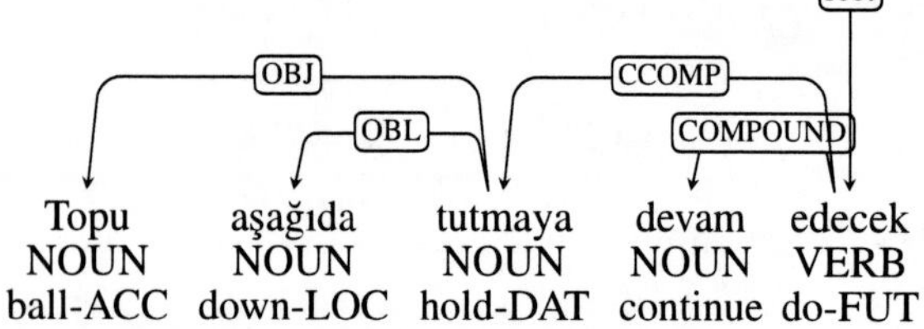

"S/he will continue to hold the ball down"

Figure 4: Clausal objects in the dependency structure

Topu	aşağıda	tutmaya	devam	edecek
NP	NP	S\NP\NP	(S\S)/(S\S)	(S\S)

Figure 5: Clausal objects in the CCGbank

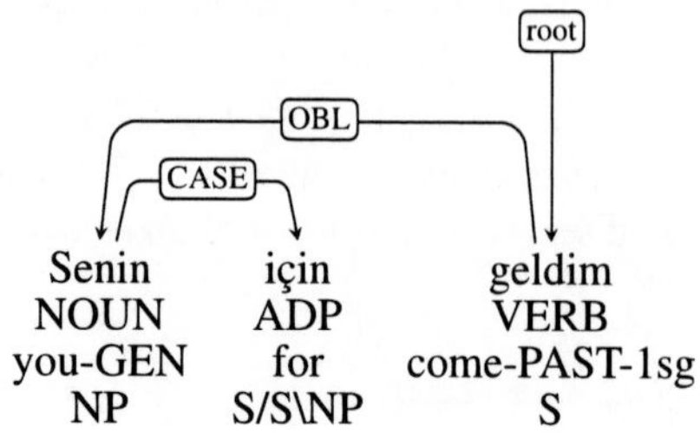

"I came for you"

Figure 6: An adposition in the dependency structure and its CCG label

4.1 Identifying Arguments

The main arguments in a sentence are identified in the first iteration. This is done by identifying the arguments of the root. Following Çakıcı (2005), we differentiated between the types of verbs according to the amount of arguments they can take and we labeled the subject NP argument as NP_{nom}. The category of the root tokens are defined in the first iteration. The algorithm counts the NSUBJ, CSUBJ, OBJ, OBL, CCOMP, and XCOMP arguments[3] that are linked to the verb root. In Çakıcı (2005), there are only three types of arguments defined, namely, subject, object, and oblique. However, the types of arguments are more detailed in the UD annotation framework, and we reflected these differences on our CCG labels. Even though the verbal nouns have the NOUN POS tag, they can take their own arguments. Figure 4 illustrates this in the dependency structure.

The algorithm may add an S instead of an NP to the argument structure of the root token as shown in Figure 5. This way, we differentiate between the verbs that take a clausal argument from the ones that take nominal arguments. The same process applies to the tokens that are linked with the PARATAXIS relation to the root token. This relation is built when two sentences occur together without any coordinator. When this happens, the main verb of the first sentence is linked to the main verb of the second sentence with the PARATAXIS relation in the UD framework. Since this token can have its own arguments, including subjects, the argument structure of such tokens is also identified in the first iteration, together with the root nodes.

[3]NSUBJ=nominal subject, CSUBJ=clausal subject, OBJ=object, OBL=oblique, CCOMP=clausal complement, XCOMP=open clausal complement
The difference between the XCOMP and CCOMP is that the former cannot have its own subject. They both define non-finite complement clauses.

4.2 Combining Adverbs

Adverbs can modify sentence heads as well as the other adjuncts such as adjectives. Çakıcı (2005) marks all of these adverbs as S/S categories in order to prevent the generation of giant categories. However, adjectives are modifiers of noun phrases and they cannot combine with an S/S category. They are type NP/NP. Anything that modifies an adjective is marked as ADVMOD. Therefore, we treated the adverbial modifiers as categories of X/X where X is the category of the modified token. The following illustrates this composition.

Daha	sağlıklı	yemekler	yedi
more	healthy	food-pl	eat-PAST
(NP/NP)/(NP/NP)	NP/NP	NP	S\NP

4.3 Adpositions

Turkish does not have any prepositions (Göksel and Kerslake, 2004). However, there are postpositions (PP's) and they are frequently used. In a phrase structure treebank, the PP heads would be the constituent heads. However, in the dependency treebanks, they are treated as the dependents of the head noun of a constituent. Postposition relations are labeled as either CASE or MARK. The former is used for the case marking elements that are connected to nouns and the latter is used for postpositions that introduce finite clauses. Figure 6 illustrates the backward relation of the postpositions to their head nouns.

We employed a type raising rule to account for the fact that the adposition is not a constituent head in the dependency structure but it actually defines

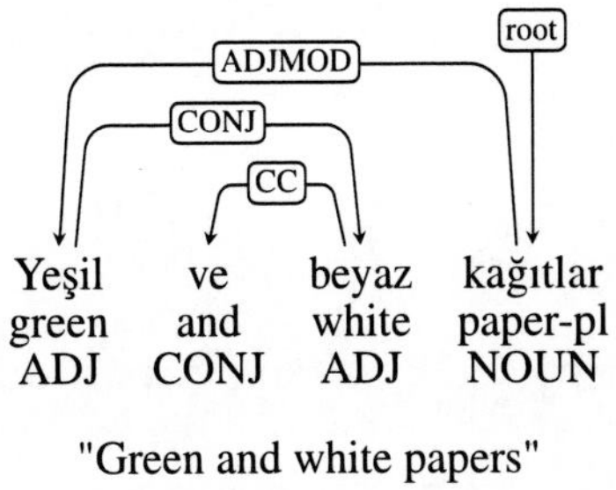

Figure 7: Conjunction in the dependency treebank

the type of relation with the main verb. Therefore, the CCG of the tokens with MARK and CASE labels are determined as S/S\X. This way, they combine with their own constituent heads, and then combine with the matrix verb.

4.4 Conjuncts

We followed Çakıcı (2005) for the conjunctions that consist of the same category. These type of conjuncts are assigned the category (X\X)/X. However, since the corpus we employed was bigger, we had to cover the cases where the types of the two conjuncts are different. In the UD framework, the head of the two conjuncts is the first one. Therefore, we labelled the conjunction as category (X\X)/Y.

The conjuncts were annotated in a nested manner. Therefore, when we combine the relations between them, the category of the conjunct becomes bigger than the average complex categories. Figure 7 illustrates the dependency annotation rule for conjuncts. The conjunct in Figure 7 is connected to the second adjective, *beyaz* and the second adjective is linked to the first one, *yeşil*. The first adjective modifies the head noun *kağıtlar*. This back and forth relation between the constituents results in some bigger categories. However, we reflected these in the conjunct to keep our CCGbank transparent to the dependency structure.

4.5 Punctuation

The punctuations are defined with the PUNCT relation in The Turkish Penn Treebank. In the CCGbank, we treated punctuations according to where they occur. The sentence final ones are given the category S\S as they modify the whole sentence. Since the sentences end up with the category S, the sentence final punctuation can take this last S to its left to modify the whole sentence. The ones that occur inside the sentence are treated as modifiers of their head categories.

5 Results

The results follow the dependency based nature of the algorithm. The bigger categories reflect the more complicated dependency relations that need to combine with each other in a CCGbank. This reflects the direct relationship between the UD-style dependency and CCG categories. The frequency of these complex categories show that they do not pose a problem for learning.

Table 2 shows the most frequent 10 word tokens along with their most common CCG categories. The category frequency is higher than the previous works on Turkish CCG induction (Çakıcı, 2005). One reason for this is that our corpus was bigger and it consists of different genres of treebanks. However, our CCGbank is not morphemic, and this should reduce the categorical frequencies. We believe results show that a dependency relation based approach is convenient for CCG induction, given that this feature of the algorithm enables it to be used in a variety of treebanks.

One thing to notice in Table 2 is that the category of "*ve*" meaning "and" consists of X's. The category of this conjunct was not left like this as explained in the previous section. Its actual category is ((NP/NP\(NP/NP))/(NP/NP))/((NP/NP\(NP/NP))/(NP/NP))\((NP/NP\(NP/NP))/(NP/NP)) and this is reduced in the table for space reasons. Each X in this category corresponds to ((NP/NP\(NP/NP))/(NP/NP)). This category is larger than others because of the complex dependency annotation rule for the conjuncts explained previously in section 4.4. The transparent relationship between the UD-style dependency relations and CCG categories sometimes creates this big structures, however, the complexity is not an indicator of rareness. These structures occur frequently and the complex CCG information they have correctly represents which constituents combine with each other.

Another thing Table 2 shows is that the punctuations have categories depending on where they occur in the sentence. For instance, a period most frequently follows a sentence and is therefore labeled as S\S while a quotation mark is labelled as the category S/S because it is mostly combined with the predicate of the quoted sentence which comes after it.

Table 2 also shows that *için*, meaning "for", is one of the most frequent postpositions in the corpus. Its category type shows that this postposition was mostly taking intransitive verbs. This is because NP$_{\text{nom}}$ marks the subjects, and the lack of a bare NP in the category signals that these verbs do not have an object. This kind of information is rendered available by the application of previous approaches in the CCGbank induction that divides the transitive verbs from the intransitive ones (Çakıcı, 2005).

token **most freq. cat.**	**freq.** **cat. freq.**
.	48274
S\S	46692
,	13110
S/S	2675
bir	10830
NP/NP	9596
ve	4506
X/X\X	993
çok	4444
S\NP$_{[nom]}$ / S\NP$_{[nom]}$	1657
bu	3605
NP/NP	3098
da /de	2795
NP$_{[nom]}$/NP$_{[nom]}$	730
için	2031
S/S\NP	856
güzeldi	1624
S\NP$_{[nom]}$	1270
ile	1574
S/S\NP	503

Table 2: The most frequent 15 tokens

Table 3 shows the 15 most frequent word categories, their frequency count and their parts of speech information in the CCGbank we created. The frequent categories reflect the translated nature of the sentences. For instance, the frequency of the verbs in pro-drop sentences is higher than the frequency of the verbs in non-pro-drop sentences. The adverb frequency also reflect this distribution. In the previous studies pro-drop sentences were also more common (Çakıcı, 2005). We think this correlation reflects the nature of the language. However, the amount of translated corpora in our study decreases the amount of pro-drop verbs. Further exploration is needed to study the effects of using translated corpora.

There are 630 different categories in this treebank. This number is only a hundred above the previous studies held in Turkish even though this corpus is 60 times bigger than the previous works.

cat. type	**freq.**	**pos**
NP/NP	94298	ADJ
NP	55580	NOUN
S\S	51707	ADV
NP$_{[nom]}$	35409	NOUN
S	25413	VERB
S \NP$_{[nom]}$	24780	VERB
S/S	22686	ADV
NP$_{[nom]}$ / NP$_{[nom]}$	18453	ADJ
S\NP$_{[nom]}$ / S\NP$_{[nom]}$	10944	VERB
S\NP	10498	VERB
NP/NP/NP/NP	6582	ADJ
S\NP/S \NP	4627	ADV
S/NP	4083	VERB
S/S \NP	3756	VERB
(S\NP$_{[nom]}$) \NP	3350	VERB

Table 3: The most frequent 15 categories

The IMST corpus used in (Çakıcı, 2005, 2009) had 60k words while the total word count of our corpus has 516k words. We think that this shows that a lexical approach that can be applied to all dependency treebanks of Turkish results in a quite convenient CCGbank corpus.

6 Conclusion

In this study, we presented the process of inducing a CCGbank for Turkish from an existing dependency treebank. We employed a transparent algorithm that can be applied to all the Turkish treebanks in the UD framework without any adjustment. We introduced the dependency treebanks used in this study along with their annotation framework. We stated the consequences of a direct induction from dependency structures to the CCG approach through certain phenomenon that was also argued in the previous literature. We also showed the similarities and differences between our algorithm and the previous studies conducted in Turkish for CCGbank induction.

This approach already results in a consistent and parsable CCG corpus. However, the Turkish annotation scheme in the UD framework becomes more morphemic in each release and we believe the adaption to the future releases of the UD annotations can easily turn our lexeme based algorithm to a morphemic one without any complication. We hope this corpus to be useful in the upcoming Turkish semantic parsing studies.

References

Burak Kerim Akkuş. 2014. Supertagging with combinatory categorial grammar for dependency parsing. Master's thesis, Middle East Technical University.

Bharat Ram Ambati, Tejaswini Deoskar, and Mark Steedman. 2018. Hindi ccgbank: A ccg treebank from the hindi dependency treebank. *Language Resources and Evaluation*, 52(1):67–100.

Nart B Atalay, Kemal Oflazer, and Bilge Say. 2003. The annotation process in the turkish treebank. In *Proceedings of 4th International Workshop on Linguistically Interpreted Corpora (LINC-03) at EACL 2003*.

Rajesh Bhatt, Bhuvana Narasimhan, Martha Palmer, Owen Rambow, Dipti Misra Sharma, and Fei Xia. 2009. A multi-representational and multi-layered treebank for hindi/urdu. In *Proceedings of the Third Linguistic Annotation Workshop (LAW III)*, pages 186–189.

Cristina Bosco, Vincenzo Lombardo, Leonardo Lesmo, and Vassallo Daniela. 2000. Building a treebank for italian: a data-driven annotation schema. In *LREC 2000*, pages 99–105. ELDA.

Sabine Brants, Stefanie Dipper, Peter Eisenberg, Silvia Hansen-Schirra, Esther König, Wolfgang Lezius, Christian Rohrer, George Smith, and Hans Uszkoreit. 2004. Tiger: Linguistic interpretation of a german corpus. *Research on language and computation*, 2(4):597–620.

Ruket Çakıcı. 2005. Automatic induction of a ccg grammar for turkish. In *Proceedings of the ACL student research workshop*, pages 73–78.

Ruket Çakıcı. 2009. Wide-coverage parsing for turkish.

Marie-Catherine De Marneffe, Bill MacCartney, Christopher D Manning, et al. 2006. Generating typed dependency parses from phrase structure parses. In *Lrec*, volume 6, pages 449–454.

Marie-Catherine de Marneffe, Christopher D Manning, Joakim Nivre, and Daniel Zeman. 2021. Universal dependencies. *Computational linguistics*, 47(2):255–308.

Aslı Göksel and Celia Kerslake. 2004. *Turkish: A comprehensive grammar*. Routledge.

Julia Hockenmaier. 2006. Creating a ccgbank and a wide-coverage ccg lexicon for german. In *Proceedings of the 21st international conference on computational linguistics and 44th annual meeting of the association for computational linguistics*, pages 505–512.

Julia Hockenmaier and Mark Steedman. 2007. Ccgbank: a corpus of ccg derivations and dependency structures extracted from the penn treebank. *Computational Linguistics*, 33(3):355–396.

Bos Johan, Cristina Bosco, and Alessandro Mazzei. 2009. Converting a dependency treebank to a categorial grammar treebank for italian. In *Eight international workshop on treebanks and linguistic theories (TLT8)*, pages 27–38. Educatt.

Aslı Kuzgun, Neslihan Cesur, Bilge Nas Arıcan, Merve Özçelik, Büşra Marşan, Neslihan Kara, Deniz Baran Aslan, and Olcay Taner Yıldız. 2020. On building the largest and cross-linguistic turkish dependency corpus. In *2020 Innovations in Intelligent Systems and Applications Conference (ASYU)*, pages 1–6. IEEE.

Mitchell P. Marcus, Beatrice Santorini, and Mary Ann Marcinkiewicz. 1993. Building a large annotated corpus of English: The Penn Treebank. *Computational Linguistics*, 19(2):313–330.

Kemal Oflazer, Bilge Say, Dilek Zeynep Hakkani-Tür, and Gökhan Tür. 2003. Building a turkish treebank. In *Treebanks*, pages 261–277. Springer.

Daniel Tse and James R. Curran. 2010. Chinese CCGbank: extracting CCG derivations from the Penn Chinese treebank. In *Proceedings of the 23rd International Conference on Computational Linguistics (Coling 2010)*, pages 1083–1091, Beijing, China. Coling 2010 Organizing Committee.

Wayne Ward. 1990. The cmu air travel information service: Understanding spontaneous speech. In *Speech and Natural Language: Proceedings of a Workshop Held at Hidden Valley, Pennsylvania, June 24-27, 1990*.

Olcay Taner Yıldız, Begüm Avar, and Gökhan Ercan. 2019. An open, extendible, and fast turkish morphological analyzer.

Reusing the Danish WordNet for a New Central Word Register for Danish a Project Report

Bolette S. Pedersen[1], Sanni Nimb[2], Nathalie Carmen Hau Sørensen[1], Sussi Olsen[1], Ida Flörke[2], Thomas Troelsgård[2]

Centre for Language Technology, NorS, University of Copenhagen[1], Society for Danish Language and Literature[2]

Emil Holms Kanal 2, 2300 Copenhagen S[1], Christian Brygge 1, 1219 Copenhagen K[2]

{bspedersen, nmp828, saolsen}@hum.ku.dk, {sn,if,tt}@dsl.dk

Abstract

In this paper we report on a new Danish lexical initiative, the Central Word Register for Danish, (COR), which aims at providing an open-source, well curated and large-coverage lexicon for AI purposes. The semantic part of the lexicon (COR-S) relies to a large extent on the lexical-semantic information provided in the Danish wordnet, DanNet. However, we have taken the opportunity to evaluate and curate the wordnet information while compiling the new resource. Some information types have been simplified and more systematically curated. This is the case for the hyponymy relations, the ontological typing, and the sense inventory, i.e. the treatment of polysemy, including systematic polysemy.

1 Introducing COR and DanNet

The Central Word Register of Danish – with the acronym COR – is a lexicon project running from 2021 to 2023 as part of a Danish governmental language technology and AI initiative. The aim of the project is to coordinate, curate, combine and extend already existing lexical NLP resources – including the Danish wordnet – in a joint initiative in order to ease the use of NLP resources and thereby help boost NLP and language-centric AI for Danish.

The COR project is funded by The Danish Agency for Digitisation and led in collaboration by three of the main dictionary and LT institutions in Denmark: i) the Danish Language Council (DSN), ii) Society for Danish Language and Literature (DSL), and iii) Centre for Language Technology (CST) at the University of Copenhagen.

One of the main ideas in COR is to assign *a unique identifier*[1] to all lemmas[2]. The main resource consists of a lexicon of the general language vocabulary with basic morphology and semantics. Syntactic and phonological information is foreseen in subsequent phases of the project.

The lemma selection as well as the morphological information, the glosses and the usage examples are based on three 'classical' dictionaries, the orthographic dictionary *Retskrivningsordbogen* from DSN, the monolingual dictionary *Den Danske Ordbog* (The Danish Dictionary, DDO) and the thesaurus *Den Danske Begrebsordbog* (The Danish Thesaurus, DDB) from DSL.

The formal semantic information in COR (labelled COR-S), in contrast, relies to a large extent on the Danish wordnet, DanNet (Pedersen et al. 2009), but also includes data from the Danish

[1] Which can be seen as a parallel to The Danish Person Register (CPR) where all Danish citizens are assigned a unique id.

[2] See also the COR description on the website of The Danish Language Council (in Danish): https://dsn.dk/nyheder-og-arrangementer/dansk-sprognaevn-med-i-stor-sprogteknologisk-satsning/

FrameNet Lexicon (Nimb et al. 2017) and the Danish Sentiment Lexicon (Nimb et al. 2022).

DanNet was originally built on DDO, meaning that, instead of compiling the wordnet as a transfer and adjustment of Princeton WordNet, it is based on monolingual grounds and subsequently linked to Princeton WordNet (cf. Pedersen et al. 2019 for a description of the linking procedure). The sense definitions from the DDO were semi-automatically transformed into wordnet relations via the genus and differentia. The rather fine-grained sense inventory of DDO was more or less taken over in DanNet with some minor adjustments, however in a 'classical' wordnet manner (Fellbaum 1998), that is, with all senses equally described at synset level and thus not capturing the structure of main and sub-senses from the DDO – and not necessarily all its senses, either. In cases of synonymy, a wordnet approach was adopted of typically including synonyms as part of the same synset.

In the following sections we describe the role of DanNet in the compilation of COR and discuss which adjustments and simplifications have been performed to make the wordnet information applicable in a resource like COR. In Section 2 we describe the overall picture of COR in relation to other existing resources. Section 3-6 goes into depth wrt. which information types have been taken over in COR-S and how. In Section 7 we discuss the consequences that our revisions may have for a future DanNet, and in Section 8 we conclude.

2 COR-S as Related to Other Danish Lexical Resources

As has been described in previous accounts (Pedersen et al. 2022 and others), all NLP resources including DanNet are linked at sense level with the sense inventory of the DDO. This means that the semantic NLP resources are all conferring to the same sense and lemma inventory and that an integration of information types is therefore more or less straight-forward.

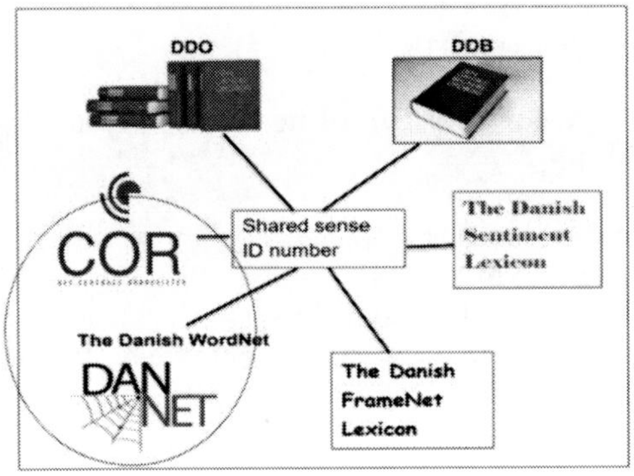

Figure 1: Danish lexical-semantic resources sharing the same sense ID number

As depicted in Figure 1, COR-S is mainly compiled on the basis of DanNet, but as mentioned above, including the integration of further information from primarily DDO, The Danish Thesaurus (surrounding words), The Danish Sentiment Lexicon (connotation polarity), and the Danish FrameNet (semantic frames on verbs and deverbal nouns).

3 Hyponymy revisited

The skeleton of the wordnet in the sense of its hyponymy structure is essentially taken over in COR, meaning that all senses in COR include a link to its most suited hypernym. Some adjustment has however taken place. For instance, very specialist taxonomies are simplified to a certain extent, reflecting now to a larger degree a layman's perspective to i.e., natural entities (e.g., plants and animals). The hypernyms of abstract and verbal entities in DanNet (denoted as 2nd and 3rd Order Entities, respectively, according to Lyons' semantic divisions (Lyons 1977) often relate to synsets that are based on highly polysemous DDO lemmas. These were therefore in some cases incorrectly assigned and have now been adjusted. For instance, the inventory of verbal hypernyms has been reduced to ensure consistency among verbs. Our goal is to cover all DanNet hypernyms in COR-S, and in the final phase to convert the synsets to the corresponding COR-S senses.

The task is somewhat complicated by the simultaneous overall reduction of senses in COR, meaning that two DanNet synsets might result in only one COR-S sense according to a set of principled reductions rules (see Section 5).

4 A Slightly Simplified Ontological Typing

DanNet contains ontological typing on all synsets conferring to the EuroWordNet Ontology (Vossen 1999) with a few extensions, such as an additional type denoting body parts, which seems to a very frequent ontological type with specific characteristics.

For COR, however, we generally aim at a much simpler and more intuitive ontology that can easily be managed and understood also by non-experts and where a high degree of consensus can be achieved in a first encoding round.

To this end, the ontology has been radically simplified, reducing the number of types by 36% from 204 to 130. For example, approx. 1/8 of the EuroWordNet ontological values were only applied 10 times or less in DanNet signaling thereby their somewhat unconsolidated status. Therefore, we decided to remove these in COR-S[3]. Since the aspectual distinction between bounded and unbounded events is rarely lexicalized in Danish (but rather determined by the surrounding adverbs, adverbial particles, or prepositional phrases), we decided to neglect this meaning component in COR-S, a fact that also reduces the number of types significantly.

DanNet	COR-S
UnboundedEvent	Event
BoundedEvent	
UnboundedEvent+Agentive	Act
BoundedEvent+Agentive	
Dynamic+Agentive	
3rdOrderEntity+Mental+Purpose	Abstract+Purpose
3rdOrderEntity+Mental+Purpose+Manner	
BoundedEvent+Agentive+Purpose+Possession	Act+Possession
BoundedEvent+Agentive+Purpose+Possession+Social	

Table 1: Ontological types in DanNet converted into simpler types in COR-S

[3] Examples of removed types are Artifact+Substance+Part, Container+Artifact+Object+Group; and 3rdOrderEntity+Relation.

Some of the most complex 2nd Order types describing several meaning components at a time in different combinations (purpose, social, as well as possession, for example) were also omitted. Instead, the lexicographer must decide on the most prominent meaning aspect when assigning a type. Finally, the names of the types were in some cases changed into more intuitive ones (3rd OrderEntity is changed to Abstract, 2ndOrderEntity+Agentive to Act and so forth). See Table 1 for examples of simplifications[4].

Where most transfer from the EuroWordNet Ontology to the COR Ontology is done fully automatically (many -> one), a few are left for manual inspection to select the most prominent meaning component among several. This is the case for instance where both the meaning components Purpose and Social are encoded in the source, and where we in COR select what we consider to be the most prominent, as in *drille* (to tease): Social.

5 A Reduced Sense Inventory Suitable for NLP

Another characteristic feature of COR-S compared to most other available lexical resources for Danish, is its *reduced sense inventory*. This feature has been suggested by NLP developers to ease word sense disambiguation and overall make the resource more directly applicable in practical NLP tasks, an approach that corresponds well to positions put forward for instance by Kilgarriff (1997), and Pedersen et al. (2018).

In Pedersen et al. (2022) we report on the lexicographical principles behind this sense reduction in COR to what we label core senses, and which can be summarized as follows:

Delete a DDO main or sub-sense if it

- is marked as rare, historic, colloquial, or slang in DDO[5]
- is marked as domain specific in DDO

[4] The entire COR-S Ontology will be released in late 2023 with the full resource.

[5] It could be argued that slang and colloquial senses would be relevant for COR, for instance for processing social media. However, it proves to be indeed very hard to keep up to date with slang meanings, and in several cases, suggested slang senses in DDO have proven to be by far outdated and thereby more confusing than helpful for NLP.

- has a low sense weight score, amounting to how much info is given about the sense in terms of examples etc.

Merge/cluster a DDO sub-sense with its main sense

- unless it diverges from the main sense in ontological typing (from DanNet) (typically concrete ontological types versus abstract types, as is the case of most figurative senses.)

The reduction is done manually for the most complex (i.e. most polysemous) part of the vocabulary[6], whereas automatic methods are used for treating the least polysemous part of the vocabulary (2-4 senses per lemma), using however, the hand-coded examples as a gold standard. We apply a rule-based method, a word2vec model (Mikolov et al. 2013) and a BERT model (Devlin et al., 2019) for our automatic merges (cf. Pedersen et al. 2022: Section 4). Since accuracy does not exceed 0.82 for any of our automatic methods, however, all merged vocabulary is carefully manually curated before admitted into COR-S.

6 Systematic Polysemy in a Reduced Sense Inventory

Systematic polysemy constitutes a particular case of ambiguity where multiple lemmas show the same, regular pattern of polysemy. The phenomenon is well described in literature (Apresjan 1973, Malmgren 1988, Pustejovsky 1995 and others) and has been dealt with in both lexicography and in linguistics more broadly, relating to whether you tend to represent the phenomenon by splitting or merging the senses – or by something in between[7]. A general aim in all approaches is to try and treat the phenomenon *consistently*, which, however, is not as easy as it sounds at least not in a fully-fledged lexicon.

For instance, the merge principles defined in Section 5 cannot really serve as guidance here since the DDO as source applies mostly extralinguistic principles for describing lemmas that are systematically polysemous, such as space principles in the original printed dictionary in combination with the frequency of the lemma[8].

Therefore, to get an overview of the phenomenon in Danish, and to subsequently outline consistent merge or split principles for COR-S (as well as to encode the pattern value as part of the semantic information for each sense), we have been through a large set of lexicographical material based on the aforementioned core vocabulary and have identified more than 20 patterns of systematic polysemy. For an in-depth account of this work, see Sørensen et al., (2023).

For each pattern we have decided whether to keep the distinction of the senses or merge them into a single sense. Here, we reused the work already done in DanNet with respect to clarifying systematic polysemy (see Pedersen et al. 2010) since the patterns become obvious both from the ontological types and from the hypernym structures. For instance, the distinction between living and non-living entities in the DanNet taxonomy reveals the ANIMAL/FOOD pattern, and these senses are maintained in COR-S since they are quite clearly distinguished in use. In addition, the frequency of a particular sense type plays a role. To this end, in the related pattern ANIMAL BODY PART/FOOD the principle says to merge due to the proportionally much higher frequency of the FOOD sense here (we only very rarely talk about e.g. chicken breasts or chicken wings outside the cooking scenario). For the PROCESS/RESULT pattern, to give another example, we only split senses when the result is a concrete artifact and thus distinguishes itself clearly from the process (as is the case for *konstruktion* 'construction').

7 COR as Feedback to DanNe

In the COR project, a lemma that is only represented in one of its senses in DanNet is considered from a *semasiological* perspective, meaning that a con-

[6] The reduction is done manually for the 3,300 lemmas in DDO of which at least one sense is linked to the so-called core concepts in PWN (https://wordnetcode.princeton.edu/standoff-files/core-wordnet.txt) via DanNet, and which constitute a highly polysemous part of the vocabulary.

[7] Pustejovsky (1995) suggests so-called 'dot types' as a means to represent under-specification in systematic polysemy.

[8] In other words: Frequent lemmas tend to be 'unfolded' in the DDO with both meanings explicitly represented, whereas rare lemmas are only provided with one sense.

siderable amount of supplementary information is encoded to it.

When the COR project ends in 2023, we will therefore consider which of this curated information should be transferred back to DanNet with the aim of improving the wordnet. The id numbers ensure that this should not be too difficult a task.

First of all, DanNet does not contain all senses of a lemma in the way that COR-S does (even if for COR-S, we merge senses). This is a flaw of DanNet, which was produced under hard time constraints and which had hypernyms with many hyponyms as a driving principle leaving sometimes quite central senses untreated.

Secondly, the DanNet senses that have being deemed rare or too domain specific via the examinations in COR-S (approx. 10%) should be labeled as such in DanNet since the information is relevant for several purposes.

Some senses in DanNet are lumped together in COR-S, and it should be considered whether also to reflect this in DanNet in some way. The validation of the hypernyms in COR-S also provides useful feedback to DanNet and calls for a similar curation in the original resource.

Last but not least, it might be fruitful to adopt the more coarse-grained version of the EuroWordNet Ontology developed in COR, and in this case also transfer the validated ontological types from COR back to DanNet to ensure a higher lexical quality of the wordnet, especially in the case of 2nd and 3rd Order Entities where the EuroWordNet Ontology has proven somewhat complex to use in practice.

Sentiment values will already be directly included in DanNet based on the underlying data of the sentiment lexicon (Nimb et al. 2022) (describing values at sense level). Finally, the integration of semantic frames in DanNet is still under consideration as a way to improve the verbal descriptions in the resource.

8 Concluding Remarks

Building a new lexical resource like COR is an expensive and extremely time-consuming task. The COR project is primarily meant to serve the NLP-related AI industry by providing an easy-to-use, open-source resource with unique identifiers. In such a case, it seems indispensable to look around in the language community for resources that can be easily reused for that particular purpose. As well as to consider lexicographical standards that can ease transfer and alignment, as underlined in the lexicographic ELEXIS infrastructure (Krek et al. 2018).

As has been shown in this paper, we have had the great advantage in the Danish language community of having several substantial semantic resources interlinked via a unified sense id structure and relying on international standards. This has enabled us to easily transfer information into the new resource. In particular, the Danish wordnet, DanNet (in combination with DDO) has proven useful for this task.

While going through DanNet for the purpose of compiling COR, we have further taken the opportunity to also consider which revisions we would like to transfer back to the wordnet at a later stage in order to improve this stand-alone resource. In this way, the COR project has given us the chance to actually curate a resource that was compiled more than 10 years ago as part of a research project with only limited resources

References

Apresjan, J. (1973). Regular polysemy. In: *Linguistics 142*, pp 5-32.

Devlin, J., Chang, M-W., Lee, K. & Toutanova, K. (2019). BERT: Pre-training of deep bidirectional transformers for language understanding. In: *Proceedings of the 2019 Conference of the North American Chapter of the Association for Computational Linguistics: Human Language Technologies*, Volume 1. pages 4171–4186, Minneapolis, Minnesota. Association for Computational Linguistics

Fellbaum, C. (ed) (1998). *WordNet – An Electronic Lexical Database.* The MIT Press, Cambridge, Massachusetts, London.

Kilgarriff, A. (1997). I Don't Believe in Word Senses. In: *Computers and the Humanities.* Vol. 31, No. 2 (1997), pp. 91-113.

Krek, S., Kosem, I., McCrae, J. P., Navigli, R., Pedersen B. S., Tiberius, C. & Wissik, T. (2018). European Lexicographic Infrastructure (ELEXIS). In : *Proceedings of the XVIII EURALEX International Congress: Lexicography in Global Contexts*, Ljubljana.

Lyons, J. (1977). *Semantics.* Cambridge University Press.

Malmgren, S. (1988). On Regular Polysemy in Swedish. In: *Studies in Computer-Aided Lexicography*, Almquist & Wiksell, Stockholm.

Mikolov, T., Yih, W. & Zweig, G. (2013). Linguistic regularities in continuous space word representations. In : *Proceedings of the 2013 conference of the north american chapter of the association for computational linguistics: Human language technologies* (pp. 746-751).

Nimb, S. (2016). Der er ikke langt fra tanke til handling. In: S. Skovgaard Boeck & H. Blicher (eds) *Danske Studier 2016*, København, Universitets-Jubilæets danske Samfund, pp. 25-59. Copenhagen.

Nimb, S., Braasch, A., Olsen, S., Pedersen, B. S., & Søgaard, A. (2017). From Thesaurus to Framenet. In: I. Kosem, C. Tiberius, M. Jakubíček, J. Kallas, S. Krek, & V. Baisa (red.), *Electronic Lexicography in the 21st Century: Proceedings of eLex 2017 conference* (s. 1-22). Lexical Computing CZ.

Nimb, S., Olsen, S., Pedersen, B. S., & Troelsgaard, T. (2022). A Thesaurus-based Sentiment Lexicon for Danish: The Danish Sentiment Lexicon. In: *Proceedings of the Language Resources and Evaluation Conference: LREC2022* (Bind 2022, s. 2826--2832). European Language Resources Association.

Pedersen, B. S., Nimb, S., Asmussen, J., Sørensen, N., Trap-Jensen, L., & Lorentzen, H. (2009). DanNet - the challenge of compiling a WordNet for Danish by reusing a monolingual dictionary. In: *Language Resources and Evaluation*, *43*, 269-299.

Pedersen, B., M. Agirrezabal, S. Nimb, I. Olsen, S. Olsen (2018). Towards a principled approach to sense clustering – a case study of wordnet and dictionary senses in Danish. In: *Proceedings of the 9th Global Wordnet Conference.* Singapore.

Pedersen, B. S., Nimb, S., Olsen, I. R., & Olsen, S. (2019). Linking DanNet with Princeton WordNet. In: *Global WordNet 2019 Proceedings, Wroclaw, Poland* Oficyna Wydawnicza Politechniki Wroclawskiej.

Pustejovsky, J. (1995). *The Generative Lexicon.* The MIT Press.

Sørensen, N., S. Nimb & B. Pedersen (2023). Validating Systematic Polysemy in WordNets by Means of Contextualized Embeddings. In: *Global WordNet Conference 2023*, Donostia, Spain.

Vossen, P. (ed.) (1997). *EuroWordNet: A multilingual database with lexical semantic networks.* Springer Verlag.

Recent Developments in BulTreeBank-WordNet (BTB-WN)

Kiril Simov and **Petya Osenova**
Institute of Information and Communication technologies
Bulgarian Academy of Sciences
kivs|petya@bultreebank.org

Abstract

The paper reports on recent developments in Bulgarian BTB-WordNet (BTB-WN). This resource is viewed as playing a central role with respect to the integration and interlinking of various language resources such as: e-dictionaries (morphological, terminological, bilingual, orthographic, etymological and explanatory, etc., including editions from previous periods); corpora (coming from outside or being internal - like the corpus of definitions as well as the corpus of examples to synset meanings); ontologies (such as CIDOC-CRM, DBpedia, etc.); sources of world knowledge (such as information from the Bulgarian Encyclopedia, Wikipedia, etc.). The paper also gives information about a number of applications built on BTB-WN. These are: the Bulgaria-centered knowledge graph, the *All about word* application as well as some education-oriented exercises.

1 Introduction

In this paper we report on the developments of the Bulgarian BTB-WordNet (BTB-WN) during the last three years (2020, 2021, 2022). The development of BTB-WN goes back to the times when an Ontology-based lexicon for Bulgarian was initially constructed (Simov and Osenova, 2010). Here we started with the concept set from the upper ontology DOLCE[1]. Then it was extended with concepts selected from the OntoWordNet (Gangemi et al., 2003), which correspond to Core WordNet and EuroWordNet Base concepts[2]. The construction of the Ontology-based lexicon - that later on evolved into the BTB-WN – was driven by the need of such a resource for some NLP applications like domain ontology text annotation, word sense disambiguation, co-reference resolution, machine translation and others. However, it turned out that each of these applications required not only available resources but also appropriate integration among them. The interface between the lexical semantics and grammar, between the lexicons and corpora has been extensively discussed from various points of view: linguistic, typological, formal, implementational, etc. Either starting point causes problems – the lexicalist-centric and the grammar-centric ones. Here we support the point of view in which the grammar is born in the lexicon, i.e. the lexicalist-centric one, without lowering the role of the grammar at all. This view is on a par with the linguistic theories that are constraint-based (such as HPSG and LFG) or are word-based (dependency theories). It is also in line with the ideas behind the flagship project in eLexicography – ELEXIS[3]. The result from this project is a roadmap in eLexicography where all the steps in the various life cycles of producing a dictionary have been studies, documented, implemented and tested. The interested reader is forwarded to (Tiberius et al., 2021).

It is well-known that WordNets are thesauri and despite providing the meaning of words grouping them within synsets and providing relations among these synsets, they are still very static, self-contained and often do not cover all parts of speech. At the same time, they are good candidates for playing a central role – like a hub – for linking grammar, other lexical data and world knowledge. Our ultimate goal however would be that users could customise their own dictionaries, examples or other material through these interlinked resources. For that reason, along with cleaning the meanings and relations within BTB-WN, we started also other tasks such as: linking lemmas to their morphosyntactic characteristics through a rich tagset and morphological/inflectional dictionary of Bulgarian; linking meanings to examples from corpora; constructing a corpus of definitions, annotated with senses from BTB-WN; adding domain

[1] http://www.loa.istc.cnr.it/dolce/overview.html

[2] http://globalWordNet.org/resources/gwa-base-concepts/

[3] https://elex.is/

terms; adding dictionaries from previous times with their specific spellings; constructing a Bulgaria-centric knowledge graph as an extension of BTB-WN; aligning different ontologies with respect to BTB-WN; using the lexical chains over the BTB-WN graph for generating correct sense detection drills for Bulgarian learners.

The extension of BTB-WN with information from the Bulgarian Wikipedia has been enhanced in three directions: adding concepts, adding instances, and adding properties. The idea behind this approach is to support the mapping of the ontology with the vocabulary of BTB-WN as well as the mapping of the BTB-WN relations to knowledge graphs created on the basis of Wikipedia, DBpedia, Wikidata, etc. Such mappings would also facilitate the knowledge extraction from the wiki media themselves. This endeavour is in line with works like (McCrae and Cillessen, 2021), where a method is presented for linking English Wordnet with Wikidata.

The paper is structured as follows: the next section outlines some related works from different perspectives and thus is not exhaustive. Section 3 describes the linking of BTB-WN with in-house and external resources. Section 4 focuses on some BTB-WN based applications. Section 5 concludes the paper.

2 Related works

It is difficult to refer to the great number of publications that discuss various parameters of integration and usage of WordNets. Also, here we do not focus on the integration and representation of WordNets through formatting standards like LEMON[4], LMF[5], etc. but rather on resource integration where the WordNet plays the main role. For that reason, only some of the many works are cited here with the aim to illustrate our work in the context of the existing research.

A lot of works have been devoted to the usage of language specific and multilingual resources such as monolingual and bilingual dictionaries for the quicker and less expensive construction of WordNets. For example, (Siegel and Bond, 2021) report on the construction of the German WordNet called OdeNet and (Fišer and Sagot, 2015) report about the creation of the Slovene WordNet. Our BTB-WN was constructed semi-automatically with the combination of both established methods - *expand* and *merge*. The automatic part was used when extracting data from Bulgarian resources and for merging it before being validated by a human.

(Bentivogli et al., 2004) share their experience on how to incorporate domain lexica in their WordNet. As expected, the main reported problems were in the synchronization of the hierarchies between the WordNet and the specialized thesaurus in the domain of architecture. In our case the inclusion of domain terms still follows the WordNet hierarchy.

(Ahmadi et al., 2020) present a method for an automatic alignment between the senses of the same lemma across two monolingual Danish dictionaries that come from two periods - modern and historic. In our case we have performed automatic lemma-based alignments among a contemporary dictionary of Bulgarian and an older one. The spellings in both resources differ. A sense alignment has not been performed yet but it is envisaged as a future task.

(Laparra et al., 2009) present a graph-based Word Sense Disambiguation algorithm for integrating WordNet with FrameNet[6]. In our case the integration considers VerbNet[7] first – through the customized mapping with the Bulgarian Valency Dictionary (BVD) (Osenova et al., 2012). FrameNet is incorporated through the inclusion of the event-evoking verbs within the Bulgarian Event Corpus (Osenova et al., 2022). These events have been annotated with named entities, roles and relations adapted from FrameNet and CIDOC-CRM ontology[8].

(Oliver, 2020) surveys various techniques for aligning Wikipedia with WordNet. The author concludes that the evaluation of alignments between the two is still an open research task. In our mapping strategy we use a rule-based approach with a post-editing validation by a human.

In (Rudnicka et al., 2022) the gaps in mapping Polish and English WordNets were identified and addressed. Such gaps are observed also in our case, and although we preserve the mappings with the Open English WordNet (OEW), we also try to make the Bulgarian hierarchy more natural to the Bulgarian cultural environment and speakers with removing the artificial intermediate nodes and with adding Bulgarian hypernyms and hyponyms.

[4]https://www.w3.org/2019/09/lexicog/

[5]https://www.iso.org/standard/68516.html

[6]https://framenet.icsi.berkeley.edu/fndrupal/

[7]https://verbs.colorado.edu/verbnet/

[8]https://www.cidoc-crm.org/

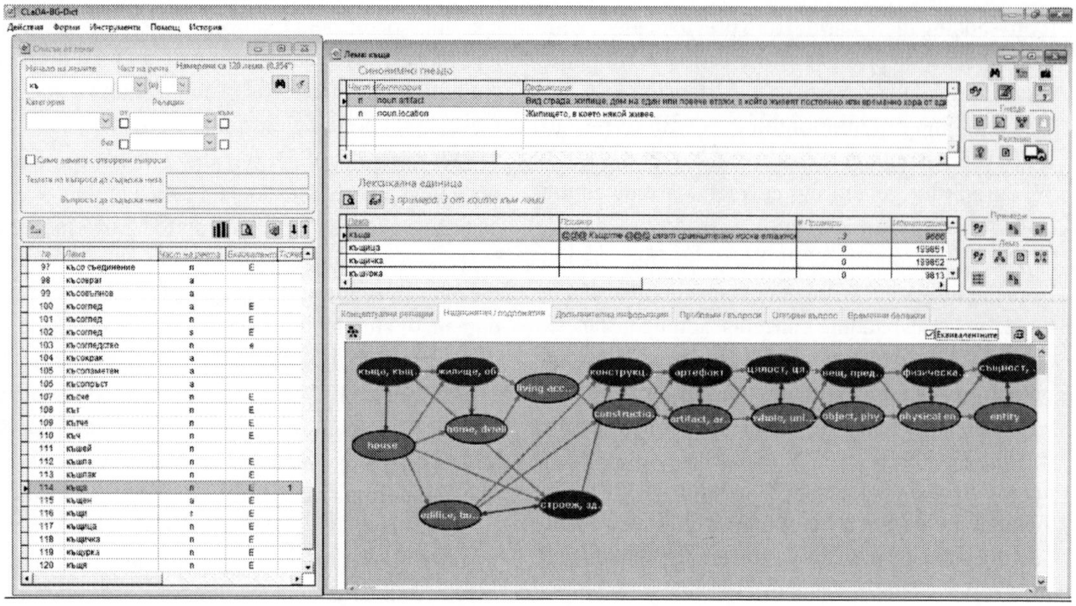

Figure 1: A screenshot of the user interface of CLaDA-BG-Dict. It shows a search of lemmas against several criteria within the current BTB-WN (on the left); A synset editor (on the right) – shows all the synsets (upper part of the window) for a selected lemma; for the selected synset it shows its category, a definition and a list of synonyms. For each lemma there are assigned examples as well as mappings to the respective inflectional paradigms. At the bottom of the window a graphic representation of a noun hierarchy is given and also the mapping to the English synsets.

3 Extending and Linking BTB-WN

One important step we performed within the period of work reported here is the switching from a tool that supported only local editing (where synsets were considered within a very limited context) to a tool that supports editing of the Wordnet data within a global context. In Fig. 1 the main user interface of the system is presented.

When a lemma is selected within BTB-WN, the following information can be accessed immediately: the number of synsets related to it with the part-of-speech as well as the numbered meanings and links to the Open English WordNet. The usage of almost each synonym within a synset is illustrated with examples. Within the system the user could consult several other sources of information. The center of the system is BTB-WordNet. The user could open as many editor forms as necessary in which to observe the synsets for different words. Similarly the Open English Wordnet is available in the system. The creation of a new Bulgarian synset could start from scratch – entering all the information, including relations to other systems. But it is also possible to create such a synset with using an equivalent English synset. In this way the relations of the English synsets are automatically transferred to BTB-WN. Also, a graphic is provided that reflects the ratio among the relations that are relevant to the synset (not visible in Fig. 1). In addition, the hypernyms and hyponyms can be observed as well.

The user can access the requested lemma in two ways: a) through writing it in the search box, or b) through finding it in the list of all lemmas. If the first option has been chosen, then the available information about the lemma is immediately presented. If the second option has been chosen, then one can see the part-of-speech and then enhance further information such as statistics of the lemma occurrence in the resource, or access the lemma information in the current representation or in a separate one. The 'Search' option provides various filters for making the inquiry more accurate. These include not only the lemma but also part-of-speech, lexicographic category, various relations. If the query is too broad for the database to return a reasonable set of examples, the user is prompted to specify it further. Another possibility to access the available lexical information is through the specific ID of the synset.

In addition to granting access to OEW, the system provides access to dictionaries that are freely available to us, among which the Bulgarian Explanatory Dictionary, our in-house Bulgarian Inflec-

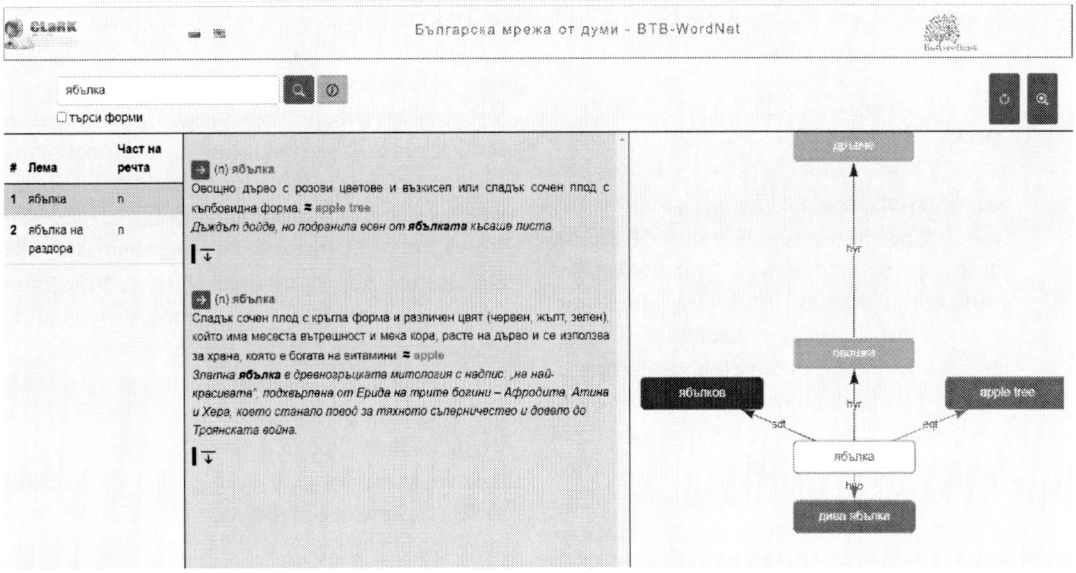

Figure 2: Information about the lemma 'apple'. This is a system providing access to the BTB-WN for external users.

tional dictionary, two Bulgarian-English dictionaries. Each of these dictionaries could be consulted in isolation or simultaneously on the base of the alignments performed through lemmas. The user could also define different lists of lemmas which to be mapped to the vocabulary of BTB-WN and to the vocabularies of the included dictionaries. In this way it can be decided which new lemmas to be included within BTB-WN, or which to be used within a given application. Currently we support vocabularies co-responding to Bulgarian learners' levels like A1-A2, B1-B2, C. Also vocabularies of two student spelling lexicons and a list of the first 10 000 ranked lemmas were added against the Bulgarian Referent Corpus. The information within dictionaries is available within the editor form under the tab labeled as 'Additional information'. When exploring regular expressions, the user could observe different patterns of lemmas within the dictionaries.

Through the lexicographic classes (such as verb.social, verb.cognition, etc.) the synsets are connected also to the Bulgarian Valency Dictionary. This linking has not been implemented in our system yet since the Valency dictionary is being curated by specialists. For example, if the verb.emotion 'worry' is considered, the Bulgarian counterpart is displayed with a definition and a valency frame where the Subject has the role of Experiencer and the complement event that causes worrying has the role of Stimulus. The link to the VerbNet frame is also given[9]. The transfer of valency frames from English to Bulgarian through an English-centered resource is not trivial. For that reason, often the initial frames are customized accordingly. As best practices for valency dictionaries we follow the Czech VALLEX (Lopatková et al., 2016) and the Polish Walenty (Przepiórkowski et al., 2014), among others.

In addition to the data access options, described above, one can search with the selected lemma in various corpora. We consider the definitions and examples already included in BTB-WN as a corpus from which to select examples for other senses. In this case we could construct sense annotated corpora similar to the (Rademaker et al., 2019). The system provides access to text corpora. For searching in the textual corpora the user has to point to a given corpus compiled from a text format where the metadata (like the source, for example) is introduced inside the text as a new line starting with a special symbol (@). The user might incrementally compile through various searches their own corpus with examples since there is an option of adding previously extracted results to the new ones.

With these functionalities, we performed a full examination of the existing version of BTB-WN (version 3.0) at the time when our working system was ready. BTB-WN contained a little more than

[9]https://verbs.colorado.edu/verbindex/vn/marvel31.3.php

19 000 synsets. Each synset was checked with respect to the following criteria:

- *Appropriateness of definitions.* We have checked the definitions for the different kinds of word classes and also per synset. This step was necessary, because in many cases the definition types in our resource differ from the ones in paper dictionaries. This holds especially for adjectives. In the traditional dictionaries the adjective is usually defined as qualifying a noun. In our case we go further and develop the definition of the adjective also to the specific features of the qualified noun. This holds especially for the relational adjectives like 'sofiyski' (Sofia-adjective). This adjective might relate to something: that originates in Sofia; is made in Sofia style; is placed in Sofia, etc.

- *Alignment to OEW.* In version 3.0 we supported as many relations as possible between the Bulgarian and English synsets. With the switch to the global view it became much more convenient to verify these mappings.

- *Missing senses.* The construction of the BTB-WN up to version 4 was mainly driven by specific NLP tasks, as it was mentioned in the Introduction. Thus, it reflected the needs of these tasks. Now we decided to check the coverage of the resource with respect to the most common and well-established senses.

- *Relations.* When a Bulgarian synset was created on the basis of the corresponding English one, the relations were transferred automatically. After the transfer the set of relations became eligible for modifications, if needed.

- *Appropriateness of examples.* The assigned examples were specially checked with respect to their appropriateness to the corresponding sense. The most frequent error was when the example did not provide enough context for the meaning, and thus the corresponding word form might have been interpreted ambiguously. In such cases the example was extended or deleted.

Besides the examination of the existing synsets we have extended BTB-WN with new synsets through the above mentioned vocabularies extracted from both types of sources - dictionaries and corpora. This was performed in line with our goal to cover the senses of the most common lemmas in Bulgarian. At the moment we completed the coverage of the core vocabulary with about 6000 lemmas. Then the following information was added: derivational sets for these lemmas such as adjectives derived from nouns, aspectual variants of Bulgarian verbs that share a common basic sense, etc. In this way, more than 14 000 synsets were added. For the addition of examples we compiled and used a concise guide. For the moment it is for our internal usage only, but it will be available also in English for better accessibility by anyone who would be interested in it. The short guide explains how the examples were selected that are connected to senses, how to better search for examples in corpora and on the net, and what the recommendation criteria are for this selection. The best examples always should reflect some of the characteristics given in the definition, or add to them. For instance, if we want to give a good example to the *noun.artifact* 'pair of trousers', we might take the following one: 'The right leg of his trousers was split to allow his plastered leg to pass through'. Here the sentence reveals the following facts: that the trousers cover legs and that the trousers have two parts.

4 BTB-WN based applications

In this section we present some of the applications of BTB-WN that were developed recently or are under development.

The first application is the role of BTB-WN in the Bulgaria-centric knowledge graph. We consider the knowledge graph a core semantic repository for Bulgarian research infrastructure related to CLARIN[10] and DARIAH[11]. For that reason BTB-WN has been further enriched with terms from various Social Sciences and Humanities domains such as history and ethnography. Here two challenges appeared. The first one is related to the introduction of terminological multiword expressions while the second one refers to the register of usage such as being archaic or dialectal, etc.

For example, let us take the Bulgarian folk units of measurement. They are linked with a hyponymy relation to the concept about the official Bulgarian folk units (such as 'pedya' (span), 'prast' (finger), 'lakat' (elbow), etc.) and the concept for linear

[10]https://www.clarin.eu/

[11]https://www.dariah.eu/

units (such as the unit for length).

The inclusion of domain terms in the WordNet would allow the annotation of domain texts with word senses. These then might be used for training domain-specific semantic taggers and would be able to contribute to the task of natural language understanding.

The contemporary terminological lexicons very often comprise detailed encyclopedic knowledge. We do not incorporate such detailed entries in BTB-WN, but just concise definitions and references to the respective terminological lexicon. This step is similar to the operation of mapping from BTB-WN to Wikipedia.

The generalization of this approach grew into the creation of a hub for a bigger net of dictionaries and resources, called in our case 'All about words'. In this application we reused the integration of dictionaries within the system for further creation of BTB-WN in order to provide as much as information as possible about the Bulgarian words. The system includes a concordancer, a Wordnet viewer, a word form analyser, a viewer for the Bulgarian inflectional dictionary, viewers for other dictionaries. Thus, the user can run the concordancer with the query expression of interest. From the returned concordance lines the users could select arbitrary word forms and require information about them. The system applies the word form analyser which returns all possible lemmas for the word form with the appropriate part of speech. For example, if we type the word 'belya', it will return three part-of-speech types: peel (verb), peel oneself (verb), white (adjective) and mischief (noun). Then the system switches to a different browser tab where the user could consult different resources via these lemmas. At the heart of these interrelated resources come BTB-WN and the Inflectional lexicon. The user could observe the paradigm of the selected lemma, its meanings in BTB-WN, brief information from other dictionaries in which the lemma is presented, and a list of examples extracted from the sense annotated treebank of Bulgarian, etc. From this tab the user could switch to other tabs in order to consult the corresponding resource in more detail. Also the user could switch back to the concordancer for searching examples about other word forms.

For example, if we choose the noun (mischief) from the above list of ambiguous lemmas, then the noun paradigm will be made visible. If one of the verbs is chosen, then the verb paradigm of present tense in all persons and numbers is made visible. All other verb forms are planned to be made available as well, irrespective of whether they are synthetic or analytic. If the user clicks on a specific wordform of the paradigm information, they can see the respective description of the grammatical characteristics like the following: for the lemma 'belya' the description is: verb, personal, imperfective, transitive, indicative, present tense, 1 person, singular; for the word form 'belyat' the description will change in the indicated places which are: 3 person, plural. When the user selects the BTB-WN visualization page, all synsets of the lemma are listed, a graphical presentation of the relational graph around the synset is visualized. Additionally, users can type another lemma and see all the synsets in which this lemma participates. When a synset is selected, also a graphical view with the available relations is shown. An example for the lemma 'apple' is given in Fig. 2.

In Fig. 2 the following information is displayed. On the left side the lemma 'apple' is given as number 1. As number 2 one can see an idiom starting with this lemma, namely 'apple of discord'. However, the first one has been selected. In the middle column both meanings of the lemma have been listed - as an apple tree and as the apple fruit - together with the mappings to Open English WordNet. The third column presents a visualization of some of the relations in which the meaning for 'apple tree' participates. These are as follows: the immediate hypernym is a 'fruit tree' and the next level hypernym is a 'tree'. There is an immediate hyponym which is a 'wild apple tree'. Through the equality relation on the right, the Bulgarian lemma is related to the English one. Last, but not least, on the left, a derivation relation is established to the adjective 'apple'.

While the above described applications serve mostly as a guide to the specifics of Bulgarian words, the next one that we discuss here is more educationally oriented. It is a newly developed application called 'Game of Meanings'. The user receives a task where they have to select the correct definition per lemma in a sentence from the examples associated with one of the synsets for this lemma. The definitions in the multiple choice task as well as the contexts in which a certain lemma was used come from BTB-WN. An example from the beta version is shown on Fig. 3. Each game

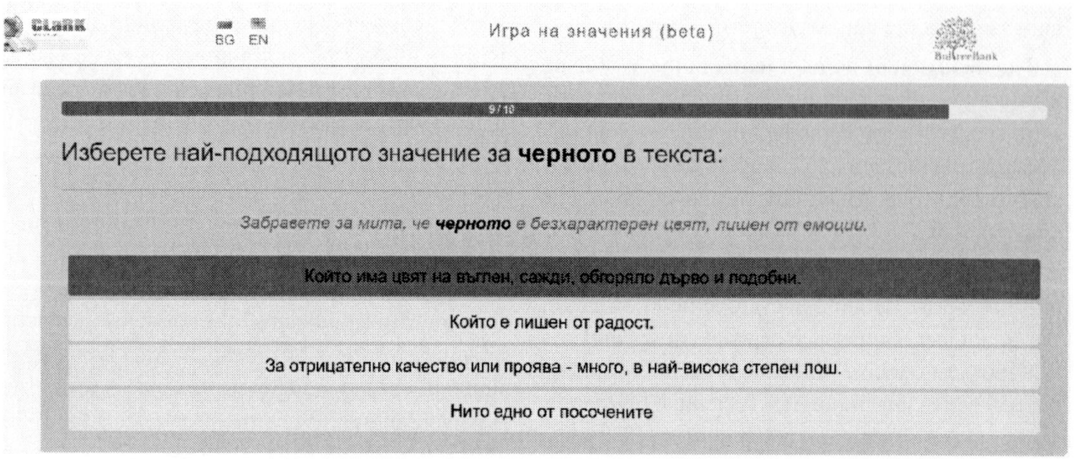

Figure 3: The multiple choice question on the color of black.

consists of a set of 10 tasks. Each task includes an example for a selected lemma in a selected synset with four alternative answers. Each answer is a definition or a message for a missing definition - the algorithm for generation of tasks is given below.

In Fig. 3 the following task is given: Select the most appropriate meaning for the word 'the black' in the text that says: *Forget the myth that 'black' is a featureless color that lacks emotion.* Four possible definitions are given to the player to select from. They are: 1. Which has the color of charcoal, soot, burnt wood and the like; 2. Which lacks joy; 3. For a negative quality or manifestation - very bad; 4. None of these.

Here the correct answer is supposed to be the first one (1). It should be noted that the more similar definitions to select from, the more difficult the task is, and vice versa.

The algorithm for generating the tasks includes these steps: a) a lemma is selected; b) a synset is chosen for this lemma; c) from this synset an example is selected; d) the available definition is given as an option to choose from. e) the other alternatives are selected over the synsets with the lexical chains navigation algorithm (Hirst and St-Onge, 1996) over the BTB-WN graph including the other synsets of the lemma, if available. In cases when there are no enough options, a string-based similarity search is performed with respect to the initial lemma.

We imagine that such a type of game would increase the ability of students but also of the whole interested community to improve their reading with understanding. It should be noted that with respect to the task of 'reading with understanding' Bulgarian students perform poorly in comparison to their peers in Europe.

5 Conclusions

In this paper we present an environment where the BTB-WN plays a central role in displaying all the available information about a lemma in Bulgarian - synsets, associated definitions and examples, grammatical information in the form of paradigms and descriptions, possibilities to search in corpora of all definitions or in external ones. Thus, our approach is lemma-based but at the same time it starts from the lexical semantics and through various linking strategies incorporates also the grammar and pieces of world knowledge.

Our future plans are to add more information of all kinds and more relations as well as relation directions among the resources. Needless to say, approaches for automation of resources enrichment and linking are also envisaged.

In addition to the presented tasks, we have been working also on generation of exercises for mastering Bulgarian grammar. Since the exercises use our dictionaries and patterns to produce as many drills as possible, very often their semantics is questionable. This fact causes a serious problem to the freedom of the underlying generating algorithms since the users should be prevented from seeing and memorizing nonsense or pedagogically and ethically flawed messages. Thus, even in automatized exercises such as drills we should be very careful about what suggestions we provide to trainees. Following this line, we plan not to stop the generating power per se but to use BTB-WN (integrated with the Bulgarian Valency Dictionary) as a semantic filter in the exercise production module.

6 Acknowledgements

The reported work has been partially supported by CLaDA-BG, the Bulgarian National Interdisciplinary Research e-Infrastructure for Resources and Technologies in favor of the Bulgarian Language and Cultural Heritage, part of the EU infrastructures CLARIN and DARIAH, Grant number DO1-301/17.12.21.

We would like to sincerely thank the three anonymous reviewers for their very valuable remarks on the initially submitted version of the paper.

References

Sina Ahmadi, Sanni Nimb, Thomas Troelsgård, John P. McCrae, and Nicolai H. Sørensen. 2020. Towards Automatic Linking of Lexicographic Data: the case of a historical and a modern Danish dictionary. Zenodo.

Luisa Bentivogli, Andrea Bocco, and Emanuele Pianta. 2004. ArchiWordNet: Integrating WordNet with Domain-Specific Knowledge. In *Proceedings of the 2nd International Global Wordnet Conference*, pages 39–47.

Darja Fišer and Benoît Sagot. 2015. Constructing a poor man's wordnet in a resource-rich world. In *Language Resources and Evaluation*, pages 601–635.

Aldo Gangemi, Roberto Navigli, and Paola Velardi. 2003. The ontowordnet project: Extension and axiomatization of conceptual relations in wordnet. In *On The Move to Meaningful Internet Systems 2003: CoopIS, DOA, and ODBASE*, pages 820–838, Berlin, Heidelberg. Springer Berlin Heidelberg.

Graeme Hirst and David St-Onge. 1996. *Lexical chains as representations of context for the detection and correction of malapropisms*. The MIT Press.

Egoitz Laparra, German Rigau, and Montse Cuadros. 2009. Exploring the Integration of WordNet and FrameNet. In *Proceedings of the 5th Global WordNet Conference*.

Markéta Lopatková, Václava Kettnerová, Eduard Bejček, Anna Vernerová, and Zdeněk Žabokrtský. 2016. *Valenční slovník českých sloves VALLEX*. Karolinum, Praha.

John P. McCrae and David Cillessen. 2021. Towards a linking between wordnet and wikidata. Zenodo.

Antoni Oliver. 2020. Aligning Wikipedia with WordNet:a review and evaluation of different techniques. In *Proceedings of the Twelfth Language Resources and Evaluation Conference*, pages 4851–4858, Marseille, France. European Language Resources Association.

Petya Osenova, Kiril Simov, Laska Laskova, and Stanislava Kancheva. 2012. A treebank-driven creation of an OntoValence verb lexicon for Bulgarian. In *Proceedings of the Eighth International Conference on Language Resources and Evaluation (LREC'12)*, pages 2636–2640, Istanbul, Turkey. European Language Resources Association (ELRA).

Petya Osenova, Kiril Simov, Iva Marinova, and Melania Berbatova. 2022. The Bulgarian event corpus: Overview and initial NER experiments. In *Proceedings of the Thirteenth Language Resources and Evaluation Conference*, pages 3491–3499, Marseille, France. European Language Resources Association.

Adam Przepiórkowski, Elżbieta Hajnicz, Agnieszka Patejuk, Marcin Woliński, Filip Skwarski, and Marek Świdziński. 2014. Walenty: Towards a comprehensive valence dictionary of Polish. In *Proceedings of the Ninth International Conference on Language Resources and Evaluation (LREC'14)*, pages 2785–2792, Reykjavik, Iceland. European Language Resources Association (ELRA).

Alexandre Rademaker, Bruno Cuconato, Alessandra Cid, Alexandre Tessarollo, and Henrique Andrade. 2019. Completing the Princeton annotated gloss corpus project. In *Proceedings of the 10th Global Wordnet Conference*, pages 378–386, Wroclaw, Poland. Global Wordnet Association.

Ewa Rudnicka, Łukasz Grabowski, Maciej Piasecki, and Tomasz Naskręt. 2022. In Search of Gaps between Languages and Wordnets: the Case of Polish-English WordNet. *International Journal of Lexicography*. Ecac005.

Melanie Siegel and Francis Bond. 2021. OdeNet: Compiling a GermanWordNet from other resources. In *Proceedings of the 11th Global Wordnet Conference*, pages 192–198, University of South Africa (UNISA). Global Wordnet Association.

Kiril Simov and Petya Osenova. 2010. Constructing of an ontology-based lexicon for Bulgarian. In *Proceedings of the Seventh International Conference on Language Resources and Evaluation (LREC'10)*, Valletta, Malta. European Language Resources Association (ELRA).

Carole Tiberius, Simon Krek, Katrien Depuyd, Polona Gantar, Jelena Kallas, Iztok Kosem, and Rundell Michael. 2021. Towards the ELEXIS data model: defining a common vocabulary for lexicographic resources. Zenodo.

Lexicalised and Non-lexicalized Multi-word Expressions in WordNet: a Cross-encoder Approach

Marek Maziarz[1], **Łukasz Grabowski**[2], **Tadeusz Piotrowski**[3], **Ewa Rudnicka**[1], and **Maciej Piasecki**[1]

[1]Wrocław University of Science and Technology, Wyspiańskiego 27, 50-370 Wrocław, Poland
[1]{marek.maziarz, ewa.rudnicka, maciej.piasecki}@pwr.edu.pl
[2]University of Opole, pl. Kopernika 11, 45-040 Opole, Poland
[2]lukasz@uni.opole.pl
[3]University of Wrocław, English Department, Kuźnicza 22, 50-138 Wrocław, Poland
[3]tadeusz.piotrowski@uwr.edu.pl

Abstract

Focusing on recognition of multi-word expressions (MWEs), we address the problem of recording MWEs in WordNet. In fact, not all MWEs recorded in that lexical database could with no doubt be considered as lexicalised (e.g. elements of wordnet taxonomy, quantifier phrases, certain collocations). In this paper, we use a cross-encoder approach to improve our earlier method of distinguishing between lexicalised and non-lexicalised MWEs found in WordNet using custom-designed rule-based and statistical approaches. We achieve F1-measure for the class of lexicalised word combinations close to 80%, easily beating two baselines (random and a majority class one). Language model also proves to be better than a feature-based logistic regression model.

1 Introduction

Recognition of multi-word expressions (MWEs) is one of the main tasks in the field of natural language processing (NLP) and lexicography, notably in the development of custom-designed MWE lexicons for various NLP tools or compilation of dictionaries, respectively (Gantar et al., 2018). However, MWEs are not homogeneous and there is a plethora of their definitions and operationalizations in specialized literature. For example, according to (Sag et al., 2002), the range of MWEs is very broad (including idioms, proper names, fixed phrases, compound nouns, collocations, to name but a few), as any "idiosyncratic interpretations that cross word boundaries (or spaces)" are considered to be MWEs. These idiosyncratic interpretations of a given word combination can be related to various linguistic criteria (formal, pragmatic, statistical or psycholinguistic ones), e.g, morphosyntactic patterns, constituent substitutability, semantic compositionality, frequent/recurrent use, reproducibility, collocational strength, conventionalization, pragmatic function (Woźniak, 2017; Gantar et al., 2018), and any idiosyncrasy/irregularity/non-standardness in those criteria may imply that we are potentially dealing with a MWE that is lexicalised.

We treat lexicalisation as a gradable syntax-to-lexicon process whereby a purely compositional word combination (a syntactic unit) comes to be treated as a single semantic or pragmatic unit (a lexical unit), exhibiting word-like behaviour (Lipka, 1990; Jezek, 2016; Constant et al., 2017), or – in other words – as "a conventionalized association of a contentful sense with a form at the level of the lexicon" (Van Rompaey et al., 2015, p.234). As we argue that lexicalisation is best described on a continuum, the range of multi-word expressions (MWEs) is rather wide, starting with purely compositional word combinations created *ad hoc* on one end, through collocations, to fixed phrases and idioms on the other end (Maziarz et al., 2022, 2023). However, in the theory and practice of lexicography, it is often difficult to determine which MWEs should or should not be recorded in a dictionary, i.e., treated as vocabulary/lexical units rather than mere word combinations created *ad hoc* in speech or writing. Lexicographers have to make a binary decision: either this is a *bona fide* lexical unit or not. Traditionally this status was indicated in a dictionary by place of an item in the entry and typography. More precisely, when making this binary choice, lexicographers rely on their linguistic intuition, linguistic experience and competence, contemporary and previous sources of information (dictionaries, books, corpora, etc.) to decide which MWEs to record in a dictionary, and these decisions may also differ across lexicographic traditions. For example, we looked into selected dictionaries of English and Polish and found that English lexicographers tend to record semantically compositional word combinations much more often than their Polish counterparts (Maziarz et al., 2023).

In this study, we assume that the same practical lexicographic problems apply to wordnets, as not all MWEs recorded in the Princeton WordNet can be indisputably considered to be lexicalised, e.g., such items as elements of the WordNet taxonomy (*biological group, animal group* etc.), quantifier phrases (*piece of furniture, article of furniture*), collocations (*rich people, psychology department*). For this reason, we need clear and operational procedures for deciding which MWEs should be included in a wordnet and which should not. By analogy to lexicography, where lexical entries in dictionaries are treated as lexical units, in this study we use the label 'multi-word lexical units' (MWLUs) for those lexicalised MWEs that should indisputably be recorded in a wordnet. Hence, our proposed procedure, combining rule-based and statistical approaches, would help us filter out MWLUs from the broad pool of MWEs recorded in WordNet (or PWN/enWN) and, in consequence, facilitate making the aforementioned dichotomous choice. The findings may help fine-tune the list of WordNet MWEs, which are often used as gold standard for NLP applications (Schneider et al., 2014; Farahmand and Martins, 2014; Riedl and Biemann, 2016). Finally, we believe that our findings will help us better understand how WordNet developers (Fellbaum, 1998) tackled the problem of recording MWEs when compiling that lexical resource.

2 Sample annotation

From Princeton WordNet and enWordNet we chose all word combinations that contained at least one space. We ruled out all proper names, as well as chemistry and biological taxonomy terms, just like we did in our previous experiment (Maziarz et al., 2022)[1]. After the filtering, we got 39,406 MWEs. Table 1 presents part of speech distribution in the dataset. 387 MWEs were randomly drawn from the remaining word combination set[2].

nouns	verbs	adjectives	adverbs
33713	4389	540	764
86%	11%	2%	1%

Table 1: POS statistics for the MWE dataset.

In order to verify the potential MWLU status of the sampled 387 word combinations, we checked how they are described in 6 dictionaries of English; we assume that if a word combination was given the headword status in the dictionaries then that indicates they are treated as multiword lexical units by native speakers of English – lexicographers – whose lexical competence surpasses that of any native speaker of English. We treat data from dictionaries thus as native speakers' response to a question: is this expression a MWLU? In other words, we believe that lexical units with headword status in dictionaries are end products of lexicalization. We are going to mention some problems with this belief below.

The dictionaries are all from established publishing houses, and will be mainly identified as such; they are: New Oxford Dictionary of English (NODE, British)[3], Merriam-Webster Collegiate (M-W, USA)[4], Collins Dictionary (CED, British)[5], New World Dictionary (N-W, USA), Collins COBUILD (COBUILD)[6], Longman Dictionary of Contemporary English (Longman)[7]. Four of those dictionaries (NODE, M-W, N-W, CED) are so-called medium, or desktop, dictionaries that are intended to be used primarily by educated native speakers of English, and two are so-called pedagogical dictionaries (COBUILD, Longman), that are intended to be used primarily by advanced learners of English or non-native speakers of English (Jackson, 2022; Cowie, 2009). We used online versions, as they are updated quite regularly in contrast to printed versions. These dictionaries were selected to ensure that we have a multi-faceted approach, and this can be shown as follows.

First, the selection was based on the needs of the intended user, as described above, but it was also based on the size and comprehensiveness of coverage. Desktop dictionaries include most of the vocabulary that educated native speakers can find

[1]We singled them out on the basis of hyponymy relation to the following top synsets: {organism 1}, {biological group 1}, {chemical element 1} and {chemical 1}.

[2]This is roughly one percent of the total 39k set. To the training set, containing 200 MWEs, used in our previous experiment (Maziarz et al., 2022), we also added 100 new MWEs as well as 50 MWEs used for final evaluation in the previous paper (already cross-checked with dictionaries). Since the 50 MWEs set represented 'MWLU' prediction class of the logistic model, we had to balance the sample to preserve the ratio of real classes. That is why additional 37 MWEs were added (recognised as non-lexicalised by the logistic classifier). We publish data sets used in this research under the CC BY 4.0 licence on GitHub (`https://github.com/MarekMaziarz/MWE-recognition-in-WN`).

[3]`lexico.com` (until August 27, 2022) and at `google.com`

[4]`www.merriam-webster.com`

[5]`www.collinsdictionary.com`

[6]`www.collinsdictionary.com`

[7]`www.ldoceonline.com`

in texts of English and which they may not know (that is why they reach for a dictionary), though they do not use them on their own. We used dictionaries that are meant to be used by both American or British English speakers. Pedagogical dictionaries include vocabulary of high frequency that native speakers have in their active vocabulary, the needs of a non-English user, especially from outside European culture, are not quite predictable. They have a balanced selection of British and American items, therefore we did not describe them as being British or American.

Each MWE in our sample was manually verified in terms of its occurrence as a lexical entry in any of the six dictionaries on the basis of elimination tests, starting with M-W, followed by Longman, COBUILD, CED, N-W, and concluding with NODE. In the sample we treated COBUILD, CED and N-W as one source. For example, if a MWE was recorded in M-W, then its occurrence was not checked in the remaining dictionaries, and its status as MWLU was labeled as True (T). Conversely, if the MWE was not recorded in any dictionary, then its MWLU status was labelled as False (F). We denote those non-lexicalised MWEs with the 'non-MWLU' label. Finally, in the 387 MWEs sample we obtained 144 non-lexicalised MWEs and 243 multi-word lexical units.

3 Methodology

We capitalize on and extend our earlier research (Maziarz et al., 2022), where we developed and applied a method (rule-based and statistical one using ridge logistic regression) of distinguishing between lexicalised ('MWLUs') and non-lexicalised word combinations in WordNet, taking into account selected lexicality features. In the rule-based approach, we used I-synonymy and cascade dictionary equivalents, while in the statistical approach we used MWE length measured in characters, the cosine of the angle between embedding vectors calculated for WordNet glosses and MWE lemmas, MWE sense ordering in WordNet, and the existence of equivalents in each constituent cascade dictionary. We extracted the subset of MWLUs from WordNet and its extension, enWordNet with high precision (> 70%), yet the completeness of both approaches varied. Using the rule-based approach, we obtained approximately 25% of all MWLUs, and using the statistical approach we extracted nearly 50% of the MWLUs, which translates into absolute

lemma	hypernym, definition	label
jest at	mock, subject to laughter or ridicule	0
take back	disown, take back what one has said	1

Table 2: Two examples from the sample passed to the cross-encoder. Zero means 'non-lexicalised multi-word expression', while one stands for 'multi-word lexical unit'.

figures as 6,4k and and 19k MWLUs respectively (ibid.). Hence, in this study we made an attempt at improving our method in order to increase the recall for extraction of the MWLU class from WordNet and enWordNet.

This time we use a cross-encoder in the task (Reimers and Gurevych, 2019), using sentence-transformers Python library.[8] The setu4993/smaller-LaBSE model (Feng et al., 2020) rather than a large language model was used, because of a relatively small size of the manually annotated sample. We used a language-agnostic model as it could be also applied to other languages (e.g. Polish) in the future. To the cross-encoder we passed separately (i) a multi-word lemma and (ii) a synset definition (preceded by lemmas of a hypernym synset) together with (iii) the label of the sequence pair (based on entries of English dictionaries). By adding hypernymic lemmas to the semantic description (given in a definition), we attempted to provide the model with the capacity to discover semantic compositionality of a MWE, cf. (Bauer, 2019, p. 52). Two exemplar word combinations together with their semantic descriptions (i.e. a hypernym plus a definition) were presented in Table 2. We trained a classifier to automatically classify word combinations recorded in WordNet as either non-lexicalised MWEs ('non-MWLU') or multi-word lexical units ('MWLUs', that is lexicalised MWEs). Tokenizer and model inputs were truncated to 48 tokens. The number was slightly bigger than the 95th percentile of the sample definition length, cf. Fig. 1.

We fine-tuned the setu4993/smaller-LaBSE pretrained model one hundred times in a loop (with four epochs in each turn) for the need of the .632 bootstrap estimator (Efron, 1983; Jiang and Simon, 2007). In each iteration, we sampled with replacement $n_{MWLU} = 243$ examples from lexicalised MWEs and $n_{nonMWLU} = 144$ examples with replacement from the set of non-lexicalised MWEs.

[8] `https://huggingface.co/sentence-transformers`

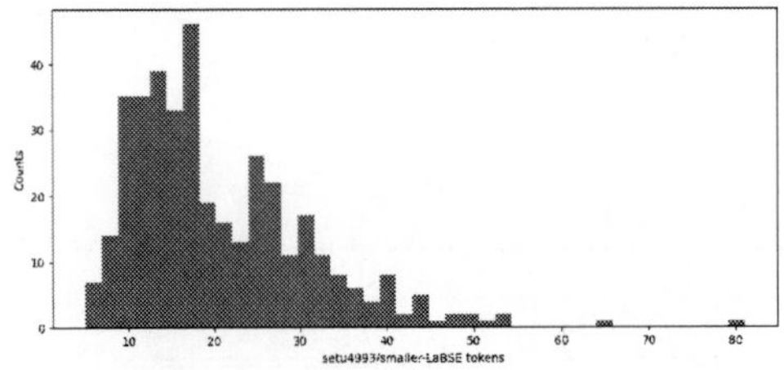

Figure 1: Histogram of lengths of sample definitions (enriched with hypernyms) in terms of LaBSE tokens. The 95th percentile for the empirical distribution equals 41, while the maximal length is 81 tokens.

In order to balance the training sample, we also additionally resampled 99 ($= 243 - 144$) examples *without* replacement from the set of just resampled non-lexicalised MWEs. The remaining (i.e. not selected) word combinations were assigned to the evaluation (testing) data set. Thus, in the training data set both classes were balanced, while in the testing data set they were not. Within the bootstrap loop, we calculated precision (P), recall (R) and F_1 measure from confusion matrices for the language model, as well as for random and majority baselines. The results were further tested for significance with the non-parametric .632 bootstrap method (Efron, 1983; Efron and Tibshirani, 1997)[9].

The confusion matrices were obtained from Efron's .632 bootstrap rule:

$$\begin{aligned} N_i(j) = n \times Pr_i(j) = \\ n \times [0.632 \times Pr_i^{test}(j) \\ +0.368 \times Pr_i^{subst}(j)], \end{aligned} \quad (1)$$

where j ($= 1, 2, 3, 4$) and i ($= 1, ..., B$) denote the j-th cell of the i-th confusion matrix, $n = 387$, i.e. the whole sample size. B is the number of bootstrap iterations, in our case it is 100. Probabilities $P_i(j)$ were calculated simply as proportions of each cell counts either in testing data (out-of-bag sample, the superscript ^{test}) or in a training sample (through substitution to the model taught on the balanced sample, the symbol ^{subst}). Before calculating each cell count, the substitution sample was checked for duplicates, which were subsequently removed.

Table 3 presents the mean values of precision, recall and F_1 measure, obtained from the corresponding $\{N_i(j)\}$ matrices ($j = 1, 2, 3, 4$). Confusion matrices presented in the table were also averaged in the following manner:

$$\begin{aligned} N(j) = \frac{\sum_{i=1}^{B} N_i(j)}{B} = \\ \frac{n \times \sum_{i=1}^{B} Pr_i(j)}{B} = \\ (n \times \sum_{i=1}^{B} [0.632 \times Pr_i^{test}(j) \\ +0.368 \times Pr_i^{subst}(j)]) \div B, \end{aligned} \quad (2)$$

where $N(j)$ stands for the j-th cell of the mean confusion matrix.

The number of epochs in each training iteration was *arbitrarily* set to 4. For BERT-like models, the number should be sufficient, although not optimal. For BERT itself, Devlin et al. (2018) recommend 2-4 epochs for fine-tuning. We selected the biggest number from that range, as we had assumed that the smaller-LaBSE model would have needed more time to optimize its weights due to a rather small annotated sample size. Our assumption was later verified with accuracy gain/loss results for each iteration (Fig. 2). The posterior evaluation revealed that setting the number of epochs to 4 almost always resulted in the highest accuracy scores. This excludes overfitting, but still our approach is prone to the problem of underfitting. We used default settings for other training parameters.

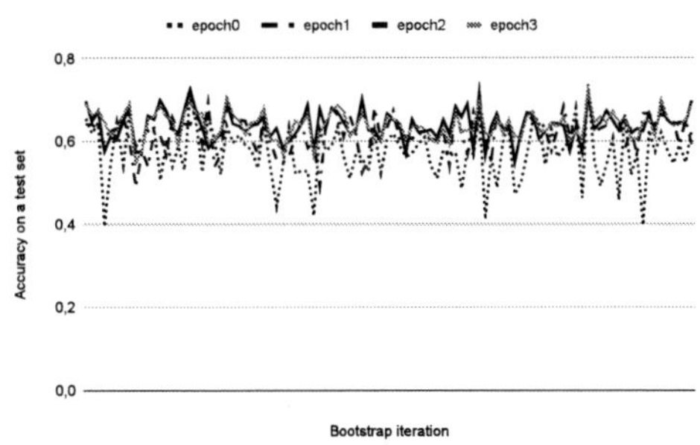

Figure 2: Accuracy gain/loss on testing sets throughout four epochs and one hundred bootstrap iterations.

4 Results

Table 3 presents the efficiency measures for the language model. In one-tailed tests the language model turned out to be better than the uniform distribution random baseline with regard to the precision, recall and F1-measure for both classes (with p-value lower than 0.01 or .025). The precision of the 'MWLU' class was also better than the majority

[9] In the same manner to (Maziarz et al., 2022).

		real		efficiency		
LaBSE model		non-MWLU	MWLU	P	R	F
prediction	non-MWLU	89.3	52.3	$\mathbf{.63}^{-}_{*}$	$\mathbf{.62}^{**}_{**}$	$\mathbf{.62}^{-}_{**}$
	MWLU	54.5	190.9	$\mathbf{.78}^{**}_{**}$	$.78_{**}$	$\mathbf{.78}_{**}$
majority baseline		non-MWLU	MWLU	P	R	F
prediction	non-MWLU	0	0	—	0	—
	MWLU	144.0	243.0	.63	$\mathbf{1}^{**}$	**.77**
random baseline		non-MWLU	MWLU	P	R	F
prediction	non-MWLU	69.7	71.9	.49	.36	.41
	MWLU	124.0	121.4	.50	.63	.55

Table 3: Confusion matrix and cross-encoder (setu4993/smaller-LaBSE) classification results for the discrimination of multi-word lexical units ("MWLUs") and non-lexicalised MWEs ("non-MWLU") in bootstrap cross-validation. Differences between the model and a random/majority baseline are statistically significant at *) <.025 or **) <.01 significance level. Comparisons with the random baseline are presented in subscript, while differences from the majority baseline are given in superscript. The presented values are averaged out over all bootstrap iteration rounds. Please note that the significance level of <0.01 was obtained when none of the bootstrap trials (out of $B = 100$ samples) found a result supporting the null hypothesis.

class baseline (with $p < 0.01$). The random baseline was obtained by sampling labels 'MWLU' and 'non-MWLU' with equal probabilities regardless real annotations, in the majority class baseline the class 'MWLU' was given to each example.

The difference between the language model and the majority class baseline was insignificant, when we compared the F1-measure for the 'MWLU' class ($p = .32$ in the test). The recall for the 'MWLU' class was, of course, lower than the 100% of the baseline. Comparing efficacy of smaller-LaBSE cross-encoder with a feature-based approach (Maziarz et al., 2022), we find that current F1 measure for the 'MWLU' class is much better (78% vs. 58%, $p<0.01$), while the measure for the 'non-MWLU' class is not worse (62% vs. 61%, $p = .31$).[10]

We retrained the model on all manual annotations and applied the fine-tuned cross-encoder to WordNet data set of 39k word combinations. Out of them, 25.5k were found to be lexicalised by the language model.

5 Conclusions

In a bootstrap cross-validation, we have found that the smaller-LaBSE cross-encoder performed very well on a manually annotated sample of nearly 400 word combinations. Both precision and recall for multi-word expressions were close to 80%, while the statistics for non-lexicalised MWEs were higher than 60%. The discrimination between lexicalised and non-lexicalised expressions worked better than two random baselines (simple uniform distribution and majority class baselines). The usage of the language model, i.e. the smaller-LaBSE cross-encoder, also improved the results obtained in (Maziarz et al., 2022) with a more traditional feature-based method. Interestingly, the cross-encoder model was given no more than bare lemmas and their synset definitions enriched only with hypernyms. No corpus frequency (a feature important in MWE recognition) was provided. We assume that the smaller-LaBSE cross-encoder (the black box *par excellance*) relied on semantic discrepancies between a word combination and its semantic description in the definition, that is, on semantic opacity/compositionality. But this assumption should be further verified in consecutive experiments in the future.

The rationale for our experiment is pivoted on lexicographic descriptions taken manually from dictionaries. A few words must be said to address possible shortcomings of this approach.

Native-speaker dictionaries are often constricted by the tradition of monolingual dictionaries in English and, what follows, by the expectations of users. This is the reservation that we voiced in Section 2: native-speaker dictionaries can include items because these items were included in some dictionaries that had been published earlier and which were quite influential. And these items are

[10]Please note that for the comparison with results from the previous experiment, we used bootstrap point estimation on mean logistic regression values, instead of paired bootstrap.

not lexical units, even though they are quite frequent in texts but the users might expect them in a dictionary. M-W and Oxford dictionaries are such influential dictionaries. In contrast, editors of pedagogical dictionaries are not constrained by tradition and one may believe that the items they include are genuine lexical items. Unfortunately, this also works in the other direction: a MWLU that is not very rare in texts may not be recorded in dictionaries because no previous dictionary recorded it. Clearly there is room for improvement both for wordnets and for "traditional" dictionaries. One obstacle for changing traditional dictionaries has been removed: they are not constrained by space, as they do not have to be printed, and may freely include MWLUs, which until recently have not been covered adequately because there was no sufficient space for them.

Acknowledgements

This research was funded by the Polish National Science Centre (NCN) under agreement no. UMO-2019/33/B/HS2/02814. Also, we would like to thank Mirosława Podhajecka for her invaluable help with data annotation.

References

Laurie Bauer. 2019. *Complex lexical units. Compounds and multi-word expressions*, chapter Compounds and multi-word expressions in English. de Gruyter.

Mathieu Constant, Gülşen Eryiğit, Johanna Monti, Lonneke van der Plas, Carlos Ramisch, Michael Rosner, and Amalia Todirascu. 2017. Survey: Multiword expression processing: A Survey. *Computational Linguistics*, 43(4):837–892.

Anthony Cowie, editor. 2009. *The Oxford History of English Lexicography. Clarendon Press*. Clarendon Press, London.

Jacob Devlin, Ming-Wei Chang, Kenton Lee, and Kristina Toutanova. 2018. Bert: Pre-training of deep bidirectional transformers for language understanding. *arXiv preprint arXiv:1810.04805*.

Bradley Efron. 1983. Estimating the error rate of a prediction rule: improvement on cross-validation. *Journal of the American statistical association*, 78(382):316–331.

Bradley Efron and Robert Tibshirani. 1997. Improvements on cross-validation: the 632+ bootstrap method. *Journal of the American Statistical Association*, 92(438):548–560.

Meghdad Farahmand and Ronaldo Teixeira Martins. 2014. A supervised model for extraction of multiword expressions, based on statistical context features. In *Proceedings of the 10th workshop on multiword expressions (MWE)*, pages 10–16.

Christiane Fellbaum, editor. 1998. *WordNet – An Electronic Lexical Database*. The MIT Press.

Fangxiaoyu Feng, Yinfei Yang, Daniel Cer, Naveen Arivazhagan, and Wei Wang. 2020. Language-agnostic bert sentence embedding.

Polona Gantar, Lut Colman, Carla Parra Escartín, and Héctor Martínez Alonso. 2018. Multiword expressions: Between lexicography and NLP. 32(2):138–162. _eprint: https://academic.oup.com/ijl/article-pdf/32/2/138/29012810/ecy012.pdf.

Howard Jackson. 2022. *The Bloomsbury Handbook of Lexicography. Second ed.* Bloomsbury Academic, London.

Elisabetta Jezek. 2016. *The Lexicon: An Introduction (Oxford Textbooks in Linguistics*. Oxford University Press, Oxford.

Wenyu Jiang and Richard Simon. 2007. A comparison of bootstrap methods and an adjusted bootstrap approach for estimating the prediction error in microarray classification. *Statistics in medicine*, 26(29):5320–5334.

Leonhard Lipka. 1990. *An Outline of English Lexicology; Lexical Structure, Word Semantics, and Word-formation*. Max Niemeyer, Tuebingen.

Marek Maziarz, Łukasz Grabowski, Tadeusz Piotrowski, Ewa Rudnicka, and Maciej Piasecki. 2023. Lexicalisation of polish and english word combinations: an empirical study. *Poznan Studies in Contemporary Linguistics*. In print.

Marek Maziarz, Ewa Rudnicka, and Łukasz Grabowski. 2022. Multi-word lexical units recognition in wordnet. In *Proceedings of the 18th Workshop on Multiword Expressions@ LREC2022*, pages 49–54.

Nils Reimers and Iryna Gurevych. 2019. Sentence-bert: Sentence embeddings using siamese bert-networks. *arXiv preprint arXiv:1908.10084*.

Martin Riedl and Chris Biemann. 2016. Impact of mwe resources on multiword recognition. In *Proceedings of the 12th Workshop on Multiword Expressions*, pages 107–111.

Ivan A. Sag, Timothy Baldwin, Francis Bond, Ann Copestake, and Dan Flickinger. 2002. Multiword expressions: A pain in the neck for NLP. In *Computational Linguistics and Intelligent Text Processing*, pages 1–15. Springer Berlin Heidelberg.

Nathan Schneider, Emily Danchik, Chris Dyer, and Noah A Smith. 2014. Discriminative lexical semantic segmentation with gaps: running the mwe gamut. *Transactions of the Association for Computational Linguistics*, 2:193–206.

Tinne Van Rompaey, Kristin Davidse, and Peter Petré. 2015. Lexicalization and grammaticalization: The case of the verbo-nominal expressions be on the/one's way/road. *Functions of Language*, 22(2):232–263.

Michał Woźniak. 2017. *Jak znaleźć igłę w stogu siana? Automatyczna ekstrakcja wielosegmentowych jednostek leksykalnych z tekstu polskiego*. IJP PAN, Kraków.

Towards an RDF Representation of the Infrastructure consisting in using Wordnets as a conceptual Interlingua between multilingual Sign Language Datasets

Thierry Declerck
DFKI GmbH
Saarland Informatics Campus
Stuhlsatzenhausweg, 3
66123 Saarbrücken
declerck@dfki.de

Thomas Troelsgård
University College
Copenhagen (KP)
Humletorvet 3
1799 Copenhagen V
ttro@kp.dk

Sussi Olsen
Centre for Language Technology,
NorS, University of Copenhagen
Emil Holms Kanal 2
2300 Copenhagen S
saolsen@hum.ku.dk

Abstract

We present ongoing work dealing with a Linked Data compliant representation of infrastructures using wordnets for connecting multilingual Sign Language data sets. We build for this on already existing RDF and OntoLex representations of Open Multilingual Wordnet (OMW) data sets and work done by the European EASIER research project on the use of the CSV files of OMW for linking glosses and basic semantic information associated with Sign Language data sets in two languages: German and Greek. In this context, we started the transformation into RDF of a Danish data set, which links Danish Sign Language data and the wordnet for Danish, DanNet. The final objective of our work is to include Sign Language data sets (and their conceptual cross-linking via wordnets) in the Linguistic Linked Open Data cloud.

1 Introduction

A final goal of our work is to represent and publish Sign Language (SL) data sets in the Linguistic Linked Data (LLOD) cloud, which is a subset of the Linked Data (LD) cloud.[1] We can observe that SL data are not represented in the data sets currently included in the LLOD cloud. And looking at the "Overview of Datasets for the Sign Languages of Europe" published by the "EASIER" European project (Kopf et al., 2022)[2] we do not see any mention of a data set being available in a Linked Data compliant format.

This shortcoming is a problematic issue, as an important type of natural language is missing from the LLOD, while the motivation behind the creation of the LLOD is that it can ease the linking of all types of natural language resources.[3]

The prerequisite for publishing linguistic data in the LLOD cloud is to have it formally represented within the Resource Description Framework (RDF).[4] And as an RDF-based de facto standard for representing lexical information, the OntoLex-Lemon specifications,[5] already exists, we investigate as a first step the re-use of this model in order to accommodate the description of Sign Language data sets. But as we can see in Figure 1, the class `ontolex:Form` covers only the representation of written languages (with the addition of the associated pronunciation information), so that there is a need to think about possible adaptations or extensions of OntoLex-Lemon.

At the same time, the OntoLex-Lemon model supports the representation of WordNet data, which are typically encoded with the SKOS[6] vocabulary, where the synsets are represented as instances of the `ontolex:LexicalConcept` subclass of the `skos:Concept` class.[7] This feature is offering us a good starting point for transforming into RDF (and OntoLex-Lemon) recent work by the EASIER project dealing with the use of shared IDs of the Open Multilingual Wordnet (OMW)[8] infrastructure for interlinking SL data sets for two languages: German and Greek, as described in (Bigeard et al., 2022).[9]

[1]Those clouds can be accessed respectively at http://linguistic-lod.org/llod-cloud and https://lod-cloud.net/

[2]Available as a public deliverable at https://www.project-easier.eu/deliverables/

[3]See (Chiarcos et al., 2012) for a first description of the motivations leading to the creation of the LLOD, and (Cimiano et al., 2020) for a more recent and much more detailed description of all aspects of the LLOD infrastructure

[4]See https://www.w3.org/TR/rdf11-primer/ for an introduction to RDF

[5]See https://www.w3.org/2016/05/ontolex/ and (McCrae et al., 2017)

[6]SKOS stands for "Simple Knowledge Organization System". see https://www.w3.org/TR/skos-primer/ for more details

[7]See for example (Declerck, 2019)

[8]See (Bond and Foster, 2013) and (Bond et al., 2016) for more details on the Open Multilingual Wordnet and the interlinking between OMW data sets

[9]The EASIER project is publishing the related data at https://www.fdr.uni-hamburg.de/record/10169#.Y1Ufs-RBzmF

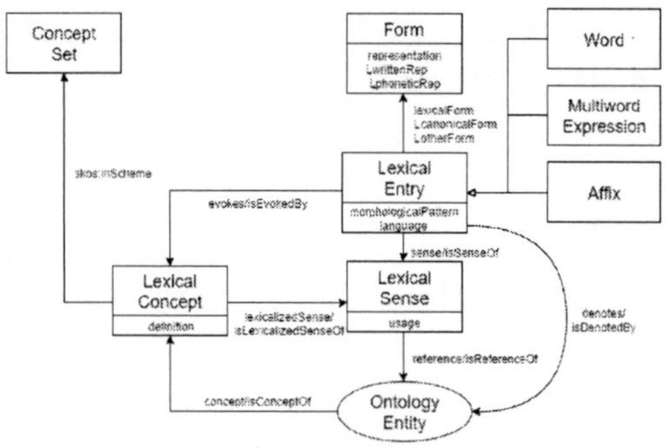

Figure 1: The core module of OntoLex-Lemon, taken from `https://www.w3.org/2016/05/ontolex/`

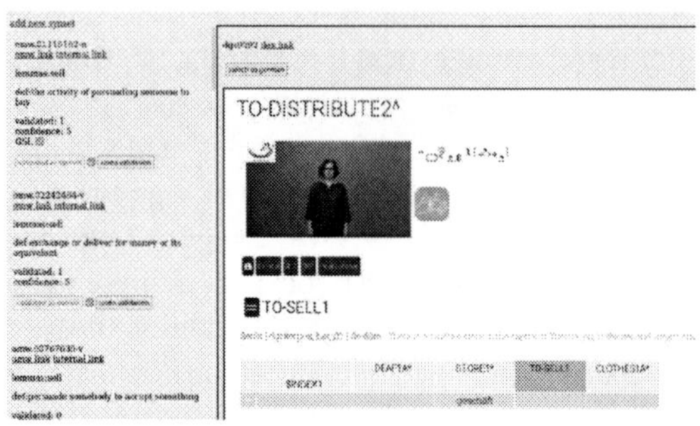

Figure 2: A screenshot showing how German and Greek Sign Language data are interlinked via a shared OMW index, as proposed by the EASIER project. Taken from `https://www.fdr.uni-hamburg.de/record/10169#.Y01WXExBzmE`, screenshot4.jpg

Figure 2,[10] displays the starting point of a video representing a sign, its related glosses (written using only capital letters, in order to distinguish them from keywords or potential lexical entries),[11] its phonetic transcription (in HamNoSys, (Hanke, 2004)), as well as its link to the OMW version of the Princeton WordNet (omw.01115162-n, with its lemma and definition).

This link to OMW is done for the German sign indexed with "dgs9292",[12] which points to the subtype (or the "sub-gloss") "TO-SELL1" of "TO-DISTRIBUTE2^". Those English glosses are in fact translations of the German glosses "VERKAUFEN1" and "VERTEILEN2^", which are used for accessing the Princeton WordNet in OMW (as the GermaNet resource (Kunze and Lemnitzer, 2002) used in EASIER is not included in OMW). It can also be seen in Figure 2 that a "GSL" box is being positively checked. "GSL" stands for "Greek Sign Language", and the positively checked abbreviation in the screenshot means that there is a corresponding synset in the Greek Wordnet available in OMW. This way, a DGS sign can be linked to a GSL sign, based on a shared OMW ID, which is much more accurate than linking only via translation of glosses.

The links between the one OMW ID and the two signs/videos IDs are available in Excel files.[13] The corresponding CSV lines are displayed in Figure 3 and Figure 4, where we can see that one OMW ID (omw.00377364-n, with the English lemma "explosion", translated to German "*Explosion*", and with the Greek lemma "*έκρηξη*") is associated with both the German and the Greek SL resources, thus establishing a conceptual link between those.

6833	dgs67339,omw.00568430-n,auto accept
6834	dgs10875,omw.14449405-n,auto accept
6835	dgs10040,omw.00377364-n,manual accept
6836	dgs10481,omw.00377364-n,manual accept
6837	dgs9882,omw.04228054-n,auto accept
6838	dgs73480,omw.07349299-n,auto accept

Figure 3: The CSV representation of the linking of OMW and a German sign, taken from `https://www.fdr.uni-hamburg.de/record/10169#.Y01WXExBzmE`

970	gsl326,omw.00988028-v,manual accept
971	gsl1049,omw.00362103-n,manual accept
972	gsl1050,omw.00377364-n,manual accept
973	gsl1050,omw.07308563-n,manual accept
974	gsl2592,omw.05128519-n,manual accept

Figure 4: The CSV representation of the linking of OMW and a Greek sign, `https://www.fdr.uni-hamburg.de/record/10169#.Y01WXExBzmE`

Those elements: videos, glosses, phonetic transcriptions, links to OMW, are the elements we are encoding in a unified and harmonized Linked Data compliant format.

[10]As stated in the web page, from which this screenshot is taken, the online interface is not yet live. But the displayed screenshot represents clearly how the linking of a German sign and an OMW ID is (will be) represented on the web.

[11]On the specificity of glosses used for naming (or labelling) SL data in corpora, see (Ormel et al., 2010)

[12]DGS stands for "Deutsche Gebärdensprache", *German Sign Language*

[13]Also made available at `https://www.fdr.uni-hamburg.de/record/10169#.Y01WXExBzmE`

2 Linked Data compliant Encoding of the Infrastructure using shared OMW IDs

As stated in the introduction, we need to transform into RDF the different types of data used for representing signs for their future publication in the LLOD cloud. We also make use of RDF(S) and OWL representation languages, as those are constitutive parts of the OntoLex-Lemon specifications and of the building of ontologies.[14]

For the RDF representation of videos included in our data set, we just introduce a class and have all videos encoded as instances of this class.

Listing 1 displays the RDF-based encoding of a video containing a German sign.[15] A partial view of the original web page is displayed in Figure 5.

Figure 5: The German sign associated with the gloss SCHUTZ1A^ in the DGS Corpus https://www.sign-lang.uni-hamburg.de/meinedgs/types/type13990_de.html

In the RDF representation of the sign, it can be seen that the video/sign is linked to two glosses, as this sign has more than one gloss related to it.

Listing 1: The RDF-based encoding of a video containing a sign

```
<http://example.org/dgs#
        SignVideos_40085921.mp4>
   rdf:type sl:SignVideos ;
   dgs:hasGLOSS dgs:GLOSS_13990 ;
   dgs:hasGLOSS dgs:GLOSS_13990-2966 ;
   sl:hasVideoAdresss
         "https://www.sign-lang.
         uni-hamburg.de/korpusdict/
         clips/4008592_1.mp4"^^rdf:HTML ;
   rdfs:label "\"Videos representing
               a sign\"" ;
.
```

Listing 2 displays the corresponding glosses (as instances of a specific class).

Listing 2: The RDF-based encoding of glosses

```
dgs:GLOSS_13990
  rdf:type dgs:GLOSS ;
  rdfs:label "\"PROTECTION1A^\""@en ;
  rdfs:label "\"SCHUTZ1A^\""@de ;
.
dgs:GLOSS_13990-2966
  rdf:type dgs:GLOSS ;
  rdfs:label "\"PROTECTION1A\""@en ;
  rdfs:label "\"SCHUTZ1A\""@de ;
.
```

The subclass/subtype relation between the glosses displayed in Listing 2 is encoded in a specific class, called "Type", as can be seen in Listing 3, which displays the subclass hierarchy between glosses (here class and subclass instances are linking to the same video), and linking the instance of the subclass to an OMW element (as instance of the class `ontolex:LexicalConcept`), establishing thus the link to the WordNet world, and to the corresponding video(s), as we can collect more than one video representing a sign.

Listing 3: Subclass hierachy of glosses linking the subgloss to OWM and to videos

```
dgs:Type_13990
  rdf:type dgs:Type ;
  dgs:hasGLOSS dgs:GLOSS_13990 ;
  dgs:hasSubType
     dgs:Subtype_13990-2966 ;
  dgs:hasVideo
     <http://example.org/dgs#
     SignVideos_40085921.mp4> ;
  dgs:hasVideo
     <http://example.org/dgs#
      SignVideos_dgs-688.mp4> ;
  rdfs:label "\"Schutz\""@de ;
  rdfs:label "\"protection\""@en ;
.

dgs:Subtype_13990-2966
  rdf:type dgs:Subtype ;
  dgs:hasGLOSS dgs:GLOSS_13990-2966 ;
  dgs:hasOMW-Link wnid:omw-00817680-n ;
  dgs:hasVideo
    <http://example.org/dgs
     #SignVideos_40085921.mp4> ;
  dgs:hasVideo
    <http://example.org/dgs
     #SignVideos_dgs-688.mp4> ;
  rdfs:label "\"Schutz\""@de ;
  rdfs:label "\"protection\""@en ;
.
```

[14]RDF(S) stands for "RDF-Schema", see https://www.w3.org/TR/rdf-schema/ for more details. OWL stands for "Web Ontology Language", see https://www.w3.org/TR/2012/REC-owl2-primer-20121211/ for more details.

[15]The original sign and all the related information are accessible at https://www.sign-lang.uni-hamburg.de/meinedgs/types/type13990_de.html (for the English translation of the page: https://www.sign-lang.uni-hamburg.de/meinedgs/types/type13990_en.html)

The OMW synset linked to in Figure 3 has the internal organisation displayed in Figure 6. Here we didn't include links to glosses or videos, as the relations to OMW described in listing 3 are inverse.

```
wnid:omw-00817680-n
  rdf:type ontolex:LexicalConcept ;
  sl:hasWnLemma "\"protection\""@en ;
  sl:hasWnLemma "\"προστασία\""@el ;
  rdfs:label "\"Schutz\""@de ;
  rdfs:label "\"protection\""@en ;
  rdfs:label "\"προστασία\""@el ;
  skos:definition "\"παρεχόμενη φροντίδα
    σε κάποιον ώστε να προφυλάσσεται από
    υπαρκτούς ή διάφορους πιθανούς
    κινδύνους\""@el ;
  skos:inScheme sl:ConceptSet_OMW-DGS ;
  wn:definition "\"a covering that is
    intend to protect from damage or
    injury\""@en ;
.
```

Figure 6: The ID omw-00817680-n of OMW

Finally, the representation of the form(s) of the sign is performed for the time being as instances of `ontolex:Form` (mediated, also for the time being, by an underspecified instance of `ontolex:LexicalEntry`). This representation, displayed in Figure 7, includes the machine-readable transcription of the HamNoSys code, in the so-called SiGML XML format (Neves et al., 2020). It also includes potential keywords or lexical entries.

```
dgs:Form_13990
  rdf:type ontolex:Form ;
  dgs:hasVideo
   <http://example.org/dgs#SignVideos
     _40085921.mp4> ;
  dgs:hasVideo
   <http://example.org/dgs#SignVideos
     _dgs-688.mp4> ;
  sl:hasGloss "\"protection\""@en ;
  sl:hasTranslationInSpokenLanguage
   "\"geschützt, Schutz, schützen\""@de ;
  sl:hasTranslationInSpokenLanguage
   "\"protection\""@en ;
  sl:hasTranslationInSpokenLanguage
   "\"προστασία\""@el ;
  rdfs:label "\"protection\""@en ;
  ontolex:representation
   "\"https://www.sign-lang.
    hamburg.de/galex/glossen/
    g13990.html\"" ;
  ontolex:writtenRep
    "\"hamsymmpar,hamparbegin,hamfist,
    hamthumbacrossmod,hamextfingerdo,
    hamextfingerol,hampalml,hamplus,
    hamfist,hamthumbacrossmod,
    hamextfingeror,hampalmdr,
    hamparend,hamparbegin,
    hamthumbside,hambetween,
    hamindexfinger,hamplus,
    hamfingerbase,hamhandback,
    hamparend,hamtouch,hamchest,
    hammovedo\" {hamnosys-sigml}" ;
.
```

Figure 7: The encoding of the form of a sign

3 Extending the EASIER Approach with additional Sign Videos per Language

We searched for other Sign Language resources in order to extend the approach described in (Bigeard et al., 2022), thus linking SL data and wordnets, and then transforming those SLs-wordnets combinations into RDF and OntoLex-Lemon.

We found a basic lexicon of 1000 concepts associated with SL data in 4 languages, English, French, German and Greek, an outcome of the past Dicta-Sign project (Matthes et al., 2012), which is available at the University of Hamburg at `https://www.sign-lang.uni-hamburg.de/dicta-sign/portal/concepts/concepts_eng.html`. This resource is directly relevant to our purposes, as the included videos are equipped with glosses and HamNoSys transcriptions, as shown in Figure 8.

In Figure 8, we observe that the gloss and the HamNoSys transcription for the German video are identical with those deployed in the data used by the EASIER project for linking SL data and wordnets, as can be seen at `https://www.sign-lang.uni-hamburg.de/meinedgs/types/type13990_de.html`, and which is also shown in Figure 5.

This concordance of gloss and HamNoSys transcriptions[16] not only allows for the association of two videos representing this German sign to one OWM ID,[17] but it also permits the addition of signs in two additional languages, English and French, extending thus the multilingual coverage of the approach described by (Bigeard et al., 2022). We just need to introduce in our RDF representation new video instances (one per language) and to link them to the same OMW ID.

[16]But we can observe that in the one case the gloss is realised as a noun and in the second case as a verb. Signs are often ambiguous with respect to PoS, and in the future we will link the videos to both the nominal and verbal synsets, if both are available in the corresponding wordnet.

[17]As the page `https://www.sign-lang.uni-hamburg.de/dicta-sign/portal/concepts/cs/cs_688.html` is linking to a more detailed lexical description of the sign, with the same gloss and HamNoSys transcription (see `https://www.sign-lang.uni-hamburg.de/galex/glossen/g13990.html`), with another video for the sign, we can in fact have 3 videos for this German sign associated with one OMW ID.

Figure 8: The concept "protect" as realised in 4 different Sign Languages. Taken from `https://www.sign-lang.uni-hamburg.de/dicta-sign/portal/concepts/cs/cs_688.html`

Thus, the transformation of this additional data into our RDF and OntoLex-Lemon representation means organising those originally disparate and heterogeneous data sources in one harmonised representation format, with OMW as the central component for the interlinking of the different data types and sources.

4 Extending the Approach to Danish WordNet and Sign Language Data

(Troelsgård and Kristoffersen, 2018) discusses approaches for ensuring consistency between (Danish) Sign Language corpus data and the dictionary of Danish signs that is described in (Kristoffersen and Troelsgård, 2010). This approach aims at getting a correspondence between the dictionary lemmas and the corpus lexicon, which consists of types introduced for lemmatising the tokens found in the annotations (glosses added to the signs) of the corpus.

The strategy being to use words and their equivalents (also found in the dictionary) to search for signs in the corpus. In order to extend the list of potential Danish equivalents that could be used for a word-based search of signs in the corpus, (Troelsgård and Kristoffersen, 2018) suggest using the Danish wordnet, DanNet, which is briefly described below and in more details in (Pedersen et al., 2009) and (Pedersen et al., 2018).

DanNet was constructed using the merge approach where the wordnet is built on a monolingual resource, in this case on the corpus-based Danish dictionary Den Danske Ordbog (DDO, (Lorentzen, 2004), see also `https://ordnet.dk/ddo`), and subsequently linked to PWN. For DanNet this linking was based on the Princeton Core wordnet, a subset containing 5,000 central concepts of English (see the file "core-wordnet.txt" in the folder "LFglosses.standoff-files.zip " under `https://wordnetcode.princeton.edu/morpholinks`) that were semi-automatically linked to DanNet. These linked elements constitute the part of DanNet available in OMW.[18]

The relations between sign identifiers and lexical elements from both DanNet and other dictionary sources are encoded in a database, out of which we got a CSV export.

In this export, we first have the signs, which are corresponding to entries in the dictionary of signs available at `www.tegnsprog.dk`.

A second type of data available in the export holds video links and information about the sign form (HamNoSys/SiGML). The HamNoSys notation, though, is rather coarse, as it is generated automatically from the dictionary's phonological descriptions.

A third type of information included in the export is dealing with the senses associated with the signs and their (form) variants.

Lastly, we also have the information from DanNet and PWN. Our work consists thus in porting all those (interlinked) resources to RDF and OntoLex-Lemon, as we did for the German and the Greek data, as presented in Section 2. In the OMW version of DanNet, we find for example the following information"00817680-n lemma beskyttelse", where the lemma corresponds to the OMW English wordnet "00817680-n lemma protection", sharing thus the same ID for the concept of "protection" as the English and Greek wordnets we have in OMW. So that we can add the Danish sign ID (and video), which we got from the database, to our infrastructure. The Danish sign associated with the wordnet

[18]Since 2018, there has been an ongoing effort to link a larger part of DanNet's more than 65,000 synsets to PWN, this time taking departure in the core Danish vocabulary, see (Pedersen et al., 2019).

lemma "beskyttelse" is displayed in Figure 9.

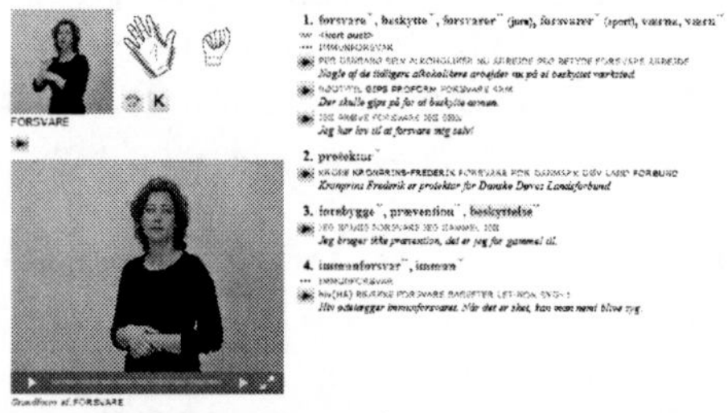

Figure 9: The Danish sign associated with the OMW ID "00817680-n", corresponding to the (highlighted) lemma "beskyttelse", here as possible lexical realisation of the Danish gloss "FORSVARE" (*defend*)

It is then straightforward to encode all those types of information on the relation between Danish SL data and DanNet into our RDF-based model. We need only to add an instance for the video displaying the sign, and its associated gloss (with language equivalents), as shown in Figure 10. The language equivalents are included, so that a danish sign can be cross-lingually searched for, using glosses in other languages.

```
dts:GLOSS_dts-1_2162
  rdf:type sl:GLOSS ;
  rdfs:label "\"FORSVARE\""@da ;
  rdfs:label "\"PROTEGER\""@fr ;
  rdfs:label "\"SCHUTZ1A^\""@de ;
  rdfs:label "\"protect(v)#1\""@en ;
  rdfs:label "\"ΠΡΟΣΤΑΤΕΥΩ\""@el ;
.
```

Figure 10: The Danish gloss (with language equivalents) associated with the video with ID dts-1_2162

Then we just have to add an `ontolex:Form` instance for the Danish sign, displayed in Figure 11 and which is linked via its corresponding lexical entry to the corresponding OMW instance, which are shown in Figure 12.

Finally, Figure 13 displays (partially) the current encoding of the OMW ID, showing the central and pivotal role of this ID for interlinking the various types of resources involved in our work.

5 Current Results

Our encoding results in a harmonised representation of data that was originally stored in different formats in different locations. Taking advantage of the work proposed by (Bigeard et al., 2022), (Troelsgård and Kristoffersen, 2018) and others, we can include the links between SL data and

```
dts:Form_1_2162
  rdf:type ontolex:Form ;
  dgs:hasVideo
    <http://example.org/dts#SignVideos_dts-t_2162.mp4> ;
  sl:hasGloss "\"FORSVARE\""@en ;
  sl:hasTranslationInSpokenLanguage "\"forsvare, beskytte,
      forsvarer, værne, værn, beskyttelse\""@da ;
  sl:hasTranslationInSpokenLanguage "\"geschützt, Schutz,
      schützen\""@de ;
  sl:hasTranslationInSpokenLanguage "\"protection\""@en ;
  sl:hasTranslationInSpokenLanguage "\"protection\""@fr ;
  sl:hasTranslationInSpokenLanguage "\"προστασία\""@el ;
  rdfs:label "\"protection, protect\""@en ;
  ontolex:representation "\"https://www.tegnsprog.dk/#
   %7Csoeg%7C'tekst'beskytte%
   7Cresultat%7C4%7Ctrestjerner%7C1%7Ctegn%7C837\"" ;
  ontolex:writtenRep "<sigml><hns_sign gloss='FORSVARE'>
   <hamnosys_manual><hamsymmlr/><hamfist/><hamparbegin/>
   <hamextfingeru/><hampalmd/><hamplus/><hamextfingerr/>
   <hampalmr/><hamparend/><hamparbegin/><hammoveu/>
   <hamthumbside/><hamtouch/><hamplus/><hamnomotion/>
   <hamparend/><hamrepeatfromstart/></hamnosys_manual>
   </hns_sign></sigml>\" {hamnosys-sigml}" ;
.
```

Figure 11: The encoding of OntoLex-Lemon form associated with the sign, where various lexical realisations of the gloss (and of the OMW ID are included, as well as the SiGML code.

```
dts:LexicalEntry_1_2162
  rdf:type ontolex:LexicalEntry ;
  rdfs:label "\"forsvare, beskytte,
    værne, værn, beskyttelse\""@da ;
  ontolex:evokes wnid:omw-00817680-n ;
  ontolex:lexicalForm dts:Form_1_2162 ;
.
```

Figure 12: The encoding of OntoLex-Lemon entry associated with the sign and its ontolex:Form, and which is linking to the corresponding OMW ID

wordnets in a harmonised representation, under the umbrella of RDF and by re-using elements of OntoLex-Lemon. The Open Multilingual Wordnet infrastructure is playing a central role in this work, as the shared OMW IDs across various languages are at the core of the interlinking of the distinct data types and sources. The resulting unified representation supports a dense linking of different types of information. Our model will be made available on Github (`https://github.com/Declerck/sl-wn-rdf-ontolex`)

6 Future Work

The next steps of our work will consist in automatising the transformation into RDF and aspects of OntoLex-Lemon so that we have all the data in the harmonised representation space. We are also planning to investigate a transformation of ASLNet (Lualdi et al., 2021) into RDF. We continue to extend our work with more data in more languages, starting with Maltese,[19] as a low resourced lan-

[19]For example, a useful dictionary resource for Maltese Sign Language is available at `https://mlrs.research.`

```
wnid:omw-00817680-n
  rdf:type ontolex:LexicalConcept ;
  sl:hasWnLemma "\"beskyttelse\""@da ;
  sl:hasWnLemma "\"forsorg\""@da ;
  sl:hasWnLemma "\"forsvar\""@da ;
  sl:hasWnLemma "\"protection\""@en ;
  sl:hasWnLemma "\"protection\""@fr ;
  sl:hasWnLemma "\"værn\""@da ;
  sl:hasWnLemma "\"προστασία\""@el ;
  rdfs:label "\"Schutz\""@de ;
  rdfs:label "\"beskyttelse\""@da ;
  rdfs:label "\"protection\""@en ;
  rdfs:label "\"protection\""@fr ;
  rdfs:label "\"προστασία\""@el ;
  skos:definition "\"παρεχόμενη φροντίδα
     σε κάποιον ώστε να προφυλάσσεται από
     υπαρκτούς ή διάφορους πιθανούς
     κινδύνους\""@el ;
  skos:inScheme sl:ConceptSet_OMW-DGS ;
  ontolex:isEvokedBy dgs:LexicalEntry_13990-2966 ;
  ontolex:isEvokedBy dts:LexicalEntry_1_2162 ;
  ontolex:isEvokedBy lsf:LexicalEntry_668-n ;
  wn:definition <http://wordnetweb.princeton.edu/
       perl/webwn?o2=&o0=1&o8=1&o1=1&o7=&o5=&o9=
       &o6=&o3=&o4=&s=protection&i=0&h=0000000#c> ;
.
```

Figure 13: The encoding of the OWM ID, linking to corresponding lexical entries, which again are linking to other elements of our data set, as can be seen in 12 for the Danish case

guage. Finally, we aim at adding other types of visual lexical data, like pictograms, as the links between such data and wordnet have been already investigated, for example in (Schwab et al., 2020).

Acknowledgements

The presented work is pursued in the context of the COST Action NexusLinguarum – European network for Web-centered linguistic data science (CA18209), 731015). We thank Thomas Hanke and Sam Bigeard from the Institute of German Sign Language and Communication of the Deaf (IDGS) at the University of Hamburg for providing links and explanations to data developed in the context of the EASIER project (https://www.project-easier.eu/de/). The work we started dealing with Maltese language is pursued in the context of the LT-BRIDGE project, which has received funding from the European Union's Horizon 2020 Research and Innovation Programme under Grant Agreement No 952194.

um.edu.mt/resources/lsm. This resource is interesting to us, as it makes use of another transcription system than HamNoSys, the SignWriting system (Sutton, 1991), so that our model will deal also with more than one transcription system.

References

Sam Bigeard, Marc Schulder, Maria Kopf, Thomas Hanke, Kiki Vasilaki, Anna Vacalopoulou, Theodoros Goulas, Athanasia-Lida Dimou, Stavroula-Evita Fotinea, and Eleni Efthimiou. 2022. Introducing Sign Languages to a Multilingual Wordnet: Bootstrapping Corpora and Lexical Resources of Greek Sign Language and German Sign Language. In *Proceedings of the LREC2022 10th Workshop on the Representation and Processing of Sign Languages: Multilingual Sign Language Resources*, pages 9–15, Marseille, France. European Language Resources Association (ELRA).

Francis Bond and Ryan Foster. 2013. Linking and extending an Open Multilingual Wordnet. In *ACL (1)*, pages 1352–1362. The Association for Computer Linguistics.

Francis Bond, Piek Vossen, John P. McCrae, and Christiane Fellbaum. 2016. CILI: the Collaborative Interlingual Index. In *Proc. of the Global WordNet Conference 2016*.

Christian Chiarcos, Sebastian Hellmann, and Sebastian Nordhoff. 2012. The Open Linguistics Working Group of the Open Knowledge Foundation. In *Linked Data in Linguistics*, pages 153–160. Springer, Heidelberg.

Philipp Cimiano, Christian Chiarcos, John P. McCrae, and Jorge Gracia. 2020. *Linguistic Linked Data - Representation, Generation and Applications*. Springer.

Thierry Declerck. 2019. Ontolex as a possible bridge between wordnets and full lexical descriptions. In *Proceedings of Global WordNet Conference 2019*.

Thomas Hanke. 2004. HamNoSys – representing sign language data in language resources and language processing contexts. In *Proceedings of the LREC2004 Workshop on the Representation and Processing of Sign Languages: From SignWriting to Image Processing. Information techniques and their implications for teaching, documentation and communication*, pages 1–6, Lisbon, Portugal. European Language Resources Association (ELRA).

Maria Kopf, Marc Schulder, and Thomas Hanke. 2022. D6.1 overview of datasets for the sign languages of europe.

Jette Kristoffersen and Thomas Troelsgård. 2010. The danish sign language dictionary. In *Proceedings of the 14th EURALEX International Congress*, pages 1549–1554, Leeuwarden/Ljouwert, The Netherlands. Fryske Akademy.

Claudia Kunze and Lothar Lemnitzer. 2002. Germanet - representation, visualization, application. In *LREC*. European Language Resources Association.

Henrik Lorentzen. 2004. The danish dictionary at large: presentation, problems and perspectives. In

Proceedings of the 11th EURALEX International Congress, pages 285–294, Lorient, France. Université de Bretagne-Sud, Faculté des lettres et des sciences humaines.

Colin Lualdi, Elaine Wright, Jack Hudson, Naomi Caselli, and Christiane Fellbaum. 2021. Implementing ASLNet V1.0: Progress and Plans. In *Proceedings of the 11th Global Wordnet Conference, GWC 2021, University of South Africa (UNISA), Potchefstroom, South Africa, January 18-21, 2021*, pages 63–72. Global Wordnet Association.

Silke Matthes, Thomas Hanke, Anja Regen, Jakob Storz, Satu Worseck, Eleni Efthimiou, Athanasia-Lida Dimou, Annelies Braffort, John Glauert, and Eva Safar. 2012. Dicta-Sign -Building a Multilingual Sign Language Corpus. In *5th Workshop on the Representation and Processing of Sign Languages: Interactions between Corpus and Lexicon. Satellite Workshop to the eighth International Conference on Language Resources and Evaluation (LREC-2012)*, Istanbul, Turkey.

John P. McCrae, Paul Buitelaar, and Philipp Cimiano. 2017. The OntoLex-Lemon Model: development and applications. In *Proc. of the 5th Biennial Conference on Electronic Lexicography (eLex)*.

Carolina Neves, Luísa Coheur, and Hugo Nicolau. 2020. HamNoSyS2SiGML: Translating HamNoSys into SiGML. In *Proceedings of the 12th Language Resources and Evaluation Conference*, pages 6035–6039, Marseille, France. European Language Resources Association.

Ellen Ormel, Onno Crasborn, Els van der Kooij, Lianne van Dijken, Ellen Yassine Nauta, Jens Forster, and Daniel Stein. 2010. Glossing a multi-purpose sign language corpus. In *Proceedings of the LREC2010 4th Workshop on the Representation and Processing of Sign Languages: Corpora and Sign Language Technologies*, pages 186–191, Valletta, Malta. European Language Resources Association (ELRA).

Bolette Sandford Pedersen, Manex Aguirrezabal Zabaleta, Sanni Nimb, Sussi Olsen, and Ida Rørmann Olsen. 2018. Towards a principled approach to sense clustering – a case study of wordnet and dictionary senses in danish. In *Proceedings of Global WordNet Conference 2018*. Global WordNet Association. Null ; Conference date: 08-01-2018 Through 12-01-2018.

Bolette Sandford Pedersen, Sanni Nimb, Jørg Asmussen, NicolaiHartvig Sørensen, Lars Trap-Jensen, and Henrik Lorentzen. 2009. DanNet — the challenge of compiling a wordnet for Danish by reusing a monolingual dictionary. *Language Resources and Evaluation*, 43(3):269–299.

Bolette Sandford Pedersen, Sanni Nimb, Ida Rørmann Olsen, and Sussi Olsen. 2019. Linking dannet with princeton wordnet. In *Global WordNet 2019 Proceedings, Wroclaw, Poland*, Poland. Oficyna Wydawnicza Politechniki Wroclawskiej.

Didier Schwab, Pauline Trial, Céline Vaschalde, Loïc Vial, Emmanuelle Esperanca-Rodier, and Benjamin Lecouteux. 2020. Providing semantic knowledge to a set of pictograms for people with disabilities: a set of links between WordNet and arasaac: Arasaac-WN. In *Proceedings of the Twelfth Language Resources and Evaluation Conference*, pages 166–171, Marseille, France. European Language Resources Association.

V. Sutton. 1991. *Lessons in Sign Writing: Textbook*. Cent. for Sutton Movement Writ.

Thomas Troelsgård and Jette Kristoffersen. 2018. Improving lemmatisation consistency without a phonological description. the Danish Sign Language corpus and dictionary project. In *Proceedings of the LREC2018 8th Workshop on the Representation and Processing of Sign Languages: Involving the Language Community*, pages 195–198, Miyazaki, Japan. European Language Resources Association (ELRA).

Semantic Parsing and Sense Tagging the Princeton WordNet Gloss Corpus

Alexandre Rademaker
IBM Research and FGV/EMAp
alexrad@br.ibm.com

Abhishek Basu
IBM

Rajkiran Veluri
IBM

Abstract

In 2008, the Princeton team released the last version of the "Princeton Annotated Gloss Corpus". In this corpus. The word forms from the definitions and examples (glosses) of Princeton WordNet are manually linked to the context-appropriate sense in WordNet. However, the annotation was not complete, and the dataset was never officially released as part of WordNet 3.0, remaining as one of the standoff files available for download. Eleven years later, in 2019, one of the authors of this paper restarted the project aiming to complete the sense annotation of the approximately 200 thousand word forms not yet annotated. Here, we provide additional motivations to complete this dataset and report the progress in the work and evaluations. Intending to provide an extra level of consistency in the sense annotation and a deep semantic representation of the definitions and examples promoting WordNet from a lexical resource to a lightweight ontology, we now employ the English Resource Grammar (ERG), a broad-coverage HPSG grammar of English to parse the sentences and project the sense annotations from the surface words to the ERG predicates. We also report some initial steps on upgrading the corpus to WordNet 3.1 to facilitate mapping the data to other lexical resources.

1 Introduction

In the "Princeton Annotated Gloss Corpus" (GlossTag), the content word forms in the definitions and examples in WordNet[1] (Fellbaum, 1998) are manually linked to the context-appropriate sense in WordNet itself. Thus, the glosses are a sense-disambiguated corpus, and WordNet is the dictionary against which the corpus was annotated. The corpus is available for download on the Princeton WordNet website as a standoff package supplementing the WordNet 3.0 release. Although it has already been recognized as a precious resource, not all words have been annotated yet. According to the statistics in the website,[2] by 2008, the corpus contains 206,711 words (including collocations and multi-word expressions) yet to be disambiguated. In (Rademaker et al., 2019), one of the authors reported initial efforts to complete the annotation of the corpus (release 2019). This paper reports the progress on this endeavor (release 2022) with improvements in the methodology and evaluation.

The glosses were introduced in WordNet around 1989 (Fellbaum, 1998); before them, senses were distinguished only by synonyms and semantic relations. From this same reference,"As the number of words in WordNet increased, it became increasingly difficult for us, purely on the basis of synonyms, to keep all the different word senses distinct."

On the other hand, introducing glosses has its problems. First, it is not always easy to write good definitions, and second, glosses introduce information redundancy.

> "In the course of incorporating this kind of explanatory information, we have all acquired greater respect for traditional lexicographers."

[1]We are using the trademark 'WordNet' for the Princeton English Wordnet.

[2]http://wordnetcode.princeton.edu/glosstag.shtml

> "The (somewhat idealistic) hope was that the definition of any word could be inferred from its position in this network of semantic relations and that definitional glosses would be redundant [...] If more distinguishing features could be indicated by pointers representing additional semantic relations, the glosses would become even more redundant. An imaginable test of the system would then be to write a computer program that would synthesize glosses from the information provided by the pointers." (Fellbaum, 1998)

Nevertheless, since its introduction, researchers have found many applications for WordNet glosses. Harabagiu and Moldovan (Fellbaum, 1998; Harabagiu et al., 1999; Moldovan and Novischi, 2004; Mihalcea and Moldovan, 2001) propose disambiguating the content words in the glosses to increase the semantic connections among the words and to establish relations among them between different syntactic categories to support common-sense reasoning. In one example, they explain how the disambiguation of the words 'eat' and 'food' in the definitions of the adjective 'hungry,' the verb 'eat,' and the noun 'refrigerator' establish a semantic path between the concepts expressed by the words. Thus, one can infer from 'being hungry' the action of 'going to the refrigerator.' Increasing the semantic connections among WordNet synsets also improves the results of many word sense disambiguation (WSD) algorithms that use the network structure of WordNet to identify the most plausible sense for the words in a context (Agirre and Soroa, 2009; Banerjee and Pedersen, 2002; Basile et al., 2007). By disambiguating the words in the glosses, we add pointers between synsets A and B whenever we annotated a word with a sense from A in B's definition. With that approach, we can increase the connectivity between the WordNet synsets by approximately an order of magnitude.

The disambiguation of words in the glosses can also improve WordNet and provide completeness and consistency. For instance, the initial versions of WordNet do not contain relations that indicate how words like 'racquet', 'ball', and 'net', and the concepts behind them, are part of another concept that can be expressed by 'court game' (Fellbaum, 1998). In WordNet 3.0 the 'domain relations' between synsets were introduced to alleviate this so-called 'tennis problem' of WordNet (Miller, 1993), but the disambiguated gloss of the synset $\{tennis, lawn\_tennis\}$ (1) would already enrich the connections among the concepts. Another desired property is that all words used in the definitions are defined in this same resource. Hopefully, this completeness could also help us ensure quality in our long-term endeavor during the expansion of WordNet to highly technical domains. Once more concepts are added or redefined, the glosses would be refined and disambiguated, forcing us to use the newly added senses in a productive cycle of editing, testing, and correcting.

(1) a game played with **rackets** by two or four players who hit a **ball** back and forth over a **net** that divides the court (00482298-n) [3]

Beyond the disambiguation of words in the glosses, (Clark et al., 2008a,b) used manually constructed logical forms from a subset of the WordNet glosses for text understanding and question answering.

In our approach, we aim at high-quality human annotation, leveraging the lessons learned and directives developed for the project in Princeton but adapting them to our tools. Data is available using the same open license used by Princeton for the initial version of the data (called GlossTag 2008). In (Rademaker et al., 2019), we reported the initial steps of data preparation, our annotation interface's implementation, and a preliminary experiment on the inter-annotator agreement. The result was called GlossTag 2019 (the 2019 release of the corpus).

[3] Glosses, definitions or examples will be followed by the corresponding synset identifiers from WordNet 3.0.

Here we present the GlossTag 2022. In Section 2, we discuss some inconsistencies in the data identified during the annotation; mainly, we ensure that GlossTag 2022 sentences are all effectively derived from the WordNet 3.0 glosses. In Section 3, we explain why we employed the English Resource Grammar (ERG) to parse the sentences into syntactic and semantic structures, hopefully more consistent than previous pre-processing annotations in GlossTag 2008 and manually constructed logical forms (Clark et al., 2008a,b; Niles and Pease, 2003; Pease and Cheung, 2018). We also explain the projection of the sense annotations from the surface words to the ERG predicates. This helped us improve consistency and facilitate sense annotation, mainly of verbs, where senses are normally related to specific syntactic valence alternations. In Section 4 we evaluated the UKB word-sense disambiguation algorithm (Agirre and Soroa, 2009) in the annotation of the GlossTag itself. The idea was to test the feasibility of having an algorithm give hints to the sense annotator and produce intermediary 'silver' versions of the data in future releases. In Section 5 we make initial considerations about the challenge to migrate the GlossTag 2022 annotations to WordNet 3.1. We presented some final considerations and future work in Section 6.

2 Data validation and preparation

As reported in (Rademaker et al., 2019), from the GlossTag 2008 XML files, we built the GlossTag 2019 JSON-Lines files with one JSON object per line for each gloss. The transformation was done mainly to facilitate the data ingestion in the backend of our annotation tool with elementary validations. In GlossTag 2019, we focused on the annotation job and assessing its complexity only. Nevertheless, the work over the last three years reveals inconsistencies, and data need to be prepared to be combined with their semantic representation obtained from the English Resource Grammar.

In (Miller and Fellbaum, 2007), the authors briefly mentioned the sense tagging of the WordNet glosses. The description is not detailed enough to conclude if they are describing the GlossTag 2008. The best documentation about the dataset is provided as comments on a DTD file that specifies the `wordnet` document type of the XML files in the 'merged' folder of the dataset.[4] Every 'synset' element in the DTD contains three 'gloss' child elements. One with the attribute 'orig', is a string that allegedly matches the gloss of this same synset in the WordNet 3.0 DB files. The second, with the attribute 'text', is also a string, with extra spaces indicating the tokenization and quotes encoded in UTF-8. The third, with the attribute 'wsd', is the one that holds the actual annotations of words and collocations in child elements.

The glosses in WordNet 3.0 can be preceded by a domain classification fragment and/or an auxiliary fragment, both usually in parenthesis and optionally followed by more auxiliary fragments and zero or more examples. For sense tagging purposes, the original annotators ignored the classification fragments, as the information is normally repeated in the usage, region, and category pointers. The auxiliary fragments are always secondary to the primary sense of the synset; they can precede or follows the definition but can also be embedded within the definition. Auxiliary fragments are tagged with 'ignore' or 'arg.' Those assigned with the tag 'ignore' are ignored for sense tagging and contain mainly grammatical or usage information, some qualifying text such as a year born, time, date range, or a chemical or other symbols.

In (2) we show the gloss of the synset $\{wash\}$ (verb) with a fragment assigned with tag 'arg', the argument or typical argument (in green), for the preceding verb (in blue). They are set off in this way so that the syntax of the definition fits that of the lemma (the defining verb is intransitive if the lemma is intransitive).

(2) to cleanse (itself or another animal) by

[4] https://wordnetcode.princeton.edu/glosstag.shtml

licking; "The cat washes several times a day" (00036178-v)

Inside the definitions and examples, we have the 'wf' (word form), 'cf' ('wf' that are part of one or more collocations), and 'mwf' elements. The 'wf' and 'cf' are marked up with parts of speech and potential lemma forms at WordNet 3.0. The collocations are marked in a way that can even indicate discontiguous forms. The 'wf' can also be annotated with some semantic classes: punctuation, year, chemical name, number, time, currency, abbreviations, or mathematical symbol. The 'mwf' are multi-word forms composed by 'wf' and 'cf' children that can also be annotated with semantic classes: date, date/numeric range, numeric form, currency, measurement, mathematical formula, and other groups of symbols. The 'wf' and 'cf' that have been disambiguated are further annotated with WordNet sense keys and the flag indicating if the annotation was done automatically or manually. Furthermore, 'wf' and 'cf' elements may contain a separator attribute with the character separating the corresponding form from the next in print. Valid values for this attribute are hyphen, empty string, and space for hyphenated words not in WordNet, contractions that get split (in 'cf' forms), and cases where no space follows the form. The default value is a space, not explicitly assigned. We should be able to reconstruct the original text of the glosses in the WordNet DB files using the separators, but this was not true for approximately 2100 glosses; we found and fixed some mismatches also caused by extra semi-colons added in the end of the examples.

We know almost nothing about how the original text of the glosses was processed to produce all these mark ups in the GlossTag 2008. What are the tokenization criteria? How were the semantic classes identified? How the definitions and examples segments were identified in a given gloss text. Moreover, some essential details are provided in the DTD. The part-of-speech (POS) tags were automatically assigned only to word forms in the definitions, not in the examples, apparently because examples were supposed to be partially annotated; according to another comment, that says 'only synset terms in examples should be sense tagged,' but we have a more ambitious goal.

Once the tokenization issues were solved, and data was confirmed to correspond to the original WordNet 3.0 DB files, we split the glosses into sentences (definitions and examples). Approximately 758 examples in WordNet 3.0 are quotes such as (3), that is, quotes followed by the author's name or source. We removed the quote marks and moved the author's name (or title of the publication) to the metadata associated with the example.

(3) "their views of life were reductive and depreciatory" - R.H.Rovere (00050446-a)

Finally, we calculated the text span of each word form (also known in the literature as token ranges) in the sentences. As we will see in the rest of the paper, once we parse the sentences with ERG to produce the semantic representations, we need to match the predicates obtained from the ERG analysis with the word forms in the GlossTag 2022 using the text spans. That is the reason for such careful considerations about tokenization. The missing POS in the examples were obtained from ERG analysis.

3 Parsing with English Resource Grammar

The English Resource Grammar (ERG) (Flickinger, 2000, 2011) is a broad-coverage, general-purpose computational grammar that, combined with specialized tools, can map running English text to highly normalized logical-form representations of meaning. ERG is a linguistically precise HPSG-based grammar of English and semantically grounded in Minimal Recursion Semantics (MRS) (Copestake et al., 2005), which is a form of flat semantic representation capable of supporting underspecification. The ERG is developed as part of the international Deep Linguistic Processing with HPSG Initiative

(DELPH-IN) [5] and can be executed by some parsing and realization systems, including the LKB grammar engineering environment (Copestake, 2002), as well as the more efficient ACE parser,[6] for applications.

We grouped the GlossTag 2022 sentences in profiles, test suites, collections of test items for judging the performance of an implemented grammar within DELPH-IN. While the original purpose of test suites is to aid in grammar development, they are more generally useful for batch processing. [incr tsdb()](Oepen, 2001) is the canonical software for managing the profiles but PyDelphin Library (Goodman, 2019) is an alternative. A profile is just a relational database. However, the data are stored in flat text files on disk instead of using a standard SQL database, and the profile is the folder. The file relations describe the database schema of this profile; its syntax is described in (Oepen, 2001). Individual relations (or tables) are stored in separate files with the same name as the relation. The SQL-like query language TSQL can be used to query profiles.

After creating the profiles with 2000 sentences each, we processed them with the Ace parser in a cluster, running each profile in parallel. It took about 30 minutes. For each sentence, we asked for the top-best analysis of ERG. GlossTag 2022 contains 165,976 sentences; from these, only 5,282 were not parsed by ERG. Using some heuristics (the most productive one is adding an extra 'X' in sentences ending with the preposition 'of', e.g. "get the votes *of X*"), we were able to parse roughly 600 more sentences (only 2% are not parsed).

Since ERG is a computational grammar and sentences are typically ambiguous, we can have hundreds or thousands of readings for each sentence. We stored only the top-best analysis according to the pretrained parsing ranking model distributed with ERG.[7] This is not to say that all analyses were the expected ones, but informal evaluation gives us some great expectations. In a future experiment, we aim to employ FFTB (Packard, 2015) for gradually treebanking all sentences. FFTB allows the selection of an arbitrary tree from the 'full forest' without enumerating/unpacking all analyses in the parsing stage. The treebanking of all sentences would ensure the data's quality and the actual evaluation of the parsing selection model. We aim to turn GlossTag 2022 into a dynamically annotated treebank (Flickinger et al., 2012; Oepen et al., 2002).

For each item (sentence) in a profile, once it was processed, we have the derivation tree and the semantic representation MRS.[8] Figure 1 presents one MRS. Predicate–argument structure is expressed in a bag of n-ary elementary predications (EP) linked together by typed variables.[9] The predicate symbols can be divided into surface predicates and abstract predicates. Surface predicates follow a naming convention where the symbol is composed of three components, called 'lemma', 'pos' (mostly align with a crude inventory of word classes (n)oun, (q)uantifier, (v)erb and (a)djective, etc), and 'sense' (coarse-grained senses, ERG only marks those sense distinctions that are morphosyntactically marked). Surface predicates, by convention, are marked by a leading underscore and are exclusively introduced by lexical entries from the grammar, whose orthography is a (possibly inflected) form of the lemma field in the predicate. The predicate `_palmately/rb_u_unknown` is a generic predicate instantiated by ERG for dealing with the unknown word.[10] The numbers following the predicate name indicate the text span to which the EP corresponds.[11]

[5] `https://github.com/delph-in/docs/wiki/`

[6] `https://github.com/delph-in/docs/wiki/AceTop`

[7] We are ignoring details about all other parameters that control the ACE parser.

[8] Among many additional information that we do not have space to describe.

[9] Eventualities (e), instances (of type x), labels or handles (of type h), and underspecified (u and i).

[10] Not explicited defined in its lexicon.

[11] The most complete and up-to-date presentation of ERG semantics can be found in `https://github.com/delph-in/docs/wiki/ErgSemantics`.

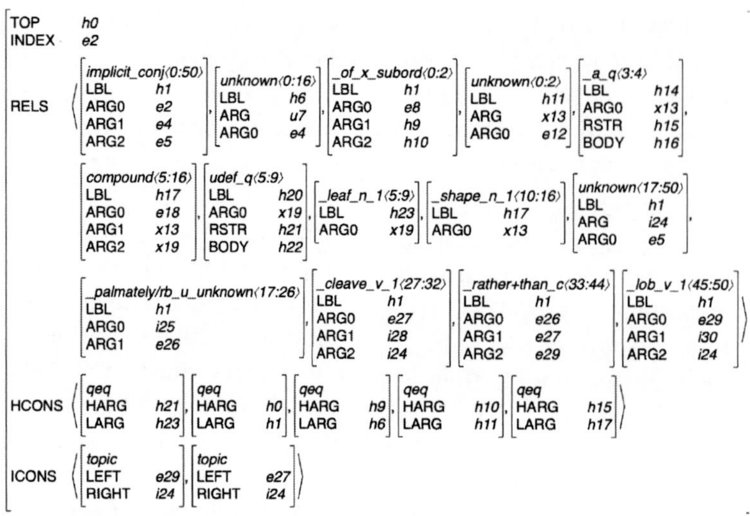

Figure 1: MRS of the definition "of a leaf shape; palmately cleft rather than lobed" (02173264-a)

4 Speeding up the annotations

Manual word sense disambiguation (WSD) is an arduous task, but many techniques for automatic WSD are being investigated. Automatic WSD methods include graph-based (or knowledge-based), supervised and unsupervised machine learning methods (Bevilacqua et al., 2021). Since GlossTag 2022 is still not wholly annotated, having an automatic method to complete the annotation or filter the most plausible senses for the human annotator is appealing. The automatic annotation would allow us to provide intermediary releases of the GlossTag, but we need to estimate the quality of such 'silver' version.

Note that the GlossTag 2008 was already used by many WSD approaches (Bevilacqua et al., 2021). It has been used as a dataset for training supervised WSD algorithms.[12] and also to increase the connectivity among synsets by (Agirre and Soroa, 2009). In this section, we used UKB (Agirre and Soroa, 2009), a graph-based approach for WSD. It applies random walks, e.g., Personalized PageRank, on the Knowledge Base (KB) graph to rank the vertices according to the given context. UKB has been shown to perform almost as well as supervised methods or even outperform them on specific domains (Agirre et al., 2018, 2009). Since UKB uses GlossTag, this creates a possible circularity, problematic for WSD evaluation but not for our goal. We took the GlossTag 2022 sentences, removed all the annotated senses, and passed the sentences to UKB. Given the results of UKB, for each word, we compare the annotations we already have in the data with the sense provided by UKB, evaluating the performance of UKB.

Figure 2 presents the GlossTag information of the same definition processed by ERG and presented in Figure 1 in a tabular format. To produce the UKB input (Figure 3), we have to consolidate the information obtained from ERG with the GlossTag annotations, which is not easy. MWE must be combined into a single token, and all tokens must have lemma and POS so that UKB can disambiguate them. But in Figure 2, tokens 9-10 are not marked as 'cf' (MWE). Token 11 was tagged as an adjective but manually disambiguated and analyzed by ERG as a verb. On the other hand, the MWE 'leaf shape' (Tokens 3-5) matches with the ERG analysis that identified the expression with the 'compound' predicate.[13]

[12]Replacing the well-known but controversial SemCor (semantic concordance), a subset of the Brown Corpus (Miller, 1993) and other small corpora used in the previous SemEval tasks.

[13]We are skipping details related to obtaining the lemmas `rather` and `leaf_shape` from the predicates

```
# text = of a leaf shape; palmately cleft rather than lobed
# id = 02173264-a
# type = def
1       wf      ignore  0:2     IN      of      of      _
2       wf      ignore  3:4     DT      a       a       _
3       glob|a  auto    _       _       _       leaf_shape%1    leaf_shape%1:25:00::
4       cf|a    un      5:9     NN      leaf    leaf%1|leaf%2   _
5       cf|a    un      10:15   NN      shape   shape%1|shape%2 _
6       wf      ignore  15:16   :       ;       _       _
7       wf      auto    17:26   RB      palmately       palmately%4     palmately%4:02:00::
8       wf      man     27:32   VBN     cleft   cleft%1|cleave%2|cleft%3        cleft%5:00:00:compound:00
9       wf      un      33:39   RB      rather  rather%4        _
10      wf      ignore  40:44   IN      than    than    _
11      wf      man     45:50   JJ      lobed   lob%2|lobed%3   lob%2:35:00::
```

Figure 2: GlossTag 2022 tabular presentation of a sentence. The lines starting with hash contains sentence metadata. Each word is presented in a line, column 1 is the identifier, column 2 is the word type, column 3 the annotation flag, column 4 the text span, column 5 the part-of-speech tag (when available), column 6 the form in the sentence, column 7 the possible WordNet 3.0 lemmas and column 8 the sense, when annotated.

Figure 3 presents the UKB inputs for the sentence from Figures 1 and 2. Two consecutive lines represent each context. The first line contains the context identifier, whereas the second one contains the words to be disambiguated. Each element in a context has four mandatory fields; lemma and POS are the most important ones. UKB then disambiguates all the words from the input in a single run. UKB can deal with partially disambiguated contexts and use the provided concept identifiers (synset identifiers) to give extra information in the disambiguation of the remaining tokens. Given that, we generated two contexts for each sentence. In the first context in Figure 3, we included one extra token, the synset identifier.

For evaluation, we only considered the words in the GlossTag which are associated with at least one sense.[14] We have looked for a match by checking if UKB generated sense is a subset of the senses provided in the annotations. The total number of words disambiguated and considered for evaluation using UKB was 819,533. Among them, the ones with senses that were also disambiguated by UKB sum up to 442,782. Table 1 shows the results for the contexts with the additional synset identifier (a) and the results for the contexts without the additional synset identifier (b).

	Total	# (a)	# (b)	% (a)	% (b)
All	442782	413546	374648	93.39	84.61
Noun	329692	308245	287033	93.49	87.06
Adj	64298	60591	52008	94.23	80.89
Verb	41520	37832	29529	91.11	71.12
Adv	7272	6878	6078	94.58	83.58

Table 1: UKB evaluation results by part-of-speech. Columns # shown the counts of matches and columns % the percentage.

The majority of the UKB errors involved words that are highly polysemic. For example, the verb 'make' has 52 senses in WordNet 3.0. Synset 00891038-v has the definition "assure the success of" and example "A good review by this critic will **make** your play!". UKB does not annotate the correct sense of 'make' in the example, even in the context where the synset identifier itself is added as an extra fake word. Finally, we have definitions such as "of or relating to taxonomy" (03018498-a) with only two content words, not enough information to UKB. After some error additional analysis, we have found some necessary improvements for further evaluation. UKB did not find many lemmas in WordNet 3.0 because they were not lower-cased properly. Many cases of MWE were not annotated in the GlossTag nor detected correctly by ERG also need to be fixed. The mapping of ERG com-

_rather+than_c, _leaf_n_1 and _shape_n_1.

[14]In our annotation guideline, the annotators can annotate more than one sense for each word.

```
ctx-02173264-a/a
leaf_shape#n#w4#1#1 palmately#r#w7#1#1 cleave#v#w8#1#1 rather#r#w9#1#1 lob#v#w11#1#1 02173264-a#a#fake1#2#1

ctx-02173264-a/b
leaf_shape#n#w4#1#1 palmately#r#w7#1#1 cleave#v#w8#1#1 rather#r#w9#1#1 lob#v#w11#1#1
```

Figure 3: UKB Input Context Example

pounds [15] and GlossTag globs needs improvements. Nevertheless, we can safely conclude that adding the synset identifier as an additional word in the context helps UKB. It seems to justify the use of UKB to automatically annotate missing senses and thus generate a 'silver' release of GlossTag 2022.

5 The ongoing update to WordNet 3.1

In the latest version of WordNet, Princeton team applied minor fixes in the texts of the glosses and removed many newly considered offensive words. Besides adding (676 senses) and removing senses (382 senses), some WordNet 3.0 senses have moved between synsets, or the corresponding synsets were changed in WordNet 3.1. Given these changes, projecting the annotations in GlossTag 2022 to the senses of WordNet 3.1 needs some careful consideration. This section presents our initial considerations and plans to make the migration.

An extra motivation for moving GlossTag 2022 to WordNet 3.1 is that other lexical resources like VerbNet (Schuler, 2005) are already mapped to WordNet 3.1. Using those mappings, one can enrich the information of verbs in WordNet, restricted to verb frames ('Somebody –s something') with additional information like valences, semantic restrictions, etc. This extra information could facilitate sense annotation. For example, the verb 'make' has 52 senses in WordNet 3.0, grouped into six classes in VerbNet. If the annotator is first presented with the information from VerbNet, it can first choose the VerbNet class by selecting the proper syntactic restrictions and later select the WordNet senses in that class.

The projection of the annotations of GlossTag to WordNet 3.1 needs to deal with the following cases. First, we need to identify which definitions and examples changed. The new sentences need to be processed by ERG and prepared for manual annotation from scratch. The removed sentences can be just removed. Next, we must consider each word in the sentences preserved in WordNet 3.1. We need to consider the annotated words only and what happens with the used sense key. If sense keys were not reused with a different meaning, we would have no problem. Unfortunately, we found cases where a given sense key got a different meaning in WordNet 3.1.

For example, in WordNet 3.1 we have the word 'Pluto' with the sense key `pluto%1:17:00::` which has the gloss "a large asteroid that was once thought to be the farthest known planet from the sun; it has an elliptical orbit" and the example "Pluto was discovered by Clyde Tombaugh in 1930". In WordNet 3.0, the same sense key `pluto%1:17:00::` is part of a synset with the definition "a small planet and the farthest known planet from the sun; it has the most elliptical orbit of all the planets". Note how the definition changed from planet to asteroid. Since the concept has changed, the relations have also changed; it is now an instance of 'asteroid' instead of 'outer planet' and 'superior planet'. In this case, it would have been more appropriate to introduce a new sense key to signify a deviation of the new definition from the old one. Another sense of 'Pluto' in WordNet 3.0 is part of the synset "(Greek mythology) the god of the underworld in ancient mythology; brother of Zeus and husband of Persephone". In WordNet 3.0, this sense of Pluto

[15] Compounding comprises a variety of (semantic) head–modifier structures that can often be paraphrased using overt prepositions.

is part of the synset "(Roman mythology) god of the underworld; counterpart of Greek Hades". In WordNet 3.0, Pluto was defined as a synonym of Hades, but WordNet 3.1 revised that definition making it part of Roman mythology and a counterpart of Hades. There are eight occurrences of 'pluto' in the WordNet 3.0 sentences. For instance, the definition "United States astronomer who discovered the planet Pluto (1906-1997))" was not updated to follow the new definitions in WordNet 3.1. This shows how hard it is to keep the glosses consistent with the WordNet structure.

Another challenge arises when a new sense is introduced in WordNet 3.1, and some words in the sentences could be better annotated with the new sense. For example, if we look at the senses of the word 'technology', we note that there is a new sense introduced in WordNet 3.1, with the synset 03707142-n and the sense key `technology%1:06:00::` with the definition "machinery and equipment developed from engineering or other applied sciences". In the GlossTag 2022 we found 53 instances of the word 'technology' annotated, and the new sense from WordNet 3.1 may be more appropriate for some of them. Upon manual inspection, we found that this is indeed the case in one of the examples of synset 08343534-n "has procured nuclear technology and delivery capabilities". In this gloss definition, 'technology' may be better mapped to the new sense at WordNet 3.1 rather than any of the other existing senses in WordNet 3.0. All annotated instances of 'technology' need to be checked manually.

We are refining the idea of sense stability. For example, for the sense `a._noam_chomsky%1:18:00::` in WordNet 3.0, we have the synset 10896452-n, which contains two co-occurring senses. In WordNet 3.1, we have the related synset 10916204-n which contains the same and no new senses. Thus, we call this sense stable. An example where the senses diverge is for the sense `constrain%2:35:00::`. In WordNet 3.0, this sense is part of the synset 01301051-v with three other senses. In WordNet 3.1, this sense was moved to synset 01304044-v. Given that, all senses of 01301051-v (WordNet 3.0) became unstable. Considering all the challenges ahead, GlossTag 2022 is still based on WordNet 3.0.

6 Conclusion

In this paper, we presented the GlossTag 2022 release. The project is hosted in the `https://github.com/own-pt/glosstag` repository, and it will be updated in the following days. As put by (Miller et al., 1993), the semantic annotation of corpora helps improve both the coverage and the precision of the semantic resource being used in the annotation. This work is thus part of our effort in expanding and improving WordNet-like resources in an application-driven and domain-specific way.

Besides continuing the manual annotation, we plan to improve the annotation interface[16] and experiment with alternative WSD methods (McCord, 2004). Concerning the annotation tool, we intend to improve its performance and make it a wordnet editor, allowing the sense annotation to influence wordnet improvements. We also aim for a workflow with feedback between annotation and ERG analysis, one supporting the other. Additionally, we also intend to develop querying and visualization tools. Finally, we need to finish the migration to WordNet 3.1 before forking it from the Princeton official release (or further mapping to (McCrae et al., 2020)) for changes driven by the annotation.

Acknowledgments The authors would like to thank the support from Francis Bond and Dan Flickinger for all their support and valuable comments and suggestions.

References

Eneko Agirre, Oier Lopez De Lacalle, Aitor Soroa, and Informatika Fakultatea. 2009. Knowledge-based wsd and specific domains: Performing better than generic supervised wsd. In *IJCAI*, pages 1501–1506.

[16]`https://github.com/own-pt/sensetion.el`

Eneko Agirre, Oier López de Lacalle, and Aitor Soroa. 2018. The risk of sub-optimal use of open source nlp software: Ukb is inadvertently state-of-the-art in knowledge-based wsd.

Eneko Agirre and Aitor Soroa. 2009. Personalizing pagerank for word sense disambiguation. In *Proceedings of the 12th Conference of the European Chapter of the Association for Computational Linguistics*, pages 33–41. Association for Computational Linguistics.

Satanjeev Banerjee and Ted Pedersen. 2002. An adapted lesk algorithm for word sense disambiguation using wordnet. In *Computational Linguistics and Intelligent Text Processing*, pages 136–145, Berlin, Heidelberg. Springer Berlin Heidelberg.

Pierpaolo Basile, Marco de Gemmis, Anna Lisa Gentile, Pasquale Lops, and Giovanni Semeraro. 2007. Uniba: Jigsaw algorithm for word sense disambiguation. In *Proceedings of the Fourth International Workshop on Semantic Evaluations (SemEval-2007)*, pages 398–401, Prague, Czech Republic. Association for Computational Linguistics.

Michele Bevilacqua, Tommaso Pasini, Alessandro Raganato, Roberto Navigli, et al. 2021. Recent trends in word sense disambiguation: A survey. In *Proceedings of the Thirtieth International Joint Conference on Artificial Intelligence, IJCAI-21*. International Joint Conference on Artificial Intelligence, Inc.

Peter Clark, Christiane Fellbaum, and Jerry Hobbs. 2008a. Using and extending wordnet to support question-answering. In *Proceedings of the 4th Global Wordnet Conference*, pages 111–119, Hungary.

Peter Clark, Christiane Fellbaum, Jerry R Hobbs, Phil Harrison, William R Murray, and John Thompson. 2008b. Augmenting wordnet for deep understanding of text. In *Semantics in Text Processing. STEP 2008 Conference Proceedings*, pages 45–57.

Ann Copestake. 2002. *Implementing typed feature structure grammars*, volume 110. CSLI publications Stanford.

Ann Copestake, Dan Flickinger, Carl Pollard, and Ivan A Sag. 2005. Minimal recursion semantics: An introduction. *Research on language and computation*, 3(2):281–332.

Christiane Fellbaum, editor. 1998. *WordNet: An Electronic Lexical Database (Language, Speech, and Communication)*. The MIT Press.

Dan Flickinger. 2000. On building a more efficient grammar by exploiting types. *Natural Language Engineering*, 6(1):15–28.

Dan Flickinger. 2011. Accuracy v. robustness in grammar engineering. In Emily M. Bender and Jennifer E. Arnold, editors, *Language from a Cognitive Perspective: Grammar, Usage and Processing*, pages 31–50. CSLI Publications, Stanford, CA.

Dan Flickinger, Yi Zhang, and Valia Kordoni. 2012. Deepbank. a dynamically annotated treebank of the wall street journal. In *Proceedings of the 11th International Workshop on Treebanks and Linguistic Theories*, pages 85–96.

Michael Wayne Goodman. 2019. A python library for deep linguistic resources. In *2019 Pacific Neighborhood Consortium Annual Conference and Joint Meetings (PNC)*, pages 1–7. IEEE.

Sanda M. Harabagiu, George A. Miller, and Dan I. Moldovan. 1999. Wordnet 2: a morphologically and semantically enhanced resource. In *Proceedings of SIGLEX99: Standardizing Lexical Resources*, pages 1–8.

Michael C McCord. 2004. Word sense disambiguation in a slot grammar framework. Technical Report RC23397, IBM.

John Philip McCrae, Alexandre Rademaker, Ewa Rudnicka, and Francis Bond. 2020. English WordNet 2020: Improving and extending a WordNet for English using an open-source methodology. In *Proceedings of the LREC 2020 Workshop on Multimodal Wordnets (MMW2020)*, pages 14–19, Marseille, France. The European Language Resources Association (ELRA).

Rada Mihalcea and Dan I. Moldovan. 2001. extended wordnet: progress report. In *Proceedings of NAACL Workshop on WordNet and Other Lexical Resources*, pages 95–100.

George A Miller. 1993. The association of ideas. *The General Psychologist*, 29:69–74.

George A Miller and Christiane Fellbaum. 2007. WordNet then and now. *Language Resources and Evaluation*, 41(2):209–214.

George A Miller, Claudia Leacock, Randee Tengi, and Ross T Bunker. 1993. A semantic concordance. In *Proceedings of the workshop on Human Language Technology*, pages 303–308. Association for Computational Linguistics.

Dan Moldovan and Adrian Novischi. 2004. Word sense disambiguation of wordnet glosses. *Computer Speech & Language*, 18(3):301–317.

Ian Niles and Adam Pease. 2003. Linking lexicons and ontologies: Mapping wordnet to the suggested upper merged ontology. In *Ike*, pages 412–416.

Stephan Oepen. 2001. [incr tsdb()] — competence and performance laboratory. User manual. Technical report, Computational Linguistics, Saarland University, Saarbrücken, Germany. In preparation.

Stephan Oepen, Kristina Toutanova, Stuart M Shieber, Christopher D Manning, Dan Flickinger, and Thorsten Brants. 2002. The lingo redwoods treebank: Motivation and preliminary applications. In *COLING 2002: The 17th International Conference on Computational Linguistics: Project Notes*.

Woodley Packard. 2015. *Full forest treebanking*. Ph.D. thesis, University of Washington.

Adam Pease and Andrew Cheung. 2018. Toward a semantic concordancer. In *Proceedings of the 9th Global Wordnet Conference*, pages 97–104, Nanyang Technological University (NTU), Singapore. Global Wordnet Association.

Alexandre Rademaker, Bruno Cuconato, Alessandra Cid, Alexandre Tessarollo, and Henrique Andrade. 2019. Completing the Princeton annotated gloss corpus project. In *Proceedings of the 10th Global Wordnet Conference*, pages 378–386, Wroclaw, Poland. Global Wordnet Association.

Karin Kipper Schuler. 2005. *VerbNet: A broad-coverage, comprehensive verb lexicon*. Ph.D. thesis, University of Pennsylvania.

Context-Gloss Augmentation for Improving Arabic Target Sense Verification

Sanad Malaysha, Mustafa Jarrar, Mohammed Khalilia
Birzeit University, Palestine
{smalaysha, mjarrar, mkhalilia}@birzeit.edu

Abstract

Arabic language lacks semantic datasets and sense inventories. The most common semantically-labeled dataset for Arabic is the *ArabGlossBERT*, a relatively small dataset that consists of 167K context-gloss pairs (about 60K positive and 107K negative pairs), collected from Arabic dictionaries. This paper presents an enrichment to the ArabGlossBERT dataset, by augmenting it using (Arabic-English-Arabic) machine back-translation. Augmentation increased the dataset size to 352K pairs (149K positive and 203K negative pairs). We measure the impact of augmentation using different data configurations to fine-tune BERT on target sense verification (TSV) task. Overall, the accuracy ranges between 78% to 84% for different data configurations. Although our approach performed at par with the baseline, we did observe some improvements for some POS tags in some experiments. Furthermore, our fine-tuned models are trained on a larger dataset covering larger vocabulary and contexts. We provide an in-depth analysis of the accuracy for each part-of-speech (POS).

1 Introduction

There are three tasks in the literature that are related to semantic understanding of natural language: *(i)* Word Sense Disambiguation (WSD), *(ii)* Target Sense Verification (TSV), and *(iii)* Word-in-Context (WiC). WSD is the most common task, which aims to disambiguate word's semantics. Given a context (i.e., sentence), a target word in the context, and a set of candidate senses (i.e., glosses, meaning definitions (Jarrar, 2006)) for the target word, the goal of the WSD task is to determine *which of these senses* is the intended meaning for the target word (Al-Hajj and Jarrar, 2022). For example, the word (جداول *ǧdāwl*) has two senses in Arabic: *tables* (شكل يحتوي على مجموعة قضايا أو معلومات) and *creek* (مجرى صغير متفرع من نهر). Thus, in the context (تمشى بين الجداول والازهار), WSD aims to determine which of the two senses is the intended meaning of (الجداول *ālǧdāwl*). The TSV task is newly proposed in the literature (Breit et al., 2020). It aims to classify a sentence pair with positive or negative. Given a context, target and gloss, TSV aims to decide whether this gloss is the intended meaning of the target. In other words, TSV does not determine which sense is the intended meaning, but rather, decides whether the context-gloss pair match (Positive) or not (Negative). For example, the sentence pair (تمشى بين الجداول والازهار - مجرى صغير متفرع من نهر) is Positive, while the pair (شكل يحتوي على مجموعة قضايا أو معلومات - تمشى بين الجداول والازهار) is Negative. WiC aims to determine whether a target word in two contexts is used in the same sense or not (Moreno et al., 2021). Although the three tasks are closely related, they are not the same, and the choice of which task to use depends on the application scenario (e.g., machine translation, information retrieval, semantic tagging, or others). Some researchers try to address these tasks using different approaches. For example, Hauer and Kondrak (2022) proposed to solve the WSD by re-formulating it as a TSV task, a WiC task and a combination of TSV and WiC tasks.

Such semantic understanding tasks have been challenging for many years, but recently gained attention due to the advances in contextualized word embedding models (Al-Hajj and Jarrar, 2022, 2021). Language models, specially BERT (Kenton and Toutanova, 2019), have made significant advancements in down-streaming NLP tasks. BERT is a transformer-based model pre-trained on huge corpora (Devlin et al., 2019). It can be fine-tuned on domain/task-specific data (e.g., POS tagging, WSD, TSV, and WiC) to update its contextualized embeddings. The TSV task has been addressed by fine-tuning BERT on context-gloss pairs as a sentence pair binary classification problem (Huang et al., 2019; Yap et al., 2020; Patel et al., 2021; Ranjbar and Zeinali, 2021; Lin and Giambi, 2021; El-Razzaz et al., 2021; Al-Hajj and Jarrar, 2022). However, the TSV task, similar to most NLP tasks, suffers from the knowledge-gain bottleneck, i.e., the lack of available quality datasets to train machine learning models.

Arabic is a low-resourced language (Darwish

et al., 2021; Jarrar et al., 2022) and the only available context-gloss pairs dataset is ArabGlossBERT (Al-Hajj and Jarrar, 2022). It consists of 167K context-gloss pairs, a relatively small dataset for fine-tuning BERT on a TSV task. The positive pairs (60K) were collected from multiple Arabic dictionaries (Jarrar and Amayreh, 2019; Jarrar, 2018; Jarrar et al., 2019; Jarrar, 2020) as well as from the Arabic Ontology (Jarrar, 2021, 2011). The pairs were cross-related to generate 106.8K negative pairs and used to fine-tune a BERT model, which achieved 84% accuracy.

This paper aims to enrich the ArabGlossBERT dataset by augmenting it using the back-translation technique, similar to the work done for English by Lin and Giambi (2021). With data augmentation, we generate new Arabic paraphrased contexts and glosses by translating the original data into English and back to Arabic, using Google Translate API. The new augmented dataset consists of 352K context-gloss pairs. To answer the question of whether the back-translation enrichment improves the TSV accuracy, we conduct 13 experiments that compare the accuracy obtained using the original dataset with the accuracy obtained using different combinations of the augmented datasets. We, also, provide an in-depth analysis of the TSV accuracy for each part-of-speech, which was not provided in (Al-Hajj and Jarrar, 2022). The main contributions of this work are:

- Augmented ArabGlossBERT using back-translation (352K pairs).
- Thirteen experiments with different dataset configurations - to measure whether the back-translation enrichment can improve TSV performance.
- In-depth analysis of the TSV accuracy for each part-of-speech.

The rest of the paper is organized as follows: Section 2 reviews the related literature, Section 3 describes the data augmentation, Section 4 presents the experiments, Section 5 presents the results and we conclude in Section 6 with limitations and future work.

2 Related Work

TSV has proven to be an effective solution for the WSD in many state-of-the-art efforts. Although some researchers did not use the term TSV, this notion was also referred to as GlossBERT or *Context-Gloss Binary Classification* (Al-Hajj and Jarrar, 2022; El-Razzaz et al., 2021). A TSV training dataset is typically a set of context-gloss pairs, each labeled with Positive or Negative. A pre-trained language model can then be fine-tuned for sentence pair binary classification. This idea was first proposed for English as GlossBERT (Huang et al., 2019), where the training pairs were generated from a known SemCor dataset (Miller et al., 1993) with the target word, in context, marked up by a BERT-specific signal to emphasize it in the learning phase.

A similar effort in (Lin and Giambi, 2021) followed the GlossBERT technique. Their addition is the use of back-translation for improving the English WSD. They used back-translation from English to German and back to English in order to bridge the knowledge-gain gap and provide more context-gloss pairs. They also used a mark-up signal to surround the target word with double quotations. Only 2% improvement was achieved using back-translation. This paper aims to evaluate this idea for Arabic. Another idea was proposed in (Yap et al., 2020), in which a learning signal (special token [TGT]) was used, and BERT was fine-tuned on sequence-pair ranking, the model selects the most related gloss given a context sentence and a list of candidate glosses. Botha et al. (2020) used different mark-up signals in the form of open and close tags to emphasize the target word [E]target[/E] within the context sentence.

For Arabic, the TSV task was addressed in (Al-Hajj and Jarrar, 2022), which presents the ArabGlossBERT, a dataset of 167K context-gloss pairs labeled with Positive or Negative. First, 60K positive pairs were extracted from different Arabic lexicons, then 106K negative pairs were generated automatically by cross-relating the positive pairs. The target word was marked-up with different learning signals. Different Arabic pre-trained models were fine-tuned, and the best model using AraBERT-V2 (Antoun et al., 2020) achieved 84% accuracy. Similar work for Arabic was proposed in (El-Razzaz et al., 2021) using a smaller dataset (15K positive and 15K negative) in which they used AraBERT-V2 and reported 89% F1-score but this performance was criticized in (Al-Hajj and Jarrar, 2022).

	Gloss	-	Context
Original (Arabic)	فكرة أو مسألة تقدم للبحث	-	جلس المسؤولون يناقشون **أطروحات** المشروع
Translated (Arabic to English)	An idea or question is progressing to research	-	Officials sat discussing project proposals
Back-Translated (English to Arabic)	فكرة أو سؤال مقدم للبحث	-	جلس المسؤولون لناقشة مقترحات الشاريع

Table 1: Example of context-gloss back-translation (Arabic-English-Arabic).

3 Data Augmentation

NLP tasks, including TSV, typically suffer from knowledge acquisition. The importance of knowledge acquisition is increasing especially because most NLP tasks are currently tackled using pre-trained neural models such as BERT, which generally requires large data to fine-tune. If the training data is not sufficient, the model will encounter the problem of unseen vocabulary and contexts, which harms model accuracy (Bevilacqua et al., 2021). The linguistic resources that can be utilized for semantic understanding tasks are limited in Arabic language. Our assumption, for the TSV task, is that the more context-gloss pairs can be used during the training phase, the more vocabulary and more contexts will be covered, thus the better TSV accuracy. This is why researchers started to try new techniques for data augmentation in order to enrich the available dataset with more knowledge (Lin and Giambi, 2021; Ranjbar and Zeinali, 2021).

For Arabic, and in order to enrich existing Arabic datasets, we propose to use the Arabic-English-Arabic back-translation, as illustrated in Table 1. It shows how the back-translation of glosses and contexts generates new paraphrased sentences with the same meaning. For back-translation we used Google Translate API, which was found to produce good quality and generally acceptable translations (De Vries et al., 2018). We did not remove diacritics since Arabic is diacritic-sensitive (Jarrar et al., 2018). Nevertheless, there are sentences that appeared with wrong or bad-quality translations, which we will discuss later. The translation was done in two phases. The glosses and contexts were translated into English, then back to Arabic. We, then, combined both the original dataset and the back-translated set.

We only back-translated the ArabGlossBERT training dataset (152,035 pairs). The testing dataset (15,172 pairs) was not back-translated, because it is used as an evaluation benchmark to compare the performance improvement between the original and augmented datasets.

Table 2 provides statistics about the original ArabGlossBERT dataset, the newly added back-translations, and the whole dataset after augmentation. The augmentation shows that the size of the original dataset was doubled as it contains the original context-gloss pairs and the translated context-gloss pairs (152,032).

The original training dataset is not balanced with 55,585 positive pairs (36.6%) and 96,450 negative pairs (63.4%). To produce a more balanced dataset, we generated an additional 32,839 positive pairs by matching the original glosses with the new back-translated glosses increasing the number of positive pairs to 144,009. The 144,009 include 55,585 pairs from the original data, 55,585 pairs from back-translation and the added 32,839 pairs, resulting in a new dataset with 42.7% positive and 57.3% negative pairs.

Observations on Google Translate: First, although the quality of Google translations was generally acceptable, there are wrong translations. However, we did not make any improvements or revisions to these translations, as the goal of this paper is to measure whether automated back-translations can improve the accuracy of the trained models. Second, the output of the Google translation API was not always complete. In some cases it translates part of the input sentence. To overcome this challenge we used two techniques: 1) add special characters (.#) at the end of each sentence, if the special characters were translated back, then we know the translation reached the end of the sentence, 2) compare the length of the original and back-translated sentences and if the difference is significant, then this is an indication of incomplete translations. Partial translations are reviewed manually.

	Original ArabGlossBERT	Back-Translation Pairs	Augmented ArabGlossBERT
Unique un-diacritized lemmas	26,169	–	26,169
Unique glosses	32,839	32,839	65,678
Unique contexts	60,272	60,272	120,544
Training pairs	152,035	152,035 + 32,839	336,909
Positive pairs	55,585	55,585 + 32,839	144,009
Negative pairs	96,450	96,450	192,900
Testing pairs	15,172	–	15,172
Positive pairs	4,738	–	4,738
Negative pairs	10,434	–	10,434
Total: Train+Test	167,207	152,035 + 32,839	352,081

Table 2: Statistics of the original and augmented datasets.

Dataset	Description	Positive Pairs	Negative Pairs	Total
D_1	The original ArabGlossBERT dataset	55,585	96,450	152,035
D_2	D_1 with target signal	55,585	96,450	152,035
D_3	D_1 with context replaced by back-translated context	55,585	96,450	152,035
D_4	D_1 + Positive pairs of D_3	111,170	96,450	207,620
D_5	$D_1 + D_3$	111,170	192,900	304,070
D_6	D_1 + Positive pairs (original gloss - back-translated gloss)	88,424	96,450	184,874
D_7	D_4 + Positive pairs (original gloss - back-translated gloss)	144,009	96,450	240,459
D_8	D_5 + Positive pairs (original gloss - back-translated gloss)	144,009	192,900	336,909
D_9	D_1 + Positive pairs (original context - back-translated gloss)	111,170	96,450	207,620
D_{10}	D_1 + Pairs of cross relating the glosses against each other	88,424	373,955	462,379
D_{11}	D_1 (excluded pairs of functional words)	54,878	92,730	147,608
D_{12}	D_1 (only the pairs of the noun POS)	36,487	37,998	74,485
D_{13}	D_1 (only the pairs of the verb POS)	18,178	54,945	73,123

Table 3: The datasets that were used for the different experiments to fine-tune AraBERT on the TSV task.

4 Experiments

This section presents 13 experiments to measure the impact of data augmentation using back-translation on TSV model accuracy. The first experiment uses the original ArabGlossBERT dataset, D_1, (as a baseline), while the other experiments are conducted with different dataset configurations. In all experiments, we used the original test dataset 15,172 pairs (4,738 positive and 10,434 negative). Table 3 presents the training datasets that we used in the experiments.

In all experiments we fine-tuned AraBERTv2 (aubmindlab/bert-base-arabertv02, CC-BY-SA) using the following hyperparameters: $\eta = 2e^{-5}$, batch size $B = 16$, max sequence length of 512, warm-up steps 1,412 and number of epochs 4.

The results of the 13 experiments are presented in Table 4, which includes precision, recall, F1-score, and accuracy. The results are presented at the POS tag level and overall. Also, note that the test dataset is the same test set used in the original ArabGlossBERT dataset because we consider ArabGlossBERT as a baseline. In the next sub-sections, we elaborate on each experiment.

4.1 Experiment 1: D_1 Dataset (Baseline)

This experiment is the baseline for results comparison. We used the original dataset ArabGlossBERT, D_1, without any augmentation and achieved the same results (83% accuracy) as reported in (Al-Hajj and Jarrar, 2022). Additionally, we evaluated the model performance per POS tag since the tokens are annotated with the POS tags (noun, verb, and functional words). While the accuracy across all tags is very similar (Table 4,), we observe a big difference in the Positive pair F1-score. For the

Dataset	Metric	All POS		Accuracy	Noun		Accuracy	Verb		Accuracy	Functional Words		Accuracy
		Positive	Negative		Positive	Negative		Positive	Negative		Positive	Negative	
D1 Baseline 152,035 pairs	**Precision**	76	85		75	85		78	85		63	84	
	Recall	66	90	83	70	88	82	65	91	83	46	92	81
	F1-Score	71	88		72	82		71	88		53	88	
D2 152,035 pairs	**Precision**	81	85		79	85		82	85		71	82	
	Recall	65	93	84	68	91	83	64	94	84	36	95	81
	F1-Score	72	89		73	88		72	89		48	88	
D3 152,035 pairs	**Precision**	68	80		65	79		70	80		55	79	
	Recall	52	88	77	54	85	75	52	90	78	19	95	77
	F1-Score	59	84		59	82		60	85		29	86	
D4 207,620 pairs	**Precision**	80	81		79	80		81	81		69	80	
	Recall	53	94	81	55	92	80	53	94	81	23	97	79
	F1-Score	64	87		65	86		64	87		34	88	
D5 304,070 pairs	**Precision**	76	82		77	79		76	84		70	80	
	Recall	57	92	81	53	92	80	62	91	82	24	97	79
	F1-Score	65	87		63	85		68	87		36	88	
D6 184,874 pairs	**Precision**	76	85		76	84		76	87		71	82	
	Recall	67	90	**83**	66	89	81	70	90	84	32	96	81
	F1-Score	71	88		71	**86**		**73**	88		44	88	
D7 240,459 pairs	**Precision**	79	82		77	81		80	83		71	79	
	Recall	56	93	81	57	91	80	58	93	82	17	98	79
	F1-Score	66	87		66	86		67	88		17	98	
D8 336,909 pairs	**Precision**	80	81		79	80		81	81		69	80	
	Recall	54	94	81	55	92	80	53	94	81	23	97	79
	F1-Score	65	87		65	86		64	87		34	88	
D9 207,620 pairs	**Precision**	78	84		77	83		78	86		73	81	
	Recall	63	92	**83**	62	91	81	66	92	84	31	96	81
	F1-Score	70	88		69	**86**		**72**	88		43	88	
D10 462,379 pairs	**Precision**	71	80		70	78		71	81		66	79	
	Recall	51	90	78	50	89	76	54	90	79	19	97	78
	F1-Score	59	85		58	83		61	85		30	87	
D11 147,750 pairs	**Precision**	80	81		79	80		81	81				
	Recall	54	94	81	55	92	80	53	94	81			
	F1-Score	65	87		65	86		64	87				
D12 74,485 pairs	**Precision**				80	82							
	Recall				60	92	81						
	F1-Score				69	87							
D13 73,123 pairs	**Precision**							74	84				
	Recall							62	90	81			
	F1-Score							68	87				

Table 4: Results, expressed as percentage, of the experiments for fine-tuning AraBERT on different combinations of the original ArabGlossBERT and augmented datasets.

functional words, the F1-score for Positive pairs is only 53%, compared to 72% and 71% for the nouns and verbs, respectively. We will notice this trend across all experiments, since functional words are highly polysemous (e.g., the preposition (في / in) has ten different glosses), and their glosses represent function and use in the sentence, rather than semantics.

4.2 Experiment 2: D_2 Dataset

The idea of this experiment is to use a learning signal by marking up the target word, in its context, with an open-close tag (<token>Target</token>) to emphasize the model learning of the target word. Thus, the dataset D_2 is the same as D_1 but with a learning signal surrounding the target words. This experiment is the same experiment conducted in (Al-Hajj and Jarrar, 2022) and we achieved the same results (84% accuracy). Overall, we see a 1% increase by using D_2 over D_1. We note that D_2 is the only dataset with the target signal added.

4.3 Experiment 3: D_3 Dataset

This experiment evaluates the model performance using D_3, which contains the back-translated context and the original gloss pairs (152,035). As shown in Table 4, the overall accuracy creased from 83% on D_1 to 77% on D_3. The 6% drop in the accuracy illustrates that the quality of the back-translations is acceptable as an augmentation to the original data.

4.4 Experiment 4: D_4 Dataset

D_4 is original dataset D_1 in addition to the 55,585 Positive back-translated pairs. The motivation of adding the Positive back-translated pairs is to balance the original dataset, D_1. Recall that D_1 contains 55,585 Positive pairs (36.6%) and 96,450 Negative pairs (63.4%) and by adding the Positive back-translated pairs, D_4 size increases to 207,620 pairs, among which 111,170 (53.5%) are positive pairs. Table 4 shows that this data configuration did not improve the model performance. On the contrary, the accuracy dropped by 2% compared to D_1 (baseline). We also note that the F1-score dropped from 71% to 64% for Positive pairs, and from 88% to 87% for Negative pairs.

4.5 Experiment 5: D_5 Dataset

D_5 consists of the original dataset D_1 in addition to its back-translation dataset D_3. Although D_5 is large (304,070 pairs), its accuracy is 81%, which is 2% lower than the baseline.

4.6 Experiment 6: D_6 Dataset

The D_6 dataset used in this experiment contains the original dataset D_1, in addition to 32,839 Positive pairs that we generated by paring an original gloss with its back-translation. We achieved the same accuracy as the baseline (83%), but we believe that the fine-tuned model on D_6 is a little better than the baseline model for two reasons. First, the the F1-score for *noun* Negative pairs increased by 4% compared to the baseline to 86%, and the F1-score for *verb* Positive pairs increased by 2% to 73%. Second, since the training dataset is larger it is assumed to cover more vocabulary.

4.7 Experiments 7-8: D_7 and D_8 Datasets

Although we increased the size of datasets in these two experiments, their model accuracy and F1-scores are very similar, but lower compared with the baseline. D_7 contains the original dataset, the Positive back-translated pairs and the Positive glosses with their back-translations. With this data, we increased the Positive pairs to be 144,009 (60%) of the dataset. In experiment 8 we used D_8, which contains the original dataset, all back-translation pairs, and the Positive gloss-gloss pairs.

4.8 Experiment 9: D_9 Dataset

D_9 contains D_1 and the 55,585 Positive pairs that we produced by pairing the original context with their back-translated gloss. The Positive pairs in D_9 account for 53.5% of the dataset. This data configuration achieved the same as the baseline (83% accuracy). Although the performance is same as the baseline, we see similar behaviour and we conclude the same as we did on the dataset D_6.

4.9 Experiment 10: D_{10} Dataset

In this experiment we did not use back-translation. However, we augmented the original dataset D_1 such that, the set of glosses of a certain lemma are cross-related and the resulting pairs are considered Negative pairs. In this way, we were able to generate 32,839 Positive pairs and 277,505 Negative pairs, a total of 310,344 pairs. We augmented these pairs with D_1 resulting in 462,379 pairs. Notice that this is the hardest dataset to model because some negative pairs are generated at the lemma level and are harder to distinguish from their positive counterparts. The idea is to fine-tune a model to be more sensitive in distinguishing positive and negative pairs, which as expected resulted in the lowest performance (78% accuracy) compared to other models.

4.10 Experiment 11: D_{11} Dataset

The goal of this experiment is to fine-tune a model excluding all pairs that are labeled with functional words. Functional words such as (إذا ،من، على ،في ،إلى) play the role of particles rather than providing core semantics. Additionally, they are frequently used in contexts and are highly polysemous. We fine-tuned a model with the D_{11} dataset, which is the same as the original dataset D_1, but it excludes 4,427 pairs of functional words. However, the performance did not improve compared to the baseline. This illustrates that keeping the pairs of functional words is better than excluding them.

4.11 Experiment 12-13: D_{12} and D_{13} Datasets

The goal of these two experiments is to evaluate the pairs labeled with *nouns* and *verbs* separately. D_{12} contains 74,485 pairs, in which targets are *nouns* only, and D_{13} contains 73,123 pairs with *verb* targets. We fine-tuned two separate models for each of the datasets and achieved similar accuracy and F1-scores, however, the performance is slightly lower compared to the baseline. Nevertheless, since both D_{12} and D_{13} achieved similar results, we believe that fine-tuning the model on data with both POS tags allows for cross learning and in turn yields better performance.

5 Discussion and Conclusions

We presented an approach to improve Arabic TSV using automatic back-translation. We augmented an existing Arabic TSV dataset, ArabGlossBERT, by doubling its size with back-translated data using Google Translate API. To measure the impact of the data augmentation, we presented 13 experiments with different data configurations. Although we did not outperform the overall performance of the baseline model, we did observe that some experiments such as D_6 outperformed the baseline on *noun* positive pair and *verb* negative pair classification. Overall, our results are close to the results presented in (Lin and Giambi, 2021), which used back-translation augmentation for English TSV and achieved only 2% F1-score improvement. Nevertheless, we would like to note the following findings:

- Fine-tuning a BERT model using only the back-translation pairs achieved 77% accuracy (experiment 3), which is only 6% less than the baseline accuracy. This illustrates that the quality of automatic translations of glosses and contexts is not high but is generally acceptable.

- The different augmentations to the original dataset achieved between 78% to 83% accuracy (see experiments 4-9), but it did not outperform the baseline model. At the same time, augmentation did not harm the performance since the results are comparable to the baseline. Nevertheless, experiments 6 and 9 have illustrated a small improvement in the F1-scores for *noun* and *verb* POS. In addition, because D_6 and D_9 are larger than the baseline D_1 dataset, the fine-tuned models are assumed to cover a larger vocabulary and more contexts.

- Looking at the F1-scores, we note that the Positive pairs are always lower than the Negative pairs in all experiments and for all POS categories. This means that all models are less accurate at predicting Positive pairs. Although we tried to augment the dataset by increasing the number of Positive pairs, the F1-scores did not improve.

- In our attempts to fine-tune different models for each POS category, we found that: (1) excluding the pairs of functional words from the dataset (experiment 11) did not improve the performance, and (2) fine-tuning a model for all POS categories allows for cross learning from different POS tagged targets and yields better performance than fine-tuning separate models for *nouns* and *verbs* (experiments 12-13).

6 Limitations and Future Works

Our data augmentation as well as the experiments are based on (1) the quality of Google Translate API, (2) the quality of the glosses and contexts in the ArabGlossBERT training dataset, and most importantly on (3) the quality and coverage of the ArabGlossBERT test dataset. Although the quality of machine translation is limited, the goal of this paper is to measure whether such limited translations can improve the accuracy of the TSV fine-tuned models. Additionally, the quality of the glosses and contexts in the ArabGlossBERT training dataset cannot be improved since they originated from Arabic lexicons. However, we believe that enriching the ArabGlossBERT by collecting more pairs from Arabic lexicons (i.e., building a rich Arabic sense inventory) will empower research on TSV and WSD tasks. More importantly, all experiments conducted in this paper used the ArabGlossBERT test dataset. Since there are no other testing datasets or benchmarks, the evaluation of our fine-tuned models is limited based on the quality and coverage of the ArabGlossBERT test dataset.

Next, we plan to develop another test dataset to evaluate our models and their generalizability. We plan to further explore other approaches for WSD task such as ranking of glosses, rather than addressing the WSD task through TSV.

Acknowledgment

We would like to thank Taymaa Hammouda and Ala Omar for the technical support on many aspects of this research.

References

Moustafa Al-Hajj and Mustafa Jarrar. 2021. Lu-bzu at semeval-2021 task 2: Word2vec and lemma2vec performance in arabic word-in-context disambiguation. In *Proceedings of the 15th International Workshop on Semantic Evaluation (SemEval-2021)*, pages 748–755, Online. Association for Computational Linguistics.

Moustafa Al-Hajj and Mustafa Jarrar. 2022. Arabglossbert: Fine-tuning bert on context-gloss pairs for wsd. In *Proceedings of the International Conference on Recent Advances in Natural Language Processing (RANLP 2021), Held Online, 1-3September, 2021*, pages 35–43.

Wissam Antoun, Fady Baly, and Hazem Hajj. 2020. Arabert: Transformer-based model for arabic language understanding. In *Proceedings of the 4th Workshop on Open-Source Arabic Corpora and Processing Tools, with a Shared Task on Offensive Language Detection*, pages 9–15.

Michele Bevilacqua, Tommaso Pasini, Alessandro Raganato, Roberto Navigli, et al. 2021. Recent trends in word sense disambiguation: A survey. In *Proceedings of the Thirtieth International Joint Conference on Artificial Intelligence, IJCAI-21*, pages 4330–4338.

Jan A Botha, Zifei Shan, and Dan Gillick. 2020. Entity linking in 100 languages. In *Proceedings of the 2020 Conference on Empirical Methods in Natural Language Processing (EMNLP)*, pages 7833–7845.

Anna Breit, Artem Revenko, Kiamehr Rezaee, Mohammad Taher Pilehvar, and Jose Camacho-Collados. 2020. Wic-tsv: An evaluation benchmark for target sense verification of words in context. In *Proceedings of the 16th Conference of the European Chapter of the Association for Computational Linguistics: Main Volume, EACL 2021, Online, April 19 - 23, 2021*, pages 1635–1645.

Kareem Darwish, Nizar Habash, Mourad Abbas, Hend Al-Khalifa, Huseein T. Al-Natsheh, Houda Bouamor, Karim Bouzoubaa, Violetta Cavalli-Sforza, Samhaa R. El-Beltagy, Wassim El-Hajj, Mustafa Jarrar, and Hamdy Mubarak. 2021. A panoramic survey of natural language processing in the arab worlds. *Commun. ACM*, 64(4):72–81.

Erik De Vries, Martijn Schoonvelde, and Gijs Schumacher. 2018. No longer lost in translation: Evidence that google translate works for comparative bag-of-words text applications. *Political Analysis*, 26(4):417–430.

Jacob Devlin, Ming-Wei Chang, Kenton Lee, and Kristina Toutanova. 2019. BERT: Pre-training of deep bidirectional transformers for language understanding. In *Proceedings of the 2019 Conference of the North American Chapter of the Association for Computational Linguistics: Human Language Technologies, Volume 1 (Long and Short Papers)*, pages 4171–4186, Minneapolis, Minnesota. Association for Computational Linguistics.

Mohammed El-Razzaz, Mohamed Waleed Fakhr, and Fahima A Maghraby. 2021. Arabic gloss wsd using bert. *Applied Sciences*, 11(6):2567.

Bradley Hauer and Grzegorz Kondrak. 2022. Wic= tsv= wsd: On the equivalence of three semantic tasks. In *Proceedings of the 2022 Conference of the North American Chapter of the Association for Computational Linguistics: Human Language Technologies, NAACL 2022, Seattle, WA, United States, July 10-15, 2022*, pages 2478–2486.

Luyao Huang, Chi Sun, Xipeng Qiu, and Xuan-Jing Huang. 2019. Glossbert: Bert for word sense disambiguation with gloss knowledge. In *Proceedings of the 2019 Conference on Empirical Methods in Natural Language Processing and the 9th International Joint Conference on Natural Language Processing (EMNLP-IJCNLP)*, pages 3509–3514.

Mustafa Jarrar. 2006. Towards the notion of gloss, and the adoption of linguistic resources in formal ontology engineering. In *Proceedings of the 15th international conference on World Wide Web (WWW2006)*, pages 497–503. ACM Press, New York, NY.

Mustafa Jarrar. 2011. Building a formal arabic ontology (invited paper). In *Proceedings of the Experts Meeting on Arabic Ontologies and Semantic Networks*. ALECSO, Arab League.

Mustafa Jarrar. 2018. Search engine for arabic lexicons. In *Proceedings of the 5th Conference on Translation and the Problematics of Cross-cultural Understanding*. The Forum for Arab and International Relations.

Mustafa Jarrar. 2020. *Digitization of Arabic Lexicons*, pages 214–217. UAE Ministry of Culture and Youth.

Mustafa Jarrar. 2021. The arabic ontology - an arabic wordnet with ontologically clean content. *Applied Ontology Journal*, 16(1):1–26.

Mustafa Jarrar and Hamzeh Amayreh. 2019. An arabic-multilingual database with a lexicographic search engine. In *The 24th International Conference on Applications of Natural Language to Information Systems (NLDB 2019)*, volume 11608 of *LNCS*, pages 234–246. Springer.

Mustafa Jarrar, Hamzeh Amayreh, and John P. McCrae. 2019. Representing arabic lexicons in lemon - a preliminary study. In *The 2nd Conference on Language, Data and Knowledge (LDK 2019)*, volume 2402, pages 29–33. CEUR Workshop Proceedings.

Mustafa Jarrar, Mohammed Khalilia, and Sana Ghanem. 2022. Wojood: Nested arabic named entity corpus and recognition using bert. In *Proceedings of the International Conference on Language Resources and Evaluation (LREC 2022)*, Marseille, France.

Mustafa Jarrar, Fadi Zaraket, Rami Asia, and Hamzeh Amayreh. 2018. Diacritic-based matching of arabic words. *ACM Asian and Low-Resource Language Information Processing*, 18(2):10:1–10:21.

Jacob Devlin Ming-Wei Chang Kenton and Lee Kristina Toutanova. 2019. Bert: Pre-training of deep bidirectional transformers for language understanding. In *Proceedings of NAACL-HLT*, pages 4171–4186.

Guan-Ting Lin and Manuel Giambi. 2021. Context-gloss augmentation for improving word sense disambiguation. *arXiv preprint arXiv:2110.07174*, abs/2110.07174.

George A Miller, Claudia Leacock, Randee Tengi, and Ross T Bunker. 1993. A semantic concordance. In *Human Language Technology: Proceedings of a Workshop Held at Plainsboro, New Jersey, March 21-24, 1993*.

Jose G Moreno, Elvys Linhares Pontes, and Gaël Dias. 2021. Ctlr@ wic-tsv: Target sense verification using marked inputs andpre-trained models. In *Proceedings of the 6th Workshop on Semantic Deep Learning (SemDeep-6)*, pages 1–6.

Nikhil Patel, James Hale, Kanika Jindal, Apoorva Sharma, and Yichun Yu. 2021. Building on huang et al. glossbert for word sense disambiguation. *arXiv preprint arXiv:2112.07089*, abs/2112.07089.

Niloofar Ranjbar and Hossein Zeinali. 2021. Lotus at semeval-2021 task 2: Combination of bert and paraphrasing for english word sense disambiguation. In *Proceedings of the 15th International Workshop on Semantic Evaluation (SemEval-2021)*, pages 724–729.

Boon Peng Yap, Andrew Koh, and Eng Siong Chng. 2020. Adapting bert for word sense disambiguation with gloss selection objective and example sentences. In *Findings of the Association for Computational Linguistics: EMNLP 2020*, pages 41–46.

The Open Cantonese Sense-Tagged Corpus

Joanna Ut-Seong Sio
Palacký University Olomouc
The Czech Republic
joannautseong.sio@upol.cz

Luis Morgado da Costa
Vrije Universiteit Amsterdam
The Netherlands
lmorgado.dacosta@gmail.com

Abstract

This paper introduces the Open Cantonese Sense-Tagged Corpus, a new and ongoing project to serve as the companion to the development of the Cantonese Wordnet. This corpus is built on top of the Cantonese Wordnet Corpus, which currently provides example sentences for most verbs in this wordnet. This paper motivates the choice of starting a sense-tagged corpus from both linguistic and educational perspectives, and discusses the current solutions to issues arisen from the sense-tagging exercise. In total, we have tagged over 5,000 concepts, with more than 3,700 direct links to the Cantonese Wordnet.

1 Introduction

This paper presents the first sense-tagged corpus for Cantonese, an open corpus being built with and alongside the development of the Cantonese Wordnet (Sio and Morgado da Costa, 2019).

Sense annotation is the task of pairing a corpus with a semantic lexicon, by linking every *substantive* word in the corpus to its correct sense (as represented in the lexicon). This kind of annotation can help identify a variety of problems in the lexicon, such as missing senses or indistinguishable definitions, and hence helps improve both the coverage and the precision of the lexicon being used in the annotation (Miller et al., 1993). And it can also contribute to the concept of attestation, which is becoming a common requirement in most large lexicographic projects. [1]

While building sense annotated corpora is an extremely time-consuming task, building better language resources (both corpora and lexicons) addresses some of the ever-increasing needs required to solve complex Natural Language Processing problems such as information retrieval, machine translation, and automatic summarization.

The earliest project attempting to do sense annotation with wordnets was SemCor (Landes et al., 1998), a companion corpus to the Princeton Wordnet (PWN, Fellbaum, 1998) – the first wordnet, and the first sense-tagged corpus. Since then, a large number of wordnets started to emerge, alongside similar sense-tagged corpora. A good summary of the existing work in this field can be found in Petrolito and Bond (2014), which reports finding more than 20 sense-annotated corpora using wordnets, in more than 10 different languages.

In addition to the reasons stated above, which would already be sufficient, our project is also motivated from an educational standpoint. Despite being widely spoken, many scholarly efforts often seem to forgo Cantonese in preference to other varieties of Chinese (e.g., Mandarin). This project is one more contribution to support this language's maintenance and preservation. We believe that, if planned properly, sense annotated corpora can serve as excellent resources for language education – especially if the data being sense-tagged is suitable to be used in educational contexts. This is also why we chose to start the annotation using the Cantonese Wordnet Corpus (Sio and Morgado da Costa, 2022) – which comprises hand-crafted examples from a variety of day-to-day, modern and culturally-appropriate contexts.

2 Methodology

This paper reports an experiment that sense-tagged 300 random sentences extracted from the Cantonese Wordnet Corpus. These sentences were segmented manually by a native Cantonese speaker studying linguistics, and revised by a second native speaker who is a senior linguist. We are aware that the notion of 'word' is a contentious issue in Chinese languages (including Cantonese) (Packard, 2000). The native speakers were instructed to segment sentences (into words) based on their intuition, while taking into consideration both on-

[1] See, e.g., `https://en.wiktionary.org/wiki/Wiktionary:Criteria_for_inclusion#Attestation`

going linguistic discussion on Chinese wordhood (e.g., freedom-of-parts, semantic and structural non-compositionality, etc., Chu-Ren et al., 2017), and previous decisions made in the process of building the Cantonese Wordnet.

The tagging is being carried out by a single native Cantonese speaker lexicographer, but annotation issues and solutions are frequently discussed with the maintainers of the Cantonese Wordnet.

We are currently using IMI – a multilingual semantic annotation environment (Bond et al., 2015)[2]. IMI was designed for multilingual sense annotation. But in addition to sense-tagging, it provides multiple layers of annotation that include lemmatization, POS tagging, sentiment annotation and interlingual-mapping. This annotation tool has been tested for a wide selection of languages (i.e., English, Mandarin, Japanese and Indonesian) while tagging the NTU Multilingual Corpus (Tan and Bond, 2014; Bond et al., 2013) – a project that heavily influenced our corpus.

IMI uses an interface to the Open Multilingual Wordnet (OMW, Bond and Foster, 2013) to show candidate senses for concepts in the corpus. Fig. 1 shows an example of how our corpus is being created. In addition to data from the Cantonese Wordnet, we also rely on data from PWN and the Chinese Open Wordnet (COW, Wang and Bond, 2013) to find the right concepts.

Because we considered this preliminary work an exercise to fool-proof future annotation efforts, we decided to tag concepts sequentially, as they appear in a sentence, instead of relying on more efficient annotation methods such as tagging all instances of the same concept all at once (see Wang and Bond, 2014).

Clicking on a word in the corpus generates a web form upon which the lexicographer can make a decision based on existing senses in the wordnet. In the example shown in Fig. 1 we see an attempt to tag the word '會' wui5 (highlighted in yellow, around the middle of the figure). This word could be tagged as any of three concepts currently in the Cantonese Wordnet (numbered from 1 to 3, on the right side). In this case, the correct tag is the concept number 3, which is shown by the selection of the appropriate bullet on the left side, below the main text. In addition to the senses provided by the wordnet, the annotator has a few other options to choose from:

- the tag **e** notes that there is some sort of error in the corpus. This can be a segmentation or orthographic mistake, or an idiomatic but separable multi-word expression – which failed to generate automatically;
- the tag **x** is used for words that should not be sense-tagged. Currently, this is only being used for punctuation. In previous projects this tag was used, e.g., to tag determiners or auxiliary verbs in English. However, with the move to adding more and more parts-of-speech to wordnets such as pronouns, interjections and classifiers (see: Seah and Bond, 2014; Morgado da Costa and Bond, 2016), this tag is used less and less;
- the tag **w** notes that the wordnet is missing the right concept to tag the word in question. In cases where the OMW hierarchy has the right concept but the Cantonese Wordnet was missing a sense, we add the missing sense using OMWEdit (Morgado da Costa and Bond, 2015) – a tool integrated into IMI which allows editing a wordnet on the fly. However, even though this tool also allows adding new concepts to the semantic hierarchy, we decided not to use this feature for the moment (see Section 4);
- the tags **Org**, **Loc**, **Per**, **Dat**, **Oth**, **Num**, and **Year** are used to tag named entities and other productive expressions (e.g., dates, time expressions) that cannot be found in the wordnet;[3]

3 Tagging Results and Release

The results from the tagging exercise are summarized in Table 1. In total, the 300 sentences discussed in the section above generated a total of 5,279 candidate concepts. This number closely reflects the work done for segmentation, where each word was considered a possible concept. The tagged corpus contains 3,728 concepts linked to the Cantonese Wordnet.

The remaining lines in Table 1 should be interpreted with reference to the discussion of Fig. 1, above. In summary, the lexicographer identified 196 errors in the corpus – comprising segmentation errors, orthographic mistakes, and instances of separable idiomatic expressions – all of which will

[2] `https://github.com/bond-lab/IMI`

[3] A fuller guide on how to use these tags can be found in: `https://github.com/bond-lab/IMI/blob/develop/docs/tagdoc.html`

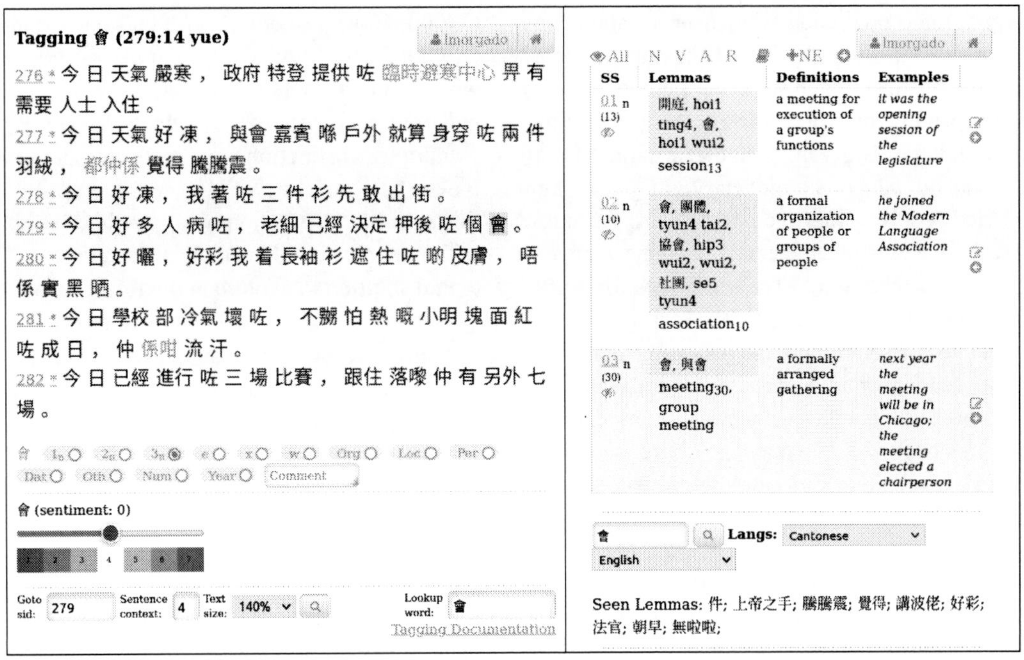

Figure 1: IMI's "Sentence Tagger" mode, in Cantonese

be further discussed in the section below. There were 658 instances where the concept was not contentful (currently only punctuation is tagged with *x*). And our corpus identified 461 instances of a missing concept in the OMW hierarchy (provided by PWN). This number excludes cases where only a sense was missing from and added to the Cantonese Wordnet – which happened 709 times.

The remainder of Table 1 shows the number of named entities found in the corpus, as well as a small amount of tags under *Other* which are currently being used to capture the use of foreign words within the corpus. Problems surrounding the use of 'foreign words', which are a mix of code-switching and loanwords, will be further discussed in the section below.

Finally, Table 1 also shows that 1,239 distinct concepts were used to tag the 3,729 contentful concepts in the corpus. This is a useful measure to show that there is a considerable semantic overlap between example sentences.

This sense-tagged corpus will be released as part of the Cantonese Wordnet Corpus, which will be released in the Cantonese Wordnet's main Github repository.[4] New senses added to the Cantonese Wordnet will be included in following releases.

Tag Type	No. of Concepts
Cantonese Wordnet	3,728
Errors in the corpus (*e*)	196
No need to tag (*x*)	658
Missing Concepts (*w*)	461
Named Organization (*org*)	79
Named Location (*loc*)	24
Named Person (*per*)	40
Number (*num*)	18
Other (*oth*)	75
Total	5,279
Distinct Concepts	1,239

Table 1: Summary of Annotation

4 Discussion and Future Work

We have encountered several noteworthy issues during the segmentation process: (i) missing concepts in the PWN; (ii) lack of distinction of senses in Cantonese; (iii) separable verbs; (iv) errors in segmentation; and (v) Other

There are many concepts that are unique to Hong Kong culture, which are (understandably) missing in the Princeton WordNet.[5] For example, '籤' cim1 refers to a piece of paper with an arbi-

[4] https://github.com/lmorgadodacosta/CantoneseWN

[5] The Cantonese Wordnet is currently built based on Hong Kong Cantonese, though in the future we plan to include also variations in different varieties of Cantonese.

trary fortune prediction written on it, something you receive in a temple by first shaking a cylindrical tube of sticks. Each stick has a unique number and depending on which stick comes out, a different prediction is given. Another example is '利是' lai6 si6, which is a monetary gift given to unmarried people by married people, during Chinese New Year and in other special occasions to anyone (married or otherwise). The same goes for typical Cantonese dishes, such as '乾炒牛河' gon1 caau2 ngau4 ho2. Even though the dish name can be decomposed into smaller meaningful units (i.e., dry-fried-beef-rice noodles), it is not just any dish that stir-fries beef with rice noodles. There is a region-based expectation as to how the dish should look like. Thus, the term is somewhat idiomatic and should be listed. There are also names for common products in Hong Kong which need to be added, e.g., '八達通' baat3 daat6 tung1, of which the official English name is 'Octopus Card' in Hong Kong. It is a reusable stored-value smart card that can be used for all kinds of electronic payment. All these concepts should and will soon be added to the Cantonese Wordnet. As mentioned above, we decided to hold off on adding new concepts for now. This decision was based on the upcoming release of the Collaborative Interlingual Index (Bond et al., 2016, CILI) – an open, language agnostic, flat-structured index that links wordnets across languages without imposing the hierarchy of any single wordnet. We would like the creation of the new concepts to happen already within CILI's context, in order to avoid having to redo this work later.

There are also many concepts which are not culturally/societally bounded, but are unique to the language. For example, '成' sing4 is the equivalent of 10%, a concept that is missing in the PWN. Other more common instances are Cantonese functional elements, such as classifiers, post-verbal particles, sentence-final particles, conjunction, prepositons, etc. The current version of the Cantonese Wordnet already has concepts for 32 post-verbal particles and 41 sortal classifiers, but more are needed.

There are cases where OMW/PWN has a much-finer sense distinction than in Cantonese – e.g., the 3rd person singular pronoun is 佢 keoi5 in Cantonese, which is not specified for gender. It is now mapped three times to the OMW[6]: to 'he/him' (77000046-n), 'she/her' (77000041-n) and 'it' (77000053-n). Another example is '多' do1, which can mean both 'numerous' (01552419-a) and 'much' (01553629-a). In other words, the count/mass distinction is not reflected in the Cantonese '多' do1. As of now, we attempt to keep this semantic distinction by tagging '多' with one of the two synsets, depending on the context. A potential solution to explore in the future is to merge synsets for senses that are not distinguished.

Many verbs in Cantonese contain two parts/characters, and they are separable in the sense that a post-verbal particle can be inserted in-between the two characters. And since the two parts are non-consecutive in the corpus (with a particle in-between), they couldn't easily be tagged as one concept without manually creating a multi-word expression. For example, '跳舞' tiu3 mou5 means 'dance' (or literally 'dance a dance') should probably be mapped to the synset for 'dance' (01894649-v) but, in the corpus, the two characters were separated by the Cantonese perfective particle '咗' (zo2). Our current solution is to tag each of characters by its literal meaning if there is some level of compositionality (even if not very strong). In this case, '跳' is tagged as the verb 'dance' (01894649-v) and '舞' is tagged as the noun 'dance' (00428270-n), functioning like a cognate object. In the future, when we add these multi-word expressions as concepts, we would like to explore keeping the two levels of annotation (with the example '跳舞' tiu3 mou5, it would be mapped as a multi-word expression to the synset of 'dance' as well as decompositonally as 'dance a dance'), since this could end up being useful for future research.

Examples where two or more characters of an idiomatic separable expression could not preserve any of its meaning if tagged literally include '挖角' waat3 gok3, which means 'headhunt'. Literally, the first character means 'dig' and the second character means 'horn'. The meaning of 'headhunt' is idiomatic. In such cases, we have marked both characters as 'errors' (as in the corpus, the two characters are not consecutive and are separated by an aspectual particle) while noting that as a whole it has an idiomatic reading. In the future, we would like to tag these cases as multi-word expressions.

Our corpus also contained some segmentation errors where the already segmented unit should be

[6]These three synsets are not officially part of the PWN, but are introduced by the OMW's pronoun expansion introduced by Seah and Bond (2014)

further segmented. The expression '今次' gam1 ci3 'this time', for example, can be further segmented into '今' (a proximal demonstrative used in classical Chinese but still appears with various nouns bearing the same meaning) and '次', which means 'time' as in 'an instance or single occasion for some event'. Given their frequency, we plan to fix many of these errors semi-automatically.

Another less common error type found in our corpus were orthographic mistakes. These are cases where a wrong character has been used when the corpus was crafted. These will have to be hand-corrected.

One final note worthy of discussion is the fact that Hong Kong Cantonese, in natural speech, contains a lot of English loanwords and instances of code switching. This is easy to understand since Hong Kong was under British rule for more than 150 years and because it still preserves English as one of its official languages. This is also reflected in our corpus (e.g., 'meet 到 target', with '到' dou2 as a post-verbal particle expressing accomplishment or successful completion of an action; the selected segment means 'succeed in meeting the target'). In such cases, the English words are tagged as 'Other', and a comment marks them as foreign words ('FW'). In the future we will need to take a closer look at these cases and decide whether there is enough reason to include some of these words as part of the Cantonese Wordnet (other examples in our corpus include 'boxing', 'sem' as in 'semester', 'app', among many others), or if we should continue to consider them as foreign words. Deciding whether specific cases are instances of loanwords or code-switching will ultimately determine the treatment these words deserve in our project. If deemed as instances of code-switching, words can most probably be either ignored or should be tagged using the a wordnet for the code-switched language (e.g., PWN, for English). However, whenever deemed as loanwords, these words should be considered as an intrinsic part of the Cantonese lexicon, and must be included in the Cantonese Wordnet (e.g., similar to how 'kindergarten' is part of the PWN, even though it is clear from its orthography that it was borrowed from German).

In addition to further researching and addressing the points raised above, we have plans to continue expanding the Cantonese Wordnet corpus by incorporating freely available data useful for educational purposes. Two such projects include Hambaanglaang,[7] a collection of open Cantonese resources created by volunteers and Tatoeba,[8] a multilingual collection of freely available sentences compiled specifically for second language learners. More specifically, we would like to adapt experiments such as the one presented in Bond et al. (2021). In this work, sense tagging is used as a tool to teach lexical semantics, and we believe similar experiments could be set for second language learners – e.g., by inviting learners of Cantonese to tag very basic texts in an attempt to help them recognize multiple senses of individual words.

5 Conclusion

This paper presented the Open Cantonese Sense-Tagged Corpus, an ongoing project seeking to improve the Cantonese Wordnet and the digital viability of Cantonese through the creation of a sense-tagged corpus.

The sense tagging process is demanding and yet useful in building linguistic sensitivity to lexical meaning and to discover interesting linguistic phenomena. We hope the work in our corpus will inspire further linguistic research for Cantonese.

In this preliminary experiment, we have tagged more than 5,000 concepts and, with it, we have raised our awareness for some key-issues that must be addressed before proceeding further. We are determined to continue pursuing this project and, with it, also continue to improve the Cantonese Wordnet.

Acknowledgments

The research described here is supported by the European Regional Development Fund - Project 'Sinophone Borderlands - Interaction at the Edges' CZ.02.1.01/0.0/0.0/16_019/0000791 and by the European Union's Horizon 2020 research and innovation programme under the Marie Skłodowska-Curie grant agreement H2020-MSCA-IF-2020 CHILL – No.101028782. We would also like to thank Dennis Ngai Wa Lam for helping with the segmentation work.

References

Francis Bond and Ryan Foster. 2013. Linking and extending an Open Multilingual Wordnet. In *51st An-*

[7] https://hambaanglaang.hk/

[8] https://tatoeba.org/en/

nual Meeting of the Association for Computational Linguistics: ACL-2013, Sofia, pages 1352–1362.

Francis Bond, Andrew Kirkrose Devadason, Rui Lin Melissa Teo, and Luis Morgado Da Costa. 2021. Teaching through tagging —interactive lexical semantics. In *Proceedings of the 11th Global WordNet Conference (GWC 2021)*, Pretoria, South Africa. Global Wordnet Association.

Francis Bond, Luís Morgado da Costa, and Tuan Anh Le. 2015. IMI – A multilingual semantic annotation environment. In *Proceedings of the 53rd Annual Meeting of the Association for Computational Linguistics and the 7th International Joint Conference on Natural Language Processing of the Asian Federation of Natural Language Processing, System Demonstrations (ACL 2015)*, pages 7–12, Beijing, China.

Francis Bond, Piek Vossen, John Philip McCrae, and Christiane Fellbaum. 2016. Cili: the collaborative interlingual index. In *Proceedings of the 8th Global WordNet Conference (GWC)*, pages 50–57.

Francis Bond, Shan Wang, Eshley Huini Gao, Hazel Shuwen Mok, and Jeanette Yiwen Tan. 2013. Developing parallel sense-tagged corpora with wordnets. In *Proceedings of the 7th Linguistic Annotation Workshop and Interoperability with Discourse*, pages 149–158.

Huang Chu-Ren, Hsieh Shu-Kai, and Chen Keh-Jiann. 2017. *Mandarin Chinese words and parts of speech: A corpus-based study*. Routledge.

Christiane Fellbaum, editor. 1998. *WordNet: An Electronic Lexical Database*. MIT Press, Cambridge, MA.

Shari Landes, Claudia Leacock, and Randee I Tengi. 1998. Building semantic concordances. *WordNet: An electronic lexical database*, 199(216):199–216.

George A Miller, Claudia Leacock, Randee Tengi, and Ross T Bunker. 1993. A semantic concordance. In *Human Language Technology: Proceedings of a Workshop Held at Plainsboro, New Jersey, March 21-24, 1993*.

Luís Morgado da Costa and Francis Bond. 2015. Omwedit - the integrated open multilingual wordnet editing system. In *Proceedings of the 53rd Annual Meeting of the Association for Computational Linguistics and the 7th International Joint Conference on Natural Language Processing of the Asian Federation of Natural Language Processing, System Demonstrations (ACL 2015)*, pages 73–78, Beijing, China.

Luís Morgado da Costa and Francis Bond. 2016. Wow! what a useful extension! introducing non-referential concepts to wordnet. In *Proceedings of the 10th edition of the International Conference on Language Resources and Evaluation (LREC 2016), Portorož, Slovenia*.

Jerome L Packard. 2000. *The morphology of Chinese: A linguistic and cognitive approach*. Cambridge University Press.

Tommaso Petrolito and Francis Bond. 2014. A survey of wordnet annotated corpora. In *Proceedings of the Seventh Global WordNet Conference*, pages 236–245.

Yu Jie Seah and Francis Bond. 2014. Annotation of pronouns in a multilingual corpus of mandarin chinese, english and japanese. In *Proceedings of the 10th Joint ISO-ACL SIGSEM Workshop on Interoperable Semantic Annotation*.

Joanna Ut-Seong Sio and Luis Morgado da Costa. 2019. Building the cantonese wordnet. In *Proceedings of the 10th Global Wordnet Conference (GWC 2019), Wroclaw, Poland*.

Joanna Ut-Seong Sio and Luis Morgado da Costa. 2022. Enriching linguistic representation in the cantonese wordnet and building the new cantonese wordnet corpus. In *Proceedings of the 13th Conference on Language Resources and Evaluation*, Marseille, France. European Language Resources Association (ELRA).

Liling Tan and Francis Bond. 2014. NTU-MC toolkit: Annotating a linguistically diverse corpus. In *Proceedings of COLING 2014, the 25th International Conference on Computational Linguistics: System Demonstrations*, page 86–89, Dublin.

Shan Wang and Francis Bond. 2013. Building the Chinese Open Wordnet (COW): Starting from core synsets. In *Proceedings of the 11th Workshop on Asian Language Resources, a Workshop at IJCNLP-2013*, pages 10–18, Nagoya.

Shan Wang and Francis Bond. 2014. Building the sense-tagged multilingual parallel corpus. In *Proceedings of the Ninth International Conference on Language Resources and Evaluation (LREC'14)*, Reykjavik, Iceland. European Language Resources Association (ELRA).

Correcting Sense Annotations Using Wordnets and Translations

Arnob Mallik and **Grzegorz Kondrak**
Alberta Machine Intelligence Institute
Department of Computing Science
University of Alberta, Edmonton, Canada
{amallik,gkondrak}@ualberta.ca

Abstract

Acquiring large amounts of high-quality annotated data is an open issue in word sense disambiguation. This problem has become more critical recently with the advent of supervised models based on neural networks, which require large amounts of annotated data. We propose two algorithms for making selective corrections on a sense-annotated parallel corpus, based on cross-lingual synset mappings. We show that, when applied to bilingual parallel corpora, these algorithms can rectify noisy sense annotations, and thereby produce multilingual sense-annotated data of improved quality.

1 Introduction

Word sense disambiguation (WSD) is the task of identifying the appropriate meaning of a word in context, from a predefined sense inventory, such as WordNet (Miller, 1995) and BabelNet (Navigli and Ponzetto, 2012). It is one of the central problems in natural language understanding (Navigli, 2018). The primary approaches to tackle the WSD problem can be divided into supervised and knowledge-based methods. Supervised WSD systems have historically achieved the best overall results on standard WSD datasets (Raganato et al., 2017). However, these systems rely on large amounts of sense-annotated data for training, which is costly and difficult to produce. In particular, there is a severe lack of high-quality annotated data for languages other than English, which is known as the *knowledge acquisition bottleneck problem* (Pasini, 2020). To address this issue, various approaches have been proposed to automate the process of annotating texts in different languages at a large scale.

Some of the automated annotation approaches operate by leveraging translations from parallel corpora. The idea of using translations for WSD was considered by Resnik and Yarowsky (1997), based on the conjecture that different translations of an ambiguous source word in a target language could serve as sense-tagged training examples. This idea was put into practice by Ng et al. (2003), and then on a large scale by Chan and Ng (2005), as they implemented a semi-automatic approach of disambiguating English nouns using distinct Chinese translations, leveraged from an English-Chinese parallel corpora. Taghipour and Ng (2015) used a similar semi-automatic approach to create a WSD training set by leveraging the Chinese-English part of the MultiUN corpus (Eisele and Chen, 2010). Delli Bovi et al. (2017) removed the bottleneck of manual intervention, as they proposed a fully automated approach of producing multilingual sense-tagged corpora by jointly disambiguating multiple languages of a parallel corpus.

Our work is inspired by the central idea of the aforementioned research that translations may provide the necessary information to disambiguate an ambiguous word. However, we focus on leveraging translations to improve the quality of an already sense-tagged parallel corpus, rather than to annotate the corpus from scratch. We propose two algorithms for correcting sense annotations in a parallel corpus. The first algorithm attempts to rectify aligned senses that belong to different multisynsets. The second algorithm considers all alignment links in a bitext to construct a one-to-one mapping between synsets in different languages. Both algorithms are based on the theory of synonymy and translational equivalence of Hauer and Kondrak (2020).

We empirically show that our algorithms achieve their goal of improving the quality of sense annotations in multiple languages. We extrinsically evaluate the proposed corrections by providing the corrected corpora as training data to a supervised WSD system. An intrinsic evaluation on a random sample of 200 corrected instances in English and Spanish confirms the improvement in the overall quality of the annotated corpora.

2 MultiWordNet (MWN) Algorithm

Algorithm 1 MWN

Input : set of aligned sense pairs (s, t)
$lex(s)$ - word of which s is a sense
$M(s)$ - multi-synset that contains sense s
$\mathcal{M}(w)$ - set of multi-synsets that contain word w

1: **for each** aligned sense pair (s, t) **do**
2:   **if** $M(s) \neq M(t)$ **then**
3:     $\mathcal{C} \leftarrow \mathcal{M}(lex(s)) \cap \mathcal{M}(lex(t))$
4:     **if** $M(s) \in \mathcal{C}$ **and** $M(t) \notin \mathcal{C}$ **then**
5:       CORRECT: $t \leftarrow (lex(t), M(s))$
6:     **if** $M(s) \notin \mathcal{C}$ **and** $M(t) \in \mathcal{C}$ **then**
7:       CORRECT: $s \leftarrow (lex(s), M(t))$

The MWN algorithm (Algorithm 1) is based on the simplifying assumption that the senses of aligned words are translationally equivalent (Hauer and Kondrak, 2020). The algorithm consults an existing multilingual wordnet (*multi-wordnet*) which is composed of multilingual synsets (*multi-synsets*) that include translationally-equivalent senses of words from both languages. Each polysemous word belongs to multiple multi-synsets. If the senses of the aligned words are found to belong to different multi-synsets, this is an indication of a possible annotation error that could be corrected.

The algorithm operates on a sense-annotated parallel corpus (*bitext*). It performs annotation corrections on individual aligned word pairs (line 1) which are annotated with different multi-synsets (line 2). Each sense in a multi-wordnet is uniquely defined as a (word, synset) tuple. When applied to a sense, the *lex* and M operators return the first and second element of the tuple, respectively. We denote as $\mathcal{C}$ the set of all multi-synsets that contains both aligned words (Line 3).

The algorithm is designed to make selective corrections only in those alignment instances where there is little doubt about the appropriate correction. At most one of the two sense annotations in each instance can be corrected. A correction is made if and only if *exactly one* of the two aligned senses is found in $\mathcal{C}$ (lines 4-7). We do not attempt a correction if either both or none of the two senses are in $\mathcal{C}$. If both senses are outside of $\mathcal{C}$, we suspect multiple errors in bitext annotations and/or the multi-wordnet. On the other hand, if both senses are within of $\mathcal{C}$, it is not clear which of the two annotations may be incorrect.

3 Bipartite (BP) Algorithm

Algorithm 2 BP

Input : set of aligned sense pairs (s, t)
$lex(s)$ - word of which s is a sense
$S(s)$ - synset that contains sense s
$\mathcal{S}(w)$ - set of synsets that contain word w

G $\leftarrow \varnothing$
for each aligned sense pair (s, t) **do**
  $weight(S(s), S(t))$++
  $weight(S(s))$++
  $weight(S(t))$++

$G' \leftarrow \varnothing$
for each edge $(S_1, S_2) \in G$ **do**
  if $weight(S_1, S_2) \div weight(S_1) > \alpha$ **and**
    $weight(S_1, S_2) \div weight(S_2) > \alpha$ **then**
    $G' \leftarrow G' \cup (S_1, S_2)$

for each aligned sense pair (s, t) **do**
  if $(S(s), S(t)) \notin G'$ **then**
    for each $S' \in \mathcal{S}(lex(t))$ **do**
      if $(S(s), S') \in G'$ **then**
        CORRECT: $t \leftarrow (lex(t), S')$

The BP algorithm (Algorithm 2) is also based on the assumption that the aligned words should express exactly the same concept. However, it differs from the MWN algorithm in that it globally considers all the alignment links in a given bitext, and makes annotation corrections based on the most frequently observed links. Another difference is that BP only corrects the annotations in language L_2, based on the annotations in the *base language* L_1, which are assumed to be always correct. The algorithm is inspired by the *concept universality principle* of Hauer and Kondrak (2020) which states that each each monolingual synset corresponds to at most one synset in another language. No access to a multi-wordnet is assumed; instead the algorithm consults two language-specific wordnets, which are composed of monolingual synsets, rather than of multi-synsets.

The BP algorithm consists of three stages: (1) construct a bipartite graph G of synsets; (2) identify its subgraph G' of degree 1; and (3) correct sense annotations that are not found in subgraph G'. In fact, the first two stages constitute a stand-alone algorithm for creating a cross-lingual mapping between synsets. We describe the three stages in more detail below.

In the first stage (lines 1-5), we construct a *weighted undirected bipartite graph* $G = (V, E, weight)$ in which nodes represent monolingual synsets, and edges represent alignment links that are observed in the bitext. The weight of an edge is equal to the number of the observed alignment links in the bitext between the senses of the corresponding synsets. The weight of a node is simply the sum of the weights of all edges incident with the node, which is equal to the number of times the corresponding synset is used in aligned sense annotations in the bitext.

In the second stage (lines 6-10), we construct a graph $G' = (V, E')$, which is a subgraph of G, such that every node has a degree of at most 1. The goal is to select the edges that represent the most frequent alignments. This is achieved by only retaining the edges with the relative weight above a threshold α (lines 8-9) in both directions. The threshold is constrained to be greater than 0.5, to guarantee that at most one edge per node is selected.

In the third stage (lines 11-15), annotation corrections are made based on the edges of the constructed bipartite graph G'. Unlike the MWN algorithm, the BP algorithm only corrects the annotations of words in language L_2. If an edge corresponding to a given alignment link is not found in G' (line 12), it attempts to correct the annotation in L_2 by following the edge in G' between the node $S(s)$, which represents the synset used to annotate the word in L_1, and the node S', which represents the synset in L_2 that expresses the same concept as $S(s)$.

4 Extrinsic WSD Evaluation

To extrinsically evaluate the algorithms, we apply them to *EuroSense* (Delli Bovi et al., 2017), an automatically constructed sense-annotated resource based on the *EuroParl* parallel corpus (Koehn, 2005). In EuroSense, words (which include non-compositional MWEs) are tagged with multilingual synsets from BabelNet 4.0 (Navigli and Ponzetto, 2012), and accompanied by their respective lemmatized forms.

We extract four sentence-aligned bitexts from EuroSense, by considering four different language pairs: English-Italian (EN-IT), English-German (EN-DE), English-French (EN-FR) and English-Spanish (EN-ES). We employ BABALIGN (Luan et al., 2020) to align the bitexts at the word level; the aligned word or phrase of each annotated token is taken as its translation.

Bitext	Sense Pairs	MWN	BP
EN → IT	4,713,589	541,326	82,685
EN → FR	5,219,146	664,253	106,023
EN → DE	3,083,325	179,400	59,446
EN → ES	5,015,140	518,488	92,634
IT → EN	4,713,589	235,087	89,798

Table 1: Number of sense corrections made by both algorithms.

The annotated translation pairs in EuroSense are filtered to remove non-existent senses, non-literal translations, and hypernym translations. A sense of a word is considered non-existent if it is not found in the respective BabelNet synset. If the aligned words have no synsets in common, they are treated as non-literal translations. Finally, we detect non-synonymous translations pairs by traversing hypernymy and hyponymy links in BabelNet (Hauer et al., 2020). In our development experiments, we found that approximately 3% of the pairs contain invalid senses, 13% are cases of non-literal translations. and 5% involve word entailment.

Following this filtering procedure, the remaining translation pairs are used as inputs to both algorithms to perform annotation corrections for each language separately. The BP threshold α is set to 0.8 on the basis of the development experiments. For IT, DE, FR and ES corrections, we use English as the base language. To perform EN corrections, we use Italian as the base language as it is reported to have good BabelNet coverage (Hauer et al., 2020). 75.3% of the English-Italian synset mappings returned by the BP algorithm match BabelNet concepts. Table 1 contains dataset and correction statistics for each of the five languages. The arrows in the leftmost column point from the base language to the corrected language.

We extrinsically evaluate the corrections by providing the corrected corpora as training data for a supervised WSD system, which is then evaluated on standard benchmark datasets. To this end, we employ IMS (Zhong and Ng, 2010), a supervised WSD system based on lexical features. To keep the corpus at a reasonable size, we consider a maximum of 10,000 randomly sampled training examples per sense. For English, in cases where

Train Set	Test Set							
	SemEval 2015			SemEval 2013				
	EN	IT	ES	EN	IT	FR	DE	ES
EuroSense	64.3	56.3	54.3	65.3	56.5	45.4	58.8	53.9
+ MWN	65.1	57.1	**55.3**	65.5	**58.3**	**48.0**	**60.0**	**56.7**
+ BP	64.5	**57.2**	**55.3**	65.4	56.7	45.9	59.1	54.1

Table 2: WSD F-score (%) of IMS trained on different corpora. A boldfaced result indicates a statistically significant improvement.

Lang.	Algorithm	original correct	algorithm correct	neither correct
English	MWN	6	**18**	26
	BP	12	18	20
Spanish	MWN	11	**33**	6
	BP	17	20	13

Table 3: Intrinsic evaluation results. A boldfaced result indicates a statistically significant improvement.

the system fails to make a prediction, we back off to the most frequent sense. For all languages, any monosemous words are automatically tagged with their single possible sense.

Table 2 presents the WSD results of IMS models trained on the corrected corpora, along with the results of models trained on the original EuroSense corpus. The evaluation is performed on benchmark multilingual datasets from SemEval-2013 task 12 (Navigli et al., 2013) and SemEval-2015 task 13 (Moro and Navigli, 2015). The results show that IMS achieves better results when trained on the corrected corpora. The MWN improvements are statistically significant ($p < 0.05$ using McNemar's test) over the results obtained by the original corpus for all languages except English. The BP improvements are smaller but consistent. This verifies the utility of the annotation corrections made by two algorithms when the information is transferred from English to less-resourced languages.

5 Intrinsic Evaluation

To intrinsically evaluate the quality of the sense annotation corrections made by the algorithms, a random sample of 200 English and Spanish instances were annotated manually. For each instance, an annotator was shown the corresponding sentence from EuroSense, and asked to decide whether the focus word is used in the original or the corrected sense (or neither). The senses were defined using BabelNet glosses and synonyms. and provided in a random order.

The results in Table 3 indicate that both algorithms improve the quality of the annotations in both languages. The improvements are statistically significant for the MWN algorithm ($p < 0.05$ with McNemar's test).

The wrong corrections may be grouped into three types:

Incomplete multi-synsets Many BabelNet synsets do not contain all possible lexicalizations of the concept that it represents. For example, the synset *bn:00109131a*, which is glossed in English as "related to the future", contains the Spanish adjective *futuro* but not its English translation *future*. Such omissions, which are frequent in BabelNet because of its semi-automatic construction method, prevent the MWN algorithm from making a correction.

Noise in the bitext The English-German bitext slice of EuroSense contains a total of 19,230 distinct English synsets, among which only 10,661 (55%) have matching German synsets in the dataset. This implies that nearly half of concepts represented in English are not expressed by German words, which makes it impossible to match concepts across languages. The issue may be related to the high frequency of nominal compound words in German, which are often translated as multi-word expressions in English (e.g., *Versicherungskaufmann* "insurance salesman").

Excessive granularity of senses Some instances involved a choice between fine-grained senses. For example, in the Spanish phrase *"la conclusión real de este fin de semana"* ("the actual conclusion of this weekend") the annotator found it difficult to decide whether the Spanish noun *conclusión* is used in the sense of "the temporal end; the concluding time" or "a concluding action."

6 Conclusion

Our extrinsic and intrinsic evaluation results constitute a strong proof-of-concept that translations and wordnets can be leveraged to make effective annotation corrections in a sense-annotated bitext. Manual analysis indicates that most of the invalid corrections can be traced to errors and omissions in existing lexical resources. In the future, we plan to investigate the use of machine translation instead of bitexts for the purpose of automatically annotating raw monolingual text corpora.

Acknowledgments

We thank Eduardo Montemayor Castillo and Dawn McKnight for help with manual annotation, We thank Bradley Hauer for comments on the final version of the paper.

This research was supported by the Natural Sciences and Engineering Research Council of Canada (NSERC), and the Alberta Machine Intelligence Institute (Amii).

References

Yee Seng Chan and Hwee Tou Ng. 2005. Scaling up word sense disambiguation via parallel texts. In *AAAI*, volume 5, pages 1037–1042.

Claudio Delli Bovi, Jose Camacho-Collados, Alessandro Raganato, and Roberto Navigli. 2017. Eurosense: Automatic harvesting of multilingual sense annotations from parallel text. In *Proceedings of the 55th Annual Meeting of the Association for Computational Linguistics (Volume 2: Short Papers)*, pages 594–600.

Andreas Eisele and Yu Chen. 2010. MultiUN: A multilingual corpus from United Nation documents. In *LREC*.

Bradley Hauer, Amir Ahmad Habibi, Yixing Luan, Arnob Mallik, and Grzegorz Kondrak. 2020. UAlberta at SemEval-2020 task 2: Using translations to predict cross-lingual entailment. In *Proceedings of the Fourteenth Workshop on Semantic Evaluation*, pages 263–269, Barcelona (online).

Bradley Hauer and Grzegorz Kondrak. 2020. Synonymy = translational equivalence. *arXiv preprint arXiv:2004.13886*.

Philipp Koehn. 2005. Europarl: A parallel corpus for statistical machine translation. In *MT Summit*, volume 5, pages 79–86.

Yixing Luan, Bradley Hauer, Lili Mou, and Grzegorz Kondrak. 2020. Improving word sense disambiguation with translations. In *Proceedings of the 2020 Conference on Empirical Methods in Natural Language Processing (EMNLP)*, pages 4055–4065.

George A Miller. 1995. WordNet: A lexical database for English. *Communications of the ACM*, 38(11):39–41.

Andrea Moro and Roberto Navigli. 2015. Semeval-2015 task 13: Multilingual all-words sense disambiguation and entity linking. In *Proceedings of the 9th International Workshop on Semantic Evaluation*, pages 288–297.

Roberto Navigli. 2018. Natural language understanding: Instructions for (present and future) use. In *IJCAI*, pages 5697–5702.

Roberto Navigli, David Jurgens, and Daniele Vannella. 2013. Semeval-2013 task 12: Multilingual word sense disambiguation. In *Proceedings of the Seventh International Workshop on Semantic Evaluation*, pages 222–231.

Roberto Navigli and Simone Paolo Ponzetto. 2012. BabelNet: The automatic construction, evaluation and application of a wide-coverage multilingual semantic network. *Artificial Intelligence*, 193:217–250.

Hwee Tou Ng, Bin Wang, and Yee Seng Chan. 2003. Exploiting parallel texts for word sense disambiguation: An empirical study. In *Proceedings of the 41st Annual Meeting of the Association for Computational Linguistics*, pages 455–462.

Tommaso Pasini. 2020. The knowledge acquisition bottleneck problem in multilingual word sense disambiguation. In *Proceedings of the Twenty-Ninth International Joint Conference on Artificial Intelligence, IJCAI-20*, pages 4936–4942.

Alessandro Raganato, Jose Camacho-Collados, and Roberto Navigli. 2017. Word sense disambiguation: A unified evaluation framework and empirical comparison. In *Proceedings of the 15th Conference of the European Chapter of the Association for Computational Linguistics: Volume 1, Long Papers*, pages 99–110.

Philip Resnik and David Yarowsky. 1997. A perspective on word sense disambiguation methods and their evaluation. In *Tagging Text with Lexical Semantics: Why, What, and How?*, pages 79–86.

Kaveh Taghipour and Hwee Tou Ng. 2015. One million sense-tagged instances for word sense disambiguation and induction. In *Proceedings of the Nineteenth Conference on Computational Natural Language Learning*, pages 338–344.

Zhi Zhong and Hwee Tou Ng. 2010. It makes sense: A wide-coverage word sense disambiguation system for free text. In *Proceedings of the ACL 2010 System Demonstrations*, pages 78–83.

A Benchmark and Scoring Algorithm for Enriching Arabic Synonyms

Sana Ghanem[1], **Mustafa Jarrar**[1], **Radi Jarrar**[1], **Ibrahim Bounhas**[2,3]
[1]Department of Computer Science, Birzeit University, Palestine
[2]LISI Laboratory of Computer Science for Industrial System, INSAT, Carthage University, Tunisia
[3]JARIR: Joint group for Artificial Reasoning and Information Retrieval, Tunisia
{swghanem, mjarrar, rjarrar}@birzeit.edu
ibrahim.bounhas@isd.uma.tn

Abstract

This paper addresses the task of extending a given synset with additional synonyms taking into account synonymy strength as a fuzzy value. Given a mono/multilingual synset and a threshold (a fuzzy value $[0-1]$), our goal is to extract new synonyms above this threshold from existing lexicons. We present twofold contributions: an algorithm and a benchmark dataset. The dataset consists of 3K candidate synonyms for 500 synsets. Each candidate synonym is annotated with a fuzzy value by four linguists. The dataset is important for (i) understanding how much linguists (dis/)agree on synonymy, in addition to (ii) using the dataset as a baseline to evaluate our algorithm. Our proposed algorithm extracts synonyms from existing lexicons and computes a fuzzy value for each candidate. Our evaluations show that the algorithm behaves like a linguist and its fuzzy values are close to those proposed by linguists (using RMSE and MAE). The dataset and a demo page are publicly available at `https://portal.sina.birzeit.edu/synonyms`.

1 Introduction and Motivation

Synonymy relationships are used in many NLP tasks and knowledge organization systems. However, automatic synonym extraction is a challenging task, especially for low-resourced and highly ambiguous languages such as Arabic (Darwish et al., 2021). There are some Arabic resources representing synonymy, such as Al-Maknaz Al-Kabīr, Arabic WordNet (Elkateb et al., 2006) and the Arabic Ontology (Jarrar, 2021, 2011); however, these resources are limited in terms of size and coverage (Helou et al., 2016; Al-Hajj and Jarrar, 2021), especially if compared with the English Princeton WordNet (Miller et al., 1990). Building such resources is expensive and challenging (Helou et al., 2014; Jarrar and Amayreh, 2019; Jarrar, 2020). In addition, the notion of synonymy itself is problematic, as it can vary from near (i.e., semantically related) to strict synonymy (Jarrar et al., 2021; Jarrar, 2005). Strict and formal synonymy is used in ontology engineering as an equivalence relation, thus its reflexive, symmetric, and transitive (Jarrar, 2021). A less formal synonymy is used in the construction of synsets in Princeton WordNet, which relies on the substitutionability of words in a sentence: "two expressions are synonymous in a linguistic context c if the substitution of one for the other in c does not alter the truth value" (Miller et al., 1990). For example, (طريق/road) and (شارع/street) are substitutionable in many contexts in Arabic, thus they can be synonyms. As will be reviewed in section 2, different approaches have been proposed for extracting synonyms automatically.

Nevertheless, one of the major challenges in extracting synonyms is that it is hard to evaluate them (Wu and Zhou, 2003) and there are no common evaluation datasets. Moreover, the substitutionability criteria are subjective, because humans do not necessarily agree on synonymy. As will be illustrated later in this paper, if different linguists are given the same words to judge whether they are synonyms, it is unlikely that they will agree on all cases. Thus, instead of relying on "the substitutionability of words in a sentence" as a criterion to judge whether two words are synonyms or not, we propose to model it with a *fuzzy value*. For example, let {confederacy, confederation} be two synonyms in the context of "a union of political organizations", and let "alliance" and "federation" be candidate additional synonyms, our goal is to assign a fuzzy value (e.g., 0.6 and 0.9) to each candidate synonym to indicate how much it is substitutionable, i.e., acceptable to be an additional third synonym.

Using such a fuzzy value is helpful for different application scenarios. For example, when constructing wordnet synsets, synonyms can be extracted with a high fuzzy value, but in the case of less sensitive information retrieval applications, a lower value might be more suitable. In a quality control scenario, one may evaluate a thesaurus by masking each synonym in a synset and assessing if its fuzzy value passes a threshold. Nevertheless, assigning a meaningful fuzzy value to each synonym in a synset is challenging. Thesauri are typically constructed based on linguists' intuition and without assigning a strength, or a fuzzy, value explicitly. To overcome this challenge, we developed a dataset of 3K synonyms, each assigned with a fuzzy value by four different linguists. We used this dataset to measure how much linguists (dis/)agree on synonymy. The dataset is also used to train our proposed algorithm (i.e., tune its fuzzy model) for extracting synonyms from dictionaries.

Task definition: The task we aim to address is defined as the following: Let S be a set of synonyms, c is a candidate synonym to S, and a dictionary D, our goal is to compute a fuzzy value f to indicate how much c is acceptable to be an addition to S. As will be elaborated in section 4, we assume D to be a set of sets of synonyms, and that S can be mono or multilingual synonyms.

Our main contributions in this paper are a dataset and an algorithm. The dataset was constructed by employing four linguists and giving them 3,000 candidate synonyms and 500 synsets from the Arabic WordNet (Elkateb et al., 2006). Each linguist was asked to score each candidate synonym in a given synset. Our proposed algorithm aims at discovering new candidate synonyms from existing linguistic resources. Given a set of synonyms, the algorithm builds a directed graph, at level *k* for all words in this set. Cyclic paths in this graph are then detected, and all words participating in these cyclic paths are considered candidate synonyms for the given synset. Each of these candidate synonyms is assigned a fuzzy value, which is calculated based on a fuzzy model that we learned from the dataset and that takes into account the connectivity of the candidate synonym in the graph. The novelty of our algorithm and our dataset is that we treat synonyms as a fuzzy relation. We evaluated the algorithm's fuzzy values by comparing them with the average of the linguists' scores (i.e., as a baseline). The Root Mean Squared Error (RMSE) between the scores of the algorithm and the average of the linguists' scores is 0.32 and the Mean Average Error (MAE) is 0.27. This means that the algorithm was behaving closely to a linguist. To evaluate the accuracy of our algorithm, we used the 10K synsets in Arabic WordNet. We masked the word with (highest, lowest, average, and random) frequency in each synset and used the algorithm to see if it could discover it again with top rank. The achieved accuracy was indeed high. For example, with the average frequency we achieved an accuracy of 98.7% at level 3 and 92% at level 4.

This paper is organized as follows: Section 2 presents related works in the field of synonym extraction. Section 3 overviews the algorithm. Section 4 summarizes and discusses the experimental results. Section 5 concludes the paper and proposes some perspectives.

2 Related Work

In what follows, we overview several approaches have been proposed to extract synonyms or build synsets. We refer to (Naser-Karajah et al., 2021) for a recent survey on this topic.

2.1 Synset Construction

New WordNets may be built by mining corpora and/or monolingual dictionaries as in (Oliveira and Gomes, 2014) for Portuguese. After extracting candidate synonym pairs, authors cluster these pairs into different clusters. Ercan and Haziyev (2019) proposed to build a multilingual synonymy graph from existing resources and wordnets, then used a supervised clustering algorithm to cluster synonyms. In both works, each cluster is then considered a synset. Neural language models, such as word embeddings, were also employed in synonymy extraction and wordnet construction (Mohammed, 2020). For example, Khodak et al. (2017) proposed to construct wordnets using the Princeton WordNet (PWN), machine translation, and word embeddings. A word is first translated into English using machine translation, and these translations are used to build a set of candidate synsets from PWN. A similarity score is used to rank each candidate synset, which is calculated using the word embedding-based method. Similarly, Tarouti and Kalita (2016) used static word embeddings to improve the quality of automatically constructed Arabic wordnet. Furthermore, Al-Matham and Al-Khalifa (2021) proposed to extract Arabic synonyms based on a static word embedding model that was created using Arabic corpora. Cosine similarity, in addition to some filters, were used to extract Synonyms.

2.2 Synonym Graph Mining

Other approaches are proposed to mine a graph from an existing resource(s) in order to discover new synonyms and translation pairs. The structure of the graph is exploited to compute ranking scores, which reflect how much two terms are likely to be synonyms (Jarrar, 2005). The main hypothesis is that some words, which are not necessarily directly connected with an edge may be semantically close. That is why cycles are widely exploited. Indeed, graphs are generic tools that may be used both for monolingual and bilingual resources and for several types of linguistic resources. For example, Flati and Navigli (2012) proposed an algorithm to find missing synonyms in the Ragazzini-Biagi English-Italian dictionary. A synonymy graph was built using this dictionary, then cyclic and quasi-cyclic paths are detected. Cyclic paths are those that have all edges in the same direction, while quasi cycles should be consecutive reverse edges. The length of a path is used to score the discovered synonyms. Discovering new translation pairs from multilingual dictionaries is also related to synonymy extraction. Villegas et al. (2016) proposed to construct a multilingual translation graph using translation pairs in the Apertium dictionaries. New translation pairs are then extracted from cyclic paths. However, wrong translations might be detected because of polysemy. The authors proposed to score the density of each path and exclude those paths with low densities. Instead of only using density, Torregrosa et al. (2019) proposed to combine it with a multi-way neural machine translation trained with parallel English and Spanish, Italian and Portuguese, and French and Romanian corpora. Their experiment shows a low recall and a reasonable precision ($25\% - 75\%$).

A recent algorithm that uses synonymy graphs was proposed by Jarrar et al. (2021). The idea is to construct an Arabic-English translation graph from a given bilingual dictionary (Jarrar et al., 2019). Terms participating in cyclic paths are extracted and consolidated, and considered synonyms. However, instead of using fuzzy values, they proposed the idea of bidirectional consolidation.

2.3 Related Notions of Fuzziness

Different notions of fuzziness were proposed in the WordNet literature. Hossayni et al. (2020) and Alizadeh-Q et al. (2021) proposed to compute the frequency of each word-sense pair in a corpus that is annotated using a WSD algorithm. The frequency is then normalized and transformed into a "possibility" value between 0 and 1 reflecting the membership degree. In (Hossayni et al., 2020), the same notion is evaluated in an interval indicating minimum and maximum values by dividing the corpus into several categories. In both cases, These membership degrees depend on the number of times a word-sense pair appeared in a given corpus. We believe that this notion of fuzziness is valuable and complements our proposed work; however, it highly depends on the coverage of the used corpora and the accuracy of the WSD algorithm, which is typically not good enough (Maru et al., 2022). Another notion of fuzziness was used in (Oliveira and Santos, 2016), to compute how likely two words are synonyms based on much they share words in their dictionary definitions. This notion of fuzziness was used to extract a Portuguese synonym network from seven resources taking into account the number of times a relation between two given words exists across resources. This notion of fuzziness, similar to (Hossayni et al., 2020), depends on text mining rather than synonyms graphs. Additionally, it computes the fuzziness between two words rather than between a word and a given synset. Most importantly, as discussed in section 3.3, our fuzzy scores are designed to reflect meaningful values, i.e., semantic truth, rather than frequency of use.

2.4 Benchmarks

As far as benchmarking and evaluation are concerned, it is hard to compare previous works, given the lack of a common gold standard. Indeed, the above-reviewed approaches were evaluated using different ways and resources, as no evaluation benchmarks are available for synonymy extraction. More precisely, and to our knowledge, there are no datasets of synonyms with ranking or fuzzy values to indicate how much a term is likely to be a synonym with a given synset.

3 Dataset Construction

This section presents a benchmarking dataset annotated with fuzzy values[1]. The dataset can be used for training and evaluating (i.e., a baseline) synonym extraction algorithms. Additionally, the construction of this dataset can also be used as an experiment to measure how much linguists (dis/)agree on synonymy.

[1]The dataset and source code are publicly available at `https://portal.sina.birzeit.edu/synonyms`

Figure 1: Example of scoring candidate synonyms.

3.1 Data Selection

First, we selected 500 synsets from the 10K synsets in Arabic WordNet. For each synset, we extracted a set of Arabic candidate synonyms, which we collected using our algorithm presented in Section 4. The total number of candidate synonyms is 3K. The 500 synsets were selected proportionally to the WordNet's distribution: 350 noun synsets, 140 verb synsets, and 10 adjective synsets. These synsets were selected randomly but we also took into account synset length and selected 142, 207, and 151 synsets of 2, 4, and 6 words in each synset, respectively. The 3K candidate synonyms were then given to four linguists to give them scores.

3.2 Experimental Setup

The four linguists who participated in this experiment are top students, who graduated recently with high distinction from the department of linguistics and translation at Birzeit University. Three training workshops were organized to explain the experiment and to emphasize the notion of synonymy. To ensure that all linguists have the same understanding of the task, we gave each linguist a small quiz (~30 synonyms) to try alone, then we discussed the results jointly. After that, each linguist was given the 3K candidate synonyms in a separate file in Google Sheet. Figure 1 illustrates an example of a synset and four candidate synonyms as scored by one of the linguists. As shown in Figure 1, the scoring is based on the linguist's understanding of the given synset (both English and Arabic synonyms), the gloss, and the context example (if available), which we extracted from the Arabic WordNet.

3.3 Scoring Guidelines

Table 1 presents our scoring schema, which is a scale from 0 to 100 representing the strength of the synonymy relation. The main factor in the scoring is the semantics, which indicates *how much the truth of a sentence is altered if the candidate synonymy is substituted with one of the given synonyms*, as defined in Miller et al. (1990). The scoring schema should not be interpreted as absolute numbers, but rather, they are used as annotation methodology to maintain a degree of consistency among linguists' scores as will be discussed next. From a semantics viewpoint, the scoring schema is divided into three categories: same ($> 60\%$), close ($60\% - 50\%$), or related/different semantics ($< 50\%$). *Same semantics* means that a word can be substituted in a sentence without altering the truth of this sentence. The four different scores inside this range are used to capture the *use*; i.e., how much it is common that a word can be used in this context. For example, the word إئْتِلاف has the same semantics as the other synonyms in the synset that means "a union of political organizations", but this word is rarely used in this context. *Close Semantics* means that it is possible to use a word (e.g., جامِعَة) with this semantics, but with some doubts, for instance, the word has an uncommon meaning or is usually employed in different contexts/with different purposes. Scores less than 40% mean different, related, or unrelated semantics, which means that the word cannot be a candidate synonym in this context. It is worth noting that this fine-grained scoring schema emerged after different iterations of discussion with the linguists in order to create sound methodological guidelines to annotate the dataset with fuzzy values.

Score	Meaning
100	Same semantics, style, use
90	Same semantics, style, less used
80	Same semantics, style, rarely used
70	Same semantics, style, not used
60	Close semantics, weak style, uncommon
50	Close semantics, not exact purpose
40	Semantically related
30	Semantically related (somehow)
20	Semantically different
10	Semantically very different
0	Semantically unrelated

Table 1: The fuzzy scoring scale - synonymy strength

3.4 Linguists Agreement Evaluation

The scoring of the 3K synonyms spanned over three months and took about 100 working hours for each linguist. The results of the four linguists are aggregated, and an average of all scores was computed.

To measure the (dis)agreements between linguists, we computed the Root Mean Squared Error (RMSE) and the Mean Average Error (MAE) between their scores (see table 2). We also computed the RMSE and MAE between the scores of each linguist with the average score for the four linguists. Later, we will use the same model (i.e., the average of answers) as a baseline to evaluate our algorithm, (see subsection 5.1). The RMSE might be more commonly used than MAE in measuring the differences between scores, but we provide both metrics in this paper. The MAE scores treat differences equally, while RMSE penalizes large variations (Wang and Lu, 2018).

As shown in table 2, linguists L_2 and L_3 have the closest RMSE to the average of all linguists. Linguists L_1 and L_4 have the highest RMSE distances if compared with the average scores. However, this does not indicate that they are more or less precise in their scores, it only shows that the scores of their answers deviate by the value stated by RMSE. Nevertheless, the RMSE of each linguist and the average ranges between 0.1 and 0.13. This indicates how much the scores of all linguists deviate from their average (i.e., which can be seen as an estimator of the standard deviation of errors between the linguist scores and the average of all linguists). It can be also noticed that the average deviation of the linguists and their average ranges between 0.31 to 0.39 from the algorithm. Though the algorithm deviates from the average score more than the individual linguists, the reported RMSE and MAE values are not considered high and further experiments are conducted to highlight if the difference between the scores is statistically significant.

To conform with this conclusion and to better understand the behavior of linguists in scoring these 3K synonyms, we perform a one-way ANOVA test (at $p < 0.05$). This test determines if the difference between the linguists' scores is generated at random or if their scores are different consistently (i.e., significantly different).

Post-hoc comparisons using the Tukey HSD test (using SPSS) indicated that the mean score for linguist L_1 (Mean = 0.4919, Standard Deviation = 0.34223) was significantly different than the other linguists (Mean = 0.4596, Standard Deviation = 0.31899). All included variables are following the normal distribution.

4 Algorithm Overview

The algorithm takes two inputs: a dictionary D, and a synset S. The output is a set of candidate synonyms C, each synonym c_i is assigned a fuzzy value f_i. The dictionary D itself is assumed to consist of set of synsets, $S_i \in D$. Each synset is a tuple $< t_1, .., t_n >$ of linguistic terms regardless of the language it belongs to. In this way, we can benefit from mono and multiple dictionaries and thesauri. In the first step, the algorithm extracts the candidate synonyms C, then it computes the fuzzy value f_i for each synonym c_i.

4.1 Candidate Synonym Extraction

For each term t_i in synset S, the algorithm finds all cyclic paths at level k, where k = 3, 4, 5,... n. That is, starting from t_i as a root, a graph is constructed using D, at level k, and all paths starting and ending with t_i are considered cyclic paths. If a term appears in any cyclic path, it is then considered a candidate synonym and is added to C.

Example: Figure 2 illustrates the synset {رَكِبَ, ride}, taken from the Arabic WordNet, and the generated graph at level 4 for each word in this synset. There are ten cyclic paths in this graph, highlighted as bold green lines, and shown below separately in Figure 3. The new terms participating in these ten cyclic paths are {إمتطى, sit}, which is the set C of candidate synonyms.

4.2 Candidate Synonym Selection

The intuition of our fuzzy model is that the more a candidate synonym appears in different cyclic paths and with different terms in S, the higher its fuzzy value, i.e., the stronger the synonymy. As such, to compute the fuzzy value f_i for each c_i in set C, we propose the following $Fuzzy$ function, which is based on two variables and two constant weights, as in the following formula:

$$Fuzzy(f_i) = \theta_1 \cdot P_i + \theta_2 \cdot Q_i$$

where P_i is the number of cyclic paths that c_i appears in, divided by the total number of cyclic paths, and Q_i is the number of root nodes t that appear in the cyclic paths of c_i, divided by the total number of terms in the synset S. θ_1 and θ_2 are two constant weights that we tuned using a 10-fold Cross-Validation (See section 4.3). The best values we found at level 3 and 4 are $(0.4, 0.6)$ and $(0.5, 0.5)$, respectively. As Figure 2 illustrates, the term (sit) appears six times among the ten cyclic paths found at the level 4, and appears in two root nodes among the two synonyms in the original synset; and similarly for (إمتطى). Therefore, their fuzzy values are:

$$Fuzzy(sit) = \frac{6}{10} \times 0.5 + \frac{2}{2} \times 0.5 = 0.8$$

$$Fuzzy(\text{إمتطى}) = \frac{6}{10} \times 0.5 + \frac{2}{2} \times 0.5 = 0.8$$

	L1		L2		L3		L4		Avg		Algorithm	
	RMSE	MAE	RMSE	MAE	RMSE	MAE	RMSE	MAE	RMSE	MAE	RMSE	MAE
L1			0.19	0.14	0.19	0.14	0.22	0.16	0.13	0.10	0.35	0.30
L2	0.19	0.14			0.16	0.12	0.20	0.15	0.10	0.11	0.31	0.26
L3	0.19	0.14	0.16	0.12			0.20	0.16	0.11	0.08	0.32	0.26
L4	0.22	0.16	0.20	0.15	0.20	0.15			0.13	0.08	0.39	0.34
Avg	0.13	0.10	0.10	0.08	0.11	0.08	0.13	0.11			**0.32**	**0.27**
Algorithm	0.35	0.30	0.31	0.26	0.32	0.26	0.39	0.34	**0.32**	**0.27**		

Table 2: The Root Mean Squared Error (RMSE) and the Mean Average Error (MAE) between the scores of each linguist, the average scores of all linguists, and the scores of the algorithm.

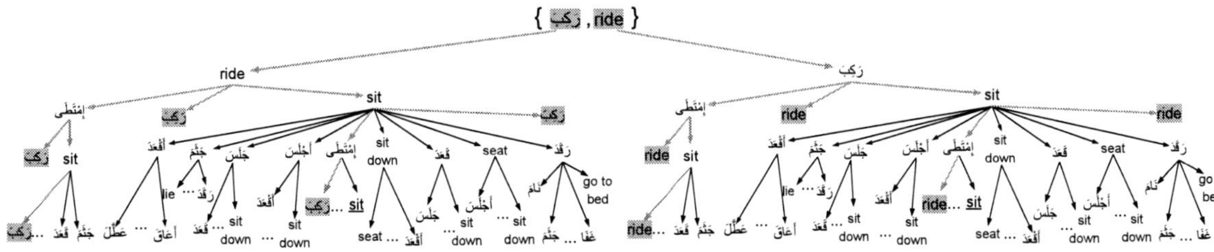

Figure 2: The cyclic paths for the {رَكِبَ , ride} synset from AWN

رَكِبَ→ride→sit→رَكِبَ
رَكِبَ→ride→sit→إمتطى→رَكِبَ
رَكِبَ→ride→رَكِبَ
رَكِبَ→ride→إمتطى→رَكِبَ
رَكِبَ→ride→إمتطى→sit→رَكِبَ
ride→رَكِبَ→sit→ride
ride→رَكِبَ→sit→إمتطى→ride
ride→رَكِبَ→ride
ride→رَكِبَ→إمتطى→ride
ride→رَكِبَ→إمتطى→sit→ride

Figure 3: The ten cyclic paths extracted from the graph generated in Figure 2.

4.3 Parameter Tuning

As our proposed $Fuzzy$ function depends on two constant weights (θ_1 and θ_2), our goal in this subsection is to find the best values of these θ_s. The best values are those that enable the $Fuzzy$ function to produce fuzzy values as close to linguists' scores as possible. Thus, we used our dataset, which contains 3K candidate synonyms, each with a fuzzy value (i.e., the average of the four linguists). To generate a model with the best results, we varied the values of the parameters θ_1 and θ_2 by selecting their values within the range of $[0.1, 0.9]$ with a step of 0.1 for each parameter. The total weight of both variables θ_1 and θ_2 should total to 1. This is because each of these variables is contributing to the score which ranges from 0 to 1.

Table 3 shows the average RMSE and the average MAE values using a 10-fold Cross-Validation of the algorithm run on all combinations of the variables. The results show that the best combination is 0.5 for θ_1 and 0.5 for θ_2 which resulted in the lowest RMSE value of 0.32, and the lowest MAE value of 0.27 at level 4. For level 3, the best combination is 0.4 for θ_1 and 0.6 for θ_2 with value of 0.35 for RMSE and 0.29 for MAE. Thus, we complete the RMSE and MAE calculations with level 4, as the RMSE and MAE values in level 4 are better than in level 3. These are the weights that are used in the algorithm evaluations in the next section.

5 Algorithm Evaluation

This section presents two experiments to evaluate the performance of our algorithm. The first experiment compares the results obtained by the algorithm with linguists' scores. The second experiment measures the accuracy of the algorithm.

5.1 Comparing the Algorithm with the Baseline

This experiment compares the results of our algorithm with the average of the linguists' scores (as a baseline) that we presented in section 3.4.

Table 2 shows 0.32 RMSE and 0.27 MAE scores

θ_1, θ_2		Level 4	Level 3
[0.1, 0.9]	RMSE	0.459	0.377
	MAE	0.375	0.319
[0.2, 0.8]	RMSE	0.408	0.362
	MAE	0.330	0.304
[0.3, 0.7]	RMSE	0.366	0.352
	MAE	0.299	0.296
[0.4, 0.6]	RMSE	0.336	**0.349**
	MAE	0.280	**0.293**
[0.5, 0.5]	RMSE	**0.321**	0.352
	MAE	**0.271**	0.296
[0.6, 0.4]	RMSE	0.323	0.363
	MAE	0.271	0.304
[0.7, 0.3]	RMSE	0.343	0.382
	MAE	0.272	0.316
[0.8, 0.2]	RMSE	0.378	0.407
	MAE	0.302	0.335
[0.9, 0.1]	RMSE	0.425	0.437
	MAE	0.335	0.357

Table 3: Average RMSE and MAE with various values of θ_1 and θ_2 obtained using 10-fold Cross-Validation

of the algorithm against the linguists' average. To understand the algorithm's 0.32 RMSE, one can notice that the RMSE difference between L_2 and L_4 is 0.20, and between L_1 and L_4 is 0.22. The RMSE difference between each pair of linguists ranges from 0.16 to 0.22. Now, the RMSE difference between the algorithm and the average of the linguists is 0.32. This means that the algorithm has only 0.10 more difference if compared with the RMSE variation between linguists.

Similarly, to understand the 0.27 MAE between the algorithm and the linguists, one can notice that the MAE between the four linguists themselves ranges from 0.12 to 0.16. Both RMSE and MAE, confirm the variation between the algorithm and the average of linguists. This illustrates that the algorithm's scores are close to the linguists' scores.

Nevertheless, as noted in section 3.4, the variations between linguists' scores, as well as the algorithm, do not tell us whether a linguist is better or more accurate than the others, which is because synonymy is a subjective notion. However, being close to the linguists' variations is a good indication that the algorithm scores are realistic. Next, we compare the behavior of the algorithm with the linguists' behavior in scoring synonyms, which provides an additional evaluation.

Testing the algorithm's *behavior*: to further understand the algorithm's behavior, we need to test whether the scores of the algorithm are statistically significant, i.e., the scores were consistent or resulted at random. In other words, we need to test whether the algorithm is consistently giving scores and behaving like a linguist - regardless of the differences in RMSE and MAE.

We performed a one-way ANOVA test (at $p < 0.05$) to check if there is a statistical difference between the algorithm and the other linguists. Before conducting this test, we first needed to check if all the linguists' and the algorithm's scores follow a normal distribution, or if there are no outliers, which are the main assumptions to conduct a one-way ANOVA test. Our result of the normality test (using SPSS) indicated that the scores of the algorithm are not normally distributed. Thus, we performed a univariate and multivariate outlier analysis. The results (using SPSS) indicated that there are no outliers, which means that the non-normality of the algorithm's scores are due to skewness in the data and not because of outliers. Therefore, the one-way ANOVA test can be applied, as explained by Tabachnick and Fidell (2001): *"it is assumed that the data has a normal distribution, however, note that violations of the normality assumption are not fatal and the result of the significant test is still reliable as long as non-normality is caused by skewness and not outliers"*.

The post-hoc comparisons (using the Tukey HSD test, in SPSS) indicated that the mean score for the algorithm (Mean = 0.4535, Standard Deviation = 0.16416) was significantly different only with linguist L_1 (Mean = 0.4919, Standard Deviation = 0.34223). This indeed confirms the findings shown in the previous section in which linguist L_1 has significantly different scores than the other linguists. In other words, the algorithm has shown to be not statistically different with the other linguists and their average (i.e., the baseline). Being not statistically different means that the algorithm's behavior in scoring synonyms is similar to the behavior of the linguists, except for linguist L_1.

To sum up, the variation between the scores of the algorithm and the linguists (using RMSE and MAE) are close to those between the linguists themselves. The one-way ANOVA test also confirms that the algorithm behaves as a linguist.

5.2 Accuracy Evaluation

We measure the accuracy of the algorithm in terms of retrieved words for each synset, by masking a synonym in a given synset, then try predicting it again. Masking is the process of removing a synonym from a synset, and then measure whether the masked term is retrieved back. The accuracy of the algorithm is determined by the rank of the masked term. Ideally, if every masked term is retrieved with the highest (i.e., top) rank, it means the accuracy is 100%.

5.2.1 Experiment Setup

We used the 10K synsets in the Arabic WordNet (AWN), and we conducted four masking experiments. For every synset in the 10K AWN's synsets, we calculated the frequency of each synonym (Arabic and English), then selected the synonyms with (highest, lowest, average, and random) frequencies in each synset to conduct the experiment. The frequency of a term is the number of synsets in which this term appears. We considered synsets that contain more than two synonyms, regardless of the language. That is, the experiment was conducted on both Arabic and English terms. Terms with the frequency of 1 (i.e., appeared in one synset only) are not selected. The number of synsets that are longer than two terms, and with a term with a frequency more than 1 are $7,219$, while the number of synsets longer than two terms, and with a term with lowest frequency are only $1,085$. Similarly, we selected synsets with average and random term frequencies, $5,207$ and $4,153$, respectively. Table 4 shows the results of the masking experiments.

The algorithm was applied individually for each synset by eliminating (i.e., masking) a term, in this synset, and retrieving back the top-ranked term using the algorithm. That is, given a term c_1 in synset s_n, c_1 will be eliminated from s_n, then we compute the fuzzy value of c_1 using our algorithm and check if the algorithm was able to retrieve it with highest fuzzy value (i.e., top rank) among other possible candidate synonyms for s_n. In this way, the algorithm is applied on synsets by masking terms with highest, lowest, average, and random frequencies, at level 3; and repeated at level 4, as shown in Table 4.

5.2.2 Results

The accuracy of the algorithm was calculated as a ratio of the correctly retrieved synonyms (i.e., top rank) from all samples. For example, the algorithm was able to retrieve 7,157 (99.1%) of the masked terms with highest frequencies at level 3 with the top ranking (i.e., highest fuzzy values).

The results in Table 4 illustrate that the lower the frequency of a term in the lexicon the lower the accuracy, which is because the connectivity of less frequent terms yields less fuzzy values by the algorithm. This does not mean that the masked terms were not retrieved by the algorithm, but rather, they are not ranked as the top (highest fuzzy values). The accuracy at level 4 decreases because the synonymy graph at this level becomes larger, and thus it contains more candidate synonyms.

It is important to remark that the algorithm was able to obtain high accuracy in this experiment but the accuracy evaluation heavily depends on the structure of the used lexicon, which is AWN in our case. Changing the dictionary, by adding more synonymy/translation relations yields to constructing a different graph, thus different accuracy is expected.

Experiment	Sample Size	Accuracy at Level 3	Accuracy at Level 4
Exp.1 (Highest)	$7,219$	99.1%	95.2%
Exp.2 (Average)	$5,207$	98.7%	92.0%
Exp.3 (Lowest)	$1,085$	88.4%	62.0%
Exp.4 (Random)	$4,153$	98.1%	89.3%

Table 4: The accuracy of the algorithm using the masking experiment with the highest, average, lowest, and random frequencies within each synset.

6 Conclusion

We presented a benchmark dataset and an algorithm to extract synonyms and fuzzy values. The benchmark dataset consists of 3K candidate synonyms for 500 synsets, each candidate synonym was annotated with a fuzzy value by four linguists. The dataset is important for measuring how much linguists disagree on synonymy, which ranged between $0.16 - 0.22$ for RMSE and $0.12 - 0.16$ for MAE. These measures were also used as a baseline to evaluate our algorithm. The algorithm presented in this paper aims to enrich a given mono/multilingual synset with more synonyms. Our evaluation shows that our algorithm behaves as linguists in producing fuzzy values, and the fuzzy scores are also close to those of the linguists. The accuracy evaluation illustrates that it is highly accurate.

7 Limitations and Future Work

The current version of our algorithm neglects the effect of diacritics in the Arabic language (Jarrar et al., 2018), so that a word with different diacritics is considered as different, like كَتب, كتَّب, even if they are the same. Thus, we plan to enhance the algorithm to consider the characteristics of the Arabic language, and consider synonyms in MSA and

Arabic dialects as described in (Haff et al., 2022; Jarrar et al., 2017, 2022).

Acknowledgment

We acknowledge the support of the Research Committee at Birzeit University (No. 2021/49), and would like to thank Taymaa Hammouda and Muhannad Yaseen for the technical and statistical support, and all students who helped in the annotation process, especially Tamara Qaimari, Asala Hamed, Ahd Muhtasib, Doa Shwiki, Shaimaa Hamayel, Hiba Zayed, Rwaa Zaid, and others.

References

Moustafa Al-Hajj and Mustafa Jarrar. 2021. Arabglossbert: Fine-tuning bert on context-gloss pairs for wsd. In *Proceedings of the International Conference on Recent Advances in Natural Language Processing (RANLP 2021)*, pages 40–48, Online. INCOMA Ltd.

Rawan N Al-Matham and Hend S Al-Khalifa. 2021. Synoextractor: a novel pipeline for arabic synonym extraction using word2vec word embeddings. *Complexity*, 2021.

Yousef Alizadeh-Q, Behrouz Minaei-Bidgoli, Sayyed-Ali Hossayni, Mohammad-R. Akbarzadeh-T., Diego Reforgiato Recupero, Mohammad Reza Rajati, and Aldo Gangemi. 2021. Interval probabilistic fuzzy wordnet. *CoRR*, abs/2104.10660.

Kareem Darwish, Nizar Habash, Mourad Abbas, Hend Al-Khalifa, Huseein T. Al-Natsheh, Houda Bouamor, Karim Bouzoubaa, Violetta Cavalli-Sforza, Samhaa R. El-Beltagy, Wassim El-Hajj, Mustafa Jarrar, and Hamdy Mubarak. 2021. A panoramic survey of natural language processing in the arab worlds. *Commun. ACM*, 64(4):72–81.

Sabry Elkateb, William Black, Piek Vossen, David Farwell, H Rodríguez, A Pease, and M Alkhalifa. 2006. Arabic wordnet and the challenges of arabic. In *Proceedings of Arabic NLP/MT Conference, London, UK*, pages 665–670.

Gonenc Ercan and Farid Haziyev. 2019. Synset expansion on translation graph for automatic wordnet construction. *Information Processing & Management*, 56(1):130–150.

Tiziano Flati and Roberto Navigli. 2012. The cqc algorithm: Cycling in graphs to semantically enrich and enhance a bilingual dictionary. *Journal of Artificial Intelligence Research*, 43:135–171.

Karim El Haff, Mustafa Jarrar, Tymaa Hammouda, and Fadi Zaraket. 2022. Curras + baladi: Towards a levantine corpus. In *Proceedings of the International Conference on Language Resources and Evaluation (LREC 2022)*, Marseille, France.

Mamoun Abu Helou, Matteo Palmonari, and Mustafa Jarrar. 2016. Effectiveness of automatic translations for cross-lingual ontology mapping. *Journal of Artificial Intelligence Research*, 55(1):165–208.

Mamoun Abu Helou, Matteo Palmonari, Mustafa Jarrar, and Christiane Fellbaum. 2014. Towards building lexical ontology via cross-language matching. In *Proceedings of the 7th Conference on Global WordNet*, pages 346–354. Global WordNet Association.

Sayyed-Ali Hossayni, Mohammad-R. Akbarzadeh-T., Diego Reforgiato Recupero, Aldo Gangemi, Esteve del Acebo, and Josep Lluís de la Rosa i Esteva. 2020. An algorithm for fuzzification of wordnets, supported by a mathematical proof. *CoRR*, abs/2006.04042.

Mustafa Jarrar. 2005. *Towards Methodological Principles for Ontology Engineering*. Ph.D. thesis, Vrije Universiteit Brussel.

Mustafa Jarrar. 2011. Building a formal arabic ontology (invited paper). In *Proceedings of the Experts Meeting on Arabic Ontologies and Semantic Networks*. ALECSO, Arab League.

Mustafa Jarrar. 2020. *Digitization of Arabic Lexicons*, pages 214–217. UAE Ministry of Culture and Youth.

Mustafa Jarrar. 2021. The arabic ontology - an arabic wordnet with ontologically clean content. *Applied Ontology Journal*, 16(1):1–26.

Mustafa Jarrar and Hamzeh Amayreh. 2019. An arabic-multilingual database with a lexicographic search engine. In *The 24th International Conference on Applications of Natural Language to Information Systems (NLDB 2019)*, volume 11608 of *LNCS*, pages 234–246. Springer.

Mustafa Jarrar, Hamzeh Amayreh, and John P. McCrae. 2019. Representing arabic lexicons in lemon - a preliminary study. In *The 2nd Conference on Language, Data and Knowledge (LDK 2019)*, volume 2402, pages 29–33. CEUR Workshop Proceedings.

Mustafa Jarrar, Nizar Habash, Faeq Alrimawi, Diyam Akra, and Nasser Zalmout. 2017. Curras: An annotated corpus for the palestinian arabic dialect. *Journal Language Resources and Evaluation*, 51(3):745–775.

Mustafa Jarrar, Eman Karajah, Muhammad Khalifa, and Khaled Shaalan. 2021. Extracting synonyms from bilingual dictionaries. In *Proceedings of the 11th International Global Wordnet Conference (GWC2021)*, pages 215–222. Global Wordnet Association.

Mustafa Jarrar, Fadi Zaraket, Rami Asia, and Hamzeh Amayreh. 2018. Diacritic-based matching of arabic words. *ACM Asian and Low-Resource Language Information Processing*, 18(2):10:1–10:21.

Mustafa Jarrar, Fadi A Zaraket, Tymaa Hammouda, Daanish Masood Alavi, and Martin Waahlisch. 2022. Lisan: Yemeni, irqi, libyan, and sudanese arabic dialect copora with morphological annotations.

Mikhail Khodak, Andrej Risteski, Christiane Fellbaum, and Sanjeev Arora. 2017. Automated wordnet construction using word embeddings. In *Proceedings of the 1st Workshop on Sense, Concept and Entity Representations and their Applications*, pages 12–23.

Marco Maru, Simone Conia, Michele Bevilacqua, and Roberto Navigli. 2022. Nibbling at the hard core of Word Sense Disambiguation. In *Proceedings of the ACL2022 (Vol.1)*, pages 4724–4737, Dublin, Ireland. ACL.

George A Miller, Richard Beckwith, Christiane Fellbaum, Derek Gross, and Katherine J Miller. 1990. Introduction to wordnet: An on-line lexical database. *International journal of lexicography*, 3(4):235–244.

Nora Mohammed. 2020. Extracting word synonyms from text using neural approaches. *International Arab Journal of Information Technology*, 17.

Eman Naser-Karajah, Nabil Arman, and Mustafa Jarrar. 2021. Current trends and approaches in synonyms extraction: Potential adaptation to arabic. In *Proceedings of the 2021 International Conference on Information Technology (ICIT)*, pages 428–434, Amman, Jordan. IEEE.

Hugo Gonçalo Oliveira and Paulo Gomes. 2014. Eco and onto.pt: A flexible approach for creating a portuguese wordnet automatically. *Language Resources and Evaluation*, 48.

Hugo Gonçalo Oliveira and Fábio Santos. 2016. Discovering fuzzy synsets from the redundancy in different lexical-semantic resources. In *Proceedings of LREC 2016*, Paris, France. ELRA.

Barbara G Tabachnick and LS Fidell. 2001. Using multivariate statististics. *Allyn &Bacon A Pearson Education Company: Boston.*

Feras Al Tarouti and Jugal Kalita. 2016. Enhancing automatic wordnet construction using word embeddings.

Daniel Torregrosa, Mihael Arcan, Sina Ahmadi, and John P McCrae. 2019. Tiad 2019 shared task: Leveraging knowledge graphs with neural machine translation for automatic multilingual dictionary generation. *Translation Inference Across Dictionaries.*

Marta Villegas, Maite Melero, Núria Bel, and Jorge Gracia. 2016. Leveraging rdf graphs for crossing multiple bilingual dictionaries. In *Proceedings of LREC2016*, pages 868–876.

Weijie Wang and Yanmin Lu. 2018. Analysis of the mean absolute error (mae) and the root mean square error (rmse) in assessing rounding model. In *IOP conference series: materials science and engineering*, volume 324. IOP Publishing.

Hua Wu and Ming Zhou. 2003. Optimizing synonym extraction using monolingual and bilingual resources. In *Proceedings of the second international workshop on Paraphrasing*, pages 72–79.

Expanding the Conceptual Description of Verbs in WordNet with Semantic and Syntactic Information

Ivelina Stoyanova
Department of
Computational Linguistics
Institute for Bulgarian Language
Bulgarian Academy of Sciences
iva@dcl.bas.bg

Svetlozara Leseva
Department of
Computational Linguistics
Institute for Bulgarian Language
Bulgarian Academy of Sciences
zarka@dcl.bas.bg

Abstract

This paper describes an ongoing effort towards expanding the semantic and conceptual description of verbs in WordNet by combining information from two other resources, FrameNet and VerbNet, as well as enriching the verbs' description with syntactic patterns extracted from the three resources. The conceptual description of verb synsets is provided by assigning a FrameNet frame which provides the relevant set of frame elements denoting the predicate's participants and props. This information is supplemented by assigning a VerbNet class and the set of semantic roles associated with it. The information extracted from FrameNet and VerbNet and assigned to a synset is aligned (semi-automatically with subsequent manual corrections) at the following levels: (i) FrameNet frame: VerbNet class; (ii) FrameNet frame elements: VerbNet semantic roles; (iii) FrameNet semantic types and restrictions: VerbNet selectional restrictions. We then link the syntactic patterns associated with the units in FrameNet, VerbNet and WordNet, by unifying their representation and by matching the corresponding patterns at the level of syntactic groups. The alignment of the semantic components and their syntactic realisations is essential for the better exploitation of the abundance of information across resources, including shedding light on cross-resource similarities, discrepancies and inconsistencies. The syntactic patterns can facilitate the extraction of examples illustrating the use of verb synset literals in corpora and their semantic characterisation through the association of the syntactic groups with the components of semantic description (frame elements or semantic roles) and can be employed in various tasks requiring semantic and syntactic description. The resource is publicly available to the community. The components of the conceptual description are visualised showing the links to the original resources each component is drawn from.

1 Introduction

The paper focuses on describing an effort at obtaining a rich semantic and syntactic description of verbs in WordNet through mapping other lexical and conceptual resources to it (FrameNet and VerbNet, in particular). This has been achieved through aligning corresponding elements of the semantic and syntactic description of the entities in these resources. We rely on existing alignments between the resources – part of the verbs in WordNet have been assigned a FrameNet frame and/or a VerbNet class on the basis of equivalent or similar meaning. After the basic units of the resources have been aligned, we implement procedures for mapping their constituent parts: frame elements with semantic roles, syntactic groups with syntactic groups or syntactic positions. This type of alignment makes it possible to study the commonalities and differences in and possibly to perfect the representation of verbs across resources and languages, on the one hand, and to obtain a richer and more reliable description for the purposes of tasks in computational linguistics, on the other.

2 Related Work

In recent years, significant efforts have been invested in harnessing the strengths of lexical, conceptual and syntactically-oriented resources through mapping them on various levels. Such efforts include works on mapping WordNet, FrameNet and VerbNet (the earliest attempt probably being made by Shi and Mihalcea (2005)) or different combinations of these resources resulting in combined resources, such as WordFrameNet[1] by Laparra and Rigau (2010) and MapNet[2] by Tonelli and Pighin (2009), other other FrameNet-to-WordNet mappings, such as the one by Ferrández et al. (2010). The further enhancement of these

[1]http://adimen.si.ehu.es/web/WordFrameNet
[2]https://hlt-nlp.fbk.eu/technologies/mapnet

resources with others has resulted in the emergence of Semlink[3] (Palmer, 2009), which unifies WordNet, FrameNet and VerbNet with PropBank, and Semlink+ that brings in a mapping to Ontonotes (Palmer et al., 2014). Efforts such as the SynSemClass lexicon[4] centre not on any of the discussed resources, but on a different one (in this case the Vallex dictionary family), which is further enriched with conceptual and syntactic information from external semantic resources (Urešová et al., 2020a), including linking to FrameNet, WordNet, VerbNet, OntoNotes and PropBank, as well as the Czech VALLEX.

As the alignment between resources is limited by the overlap between the lexis covered by them, a major effort has been to expand the coverage of the mapping across resources by way of generalisation and transfer of existing descriptions from already described items (literals, synsets, lexical units, verbs in verb classes, etc.) to other units that share the same semantic and syntactic properties. VerbAtlas[5], proposed by Di Fabio et al. (2019) has adopted a representation of synsets as clusters with prototypical argument structures presented as frames (to a large extent inspired by VerbNet roles and semantic restrictions). The clustering leads to a significant expansion encompassing the entire verb inventory (13,767 synsets).

Another approach, adopted by (Leseva et al., 2018a) and further refined in (Leseva and Stoyanova, 2019, 2020), involves the mapping of FrameNet frames to WordNet synsets on the basis of the inheritance of conceptual features in hypernym trees, i.e., by assigning frames from hypernyms to hyponyms where possible and implementing a number of validation procedures based on the structural properties of the two resources, primarily the relations encoded in them. This has resulted in 13,104 automatic alignments, of which 6,000 have been validated and corrected manually in the framework of this project and previous initiatives.

Another venue of research has been to map relevant information representing fragments of meaning associated with lexical units across resources, especially essential components of the semantic and the syntactic description such as semantic roles or their counterparts in the respective resources (e.g. frame elements, argument positions, valency slots). Alignments at the verb arguments' level have been carried out as part of the Semlink project and its more recent version Semlink 2.0. (Stowe et al.). The alignments described there include PropBank to VerbNet mappings (PropBank roleset – VerbNet senses, PB arguments – VerbNet semantic roles) as well as VerbNet to FrameNet mappings (VerbNet senses – FrameNet frames, VerbNet semantic roles – FrameNet frame elements). Another similar task, which makes use of the linking of various semantic resources (FrameNet, WordNet, VerbNet, OntoNotes and PropBank), has been implemented in the development of the SynSemClass Lexicon (Urešová et al., 2020a,b): the more general SynSemClass valency slots have been mapped to relevant FrameNet frame elements.

It has long been discussed that combining WordNet and other lexical and conceptual resources such as FrameNet produces a more complete semantic and syntactic representation of the meaning lexical entries (Baker and Fellbaum, 2009; Schneider, 2012) which expands the possible application of the resources for the purpose of syntactic and semantic parsing.

Our current effort builds on our previous work described in (Leseva et al., 2018b,a) and further refined in (Leseva and Stoyanova, 2019, 2020)[6], and proceeds onwards. Our interests lie in both: (i) expanding the alignment between the most lexically populated resource, WordNet, the rich conceptual apparatus and the more generalised argument-structure descriptions of FrameNet and VerbNet, respectively, and the syntactic descriptions available in the three resources; (ii) mapping the basic building blocks across resources, where possible, i.e. frame elements and semantic roles and respectively – their syntactic expressions.

In this paper we particularly focus on the latter: extending the description of WordNet verbs by mapping semantic and conceptual components of the description extracted from the three resources employed in the study, and supplementing it with syntactic patterns by combining and aligning the available syntactic information.

The proposed enhancements are directed to: (a) improving the existing mappings by aligning FrameNet frames and VerbNet verb classes assigned to the same synset; (b) enhancing the conceptual description of synsets with additional infor-

[3] https://verbs.colorado.edu/semlink/

[4] https://ufal.mff.cuni.cz/synsemclass

[5] http://verbatlas.org/

[6] The resource is distributed as a standoff file under CC by 4.0 license: https://dcl.bas.bg/semantic-relations-data/.

mation about the syntactic realisation of FrameNet frame elements and VerbNet semantic roles; and (c) suggesting further procedures for verification and improvements of conceptual descriptions of verb synsets in WordNet.

3 Lexical and Conceptual Resources

Below we describe in brief the used resources and how they are integrated with each other.

3.1 WordNet

WordNet[7] (Miller, 1995; Fellbaum, 1998) is a large lexical database that represents comprehensively conceptual and lexical knowledge in the form of a network whose nodes denote cognitive synonyms (synsets) linked by means of a number of conceptual-semantic and lexical relations such as hypernymy, meronymy, antonymy, etc. Of the three resources employed in this work, WordNet provides the greatest lexical coverage; the verbs represented in it are organised in 14,103 synsets (including verb synsets specific for Bulgarian). We use both the Princeton WordNet and the Bulgarian WordNet, which are aligned at the synset level by means of unique synset identifiers.

WordNet verb synsets are supplied with generalised sentence frames which specify the subcategorisation features of the verbs in the synset by indicating the kinds of sentences they can occur in (Fellbaum, 1990, 1999). The main purpose of these frames is to allow the identification of synsets sharing one or more syntactic frames, which facilitates the analysis of the syntactic realisation of semantically related verbs (e.g., verbs belonging to the same semantic class expressed by the semantic primitive, or synsets in the same hypernym tree).

There are 35 generic sentence frames illustrating the use of the literals in the synsets[8], e.g., (8) Somebody —-s something, (16) Somebody —-s something from somebody, (22) Somebody —-s PP, etc. As the syntactic frames describe the properties of individual verbs (literals), the generalised frames in WordNet can be applicable to all or only some of the literals in the synset.

Besides the rich lexical description (glosses, examples, semantic primitive) and the encoded relations, WordNet's main contribution to this work is the rich lexical coverage of verbs, including information about the membership of synsets to the so-called base concepts – a cross-lingual selection of synsets which we use as an approximation (together with other selection criteria) for establishing a set of general lexis verbs.

[7]https://wordnet.princeton.edu/

[8]https://wordnet.princeton.edu/documentation/wninput5wn

3.2 FrameNet

FrameNet[9] (Baker et al., 1998; Baker, 2008) is a lexical semantic resource which couches lexical and conceptual knowledge in the terms of frame semantics. Frames are conceptual structures describing types of objects, situations, or events along with their components (frame elements) (Baker et al., 1998; Ruppenhofer et al., 2016). Depending on their status, frame elements (FEs) may be core, peripheral or extra-thematic (Ruppenhofer et al., 2016). In terms of the conceptual description, we deal primarily with core FEs, which instantiate conceptually necessary components of a frame, and which in their particular configuration make a frame unique and different from other frames.

FrameNet frames represent conceptual rather than lexical knowledge and thus are to a large extent language independent. FrameNet frames apply at synset (sense) level and in most cases cover all literals. Each frame is associated with a set of syntactic patterns showing the realisation of different configurations of the FEs in sentences. Here, we consider the configurations of core FEs which describe the obligatory participants in the situation. Example 1 shows the FrameNet frame *Cause_motion* and its description.

Example 1. FrameNet frame *Cause_motion* and its description.

Frame definition: An Agent causes a Theme to move from a Source, along a Path, to a Goal.

Frame elements: Agent (Sentient); Cause; Theme; Source; Goal; Path; Initial_state; Area; Result.

Syntactic patterns (total of 116 patterns):
NP (Agent) V NP (Theme);
NP (Agent) V INI (Goal) NP (Theme);
NP (Agent) V PP[off] (Source) NP (Theme);
NP (Agent) V PP[into] (Goal) PP[across] (Path) NP (Theme);
NP (Theme) V PP[around] (Area) PP[by] (Cause);
NP (Theme) V PP[by] (Agent) NP (Path); etc.

Examples: She$_{\text{Agent}}$ THREW {her shoes}$_{\text{Theme}}$ {into the dryer}$_{\text{Goal}}$.

Croquet$_{\text{Theme}}$ was PUSHED out$_{\text{Source}}$ by tennis$_{\text{Cause}}$.

[9]https://framenet.icsi.berkeley.edu/fndrupal/

The storm$_{\text{Cause}}$ TOSSED the sailor$_{\text{Theme}}$ from the boat$_{\text{Source}}$.

3.3 VerbNet

VerbNet (Kipper-Schuler, 2005; Kipper et al., 2008) is a hierarchical network of English verbs which represents their syntactic and semantic patterns[10]. It is organised into 274 classes extending Levin's classification (Levin, 1993) through refining and adding subclasses so as to provide better syntactic and semantic coherence among members of a class. VerbNet explicitly projects semantic relations onto syntactic structures and encodes information about thematic roles, arguments' selectional restrictions and syntactic frames. While the syntactic dimension of the resource is more specific to English, the semantic roles and the selectional restrictions employed provide well-motivated semantic generalisations.

Each VerbNet class is associated with a number of syntactic patterns which have a generalised form and express the configurations in which the thematic roles appear in sentences. Unlike FrameNet patterns, the VerbNet patterns do not account for syntactic transformations such as passivisations, etc. Example 2 shows the VerbNet class *run-51.3.2* with its corresponding description.

Example 2. VerbNet class *run-51.3.2* and its description.

Roles: Theme [+animate | +machine]; Trajectory [+concrete]; Initial_Location [+concrete]; Destination [+concrete].
Syntactic patterns (total of 6 patterns): NP V
NP V PP.location
NP V PP.location
There V PP NP
There V NP PP
PP.location V NP
Syntax: Theme VERB
Examples: The horse$_{\text{Theme}}$ RAN.
The horse$_{\text{Theme}}$ RAN to the barn$_{\text{Destination}}$.
The horse$_{\text{Theme}}$ JUMPED {over the fence}$_{\text{Trajectory}}$.
{Out of the box}$_{\text{Initial\_location}}$ JUMPED {a little white rabbit}$_{\text{Theme}}$.

[10] https://verbs.colorado.edu/verbnet/

4 Alignment between Resources

4.1 Mapping VerbNet classes and FrameNet frames to WordNet synsets

The alignment between WordNet, FrameNet and VerbNet results in a rich semantic and syntactic description of verbs in terms of:

(i) a set of semantic relations between verbs (lexical entries), including hypernymy and hyponymy, synonymy, causativity, etc.; as well as derivational and morphosemantic relations between verb and noun synsets;

(ii) frames, frame elements and semantic restrictions associated with FrameNet lexical units and assigned to WordNet synsets, thus providing detailed valency patterns for the syntactic realisation of the frame elements for each verb (in the form of annotated sentençes);

(iii) a set of frame-to-frame hierarchical and non-hierarchical relations, which are translated into relations of inheritance, specialisation, etc. both between pairs of frames and between pairs of frame elements; these relations are also reflected in the alignment between WordNet synsets and FrameNet frames;

(iv) verb classes, predicate-argument structures (in the form of semantic role configurations), selectional restrictions and syntactic patterns realising the arguments of the verbs pertaining to the classes defined in the VerbNet lexicon which are also assigned to WordNet synsets and literals;

(v) aligned VerbNet classes and FrameNet frames providing correspondence between semantic roles and frame elements applicable to lexical units.

By aligning the lexical items in FrameNet and VerbNet we focus particularly on mapping core frame elements as they are most likely to represent a verb's arguments and hence – constitute counterparts of the semantic roles. Differences between frames' core FEs sets and corresponding predicate argument structures reveal valuable language- and resource-specific features of the semantic and syntactic description.

The three resources have been aligned automatically using existing mappings (see Section 2) on top of which further mapping procedures have been implemented. In particular, the following resources have been employed: a mapping of the VerbNet 3.4 verb classes to WordNet 3.0 synsets, as well as two types of mappings of the frames in FrameNet and the synsets in WordNet 3.0[11]: indirectly via SemLink and directly through the system described by Laparra and Rigau (2010). These mappings have resulted in the assignment of FrameNet frames to 4,306 verb synsets.

The number of synsets that are assigned a FrameNet frame have been supplemented using the expanded synset-to-FrameNet frame mapping described in (Leseva et al., 2018a) and further refined in (Leseva and Stoyanova, 2019, 2020) which involves the mapping of FrameNet frames to WordNet synsets on the basis of the inheritance of conceptual features in hypernym trees, i.e., by assigning frames from hypernyms to hyponyms where possible and implementing a number of validation procedures based on the structural properties of the two resources, primarily the relations encoded in them. This has resulted in 13,104 automatic alignments, of which over 6,000 have been validated and corrected manually in the framework of this project and previous initiatives. VerbNet class-to-FrameNet frame alignments have not been separately validated.

Example 3 represents the different blocks of information obtained from the three resources through the mapping. Figure 1) exemplifies the successful mapping of the hierarchical structure of FrameNet and WordNet and their coarser-grained correspondence in VerbNet. In particular, the example illustrates a hypernym–hyponym pair of synsets, with the appropriate FrameNet frames assigned to them, which are themselves related by means of an inheritance relation (Cause_change_of_position_on_a_scale being an elaboration of the mother frame Cause_change). Both synsets are described by the *other_cos-45.4* class in VerbNet; respectively, for these particular synsets a correspondence between the pair of FrameNet frames and the *other_cos-45.4* VerbNet class is established.

Example 3. Alignment between FrameNet frames and VerbNet classes (Figure 1).

(a) **WordNet synset:** *eng-30-00126264-v change; alter; modify* verb.change 'cause to change; make different; cause a transformation'
FrameNet frame: *Cause_change*: Agent (Sentient); Entity (Entity); Initial_category; Final_category; Initial_value; Final_value; Attribute [unexpressed]; Cause [unexpressed]

[11]Additional mappings between WordNet versions were also involved.

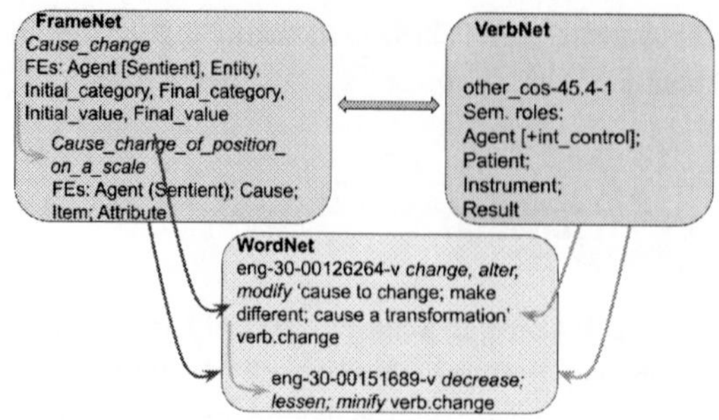

Figure 1: Frames inheritance (Cause_change → Cause_change_of_position_on__scale) reflected in synset hypernym / hyponym relations (*change → decrease*)

VerbNet class: *other_cos-45.4*: Agent [+int_control]; Patient; Instrument; Result

(b) **WordNet synset:** *eng-30-00151689-v decrease; lessen; minify* 'make smaller'
FrameNet frame:*Cause_change_of_position _on_a_scale*: Agent (Sentient); Cause; Item; Attribute
VerbNet class: *other_cos-45.4*: Agent [+int_control]; Patient; Instrument; Result.

4.2 Mapping FrameNet frame elements to VerbNet semantic roles

The mapping between FrameNet frame elements and VerbNet semantic roles is based on extracting semantic information from the two resources: (i) establishing correspondence between frame elements and semantic roles, where possible, and (ii) inferring knowledge from the structure of FrameNet, many frame elements being more specific than VerbNet semantic roles. The former case (i) involves heuristic procedures such as establishing identity, similarity or correspondences in the naming of elements and roles, and possibly comparing their definitions. Example 4 shows a FrameNet frame–VerbNet class alignment where the frame *Breathing* has been automatically aligned to the VerbNet class *breathe-40.1.2*. The frame elements and semantic roles Agent and Source have been aligned on the basis of their identical names. In addition, the frame element Goal has been aligned to the role Destination based on established general (frame/class non-specific) correspondences in the naming conventions adopted in the two resources. The latter case (ii) involves knowledge about the relations between more general and more concrete frame elements, which is obtained from a shallow hierarchy of frame elements based on inheritance

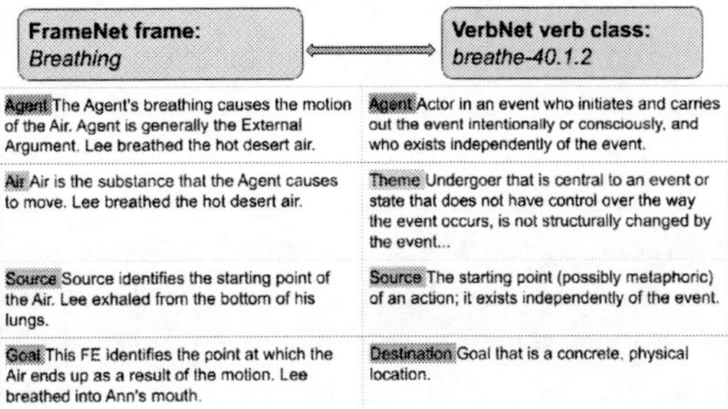

Figure 2: Frame inheritance reflected in the hypernym/hyponym relation between synsets.

between frames (Leseva et al., 2018b). *Breathing* inherits its properties from a series of frames that form a chain of inheritance from a more specific to a more general frame – *Breathing > Fluidic_motion > Motion*. The frame-to-frame relations help identify corresponding inheritance relations between the relevant frame elements in these frames: *Air > Fluid > Theme*. The FE-to-FE relations are obtained semi-automatically based on their syntactic expression and/or similarity of definitions. After establishing inheritance chains, we try to map the more general FEs to relevant roles in the semantic role set of the VerbNet verb class aligned with the respective frame. As a result, the Breathing *Air* is mapped to the *Theme* in the VerbNet class *breathe-40.1.2*.

Example 4. FrameNet frame *Breathing* aligned to VerbNet class *breathe-40.1.2* along with the alignment between frame elements and semantic roles (Figure 2).

WordNet synset: *eng-30-00001740-v breathe; take a breath; respire; suspire* verb.body 'draw air into, and expel out of, the lungs'
FrameNet frame: *Breathing*: Agent (Sentient); Air; Source; Goal
VerbNet class: *breathe-40.1.2*: Agent [+int_control]; Theme; Source; Destination

While often there is no full frame-to-verb class equivalence, the greater the correspondence between the frame elements and semantic roles in terms of their number and semantics, the better the match is.

5 Corpus Resources

The semantically annotated corpus SemCor (current version 3.0) (Miller et al., 1993; Landes et al., 1998) is compiled by the Princeton WordNet team and covers texts excerpted from the Brown Corpus. SemCor is supplied with POS and grammatical tagging and all open-class words (both single words and multiword expressions, as well as named entities) are semantically annotated by assigning each word a unique WordNet sense (synset ID).

BulSemCor (Koeva et al., 2010, 2011) has been generally modelled on the SemCor methodology and structure. While only open-class words are annotated with WordNet senses in SemCor, all lexical units in BulSemCor have been annotated; for that purpose the Bulgarian wordnet has been expanded with closed-class words (Koeva et al., 2010).

We use SemCor and BulSemCor to extract usage examples for the syntactic patterns in which literals in the corresponding synsets appear in corpora. The extracted examples in English are analysed with a view to the differences in the syntactic patterns applicable to different literals. Examples from BulSemCor serve the purpose to provide material for the investigation of the possible syntactic knowledge transfer from English to Bulgarian.

6 Compilation of Syntactic and Semantic Description of Verbs in WordNet

After aligning FrameNet frames to VerbNet classes (assigned to synsets or groups of synsets), and FrameNet frame elements to VerbNet roles, we move towards mapping syntactic patterns from the resources to the end of providing a new, syntactic layer to the conceptual description of the verbs in WordNet. In order to make the alignment between the patterns obtained from VerbNet and FrameNet as precise as possible, we perform this procedure at the literal level and then transferred onto the the FrameNet frame and VerbNet class pair, i.e. for each literal in a synset which is mapped to a lexical unit in FrameNet and an entry in VerbNet, the corresponding patterns from the two resources are aligned according to several criteria. These include:

- correspondence in the number of elements or roles expressed in a syntactic pattern;
- correspondence between the frame element and the semantic role mapped to it as part of the previous task;
- correspondence in the syntactic restrictions (PP heads, clause types or subordinating elements) defined for the mapped frame elements and semantic roles;

- correspondence between the syntactic expression of each mapped frame element and semantic role – both in terms of the type of syntactic phrase by means of which they are expressed (NP, PP, etc.), and the syntactic position in which they are projected (e.g. subject, object).

The syntactic pattern alignment procedure is implemented as a set of mapping rules. As a result of their application, we obtain a list of the equivalent syntactic models for a given FrameNet frame and VerbNet class pair (Examples 5, 6 and 7). Where no correspondence is discovered, the table cell is marked as NONE.

Example 5. Aligned syntactic patterns for the WordNet synset *eng-30-00001740-v breathe; take a breath; respire; suspire*, FrameNet frame *Breathing* and the VerbNet class *breathe-40.1.2*. (FN syntactic patterns with frequency of 3+ are labelled by a *.)

WN	Somebody	–s	
VN	NP(Agent)	V	
FN	*NP.Ext(Agent)	V	
WN	Somebody	–s	
VN	NP(Agent)	V	PP.destination[on,onto] (Destination)
FN	*NP.Ext(Agent)	V	INC(Air) PP[in,on](Goal)
WN	Somebody	–s	something
VN	NP(Agent)	V	NP(Theme)
FN	*NP.Ext(Agent)	V	NP(Air)
WN	Somebody	–s	something
VN	NP(Agent)	V	NP(Theme) PP.destination[on,onto] (Destination)
FN	*NP.Ext(Agent)	V	NP(Air) PP[in,on](Goal)
WN	Somebody	–s	
VN	NONE		
FN	NP.Ext(Agent)	V	INC(Air) PP[down] (Path)
	NP.Ext(Agent)	V	INC(Air) PP[in] (Place)
	*NP.Ext(Agent)	V	INC(Air) PP[at] (External_cause)
	*NP.Ext(Agent)	V	INC(Air) AVP (Manner)
	NP.Ext(Agent)	V	INC(Air) PP[by,without] (Means)
	NP.Ext(Agent)	V	INC(Air) PP[as] (Depictive)
	NP.Ext(Agent)	V	INC(Air) PP[from,out] (Source)
	NP.Ext(Agent)	V	INC(Air) VPto (Purpose)
WN	Somebody	–s	something
VN	NONE		
FN	NP.Ext(Agent)	V	NP(Air) PP[down] (Path)
	NP.Ext(Agent)	V	NP(Air) AVP (Manner)
	NP.Ext(Agent)	V	NP(Air) PP[in](Goal) PP[from,out] (Source)
	NP.Ext(Agent)	V	NP(Air) PP[in](Goal) PP[through] (Instrument)

Example 5 shows the alignment of the syntactic patterns between the frame *Breathing* and the class *breathe-40.1.2* following the mapping between the frame elements and semantic roles (Agent – Agent, Air – Theme, Source – Source, Goal–Destination). Misalignment occurs in the cases of additional semantic roles that are not considered core FEs (e.g., Path, Manner, etc.) which have no correspondence to VerbNet roles and participants in WordNet basic sentence frames.

Example 6. Aligned syntactic patterns for the FrameNet frame *Killing* and the VerbNet class *murder-42.1* for the synset eng-30-01323958-v *kill* 'cause to die; put to death, usually intentionally or knowingly'.

WN	Somebody	–s	somebody	
VN	NP(Agent)	V	NP(Patient)	
FN	NP.Ext(Killer)	V	NP.Obj(Victim)	
WN	Somebody	–s	somebody	
VN	NP(Agent)	V	NP(Patient)	{with} PP.instrument (Instrument)
FN	NP.Ext(Killer)	V	NP.Obj(Victim)	PP[with].Dep (Instrument)
WN	Something	–s	somebody	
VN	NP.instrument (Instrument)	V	NP(Patient)	
FN	NP.Ext (Instrument)	V	NP.Obj(Victim)	
WN	Something	–s	somebody	
VN	NONE			
FN	NP.Ext(Cause)	V	NP.Obj(Victim)	

Example 7. Aligned syntactic patterns for the FrameNet frame *Killing* and the VerbNet class *suffocate-40.7* (e.g., *asphyxiate, choke, suffocate*, etc.).

WN	Somebody	–s	somebody	
VN	NP(Agent)	V	NP(Patient)	
FN	NP.Ext(Killer)	V	NP.Obj(Victim)	
WN	Somebody	–s	somebody	
VN	NP(Agent)	V	NP(Patient)	{with} PP.instrument (Instrument)
FN	NP.Ext(Killer)	V	NP.Obj(Victim)	PP[with].Dep (Instrument)
WN	Something	–s	somebody	
VN	NONE			
FN	NP.Ext (Instrument)	V	NP.Obj(Victim)	
WN	Something	–s	somebody	
VN	NONE			
FN	NP.Ext(Cause)	V	NP.Obj(Victim)	
WN	Somebody	–s	somebody	
VN	NP(Agent)	V	NP(Patient)	{to, into} PP.result(Result)
FN	NONE			

Examples 6 and 7 show different degrees of misalignment between the syntactic patterns of the corresponding frames and verb classes. The frame *Killing* allows for the Instrument to appear as an external argument NP which matches a syntactic pattern within the verb class *murder-42.1* but not the verb class *suffocate-40.7*. Further, while the verbs evoking the frame *Killing* incorporate the result (the death of the Patient / Victim), the verb class *suffocate-40.7* also allows for a different Result as shown in the last row of the table in Example 7 (e.g., *suffocate to/into unconsciousness*).

Further, in order to increase the number of mapped frames we generalise some unmapped FrameNet frames by excluding optional or unexpressed arguments, thus reducing the pattern to a more basic form.

The asymmetries in the syntactic patterns covered by matched FrameNet frames and VerbNet classes for particular WordNet synsets are indicative of the need for more detailed syntactic analysis and the study of both the alignment between frame elements and semantic roles and their syntactic realisation.

Example 8 shows sentences featuring the literals from a given synset which are extracted from SemCor.

Example 8. Corpus data for the FN frame – VN class pair <Becoming_aware : see-30.1> on synset eng-30-00598954-v verb.cognition *learn; hear; get word; get wind; pick up; find out; get a line; discover; see* 'get to know or become aware of, usually accidentally'

Most frequent aligned patterns:

VN: NP (Experiencer) V NP (Stimulus)
FN: NP (Cognizer) V NP (Phenomenon)

VN: NP (Experiencer) V PP.stimulus[about,of] (Stimulus)
FN: NP (Cognizer) V PP (Phenomenon)

VN: NP (Experiencer) V S[that,wh*,∅] (Stimulus)
FN: NP (Cognizer) V S[that,wh*,∅] (Phenomenon)

Corpus examples:

*We **learned** this year that our older son, Daniel, is autistic.*
*Have you ever **heard** of thuggee?*
*We had merely been **discovered** by the pool sharks.*
*We want to **find_out** who knew about it.*
*Williams is **learning** the difficulties of diplomacy rapidly.*
*I was anxious to **hear** about those dazzling days on the Great_White Way.*
*What obsessions had she **picked_up** during these long nights of talk?*

As illustrated by the examples: (a) some literals appear more frequently in the data while others do not appear at all (e.g., *get wind*) and for the latter we cannot draw any conclusions; (b) some literals have a restricted number of patterns applicable to them (e.g., multiword expressions such as **get word** cannot have a Phenomenon as a direct object) or accept particular lexical entries (e.g., prepositions *hear of* but **pick_up of*).

7 Results

The processing of the data included the following key procedures:

(1) Identifying FrameNet-frame-to-WordNet-synsets alignments and selecting only manually validated ones so as to ensure the quality of the dataset.

(2) Identifying VerbNet-class-to-WordNet-synsets alignments. Out of these, as a matter of validation, we select only those that have been aligned to FrameNet frames.

(3) The resulting dataset covers 1,121 WordNet synsets and a total of 5,264 verb literals. Each synset is assigned a pair <FN frame : VN class>. There are a total of 329 such pairs involving 195 FrameNet frames and 165 VerbNet classes. As already illustrated (e.g., Example 3), there are VerbNet classes that correspond to more than one pair of alignments, as well as FrameNet frames that correspond to more than one class (e.g., Examples 6 and 7).

The VerbNet classes represented in the dataset include 32 unique semantic roles which are matched to a total of 217 FrameNet frame elements.

The synsets in the dataset cover 29 (out of the 35) generalised WordNet sentence frames. These are aligned to 451 VerbNet syntactic patterns and 13,884 FrameNet syntactic patterns. The greater number of FrameNet syntactic realisations is due to: (a) the large number of peripheral and extra-thematic frame elements[12] and the variety of configurations they enter in the different realisations; and (b) the representations of alternations and variations (e.g., passives, incorporation of FEs, various prepositions in PPs, etc.). The FrameNet patterns

[12]Although we focus on the core FEs, the syntactic patterns include some peripheral and extra-thematic elements with high frequency.

have been filtered based on frequency (of examples exhibiting the pattern included in the FrameNet dataset), which has resulted in 811 FrameNet syntactic patterns with frequency of 3 or more.

The dataset is supplemented with a set of 16,059 corpus examples illustrating the annotated synsets (on average, 14 examples per synset). Additionally, we have also included the usage examples provided in all of the resources – WordNet examples (which are often not full sentences but phrases) and FrameNet and VerbNet illustrative examples.

The newly developed resource containing pairs of a FrameNet frame and a VerbNet class with their corresponding syntactic patterns for realisation of FEs and semantic roles is distributed under a CC by 4.0 license[13].

7.1 Towards Literal-Specific Description

Our efforts are aimed at expanding the description of WordNet synsets towards a complex conceptual and syntactic representation. While the conceptual description applies to a large extent to the whole synsets, the considered syntactic patterns are relevant to individual literals in the synset. The corpus examples provide material to confirm the syntactic patterns valid for certain literals. However, for some literals there are insufficient number of examples or no examples at all. These will require the use of a general corpus with no semantic annotation where ambiguity also needs to be taken into account. However, the syntactic models applying to some of the literals in the synset can serve to extract detailed semantic description of the semantic roles and frame elements co-occuring with the particular use of the verb and its subcategorisation frame, and this knowledge can inform algorithms for synonym detection in a general corpus and identifying verbs belonging to the same synset and analysing their syntactic realisation.

7.2 Towards a Cross-Language Description

Further, efforts can be invested into the cross-language transfer of knowledge in order to develop conceptual and syntactic description of synsets for other languages, especially under-resourced languages such as Bulgarian. For this purpose, once again, we consider the applicability of the conceptual description contained in FrameNet frames and VerbNet classes as largely language-independent, which can be transferred and / or adapted. The syntactic patterns need further examination and filtering in order to match the Bulgarian data. We have extracted a dataset of 6,249 sentences from the BulSemCor corpus containing instances of the synsets under analysis. Some of the syntactic patterns can be directly transferred to Bulgarian, while others need adaptation (e.g., considering prepositions or other lexical information), or are not relevant (e.g., constructions such as 'THERE (Aux) is / are ...' which are not found in Bulgarian).

In the future our efforts will be focused on validating the syntactic description for Bulgarian and expanding the dataset of examples in order to provide more linguistic material for reliable decisions on the syntactic realisation of verbs and their subcategorisation frames.

8 Conclusions

In this paper we present a dataset of WordNet synsets supplied with extensive semantic, conceptual and syntactic information obtained by combining (i) WordNet's description and semantic relations with (ii) the conceptual information from the relevant FrameNet frame (including the frame elements and the specific semantic restrictions) and VerbNet class assigned to the synsets and (iii) the syntactic patterns compiled from all the three resources and aligned both in terms of the syntactic realisation and the frame element or semantic role of each component.

The combination of semantic and syntactic information is seen as a possible way to transfer knowledge across languages (e.g., from English to Bulgarian) by relying on the universality of semantic description. Various annotated corpora will be further used in studying the syntactic properties of verbs to the end of: enhancing their applicability to NLP tasks such as semantic role labelling, word sense disambiguation, etc. Another promising venue of research is related to facilitating the more precise identification of the participants in the situations described by verbs, thus enabling better information extraction, text recognition and generation, question answering, machine translation.

9 Acknowledgments

This paper is carried out as part of the scientific programme under the project *Enriching the Semantic Network Wordnet with Conceptual Frames* funded by the Bulgarian National Science Fund (Grant Agreement No. KP-06-N50/1 of 2020).

[13]https://dcl.bas.bg/enriching-wordnet-results/

References

Collin F. Baker. 2008. FrameNet, present and future. In *The First International Conference on Global Interoperability for Language Resources*, Hong Kong. City University, City University.

Collin F. Baker and Christiane Fellbaum. 2009. WordNet and FrameNet as complementary resources for annotation. In *Proceedings of the Third Linguistic Annotation Workshop (LAW III)*, pages 125–129, Suntec, Singapore. Association for Computational Linguistics.

Collin F. Baker, Charles J. Fillmore, and John B. Lowe. 1998. The Berkeley FrameNet project. In *COLING-ACL '98: Proceedings of the Conference. Montreal, Canada*, pages 86–90.

Andrea Di Fabio, Simone Conia, and Roberto Navigli. 2019. Verbatlas: a novel large-scale verbal semantic resource and its application to semantic role labeling. In *Proceedings of the 2019 Conference on Empirical Methods in Natural Language Processing and the 9th International Joint Conference on Natural Language Processing, Hong Kong, China, November 3 – 7, 2019*, page 627 – 637. Association for Computational Linguistics.

Christiane Fellbaum. 1990. English Verbs as a Semantic Net. *International Journal of Lexicography*, 3(4):278–301.

Christiane Fellbaum, editor. 1998. *WordNet: an electronic lexical database*. MIT Press, Cambridge, MA.

Christiane Fellbaum, editor. 1999. *WordNet: an Electronic Lexical Database*. MIT Press, Cambridge, MA.

Óscar Ferrández, Michael Ellsworth, Rafael Muñoz, and Collin F. Baker. 2010. Aligning FrameNet and WordNet based on semantic neighborhoods. In *Proceedings of the 7th Conference on Language Resources and Evaluation (LREC 2010), May 17-23, Valletta, Malta*, pages 310 – 314.

Karin Kipper, Anna Korhonen, Neville Ryant, and Martha Palmer. 2008. Language resources and evaluation. *Communications. ACM*, 42(1):21–40.

Karin Kipper-Schuler. 2005. *VerbNet: A broad-coverage, comprehensive verb lexicon. PhD Thesis*. Computer and Information Science Dept., University of Pennsylvania. Philadelphia, PA.

S. Koeva, S. Leseva, B. Rizov, E. Tarpomanova, T. Dimitrova, H. Kukova, and M. Todorova. 2011. Design and development of the Bulgarian Sense-Annotated Corpus. In *Proceedings of the Third International Corpus Linguistics Conference (CILC), 7-9 April 2011, Valencia, Spain*, pages 143–150. Universitat Politecnica de Valencia.

Svetla Koeva, Svetlozara Leseva, Ekaterina Tarpomanova, Borislav Rizov, Tsvetana Dimitrova, and Hristina Kukova. 2010. Bulgarian Sense-Annotated Corpus – results and achievement. In *Proceedings of the 7th International Conference of Formal Approaches to South Slavic and Balkan Languages (FASSBL-7)*, pages 41–49.

Shari Landes, Claudia Leacock, and Rundee Tengi. 1998. Building semantic concordances. In Christiane Fellbaum, editor, *WordNet: An electronic lexical database*, chapter 8.

Egoitz Laparra and German Rigau. 2010. eXtended WordFrameNet. In *Proceedings of LREC 2010*, pages 1214–1219.

Svetlozara Leseva and Ivelina Stoyanova. 2019. Enhancing conceptual description through resource linking and exploration of semantic relations. In *Proceedings of 10th Global WordNet Conference, 23 – 27 July 2019, Wroclaw, Poland*, pages 229–238.

Svetlozara Leseva and Ivelina Stoyanova. 2020. Beyond lexical and semantic resources: linking WordNet with FrameNet and enhancing synsets with conceptual frames. In *Towards a Semantic Network Enriched with a Variety of Semantic Relations*. Prof. Marin Drinov Academic Publishing House of the Bulgarian Academy of Sciences.

Svetlozara Leseva, Ivelina Stoyanova, Hristina Kukova, and Maria Todorova. 2018a. Integration of subcategorisation information in WordNet's relational structure. *Balgarski ezik*, 65(2):11–40.

Svetlozara Leseva, Ivelina Stoyanova, and Maria Todorova. 2018b. Classifying verbs in WordNet by harnessing semantic resources. In *Proceedings of CLIB 2018, Sofia, Bulgaria*.

Beth Levin. 1993. *English verb classes and alternations: A preliminary investigation*. Chicago and London: The University of Chicago Press.

George A. Miller. 1995. WordNet: A lexical database for English. *Commun. ACM*, 38(11):39–41.

George A. Miller, Claudia Leacock, Randee Tengi, and Ross T. Bunker. 1993. A semantic concordance. In *Human Language Technology: Proceedings of a Workshop Held at Plainsboro, New Jersey, March 21-24, 1993*.

Martha Palmer. 2009. Semlink: linking PropBank, VerbNet and FrameNet. In *Proceedings of the Generative Lexicon Conference*. 9–15.

Martha Palmer, Claire Bonial, and Diana McCarthy. 2014. SemLink+: FrameNet, VerbNet and event ontologies. In *Proceedings of Frame Semantics in NLP: A Workshop in Honor of Chuck Fillmore (1929–2014), Baltimore, Maryland USA, June 27, 2014*, pages 13–17. Association for Computational Linguistics.

Josef Ruppenhofer, Michael Ellsworth, Miriam R. L. Petruck, Christopher. R. Johnson, Collin. F. Baker, and Jan Scheffczyk. 2016. *FrameNet II: extended theory and practice*. International Computer Science Institute, Berkeley, California.

Gerold Schneider. 2012. Using semantic resources to improve a syntactic dependency parser. In *LREC 2012 Conference Workshop "Semantic Relations II", Istanbul, Turkey, 22 May 2012*, pages 67–76.

Lei Shi and Rada Mihalcea. 2005. Putting pieces together: combining FrameNet, VerbNet and WordNet for robust semantic parsing. In A. Gelbukh, editor, *Computational Linguistics and Intelligent Text Processing. CICLing 2005. Lecture Notes in Computer Science*, volume 3406. Springe, Berlin, Heidelbergr.

Kevin Stowe, Jenette Preciado, Kathryn Conger, Susan Brown, Ghazaleh Kazeminejad, James Gung, and Martha Palmer. Semlink 2.0: chasing lexical resources. In *Proceedings of the 14th International Conference on Computational Semantics, pages 222–227 June 17–18, 2021*, pages 222–227. Association for Computational Linguistics.

Sara Tonelli and Daniele Pighin. 2009. New features for Framenet – Wordnet mapping. In *Proceedings of the Thirteenth Conference on Computational Natural Language Learning (CoNLL'09), Boulder, USA*.

Zdenka Urešová, Eva Fucíková, Eva Hajičová, and Jan Hajič. 2020a. SynSemClass linked lexicon: Mapping synonymy between languages. In *Proceedings of the Globalex Workshop on Linked Lexicography, Language Resources and Evaluation Conference (LREC 2020), Marseille, 11–16 May 2020*, pages 10 – 19.

Zdenka Urešová, Eva Fučíková, Eva Hajičová, and Jan Hajič. 2020b. Syntactic-semantic classes of context-sensitive synonyms based on a bilingual corpus. In *Human Language Technology. Challenges for Computer Science and Linguistics*, pages 242–255. Springer International Publishing.

An Experiment: Finding Parents for Parentless Synsets by Means of CILI

Ahti Lohk[1], **Martin Rebane**[2] and **Heili Orav**[3]

[1]Department of Software Science, Tallinn University of Technology, Tallinn, Estonia
[2]School of Engineering, University of Warwick, Coventry, United Kingdom
[3] Department of Computer Science, University of Tartu, Tartu, Estonia

<ahti.lohk@taltech.ee,
martin.rebane@warwick.ac.uk,
heili.orav@ut.ee>

Abstract

Identifying and correcting inconsistencies in wordnets is a natural part of their development. Focusing only on the sub-problem of *missing links*, we aim to find automatically possible parents for parentless synsets in IS-A hierarchies of a target wordnet by means of source wordnets where target and source wordnets are in XML-format and equipped with Collaborative Interlingual Index (CILI).
In this paper, we describe the algorithm and provide statistics on the possible parents of parentless synsets of the wordnets included in the study. Additionally, we investigate the suitability of the proposed potential parent synsets for correcting noun and verb synsets within the Estonian wordnet.

1 Introduction

One of the main goals of wordnet (Fellbaum 1998) development is to make it accessible while ensuring its correctness.

The developer must consider that wordnet errors can be formal, semantic, or structural, where **formal errors** are related to the source file structure or data presentation in it, **semantic errors** are related to wordnet semantics and **structural errors** are related to wordnet as a graph (Piasecki et al., 2013). The category of structural errors is set apart from formal and semantic errors in that it doesn't require any knowledge of the wordnet language, but correcting it requires the assistance of a lexicographer (Lohk 2015).

Structural errors often result in **missing links** between wordnet synsets, which is one of the most obvious problems. This type of problem can appear either as 1) synsets that are completely lacking semantic relationships, as 2) small separate hierarchies, or as 3) a big number of parentless synsets.

In identifying parentless synsets for noun and verb synsets, it must be considered that the synsets named as root concepts (or unique beginners) cannot have parents[1]. For example, only one root concept of the IS-A noun hierarchy - {entity} - has been considered correct for the Princeton WordNet. On the Dutch wordnet Cornetto (version 2)[2], however, the corresponding number is two. The same number of root concepts is also assigned to verb hierarchies of Cornetto. (Lohk, 2015). These three examples point to a situation where there is no problem with parentless synsets. Nevertheless, this problem is common to all wordnets tested by us in this experiment. For example, the verb hierarchies of Open English WordNet (OEWN) contain as many as 574 parentless synsets (see Table 1).

The fact that there are synsets with missing links in wordnet has been pointed out by other authors (Smrž, 2004, Richens, 2011). However, to the best of the authors' knowledge, no solution has been proposed that automatically provides a possible parent for a parentless synset. This article tries to partially fill this gap, focusing primarily on such missing links, where synset lacks a parent or higher-level concept (superordinate). An additional refinement of the proposed approach comes from

[1] An exception is synsets, which are labeled as nouns but are names in terms of content.

[2] http://www.cltl.nl/projects/previous-projects/cornetto/

the fact that we take advantage of the information available on wordnets equipped with Collaborative Interlingual Index (CILI) (Bond et al., 2016).

To conduct the experiment, we utilize the following wordnets: Estonian wordnet (EstWN, version 2.5)[3] (Orav et al., 2018), Open English WordNet (OEWN, version 2021)[4] and six wordnets downloaded from the Open Multilingual Wordnet[5] website: Open German WordNet (Odenet)[6], Open Dutch WordNet (ODWN) (Postma et al., 2016), Finnish WordNet (FinWN)

Wordnet (language)	Parentless synsets	
	noun	verb
OEWN (English)	8	574
EstWN (Estonian)	190	13
Odenet (German)	3 433	2 583
ODWN (Dutch)	0	87
FinWN (Finnish)	172	559
LSG (Irish)	6 000	1 468
OWN-PT (Portuguese)	18 577	7 143
NTU-JPN (Japanese)	5 766	420

Table 1: Number of parentless synsets in wordnets.

(Lindén et al., 2010), Irish Language Semantic Network (LSG)[7], Open Brazilian Wordnet (WN-PT) (de Paiva et al., 2012), Japanese Open Wordnet (NTU-JPN) (Isahara et al., 2008). All eight wordnets are in XML-format and many of their synsets are CILI- equipped.

The main idea behind our approach is to provide possible parents for parentless synsets in target wordnet using other wordnets. More specifically, this means that a possible parent can only be provided if both the target wordnet synset and its possible parent are equipped with a CILI, and so are the synsets from other wordnets corresponding to the same CILIs.

The paper is organized in the following manner: Section 2 formulates the algorithm to find parents for parentless synsets by means of CILI. Next, Section 3 describes the format for reporting the results and provides descriptive statistics about the results obtained. Section 4 focuses on the case study of Estonian Wordnet. Section 5 concludes the paper and its findings.

2 Algorithm

Each wordnet w contains a set of synsets S. Each synset $s \in S$ has a unique ID number i and might have an optional Collaborative Inter Lingual Index (CILI) $c \in C$ where C is a set of all CILIs. ID i is unique with a wordnet, but each wordnet uses its own set of ID numbers. CILI c is also unique within a wordnet but all wordnets use the same c for equivalent synsets. Additionally, most (but not all) synsets have hierarchical parent-child relationship structure. However, such relationship might exist in a language but be missing in the wordnet. CILIs make it possible to use one wordnet w_{src} as a source to estimate the hierarchical parent-child relationship of the other wordnet w_{tgt} (target). The algorithm in this Section does this by using a set of CILIs C_{src} of w_{src}, a set of CILIs C_{tgt} of w_{tgt}, parent-child relationship map M_{src} Msrc of w_{src} for computing a parent-child relationship map M_{tgt} for w_{tgt}. Each CILI c in C_{src} has an associated set of parent CILIs P_c. Each CILI $c \in C$ also has an associated ID number i. Therefore, it is possible to construct a map M_{tgt} that represents estimated parent-child relationships for target wordnet w_{tgt}based on similar relations in w_{src}. We introduce Algorithm 1 to construct such map.

Algorithm 1 Synset Sync

```
Input: map : M_src, set : C_src, set : C_tgt
M_tgt = map : ∅
for all c ∈ C_tgt do
    P_c ← getParentCilis(c, M_src)
    for all c_parent ∈ P_c do
        i_child = getSynsetIdByCili(c, C_tgt)
        i_parent = getSynsetIdByCili(c_parent, C_tgt)
        relation : r =< i_child, i_parent >
        M_tgt = M_tgt ∪ {r | r ∉ M_tgt}
    end for
end for
return M_tgt
```

We assume that it is trivial to map CILI c to a corresponding ID i and will represent this operation as a function $getSynsetIdByCili(cili : c, set : C)$. Finding parents using a map data structure is also a standard procedure in every programming language, hence we represent this as

[3]https://gitlab.keeleressursid.ee/avalik/data/-/tree/master/estwn/estwn-et-2.5

[4]https://en-word.net/

[5]https://github.com/globalwordnet/OMW

[6]https://ikum.mediencampus.h-da.de/projekt/open-de-wordnet-initiative

[7]https://cadhan.com/lsg/index-en.html

a function $getParentCilis(cili : c, map : M)$. The resulting map M_{tgt} contains all found parent-child relations for w_{tgt} based on similar relations in w_{src}. Therefore, it does not limit the depth of hierarchy, i.e., the algorithm is able to find and store complex and deep hierarchical relations.

3 Results

Within this section, we describe the format for reporting the results and provide descriptive statistics about the results obtained.

3.1 Presentation format of results

The examples presented in **Appendices A-D** give an idea of the format for presenting the results. Here we provide a detailed overview of the structure of the presentation format.

Appendices A-D represent four categories of results, which are explained in more details in Section 4.

Each case of a parentless synset begins with a **sequence number**. The rest of the information is distributed among five fields. We will explain their content in more thoroughly below.

1) **Without parent**
   A target wordnet synset with no parent is displayed under "WITHOUT PARENT". Along with the synset, synset ID, and the OEWN equivalent synset are presented through CILI.
2) **Possible parent(s)**
   Finding possible parents is based on the CILIs identified under "PARENTS FROM OTHER WORDNET(S):" which refers to parents in other wordnets. "POSSIBLE PARENT(S)" is presented above because this information is more important to the lexicographer. If no parent is found for the target wordnet parentless synset through CILI, the text "No possible parent(s) through CILI" is returned.
3) **Parents from other wordnet(s)**
   This structure field gets its content based on the CILI given in the "WITHOUT PARENT" field. There are as many lines in this field as there are wordnets among the source wordnets that input CILI finds parent with CILI. Each line contains information about the CILI of the synset without a parent, the CILI of the synset with its corresponding parent, the synset ID given to the parent of the CILI in a particular wordnet, and the equivalent synset in the OEWN. The latter is added so that the content of synsets can be quickly captured. If no parent is found in source wordnets, the text "No possible parent(s) through CILI" is returned.
4) **Possible grandparent(s)**
   To get a broader background of the problem situation, we added possible grandparents in addition to possible parents. Finding possible grandparents is based on the CILIs identified under "GRANDPARENTS FROM OTHER WORDNET(S):" which refer to grandparents in other wordnets. If no grandparent is found for the target wordnet parentless synset through CILI, the text "No possible parent(s) through CILI" is returned.
5) **Grandparents from other wordnet(s)**
   The content of this field is derived like the "PARENTS FROM OTHER WORDNET(S)" field. The difference is that the CILIs used as input are the same as those given in the "Possible parents" field.

3.2 Statistics

Just as in Table 1, only synsets whose first, last and second member (lexical unit) does not start with a capital letter are considered in Table 2 to avoid synsets, which are defined by nouns, but which are names in terms of content. In the last column of the Table 2, the first two numbers represent cases where parents were found in the source wordnets regardless of whether a parent was also found in the target wordnet. Many of the figures seen in the table are very large. One reason for this is that the result contains both synsets with subordinates and those without (so called orb synsets). In the case of the EstWN, the number of synsets without parents is low as expected, since its structure has been validated with various graph methods in the last ten years (Lohk, 2015).

For our study, it is important to know in how many cases it is possible to obtain additional information for parentless synsets. This information can be obtained by dividing the last number in the third column (possible simultaneous absence of parents and grandparents) by the first number in the second column (number of synsets equipped with CILI and without parents). The resulting quotient gives an idea of how large amount of synsets lack a parent and/or grandparent. Parents and grandparents found through CILI seem to benefit the most in the case of the OWN-PT, where possible parents/grandparents information is missing only in 0.8% of the cases (194/25660 x 100). It is followed by the Irish wordnet and EstWN, where these numbers are 1.5% and 12.2% respectively.

By comparing the number of parentless synsets in Tables 1 and 2, we can see in Figure 1 the extent to which parentless synsets are endowed with CILI.

Wordnet/ Language	Nr of parentless synsets with CILI total|noun|verb	Nr of possible parents| grandparents| no parents & grandparents
OEWN (English)	572|7|565	268|250|300
EstWN (Estonian)	41|35|6	36|36|5
Odenet (German)	2052|1313|739	1178|1140|874
ODWN (Dutch)	87|0|87	38|31|49
FinWN (Finnish)	730|171|559	410|390|319
LSG (Irish)	7454|5989|1465	7337|7258|114
OWN-PT (Portuguese)	25660|18517|7143	25457|25020|194
NTU-JPN (Japanese)	5950|5530|420|	5211|5192|739

Table 2: Descriptive statistics of results

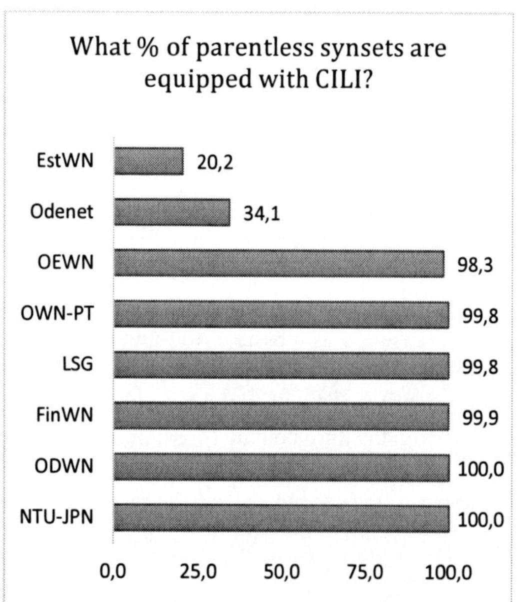

Figure 1: CILI proportions in parentless synsets in different wordnets

4 Case Study of Estonian Wordnet (EstWN)

In the EstWN analysis, our program found 41 parentless and CILI-equipped synsets. The noun synsets were represented 35 times and the verb synsets 6 times. In 7 cases out of 41 it was not necessary to determine a parent, as the synsets represented root concept.

After a closer examination of each of the 41 cases by the lexicographer, it was found that the decisions that had to be made in solving them fell into four categories (for each category, one example is given in the appendices):

1) The suggested possible parent was suitable for the parentless synset. **10 cases**. (See Appendix A)
2) The suggested possible grandparent was suitable for the parentless synset. **4 cases**. (See Appendix C)
3) The parentless synset turned out to be a root concept. **7 cases** (3 nouns + 4 verbs). (See Appendix B).
4) A parentless synset receives a parent that was not present in either the possible parents or grandparents. **21 cases**. (See Appendix D)

All root concepts classified under category 3 are not root concepts in any other language. This becomes obvious when comparing the EstWN root concepts with the corresponding synsets of OEWN. It turns out that two out of three EstWN noun root concepts have parent in the OEWN. That means, if the EstWN has ['existence', 'existence', ...] (['existence', 'being', '...']) as a root concept, then in the OEWN its parent is ['state']. Also, if the EstWN has ['fenomen', 'ilming', '...'] (['phenomenon'] as a root concept, then in the OEWN its parent is ['process', 'physical process'].

With four EstWN verb root concepts, it is noteworthy that no single source wordnet (including OEWN) offers any parents for them.

In the EstWN, root concepts for nouns and verbs are as follows:

1) (n) ['olev'] (['entity'], oewn-00001740-n)
2) (n) ['eksisteerimine', 'eksistents', 'olelu', '...'] (['existence', 'being', 'beingness', '...'], oewn-13977471-n)
3) (n) ['fenomen', 'ilming', 'nähe', '...'] (['phenomenon'], oewn-00034512-n)
4) (v) ['modifitseeruma', 'muutuma', '...'] (['switch', 'change', ...], oewn-00551194-v)

5) (v) ['sooritama', 'tegema'] (['do', 'execute', 'perform'], oewn-01716563-v)
6) (v) ['eksisteerima', 'olema', '...'] (['exist', 'be'], oewn-02609706-v)
7) (v) ['olema'] (['be'], oewn-02610777-v)

Summarizing the results of the four categories, it is easy to decide about a parentless synset in approximately half of the cases. Such cases belong to categories 1 to 3. Most efforts should be made to resolve Category 4 cases where possible parents and/or grandparents have been suggested but are not suitable.

Hereby we give some examples where the suggested parent was unsuitable for the EstWN. Briefly, these cases can be summarized on the grounds that, although a parentless synset is related via CILI to synsets in other language wordnets, its semantic field is sufficiently different to be assigned the same parents as in other wordnets.

Example 1:
Parentless synset:
['smugeldamine', '...'] (['smuggling'])
Suggested parent:
['import', '...'] (['importation', 'importing'])
Correct parent:
[transport, '...'] ([['transport', 'transfer', '...'])
Argument:
smuggling in Estonian does not mean only import but also export

Example 2:
Parentless synset:
['möirataja', '...'] (['screamer', 'shouter', '...'])
Suggested parent:
['suhtleja'] (['communicator'])
Correct parent:
['hääletegija'] (*voice maker*). No corresponding CILI.
Argument:
'screamer' is not necessarily only a person in Estonian.

Example 3:
Parentless synset:
['amatörism'] (['amateurism'])
Suggested parent:
['conviction', 'articleoffaith', 'strongbelief']
Correct parent:
['harrastus'] (['avocation', 'by-line', 'hobby', '...']
Argument:
'amateurism' in Estonian is more of a hobby than conviction.

Example 4:
Parentless synset:
['foneetika', '...'] ([' phonetics'])
Suggested parent:
['akustika', 'heliõpetus'] (['acoustics'])
Correct parent:
[lingvistika, '...'] ([['linguistics'])
Argument:
The authoritative dictionary of the Estonian language (Sõnaveeb [8]) declares that phonetics is a part of linguistics.

5 Conclusion

The present study proposed an approach for identifying potential parents for parentless synsets equipped with the Collaborative Interlingual Index (CILI) feature using source wordnets. The method is applicable to all wordnets with different languages that have specific XML formats and CILI-equipped synsets and has the potential to enhance the quality of wordnets.

The experiment revealed that seven out of the eight wordnets analyzed contained a significant number of parentless synsets. However, the majority of these synsets, six out of eight wordnets, had 98% or more parentless synsets that were also equipped with a designated CILI. Possible parents and grandparents were automatically found for 43% to 99% of the parentless synsets across different wordnets, with 87% or more of the synsets having possible parents in half of the cases.

The study indicates that lexicographer involvement may be necessary to correct the identified inconsistencies (missing parents), and that synsets connected through CILI in different languages may have different meanings.

The proposed approach could also be applied to detect inconsistencies in synsets that already have parents in the future. Overall, the method presented in this study provides a useful tool for improving the quality of wordnets across various languages.

References

Fellbaum, D. C. 1998. *WordNet: An Electronic Lexical Database*. Cambridge: MIT Press

Bond, F., Vossen, P. Th. J. M., McCrae, J. P. and Fellbaum, C. D., 2016. CILI: the collaborative interlingual index. In *Proceedings of the 8th Global WordNet Conference (GWC2016)*, pp. 50-57. https://aclanthology.org/2016.gwc-1.9/

[8] https://sonaveeb.ee/

Isahara, H., Bond, F., Uchimoto, K., Utiyama, M. and Kanzaki, K., 2008. Development of the Japanese WordNet. *In Proceedings of the Sixth International Conference on Language Resources and Evaluation (LREC'08),* pp. 2420-2423. https://aclanthology.org/L08-1269/

Lindén, K. and Carlson, L., 2010. *FinnWordNet–finnish wordnet by translation.* LexicoNordica–Nordic Journal of Lexicography, 17, pp.119-140.

Lohk, A. 2015. *A System of Test Patterns to Check and Validate the Semantic Hierarchies of Wordnet-type Dictionaries*. Tallinn, Estonia: TalTech Press.

McCrae, J.P., Rademaker, A., Bond, F., Rudnicka, E. and Fellbaum, C., 2019, July. English WordNet 2019 – An Open-Source WordNet for English. *In Proceedings of the 10th Global WordNet Conference (GWC2019),* pp 245-252.

de Paiva, V., Rademaker, A., de Melo, G. 2012. OpenWordNet-PT: An Open Brazilian Wordnet for Reasoning. *In Proceedings of COLING 2012: Demonstration Papers*. Mumbai, India, pp. 353-360.

Orav, H., Vare, K. and Zupping, S., 2018, January. Estonian Wordnet: Current State and Future Prospects. *In Proceedings of the 9th Global Wordnet Conference*, pp. 347-351.

Piasecki, M., Burdka, L., Maziarz, M., 2013. Wordnet Diagnostics in Development, *In Human Language Technologies as a Challenge for Computer Science and Linguistics*. Poznań, Poland, pp. 268–272.

Postma, M., Van Miltenburg, E., Segers, R., Schoen, A. and Vossen, P., 2016. Open Dutch WordNet. *In Proceedings of the 8th Global WordNet Conference (GWC2016)*, pp. 302-310.

Richens, T., 2008. Anomalies in the Wordnet Verb Hierarchy, *In Proceedings of the 22nd International Conference on Computational Linguistics-Volume 1. Association for Computational Linguistics (ACL)*, pp. 729–736.

Smrž, P., 2004. Quality control for wordnet development. *In Proceedings of the Second International WordNet Conference (GWC2004),* pp. 206-212.

Appendix A. The suggested possible parent which was suitable for parentless synset

```
-----------------------------------------------------------------------------------
26 # Correct parent for ['puuderdama'] (['powder']) is ['maalima', 'meikima', 'minkima',
'...'] (['makeup'])
-----------------------------------------------------------------------------------
WITHOUT PARENT
       i21979 estwn-et-19703-v|['puuderdama']
       (OEWN equivalent: oewn-00041904-v|['powder'])

POSSIBLE PARENT(S):
       i21972 estwn-et-5410-v|['maalima', 'meikima', 'minkima', '...']

PARENTS FROM OTHER WORDNET(S):
       (i21979)->i21972 cow-00040928-v oewn-00040659-v|['makeup']
        ...
       (i21979)->i21972 lsg-00040928-v oewn-00040659-v|['makeup']
       (i21979)->i21972 oewn-00040659-v oewn-00040659-v|['makeup']

POSSIBLE GRANDPARENT(S):
       i30124 estwn-et-70-v|['dekoorima', 'dekoreerima', 'ehtima', '...']
       i21970 estwn-et-173-v|['kohendama', 'kordaseadma', 'korrastama']

GRANDPARENTS FROM OTHER WORDNET(S):
       (i21972)->i21970 cow-00040353-v oewn-00040084-v|['neaten', 'groom']
        ...
       (i21972)->i21970 oewn-00040084-v oewn-00040084-v|['neaten', 'groom']
       (i21972)->i21970 slownet-eng-30-00040353-v oewn-00040084-v|['neaten', 'groom']
```

Appendix B. The parentless synset which turned out to be the root concept

```
-----------------------------------------------------------------------------
31 # Synset ['olema'] (['be']) is a root concept
-----------------------------------------------------------------------------
WITHOUT PARENT
     i34713 estwn-et-148-v|['olema']
     (OEWN equivalent: oewn-02610777-v|['be'])

POSSIBLE PARENT(S):
     No possible parent(s) through CILI

PARENTS FROM OTHER WORDNET(S):
     No possible parent(s) through CILI

POSSIBLE GRANDPARENT(S):
     No possible grandparent(s) through CILI

GRANDPARENTS FROM OTHER WORDNET(S):
     No possible grandparent(s) through CILI
```

Appendix C. The suggested possible grandparent which was suitable for parentless synset

```
--------------------------------------------------------------------------------
8 # Correct parent for ['akkommodatsioon'] (['accommodation']) is possible
  grandparent ['acquisition', 'learning'] as ['developmentallearning'] is not use in
  Estonian
--------------------------------------------------------------------------------
WITHOUT PARENT
     i67146 estwn-et-51697-n|['akkommodatsioon']
     (OEWN equivalent: oewn-05763483-n|['accommodation'])

POSSIBLE PARENT(S):
     i67135 not in ESTWN

PARENTS FROM OTHER WORDNET(S):
     (i67146)->i67135 cow-05753207-n oewn-05761204-n|['developmentallearning']
     …
     (i67146)->i67135 fiwn-05753207-n oewn-05761204-n|['developmentallearning']
     (i67146)->i67135 oewn-05761204-n oewn-05761204-n|['developmentallearning']

POSSIBLE GRANDPARENT(S):
     i67133 not in ESTWN

GRANDPARENTS FROM OTHER WORDNET(S):
     (i67135)->i67133 cow-05752544-n oewn-05760541-n|['acquisition', 'learning']
     …
     (i67135)->i67133 oewn-05760541-n oewn-05760541-n|['acquisition', 'learning']
     (i67135)->i67133 wnja-05752544-n oewn-05760541-n|['acquisition', 'learning']
```

Appendix D. A parentless synset which received a parent that was not present in either the possible parents or grandparents

```
--------------------------------------------------------------------------------
13 # Correct parents for ['hüpnopeedia'] (['hypnopedia', 'sleep-learning']) is
   ['õppimine', 'tudeerimine', 'õpe'] (['acquisition', 'learning'])
--------------------------------------------------------------------------------
WITHOUT PARENT
     i40094 estwn-et-31344-n|['hüpnopeedia']
     (OEWN equivalent: oewn-00894218-n|['hypnopedia', 'sleep-learning'])

POSSIBLE PARENT(S):
     i40057 estwn-et-9263-n|['haridustegevus', 'õpetamine']

PARENTS FROM OTHER WORDNET(S):
     (i40094)->i40057cow-00887081-n oewn-00888759-n|['pedagogy','teaching', '…']
     …
     (i40094)->i40057 oewn-00888759-n oewn-00888759-n|['pedagogy', 'teaching', '…']
     (i40094)->i40057 wnja-00887081-n oewn-00888759-n|['pedagogy', 'teaching', '…']

POSSIBLE GRANDPARENT(S):
     i37550 estwn-et-677-n|['talitlus', 'tegevus', 'tegutsemine', '...']
     i68339 not in ESTWN
     i38639 not in ESTWN
     i36822 not in ESTWN

GRANDPARENTS FROM OTHER WORDNET(S):
     (i40057)->i38639 cow-00611433-n oewn-00612720-n|['education']
     (i40057)->i37550 estwn-et-677-n oewn-00408356-n|['activity']
     …
     (i40057)->i36822 plwn-pls-27941 oewn-00271644-n|['coaching', 'coachingjob']
     (i40057)->i68339 trwn-0103020 oewn-06008975-n|['science', 'scientificdiscipline']
```

Extending the Usage of Adjectives in the Zulu AfWN

Laurette Marais
Voice Computing
NextGen Enterprises and Institutions
CSIR
South Africa
lmarais@csir.co.za

Laurette Pretorius
Division of Computer Science,
Department of Mathematical Sciences
Stellenbosch University
South Africa
lpretorius@sun.ac.za

Abstract

The African languages Wordnet (AfWN) for Zulu (ZWN) was built using the expand approach, which relies on the translation of concepts in the Princeton WordNet (PWN), while retaining their PWN lexical categories. In this paper the focus is on the adjective as PWN lexical category. What is considered adjectival information (provided both attributively and predicatively) in English, is usually verbalised quite differently in Zulu - often as verb or copulative constructions - as may be seen by inspecting the Zulu written forms in "adjective" entries in ZWN. These written forms are not complete Zulu verb or copulative constructions and in order for them to be useful, tense, polarity and agreement have to be added. This paper presents a grammar-based approach to recover important morphosyntactic information implicit in the ZWN "adjective" written forms in order to derive a tool that would assist a user of the ZWN to render and analyse correct full forms automatically as desired by the context in which an "adjective" is used.

1 Introduction

The central role that the PWN has come to play in computational lexical semantics and meaning representation is well known and has given rise to the development of wordnets for many languages, including the African languages, with the expectation that they would play a similar role in the natural language processing (NLP) of these languages. From the outset, the developers of AfWN were confronted with, amongst others, the structural discrepancies that arise in creating "adjective" entries (Mojapelo, 2014). This resulted in "adjective" entries that are mostly based on word categories other than Zulu adjectives - categories that exhibit their own complex morphosyntactic structure. For this reason, these entries pose unique challenges for the potential users of the AfWN, creating the need for computational tools and methods for using them. We are not aware of any language other than those of the AfWN that exhibit this characteristic and has a wordnet. Indeed, dealing with this issue has not been discussed elsewhere except for Northern Sotho in (Mojapelo, 2014).

In this paper we propose a novel approach for extending the usage of "adjective" entries in the ZWN and we provide a tool that could in due course support applications of the ZWN.

2 Background

It is often stated that the expand model, by "which the source wordnet, usually the English PWN, is translated into the target language, relies on the assumption that the new language shares an underlying structure with the PWN" (Griesel and Bosch, 2020). It is also widely stated that this model is often used in cases where the target language is under-resourced. The AfWN developers adopted the expand model, mainly on the basis of the under-resourcedness of the African languages. What has received less attention is the extent to which the African languages "share an underlying structure with the PWN". The PWN has four main lexical categories: nouns, verbs, adjectives and adverbs. In this article we focus on what is known as the "adjective" (as noun qualifier) in the PWN and how noun qualification in Zulu presents unique challenges for "adjective" entries in the ZWN.

English adjectives (PWN) seldom map to adjectives in Zulu. Zulu employs qualificatives to modify nouns, namely the adjective, the descriptive possessive, the verbal relative, copulative relative and the enumerative[1] (Poulos and Msimang, 1998). The question arises how the ZWN should apply the expand model in this situation. Mojapelo (2014) notes that for Northern Sotho, "[t]he challenge ... is that while they are all meaning equivalents of the same English word category, they straddle a

[1] There are only four enumeratives in Zulu, so we disregard them here.

number of morphosyntactic categories in Northern Sotho, which nevertheless share a semantic function." This also applies to Zulu in that the written forms of the "adjective" entries in the ZWN represent a diverse set of complex mophosyntactic constructions.

Our aim in this paper is to use a computational grammar to recover these implicit constructions of the ZWN written forms and to use this information to generate and analyse all full forms for varying tense, polarity and agreement. We describe how this generation and analysis can be exposed via an end-user command line tool.[2]

The structure of the paper is as follows; In Section 3 we briefly discuss the AfWN, noting aspects of the ZWN that are applicable to our work. In Section 4 we focus on noun qualification and the "adjective" as lexical entry. More specifically, we discuss the challenges and limitations surrounding the choice of written forms to represent complex morphosyntactic constructions in Zulu. Section 5 introduces the GF Zulu resource grammar (ZRG): we explain how the verb phrase is modelled and how it facilitates the rendering of specific full forms of verb phrases. The extension procedure using the ZRG in Section 6 sets out the main contribution. Section 7 presents an evaluation as well as a discussion of the results.

3 The AfWN

Development of the AfWN started in 2008 by following the expand approach - considered the preferred approach (as opposed to the merge approach) for under-resourced languages, using the CBC.[3] Over time the need to be more African focused was recognised, which led to the use of the SIL-CAWL,[4] consisting of 1700 terms which resulted from linguistic research in Africa. Although the PWN includes four open lexical categories (noun, verb, adjective and adverb), the publications of the AfWN, more specifically the ZWN, have up to now addressed predominantly nouns and verbs (see, for example, (Griesel and Bosch, 2020)). These two lexical categories are known to allow for a mostly well-behaved mapping between the nouns and verbs of English and Zulu, provided that the concepts are lexicalised in both languages. The lexical category of adjective, however, does not allow for an equally well-behaved mapping. This has important consequences for the structure and subsequent use of ZWN entries that are labelled as "adjective", as will be explicated in subsequent sections.

4 Noun Qualification

4.1 English

While noun modification in English is achieved through a variety of word categories and constructions,[5] our focus is on the adjective as it occurs in the PWN. Broadly speaking, an adjective in English is a word that defines, qualifies or modifies the meaning of a noun.[6] The use of an adjective in English is either attributive or predicative. The attributive use is the most common use with the adjective almost always coming before the noun. Adjectives are said to be predicative when they are used as the complement of the verb *to be*, or other similar verbs such as *get*, *become*, *grow*, etc. In Tables 1 and 2 we see that no matter how the adjective is used (attributively or predicatively in any tense and polarity), its form (*accessible*, *blind*, etc.) remains basically unchanged. This is, however, not the case when modifying nouns in Zulu and the other languages of the AfWN.

4.2 Zulu

In Zulu, noun qualification is essentially achieved by means of not only the adjective, but also the descriptive possessive, the verbal relative and the copulative relative (see, for example PoulosMsimang). These so-called qualificatives differ in terms of morphosyntactic structure, which raises the question of how they should be handled in the ZWN given the expand model.

Mojapelo (2014) notes for Northern Sotho that "[t]he immediate issue, first of all, is the absence of a one-to-one correspondence between the adjective in English and that in Northern Sotho ... The issue is that a lexicalised equivalent of the sense expressed by an English adjective cannot be ignored on the grounds that it is not an adjective, nor can it be categorized as an adjective while it not". She

[2]Available at: `https://github.com/LauretteM/gf-afwn`

[3]`http://globalwordnet.org/resources/gwa-base-concepts/`

[4]`https://www.sil.org/resources/archives/7882`

[5]For example, the adjective, adjectival phrase, noun, genitive, participle, and even adverbs and sentences.

[6]In English an attributive noun functioning as an adjective qualifying a noun is often used instead of the genitive case or the dative case as in many other languages.

concludes: "The proposal is that while it is understandable that only stems be considered, invariant parts that are separate from the stem but that will help to disambiguate it be retained". It is clear that this approach was also followed by the developers of the ZWN, although the conjunctive orthography of Zulu presents challenges with regards to isolating invariant parts.

For the purpose of this paper, we refer to qualificatives that are employed in Zulu in contexts where English employs an adjective, as adjective-like qualificatives.

Some adjective-like qualificatives, namely the verbal and copulative constructions occur in various tenses and polarities. It is also important to note that an adjective in English, stated positively, is often lexicalised in Zulu by means of a negative predicate-based construction (see Section 4.2.2). Polarity is therefore often an inherent aspect of the lexicalisation of an English adjective as a Zulu qualificative. Descriptive possessives, on the other hand, do not exhibit tense and polarity.

While an exposition of Zulu linguistics, including the nominal classification and concordial agreement systems, falls outside the scope of this article (see, for example, (Poulos and Msimang, 1998) and (Taljaard and Bosch, 1988)), we give a short overview of the adjective-like qualificative constructions found in the ZWN.

4.2.1 Constructions Based on Adjective Stems and Primitive Relative Stems

There are a limited number of so-called adjective stem and primitive relative stems in Zulu.[7] For example, in Zulu, 'the big house' and 'the house that is big' are expressed using the same construction, namely the relative descriptive copulative in the present, positive: *indlu enkulu*. In fact, strictly speaking Zulu does not have an attributive form of the adjective. Rather, nouns are either modified by adjectives in relative clauses or in main clauses. This usage roughly corresponds to what is typically meant by attributive and predicative, and so for the purpose of this paper, we will refer to any relative construction as the attributive form of a qualificative, and to the main clause predicate construction as the predicative form.

[7]For a list of the most common ones, see for example (Poulos and Msimang, 1998, pp.142)

4.2.2 Verbal Constructions

Almost any verb stem can be used to form a qualificative in the form of a verbal relative.

The so-called direct verbal relative[8] represents the attributive use of the English PWN adjective to which it is mapped. Table 1 lists some forms of the verb root *-ngenek-*, which means 'to be accessible'. The ZWN written form for 'accessible' is *ngenekayo*, which is clearly derived from the present positive relative form of the verb. Each entry in the table shows in bold the part of the verb form that also appears in the written form. We see that the full written form appears only once, with *ngeneka* appearing more often and in some cases only *ngenek* is found in the table entry.

The relative suffix *-yo* that is often used in the long form of the verb, is optional, and this can be seen from the Zulu written forms *mangalisa* for 'fabulous', *mangalisayo* for 'amazing'. The choice to include the *-yo* is purely stylistic and the two English senses are in fact lexicalised by the same Zulu construction. However, in some contexts the *-yo* may not be used, as seen in the written form *mangalisa kakhulu* for 'thundering'. Similarly, long and short forms exist for the present and past positive predicative forms. For example, in the presence of an adverb, the short form is typically required, as can be seen in the table.

Sometimes, the English adjective is lexicalised in the ZWN in the negative, such as *ngaboni* for 'blind', which is clearly derived from the present negative relative form of the verb *-bon-*, which means 'to see'. In such cases, however, the written form is even less clearly related to the various other forms of the verb, as can be seen in Table 2. The table lists some forms of the verb root *-bon-*, but the polarity of the Zulu verb is flipped. To be specific, in Zulu, 'to be blind' is lexicalised as 'not to see'. The negation of the verb in the ZWN written form is essential to communicate the correct meaning, but the negative morpheme *nga* is only found in relative constructions, i.e. the attributive forms. Different negative morphemes appear in the predicative forms.

From these examples it is clear that the written forms in the ZWN do not readily allow for the generation of all forms of the Zulu qualificatives that they represent. Not only must additional morphemes be supplied to express the correct agree-

[8]The indirect relative construction falls outside the scope of this article.

ment, tense and polarity, but as we have seen, it is necessary to have knowledge of the internal structure of the written form in order to know how it, or substrings of it, can be used.

4.2.3 Identifiying and associative copulative constructions

The identifying copulative in Zulu is translated in English with the verb 'to be', for example *umuntu nguthisha* ('the person is a teacher'). It is used in the ZWN to lexicalise a small number of adjectives. For example, the written form for 'false' is given as *ngamanga*, which is derived from the relative clause that means 'which is a lie', as in *impendulo engamanga* ('the answer that is a lie').

The associative copulative in Zulu is translated in English with the verb 'to have', for example *umuntu unemoto* ('the person has a car'). It is often used in the ZWN to lexicalise adjectives. For example, the written form for 'believable' is given as *nokukholwa*, which is derived from the relative clause that means 'which has belief', as in *impendulo enokukholwa* ('the answer that has belief').

These copulative constructions are used attributively and predicatively in the various tenses and polarities, as can be seen in the example in Table 3.

4.2.4 Descriptive possessives

Descriptive possessives are inherently attributive in nature and meaning equivalent predicates cannot be derived in a predictable way. This is in contrast to verbal and copulative (predicate-based) constructions that can express the same meaning in the attributive and predicative use by means of relative clauses and predicates in main clauses, respectively. Our focus in this paper is therefore on the predicate-based qualificatives found in the ZWN.

4.3 Problem Statement

A valuable contribution, namely that of mapping English adjectives to Zulu qualificatives, has been achieved in the ZWN. This was done by implicitly capturing the morphosyntactic constructions that represent the lexicalisations of the English senses in Zulu. However, it is clear from the discussion above that there is a gap between what the ZWN provides in its written forms and what would be required by language processing applications. A sophisticated computational solution is required to effectively deal with the complexity of the adjective-like qualificatives in the ZWN.

5 The GF Zulu Resource Grammar

Grammatical Framework is a computational grammar framework and programming language for writing multilingual grammars. A GF multilingual grammar has an abstract syntax as interlingua and one or more concrete syntaxes, one for each language. The abstract syntax defines categories and functions which are implemented in the concrete syntaxes as linearisation categories and linearisation functions. By defining the linearisation categories and functions of a language, the GF runtime is enabled to linearise abstract syntax trees into natural language strings or to parse natural language strings into abstract syntax trees (Ranta, 2011).

A central project of Grammatical Framework has been the development of a Resource Grammar Library (RGL), the core of which is a common abstract syntax that defines linguistic structures found in most languages. For example, it includes categories for nouns and verbs and functions for predication and noun modification.

The original intent of the RGL was to serve as a linguistic software library to enable rapid development of application specific grammars (Ranta, 2009). Implementing the RGL categories and functions for a language would once and for all capture the general morphology and syntax of the language, to be reused by grammars aimed at a specific use case or application. More recently, however, attempts have been made to employ the general use grammars of the RGL towards wide-coverage parsing (Ranta et al., 2020). The RGL supports close to 40 languages and has, for example, been used to develop a parallel Swedish and Bulgarian Wordnet resource (Angelov, 2020).

The Zulu Resource Grammar (ZRG) models the morphology and syntax of Zulu. This is achieved by the implementation of a deliberate selection of functions from the common abstract syntax, in addition to a set of extra language specific abstract functions.[9] A large lexicon and an extension that defines chunks have been developed to enable the use of the ZRG as a wide-coverage Zulu parser.

In the GF RGL, as in the ZRG, the `VP` category is used to model generalised predicates for which tense, polarity and agreement is not yet fixed. `VP`s are used in two main ways, namely to supply the predicate in main clauses and to construct relative

[9] See the README at `https://github.com/GrammaticalFramework/gf-rgl/blob/master/src/zulu/README.md`

Use	Tense	Pol.	Zulu	English
Attr.	Pres.	Pos.	*indlu* ***engeneka(yo)***	the house that is accessible
		Neg.	*indlu enga**ngeneki***	the house that is not accessible
	Past	Pos.	*indlu* ***engenekile(yo)***	the house that was accessible
		Neg.	*indlu enga**ngenek**anga*	the house that was not accessible
	Fut.	Pos.	*indlu ezo**ngeneka***	the house that will be accessible
		Neg.	*indlu engazuku**ngeneka***	the house that will not be accessible
Pred.	Pres.	Pos.	*indlu iya**ngeneka***	the house is accessible
	Pres.	Pos.	*indlu* ***ingeneka*** *kakhulu*	the house is very accessible
		Neg.	*indlu ay**ingeneki***	the house is not accessible
	Past	Pos.	*indlu* ***ingenek**ile*	the house was accessible
	Past	Pos.	*indlu* ***ingenek**e kakhulu*	the house was very accessible
		Neg.	*indlu ay**ingenek**anga*	the house was not accessible
	Fut.	Pos.	*indlu izo**ngeneka***	the house will be accessible
		Neg.	*indlu ayizuku**ngeneka***	the house will not be accessible

Table 1: Examples of Zulu qualificatives derived from the Zulu written form *ngenekayo* ('accessible')

Use	Tense	Pol.	Zulu	English
Attr.	Pres.	Pos.	*umuntu* ***ongaboni***	the person who is blind
		Neg.	*umuntu* ***obona****(yo)*	the person who is not blind
	Past	Pos.	*umuntu* ***ongabon**anga*	the person who was blind
		Neg.	*umuntu* ***obonile****(yo)*	the person who was not blind
	Fut.	Pos.	*umuntu* ***onga**zuku**bona***	the person who will be blind
		Neg.	*umuntu ozo**bona***	the person who will not be blind
Pred.	Pres.	Pos.	*umuntu aka**boni***	the person is blind
		Neg.	*umuntu uya**bona***	the person is not blind
	Past	Pos.	*umuntu aka**bon**anga*	the person was blind
		Neg.	*umuntu* ***ubon****(il)e*	the person was not blind
	Fut.	Pos.	*umuntu akazuku**bona***	the person will be blind
		Neg.	*umuntu uzo**bona***	the person will not be blind

Table 2: Examples of Zulu qualificatives derived from the Zulu written form *ngaboni* ('blind')

clauses. In the former case, the agreement is fixed by the subject noun phrase, while in the latter case, it is fixed by the noun phrase being modified.

In the ZRG, the `VP` linearisation category contains a table with all full forms of the predicate as it appears in the main clause and the relative clause, for every tense, polarity and agreement value, and also, if applicable, distinguishing between a long and a short form. Figure 1 shows a snippet of the code defining the `VP` linearisation category, along with the parameters that define the dimensions of this table. For example, in the `VP` for the verb `bon_V` ('to see'), we can obtain the indicative, present, positive by selecting the values `MainCl`, `Third C1_2 Sg`, `Pos`, `PresTense` and `True`, which will yield the form *uyabona* ('sees'). Implementing a function that takes a `VP` as argument therefore involves making the appropriate selections based on the context in which the `VP` is used.

6 Extending the Usage of ZWN Adjectives

The ZWN is under active development and a second release is expected soon. For this publication, our work was based on preliminary data acquired from the developers ahead of the new release. Due to the status of development at the time, the data dump did not include links to the senses of PWN 3.1 or the Zulu usage examples. However, inspection of the data showed that a significant number of adjective entries had remained essentially in tact from the first version (1338 out of 1590). We therefore decided to focus on the adjective entries in the preliminary data of the new release that also appeared in the first release. In this way, we could ensure that the ZWN written forms in our dataset were as current as possible, while their English senses could be obtained via the first release's links to PWN 2.0.

Our contribution is three-fold: we recover implicit morphosyntactic constructions from the written forms by parsing them using the ZRG; we provide functionality to generate and analyse full forms of these constructions; we do this via a mostly automatic process, which can be reused for future versions of the ZWN, and for the other languages in the AfWN once resource grammars for these languages are available.

The notion of using a fully fledged syntax parser for parsing mostly single token written forms of a wordnet seems incongruous at first glance. However, as an agglutinating language with a conjunc-

Use	Tense	Pol.	Zulu	English
Pred.	Pres.	Pos.	*impendulo **ingamanga***	the answer is a lie
		Neg.	*impendulo ay**ingamanga***	the answer is not a lie
	Past	Pos.	*impendulo ib**ingamanga***	the answer was a lie
		Neg.	*impendulo ibinge**ngamanga***	the answer was not a lie
	Fut.	Pos.	*impendulo izoba **ngamanga***	the answer will be a lie
		Neg.	*impendulo ayizukuba **ngamanga***	the answer will not be a lie
Pred.	Pres.	Pos.	*impendulo **inokukholwa***	the answer has belief
		Neg.	*impendulo ayina**kukholwa***	the answer does not have belief
	Past	Pos.	*impendulo ibi**nokukholwa***	the answer had belief
		Neg.	*impendulo ibingena**kukholwa***	the answer did not have belief
	Fut.	Pos.	*impendulo izoba **nokukholwa***	the answer will have belief
		Neg.	*impendulo ayizukuba na**kukholwa***	the answer will not have belief

Table 3: Examples of Zulu qualificatives derived from the Zulu written forms *ngamanga* ('false') and *nokukholwa* ('believable')

```
param
 CType = MainCl | RelCl ;
 Agr = First Number | Second Number | Third ClassGender Number ;
 Polarity = Pos | Neg ;
 BasicTense = PresTense | FutTense | PastTense | RemFutTense | RemPastTense ;

VP = {
 s :  CType => Agr => Polarity => BasicTense => Bool => Str ;
 ...
}
```

Figure 1: Code snippet of `VP` linearisation category with the field `s` as a table of full form strings

tive orthography, single tokens in Zulu may represent full sentences or clauses. The morphosyntactic discrepancies between English adjectives and Zulu qualificatives, in fact, has resulted in such clauses being included routinely as written forms of lemmas, as discussed in Section 4.2. In order to benefit from the lexical semantic contribution of the ZWN, a sufficiently powerful method for identifying and manipulating the relevant constructions is needed. Our contention is that a syntax parser and lineariser, such as provided by GF, is a minimum requirement for taking full advantage of the ZWN.

6.1 Preparing to Parse

The ZulMorph[10] morphological analyser (Pretorius and Bosch, 2003) was used to perform a first pass through the written forms, since it is the state-of-the-art morphological analyser for Zulu and contains a large lexicon (Bosch, 2020). It was found that 501 of the 1338 written forms contained at least one token that could not be analysed by ZulMorph, and these written forms were consequently not considered. An inspection of the failures showed that the majority of tokens that failed to analyse contained an error, although in a number of cases the absence of the relevant root or stem in the ZulMorph lexicon caused the failure. This left 837 written forms to be parsed.

The lexicon for parsing was also prepared with the help of ZulMorph. The morphological analysis is done per token, and the analyser provides all possible analyses. All these analyses of the tokens in the written forms under consideration were used to identify roots and stems for inclusion in a GF lexicon module. No attempt was made to select the applicable analyses from among the various possibilities – all roots and stems were included, leaving the disambiguation step to the parser.

6.2 Parsing the Written Forms

The focus in this paper is on predicate-based qualificatives, and as shown in Section 4.2, they have typically been captured in the ZWN as incomplete relative constructions. Using the GF runtime, it is possible to restrict parsing to a certain syntax category. Our parsing strategy consisted of making several attempts on each written form, each time with a different category restriction. This included relative clauses, verb phrases, noun phrases, adverbs and locative nouns. We also used a fallback strategy for relative clauses, where if parsing failed on the written form as is, we attempted to parse it again after prefixing a relative agreement morpheme. The GF runtime returns an iterator through which all possible parses can be accessed. Our three-step heuristic for selecting from these

[10]Available at: `https://portal.sadilar.org/FiniteState/demo/zulmorph/`

a single parse for each written form was to select present tense relative clause parses, then to favour long verb roots where applicable,[11] and finally to revert to the tree with fewest nodes.

This automatic parsing and selection strategy, which admittedly involves quite a bit of guesswork, is an attempt to recover implicit linguistic information from the written forms alone, with no reference to the corresponding usage examples. When these become available in the new release, the accuracy of parsing and selecting will improve due to the additional available context.

As it is, however, of the 837 written forms, we were able to obtain at least one parse for 783. We further excluded written forms for which the selected parse included possibly spurious object agreement morphemes. Consequently, we were able to select a present tense relative clause parse for 628 written forms. Of the remaining written form parses, 104 were direct parses of noun phrases (including those in locative forms), adverbs or locative nouns. We are therefore relatively confident that these written forms do not represent relative constructions and hence fall outside the scope of this work. In total, therefore, our success rate at obtaining a plausible parse for the ZWN "adjective" written forms can be estimated as $(628 + 104)/837 = 0.879$.

6.3 An Adjective Application Grammar

The purpose of the adjective application grammar is to simplify the manipulation of Zulu qualificatives by providing a mapping between English adjective senses and the ZRG functions that define them.

In the GF RGL, a technical distinction is made between a relative clause (`RCl`) and a relative sentence (`RS`): the former is not fixed with regards to tense and polarity, while the latter is. When parsing the written forms, we used the `RS` category in order to capture tense and polarity information. Our selected parses all reflect the present tense, but differing inherent polarity (see the discussion in Section 4.2.2). It is this inherent polarity and the description of the predicate as a `VP` that can be re-used to construct ZRG trees to express all full forms of the ZWN written form.

The 628 parsed written forms together with their linked English senses, constitute 881 unique (English sense, Zulu written form) pairs. Table 4 gives some examples, showing how each pair (columns 1 and 2) gives rise to a function name, a ZRG `VP` and an inherent polarity value (columns 3, 4 and 5). This forms the basis of the adjective grammar.

Table 4 gives some examples of mapping between English adjective senses and the Zulu syntax elements that have been recovered from the ZWN written forms.

The function names in the abstract syntax of the adjective grammar are derived from the English senses, while the linearisation functions of the Zulu concrete syntax make use of the associated `VP` and inherent polarity value. In the code snippet in Figure 2, we show the linearisation category of `ZWN_APred`, as well as an example of a function definition for obtaining a `ZWN_APred`, and its corresponding linearisation function definition.

In the adjective grammar, agreement information is manipulated via the `ZWN_Pron` category, which encapsulates pronouns modeled in the ZRG. This is convenient because Zulu is a pro-drop language, which means that the relative and main clauses can be linearised alongside pro-dropped pronouns (which are linearised as empty strings) to obtain only the qualificative strings.

Figure 3 in Appendix A shows an attributive example of an adjective grammar tree, which effectively constructs a ZRG tree that contains a relative clause, shown in Figure 4. Figures 5 and 6 give the corresponding predicative case, which involves main clause predication. The adjective grammar trees are simple, while exhibiting the full morphosyntactic behaviour of relative and main clauses in Zulu by making use of the ZRG.

6.4 A Grammar-based Tool for Extending Use of the ZWN

Our command line tool shows how the adjective grammar can be used to generate and analyse the adjective-like qualificatives of the ZWN. The tool is presented as an end-user tool, but the core functionality could just as easily be embedded into an NLP pipeline.

By making use of the linearisation functionality in the GF runtime, it allows a user to specify the English adjective, along with the required tense, polarity and agreement information in order to obtain the correct form of the corresponding Zulu qualificative(s). Each of these command line parameters map in a straight forward way to a function in the adjective grammar, which is used to construct

[11] For the purposes of this work, verb root extensions were considered as part of the root.

English sense	ZWN Written form	Function	ZRG VP	Inherent polarity
articulate	cacile	articulate_1_A	UseVStative cac_V	Pos
decided	cacile	decided_1_A	UseVStative cac_V	Pos
accessible	ngenekayo	accessible_1_A	UseV ngenek_V	Pos
accessible	finyelelekayo	accessible_2_A	UseV finyelelek_V	Pos
amazing	mangalisayo	amazing_1_A	UseV mangalis_V	Pos
fabulous	mangalisa	fabulous_1_A	UseV mangalis_V	Pos

Table 4: Examples of mappings between English adjective senses and Zulu qualificative constructions

```
- linearisation category
ZWN_APred = { vp :  VP ; pol :  ZPol } ;

- function
thundering_1_A : ZWN_APred ;

- linearisation function
thundering_1_A = { vp = AdvVP (UseV mangalis_V) kakhulu_Adv ; pol = ZPos } ;
```

Figure 2: Implementing an English adjective as a Zulu qualificative

the correct tree. The tool also allows the use of wild cards, in which case the linearisations for all possible values (and combinations of values) are given. Example output is shown in Figure 7 in Appendix A.

Conversely, the tool allows the user to provide a Zulu qualificative string in order to obtain its corresponding English adjective(s), along with the tense, polarity and agreement information. The input is parsed to obtain a tree, whose nodes contain the required information. Example output is shown in Figure 8 in Appendix A.

In contrast to Angelov (2020), where full forms were included as tables in the wordnet resource, our decision to instead provide a computational tool is based on the sheer number of full forms of the Zulu qualificatives, which could be as many as 384.

7 Evaluation and Discussion

As noted in Section 6.2, when considering those written forms for which a morphological analysis could be found for each token, a plausible parse for 87.9% of written forms could be obtained. This was used the basis for an application grammar and wrapper tool that could generate and analyse full forms of adjectives with different tense, polarity and agreement values, as well as form, whether attributive or predicative.

This is a novel contribution. The Zulu resource grammar along with the GF runtime system is the foundation of this generation and analysis capability. While some work has been done to develop GF resource grammars for other African languages (Ng'ang'a, 2012; Kituku et al., 2021), these grammars have not yet been demonstrated to support the kind of application grammar development presented here. As such, there is no baseline to compare our work to, which presents a challenge for evaluation.

The only comparable computational tool, in terms of accuracy and scope, is the ZulMorph morphological analyser, which is an FST that can be applied to surface forms in order to obtain full morphological analyses and vice versa. While it cannot disambiguate analyses for multitoken expressions and hence is not suitable for the generation and analysis task presented here, it can be utilised in the evaluation of the output of the Zulu resource grammar, as mediated by the adjective application grammar.

7.1 Evaluation

The following methodology was implemented to evaluate our system:

1. From the mappings (see examples in Table 4), randomly select 50 entries in order to obtain ZRG VPs.

2. For each ZRG VP, randomly select a value for tense, polarity, agreement, form and length (long form or short form), and construct the relevant full abstract syntax tree as done in the application grammar.

3. For each tree, linearise the tree into a string, and obtain ZulMorph analyses for each token in the string.

4. Using the information given by the abstract syntax tree and the (possibly multiple) morphological analyses per token, attempt a selection of ulMorph analyses that correspond to the abstract syntax tree.

Qualificative property	% of Total
Verb	61.5%
`UseV, UseVStative, ComplV2`	
Associative copulative	18.6%
`CopNPAssoc`	
Locative copulative	2.2%
`CopLocative`	
Adjective/primitive relative	2.0%
`CopAP`	
Identifying copulative	1.6%
`CopNP`	
Negative	9.3%
`PNeg`	

Table 5: Properties of adjective-like qualificative constructions in the "adjective" entries of the ZWN

5. If and only if such a selection is possible for all tokens in the generated form, generation is accepted as correct.

Figure 9 in Appendix A shows a snippet of the simple web based tool that was used to visualise and select ZulMorph analyses given a ZRG abstract syntax tree. It was found that ZulMorph lacked sufficient coverage of, for example, contracted past tense forms. Hence, in 9 out of the 50 entries, the tokens generated by the ZRG could not be analysed. These were analysed manually to confirm their correctness. Out of the 50 entries selected, only 2 were determined not to have been generated correctly. This was, however, not due to errors made by the ZRG, but due to incorrect parses obtained for the ZWN written forms initially. Consequently, we estimate that our tool has an accuracy of $48/50 = 0.96$.

7.2 Discussion

This high degree of accuracy allows us to make a few quantitative observations about adjective-like qualificatives in Zulu, especially with regards to relative constructions. Such an analysis is, to our knowledge, in itself a novel contribution.

Of the adjective-like Zulu qualificatives for which a parse could be selected, 628 (85.8%) represent relative, or predicate-based, constructions, while the remaining 104 (14.2%) represent descriptive possessives or adverbs. This confirms the importance of being able to process the predicate-based qualificatives effectively.

The summary in Table 5 shows the representation of certain properties of predicate-based qualificatives in the data. The properties correspond to functions in the ZRG parses, used to arrive at the percentages. We see, for example, that verbal constructions constitute a large majority of adjective-like qualificatives, namely 61.5%. The second largest group are the associative copulatives (18.6%), while constructions based on adjective and primitive relative stems make up only 2.0% of the total. We also see that 9.3% of adjective-like qualificatives inherently exhibit negative polarity.

8 Conclusion

The analysis in the previous section illustrates the morphosyntactic diversity of the adjective-like Zulu qualificatives. We have shown how a computational grammar-based approach can overcome the challenge this poses in order to take full advantage of the ZWN by facilitating its potential use in NLP applications for Zulu.

The process we have developed could be repeated whenever new versions of the ZWN are released. Moreover, as shown in the previous section, the adjective-like qualificatives in the ZWN typically represent constructions based on verbs and nouns. Future work will include developing functionality to similarly generate and analyse full forms of verb and noun entries of the ZWN, as well as replicating the work for other languages in the AfWN once resource grammars for them are developed.

Acknowledgements

This work has been funded by the South African Centre for Digital Language Resources (SADiLaR).

References

Krasimir Angelov. 2020. A parallel WordNet for English, Swedish and Bulgarian. In *Proceedings of the 12th Language Resources and Evaluation Conference*, pages 3008–3015, Marseille, France. European Language Resources Association.

Sonja Bosch. 2020. Computational morphology systems for Zulu–a comparison. *Nordic Journal of African Studies*, 29(3):28–28.

Marissa Griesel and Sonja Bosch. 2020. Navigating challenges of multilingual resource development for under-resourced languages: The case of the African Wordnet project. In *Proceedings of the first workshop on Resources for African Indigenous Languages*, pages 45–50, Marseille, France. European Language Resources Association (ELRA).

Benson Kituku, Wanjiku Nganga, and Lawrence Muchemi. 2021. Grammar engineering for the ekegusii language in grammatical framework.

Mampaka Lydia Mojapelo. 2014. Morphosyntactic discrepancies in representing the adjective equivalent in African WordNet with reference to Northern Sotho. In *Proceedings of the Seventh Global Wordnet Conference*, pages 355–362, Tartu, Estonia. University of Tartu Press.

Wanjiku Ng'ang'a. 2012. Building swahili resource grammars for the grammatical framework. In *Shall We Play the Festschrift Game?*, pages 215–226. Springer.

George Poulos and Christian T. Msimang. 1998. *A Linguistic Analysis of isiZulu*. Via Afrika, Cape Town, South Africa.

Laurette Pretorius and Sonja E Bosch. 2003. Finite-state computational morphology: An analyzer prototype for Zulu. *Machine Translation*, 18(3):195–216.

Aarne Ranta. 2009. The GF Resource Grammar Library. *Linguistic Issues in Language Technology*, 2.

Aarne Ranta. 2011. *Grammatical framework: Programming with multilingual grammars*, volume 173. CSLI Publications, Center for the Study of Language and Information Stanford.

Aarne Ranta, Krasimir Angelov, Normunds Gruzitis, and Prasanth Kolachina. 2020. Abstract Syntax as Interlingua: Scaling Up the Grammatical Framework from Controlled Languages to Robust Pipelines. *Computational Linguistics*, 46(2):425–486.

P. C. Taljaard and S. E. Bosch. 1988. *Handbook of IsiZulu*. J. L. Van Schaik, Pretoria, South Africa.

A Additional Examples

A.1 Obtaining Full Forms via an Adjective Grammar

Figures 3 and 5 show application grammar trees for expressing 'thundering' in a specified syntactic context. Figures 4 and 6 show how the same full forms are represented as trees in the ZRG.

A.2 Generating Full Forms via the Command Tool

Figure 7 shows an example of output from the command line tool. This was obtained by the following request: `python3 afwn_adjectives.py generate ? Pos 2 ? blind`

Figure 8 shows an example of output from the command line tool. This was obtained by the following request: `python3 afwn_adjectives.py analyze awubonanga`

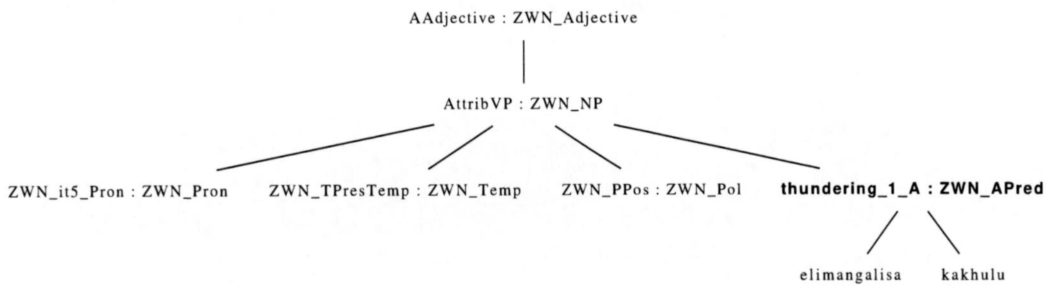

Figure 3: The adjective grammar tree for expressing 'thundering' in the attributive form in the present, positive and modifying the pronoun 'it' of class 5

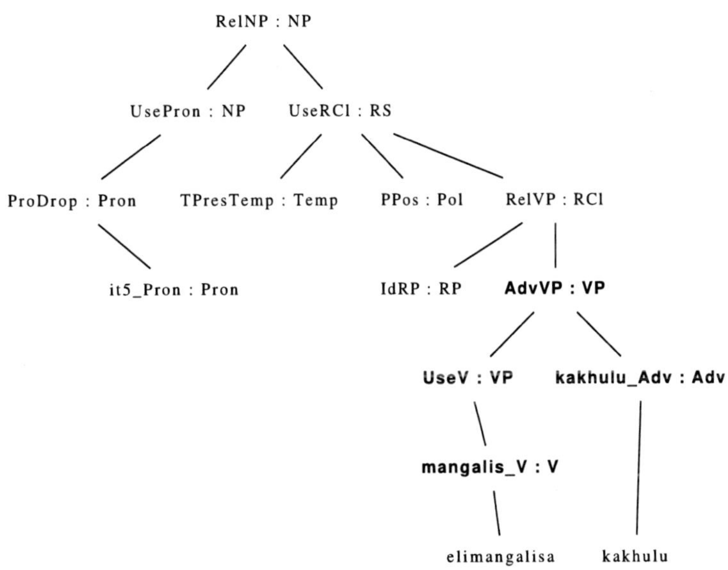

Figure 4: The resource grammar tree for expressing the concept of 'thundering' attributively as a present, positive relative clause modifying the pro-dropped pronoun 'it' of class 5.

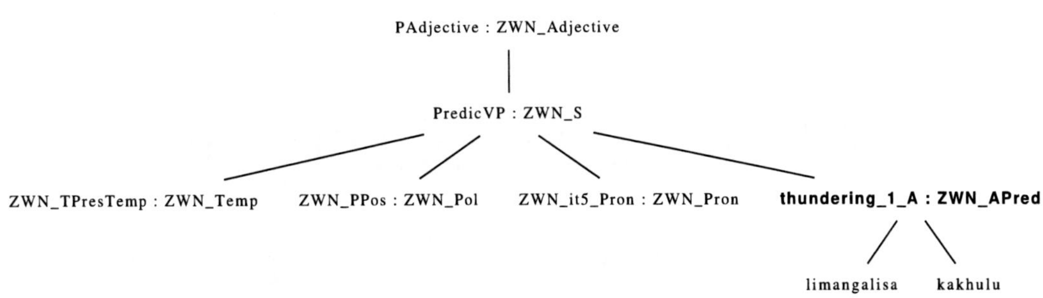

Figure 5: The adjective grammar tree for expressing 'thundering' in the predicative form in the present, positive with the pronoun 'it' of class 5 as subject

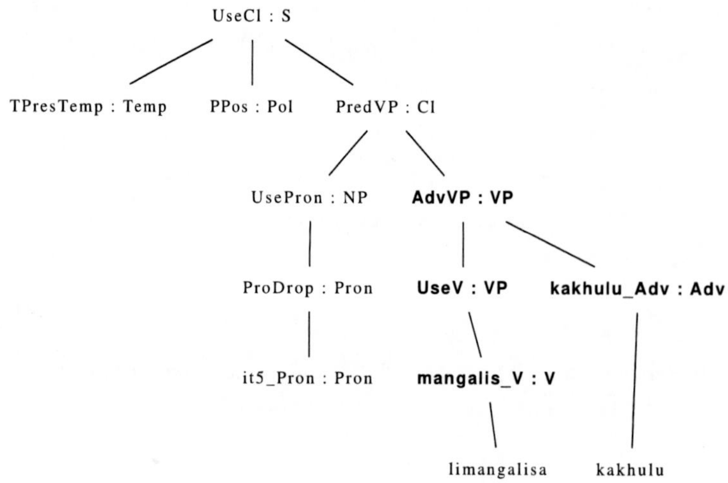

Figure 6: The resource grammar tree for expressing the concept of 'thundering' predicatively as a present, positive clause with pro-dropped pronoun 'it' of class 5 as subject.

Tense	Polarity	Class	Form	Long/short	Qualificative
Fut	Pos	2	Attr		abangazukubona
Fut	Pos	2	Pred		abazukubona
Past	Pos	2	Attr		abangabonanga
Past	Pos	2	Pred		ababonanga
Pres	Pos	2	Attr		abangaboni
Pres	Pos	2	Pred		ababoni
RemFut	Pos	2	Attr		abangayukubona
RemFut	Pos	2	Pred		abayukubona
RemPast	Pos	2	Attr		abangabonanga
RemPast	Pos	2	Pred		ababonanga

Figure 7: Output of the command line tool when requesting all positive forms of 'blind' when modifying a plural noun of class 2, such as *abafundi* ('pupils').

Tense	Polarity	Class	Form	Long/short	Adjective
Past	Neg	3	Pred		conscious
Past	Pos	3	Pred		blind
RemPast	Neg	3	Pred		conscious
RemPast	Pos	3	Pred		blind

Figure 8: Output of the command line tool when requesting an analysis of *awubonanga*

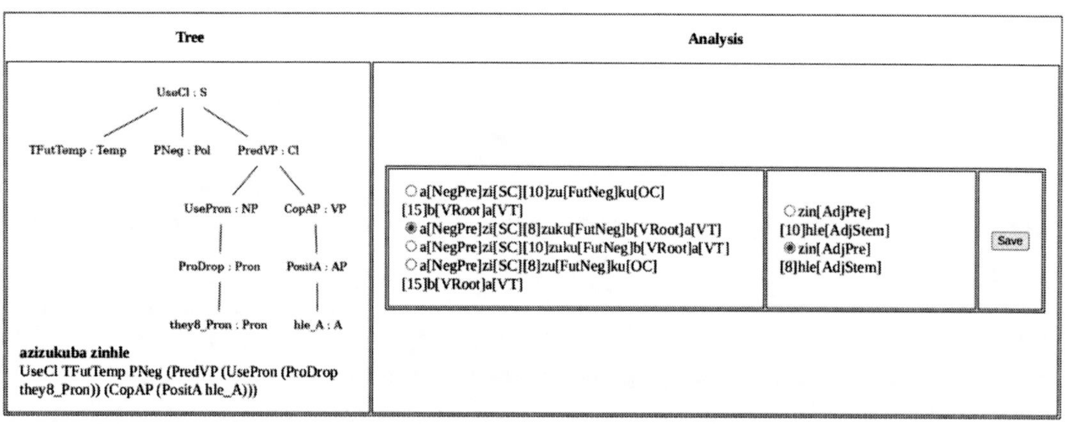

Figure 9: Example of selecting ZulMorph analyses to correspond with the ZRG abstract syntax tree

Linking SIL Semantic Domains to Wordnet and Expanding the Abui Wordnet through Rapid Word Collection Methodology

Luis Morgado da Costa[1], **František Kratochvíl**[2], **George Saad**[2], **Benidiktus Delpada**[3], **Daniel Simon Lanma**[3], **Francis Bond**[2], **Natálie Wolfová**[2], and **A.L. Blake**[4]

[1]Vrije Universiteit Amsterdam, the Netherlands
[2]Palacký University Olomouc, Czech Republic
[3]Universitas Tribuana Kalabahi, Indonesia
[4]University of Hawai'i at Mānoa, USA

Abstract

In this paper we describe a new methodology to expand the Abui Wordnet through data collected using the Rapid Word Collection (RWC) method – based on SIL's Semantic Domains. Using a multilingual sense-intersection algorithm, we created a ranked list of concept suggestions for each domain, and then used the ranked list as a filter to link the Abui RWC data to wordnet. This used translations from both SIL's Semantic Domain's structure and example words, both available through SIL's Fieldworks software and the RWC project. We release both the new mapping of the SIL Semantic Domains to wordnet and an expansion of the Abui Wordnet.

1 Introduction

In this paper we describe the second phase of the Abui Wordnet construction which merges the data collected through the Rapid Word Collection method (RWC), as described in Section 2.2, into the Abui Wordnet v1.0 (see Section 1.1). The RWC method is built around the SIL Semantic Domains ontology, discussed in detail in Section 2.1. Much of the work discussed in this paper is related to the necessity of providing structure to data collected using common methods in Field Linguistics. The SIL Semantic Domains, and the Rapid Word Collection methodology in particular, support lexicographic work on endangered languages and significantly accelerate dictionary production. This paper looks into solving these issues by providing support to link unstructured types of data collected on the field to the Abui Wordnet.

1.1 Abui Wordnet

The Abui Wordnet was developed following the expansion approach (Kratochvíl and Morgado da Costa, 2022). Through a naive multilingual sense intersection algorithm, described in Section 3, we linked the data collected over the last two decades through the traditional descriptive workflow for which English, Indonesian, and Alor Malay glosses exist in the Abui dictionary (Kratochvíl and Delpada, 2014). The first version of the Abui Wordnet contained 1,475 synsets and 3,606 senses, and was entirely hand-checked by B. Delpada, who is a native speaker of Abui and one of the authors of this paper. This wordnet is released under the open CC-BY 4.0 license.[1]

2 Data Collection

In this section we provide an introduction to the structure and method for collecting our Abui data.

2.1 SIL Semantic Domains: Structure and Use

The SIL Semantic Domains[2] (SemDoms) is an ontology created by the Summer Institute of Linguistics linguist, Ronald Moe, to help investigate relationships among words. It builds on the long tradition of ontologies and thesauri developed in comparative linguistics and theology (see, e.g., Buck, 1949; Louw and Nida, 1992).

SemDoms are organized in an associative way, grouping words used to talk about a topic, regardless of their subtle differences. For example, as shown in Figure 1, the SemDom 1.3 Water is linked with two more SemDoms (6.6.7 Working with water and 7.2.4.2 Travel by water), which contain water-related action verbs. Each SemDom includes questions that elicit synonyms, such as *water*, H_2O, and *moisture*. The ontology also tracks associated properties such as *watery*, *aquatic*, or *amphibious*, and even loosely associated *waterproof* and *watertight*. Subdomains describe bodies of water, water movement, etc.

SemDoms facilitate dictionary building and have been incorporated and supported in various SIL

[1]https://github.com/fanacek/abuiwn
[2]http://semdom.org/

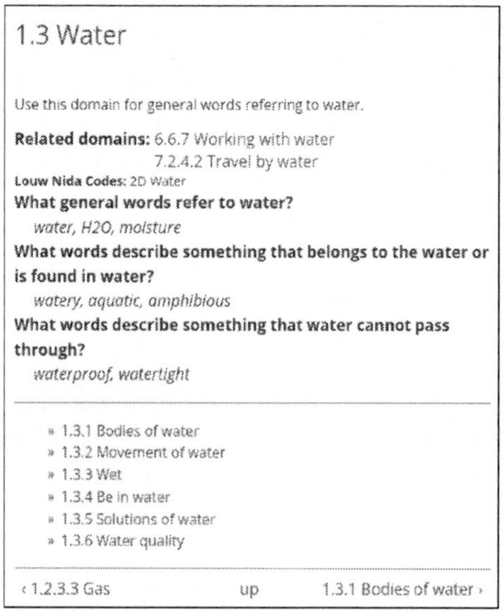
1.3 Water

Use this domain for general words referring to water.

Related domains: 6.6.7 Working with water
7.2.4.2 Travel by water

Louw Nida Codes: 2D Water

What general words refer to water?
water, H2O, moisture

What words describe something that belongs to the water or is found in water?
watery, aquatic, amphibious

What words describe something that water cannot pass through?
waterproof, watertight

- 1.3.1 Bodies of water
- 1.3.2 Movement of water
- 1.3.3 Wet
- 1.3.4 Be in water
- 1.3.5 Solutions of water
- 1.3.6 Water quality

‹ 1.2.3.3 Gas up 1.3.1 Bodies of water ›

Figure 1: SIL Semantic Domain for 1.3 Water

Languages	SemDom Titles	SemDom Words	Total
French	2,005	47,706	49,711
Spanish	2,056	45,801	47,857
English	2,013	41,494	43,507
Hindi*	2,202	34,544	36,746
Chinese	1,514	31,230	32,744
Portuguese	1,746	27,121	28,867
Indonesian	2,043	20,522	22,565
Nepalese*	2,061	17,770	19,831
Farsi	1,323	17,949	19,272
Urdu*	2,235	11,724	13,959
Bengali*	1,899	951	2,850
Russian*	2,673	3	2,676
Khmer*	2,120	0	2,120
Thai	1,555	1	1,556
Total	27,445	296,816	324,261

Table 1: SemDom data extracted from SIL FieldWorks, sorted by total number of data points per language; Data for Portuguese and Persian existed even though it was not properly advertised by SIL; Languages marked with * were missing from the OMW

software tools for language documentation, such as the SIL Toolbox, SIL Fieldworks (corpus, lexicon, parser), SIL Lexique Pro, and WeSay (dictionary).[3]

Multilingual versions of SIL Semantic Domains exist for 14 world languages,[4] including Chinese, French, Indonesian, Malay, Spanish, Swahili, and Urdu. However, not all translations are equally extensive, as shown in Table 1.

2.2 Rapid Word Collection Workshops

The Rapid Word Collection (RWC) method accelerates the lexicographic work by involving language communities, and has been used in over a hundred communities by untrained native speakers. It relies on a set of questions, derived from the SIL Semantic Domains, described above. The method exploits the brain's ability to rapidly recall words belonging to the same semantic domain. Speakers typically do not find this tiring and enjoy the process.

The questions are accompanied by answer sheets to record the semantic domain number, speaker details, and the vernacular word with their translations. Participants work in small groups or individually, according to their individual preference.

According to the RWC website,[5] two-week workshops consistently achieve 10,000 or more raw entries. This surpasses the 4,000 to 5,000 words collected over several years by a single language worker.

The RWC workflow yields a lexicon where most unique lexical entries have multiple senses, as is the case in dictionaries of resource-rich languages. The coverage is also not biased by a corpus, which is a big problem in the standard descriptive workflow. It is extremely difficult to reach the lexical breadth the RWC workshops can provide. Corpus-based methods are slow to elicit new words. One would need a corpus of upwards of one million words to collect a dictionary comparable to a two-week RWC workshop.

The RWC workshops demonstrate the wealth of lexical knowledge accumulated in minority languages and boost participants' confidence as well as language awareness. Realizing that some of the words may not be known by younger speakers, participants are challenged to assess the vitality of their language and their own commitment to promoting their language and culture. Finally, these workshops provide detailed information on community's orthographic preferences. A practical orthography may also be designed based on the RWC input.

2.3 RWC Workshops on Abui

So far, we have held three RWC Workshops for Abui (in 2013, 2014, and 2016). In total they lasted 10 working days, with 25 people involved, on average, on any day. In total 67 Abui men and 21 Abui

[3] All available here: https://software.sil.org/

[4] https://rapidwords.net/resources (provides an incomplete list)

[5] https://rapidwords.net/

Figure 2: Abui participants of the Rapid Word Collection workshop, July 22-26, 2013

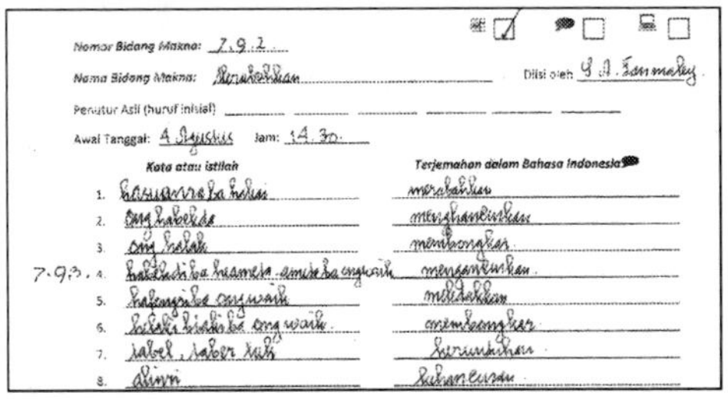

Figure 3: Rapid Word Collection worksheet example: domain 7.9.2 Tear down by S.A. Fanmaley

women participated, representing the Takalelang dialect and the adjacent areas, and contributing more than 17,000 raw entries. Figure 2 shows the Abui participants at work, writing or recording.

The participants recorded their answers on paper forms, indicating the Semantic Domain number, Abui words, and their Indonesian or Malay equivalents, as shown in Figure 3. Several Abui university students with adequate computer skills helped digitize the hand-written entries (including creating audio recordings and spreadsheets). This digitization work is still ongoing, with a small team working on the Indonesian and English translations, with about 12,300 words digitized to date.

3 Methodology

The work presented in this paper uses and extends the idea of Multilingual Sense Intersection (Bond et al., 2008; Bonansinga and Bond, 2016). The methodology is illustrated in Figure 4: it attempts to perform Word Sense Disambiguation (WSD) — i.e., to determine the most likely sense of a word with reference, e.g., to a wordnet hierarchy — by restricting the available semantic space through the intersection of semantic spaces of aligned translations of that same word. This method has been used to create new wordnets, such as the Coptic Wordnet (Slaughter et al., 2019) and, most recently, also to

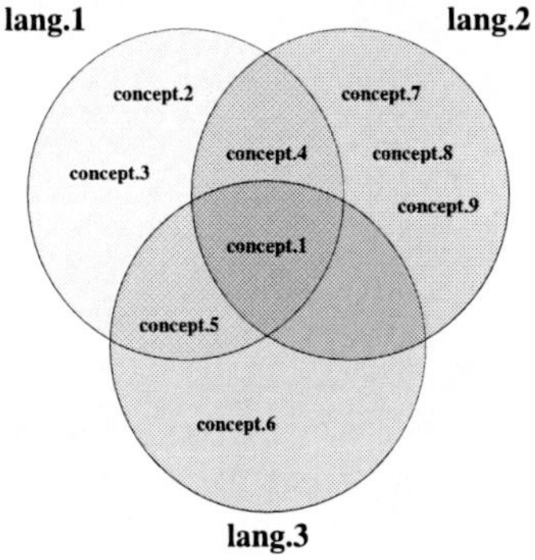

Figure 4: Sense Intersection visualization: each colored circle represent a different language (lang.1-3); concepts (concept.1-9) represent the ambiguity of a single lemma within that language; The higher the number of languages, the smaller the intersected space – yielding fewer and fewer sense candidates;

kick-start the development of the Abui Wordnet from field data (Kratochvíl and Morgado da Costa, 2022).

In this work, we employ this same concept in two ways: i) we use Multilingual Sense Intersection to perform WSD to map the SIL SemDoms data to the Open Multilingual Wordnet (OMW, Bond and Foster, 2013); ii) we use the results of the previous step as a pivot to map Abui data collected through RWC Workshops to the Abui Wordnet.

3.1 Linking SIL Semantic Domains to OMW

The idea of linking SIL SemDoms to wordnet was first proposed by Rosman et al. (2014).

As discussed in Section 2.1, SemDoms are mostly used for language documentation. To this end, there has been a considerable community effort to translate this resource. Translations of this resource are most commonly released as localization packages[6] for SIL FieldWorks[7] – an open-source project designed to help collect and publish dictionary data, including support dictionary development through SemDoms. It also supports interlinearization of texts and morphological analysis.

Our primary goal to link SemDoms to OMW was to be able to pivot this information to improve our ability to better link the Abui data collected using the RWC Workshop method, described in Section 2.3. To achieve this, we wanted to link not only the SemDom titles (as referred within FieldWords)

[6] https://software.sil.org/fieldworks/download/localizations/

[7] https://github.com/sillsdev/FieldWorks

```
<rt class="CmDomainQ" guid="6fa93eab-71e0-4880-9a78-0b2a81382880" ownerguid="60364
974-a005-4567-82e9-7aaeff894ab0">
<ExampleWords>
<AUni ws="en">water, H2O, moisture</AUni>
<AUni ws="es">agua, H2O, humedad, preciado liquido</AUni>
<AUni ws="fa">آب رطوبت نم خیس</AUni>
<AUni ws="fr">eau, H2O, humidité</AUni>
<AUni ws="hi">पानी, H2O, नमी</AUni>
<AUni ws="id">air, H2O, embun</AUni>
<AUni ws="ne">पानी, जल, नीर, तरल</AUni>
<AUni ws="pt">água, H2O, humidade</AUni>
<AUni ws="ur">پانی، آب</AUni>
<AUni ws="zh-CN">水、H2O</AUni>
</ExampleWords>
<Question>
<AUni ws="bn">(১) পানি বোঝাতে সাধারণত কি কি শব্দ ব্যবহার করা হয়?</AUni>
<AUni ws="en">(1) What general words refer to water?</AUni>
<AUni ws="es">(1) ¿Cómo se le llama generalmente al agua?</AUni>
<AUni ws="fa">چه واژگانی به آب مربوط می‌شوند؟</AUni>
<AUni ws="fr">(1) Quels sont les termes génériques qui désignent l'eau ?</AUni>
<AUni ws="hi">(1) पानी?</AUni>
<AUni ws="id">(1) Kata-kata umum apa yang digunakan untuk menyebut air?</AUni>
<AUni ws="ne">(१) साधारण कुन-कुन शब्दहरूले पानी जनाउँछ?</AUni>
<AUni ws="pt">Que palavras gerais referem à água?</AUni>
<AUni ws="ru">(1) Какие основные слова относятся к воде?</AUni>
<AUni ws="th">คำทั่วไปคำใดที่หมายถึงน้ำ? น้ำ, ความชุ่มชื้น, เหลว</AUni>
<AUni ws="ur">پانی کے لئے عام کونسے الفاظ استعمال کئے جاتے ہیں؟</AUni>
<AUni ws="zh-CN">通常说到水，你会怎么说？</AUni>
</Question>
</rt>
```


Figure 5: XML data extracted from SIL Fieldworks for the first question of SemDom 1.3 Water

but also – and most importantly – we wanted to link the answers to the questions within each SemDom (see Figure 1), as this is the primary data collected during the RWC workshops. These words are referred to as example words within FieldWorks, so this is the nomenclature we will use.

This is one of the main differences between our work and Rosman et al. (2014). In their work, only SemDom titles are linked to Wordnet. For our goals, this would not be enough. As noted by Rosman et al. (2014), even relations between domains and their subdomains are not typed in the same way as you would find in wordnets – making reference to the so-called 'Tennis Problem', which describes the fact that wordnets do not link clearly related words such as *tennis*, *racket*, *ball*, and *net*. This problem would most certainly be exacerbated when considering the relation between SemDom titles and example words – which are the basis of the RWC method.

The second main difference with the previous work mapping SemDoms was the number of languages used to attempt the mapping. While the previous work only had access to English and Indonesian data at the time of publication, we had access to a much larger collection of languages.

We created a new project on FieldWorks and imported all languages known to contain translations for SemDoms (including only partial translations). This generated an XML file containing parallel data in all available languages. This data is split into data concerning the SemDom titles, and data concerning questions and answers within a SemDom. Figure 5 shows an example of how the data is organized for the first question of the SemDom 1.3 Water – see also Figure 1, for reference.

The results of this data extraction were summarized in Table 1. In total, we extracted over 324,000 expressions (including words and multi-word-expressions), about 8.5% of which were related to SemDom titles, and the remainder to SemDom example words. We were able to extract data for 14 languages. French was the language with most words, followed by Spanish, English, Hindi and Chinese. Some languages only had a partial translation for the full SemDom hierarchy. The reason why some languages seem to have more titles than there are SemDoms is due to the fact that some semantic domains actually include a list of words in their title (e.g. SemDom 1.5.4 Moss, fungus, algae). Both titles and example words were split on commas (which were different Unicode characters for different languages).

This data was then mapped to wordnet using the data from the OMW (Bond and Foster, 2013).

3.2 Expanding the OMW

The Open Multilingual Wordnet (OMW 1.0: Bond and Foster, 2013) links dozens of open wordnets projects in a massively multilingual database, using the Princeton WordNet (Fellbaum, 1998) as the pivot structure.

Fortunately, in addition to the English Princeton WordNet, the OMW already included wordnet projects for many of the necessary languages, including: WOLF (Sagot and Fišer, 2008), for French; the Multilingual Central Repository (Gonzalez-Agirre et al., 2012), for Spanish; the Chinese Wordnet (Huang et al., 2010) and the Chinese Open Wordnet (Wang and Bond, 2013), for Mandarin Chinese; the OpenWordnet-PT (de Paiva and Rademaker, 2012), for Portuguese; the Wordnet Bahasa (Mohamed Noor et al., 2011), for Indonesian and Malay; the Persian Wordnet (Montazery and Faili, 2010), for Farsi; and the Thai Wordnet (Thoongsup et al., 2009).

The OMW was missing data for Hindi, Nepalese, Urdu, Bengali, Russian and Khmer. For Khmer, even through there are reports detailing the construction of the Khmer WordNet (Phon and Pluempitiwiriyawej, 2020), we were not able to find or access the data. Since there were no SemDom example words for this language, we decided it was not worth pursuing it further.

For the remaining languages, there were actually wordnets being actively maintained, but they were not part of the OMW due to their restrictive licensing constraints (i.e. NonCommercial). Since this did not impede our work, we added the missing languages to our own local copy of the OMW.

Data for Hindi, Nepalese, Urdu and Bengali was provided by the IndoWordnet (Bhattacharyya, 2010), and its IndoWordnet-English Wordnet Mapping (Kanojia et al., 2018). Data for Russian was provided by the Russian Wordnet (Loukachevitch et al., 2016), which also includes a mapping to the PWN (Loukachevitch and Gerasimova, 2019).

It is also important to note that, for the work presented here, we used an extended version of the OMW which includes additions to the PWN's hierarchy through the annotation of the NTU-MC sense-tagged corpus (Tan and Bond, 2014; Bond et al., 2013; Wang and Bond, 2014; Bond et al., 2021), as well as other extensions including pronouns (Seah and Bond, 2014) and exclamatives (Morgado da Costa and Bond, 2016). As a result, our released data contains some offsets that do not directly map to the PWN.

With all the data in a single repository, the expanded OMW was used to map the SIL SemDom data using the method described above – multilingual sense intersection. The results of this experiment are discussed in Section 4.1.

3.3 Linking RWC data to the Abui Wordnet

After creating the mapping between the SemDoms and the OMW, we used it to help us link the Abui RWC data to the Abui Wordnet.

Even though previous work on the Abui Wordnet showed promising results using word sense intersection to find candidate senses, this method presupposed the data was provided (at least) in three languages. The problem with the Rapid Word Collection data was that we had only a limited number of translations for each Abui word.

For the 12,331 Abui words digitized to date, 12,324 words were translated to Indonesian, 9,078 words were translated to Alor Malay, and only 5,846 were translated to English. About 11,000 words were used for the linking described in Section 4.2, the additional 1,300 words were digitized since. However, each Abui word was also linked to the SemDom identifier that prompted the native speaker to provide that word. SemDoms were used at the level of identifier (i.e., they were not linked to a specific question within that identifier).

What we wanted to verify was if, after properly linking the SemDoms to the OMW, we could use this mapping to further filter the data provided by RWC. To do this, first, we performed multilingual sense intersection using only the data provided through the RWC method, as described in Section 4.1. We then used the data provided by our SemDom mapping (with different kinds of confidence level), to check if intersecting these two mappings could be used to reliably increase the quality of new senses suggested for the Abui Wordnet. The results for these experiments are detailed in Section 4.2.

4 Results and Evaluation

In this section we discuss three different things: i) the results of mapping the SemDoms to the OMW using the data extracted from SIL FieldWorks; ii) the results of producing sense candidates for the Abui Wordnet through multilingual sense intersection using the RWC method with and without using i) as as filtering step; and iii) the results of hand-checking sense candidates produced in ii) by a group of linguists and native speakers.

4.1 Mapping SIL Semantic Domains to OMW

Using the data presented in Table 1, we extracted data for all 1,792 different SemDom identifiers. Using the method briefly described in Section 3, we performed multilingual sense intersection for each level of the SemDom hierarchy. However, we split this intersection into two parts: i) using data pertaining only to SemDom titles; and ii) using data pertaining only to SemDom example words (i.e., answers to the questions in that SemDom).

The reason to separate these two sets of data is quite intuitive. For i), we are trying to link the actual SemDom to the OMW. While this could well be a many-to-one mapping (i.e., many wordnet senses mapped to a single SemDom), there is a finite/correct set of links that should be made between these two resources. For ii), however, this is not true. The large majority of SemDom questions are open ended (e.g., 'What utensils are used to cut food?', from SemDom 5.2.1.3 Cooking utensil). The work of translating the SemDom is not strictly to translate example words that have been included in previous languages, and people are welcome to include more/different examples. We have noticed, for example, that both French and Spanish go well beyond the list of words provided for English (the original language).

Intersected Languages	SemDom Titles	SemDom Words
1 lang	29,986	293,821
2 langs	6,233	58,320
3 langs	2,524	23,074
4 langs	1,355	10,782
5 langs	804	5,595
6 langs	466	2,403
7 langs	267	317
8 langs	108	-
9 langs	8	-
Total	41,751	394,312
>3 langs	5,532	42,171

Table 2: Number of candidate concepts for the mapping SIL SemDoms to OMW, organized by number languages suggesting each candidate

Intersected Langs.	Candidate Senses
1 lang	75,188
2 langs	5,065
3 langs	1
Total	80,254

Table 3: Number of sense candidates generated by the data collected using the RWC method

	SemDom 3 langs	SemDom 4-5 langs	SemDom >5 langs	Total
RWC 1 lang	4,821	4,146	1,048	10,015
RWC 2 langs	282	333	150	765
Total	5,103	4,479	1,198	10,780

Table 4: Number of sense candidates generated by the data collected using the RWC method after applying the filtering step of belonging to the SemDom mappings

The results for the intersection experiments are summarized in Table 2. We provide the number of candidate concepts, sorted by number of languages intersected. Using any number of intersected languages, we collected about 41,700 candidates from SemDom titles, and about 394,000 candidates for SemDom example words. Some of these candidate concepts were suggested by as many as nine languages, although the large majority was suggested by either one or two languages.

However, we know from previous work that quality really spikes at a minimum of three intersected languages. Slaughter et al. (2019) reported that senses triangulated by three or more languages were shown to be correct as high as 98% of the time. Similarly, Kratochvíl and Morgado da Costa (2022) reported 99% accuracy for senses suggested by intersecting three languages, when building the Abui Wordnet. For this reason, we pruned the results of our mapping to only those provided by the intersection of three or more languages.

Our pruned results yielded over 5,500 OMW concepts linked to SemDom titles, and over 42,000 concepts linked to SemDom example words. These numbers are distributed over 1,173 SemDom titles with at least one link to OMW, and over 1,671 SemDom identifiers with at least one example word linked to OMW. We did not expect to provide mappings to all 1,792 SemDom identifiers. This is because because many SemDom titles and example words are, in fact, phrases and not words (e.g. SemDom 2.5.6 Symptom of disease, or 5.8 Manage a house). The fact that some SemDom idenfitiers did not link to OMW is a good sign of quality.

4.2 Linking RWC data to the Abui Wordnet

In order to link the Abui data gathered from the RWC method, we started by performing sense intersection on the existing data. The results of this intersection is shown in Table 3.

As mentioned in Section 3.3, this data comprised about 11,000 Abui words, almost fully translated into Indonesian, but only partially translated into Malay and English. This resulted in a very limited ability to generate high levels of intersection. As shown in Table 3, only a single word was intersected by three languages.[8]

We knew from previous work that two-way intersection yields an accuracy of about 50%. While arguably useful, this score was lower than what we wanted to work with. The way we proposed to raise the confidence score was to use the mapping between SemDom titles and example words to OMW as a filter for the data presented in Table 3.

Since every Abui word collected through the RWC method was linked to a SemDom identifier, we were able to exclude senses that had not been predicted as likely members of that SemDom identifier using the mappings we created. We used the mappings for both the SemDom titles and the example words. This greatly reduced the number of candidate senses. A summary of the results after this filtering step can be see in Table 4.

As mentioned previously, the final mappings between SemDom titles and example words contained only concepts suggested by the intersection of three or more languages. In total, after the filtering step, 10,780 candidate senses remained. However, Ta-

[8]This word was the word for 'yes'.

ble 4 shows a more in-depth distribution of the data. In total the data was distributed into six groups divided into two axes: i) whether the sense candidate was suggested by one or by two languages during the intersection of the RWC data; and ii) whether the SemDom mappings had been suggested by the intersection of three languages, either four or five languages, or by more than five languages.

In general we assumed that the higher the intersection level of both axes, the higher the quality of the suggested senses. While this was not strictly true, hand-checking part of this data confirmed that our method was quite promising.

4.3 Hand-Checked Evaluation

Following the discussion for Table 3, above, we decided to hand-check a portion of each of the six classes of candidate senses, as listed in Table 4. The checking was performed by B. Delpada and D. Lanma (Abui native speakers and linguists) and F. Kratochvíl and G. Saad (linguists working on Abui). We believe that the use of this evaluation is two-fold: i) it directly evaluates the quality of candidate senses for the Abui Wordnet; and ii) it indirectly evaluates the quality of the SemDom mappings, because all candidate senses were filtered by this mapping.

We decided to hand-check 250 candidate senses from each of the six groups discussed above.[9] The results of this evaluation are provided in Table 5.

As is shown, all six groups show a fairly high accuracy of between 87.6% and 99.6%. We had assumed that the higher the intersection level of both axes, the higher the quality of the suggested senses. However, even though the data doesn't fully confirm our assumption, we believe we know why this happened. It has to do, in great part, with the quality of the Wordnet Bahasa – which contains data for both Indonesian and Malay (developed in parallel), two of the three languages contained in the Abui RWC data.

The sense candidates generated for RWC data intersection by two languages was quite limited. And it so happened that among the candidate senses for the groups with lowest accuracy were Abui words translated with words that contained a lot of incorrect data in these two wordnets. Since these two languages are very closely related, and the Wordnet Bahasa used the same methods to develop both languages, some of these errors have a bigger impact than they should.

One simple example to illustrate this problem is the Abui word 'bilengra', which has been glossed with the word 'melukis' for Indonesian and 'draw' for English. The problem that follows is that the lemma 'melukis' has 26 senses in the Wordnet Bahasa (Indonesian). Many of these senses are, in fact, incorrect. KBBI defined 'melukis' as a verb with the gloss 'make drawings using pencils, pens, brushes, and so on, whether with color or not'.[10] However, in the Wordnet Bahasa, this lemma includes senses glossed as 'bring, take, or pull out of a container or from under a cover' (01995211-v), 'suck in or take (air)' (01199009-v), 'cause to move in a certain direction by exerting a force upon, either physically or in an abstract sense' (02103162-v) or 'take liquid out of a container or well' (01854132-v). It is not surprising that the PWN (correctly) adds the lemma 'draw' to all these concepts, hinting at why the Wordnet Bahasa may have included these incorrect senses, and showing the limitations of automatically built wordnets without incorporating a strong review cycle.

Despite some of these limitations, we are satisfied with the results we have achieved. The methodology we developed is robust enough to deal even with somewhat noisy data.

For the future, however, it is important to note that both Indonesian and Malay are essential languages in the production of language resources for Abui, since these are a few of the only other languages speakers of Abui can speak fluently. As such, working towards the improvement and maintenance of the Wordnet Bahasa is well in the interest of the Abui Wordnet and other minority languages of Indonesia.

5 Release Notes

This paper releases two new sets of data: i) the mapping of SIL Semantic Domains to OMW (through PWN 3.0 offsets); and ii) a new extension to the Abui Wordnet.

The mapping of SIL Semantic Domains to OMW will be shared under a Creative Commons Attribution-ShareAlike 4.0 license (following the original license for this resource). In the future, we will attempt to liaise with SIL and open the license further. This data will be released as two TSV files, one for the SemDom identifier titles, and another

[9] Except where mentioned in the table.

[10] Free translation from https://kbbi.kemdikbud.go.id/entri/melukis

	SemDom 3 langs	SemDom 4-5 langs	SemDom >5 langs
RWC 1 lang	0.956♠	0.952	0.996
RWC 2 langs	0.876*	0.932	0.913*

Table 5: Shows the accuracy of the matches, based on a sampled section of the data comprising 250 senses per condition (except cells marked with * for which all suggested senses were checked, see Table 4); After this initial evaluation (of 250 candidate senses per condition), and before the camera-ready version of this paper was submitted, all 4,821 members of the class marked with ♠ were hand-checked, yielding an updated accuracy score of 0.964 (i.e., higher than initially predicted)

file for example words within each identifier. The files contain the following information: SemDom identifier, suggested PWN 3.0 offset, number of languages intersected for this suggestion, and list of language names. This new dataset will be made available on GitHub.[11]

The second set of data concerns new sense candidates for the Abui Wordnet. Interestingly enough, of the 10,780 newly generated candidate senses, only 248 already existed in the Abui Wordnet. All data that has been hand-checked will be included in future version of the Abui Wordnet. The remainder of the data will also be released as separate files and incorporated into the Wordnet after it has been hand-checked (see Section 6). Both sets of data will be released in the existing Abui Wordnet GitHub repository,[12] and released under this wordnet's license – Creative Commons Attribution 4.0 International License.[13]

6 Future Work

This paper presents one of many steps towards the improvement of the Abui Wordnet and the wordnet infrastructure in general.

A natural next step is to finish hand-checking the list of candidate senses generated in this paper. Our hand-checking evaluation has checked 1,432 out of the existing 10,780 generated senses – leaving around 9,300 candidate senses that need to be checked. We hope to be able to do this with the help of the Abui community in the very near future.

Another natural step is to find ways to work with SIL directly and to produce a hand-checked mapping of SemDoms (titles and example words) to OMW. Once this is done, the multilingual nature of OMW could be used to produce official language translations for all available languages in the OMW – centralizing and accelerating the work that is now performed by individual groups of translators, for each language. If properly linked to the OMW, the PWN's semantic hierarchy could even be used to slightly expand the SemDoms by adding new example words to certain semantic classes that are well encoded in PWN's semantic hierarchy (e.g. animals, trees, professions, etc.).

An interesting idea we would like to pursue further is to push the sense-intersection one step forward and start investigating which languages yield best results when intersected. While the underlying idea that the more languages the better the candidate senses produced will undoubtedly hold truth, the quality of candidate senses produced by a 2-way or 3-way intersection may depend highly on which languages are involved. Languages that are closely related, such as Spanish and Portuguese, will arguably share more non-literal meaning extensions than other pairs of less related languages such as Spanish and Chinese. We believe that exploring our intersection methodology using languages from different families or languages that do not share a lot of their cultural background could be a great start for this future research direction.

Finally, we would like to exploit the mappings we provide for SemDom titles and example words to enrich the semantic hierarchy of wordnet projects. We believe that the association-based methodology inherent to SemDoms (and successfully exploited by the RWC method) is directly related to Common Sense Reasoning. Currently, the wordnet hierarchy is known to be both too fine-grained (Hayashi, 2022) and also lacking sufficient semantic relations (Di Caro and Boella, 2016) for tasks involving Common Sense reasoning. We believe our work mapping SemDoms to the OMW could be a good start for a project looking into these two issues.

7 Conclusion

In this paper we have used the idea of multilingual sense intersection for two ends: i) to create a new language resource – a mapping of SIL Semantic Domains to the structure of the Open Multilingual Wordnet; and ii) to use this new semantic resource

[11] https://github.com/lmorgadodacosta/sil-semantic-domains-wordnet-mapping

[12] https://github.com/fanacek/abuiwn

[13] https://creativecommons.org/licenses/by/4.0/

as a filter to expand the Abui Wordnet with data collected using the Rapid Word Collection method (which relies on the SIL Semantic Domains).

We have yielded very positive results for both goals. We have linked more than 47,500 OMW concepts to the SIL Semantic Domains (with a high confidence score), and we have generated more than 10,500 new sense candidates for the Abui Wordnet. Human evaluation has offered a confidence score for these sense candidates between 87.6% and 99.6%.

We hope our work inspires other linguists with data linked to SIL Semantic Domains to follow in our footsteps and to link their data to structures such as the OMW. We hope that lexicographic work on low-resource languages may benefit from both the OMW structure and the SIL experience in rapid lexicographic work involving language communities.

Acknowledgments

The authors acknowledge the generous support of the Czech Science Foundation grant 20-18407S Verb Class Analysis Accelerator for Low- Resource Languages - RoboCorp (PI Kratochvíl) and the EU's Horizon 2020 Marie Skłodowska-Curie grant H2020-MSCA-IF-2020 CHILL – No.101028782 (PI Morgado da Costa).

The authors contributed to the paper in the following way: i) Kratochvíl, Bond, Delpada, Lanma, and Saad conducted the Rapid Word Collection workshops and digitised the data, provided translations into Malay, Indonesian and English (Wolfová contributed many English translations); ii) Blake contributed an extensive ethnobotanical dataset to the database; iii) Morgado da Costa was responsible for extracting the data from SIL FieldWorks, implementing the sense intersection algorithm that produced the SIL mappings to OMW and a new list of sense candidates for the Abui Wordnet and, together with Kratochvíl, was the lead writer of this manuscript.

References

Pushpak Bhattacharyya. 2010. Indowordnet. In *Proceedings of the Seventh International Conference on Language Resources and Evaluation (LREC'10)*.

Giulia Bonansinga and Francis Bond. 2016. Multilingual sense intersection in a parallel corpus with diverse language families. In *Proc. of the 8th Global WordNet Conference*, pages 44–49.

Francis Bond and Ryan Foster. 2013. Linking and extending an open multilingual Wordnet. In *Proceedings of the 51st Annual Meeting of the Association for Computational Linguistics (Volume 1: Long Papers)*, pages 1352–1362, Sofia, Bulgaria. Association for Computational Linguistics.

Francis Bond, Hitoshi Isahara, Kyoko Kanzaki, and Kiyotaka Uchimoto. 2008. Boot-strapping a WordNet using multiple existing WordNets. In *Sixth International Conference on Language Resources and Evaluation (LREC 2008)*, Marrakech.

Francis Bond, Andrew Kirkrose Devadason, Rui Lin Melissa Teo, and Luis Morgado Da Costa. 2021. Teaching through tagging — interactive lexical semantics. In *Proceedings of the 11th Global WordNet Conference (GWC 2021)*, Pretoria, South Africa. Global Wordnet Association.

Francis Bond, Shan Wang, Eshley Huini Gao, Hazel Shuwen Mok, and Jeanette Yiwen Tan. 2013. Developing parallel sense-tagged corpora with wordnets. In *Proceedings of the 7th Linguistic Annotation Workshop and Interoperability with Discourse*, pages 149–158.

Carl Darling Buck. 1949. *A dictionary of selected synonyms in the principal Indo-European languages : a contribution to the history of ideas.* Chicago University Press, Chicago.

Valeria de Paiva and Alexandre Rademaker. 2012. Revisiting a Brazilian wordnet. In *Proceedings of the 6th Global WordNet Conference (GWC 2012)*, Matsue.

Luigi Di Caro and Guido Boella. 2016. Automatic enrichment of wordnet with common-sense knowledge. In *10th International Conference on Language Resources and Evaluation, LREC 2016*, pages 819–822. European Language Resources Association (ELRA).

Christiane Fellbaum, editor. 1998. *WordNet: An Electronic Lexical Database.* MIT Press, Cambridge, MA.

Aitor Gonzalez-Agirre, Egoitz Laparra, and German Rigau. 2012. Multilingual central repository version 3.0: upgrading a very large lexical knowledge base. In *Proceedings of the 6th Global WordNet Conference (GWC 2012)*, Matsue.

Yoshihiko Hayashi. 2022. Towards the detection of a semantic gap in the chain of commonsense knowledge triples. In *Proceedings of the Thirteenth Language Resources and Evaluation Conference*, pages 3984–3993.

Chu-Ren Huang, Shu-Kai Hsieh, Jia-Fei Hong, Yun-Zhu Chen, I-Li Su, Yong-Xiang Chen, and Sheng-Wei Huang. 2010. Chinese wordnet: Design and implementation of a cross-lingual knowledge processing infrastructure. *Journal of Chinese Information Processing*, 24(2):14–23. (in Chinese).

Diptesh Kanojia, Kevin Patel, and Pushpak Bhattacharyya. 2018. Indian Language Wordnets and their Linkages with Princeton WordNet. In *Proceedings of the Eleventh International Conference on Language Resources and Evaluation (LREC 2018)*, Miyazaki, Japan. European Language Resources Association (ELRA).

František Kratochvíl and Benidiktus Delpada. 2014. Abui-English-Indonesian Dictionary. 2nd. edition.

František Kratochvíl and Luís Morgado da Costa. 2022. Abui Wordnet: Using a toolbox dictionary to develop a wordnet for a low-resource language. In *Proceedings of the first workshop on NLP applications to field linguistics*, pages 54–63, Gyeongju, Republic of Korea. Association for Computational Linguistics.

Natalia Loukachevitch and Anastasia Gerasimova. 2019. Linking Russian Wordnet RuWordNet to WordNet. In *Proceedings of the 10th Global Wordnet Conference*, pages 64–71, Wroclaw, Poland. Global Wordnet Association.

Natalia V Loukachevitch, German Lashevich, Anastasia A Gerasimova, Vladimir V Ivanov, and Boris V Dobrov. 2016. Creating russian wordnet by conversion. In *Computational Linguistics and Intellectual Technologies: papers from the Annual conference "Dialogue*, pages 405–415.

Johannes P Louw and Eugene Albert Nida. 1992. *Lexical Semantics of the Greek New Testament: A Supplement to the Greek-English Lexicon of the New Testament Based on Semantic Domains*, volume Resources for Biblical Study of *Society of Biblical Literature*. Scholars Press, Atlanta.

Nurril Hirfana Mohamed Noor, Suerya Sapuan, and Francis Bond. 2011. Creating the open Wordnet Bahasa. In *Proceedings of the 25th Pacific Asia Conference on Language, Information and Computation (PACLIC 25)*, pages 258–267, Singapore.

Mortaza Montazery and Heshaam Faili. 2010. Automatic Persian wordnet construction. In *23rd International conference on computational linguistics*, pages 846–850.

Luís Morgado da Costa and Francis Bond. 2016. Wow! What a useful extension! Introducing non-referential concepts to WordNet. In *Proceedings of the 10th edition of the International Conference on Language Resources and Evaluation (LREC 2016)*, pages 4323–4328, Portorož, Slovenia.

Udorm Phon and Charnyote Pluempitiwiriyawej. 2020. Khmer wordnet construction. In *2020 - 5th International Conference on Information Technology (InCIT)*, pages 122–127.

Muhammad Zulhelmy bin Mohd Rosman, František Kratochvíl, and Francis Bond. 2014. Bringing together over- and under- represented languages: Linking WordNet to the SIL Semantic Domains. In *Proceedings of the Seventh Global Wordnet Conference*, pages 40–48, Tartu, Estonia. University of Tartu Press.

Benoît Sagot and Darja Fišer. 2008. Building a free French wordnet from multilingual resources. In *Proceedings of the Sixth International Language Resources and Evaluation (LREC'08)*, Marrakech, Morocco.

Yu Jie Seah and Francis Bond. 2014. Annotation of pronouns in a multilingual corpus of Mandarin Chinese, English and Japanese. In *Proceedings 10th Joint ISO-ACL SIGSEM Workshop on Interoperable Semantic Annotation*, pages 82–88.

Laura Slaughter, Luis Morgado Da Costa, So Miyagawa, Marco Büchler, Amir Zeldes, Hugo Lundhaug, and Heike Behlmer. 2019. The Making of Coptic Wordnet. In *Proceedings of the 10th Global WordNet Conference (GWC 2019)*, Wroclaw, Poland.

Liling Tan and Francis Bond. 2014. NTU-MC toolkit: Annotating a linguistically diverse corpus. In *Proceedings of COLING 2014, the 25th International Conference on Computational Linguistics: System Demonstrations*, pages 86–89.

Sareewan Thoongsup, Thatsanee Charoenporn, Kergrit Robkop, Tan Sinthurahat, Chumpol Mokarat, Virach Sornlertlamvanich, and Hitoshi Isahara. 2009. Thai wordnet construction. In *Proceedings of The 7th Workshop on Asian Language Resources (ALR7), Joint conference of the 47th Annual Meeting of the Association for Computational Linguistics (ACL) and the 4th International Joint Conference on Natural Language Processing (IJCNLP),*, Suntec, Singapore.

Shan Wang and Francis Bond. 2013. Building the Chinese Open Wordnet (COW): Starting from core synsets. In *Sixth International Joint Conference on Natural Language Processing*, pages 10–18.

Shan Wang and Francis Bond. 2014. Building the sense-tagged multilingual parallel corpus. In *Proceedings of the Ninth International Conference on Language Resources and Evaluation (LREC'14)*, Reykjavik, Iceland. European Language Resources Association (ELRA).

Wordnet-oriented Recognition of Derivational Relations

Wiktor Walentynowicz, Maciej Piasecki
Wrocław University of Science and Technology
{wiktor.walentynowicz|maciej.piasecki}@pwr.edu.pl

Abstract

Derivational relations are an important element in defining meanings, as they help to explore word-formation schemes and predict senses of derivates (derived words). In this work, we analyse different methods of representing derivational forms obtained from WordNet – from quantitative vectors to contextual learned embedding methods – and compare ways of classifying the derivational relations occurring between them. Our research focuses on the explainability of the obtained representations and results. The data source for our research is plWordNet, which is the wordnet of the Polish language and includes a rich set of derivation examples.

1 Introduction

Word formation processes can be observed in many, if not all natural languages: *derivatives* are formed from *derivational bases* by means of language specific derivational mechanisms, e.g. *a teacher* from *to teach*, *a duchess* from *a duke* or, from the Polish language, *domeczek* ≈'a nice, little house' from *dom* 'a house', *białość* ≈'a state of being white' from *biały* ≈'white'. In some natural languages, especially in the case of inflectional ones, e.g. Slavic languages, such mechanisms constitute a very productive system. That is why native speakers can recognise a new derived word forms (derivatives) as a language unit and identify their derivational bases with high precision. What is more, derivational relations, in contrast to morpho-syntactic word formation processes (e.g. different forms of nouns related to the grammatical cases or verb forms representing persons), signal a meaning change between a basis and the derivative. Such lexical meaning transformations are also predictive to a very large extent, e.g. *palarnia* ≈ 'a place for smoking' derived from *palić* 'to smoke'. Due to this property, such a class of derivational relations, described in lexico-semantic networks, is called *morphosemantic relations* (Fellbaum et al., 2007).

It is worth to notice that morphosemantic relations combine two transformations: one between word forms and, the second, in parallel, between lexical meanings, that are tightly coupled: different types of word form transformations are characteristic for some types of semantic derivations, e.g. *kierowniczka* ≈ 'a female head or manager' derived from *kierownik* 'a head or manager' primarily by the suffix *-ka*. Derivation rules can be described to some extent by a combination of suffixes, prefixes and inside stem alternations. However such word form level rules are semantically, ambiguous with respect to the meaning derivation. e.g., the suffix *-ka* mostly signals: a transformation from `+Male` → `+Female`, but it appears in tool name derivation, too: *wiercić* 'to drill' → *wiertarka* 'a driller', and can be also misleading: *pierwiastka* 'a woman giving birth for the first time' is not a female form of *pierwiastek* 'root', in spite of '*ka*'. Thus proper recognition and interpretation of derivational requires taking into account both types of transformations: morphological and semantic.

The general objective of our work is to developed a mechanism for recognition and interpretation of derivatives in a way combining morphological and lexico-semantic level. For a given word, a potential derivative, we want to recognise not only a set of words with which it is in a certain lexico-semantic relation, and also a word from which it has been morphologically derived – its derivational basis. We study machine learning means taking into account both levels: word form and semantic. The unique feature of our approach is a combination of transformer-based neural architecture for modelling derivational patterns tightly coupled with recognition of lexico-semantic relations based on non-contextual word embeddings as semantic representation. We focus on the Polish language for which a large and rich model of morphosemantic relations is included in plWordNet (Dziob et al., 2019). Contrary to many other wordnets and derivational dictionaries, the plWordNet morphosemantic relations link particular senses of two words, not the word forms. In addition, these relations are always directed according to the derivational processes in Polish: from a derivational basis to the derivative.

Derivational relations are often described in morphological dictionaries as links between lemmas[1] e.g. (Kanuparthi et al., 2012), (Šnajder, 2014) or a very large morphological and derivational network DeriNet (Vidra et al., 2019), only later automatically classified to 5 very coarse-grained semantic classes (Ševčíková and Kyjánek, 2019). In (Ševčíková and Kyjánek, 2019) the training data were pairs of words (not senses) and classification was based on morphological features of word forms. Semantic annotation of word pairs was adopted for wordnets (lexico-semantic networks), e.g. RoWordNet (Mititelu, 2012), BulNet (Mititelu, 2012; Dimitrova et al., 2014) or CroWN (Šojat and Srebačić, 2014). However, in wordnets, links between lemmas are additionally labelled with semantic relations, i.e. mapped onto morphosemantic relations. plWordNet (Dziob et al., 2019) showed that such an approach is simplification and prone to errors, as different morphosemantic relations may be valid only for selected senses of lemmas. Thus, we focus on morphosemantic relations as linking senses, but signalled by derivational associations.

In (Piasecki et al., 2012) two character-level transducers were built on the basis from training data (with post-pruning generalisation) and combined with internal stem alternations. Relations suggested by transducers were next filtered by grammatical patterns, corpus frequency and semantic classifiers for word pairs. trained a combination of features describing word distributions in a large corpus. The best results were reported for the set of 9 most populated relations: 36.84 (the young being relation) up to 97.19 (femininity) of F1. However, it should be emphasised that in this case wordnet-internal knowledge about assignment of lemmas to WordNet domains (Fellbaum, 1998) was utilised. We do not use such knowledge in our approach. In a similar approach (Koeva et al., 2016), but much more supported by hand-crafted knowledge F1=0.682 was achieved for verb and noun synset pairs in BulNet. A sequential pattern mining technique based on regular expressions as features for ML was proposed in (Lango et al., 2018) and tested on Polish and Spanish. It was trained on "1500 pairs of base words with their derivatives". However, the annotation guidelines are unknown, semantics of the links was not taken into account, as well as the direction of derivation. Finally, the accuracy of 82.33% was achieved with "53.5 thousand links in the network".

Word embeddings (word2vec and neural language models) were investigated in (Musil et al., 2019) for the Czech coarse-grained derivational relations. Neural character encoder–decoder was applied to predict a derivative from a derivational base in (Vylomova et al., 2017). It used occurrence context too, but was limited to deverbal nouns.

1.1 Contribution

Our main contribution is a method for recognition of morphosemantic relations and a comparison of several different representations of word forms in this task. The analysed method allows for detecting derivational relations between lexical units (word senses) in any wordnet as our method does not depend on any language-specific knowledge resource, except a training set of relation instances.

1.2 Data & Features

The data used in the experiments comes from the plWordNet[2] (Dziob et al., 2019) – precisely from the database dump from version 4.2. The dataset consists of samples represented as triples: a derivational base, a derivational relation and a derivative. Each triple originate from a morphosemantic, derivational, relation linking concrete lexical units (word senses), not lemmas, that have been manually edited and recently carefully manually verified by a separate team of lexicographers.

Statistics of the morphosemantic relations in plWordNet with respect to coarse and fine grained levels of classification is presented in Table 1. The acquired dataset consists of 134,201 triples, of which 77,122 are triples containing a single word lexical unit. The data has been divided into 5 equal numbered split folds. On the basis of the division into folds, five pairs of training and test sets were created. The training and test sets are lexically separable, what means in this case that the same derivational bases do not occur in both sets simultaneously. For the relation classification task, we

[1]Basic morphological word forms selected to represents sets of word forms that differ in the values of grammatical categories, but not meaning.

[2]`http://plwordnet.pwr.edu.pl`

Coarse-grained	Fine-grained	Cardinality
aspectuality	pure aspectuality	31030
	secondary aspectuality	7457
characteristic	characteristic	5366
markedness	diminutives	4184
	augmentatives	886
	young being	83
markedness-intensity	markedness-intensity	996
state/feature bearer	state/feature bearer	1410
similarity	similarity	2171
predisposition	habituality	120
	quantification	15
	appreciation	21
	potential	334
role	agent	153
	time	36
	location	25
	instrument	299
	patient	1039
	product	1521
	agent of hidden predicate	10
	location of hidden predicate	250
	product of hidden predicate	3762
role ADJ-V	agent	1694
	time	167
	location	937
	instrument	322
	patient	306
	product	85
	cause	427
role material	material	1315
state/feature	state/feature	1410
cross-categorial synonymy	ADJ-N	4507
	ADV-ADJ	11355
	N-ADJ	4506
	N-V	30262
	V-N	30262
	for relational	17069
role inclusion	agent inclusion	124
	time inclusion	38
	location inclusion	46
	instrument inclusion	515
	patient inclusion	234
	product inclusion	786
femininity	femininity	3789

Table 1: Relationships found in plWordNet at different granularities.

restricted the list of relations to those with a minimum of 150 examples in the dataset.

2 Embedding methods

In our experiments, we wanted to compare different methods for representing words (in fact lemmas) by vector spaces for the needs of recognition of semantic relations linking them, where all relations of interest are associated also with some relation between the word forms. First of all we used word embedding vectors, i.e. representation of words in dense spaces of real number vectors. Word embeddings were often used in recognition of lexical semantic relations. We conducted experiments with both context-free methods and those that use word context information (acquired during the learning process). We also tried to model words using vectors representing their character structure.

Concerning the latter, we call such a representation *Bag of Characters* (henceforth BoC). The vector for a word is simply constructed by counting the occurrences of different characters from the dictionary – i.e. simply letters of the Polish alphabet. Such a representation is an analogue of Bag of Words model used in Information Retrieval. It is relatively simple, but looses a lot of information related to object structures: documents and words in our case. It is known to be inferior in comparison to representations based on embeddings, so we expected it to be a kind of informative baseline.

A Bag of Characters vector of is easily interpretable in terms of its values, but unfortunately it is insensitive to the order of occurrence of the elements, i.e. character sequences that are very important in expressing derivational changes and morphems. Nevertheless, we wanted to check to what extent such an simplified representation is sufficient in representing derivational relations, which are characterised by relatively regular exchanges of characters in words. An example of such a vector is presented in Figure 1.

fastText (Bojanowski et al., 2017) is a word vectorisation model similar to *word2vec* (Mikolov et al., 2013), a kind of non-contextual word embedding model. The main difference is the use of orthographic representation in the vector creation process. The method learns the representation of character n-grams in text contexts and then constructs a vector of a given word as average of

	BoG Diff DT		BoG Diff RF		BoG Diff MLP		BoG 3-way DT		BoG 3-way RF		BoG 3-way MLP	
	Macro	Weighted	Macro	Weighted	Macro	Weighted	Macro	Weighted	Macro	Weighted	Macro	Weighted
Fold 0	0,60	0,83	0,60	0,83	0,58	0,83	0,56	0,80	0,57	0,82	0,59	0,83
Fold 1	0,61	0,83	0,61	0,83	0,61	0,83	0,56	0,80	0,59	0,82	0,59	0,82
Fold 2	0,60	0,82	0,60	0,83	0,60	0,83	0,56	0,79	0,59	0,82	0,57	0,82
Fold 3	0,60	0,82	0,61	0,82	0,60	0,82	0,55	0,79	0,57	0,81	0,58	0,82
Fold 4	0,60	0,83	0,61	0,83	0,59	0,82	0,56	0,79	0,59	0,82	0,59	0,82
Avg	***0,602***	***0,826***	***0,606***	***0,828***	***0,596***	***0,826***	***0,558***	***0,794***	***0,582***	***0,818***	***0,584***	***0,822***
St. dev	***0,004***	***0,005***	***0,005***	***0,004***	***0,011***	***0,005***	***0,004***	***0,005***	***0,011***	***0,004***	***0,009***	***0,004***
	FT 100 Diff		**FT 100 3-way**		**FT 300 Diff**		**FT 300 3-way**		**COMB 100**		**COMB 300**	
	Macro	Weighted	Macro	Weighted	Macro	Weighted	Macro	Weighted	Macro	Weighted	Macro	Weighted
Fold 0	0,58	0,82	0,61	0,83	0,60	0,83	0,63	0,85	0,61	0,83	0,62	0,84
Fold 1	0,57	0,81	0,61	0,83	0,60	0,83	0,63	0,84	0,60	0,83	0,64	0,85
Fold 2	0,57	0,81	0,61	0,83	0,61	0,83	0,62	0,84	0,60	0,83	0,64	0,84
Fold 3	0,59	0,82	0,61	0,83	0,59	0,82	0,64	0,84	0,60	0,83	0,63	0,84
Fold 4	0,57	0,82	0,61	0,83	0,61	0,83	0,61	0,84	0,61	0,83	0,62	0,84
Avg	***0,576***	***0,816***	***0,610***	***0,830***	***0,602***	***0,828***	***0,626***	***0,842***	***0,604***	***0,830***	***0,630***	***0,842***
St. dev	***0,009***	***0,005***	***0,000***	***0,000***	***0,008***	***0,004***	***0,011***	***0,004***	***0,005***	***0,000***	***0,010***	***0,004***

Table 2: Experimental results on the classifier. F-1 score measure. *DT – Decision Tree; RF – Random Forest; MLP – Multi Layer Perceptron; FT – fastText; COMB – Combination of FT and BoG vectors*

Word form: kotek *(ang. little cat)*

a	...	e	...	k	l	m	n	o	...	t	...	z
0	...	1	...	2	0	0	0	1	...	1	...	0

Figure 1: Example of bag-of-character vector for word "kotek".

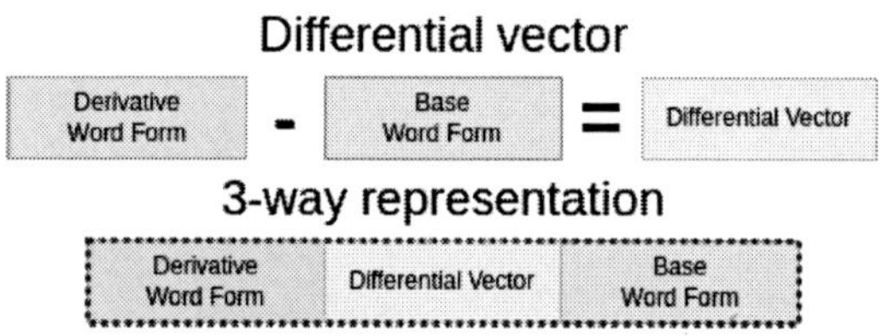

Figure 2: (Top) The way the differential vector is formed. (Bottom) The vector in the second phase of the experiments is formed by concatenating three basis vectors.

representations of the n-grams that constitute it. This process of building vectors goes around the problem of out-of-vocabulary words. The *fastText* based representation showed improvement in several NLP tasks in relation to inflectional languages, e.g. syntactic tasks relative to traditional *word2vec*, but also text classification and recognition of semantic relations.

3 Classification experiments

In order to compare the effectiveness of using different vector representations for the task of classifying derivational relations, we first used all vector versions to train a multi-class classifier based on an MLP neural network, as a classification model that seem to be in good balance between expressiveness and requirements for the size of a data set that is limited in our case (e.g. especially coverage for different relation types). We used the package default settings during learning the classifier, because our main focus was on different vector representations of examples.

Since Bag of Characters vectors are discrete in nature and their singular values are interpretable, we also decided to train classifiers using directly this representation, i.e. Decision Trees, both a single tree method and a Random Forest approach. In our experiments, we followed a multi-class classifier scheme. Each example in the training and test data subsets is an instance of a derivational relation (i.e. a pair of lemmas: a derivational basis and a derivative) so in the experiments we did not assume the possibility of labelling a pair with the label 'no relation'.

We examined each prepared vector representation in the following configurations:

1. differential vector of the derivation form and the base form;

2. concatenated vectors of a derivational form, a base form and a differential vector.

We called this vector a 3-way vector. This is shown in Figure 2. The 3-way representation was shown to be effective in recognition of wordnet relations, especially in combination with fastText representation, e.g. (Czachor et al., 2018). It is meant to represent semantic characteristic of both elements, but also to emphasise differences between them, together with the directions of the differences. The directions are potentially important for plWordNet morphosemantic relations, as they are all defined and edited in the direction from a derivational basis to the derivate (the derived word).

For the final experiment, we also analysed combination of the two different representations. Whole words were embedded using *fastText* vectors and concatenated together with a difference vector obtained using the Bag-of-Characters technique. The aim of this experiment was to test whether combining a semantic representation based on word vectors and a discrete representation associated with an orthographic form would result in an improvement in the classification task.

We implemented the classifier models for all experiments using the *scikit-learn* library (Pedregosa et al., 2011).

3.1 Results

The obtained results are shown in Table 2. All experiments yielded approximately the same results – the differences are statistically non-significant – regardless of the representation method applied. These results are quite surprising in two aspects: lack of superiority of semantically-informed representation based on fastText and no preference for MLP representation.

Classifiers from the tree family, did not differ much in their results with respect to the neural network classifier, which may also suggest saturation of the problem rather than a specific classification method. Only increasing the size of the fastText vector improved the measure by ~1.5 percentage points in 3-way representation case. This can be also an effect of learning the association of some relation types with specific semantic dimensions. However, it is worth to emphasise that we applied a technique of lexical split in selecting folds, i.e. the same words were not selected for both the training and test subsets (needless to say that relations instances are obviously not repeating between both subsets). Such a split is known to prevent a classifier for memorising prototypes for relation instances. Such conformity of the classifier may indicate that a limit with respect to the efficiency of the method has been reached, which will not be exceeded without changing the assumptions of the problem.

A major limiting factor for further progress, we suggest, is the scheme in which the classification is performed out of use context. In tasks where semantics matter (for example WSD, NER) context is a strong stimulus for classification methods. Moreover, most of the lemmas we are working here with – relations link lexical units (word senses), but representations are built for lemmas – are polysemous. What is worse, in some number of cases a given morphosemantic relations links only selected lexical units from lemmas, depending on the meaning of these lexical units. It is also worth to notice that a representation based on word embeddings is a not only a mixture of several lexical meaning per a word, but also only more salient meanings dominates in it and less frequent meanings are often hard to trace in a vector. Thus, when we work with ambiguous, lemma-based representations that make the picture very blurred from the point of view of classifiers. In this task of recognition of morphosemantic relations, we need a shift in paradigm from context-less into analysing representations of lexical units in their use contexts, in order to make further progress. The task must be somehow combined with Word Sense Disambiguation and Word Sense Induction.

4 Conclusions

Our research has shown that the limit of context-free classification of derivational relations lies not in the representation of examples, but in the absence of any other source of information for the classifier. In the final version of the system for context-free classification of derivational relations, we decided to stay with Bag of Characters vectors, due to their simple human interpretability. We want to direct our further research to the study of derivation in the context of – both the preparation of datasets (such as a corpus) and methods for detecting and classifying relations.

References

Piotr Bojanowski, Edouard Grave, Armand Joulin, and Tomas Mikolov. 2017. Enriching word vectors with subword information. *Transactions of the Association for Computational Linguistics*, 5:135–146.

Gabriela Czachor, Maciej Piasecki, and Arkadiusz Janz. 2018. Recognition of lexico-semantic relations in word embeddings for polish. In *Proceedings of the 9th Global Wordnet Conference, Singapore, 8-12 January 2018*. Global WordNet Association.

Tsvetana Dimitrova, Ekaterina Tarpomanova, and Borislav Rizov. 2014. Coping with derivation in the bulgarian wordnet. In *Proceedings of the Seventh*

Global Wordnet Conference, pages 109–117. University of Tartu Press.

Agnieszka Dziob, Maciej Piasecki, and Ewa Rudnicka. 2019. plWordNet 4.1 - a linguistically motivated, corpus-based bilingual resource. In *Proceedings of the 10th Global Wordnet Conference*, pages 353–362, Wroclaw, Poland. Global Wordnet Association.

Christiane Fellbaum, editor. 1998. *WordNet – An Electronic Lexical Database*. The MIT Press.

Christiane Fellbaum, Anne Osherson, and Peter E. Clark. 2007. Putting semantics into wordnet's "morphosemantic" links. In *Human Language Technology. Challenges of the Information Society, Third Language and Technology Conference, LTC 2007, Poznan, Poland, October 5-7, 2007, Revised Selected Papers*, volume 5603 of *Lecture Notes in Computer Science*, pages 350–358. Springer.

Nikhil Kanuparthi, Abhilash Inumella, and Dipti Misra Sharma. 2012. Hindi derivational morphological analyzer. In *Proceedings of the Twelfth Meeting of the Special Interest Group on Computational Morphology and Phonology*, pages 10–16. Association for Computational Linguistics.

Svetla Koeva, Svetlozara Leseva, Ivelina Stoyanova, Tsvetana Dimitrova, and Maria Todorova. 2016. Automatic prediction of morphosemantic relations. In *Proceedings of the 8th Global WordNet Conference (GWC)*, pages 169–177. Global Wordnet Association.

Mateusz Lango, Magda Ševčíková, and Zdeněk Žabokrtský. 2018. Semi-automatic construction of word-formation networks (for polish and spanish). In *Proceedings of the Eleventh International Conference on Language Resources and Evaluation (LREC 2018)*. European Language Resources Association (ELRA).

Tomas Mikolov, Ilya Sutskever, Kai Chen, Greg S Corrado, and Jeff Dean. 2013. Distributed representations of words and phrases and their compositionality. *Advances in neural information processing systems*, 26.

Verginica Barbu Mititelu. 2012. Adding morpho-semantic relations to the romanian wordnet. In *Proceedings of the Eighth International Conference on Language Resources and Evaluation (LREC'12)*, pages 2596–2601. European Language Resources Association (ELRA).

Tomáš Musil, Jonáš Vidra, and David Mareček. 2019. Derivational morphological relations in word embeddings. In *Proceedings of the 2019 ACL Workshop BlackboxNLP: Analyzing and Interpreting Neural Networks for NLP*, pages 173–180. Association for Computional Linguistics.

F. Pedregosa, G. Varoquaux, A. Gramfort, V. Michel, B. Thirion, O. Grisel, M. Blondel, P. Prettenhofer, R. Weiss, V. Dubourg, J. Vanderplas, A. Passos, D. Cournapeau, M. Brucher, M. Perrot, and E. Duchesnay. 2011. Scikit-learn: Machine learning in Python. *Journal of Machine Learning Research*, 12:2825–2830.

Maciej Piasecki, Radosław Ramocki, and Marek Maziarz. 2012. Recognition of polish derivational relations based on supervised learning scheme. In *Proceedings of the Eight International Conference on Language Resources and Evaluation (LREC'12)*, pages 916–922. European Language Resources Association (ELRA).

Jonáš Vidra, Zdeněk Žabokrtský, Magda Ševčíková, and Lukáš Kyjánek. 2019. DeriNet 2.0: Towards an all-in-one word-formation resource. In *Proceedings of the Second International Workshop on Resources and Tools for Derivational Morphology*, pages 81–89, Prague, Czechia. Charles University, Faculty of Mathematics and Physics, Institute of Formal and Applied Linguistics.

Ekaterina Vylomova, Ryan Cotterell, Timothy Baldwin, and Trevor Cohn. 2017. Context-aware prediction of derivational word-forms. In *Proceedings of the 15th Conference of the European Chapter of the Association for Computational Linguistics: Volume 2, Short Papers*, volume 2, pages 118–124. Association for Computational Linguistics.

Magda Ševčíková and Lukáš Kyjánek. 2019. Introducing semantic labels into the derinet network. *Journal of Linguistics/Jazykovedný casopis*, 70(2):412–423.

Jan Šnajder. 2014. Derivbase.hr: A high-coverage derivational morphology resource for croatian. In *Proceedings of the Ninth International Conference on Language Resources and Evaluation (LREC'14)*, pages 3371–3377. European Language Resources Association (ELRA).

Krešimir Šojat and Matea Srebačić. 2014. Morphosemantic relations between verbs in croatian wordnet. In *Proceedings of the Seventh Global Wordnet Conference*, pages 262–267. University of Tartu Press.

What do Language Models know about word senses? Zero-Shot WSD with Language Models and Domain Inventories

Oscar Sainz , Oier Lopez de Lacalle , Eneko Agirre , German Rigau

HiTZ Basque Center for Language Technologies - Ixa NLP Group
University of the Basque Country UPV/EHU
{oscar.sainz, oier.lopezdelacalle, e.agirre, german.rigau}@ehu.eus

Abstract

Language Models are the core for almost any Natural Language Processing system nowadays. One of their particularities is their contextualized representations, a game changer feature when a disambiguation between word senses is necessary. In this paper we aim to explore to what extent language models are capable of discerning among senses at inference time. We performed this analysis by prompting commonly used Languages Models such as BERT or RoBERTa to perform the task of Word Sense Disambiguation (WSD). We leverage the relation between word senses and domains, and cast WSD as a textual entailment problem, where the different hypothesis refer to the domains of the word senses. Our results show that this approach is indeed effective, close to supervised systems.

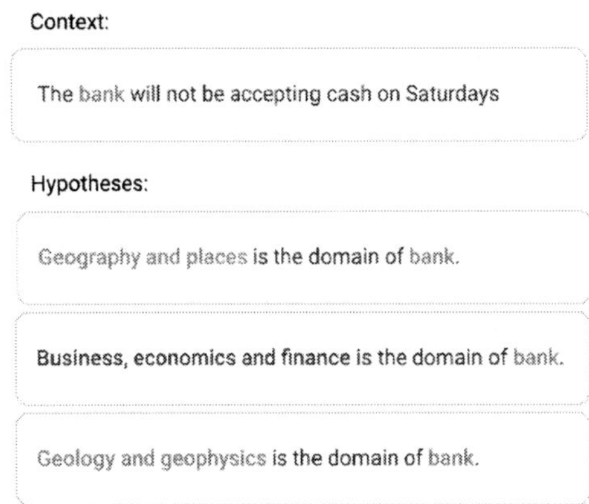

Figure 1: An example of the Word Sense Disambiguation task converted to Textual Entailment, where the hypothesis refer to the possible domains of word senses. To solve the task a model would be asked to select the most probable hypothesis based on the context.

1 Introduction

It is undeniable that Language Models (LM) have drastically changed the Natural Language Processing (NLP) field (Min et al., 2021). More recently, those LM have also shown to be capable of performing NLP tasks with just few examples given in the context (Brown et al., 2020), using the so called *prompting*. One of their particularities, and the key difference with previous approaches, is their contextualized token representation. Allowing the model to adopt different representations for words (tokens) depending on the context has supposed a huge advantage when sense disambiguation is required for a given inference. But, **to what extent do LM actually know about word senses?** In this work, we tried to answer that question by evaluating LMs directly on the Word Sense Disambiguation (WSD) task via prompting.

Word Sense Disambiguation is the task of identifying the correct sense of a word in a given context. Current state-of-the-art on WSD involves fine-tuning a LM on SemCor (Miller et al., 1994) to predict the correct among all possible sense glosses of the word in the given context. Other methods leverage the contextual representations of LM to perform WSD with a simple K-NN algorithm on the embedding space. Lately, the use of domain inventories was proposed to alleviate the high granularity of knowledge-bases (Lacerra et al., 2020). Recent studies that worked on zero-shot WSD refer to the task of predicting the senses of new lemmas not seeing during training as zero-shot (Lacerra et al., 2020) WSD, however we aim for a completely zero-shot evaluation, where no annotated data is available for any lemma.

Despite the knowledge already encoded in the LM, training data is used in one way or another to introduce knowledge about the task. To avoid drawing noisy conclusions, we evaluated the LM as they are, without further fine-tuning on or using any kind of WSD training data. To that end, we prompted LMs like BERT (Devlin et al., 2019) and RoBERTa (Liu et al., 2019) to perform a task

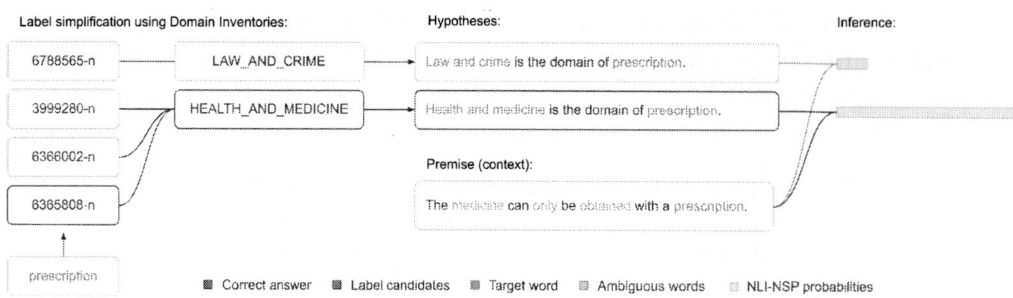

Figure 2: Graphical description of the zero-shot WSD approach using Domain Inventories.

that requires WSD knowledge to be successfully solved.

Figure 1 shows an example of how a model can be prompted to solve WSD using Textual Entailment as a proxy. On this example we consider that the word bank has senses from three different domains: *Geography and places*, *Business, economics and finance* and *Geology and geophysics*. The three possible domains are converted to hypothesis using predefined prompts. Finally, a supervised Textual Entailment model is used to perform the inference. More details on of the approach are discussed in Section 2.

In this work we first evaluated commonly used LMs as a zero-shot domain labelers with 3 different domain inventories. Then, following (Lacerra et al., 2020) we addressed the WSD using domain inventories and evaluated the LMs on them. We showed that LMs have some notion of senses as they perform zero-shot WSD significantly better than a random baseline and sometimes close to the supervised state-of-the-art. We also provided different analysis comparing different prompts and performing an error analysis over the two evaluated tasks.

2 Prompting Language Models

Since the past few years, prompting has become the *de facto* approach to probe language models (Li et al., 2022b). Min et al. (2021) defined prompting as the practice of adding natural language text, often short phrases, to the input or output to encourage pre-trained models to perform specific tasks. However, due to its wide definition, several different ways of prompting exists, such as *instruction based*, *template-based* or *proxy-task based*. For more information about prompting we encourage the reader to read the Liu et al. (2022a) survey.

In this work we focused on the *proxy-task based* approach, more precisely, we made use of the Next Sentence Prediction (NSP) and Textual Entailment (TE) tasks as a proxy. The TE is also known as Natural Language Inference (NLI), we will use both terms interchangeably. The choice of this approach was made based on previous works on zero-shot domain labelling (Sainz and Rigau, 2021).

Both, NSP and TE are sentence-pair classification tasks: the first attempts to predict whether a sentence is followed by another and the second aims to predict if an entailment relation exists between both sentences (premise and hypothesis). Figure 2 shows an example of how to perform WSD using NSP or TE models. The process can be briefly summarized as follows: (1) for each possible sense s of the target word w we obtain their corresponding domain d using a domain inventory D (domain inventories are discussed in more detail in Section 3). (2) predefined prompts are used to generate verbalizations that will serve as possible continuations (on NSP) or hypothesis (on TE) h. (3) a pretrained NSP or TE model is used to obtain a probability for each sentence/hypothesis and therefore, to each domain. Formally, for a TE model we defined the probability of word w being from domain $d_i \in D^w$ in context c as follows:

$$P(d_i|c, w) = P(\text{entailment}|c, h_{wi}) \qquad (1)$$

where h_{wi} is the hypothesis generated using a predefined prompt, the domain label d_i and the word w. Similarly, for a NSP model the probability is defined as follows:

$$P(d_i|c, w) = P(\text{is\_next}|c, h_{wi}) \qquad (2)$$

Table 2 shows the prompts used for probing Language Models in Domain Labelling and Word

Sense	BabelDomains	CSI	WN Domains	Gloss
00006484-n	Biology	Biology	biology	The basic structural and functional unit of all organisms; ...
02991048-n	Chemistry and mineralogy	Craft, Engineering and Technology	electronics	A device that delivers an electric current as the result of a chemical reaction.
02992529-n	Computing	Craft, Engineering and Technology	electricity telephony	A hand-held mobile radiotelephone for use in an area divided into small sections, each with its own short-range transmitter/receiver

Table 1: Example of Domain inventories for 3 senses of the word *cell*.

Sense Disambiguation tasks.

3 Domain Inventories

A domain inventory is a set of domain labels such as *Health and Medicine*, *Culture* or *Business and economics* that aims to cover the wider spectrum of domains as possible with a specific granularity level. Actually, these domain inventories are used to label synsets from knowledge-bases like WordNet (Fellbaum, 1998) and BabelNet (Navigli and Ponzetto, 2012). Examples of WordNet synset annotations from different domain inventories are shown in the Table 1. Recent studies (Lacerra et al., 2020) suggest to use domain inventories to address the high granularity problem that affects WSD tasks. In this section we describe the three domain inventories on which we evaluated the Language Models.

BabelDomains (Camacho-Collados and Navigli, 2017) is a unified resource that includes domain information for Wikipedia, WordNet and BabelNet. It inherits the domains from Wikipedia domains of knowledge, a total of 34 coarse labels. Although it is semi-automatically annotated, two gold standard datasets (for WordNet and Wikipedia) are provided for evaluation.

Coarse Sense Inventory (CSI) (Lacerra et al., 2020) was created to reduce the level of granularity of WordNet synsets while maintaining their expressiveness. It contains a total of 45 labels shared across the lexicon. Compared to previous alternatives, CSI provided a higher agreement among annotators. Also it was already proven to be useful for the WSD task.

WordNet Domains (Bentivogli et al., 2004) is a fine-grained domain inventory containing about 160 labels. It is organised in a hierarchical way, from global concepts such as *pure_science* to specific concepts as *oceanography*. This inventory provides a domain label to each synset in WordNet. Due to the hierarchical nature and fine granularity, in our experiments we kept only the domain labels until the third level, mapping all the labels below to the closest available domain. We end up with 60 domain labels.

4 Experimental Setup

In this section we describe the models we evaluated, and the Domain Labelling and Word Sense Disambiguation tasks we used for evaluation.

Models. For the experiments we decided to evaluate two very commonly used models: BERT and RoBERTa. We followed previous works on zero-shot domain labelling (Sainz and Rigau, 2021) for approach and model selection. As explained in Section 2 we required that the models were already fine-tuned to perform sentence pair classifications. In the case of the BERT models, we used the LM itself with the NSP head that was trained during pre-training, in the tables it is shown as NSP. For the case of RoBERTa, as it has not been pre-trained for any sentence classification task, we evaluated two checkpoints that were also fine-tuned with TE data: NLI and NLI*. The main difference between both checkpoints is the variety of data on which the models were trained. We evaluated the *large* variant of those models. The NLI variation was trained just on MultiNLI (Williams et al., 2018) dataset and NLI* variations was also trained on SNLI (Bowman et al., 2015), Fever-NLI (Thorne et al., 2018) and Adversarial-NLI (Nie et al., 2020). Both models are publicly available at HuggingFace Model Hub (Wolf et al., 2020).

Domain Labelling task is the task of classifying some text t into a set of domain labels D. In

Task	Prompt
Domain Labelling	{gloss} I The domain of the sentence is about {label}.
Word Sense Disambiguation	{context} I The domain of the sentence is about {label}.
	{context} I {label} is the domain of {word}.

Table 2: Prompts used for probing Language Models.

our case, the text to classify are WordNet synset glosses and the domain labels are the ones defined by the domain inventories. The task was evaluated on a small manually annotated dataset released by Camacho-Collados and Navigli (2017). The dataset consist of domain annotations for 1540 WordNet synsets using BabelDomains inventory. For those 1540 synsets we also collected the domain information from CSI and WordNet Domains. The 3 checkpoints described above were evaluated with each domain inventory. To evaluate the models on domain labelling data we used the prompts described in Table 2 to convert domain labelling examples into NLI or NSP examples. The prompt is used to generated as many hypotheses as labels are in the inventory, by replacing the *gloss* placeholder with the synset's gloss and the *label* placeholder with the corresponding label each time.

> Cell: **(biology)** the basic structural and functional unit of all organisms; ...

Figure 3: An example of WordNet gloss. The hint in the gloss is highlighted.

WordNet glosses sometimes contains domain information inside them. For example, in the gloss shown in Figure 3 the domain information is highlighted in bold. We will call them domain *hints*. As we are using those glosses as inputs to predict the domain of the synsets, the hints give a huge advantage to the models. Therefore, for the evaluation we considered two alternatives: with and without hints.

WSD task is the task of identifying the correct sense s a word w withing a context c among all its possible senses $s \in S^w$. In this case, and following recent works we reframed the task from predicting senses to more coarse set of labels (domains) (Lacerra et al., 2020). Therefore, the task aims to classify the domain of the correct sense d_s among the domains of the possible senses D^w. As senses in WordNet are very fine-grained, several senses of the same domain may coexist, after replacing them with their domain the set of possible labels might be reduced, therefore $|D^w| \leq |S^w|$. An example of two senses from the same domain is shown in Table 3. The task was evaluated on the standard commonly known SemEval (Pradhan et al., 2007; Navigli et al., 2013; Moro and Navigli, 2015) and Senseval (Edmonds and Cotton, 2001; Snyder and Palmer, 2004) datasets. For each model, we also compared two different prompts shown in Table 2: the first is the same as the one used for Domain Labelling and is used to predict the domain of the whole context; the second instead adds a reference to the target word, and is intended to focus the model to predict the domain of the given word withing the context. Finally, we report a random guessing baseline and a supervised upper-bound from Lacerra et al. (2020).

5 Results

In this section we discuss the results obtained on each experiment. First we discuss the results obtained on the Domain Labelling task. Then, we show the results from Word Sense Disambiguation. And finally we analyze the correlation between both tasks as they share the label space.

Are Language Models able to discriminate domains in sense glosses? Figure 4 shows the results obtained for the Domain Labelling task. As a general overview, the three models obtain decent results considering no data for training was provided. Comparing NLI models vs the NSP model, we can conclude that NLI based models perform better in all cases, in concordance with previous works (Wang et al., 2021a). However, additional TE data (NLI vs NLI*) does not seem to be very useful for the task. Finally, the results shows that the domain hints in the gloss affects significantly to the performance, specially in WordNet Domains, where the labels are very fine-grained.

Do Language Models know about Word Senses? Figure 5 shows the results for each of the WSD

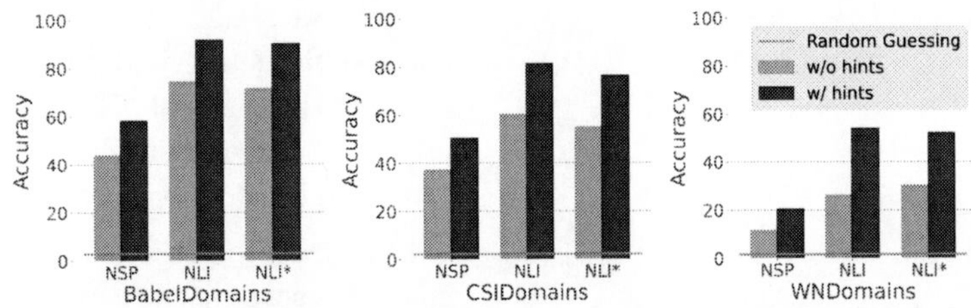

Figure 4: Results on Domain Labelling task for three different domain inventories.

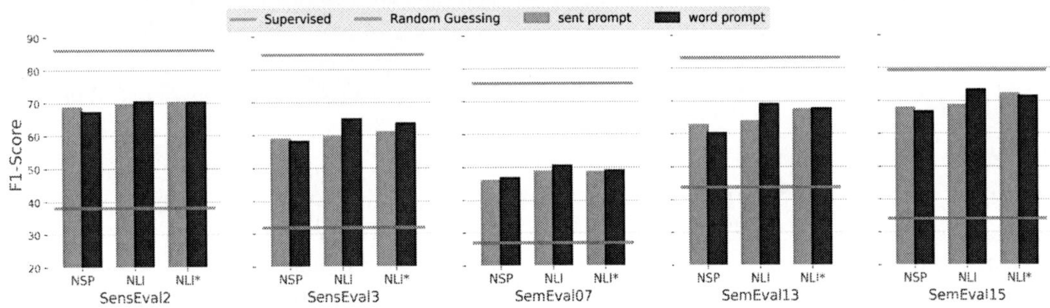

Figure 5: Word Sense Disambiguation results for the three systems in the 5 evaluation datasets. The red line indicates the state-of-the-art supervised scores and the blue line the scores obtained by random guessing.

datasets along with random and supervised baselines. In general, the results suggest that **in fact the Language Models know about senses**. While still far from a supervised upper-bound, the three models have shown significantly better performance than a random classifier. Moreover, for the SemEval-15 task the models achieve a performance close to the upper-bound. Comparing the NSP model against the NLI models, the same pattern as in the Domain Labelling task occur, the NLI models are better in all scenarios. If we compare both TE models, both perform similarly when the *sentence prompt* is used, for the *word prompt* instead the NLI model shows slightly better results. Overall, the best combination is NLI model with the *word prompt*.

Do Language Models perform differently depending on the word category? To answer this question we report the results grouped by the word category in the Table 3. The table reports the same results as Figure 5 except for the supervised upper-bound which has not been reported by Lacerra et al. (2020) under this setting. We also report the *micro-averaged* F1-Score for all categories, allowing us to clearly compare all the systems. Considering the results, the NLI model with the *word prompt* is again the best performing system across all word categories. Comparing the NLI_{word} model against the random baseline we can observe a high correlation in the scores, which suggest that the errors on each category depend more on the task difficulty rather than specific language model issues.

Model	Noun	Adj	Verb	Adv	All
Random	40.7	48.4	23.7	59.1	38.8
Sentence prompt					
NSP	60.3	84.9	50.4	86.6	62.6
NLI	64.3	86.2	54.8	86.4	66.1
NLI*	65.0	85.9	55.0	85.3	66.4
Word prompt					
NSP	59.4	84.8	50.2	86.4	61.9
NLI	**66.2**	**86.8**	**57.0**	**87.3**	**67.8**
NLI*	65.3	85.5	55.7	85.5	66.8

Table 3: F1-Scores per word category

To what extent does the performance on Domain Labelling affects WSD? As we are framing WSD as a Domain Labelling problem, it is intuitive to think that the performance on Domain Labelling can affect the performance on WSD. The evaluation we carried out in both tasks have a common label space, and therefore, we can compute the correlation between label scores. For each label,

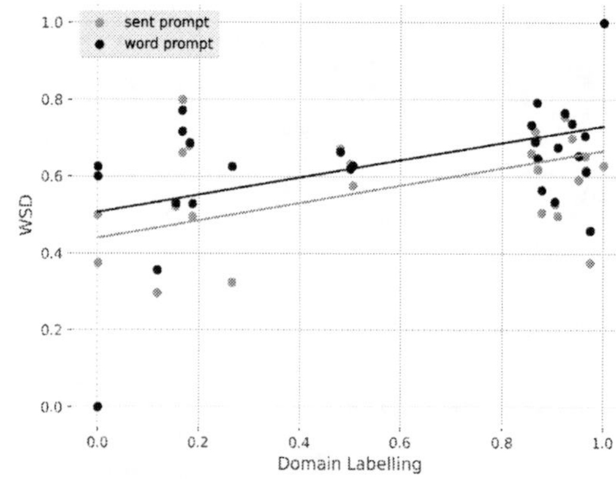

Figure 6: F1 correlation between Domain Labelling and WSD tasks.

	Dom Lab.	WSD_{sent}	WSD_{word}
Dom Lab.	1.00	0.32	0.41
WSD_{sent}	0.32	1.00	0.81
WSD_{word}	0.41	0.81	1.00

Table 4: Spearman's correlation of F1-Scores between tasks using shared labels. The scores correspond to the NLI model.

we compared the F1-score obtained on Domain Labelling and WSD tasks. Figure 6 shows the per-domain F1 scores on Domain Labelling and WSD tasks, each point represents the F1 obtained on a specific label. In the figure, we included the F1 for both *sentence prompt* and *word prompt* systems. The results shows **very little correlation** between both tasks. The Table 4 shows the Spearnman's correlation for each task pair. The results again shows that both tasks are poorly correlated, even when we use the same prompt. However, this comparison might not be completely fair, there are 2 main reasons that could affect the results: the Domain Labelling glosses have a particular structure and different from WSD contexts, also, on WSD the system needs to predict the correct among **possible** labels rather than all the label space as in Domain Labelling. We should take into consideration those differences at the time of interpreting the results.

6 Related Work

Word Sense Disambiguation Approaches to WSD range from supervised that only use annotated data (Agirre et al., 2014; Hadiwinoto et al., 2019; Bevilacqua and Navigli, 2019) to knowledge-based (Moro et al., 2014; Agirre et al., 2014; Scozzafava et al., 2020), as well as approaches that combine supervised and knowledge-based approaches (Kumar et al., 2019; Bevilacqua and Navigli, 2020; Blevins and Zettlemoyer, 2020; Conia and Navigli, 2021; Barba et al., 2021).

Knowledge-based approaches employ graph algorithms on a semantic network (Moro et al., 2014; Agirre et al., 2014; Scozzafava et al., 2020), in which senses are connected through semantic relations and are described with definitions and usage examples. Unfortunately, their independence from annotated data comes at the expense of performing worse than supervised models (Pilehvar and Navigli, 2014).

Supervised approaches frame the task as a classification problem and use available annotated data to learn mapping the words in context to senses. Before supervised neural models emerged as state of the art in NLP, the task of supervised WSD was performed based on a variety of lexico-syntantic and semantic feature representations that are fed to a supervised machine learning classifier (Zhong and Ng, 2010). Instead, current state-of-the-art supervised models rely on the use of pretrained Transformers as core architecture of the model. Among these models we can find approaches that exclusively use annotated data to learn effective representations of the target word in context and feed it to some classification head (Raganato et al., 2017; Hadiwinoto et al., 2019; Bevilacqua and Navigli, 2019; Conia and Navigli, 2021).

Some approaches have shown that an effective way to improve sense representation is to exploit the glosses provided by the sense inventories. Gloss representation are then incorporated to the sense embedding (Peters et al., 2018), in which the most probable sense is retrieve according to the similarity with the given context. Multiple works have been shown effective in WSD such as LMSS (Loureiro and Jorge, 2019), SensEmBERT (Scarlini et al., 2020a), ARES (Scarlini et al., 2020b), SREF (Wang and Wang, 2020), EWISE (Kumar et al., 2019) and EWISER (Bevilacqua and Navigli, 2020), among many others. Glosses have also been exploited in sequence-tagging approaches (Huang et al., 2019; Yap et al., 2020), where the task is framed as sequence classification problem (Barba et al., 2021). In a similar manner, (Bevilacqua and Navigli, 2020) propose a generative approach to cast WSD as sequence classification problem. In adition to glosses, other approaches presented ways to make use of the knowledge encoded in KBs such as WordNet. For instance, (Loureiro and Jorge, 2019; Wang and Wang, 2020) propagate sense embeddings using WordNet as a graph. Please refer to (Bevilacqua et al., 2021) to obtain further details of the recent trends in WSD.

Prompting Language Models has changed the paradigm of how Language Models can be used to extract even more potential from them. Initially with very large LM like GPT-3 (Brown et al., 2020) and later with smaller ones (Gao et al., 2021) prompts allowed the models to perform zero or few-shot classifications with simple natural language. This ability also allowed models to improve performance on data-scarce problems by large margin (Le Scao and Rush, 2021; Min et al., 2021; Liu et al., 2022a). These prompts can be discrete (Gao et al., 2021; Schick and Schütze, 2021a,b,c) close to natural language or continuous (Liu et al., 2022b) close to other efficient deep learning methods like Adapters (Pfeiffer et al., 2020). Closer to our work, Textual Entailment (Dagan et al., 2006) has been used as a source of external supervision to solve several text classification tasks (Yin et al., 2019, 2020; Wang et al., 2021b; Sainz and Rigau, 2021; McCann et al., 2018; White et al., 2017), Named Entity Recognition (Li et al., 2022a; Poliak et al., 2018; Yang et al., 2022), Relation Extraction (Levy et al., 2017; Sainz et al., 2021), Event Extraction (Lyu et al., 2021), Event Argument Extraction (Sainz et al., 2022a,b), Intent Classification (Xia et al., 2021), Aspect-based Sentiment Analysis (Shu et al., 2022) and many more.

Domain Inventories. Domain information was added to Princeton WordNet (Fellbaum, 1998) since version 3.0. In total 440 topics were represented as a synsets in the graph. The topic label assignment was achieved through pointers from source synsets to target synsets. Being the most frequent topic is LAW, JURISPRUDENCE. However, the manual assignment of topic labels to synsets in WordNet is very costly. As a consequence, semi-automatic methods were developed. For instance, WordNet Domains (Bentivogli et al., 2004) is a semi-automatically annotated domain inventory that labels WordNet synsets with 165 hierarchically organised domains. The use of domain inventories such as WordNet Domains, allowed to reduce polysemy degree of WordNet synsets by grouping those that belong to the same domain (Magnini et al., 2002). However, far from being perfect, many synsets were labelled as FACTOTUM, meaning that the synset cannot be labelled with a particular domain. Several works were proposed to improve WordNet Domains, such as eXtended WordNet Domains (González-Agirre et al., 2012; González et al., 2012), that applied graph-based methods to propagate the labels through the WordNet structure.

Domain information is not only available in WordNet, for example IATE[1] is a European Union inter-institutional terminology database. The domain labels of IATE are based on the Eurovoc thesaurus[2] and were introduced manually. More recently, several new domain inventories appeared, such as BabelDomains (Camacho-Collados and Navigli, 2017) or Coarse Sense Inventory (Lacerra et al., 2020).

7 Conclusions

In this work we present an evaluation approach to test Language Models on the tasks of Domain Labelling and Word Sense Disambiguation without annotated data requirements. For the WSD task we followed Lacerra et al. (2020) to reduce the granularity level. Our results showed that the Language Models we tested here **have some notion of word senses**. They easily outperformed the baseline, and sometimes almost reached to supervised systems performance. In addition, our further analysis shows that there is very low error propagation from Domain Labelling to WSD as their errors are poorly correlated. For the future, we plan to evaluate larger Language Models on the task to try to understand to what extent scaling these LMs affects to sense recognition.

Acknowledgments

Oscar is funded by a PhD grant from the Basque Government (PRE_2020_1_0246). This work is based upon work partially supported via the IARPA BETTER Program contract No. 2019-19051600006 (ODNI, IARPA), DeepKnowledge (PID2021-127777OB-C21) project funded by MCIN/AEI/10.13039/501100011033 and by FEDER Una manera de hacer Europa,

[1] `http://iate.europa.eu/`

[2] `https://op.europa.eu/en/web/eu-vocabularies/th-dataset/-/resource/dataset/eurovoc`

AWARE (TED2021-131617B-I00) project funded by MCIN/AEI/10.13039/501100011033 and by European Union NextGeneration EU/ PRTR, and by the Basque Government (IXA excellence research group IT1570-22).

References

Eneko Agirre, Oier López de Lacalle, and Aitor Soroa. 2014. Random walks for knowledge-based word sense disambiguation. *Computational Linguistics*, 40(1):57–84.

Edoardo Barba, Tommaso Pasini, and Roberto Navigli. 2021. ESC: Redesigning WSD with extractive sense comprehension. In *Proceedings of the 2021 Conference of the North American Chapter of the Association for Computational Linguistics: Human Language Technologies*, pages 4661–4672, Online. Association for Computational Linguistics.

Luisa Bentivogli, Pamela Forner, Bernardo Magnini, and Emanuele Pianta. 2004. Revising the Wordnet domains hierarchy: semantics, coverage and balancing. In *Proceedings of the Workshop on Multilingual Linguistic Resources*, pages 94–101, Geneva, Switzerland. COLING.

Michele Bevilacqua and Roberto Navigli. 2019. Quasi bidirectional encoder representations from transformers for word sense disambiguation. In *Proceedings of the International Conference on Recent Advances in Natural Language Processing (RANLP 2019)*, pages 122–131, Varna, Bulgaria. INCOMA Ltd.

Michele Bevilacqua and Roberto Navigli. 2020. Breaking through the 80% glass ceiling: Raising the state of the art in word sense disambiguation by incorporating knowledge graph information. In *Proceedings of the 58th Annual Meeting of the Association for Computational Linguistics*, pages 2854–2864, Online. Association for Computational Linguistics.

Michele Bevilacqua, Tommaso Pasini, Alessandro Raganato, and Roberto Navigli. 2021. Recent trends in word sense disambiguation: A survey. In *Proceedings of the Thirtieth International Joint Conference on Artificial Intelligence, IJCAI-21*, pages 4330–4338. International Joint Conferences on Artificial Intelligence Organization. Survey Track.

Terra Blevins and Luke Zettlemoyer. 2020. Moving down the long tail of word sense disambiguation with gloss informed bi-encoders. In *Proceedings of the 58th Annual Meeting of the Association for Computational Linguistics*, pages 1006–1017, Online. Association for Computational Linguistics.

Samuel R. Bowman, Gabor Angeli, Christopher Potts, and Christopher D. Manning. 2015. A large annotated corpus for learning natural language inference. In *Proceedings of the 2015 Conference on Empirical Methods in Natural Language Processing*, pages 632–642, Lisbon, Portugal. Association for Computational Linguistics.

Tom B. Brown, Benjamin Mann, Nick Ryder, Melanie Subbiah, Jared Kaplan, Prafulla Dhariwal, Arvind Neelakantan, Pranav Shyam, Girish Sastry, Amanda Askell, Sandhini Agarwal, Ariel Herbert-Voss, Gretchen Krueger, Tom Henighan, Rewon Child, Aditya Ramesh, Daniel M. Ziegler, Jeffrey Wu, Clemens Winter, Christopher Hesse, Mark Chen, Eric Sigler, Mateusz Litwin, Scott Gray, Benjamin Chess, Jack Clark, Christopher Berner, Sam McCandlish, Alec Radford, Ilya Sutskever, and Dario Amodei. 2020. Language models are few-shot learners.

Jose Camacho-Collados and Roberto Navigli. 2017. BabelDomains: Large-scale domain labeling of lexical resources. In *Proceedings of the 15th Conference of the European Chapter of the Association for Computational Linguistics: Volume 2, Short Papers*, pages 223–228, Valencia, Spain. Association for Computational Linguistics.

Simone Conia and Roberto Navigli. 2021. Framing word sense disambiguation as a multi-label problem for model-agnostic knowledge integration. In *Proceedings of the 16th Conference of the European Chapter of the Association for Computational Linguistics: Main Volume*, pages 3269–3275, Online. Association for Computational Linguistics.

Ido Dagan, Oren Glickman, and Bernardo Magnini. 2006. The pascal recognising textual entailment challenge. In *Machine Learning Challenges. Evaluating Predictive Uncertainty, Visual Object Classification, and Recognising Tectual Entailment*, pages 177–190, Berlin, Heidelberg. Springer Berlin Heidelberg.

Jacob Devlin, Ming-Wei Chang, Kenton Lee, and Kristina Toutanova. 2019. BERT: Pre-training of deep bidirectional transformers for language understanding. In *Proceedings of the 2019 Conference of the North American Chapter of the Association for Computational Linguistics: Human Language Technologies, Volume 1 (Long and Short Papers)*, pages 4171–4186, Minneapolis, Minnesota. Association for Computational Linguistics.

Philip Edmonds and Scott Cotton. 2001. SENSEVAL-2: Overview. In *Proceedings of SENSEVAL-2 Second International Workshop on Evaluating Word Sense Disambiguation Systems*, pages 1–5, Toulouse, France. Association for Computational Linguistics.

Christiane Fellbaum, editor. 1998. *WordNet: An Electronic Lexical Database*. Language, Speech, and Communication. MIT Press, Cambridge, MA.

Tianyu Gao, Adam Fisch, and Danqi Chen. 2021. Making pre-trained language models better few-shot learners. In *Proceedings of the 59th Annual Meeting of the Association for Computational Linguistics and the 11th International Joint Conference on Natural Language Processing (Volume 1: Long Papers)*, pages 3816–3830, Online. Association for Computational Linguistics.

Aitor González, German Rigau, and Mauro Castillo. 2012. A graph-based method to improve wordnet domains. In *International Conference on Intelligent Text Processing and Computational Linguistics*, pages 17–28. Springer.

Aitor González-Agirre, Mauro Castillo, and German Rigau. 2012. A proposal for improving WordNet domains. In *Proceedings of the Eighth International Conference on Language Resources and Evaluation (LREC'12)*, pages 3457–3462, Istanbul, Turkey. European Language Resources Association (ELRA).

Christian Hadiwinoto, Hwee Tou Ng, and Wee Chung Gan. 2019. Improved word sense disambiguation using pre-trained contextualized word representations. In *Proceedings of the 2019 Conference on Empirical Methods in Natural Language Processing and the 9th International Joint Conference on Natural Language Processing (EMNLP-IJCNLP)*, pages 5297–5306, Hong Kong, China. Association for Computational Linguistics.

Luyao Huang, Chi Sun, Xipeng Qiu, and Xuanjing Huang. 2019. GlossBERT: BERT for word sense disambiguation with gloss knowledge. In *Proceedings of the 2019 Conference on Empirical Methods in Natural Language Processing and the 9th International Joint Conference on Natural Language Processing (EMNLP-IJCNLP)*, pages 3509–3514, Hong Kong, China. Association for Computational Linguistics.

Sawan Kumar, Sharmistha Jat, Karan Saxena, and Partha Talukdar. 2019. Zero-shot word sense disambiguation using sense definition embeddings. In *Proceedings of the 57th Annual Meeting of the Association for Computational Linguistics*, pages 5670–5681, Florence, Italy. Association for Computational Linguistics.

Caterina Lacerra, Michele Bevilacqua, Tommaso Pasini, and Roberto Navigli. 2020. CSI: A coarse sense inventory for 85% word sense disambiguation. In *Proceedings of the 34th Conference on Artificial Intelligence*, pages 8123–8130. AAAI Press.

Teven Le Scao and Alexander Rush. 2021. How many data points is a prompt worth? In *Proceedings of the 2021 Conference of the North American Chapter of the Association for Computational Linguistics: Human Language Technologies*, pages 2627–2636, Online. Association for Computational Linguistics.

Omer Levy, Minjoon Seo, Eunsol Choi, and Luke Zettlemoyer. 2017. Zero-shot relation extraction via reading comprehension. In *Proceedings of the 21st Conference on Computational Natural Language Learning (CoNLL 2017)*, pages 333–342, Vancouver, Canada. Association for Computational Linguistics.

Bangzheng Li, Wenpeng Yin, and Muhao Chen. 2022a. Ultra-fine entity typing with indirect supervision from natural language inference. *Transactions of the Association for Computational Linguistics*, 10:607–622.

Jiaoda Li, Ryan Cotterell, and Mrinmaya Sachan. 2022b. Probing via prompting. In *Proceedings of the 2022 Conference of the North American Chapter of the Association for Computational Linguistics: Human Language Technologies*, pages 1144–1157, Seattle, United States. Association for Computational Linguistics.

Pengfei Liu, Weizhe Yuan, Jinlan Fu, Zhengbao Jiang, Hiroaki Hayashi, and Graham Neubig. 2022a. Pretrain, prompt, and predict: A systematic survey of prompting methods in natural language processing. *ACM Comput. Surv.* Just Accepted.

Xiao Liu, Kaixuan Ji, Yicheng Fu, Weng Tam, Zhengxiao Du, Zhilin Yang, and Jie Tang. 2022b. P-tuning: Prompt tuning can be comparable to fine-tuning across scales and tasks. In *Proceedings of the 60th Annual Meeting of the Association for Computational Linguistics (Volume 2: Short Papers)*, pages 61–68, Dublin, Ireland. Association for Computational Linguistics.

Yinhan Liu, Myle Ott, Naman Goyal, Jingfei Du, Mandar Joshi, Danqi Chen, Omer Levy, Mike Lewis, Luke Zettlemoyer, and Veselin Stoyanov. 2019. Roberta: A robustly optimized bert pretraining approach.

Daniel Loureiro and Alípio Jorge. 2019. Language modelling makes sense: Propagating representations through WordNet for full-coverage word sense disambiguation. In *Proceedings of the 57th Annual Meeting of the Association for Computational Linguistics*, pages 5682–5691, Florence, Italy. Association for Computational Linguistics.

Qing Lyu, Hongming Zhang, Elior Sulem, and Dan Roth. 2021. Zero-shot event extraction via transfer learning: Challenges and insights. In *Proceedings of the 59th Annual Meeting of the Association for Computational Linguistics and the 11th International Joint Conference on Natural Language Processing (Volume 2: Short Papers)*, pages 322–332, Online. Association for Computational Linguistics.

Bernardo Magnini, Carlo Strapparava, Giovanni Pezzulo, and Alfio Gliozzo. 2002. The role of domain information in word sense disambiguation. *Natural Language Engineering*, 8(4):359–373.

Bryan McCann, Nitish Shirish Keskar, Caiming Xiong, and Richard Socher. 2018. The natural language decathlon: Multitask learning as question answering.

George A. Miller, Martin Chodorow, Shari Landes, Claudia Leacock, and Robert G. Thomas. 1994. Using a semantic concordance for sense identification. In *Human Language Technology: Proceedings of a Workshop held at Plainsboro, New Jersey, March 8-11, 1994*.

Bonan Min, Hayley Ross, Elior Sulem, Amir Pouran Ben Veyseh, Thien Huu Nguyen, Oscar Sainz,

Eneko Agirre, Ilana Heinz, and Dan Roth. 2021. Recent advances in natural language processing via large pre-trained language models: A survey.

Andrea Moro and Roberto Navigli. 2015. SemEval-2015 task 13: Multilingual all-words sense disambiguation and entity linking. In *Proceedings of the 9th International Workshop on Semantic Evaluation (SemEval 2015)*, pages 288–297, Denver, Colorado. Association for Computational Linguistics.

Andrea Moro, Alessandro Raganato, and Roberto Navigli. 2014. Entity linking meets word sense disambiguation: a unified approach. *Transactions of the Association for Computational Linguistics*, 2:231–244.

Roberto Navigli, David Jurgens, and Daniele Vannella. 2013. SemEval-2013 task 12: Multilingual word sense disambiguation. In *Second Joint Conference on Lexical and Computational Semantics (*SEM), Volume 2: Proceedings of the Seventh International Workshop on Semantic Evaluation (SemEval 2013)*, pages 222–231, Atlanta, Georgia, USA. Association for Computational Linguistics.

Roberto Navigli and Simone Ponzetto. 2012. Babelnet: The automatic construction, evaluation and application of a wide-coverage multilingual semantic network. *Artificial Intelligence*, 193:217–250.

Yixin Nie, Adina Williams, Emily Dinan, Mohit Bansal, Jason Weston, and Douwe Kiela. 2020. Adversarial NLI: A new benchmark for natural language understanding. In *Proceedings of the 58th Annual Meeting of the Association for Computational Linguistics*, pages 4885–4901, Online. Association for Computational Linguistics.

Matthew E. Peters, Mark Neumann, Mohit Iyyer, Matt Gardner, Christopher Clark, Kenton Lee, and Luke Zettlemoyer. 2018. Deep contextualized word representations. In *Proceedings of the 2018 Conference of the North American Chapter of the Association for Computational Linguistics: Human Language Technologies, Volume 1 (Long Papers)*, pages 2227–2237, New Orleans, Louisiana. Association for Computational Linguistics.

Jonas Pfeiffer, Andreas Rücklé, Clifton Poth, Aishwarya Kamath, Ivan Vulić, Sebastian Ruder, Kyunghyun Cho, and Iryna Gurevych. 2020. AdapterHub: A framework for adapting transformers. In *Proceedings of the 2020 Conference on Empirical Methods in Natural Language Processing: System Demonstrations*, pages 46–54, Online. Association for Computational Linguistics.

Mohammad Taher Pilehvar and Roberto Navigli. 2014. A large-scale pseudoword-based evaluation framework for state-of-the-art word sense disambiguation. *Computational Linguistics*, 40(4):837–881.

Adam Poliak, Aparajita Haldar, Rachel Rudinger, J. Edward Hu, Ellie Pavlick, Aaron Steven White, and Benjamin Van Durme. 2018. Collecting diverse natural language inference problems for sentence representation evaluation. In *Proceedings of the 2018 Conference on Empirical Methods in Natural Language Processing*, pages 67–81, Brussels, Belgium. Association for Computational Linguistics.

Sameer Pradhan, Edward Loper, Dmitriy Dligach, and Martha Palmer. 2007. SemEval-2007 task-17: English lexical sample, SRL and all words. In *Proceedings of the Fourth International Workshop on Semantic Evaluations (SemEval-2007)*, pages 87–92, Prague, Czech Republic. Association for Computational Linguistics.

Alessandro Raganato, Claudio Delli Bovi, and Roberto Navigli. 2017. Neural sequence learning models for word sense disambiguation. In *Proceedings of the 2017 Conference on Empirical Methods in Natural Language Processing*, pages 1156–1167, Copenhagen, Denmark. Association for Computational Linguistics.

Oscar Sainz, Itziar Gonzalez-Dios, Oier Lopez de Lacalle, Bonan Min, and Eneko Agirre. 2022a. Textual entailment for event argument extraction: Zero- and few-shot with multi-source learning. In *Findings of the Association for Computational Linguistics: NAACL 2022*, pages 2439–2455, Seattle, United States. Association for Computational Linguistics.

Oscar Sainz, Oier Lopez de Lacalle, Gorka Labaka, Ander Barrena, and Eneko Agirre. 2021. Label verbalization and entailment for effective zero and few-shot relation extraction. In *Proceedings of the 2021 Conference on Empirical Methods in Natural Language Processing*, pages 1199–1212, Online and Punta Cana, Dominican Republic. Association for Computational Linguistics.

Oscar Sainz, Haoling Qiu, Oier Lopez de Lacalle, Eneko Agirre, and Bonan Min. 2022b. ZS4IE: A toolkit for zero-shot information extraction with simple verbalizations. In *Proceedings of the 2022 Conference of the North American Chapter of the Association for Computational Linguistics: Human Language Technologies: System Demonstrations*, pages 27–38, Hybrid: Seattle, Washington + Online. Association for Computational Linguistics.

Oscar Sainz and German Rigau. 2021. Ask2Transformers: Zero-shot domain labelling with pretrained language models. In *Proceedings of the 11th Global Wordnet Conference*, pages 44–52, University of South Africa (UNISA). Global Wordnet Association.

Bianca Scarlini, Tommaso Pasini, and Roberto Navigli. 2020a. Sensembert: Context-enhanced sense embeddings for multilingual word sense disambiguation. *Proceedings of the AAAI Conference on Artificial Intelligence*, 34(05):8758–8765.

Bianca Scarlini, Tommaso Pasini, and Roberto Navigli. 2020b. With more contexts comes better performance: Contextualized sense embeddings for all-round word sense disambiguation. In *Proceedings of the 2020 Conference on Empirical Methods in Natural Language Processing (EMNLP)*, pages 3528–3539, Online. Association for Computational Linguistics.

Timo Schick and Hinrich Schütze. 2021a. Exploiting cloze-questions for few-shot text classification and natural language inference. In *Proceedings of the 16th Conference of the European Chapter of the Association for Computational Linguistics: Main Volume*, pages 255–269, Online. Association for Computational Linguistics.

Timo Schick and Hinrich Schütze. 2021b. Few-shot text generation with natural language instructions. In *Proceedings of the 2021 Conference on Empirical Methods in Natural Language Processing*, pages 390–402, Online and Punta Cana, Dominican Republic. Association for Computational Linguistics.

Timo Schick and Hinrich Schütze. 2021c. It's not just size that matters: Small language models are also few-shot learners. In *Proceedings of the 2021 Conference of the North American Chapter of the Association for Computational Linguistics: Human Language Technologies*, pages 2339–2352, Online. Association for Computational Linguistics.

Federico Scozzafava, Marco Maru, Fabrizio Brignone, Giovanni Torrisi, and Roberto Navigli. 2020. Personalized PageRank with syntagmatic information for multilingual word sense disambiguation. In *Proceedings of the 58th Annual Meeting of the Association for Computational Linguistics: System Demonstrations*, pages 37–46, Online. Association for Computational Linguistics.

Lei Shu, Hu Xu, Bing Liu, and Jiahua Chen. 2022. Zero-shot aspect-based sentiment analysis.

Benjamin Snyder and Martha Palmer. 2004. The English all-words task. In *Proceedings of SENSEVAL-3, the Third International Workshop on the Evaluation of Systems for the Semantic Analysis of Text*, pages 41–43, Barcelona, Spain. Association for Computational Linguistics.

James Thorne, Andreas Vlachos, Christos Christodoulopoulos, and Arpit Mittal. 2018. FEVER: a large-scale dataset for fact extraction and VERification. In *Proceedings of the 2018 Conference of the North American Chapter of the Association for Computational Linguistics: Human Language Technologies, Volume 1 (Long Papers)*, pages 809–819, New Orleans, Louisiana. Association for Computational Linguistics.

Ming Wang and Yinglin Wang. 2020. A synset relation-enhanced framework with a try-again mechanism for word sense disambiguation. In *Proceedings of the 2020 Conference on Empirical Methods in Natural Language Processing (EMNLP)*, pages 6229–6240, Online. Association for Computational Linguistics.

Sinong Wang, Han Fang, Madian Khabsa, Hanzi Mao, and Hao Ma. 2021a. Entailment as few-shot learner.

Sinong Wang, Han Fang, Madian Khabsa, Hanzi Mao, and Hao Ma. 2021b. Entailment as few-shot learner.

Aaron Steven White, Pushpendre Rastogi, Kevin Duh, and Benjamin Van Durme. 2017. Inference is everything: Recasting semantic resources into a unified evaluation framework. In *Proceedings of the Eighth International Joint Conference on Natural Language Processing (Volume 1: Long Papers)*, pages 996–1005, Taipei, Taiwan. Asian Federation of Natural Language Processing.

Adina Williams, Nikita Nangia, and Samuel Bowman. 2018. A broad-coverage challenge corpus for sentence understanding through inference. In *Proceedings of the 2018 Conference of the North American Chapter of the Association for Computational Linguistics: Human Language Technologies, Volume 1 (Long Papers)*, pages 1112–1122, New Orleans, Louisiana. Association for Computational Linguistics.

Thomas Wolf, Lysandre Debut, Victor Sanh, Julien Chaumond, Clement Delangue, Anthony Moi, Pierric Cistac, Tim Rault, Remi Louf, Morgan Funtowicz, Joe Davison, Sam Shleifer, Patrick von Platen, Clara Ma, Yacine Jernite, Julien Plu, Canwen Xu, Teven Le Scao, Sylvain Gugger, Mariama Drame, Quentin Lhoest, and Alexander Rush. 2020. Transformers: State-of-the-art natural language processing. In *Proceedings of the 2020 Conference on Empirical Methods in Natural Language Processing: System Demonstrations*, pages 38–45, Online. Association for Computational Linguistics.

Congying Xia, Wenpeng Yin, Yihao Feng, and Philip Yu. 2021. Incremental few-shot text classification with multi-round new classes: Formulation, dataset and system. In *Proceedings of the 2021 Conference of the North American Chapter of the Association for Computational Linguistics: Human Language Technologies*, pages 1351–1360, Online. Association for Computational Linguistics.

Zeng Yang, Linhai Zhang, and Deyu Zhou. 2022. SEE-few: Seed, expand and entail for few-shot named entity recognition. In *Proceedings of the 29th International Conference on Computational Linguistics*, pages 2540–2550, Gyeongju, Republic of Korea. International Committee on Computational Linguistics.

Boon Peng Yap, Andrew Koh, and Eng Siong Chng. 2020. Adapting BERT for word sense disambiguation with gloss selection objective and example sentences. In *Findings of the Association for Computational Linguistics: EMNLP 2020*, pages 41–46, Online. Association for Computational Linguistics.

Wenpeng Yin, Jamaal Hay, and Dan Roth. 2019. Benchmarking zero-shot text classification: Datasets, evaluation and entailment approach. In *Proceedings of the 2019 Conference on Empirical Methods in Natural Language Processing and the 9th International*

Joint Conference on Natural Language Processing (EMNLP-IJCNLP), pages 3914–3923, Hong Kong, China. Association for Computational Linguistics.

Wenpeng Yin, Nazneen Fatema Rajani, Dragomir Radev, Richard Socher, and Caiming Xiong. 2020. Universal natural language processing with limited annotations: Try few-shot textual entailment as a start. In *Proceedings of the 2020 Conference on Empirical Methods in Natural Language Processing (EMNLP)*, pages 8229–8239, Online. Association for Computational Linguistics.

Zhi Zhong and Hwee Tou Ng. 2010. It makes sense: A wide-coverage word sense disambiguation system for free text. In *Proceedings of the ACL 2010 System Demonstrations*, pages 78–83, Uppsala, Sweden. Association for Computational Linguistics.

Resolving Multiple Hyperonymy

Svetla Koeva
Institute for Bulgarian language
Bulgarian Academy of Sciences
svetla@dcl.bas.bg

Dimitar Hristov
Institute for Bulgarian language
Bulgarian Academy of Sciences
d.hristov@dcl.bas.bg

Abstract

WordNet contains a fair number of synsets with multiple hyperonyms. In parent–child relations, a child can have only one parent (ancestor). Consequently, multiple hyperonymy represents distinct semantic relations. In order to reclassify the multiple hyperonyms, we define a small set of new semantic relations (such as **function**, **origin** and **form**) that cover the various instances of multiple hyperonyms. The synsets with multiple hyperonyms that lead to the same root and belong to the same semantic class were grouped automatically, resulting in semantic patterns that serve as a point of departure for the classification. The proposed changes are based on semantic analysis and may involve the redefinition of one or several multiple hyperonymy relations to new ones, the removal of one or several multiple hyperonymy relations, and rarely the addition of a new hyperonymy relation. As a result, we incorporate the newly defined semantic relations that resolve the former multiple hyperonymy relations and propose an updated WordNet structure without multiple hyperonyms. The resulting WordNet structure without multiple hyperonyms may be used for a variety of purposes that require proper inheritance.

1 Introduction

WordNet (Miller et al., 1990; Fellbaum, 1998) is a lexical semantic network that encodes human knowledge about synonyms – words (or multi-word expressions) denoting the same concept – and the semantic relationships between the concepts. The nodes of the semantic network are synonym sets (synsets), which are connected by arcs representing semantic relations.

The **hyperonymy** relation (and its inverse relation, **hyponymy**) connects more general concepts to more specific ones and organizes noun synsets in hierarchies, with the most abstract concepts at the root of the trees and the most specific concepts at the leaves of the trees (Miller et al., 1990). Hyperonymy and hyponymy relations satisfy properties for asymmetry and transitivity (Lyons, 1977; Miller et al., 1990). For instance, if *bird* is a hyperonym of *parrot*, then *parrot* is not a hyperonym of *bird*; similarly, if *parrot* is a hyponym of *bird*, then *bird* is not a hyponym of *parrot*. Another example illustrates the transitivity: if *bird* is a hyperonym of *parrot* and *parrot* is a hyperonym of *cockatoo*, then *bird* is a hyperonym of *cockatoo*. And vice versa, if *cockatoo* is a hyponym of *parrot* and *parrot* is a hyponym of *bird*, then *cockatoo* is a hyponym of *bird*.

The structure of nouns in WordNet is a cycle-free directed connected graph whose root is an abstraction that refers to all concepts included in the hierarchy and is therefore a hyperonym of all other synsets. A unique path exists between two nodes in the tree. A hyperonym may have multiple hyponyms, and a hyponym should have exactly one hyperonym.

However, a common practice in wordnets is to use multiple hyperonyms. Multiple hyperonyms can be exclusive (*albino* is either an *animal* or a *human*), conjunctive (*spoon* is both *cutlery* and *container*) or nonexclusive (*knife* can be *cutlery*, a *weapon*, or both) (EAGLES, 1999).

Disjunctive (exclusive) hyperonymy is related to polysemy in that different meanings of the same word can have different hyperonyms; thus, disjunctive multiple hyperonyms should not be present in the WordNet. Actually, in WordNet, the hyperonym of *albino* with the meaning ‘a person with congenital albinism: white hair and milky skin; eyes are usually pink’ is one – *person*. This suggests that for an albino animal, there must be another concept in the WordNet structure that refers only to an animal with the relevant anomaly.

Conjunctive multiple hyperonyms have a common hyperonym (usually not the direct one). In fact, conjunctive hyperonymy exemplifies the cases in which different types of semantic relations can be defined to replace multiple hyponymy relations.

The so-called non-exclusive hyperonymy allows both disjunctive and conjunctive relations, and such cases should not occur in WordNet because different senses could not be encoded in one and the same synset. For example, *hatmaker* defined as 'someone who makes and sells hats' has two hyperonyms: *maker* – 'a person who makes things' and *merchant* – 'a businessperson engaged in retail trade'.

Our work aims to investigate and resolve multiple hyperonymy relations in WordNet, which can be accomplished in one of two ways: either by defining new relations in place of some hyperonymy relations (since multiple hyperonymy may encompass several semantic relations that can be further specified) or by deleting hyperonymy relations (if appropriate). In our study, we define a small set of new semantic relations (such as **function**, **origin** and **form**) that will cover the different instances of multiple hyperonymy relations, and we classify these relations according to the defined set.

The paper is organised as follows. Section 2 explains the motivation behind our work. Section 3 places our work in the context of related studies. Section 4 presents our approach. In Subsection 4.1 we show how the synsets with multiple hyperonyms were grouped automatically, such as to form semantic patterns appropriate for the next semantic analysis. We propose an updated WordNet structure that eliminates multiple hyperonymy and incorporates the newly defined relations between the respective synsets (Subsection 4.2). Then, in Section 5, we propose a brief description of the new relations, followed by conclusions and future work (Section 6).

The resulting WordNet structure without multiple hyperonyms may be used for a variety of purposes that require proper inheritance.

2 Motivation

The hyperonymy relation is exploited in many implementations related with word sense disambiguation (Otegi et al., 2022), taxonomy extraction (Pontiki et al., 2015) or ontology learning (Lourdusamy and Abraham, 2020; Wątróbski, 2020), knowledge mining (Chen et al., 2020), etc. Thus, the unambiguous definition of hyperonymy is important for many language processing tasks.

Our motivation stems from the use of semantic classes for nouns and their inheritance from hyponyms when encoding the syntagmatic combinations of verbs and nouns. Nouns and verbs are grouped in WordNet into more specific semantic classes (Miller et al., 1990, p. 16), (Fellbaum, 1998, p. 41), describing their general meaning: noun.person, noun.animal, noun.cognition; verb.cognition, verb.change, etc. Nouns are classified into twenty-five semantic classes and verbs – into fifteen semantic classes. For example, the verbs *cook*; *fix*; *prepare* with a definition 'prepare for eating by applying heat' can be combined with nouns classified as noun.person: *the mother cooks dinner*. However, not all nouns from the class noun.person can collocate with these verbs as their subject and not every noun that is not classified as a noun.person can be their object (*the exspouse*, ?*the neoliberal*, **the infant cooks dinner*, ?*elephant*, **books*). In other words, the WordNet noun semantic classes could be further specified in order to correlate precisely with the verb-noun selectional preferences.

In a previous work we mapped 253 Corpus Pattern Analysis semantic types to the appropriate WordNet noun synsets (Koeva et al., 2018). For example, the semantic type [Permission] is mapped to the synset *permission* 'approval to do something', the semantic type [Dispute] is mapped to the synset *disagreement* 'the speech act of disagreeing or arguing or disputing', and so on. 55 semantic classes are employed so far in our work aiming at defining Conceptual frames (Koeva and Doychev, 2022), and 28 new specific semantic classes are added to encode verb-noun compatibility. The mapping of hyponym synsets to the semantic class of their hyperonym is done automatically. For this purpose, eliminating multiple hyperonyms is critical for inheriting the detailed semantic classes we employ.

3 Related work

WordNet is an **inheritance (is-a)** based semantic resource, although inheritance is only one of the semantic relations in the network. In WordNet, a hyponym inherits all the features of the more generic concept and adds at least one feature that distinguishes it from its superordinate and from any other hyponyms of that superordinate (Miller et al.,

1990). In order to use the inheritance relation in WordNet, the paths along the hyperonymy – hyponymy trees should be unambiguous, or, in other words, multiple hyperonymy should be resolved where possible.

Inheritance is important in the way that all noun synsets that are hyponyms of a synset representing a particular semantic class should inherit the properties of this class. This is generally true, and if the inheritance relations of nouns are further specified by assigning more particular semantic classes, noun synset hierarchies can serve as sets of words eligible to fill in particular verb predicate slots.

D. Alan Cruse proposes a three-category hyponymy model that includes natural kinds, nominal kinds, and functional kinds (Cruse, 2002, p. 18–19). **Natural kinds** are classifications of objects such as chemical elements, biological species, and so on, for example: *a dog is an animal*, *a violin is a musical instrument*. Sets of features can express the relations between natural kinds and their hyperonyms. In contrast, the relations between **nominal kinds** and their hyperonyms can be expressed as a single distinguishing feature: *mare is a female horse*, *kitten is a small cat*, *blonde is a blond woman*, and so on. **Functional kinds** are groups of entities that are linked together by a common function, i.e., their activities and causal roles. Inherent functional kinds are typical kinds of their hyperonyms, such as *gun is a type of weapon*, *hammer is a type of tool*, *jacket is a type garment*, and so on (Cruse, 2002, p. 19).

The proposed distinction is used to create wordnets for languages other than English, emphasizing the distinction between natural kinds and functional kinds as taxonomic relations on the one hand, and nominal kinds as a non-taxonomic relation on the other (Pederson and Sørensen, 2006).

The inheritance properties are part of the inclusion relations, which connect a more general entity to a more specific entity. Class inclusion is described as follows: X's are a type of Y, X's are Y's, X is a type of Y, and X is a Y, for example: *Cars are a type of vehicle*; *Roses are a type of flower*; *Theft is a type of crime*; and *Employee is a person* (Winston et al., 1987). V. Storey (Storey, 1993) describes several types of inclusion: classification, which relates an entity occurrence to an entity type; generalisation, in which an entity type is the union of non-overlapping subtypes; specialisation, which is defined as the inverse of generalisation; and subset hierarchy, in which potentially overlapping subtypes exist. The inheritance principle of **is-a relations** states that anything that is true about the generic entity type A, must also be true of the specific entity type B. Therefore, any attributes of A are also attributable to B (but not necessarily vice versa). Similarly, in any relations in which A can participate, B can also participate (Storey, 1993).

Other authors divide inclusion into two categories: those that relate generic to generic concepts (subset and superset, generalization and specialization, a kind of, conceptual containment, role value restrictions, sets and their characteristic types) and those that relate generic to individual concepts (set membership, predication, conceptual containment, abstraction) (Brachman, 1983). According to this analysis, the inclusion hierarchy of noun synsets may be divided into different hierarchies depending on the type of inclusion. Our goal is not to achieve this; instead, we will concentrate on cases of multiple hyperonymy and propose changing one or more hyperonymy relations based on the semantics of the relations between the synsets.

The hyponymy relation has been approached from a qualia-based perspective, yielding two types of hyponymy (Mendes and Chaves, 2001). Briefly, the level of representation at which the semantic content of a lexical item is encoded through the properties and events that define it is referred to as the Qualia structure. Four fundamental qualia roles determining the lexical-semantic structure of words have been defined (Pustejovsky, 1995):

- Constitutive: conveying the relations between an object and its components;
- Formal: expressing the characteristics that set an entity apart within a bigger domain;
- Telic: expressing an object's purpose and function;
- Agentive: showing the factors involved in the origin or emergence of an object.

It was noticed that two distinct sets of hyponyms can be distinguished: those that share the same constitutive role and those that show more specific information about this role. Based on this assumption, a distinction between true taxonomic hyponymy and functional hyponymy has been proposed (Mendes and Chaves, 2001).

Hyperonymy and hyponymy in WordNet refer to the Formal quale, meronymy relations – to the Constitutive quale, cause relations – to the Agentive quale (Pederson and Sørensen, 2006). To systematically capture all qualia roles, the EuroWordNet relations were extended with two relations (Vossen, 1998): **results (originates) from** and **has as function (goal)** (Amaro et al., 2010).

The fact that the multiple hyperonymy (or multiple inheritance) relations (in many cases) encode other relations or are used to indicate something other than the conjunction of two properties has already been pointed out (Kaplan and Schubert, 2001; Gangemi et al., 2001). So far, the investigations into multiple inheritance in WordNet have been directed mainly at validating the WordNet structure. For example, multiple inheritance test patterns were created to check and validate the semantic hierarchies of the Estonian WordNet (Lohk, 2015).

There is general agreement that hyponymy is a complicated concept and that the relation can be separated into several relations based on the hyponym's intrinsic features and the conveyed semantic relation with the hyperonym. The presence of multiple hyperonyms indicates that the WordNet hyperonymy (and its properties) exhibits a wide range of cases.

The goal of presented study is to resolve multiple hyperonymy, and we achieve it by: a) removing superfluous hyperonyms; b) replacing some inappropriate hyperonymy relations with holonymy ones; c) adding missing hyperonymy relations; and d) formulating new semantic relations to replace the multiple hyperonymy.

4 Description of the approach

We assume that multiple conjunctive hyperonyms do not represent the same relations. In addition to hyperonymy in this case, other semantic relations are also expressed. Because of the various relations, the conjunction of several hyperonyms is feasible, i.e., two or more general concepts might refer to the more specific one at the same time. We use the term **true hyperonymy**, or simply – **hyperonymy**, by which we mean a hyperonymy that expresses only the **is a** relation between more general and more specific concepts. In conjunctive multiple hyperonymy, one of the hyperonyms expresses the true hyperonymy relation, and the second hyperonym (and subsequent ones) express another semantic relation.

Following the general division of hyponyms (Cruse, 2002), the properties of the Qualia structure (Pustejovsky, 1995), and their application so far in the WordNet (Vossen, 1998), we have identified the following three groups of relations that replace multiple hyperonyms:

- **Property** (here we have distinguished three relations depending on the intrinsic properties of the hyponym):
  - **characteristic** – what feature distinguishes a given entity;
  - **origin** – what is the source of a given entity: natural object, living organism (human, animal), etc.;
  - **form** – what is the form of existence of a given entity: gas, liquid, solid body, material body, etc.
- **Application** (here we have also distinguished three relations depending on the intrinsic properties of the hyponym):
  - **function** – what is the function of a given entity: tool, container, building, etc.;
  - **purpose** – what is the purpose of a given entity;
  - **use** – what is an entity used for.
- **Composition** – what is the composition of a given entity (composition is included since many of the multiple hyperonyms express meronymy relations):
  - **member** – a member to a set;
  - **part** – a part of a whole;
  - **portion** – a portion of a whole.

The following is a description of the data preparation steps that are taken before performing the multiple hyperonymy resolving procedure.

4.1 Data preparation

For the purposes of our study, we used an XML-encoded version of the Princeton WordNet 3.0. This version of WordNet contains 82,114 noun synsets, each assigned with a WordNet semantic class. Out of these, 7,725 synsets are linked only with instance hyperonymy relations (Table 1), while 1,421 synsets have multiple hyperonyms, with the latter defining the scope of our work. Additionally, out of the 13,767 verb synsets, 31 have multiple hyperonyms.

Group	Count
With hyperonyms	74,388
With instance hyperonyms	7,725
With no hyperonyms	1
Total	82,114

Table 1: Noun synset groups based on hyperonymy type

Our interest is focused on the hyperonymy relations of the noun synsets with multiple hyperonyms, taking into consideration all their ancestors (indirect hyperonyms) up to the top level synset {*entity*:1}, which has no hyperonyms (Table 2).

Group	Count
With 2 hyperonyms	1,387
With 3 hyperonyms	30
With 4 hyperonyms	3
With 5 hyperonyms	1
Total	1,421

Table 2: Counts of synsets with multiple hyperonyms

In order to easily analyse the cases of multiple hyperonymy and identify classes of its occurrence, the synsets with multiple hyperonyms were divided non-exclusively into groups based on common hyperonyms. Two types of grouping were performed – defining groups using one common hyperonym (further called single groups) and two common hyperonyms (further called double groups). As synsets with multiple hyperonyms have at least two and up to five hyperonyms, we then expect each synset to be present in as many single groups as the number of its hyperonyms and in as many double groups as the number of its hyperonyms' pairs.

These grouping resulted in 1,814 single groups, of which 512 have 2 or more members and 66 have 5 or more members, and 1,305 double groups, of which 121 have 2 or more members and 40 have 3 or more members. We take particular interest in single groups of 5 or more synsets and double groups of 3 or more synsets, as these suggest larger classes suitable for our analysis. Tables 3 and 4 show the sizes of the 10 largest single and double groups, respectively (in number of hyponyms).

Common hyperonym	Size
{*transparent gem*:1}	20
{*gas*:7}	20
{*chemical element*:1; *element*:6}	18
{*woman*:3; *adult female*:1}	17
{*mineral*:3}	12
{*heresy*:1; *unorthodoxy*:2}	11
{*autoimmune disease*:1; *autoimmune disorder*:1}	10
{*monogenic disorder*:1; *monogenic disease*:1}	10
{*theological doctrine*:1}	10
{*food fish*:1}	10

Table 3: 10 largest single groups

Common hyperonyms	Size
{*dynasty*:1} {*royalty*:1; *royal family*:1; *royal line*:1; *royal house*:1}	9
{*heresy*:1; *unorthodoxy*:2} {*theological doctrine*:1}	9
{*clergyman*:1; *reverend*:2; *man of the cloth*:1} {*Holy Order*:1; *Order*:1}	7
{*chemical element*:1; *element*:6} {*gas*:7}	6
{*chemical element*:1; *element*:6} {*noble gas*:1; *inert gas*:1; *argonon*:1}	6
{*athlete*:1; *jock*:2} {*player*:3; *participant*:2}	6
{*chemical element*:1; *element*:6} {*halogen*:1}	5
{*school*:7} {*artistic movement*:1; *art movement*:1}	5
{*edible fruit*:1} {*drupe*:1; *stone fruit*:1}	5
{*musical composition*:1; *opus*:1; *composition*:8; *piece*:13; *piece of music*:1} {*passage*:9; *musical passage*:1}	5

Table 4: 10 largest double groups

Thematic groups were distinguished within the two large groups (single and double) based on the general thematic class of the hyponym: for example, musical instruments, chemical elements, diseases, and so on. Our hypothesis is that the resolution of multiple hyperonymy will (in many cases) be identical within thematic groups.

In order to aid the manual resolution of multiple hyperonymy, we generated visualisations of the hyperonymy graphs of all synsets with multiple hyperonyms, displaying all direct and indirect hyperonyms up to {*entity*:1}. These display the synset ID in WordNet 3.0 and literals for each synset in the graph. The visualisations were generated using graphviz (Gansner and North, 2000).

Figure 1 shows an example of one such graph visualisation for the synset {*person*:1; *individual*:1; *someone*:1; *somebody*:1; *mortal*:1; *soul*:1}, which has two hyperonyms – {*organism*:1; *being*:1} and {*causal agent*:1; *cause*:1; *causal agency*:1}. The figure displays all direct and indirect hyperonyms of {*person*:1; *individual*:1; *someone*:1; *somebody*:1; *mortal*:1; *soul*:1} up to {*entity*:1} and the hyperonymy relations between them.

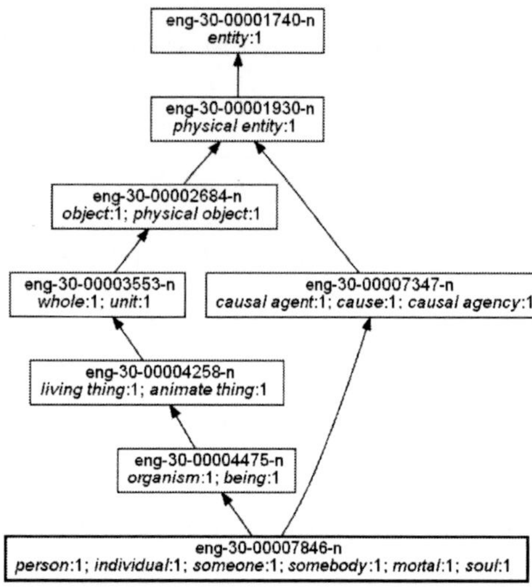

Figure 1: Graph for synset {*person*:1}

4.2 Resolving multiple hyperonymy

Initially, we focused on the 40 double groups of synsets with multiple hyperonyms with 3 or more members, as well as on some large single groups. We then expanded the scope to all 1,421 synsets with multiple hyperonyms. Our proposed changes include:

- Changing a multiple hyperonymy relation to one of 9 other relation types, 6 of which are newly defined;
- Removing a hyperonymy relation in rare cases where it is not properly connected;
- Adding a new hyperonymy relation where none of the currently linked hyperonyms is deemed suitable.

As a result of our efforts, we proposed resolving multiple hyperonymy for 1,421 synsets, with 1,638 changes to relations[1]. Table 5 presents the proposed actions and their count within the scope of the effort. As of the submission of this paper, validation of the proposed changes is ongoing, so the numbers presented are indicative.

Action	**Count**
Remove relation	66
Change relation to **characteristic**	388
Change relation to **origin**	19
Change relation to **form**	122
Change relation to **function**	431
Change relation to **purpose**	117
Change relation to **use**	123
Change relation to **member**	13
Change relation to **part**	76
Change relation to **portion**	23
Add new hyperonymy relation	76
Remove relation of a hyperonym	11
Change relation type of a hyperonym	1
Add relation of a hyperonym	14

Table 5: Proposed action types

The changes affecting the hyperonyms and their relations to next-level hyperonyms are shown in the last three rows of Table 5. They are a result of the change in the WordNet structure that removes multiple hyperonyms, and they represent the removal of an incorrect link or the addition of a missing link.

As an illustrative example, we will present the proposed changes for synsets with a common multiple hyperonym {*chemical element*:1; *element*:6}. For this hyperonym synset there are three large double groups and one single group.

Double group 1 has 6 members, which share the following multiple hyperonyms:

- {*chemical element*:1; *element*:6}
- {*noble gas*:1; *inert gas*:1; *argonon*:1}

The group includes synsets for noble gas elements such as {*helium*:1; *He*:2; *atomic number 2*:1} and {*neon*:1; *Ne*:2; *atomic number 10*:1}. The proposed change is:

- Remove the hyperonym {*chemical element*:1; *element*:6}, as it is already a hyperonym of {*noble gas*:1; *inert gas*:1; *argonon*:1}.

[1]The results are available online at https://github.com/DCL-IBL/SemNet

Double group 2 has 5 members with the following multiple hyperonyms:

- {*chemical element*:1; *element*:6}
- {*halogen*:1}

The group includes synsets for halogen elements, such as {*chlorine*:1; *Cl*:2; *atomic number 17*:1}, {*bromine*:1; *Br*:1; *atomic number 35*:1} and {*fluorine*:1; *F*:6; *atomic number 9*:1}, halogens that are usually gasses, covered also in the group 3 of this topic. The proposed changes for group 2 are:

- Change the hyperonym of {*halogen*:1} from {*group*:1; *grouping*:1} to {*chemical element*:1; *element*:6};
- Remove the hyperonym {*chemical element*:1; *element*:6} as it is already a hyperonym of {*halogen*:1};
- Change the hyperonym relations from {*chlorine*:1; *Cl*:2; *atomic number 17*:1} and {*fluorine*:1; *F*:6; *atomic number 9*:1} to {*gas*:7} to **form**;
- Add a relation **form** from {*bromine*:1; *Br*:1; *atomic number 35*:1} to {*gas*:7}.

Double group 3 has 6 members with the following common hyperonyms:

- {*chemical element*:1; *element*:6}
- {*gas*:7}

The group includes synsets for elements that usually take the form of a gas, such as {*oxygen*:1; *O*:4; *atomic number 8*:1} and {*nitrogen*:1; *N*:8; *atomic number 7*:1}. The proposed change is:

- Change the hyperonymy relation to {*gas:7*} to the relation **form**.

There are 3 more synsets in the single group with common hyperonym {*chemical element*:1; *element*:6}, not covered as members of the above double groups. These are:

- {*germanium*:1; *Ge*:3; *atomic number 32*:1} with hyperonyms:
  - {*chemical element*:1; *element*:6};
  - {*semiconductor*:2; *semiconducting material*:1} (This hyperonymy relation's proposed change is to **function**.)
- {*silicon*:1; *Si*:2; *atomic number 14*:1} with hyperonyms:
  - {*chemical element*:1; *element*:6};
  - {*semiconductor*:2; *semiconducting material*:1} (This hyperonymy relation's proposed change is to **function**.)
- {*selenium*:1; *Se*:1; *atomic number 34*:1} with hyperonyms:
  - {*chemical element*:1; *element*:6};
  - {*antioxidant*:1} (This hyperonymy relation's proposed change is to **function**.)

As a result of the proposed changes, for these synsets the following is observed:

- Each synset has only one hyperonymy relation, which is to {*chemical element*:1; *element*:6};
- A synset may have a relation **function** to a synset which was previously marked as a hyperonym;
- A relation **form** to {*gas*:7} may be inserted to keep uniformity with the rest of the chemical elements existing in gas form.

In some cases, such as with the synset {*halogen*:1}, an appropriate restructuring of the hyperonymy tree (immediately above the considered synset with multiple hyperonymy) may be required to properly resolve multiple hyperonymy. Figures 2 and 3 visualise the state of the WordNet structure immediately above the synset {*chlorine*:1; *Cl*:2; *atomic number 17*:1} before and after the proposed changes to relations.

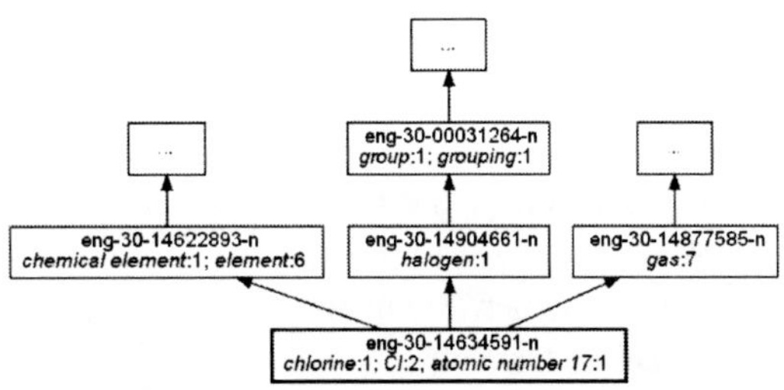

Figure 2: Local graph for synset {*chlorine*:1; *Cl*:2; *atomic number 17*:1} without the proposed changes

The synset {*chlorine*:1; *Cl*:2; *atomic number 17*:1} was originally related with three hyperonyms, two of which have a common hyperonym {*abstraction*:1; *abstract entity*:1}, and all three are finally related to the hyperonym {*entity*:1}.

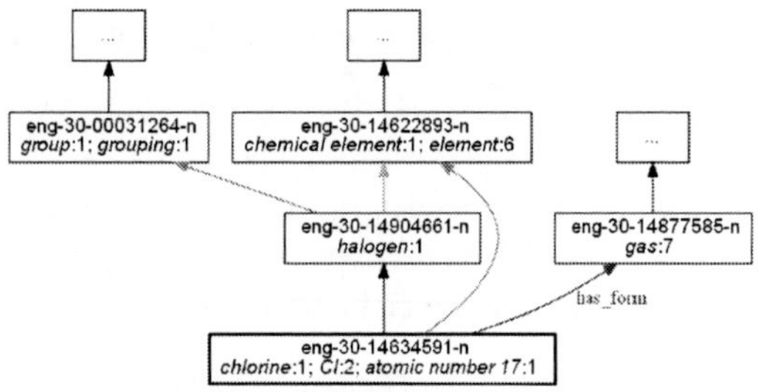

Figure 3: Local graph for synset {*chlorine*:1; *Cl*:2; *atomic number 17*:1} with the proposed changes – blue lines are changed relations, green line is added relation, red lines are removed relations

5 A brief description of the new relations

Conjunctive multiple hyperonyms are assumed not to indicate the same relation. Other semantic relations are formulated in addition to true hyperonymy, allowing a conjunction between several "hyperonyms", or when two or more more general concepts relate to a more specific one at the same time. Conjunctive multiple hyperonymy represents the newly proposed semantic relations and the true hyperonym, which reflects the genuine hyperonymy relation.

The new relations are antisymmetric and intransitive and the direction of the relations is important for expressing their semantics. Inverse relations with analogous properties are defined: has characteristic, is characteristic of, has origin, is origin for, has form, is form for, has function, is function for, uses, is used for, has member, is member of, has part, is part of, has portion, is portion of.

Following existing approaches (Alonge et al., 1998) we formulated diagnostic tests for the new relations. Let we consider the synset {*hydrogen*:1; *H*:7; *atomic number 1*:1}, currently linked with two hyperonyms: {*chemical element*:1; *element*:6} and {*gas*:7}. The relation to {*gas*:7} is redefined as **form**: hydrogen has form of gas.

We can apply the following tests to detect the relation **form** between nouns:

X has the form of Y.

If it is X, then it must have the form of Y.

Examples:

Hydrogen has the form of a gas.

? A gas has the form of hydrogen.

It is hydrogen, therefore it has the form of a gas.

? It is a gas, therefore it has the form of hydrogen.

If it is hydrogen, then it must have the form of a gas.

? If it is a gas, then it must have the form of hydrogen.

An application of the hyperonymy test shows that the relation **form** also expresses the semantics of the hyperonymy:

It is hydrogen, therefore it is also a gas.

? It is a gas, therefore it is also hydrogen.

If it is hydrogen, then it must be a gas.

? If it is a gas, then it must be hydrogen.

The hyperonymy test is applicable to true hyperonyms, but the **form** test is not:

It is hydrogen, therefore it is also a chemical element.

? It is a chemical element, therefore it is also hydrogen.

? Hydrogen has the form of a chemical element.

? A chemical element has the form of hydrogen.

? It is hydrogen, therefore it has the form of a chemical element.

? It is a chemical element, therefore it has the form of hydrogen.

The newly introduced semantic relations obey the formal tests of true hyperonymy, while the reverse is not true.

6 Conclusion and future work

Based on the hypothesis that one synset cannot be related to more than one hyperonym, other semantic relations are defined in the scope of multiple hyperonymy. Tests for the identification of new relations can be formulated following the pattern of the tests for other relations. The overall conclusion is that multiple hyperonymy embraces several semantic relations which, in turn, are only partially shown within the WordNet structure. Relations such as **origin**, **form**, **function**, etc. bear additional semantics and where they exist, they can be defined regardless of resolving multiple hyperonymy occurrences. Such specification would better outline the subsets of nouns that saturate semantic preferences of a verb predicate within the semantic classes of nouns, which are propagated through the inheritance (hyperonymy) relation.

We intend to use the **is-a** inheritance relation to subclassify the semantic classes of noun synsets to more specific groups depending on verb-noun combinability in sentences. We will demonstrate how the mapping of detailed semantic classes of nouns can benefit from a proper taxonomic tree structure.

Acknowledgments

This research is carried out as part of the project *Enriching Semantic Network WordNet with Conceptual frames* funded by the Bulgarian National Science Fund, Grant Agreement No. KP-06-H50/1 from 2020.

References

Antonietta Alonge, Nicoletta Calzolari, Piek Vossen, Laura Bloksma, Irene Castellón, Maria Antònia Martí, and Wim Peters. 1998. The linguistic Design of the EuroWordNet Database. *Computers and the Humanities*, 32(2-3):91–115.

Raquel Amaro, Sara Mendes, and Palmira Marrafa. 2010. Lexical-Conceptual Relations as Qualia Role Encoders. In *Text, Speech and Dialogue*, pages 29–36, Berlin, Heidelberg. Springer Berlin Heidelberg.

Ronald J. Brachman. 1983. What IS-A is and isn't: An analysis of taxonomic links in semantic networks. *Computer*, 16(10):30–37.

Mingda Chen, Zewei Chu, Karl Stratos, and Kevin Gimpel. 2020. Mining knowledge for natural language inference from Wikipedia categories. In *Findings of the Association for Computational Linguistics: EMNLP 2020*, pages 3500–3511, Online. Association for Computational Linguistics.

D. Alan Cruse. 2002. Hyponymy and its varieties. In Rebecca Green, Carol A. Bean, and Sung Hyon Myaeng, editors, *The Semantics of Relationships: An Interdisciplinary Perspective*, pages 3–21. Springer Netherlands, Dordrecht.

EAGLES. 1999. *Preliminary Recommendations on Lexical Semantic Encoding. Final report.*

Christiane Fellbaum, editor. 1998. *WordNet: An Electronic Lexical Database*. Language, Speech, and Communication. MIT Press, Cambridge, MA.

Aldo Gangemi, Nicola Guarino, and Alessandro Oltramari. 2001. Conceptual Analysis of Lexical Taxonomies: The Case of WordNet Top-Level. *CoRR*, cs.CL/0109013.

Emden R. Gansner and Stephen C. North. 2000. An open graph visualization system and its applications to software engineering. *Software: Practice and Expirience*, 30(11):1203–1233.

Aaron Kaplan and Lenhart Schubert. 2001. Measuring and improving the quality of world knowledge extracted from wordnet.

Svetla Koeva, Tsvetana Dimitrova, Valentina Stefanova, and Dimitar Hristov. 2018. Mapping WordNet concepts with CPA ontology. In *Proceedings of the 9th Global Wordnet Conference*, pages 69–76, Nanyang Technological University (NTU), Singapore. Global Wordnet Association.

Svetla Koeva and Emil Doychev. 2022. Ontology supported frame classification. In *Proceedings of the 5th International Conference on Computational Linguistics in Bulgaria (CLIB 2022)*, pages 203–213, Sofia, Bulgaria. Department of Computational Linguistics, IBL – BAS.

Ahti Lohk. 2015. *A System of Test Patterns to Check and Validate the Semantic Hierarchies of Wordnet-type Dictionaries*. Tallin: Tallin University of Technology.

Ravi Lourdusamy and Stanislaus Abraham. 2020. A Survey on Methods of Ontology Learning from Text. In Lakhmi C. Ain, Sheng-Lung Peng, Basim Alhadidi, and Souvik Pal, editors, *Intelligent Computing Paradigm and Cutting-edge Technologies*, pages 113–123. Springer International Publishing.

John Lyons. 1977. *Semantics. 2 vols.* New York: Cambridge University Press.

Sara Mendes and Rui Pedro Chaves. 2001. Enriching WordNet with Qualia Information. In *Proceedings of NAACL 2001 Workshop on WordNet and Other Lexical Resources*.

George A. Miller, Richard Beckwith, Christiane. Fellbaum, Derek Gross, and Katherine Miller. 1990. Introduction to WordNet: An On-line Lexical Database. *International journal of lexicography*, 3(4):235–244.

Arantxa Otegi, Iñaki San Vicente, Xabier Saralegi, Anselmo Peñas, Borja Lozano, and Eneko Agirre. 2022. Information retrieval and question answering: A case study on COVID-19 scientific literature. *Knowl. Based Syst.*, 240:57–84.

Bolette Pederson and Nikolai Hartvig Sørensen. 2006. Towards Sounder Taxonomies in WordNets. In *Ontolex2006*, pages 9–16.

Maria Pontiki, Dimitris Galanis, Haris Papageorgiou, Suresh Manandhar, and Ion Androutsopoulos. 2015. SemEval-2015 task 12: Aspect based sentiment analysis. In *Proceedings of the 9th International Workshop on Semantic Evaluation (SemEval 2015)*, pages 486–495, Denver, Colorado. Association for Computational Linguistics.

James Pustejovsky. 1995. *The Generative Lexicon*. MIT Press.

Veda C. Storey. 1993. Understanding semantic relationships. *VLDB J.*, 2(4):455–488.

Piek Vossen, editor. 1998. *EuroWordNet: A Multilingual Database with Lexical Semantic Networks*. Kluwer Academic Publishers, USA.

Morton E. Winston, Roger Chaffin, and Douglas Herrmann. 1987. A Taxonomy of Part-Whole Relations. *Cognitive Science*, 38(11):417–444.

Jarosław Wątróbski. 2020. Ontology learning methods from text – an extensive knowledge-based approach. *Procedia Computer Science*, 176:3356–3368.

Towards the integration of WordNet into ClinIDMap

Elena Zotova
SNLT group at Vicomtech Foundation,
Basque Research and Technology Alliance (BRTA) /
Mikeletegi Pasealekua 57,
20009, Donostia/San-Sebastián, Spain
and
Department of Languages and Computer Systems, University of the Basque Country (UPV-EHU) /
Paseo Manuel de Lardizábal, 1,
20018, Donostia/San-Sebastián, Spain
ezotova@vicomtech.org

Montse Cuadros
SNLT group at Vicomtech Foundation,
Basque Research and Technology Alliance (BRTA) /
Mikeletegi Pasealekua 57,
20009, Donostia/San-Sebastián, Spain
mcuadros@vicomtech.org

German Rigau
Department of Languages and Computer Systems, University of the Basque Country (UPV-EHU)
and
HiTZ Basque Center for Language Technologies
Paseo Manuel de Lardizábal, 1,
20018, Donostia/San-Sebastián, Spain
german.rigau@ehu.eus

Abstract

This paper presents the integration of WordNet knowledge resource into ClinIDMap tool, which aims to map identifiers between clinical ontologies and lexical resources. ClinIDMap interlinks identifiers from UMLS, SMOMED-CT, ICD-10 and the corresponding Wikidata and Wikipedia articles for concepts from the UMLS Metathesaurus. The main goal of the tool is to provide semantic interoperability across the clinical concepts from various knowledge bases. As a side effect, the mapping enriches already annotated medical corpora in multiple languages with new labels. In this new release, we add WordNet 3.0 and 3.1 synsets using the available mappings through Wikidata. Thanks to cross-lingual links in MCR we also include the corresponding synsets in other languages and also, extend further ClinIDMap with different domain information. Finally, the final resource helps in the task of enriching of already annotated clinical corpora with additional semantic annotations.

1 Introduction

The main goal of the ClinIDMap mapping tool (Zotova et al., 2022) is to align different types of clinical identifiers (IDs, codes) from different knowledge bases (KB) such as UMLS (Bodenreider, 2004), ICD-10 (World Health Organization (WHO), 2004), SNOMED-CT (Donnelly et al., 2006) and others. The alignment uses the actual IDs of the KBs from the official mapping resources developed by the authors of SNOMED-CT and UMLS. The alignment allows to enrich manually annotated corpora with extra clinical codes and to obtain multilingual inter-operable corpora annotated with various coding systems. For instance, if we have a corpus annotated in UMLS codes we can map each code to ICD-10-CM and ICD-10-PSC codes in order to derive automatically a new version of the corpus with ICD-10 annotations. And vise versa, corpus annotated with ICD-10 codes can be used to derive automatically new corpora annotated with UMLS codes, semantic types or groups. Moreover, ClinIDMap enriches the annotated concepts with multilingual terms and descriptions of its available Wikidata and Wikipedia articles, allowing to expand brief code descriptions to detailed information in multiple languages.

Now, we introduce the functionality of mapping those clinical concepts to WordNet (Miller, 1998). WordNet (WN) is a widely used lexical knowledge resource, which contains information about lexical relations, such as synonyny and super-subordinate relation (hyperonymy, hyponymy). In addition, WordNet is used as a backbone of many other lexical resources. The alignment allows us to enrich manually annotated corpora with extra clinical codes and to obtain multilingual inter-operable corpora annotated with various coding systems. For instance, if we have a corpus annotated in UMLS codes we can map each code to ICD-10-CM and ICD-10-PSC codes in order to derive automatically a new version of the corpus. And vise versa, a corpus annotated with ICD-10 codes can be used to derive automatically new corpora annotated with UMLS codes, semantic types or groups.

Thus, this paper focuses on two tasks: (1) extending ClinIDMap to include WordNet information, and (2) annotating automatically clinical corpora with new labels related to information associated to WordNet. Concretely, we present the integration of WordNet mapping with clinical identifiers such as UMLS, SNOMED-CT, ICD-10, MeSH a for Spanish, English and other languages. Using this tool, we derive multiple datasets annotated with different coding systems on the base of existing annotated corpora. The previous version of the tool is described in detail in Zotova et al. (2022) and the tool is publicly available[1].

For instance, a Spanish sentence from E3C corpus (Magnini et al., 2020) annotated with a UMLS code is given below.

> Durante los 5 años que permaneció en DP sufrió 10 **peritonitis** [C0031154], 8 por Staphilococcus aureus.
>
> Translation: *During the 5 years on PD he suffered 10* ***peritonitis*** *[C0031154], 8 of which were because of Staphylococcus aureus.*

The code *C0031154* corresponding to the Spanish term *peritonitis* can be mapped to the SNOMED CT code *235983003*, to the ICD-10-CM code *K65*, to the corresponding Wikipedia articles in 48 languages, to synset *14376092-n* in WordNet 3.1. and synset *14352687-n* in WordNet 3.0.

The paper is organized as follows. Section 2 describes previous attempts of mapping clinical codes and also using WordNet in the clinical domain; Section 3 is dedicated to the databases used to develop ClinIDMap—clinical ontologies, mapping schema and general purpose lexical resources; in Section 4 we describe (1) the method of aligning WordNet synsets to clinical codes, WordNet Domains and WordNets in different languages (Subsection 4.1) and (2) semi-automatic method of annotating of the clinical corpora (Subsection 4.2).Finally, Section 5 concludes the paper and presents the future work.

2 Related Work

2.1 Aligning Clinical Codes

There are two main parts of clinical codes mapping: (1) concept alignment, or ontology alignment (also known as ontology matching); (2) applications that use the resulting concept mapping to process biomedical text.

Ontology matching finds semantically related entities in different knowledge bases (KB). For instance, the OAEI Campaign (Ontology Alignment Evaluation Initiative) [2] organizes every year an ontology matching evaluation shared task. The applied methods combine multiple strategies such as lexical matching, structural matching and logical reasoning (Ochieng and Kyanda, 2018). Novel machine learning and deep learning methods are also applied to ontology alignment (Chen et al., 2021). ClinIDMap uses already aligned clinical KBs.

Most applications are designed to enrich clinical text with clinical concepts and relations. MetaMap (Aronson and Lang, 2010; Aronson, 2001) is an application for mapping biomedical text to the UMLS Metathesaurus or, equivalently, to discover UMLS concepts referred in the text. MetaMap uses a knowledge-intensive approach based on symbolic, NLP and computational-linguistic techniques to provide a link between the text of biomedical literature and the KB, including synonymy relationships, embedded in the Metathesaurus. The input of the application is English text.

I-MAGIC is an application, implemented by US National Library of Medicine, that visualises clinical IDs mappings. A demo version of the application is also available[3]. Using the rule-based SNOMED-CT to ICD-10-CM Mapping (Fung and Xu, 2012), the algorithm determines whether a valid ICD-10-CM code can be found based on the SNOMED-CT term and patient context information (age and gender). The application allows to search a term in SNOMED-CT. However, it is limited to a literal search. The tool does not consider synonyms, nor other language than English.

Rahimi et al. (2020) proposes to match UMLS concepts to Wikidata using a cross-lingual neu-

[1] https://github.com/Vicomtech/ClinIDMap

[2] http://oaei.ontologymatching.org/2021/

[3] https://imagic.nlm.nih.gov/imagic/code/map

ral re-ranking model which is based on a pre-trained contextual encoding. As the UMLS descriptions are brief and the medical entity pages in Wikipedia provide detailed descriptions (also enriched with the Wikidata knowledge graph), they use the UMLS concept description to query the Wikidata entity aliases to retrieve the best matching Wikipedia pages. Instead, ClinIDMap exploits available manual mappings between the different lexical resources.

2.2 WordNets for the Clinical Domain

There were various attempts to create domain specific WordNets such as the Medical WordNet (Smith and Fellbaum, 2004) with the goal of linking different terms, both professional terminology and general language. These resources should also be ready for NLP automatic applications such as relation extraction, entity linking, and automatic clinical coding.

WordNet was proposed as a method for giving patients interpretative support when annotating foreign word-meanings with the corresponding Norwegian synset (Ingvaldsen and Veres, 2004). This was supposed to be an add-on for the electronic medical record systems that will help regular patients in getting insight to their diagnoses. The add-on service is based annotating polysemous and foreign terms with WordNet synsets and then use the relationships established in WordNet to return definitions and hypernymy, meronymy and entailment meanings of a term.

WordNet was used to improve the direct mapping of data elements during the integration of biomedical resources in the study of Mougin et al. (2006). WordNet contributes external information useful for disambiguation and validation of UMLS direct mappings. WordNet can also help identify indirect mappings of DEs to the UMLS. Also, WordNet synsets help identify indirect mappings to the UMLS when no direct UMLS mapping was found.

There were also studies of how to align WordNet domains and Wikipedia categories to obtain domain specific corpora (Gella et al., 2014). The authors expected that the multilingual, and comparable, domain-specific corpora have the potential to enhance research in word-sense disambiguation and terminology extraction in different languages, which could enhance the performance of various NLP tasks.

3 Background

This section describes the resources and databases used to build ClinIDMap. It includes a brief information about the clinical and general knowledge bases used and the resources exploited for mapping the different codes.

3.1 Clinical Knowledge Bases

The following medical knowledge bases are used to build ClinIDMap. Each of them consists of a set of identifiers (IDs) in alphanumeric format and a brief description.

The UMLS, or Unified Medical Language System[4], is a set of files and software that brings together 102 health and biomedical vocabularies and standards and includes 4 million terms to enable interoperability between computer systems. UMLS consists of three parts: the Metathesaurus, a Semantic Network and the SPECIALIST Lexicon. This database is our main source of mapping information.

MeSH[5] stands for Medical Subject Headings (MeSH) thesaurus which is a controlled and hierarchically-organized vocabulary produced by the National Library of Medicine. It is used for indexing, cataloging, and searching of biomedical and health-related information. MeSH includes the subject headings appearing in MEDLINE/PubMed, the National Library of Medicine[6] (NLM) Catalog, and other NLM databases.

Spanish SNOMED-CT[7] is the Spanish translation of SNOMED-CT. It includes the National Extension for Spain, updated and maintained by the SNOMED CT National Reference Centre for Spain, Ministry of Health, Consumer Affairs and Social Welfare. Spanish SNOMED-CT contains 199,961 unique codes.

ICD-10-CM (International Statistical Classification of Diseases and Related Health Problems) establishes a standardized coding that allows the statistical analysis of mortality and morbidity of patients in healthcare services. It consists of 99,000 codes which are organized hierarchically. The corresponding Spanish version is called CIE-10-ES.

[4]https://www.nlm.nih.gov/research/umls/index.html

[5]https://meshb.nlm.nih.gov/

[6]https://www.nlm.nih.gov/

[7]https://www.mscbs.gob.es/profesionales/hcdsns/areaRecursosSem/snomed-ct/areaDescarga.htm

ClinIDMap uses the official Spanish version of the CIE-10 from July 2020[8].

ICD-10-PCS (Procedure Coding System)[9] is an international system of medical classification used for procedural coding, it consists of 80,000 codes, organized hierarchically. ICD-10-PCS is a result of separation of a chapter from ICD-9 which contained procedures codification. ClinIDMap uses the official Spanish version of the ICD-10-PCS from January 2020.

3.2 Clinical Codes Mapping Resources

To interconnect the different identifiers from the knowledge bases of interest ClinIDMap uses the existing mappings created by clinical experts. The mapping schemes are the following:

UMLS Metathesaurus[10]. This database has been derived from the 2021AB UMLS Metathesaurus Files which contains approximately 4.54 million concepts from 220 source vocabularies, including ICD-10-CM, MeSH, and SNOMED-CT, Hierarchies, definitions, and other relationships and attributes. The Metathesaurus is the biggest component of the UMLS. It is organised as a set of Concept Unique Identifiers (CUI) which links all the names from all of the source vocabularies that have the same meaning (synonyms). A single CUI can have several definitions in different languages. The Metathesaurus assigns several types of unique, permanent identifiers to the concepts and concept names it contains, in addition to retaining all identifiers that are present in the source vocabularies. The Metathesaurus concept structure includes concept names, their identifiers, and key characteristics of these concept names (e.g., language, vocabulary source, name type). The entire concept structure appears in a single file in the Rich Release Format (MRCONSO.RRF).

The Semantic Network from UMLS is used for grouping CUIs. Examples of the semantic groups are Organisms, Anatomical structures, Biologic function, Chemicals, Events, Physical objects, Concepts or Ideas. These types are suitable for corpus annotation and training sequence labeling models and further linking to UMLS.

SNOMED-CT to ICD-10-CM Mapping[11]. The main purpose of the SNOMED-CT to ICD-10-CM mapping is to support semi-automated generation of ICD-10-CM codes from clinical data encoded in SNOMED-CT for reimbursement and statistical purposes. It is designed as a directed set of relationships from SNOMED-CT source concepts to ICD-10-CM target classification codes. This mapping is curated by trained terminology specialists, and it is more comprehensive than the Metathesaurus CUI linking. About a third part of all active SNOMED-CT concepts are within the scope of the mapping, about 125,000 SNOMED-CT codes from the international version are mapped to ICD-10-CM codes. About 57,000 codes from the Spanish SNOMED-CT are included in the mapping (around 30% of all Spanish SNOMED-CT codes). Due to the differences in granularity, emphasis and organizing principles between SNOMED-CT and ICD-10-CM, it is not always possible to have one-to-one mappings between a SNOMED-CT concept and an ICD-10-CM code. In addition, not all ICD-10-CM codes will appear as targets.

3.3 Lexical Resources

ClinIDMap has been enriched with general purpose lexical resources in order to include terminology descriptions in different languages. The following lexical resources are included.

Wikidata[12] (Vrandečić and Krötzsch, 2014) is a free and open knowledge base that can be consulted and edited by both humans and machines. Wikidata acts as central repository for the structured data of its Wikimedia sister projects including Wikipedia, Wikivoyage, Wiktionary, Wikisource, and others. The Wikidata repository consists mainly of items, each one having a label, a description and a number of aliases. Wikidata items related to clinical concepts are annotated with UMLS ID (CUI), Medical Subject Headings (MeSH) (Rogers, 1963) and other clinical taxonomies, so Wikidata can be used to extract the corresponding articles in all available languages.

Wikipedia[13] is used as a multilingual online encyclopedia of clinical concepts. Wikipedia provides extensive description of clinical concepts in many languages.

[8] https://eciemaps.mscbs.gob.es/ecieMaps/browser/index_10_mc.html

[9] https://www.cms.gov/Medicare/Coding/ICD10/2020-ICD-10-PCS

[10] https://www.nlm.nih.gov/research/umls/knowledge_sources/metathesaurus/index.html

[11] https://www.nlm.nih.gov/research/umls/mapping_projects/snomedct_to_icd10cm.html

[12] https://www.wikidata.org

[13] https://www.wikipedia.org/

WordNet 3.1[14] (Fellbaum, 2005) is the latest version of a lexical database of English. Nouns, verbs, adjectives and adverbs are grouped into sets of cognitive synonyms (synsets), each expressing a distinct concept. Synsets are interlinked by means of conceptual-semantic and lexical relations. This version contains 155,327 words organized in 175,979 synsets for a total of 207,016 word-sense pairs.

WordNet 3.0 [15] (Fellbaum, 2005) is the previous release of the lexical database. The WordNet 3.0 release has 117,798 nouns, 11,529 verbs, 22,479 adjectives, and 4,481 adverbs. The average noun has 1.23 senses, and the average verb has 2.16 sense. In total there are 206,941 sense keys. As far as we know, no direct mapping between WN 3.0 and WN 3.1. exists.

WordNet Domains[16] (Magnini and Cavaglià, 2000) is a lexical resource created in a semi-automatic way by augmenting WordNet with domain labels. WordNet synsets have been annotated with at least one semantic domain label, selected from a set of 170 labels structured according the WordNet Domain Hierarchy. There are various domains related to health and medicine. It is unclear what type of relations among the relevant domains is established. For instance, arguably, surgery and pharmacy may be included in the broader domain of medicine or health. We manually select a set of domains:

```
medicine, anatomy, pharmacy,
health, biochemistry, surgery,
physiology, genetics,
psychological_features, psychology,
radiology, genetics, dentistry,
psychiatry, optics, chemistry
```

We use these domains for semi-automatic data annotation.

WordNet extended Domains (Gonzalez-Agirre et al., 2012b) is a resource aiming to improve WordNet Domains. The original domain labels have been projected to WordNet 3.0 using automatic mappings across WordNet versions (Daude et al., 2003). Since the automatic mapping is not complete due to new synsets, changes in the structure, etc., many synsets were left unlabeled. The extended WordNet domains were elaborated by an expansion process through the graph of WordNet. This resource consists of 170 files, one for each of the original WordNet Domains. Each file contains a vector of 117,536 synsets sorted by weight, from highest lo lowest. Thus, the most representative synsets for a given domain are at the top positions. For instance, the first four lines of the file *health.ppv* correspond to the first synset-weight pairs (we have added the variants):

```
00624738-n 0.00771299 exercise_1
14049711-n 0.00561771 good_health_1
01017738-a 0.00504791 unfit_2
05216365-n 0.00492294 body_1
```

Multilingual Central Repository (MCR) 3.0 (Gonzalez-Agirre et al., 2012a) integrates using the EuroWordNet framework, WordNets from six different languages: English, Spanish, Catalan, Basque, Galician and Portuguese. The Inter-Lingual-Index (ILI) allows the connection from words in one language to equivalent translations in any of the other languages thanks to the automatically generated mappings among WordNet versions. The current ILI version corresponds to WordNet 3.0.

Coarse Sense Inventory (CSI) (Lacerra et al., 2020) is a coarse-grained sense inventory where semantic labels are shared across the lexicon of WordNet. There are 46 labels in total and we select the class *HEALTH_AND_MEDICINE_* to filter clinical identifiers.

4 Methodology

4.1 WordNets Mapping

Items in Wikidata are annotated manually by Wikidata experts. However, there may be variations and mismatches with respect the UMLS or SNOMED CT to ICD-10 mappings described in Subsection 3.2.

Step 1. Collect all Wikidata items. First of all, we need to gather all the Wikidata items including WordNet 3.1 synsets, optionally adding their corresponding clinical IDs, such as UMLS CUI, SNOMED CT, MeSH and ICD-10.

Step 2. WordNets 3.1 and WordNet 3.0 mapping. Resources such as WordNet Domains, CSI and MCR are aligned with WordNet 3.0, while Wikidata items use WordNet 3.1. To obtain the corresponding domains and CSI codes we need to map WordNet 3.1 offsets to those of WordNet 3.0. We use the sense key index for this mapping. According to Kafe (2018), 99,4% of sense keys from WordNet 3.0 persist in WordNet 3.1–716 KSI were

[14] https://wordnet.princeton.edu/

[15] https://wordnetcode.princeton.edu/3.0/WordNet-3.0.tar.gz

[16] https://wndomains.fbk.eu/

added and 1,304 KSI were removed. Each version of WordNet distribution contains a file *index.sense* which includes all senses with their corresponding offsets. These sense keys are coded as follows. For instance, the sense key "adenoma%1:26:00::" contains a lemma of the synset "adenoma". The first number refers to the part of speech (1 is noun, 2 is verb, 3 is adjective, 4 is adverb, 5 is adjective satellite). The second two-digit code is representing the name of the lexicographer file (e.g. part of speech and its attribute, such as time, person, body—44 names in total). The third two-digit code refers to ID in lexicographical file. We use the whole sense key to match senses across the different WordNet versions.

Step 3. WordNet 3.0 to WNDomains, CSI and MCR mapping. Once having the WordNet 3.0 synsets, we can easily access the rest of the KBs –Domains, CSI and MCR. The resulting table is used as establish the mapping between the clinical codes and the WordNet synsets.

For instance, below is an example of 14235793-n synset (*adenoma*) and its five most probable WN-Domains.

```
14235793-n  0.00010198  medicine
14235793-n  0.00005412  veterinary
14235793-n  0.00003494  anatomy
14235793-n  0.00001745  radiology
14235793-n  0.00001649  cycling
```

There are about 27,500 Wikidata items annotated with WordNet 3.1 synsets. As we see in Table 1, only a small part of Wikidata items (approximately 1 to 10%) annotated with WordNet synsets is also annotated with clinical codes. Some of the items are annotated with multiple synsets, the distribution of the multiple synsets across the Wikidata items is shown in Table 2. Table 5 shows some examples of some Wikidata items connected to various clinical identifiers. This database can be used to connect clinical codes to WordNet synsets. +

Database	Unique items
Wikidata items	27,516
WordNet 3.1	26,953
WordNet 3.0 (mapped)	26,938
UMLS CUI	2,076
ICD-10	833
SNOMED CT	282

Table 1: Numbers of Wikidata items annotated with both WordNet synsets and clinical IDs.

#Wikidata items	#synsets
5	6
10	5
38	4
265	3
1,663	2
25,535	1

Table 2: Number of Wikidata items annotated with various WordNet synsets.

We also map all the Wikidata items to extended WordNet domains and to the CSI domains. For each synset, we select the 5 most probable domains from the extended WordNet domains that contain a clinical domain. Table 3 shows the number of Wikidata items with clinical codes from extended WordNet domains and from CSI, and its overlapping.

Database	Wikidata items
CSI	3,133
WordNet clinical domains	3,396
Total clinical domain only	2,398

Table 3: Number of Wikidata items annotated with clinical domains (from CSI and Extended WordNet Domains).

WordNet 3.0 offsets are also used for gathering the non-English synsets included into the MCR.

4.2 Corpora annotation with WordNet synsets

After building the new version of ClinIDMap, now integrating WordNet synsets, we study how many clinical IDs from the domain corpora (see the description of the used corpora in (Zotova et al., 2022)) can be mapped to the WordNet synsets and its corresponding domains. Four corpora of various types were selected for the experiments: CodiEsp 2020 (clinical narratives in Spanish, annotated with ICD-10 codes), E3C (clinical narratives in Spanish), CT-EBM-SP (clinical trials in Spanish annotated with CUI), MedMentions (biomedical papers in English annotated with CUI). Then, we annotate the corpora with two types of labels: (1) WordNet domains; (2) CSI labels.

As shown in the Table 4, about 5-20% percent of the clinical annotations are mapped to WordNet synsets, possibly not only from the clinical domain. The variety of the unique synsets in the corpus depends, first, on its size, and on the na-

Corpus	Tokens	Annotated CUI	Mapped WN	Unique WN
E3C ES (Magnini et al., 2020)	28,815	2,268	422	107
MedMentions (Mohan and Li, 2019)	1,258,847	540,138	24,754	841
Mantra (Kors et al., 2015)	3,492	1,058	117	62
CT-EBM-SP (Campillos-Llanos, 2019)	141,158	23.264	5,786	431
CodiEsp 2020 (Miranda-Escalada et al., 2020)	401,010	32,902	11,464	399

Table 4: Number of tokens annotated with both WN synsets and clinical IDs using mapping of UMLS CUI to WN synsets.

item	label	MESH	CUI	ICD-10	SNOMED-CT	WN 3.1	WN 3.0	sense	domain	CSI
Q272741	adenoma	D000236	C0001430	D35.0	32048006	14259275-n	14235793-n	adenoma%1:26:00::	medicine	HEALTH_AND_MEDICINE_
Q272741	adenoma	D000236	C0334389	D35.2	32048006	14259275-n	14235793-n	adenoma%1:26:00::	medicine	HEALTH_AND_MEDICINE_
Q7365	muscle organ	D009132	C0026845			05296796-n	05289297-n	musculus%1:08:00::	health	BIOLOGY_
Q84133	myocardium	D009206	C0027061			05398343-n	05391000-n	myocardium%1:08:00::	anatomy	HEALTH_AND_MEDICINE_
Q223102	peritonitis	D010538	C0029823	K65		14376092-n	14352687-n	peritonitis%1:26:00::	medicine	HEALTH_AND_MEDICINE_

Table 5: Examples of WordNets mapped with clinical IDs, WordNet domains and CSI.

ture of the data. Here, the corpus MedMEntions compiled from English biomedical papers has the largest number of mappings to WordNet synsets, but the Spanish part of E3C has in proportion the largest number of distinct mappings.

Using the new version of ClinIDMap, now including WordNet synsets we can also project all these annotations to other resources associated to WordNet such as WordNet Domains and CSI domains. Table 6 presents the distribution of medical WordNet Domain labels as there are also entities annotated with CUIs not belonging to the medical domain. Now, with the new version of ClinIDMap we can select those annotations belonging to the clinical domain. As we can see in the number of domains differs from corpus to corpus and is also related to the data type—clinical narratives contain less labels than scientific papers or trials.

We also derive a new corpora annotated with CSI labels. Table 7 shows the distribution of CSI labels across the different corpora. If various CSI domains are assigned to a token, the most frequent one is selected. Again, the distributions of the labels across the tokens is not balanced. The larger corpus (MedMentions) is annotated with 23 labels while the E3C is annotated with only four. As expected, the prevalence of health-related labels is high. Nevertheless, the texts also contain labels not related to the medical domain.

WND	MM	CT	E3C	CE
NULL	1,239,202	136,287	28,480	393,580
medicine	4,349	1,450	285	5,185
anatomy	3,001	928		72
biochemistry	3,821	807		21
pharmacy	1,922	842	29	569
radiology	529	408	3	308
psychiatry	1,678	257	37	361
optics	380	161	8	130
physiology	230	134	9	322
surgery	254	81	8	43
health	394	62	18	175
genetics	1,018	49	3	97
chemistry	974	24		30
dentistry	159	15	2	80
psychology		14	6	34

Table 6: Number of tokens annotated with WordNet domains (WN-D) using the mapping method from MedMentions (MM), CT-EBM-SP (CT), E3C, CodiEsp 2020 (CE).

5 Conclusions

In this paper we present an extension of ClinIDMap now integrating WordNet synsets in different languages and its domain information. We also use the new medical resource to provide different prespectives to the annotated data. As a future work we plan to experiment with the annotated corpora and train deep learning models for sequence labeling of WN domains and CSI labels. We also plan to use other WordNet relations and associated knowledge. We would also like to add new clinical and lexical resources to ClinIDMap such as additional knowledge from different Wikipedia.

References

Alan Aronson. 2001. Effective Mapping of Biomedical Text to the UMLS Metathesaurus: The MetaMap Program. *Proceedings / AMIA ... Annual Symposium. AMIA Symposium*, 2001:17–21.

Alan R Aronson and François-Michel Lang. 2010. An overview of MetaMap: historical perspective and recent advances. *Journal of the American Medical Informatics Association*, 17(3):229–236.

Olivier Bodenreider. 2004. The Unified Medical

CSI Label	MM	CT	E3C	CE
NULL	1,234,315	135,402	28,396	393,252
HEALTH_AND_MEDICINE_	15,796	4,379	370	7,758
BIOLOGY_	5,907	1,231	30	
CHEMISTRY_AND_MINERALOGY_	1,743	119		
MATHEMATICS_	470			
FOOD_DRINK_AND_TASTE_	112	2		57
EVALUATION_	100	17	17	
TIME_	92			
BUSINESS_ECONOMICS_AND_FINANCE_	47			
POLITICS_GOVERNMENT_AND_NOBILITY_	46			
SEX_	39	1		48
METEOROLOGY_	37			
PHILOSOPHY_PSYCHOLOGY_AND_BEHAVIOR_	36	2		305
EDUCATION_AND_SCIENCE_	26			
CULTURE_ANTHROPOLOGY_AND_SOCIETY_	20			
PHYSICS_AND_ASTRONOMY_	14	3		11
GEOGRAPHY_AND_PLACES_	11			
FARMING_	9			
COMPUTING_	7			
CRAFT_ENGINEERING_AND_TECHNOLOGY_	6			
VISUAL_	5		2	59
LANGUAGE_AND_LINGUISTICS_	5			
ART_ARCHITECTURE_AND_ARCHAEOLOGY_	2			
EMOTIONS_	1			15
WARFARE_DEFENSE_AND_VIOLENCE	1	2		

Table 7: Number of tokens annotated with CSI labels using the mapping method using the mapping method from MedMentions (MM), CT-EBM-SP (CT), E3C, CodiEsp 2020 (CE).

Language System (UMLS): integrating biomedical terminology. *Nucleic Acids Res.*, 32(Database-Issue):267–270.

Leonardo Campillos-Llanos. 2019. First steps towards building a medical lexicon for Spanish with linguistic and semantic information. In *Proceedings of the 18th BioNLP Workshop and Shared Task*, pages 152–164, Florence, Italy. Association for Computational Linguistics.

Jiaoyan Chen, Ernesto Jiménez-Ruiz, Ian Horrocks, Denvar Antonyrajah, Ali Hadian, and Jaehun Lee. 2021. Augmenting ontology alignment by semantic embedding and distant supervision. In *European Semantic Web Conference*, pages 392–408. Springer.

Jordi Daude, Lluis Padro, and German Rigau. 2003. Validation and tuning of wordnet mapping techniques. In *Proceedings of RANLP*, pages 117–123.

Kevin Donnelly et al. 2006. SNOMED-CT: The advanced terminology and coding system for eHealth. *Studies in health technology and informatics*, 121:279.

Christiane Fellbaum. 2005. Wordnet and wordnets. In *Encyclopedia of Language and Linguistics*, pages 665–670, Oxford.

Kin Wah Fung and Junchuan Xu. 2012. Synergism between the Mapping Projects from SNOMED CT to ICD-10 and ICD-10-CM. *AMIA ... Annual Symposium proceedings. AMIA Symposium*, 2012:218–227.

Spandana Gella, Carlo Strapparava, and Vivi Nastase. 2014. Mapping WordNet domains, WordNet topics and Wikipedia categories to generate multilingual domain specific resources. In *Proceedings of the Ninth International Conference on Language Resources and Evaluation (LREC'14)*, pages 1117–1121, Reykjavik, Iceland. European Language Resources Association (ELRA).

Aitor Gonzalez-Agirre, Egoitz Laparra, and German Rigau. Multilingual central repository version 3.0: upgrading a very large lexical knowledge base. *Proceedings of the 6th Global WordNet Conference (GWC'12) ISBN 978-80-263-0244-5.*

Aitor Gonzalez-Agirre, Egoitz Laparra, and German Rigau. 2012a. Multilingual central repository version 3.0. In *Proceedings of the Eighth International Conference on Language Resources and Evaluation, LREC 2012, Istanbul, Turkey, May 23-25, 2012*, pages 2525–2529. European Language Resources Association (ELRA).

Aitor Gonzalez-Agirre, German Rigau, and Mauro Castillo. 2012b. A graph-based method to improve wordnet domains. In *Computational Linguistics and Intelligent Text Processing - 13th International Conference, CICLing 2012, New Delhi, India, March*

11-17, 2012, Proceedings, Part I, volume 7181 of *Lecture Notes in Computer Science*, pages 17–28. Springer.

Jon Espen Ingvaldsen and Csaba Veres. 2004. Using the wordnet ontology for interpreting medical records. In *CAiSE Workshops*.

Eric Kafe. 2018. Persistent semantic identity in wordnet. *Cognitive Studies*, 2018.

Jan A Kors, Simon Clematide, Saber A Akhondi, Erik M van Mulligen, and Dietrich Rebholz-Schuhmann. 2015. A multilingual gold-standard corpus for biomedical concept recognition: the Mantra GSC. *Journal of the American Medical Informatics Association*, 22(5):948–956.

Caterina Lacerra, Michele Bevilacqua, Tommaso Pasini, and Roberto Navigli. 2020. CSI: A coarse sense inventory for 85% word sense disambiguation. In *Proceedings of the 34th Conference on Artificial Intelligence*, pages 8123–8130. AAAI Press.

Bernardo Magnini, Begoña Altuna, Alberto Lavelli, Manuela Speranza, and Roberto Zanoli. 2020. The E3C Project: Collection and Annotation of a Multilingual Corpus of Clinical Cases.

Bernardo Magnini and Gabriela Cavaglià. 2000. Integrating subject field codes into WordNet. In *Proceedings of the Second International Conference on Language Resources and Evaluation (LREC'00)*, Athens, Greece. European Language Resources Association (ELRA).

George A Miller. 1998. *WordNet: An electronic lexical database*. MIT press.

Antonio Miranda-Escalada, Aitor Gonzalez-Agirre, Jordi Armengol-Estapé, and Martin Krallinger. 2020. Overview of automatic clinical coding: annotations, guidelines, and solutions for non-english clinical cases at codiesp track of CLEF eHealth 2020.

Sunil Mohan and Donghui Li. 2019. MedMentions: A Large Biomedical Corpus Annotated with UMLS Concepts. *ArXiv*, abs/1902.09476.

Fleur Mougin, Anita Burgun, and Olivier Bodenreider. 2006. Using wordnet to improve the mapping of data elements to umls for data sources integration. In *AMIA Annual Symposium Proceedings*, volume 2006, page 574. American Medical Informatics Association.

Peter Ochieng and Swaib Kyanda. 2018. Large-scale ontology matching: State-of-the-art analysis. *ACM Comput. Surv.*, 51(4).

Afshin Rahimi, Timothy Baldwin, and Karin Verspoor. 2020. WikiUMLS: Aligning UMLS to Wikipedia via Cross-lingual Neural Ranking. *arXiv preprint arXiv:2005.01281*.

Frank Rogers. 1963. Medical subject headings. *Bulletin of the Medical Library Association*, 51:114–116.

Barry Smith and Christiane Fellbaum. 2004. Medical wordnet: A new methodology for the construction and validation of information resources for consumer health. In *Proceedings of the 20th International Conference on Computational Linguistics*, COLING '04, page 371es, USA. Association for Computational Linguistics.

Denny Vrandečić and Markus Krötzsch. 2014. Wikidata: A Free Collaborative Knowledgebase. *Commun. ACM*, 57(10):7885.

World Health Organization (WHO). 2004. *ICD-10 : international statistical classification of diseases and related health problems : tenth revision*, 2nd ed edition. World Health Organization.

Elena Zotova, Montse Cuadros, and German Rigau. 2022. ClinIDMap: Towards a clinical IDs mapping for data interoperability. In *Proceedings of the Thirteenth Language Resources and Evaluation Conference*, pages 3661–3669, Marseille, France. European Language Resources Association.

A Appendix. Output mappings


```
{
    "source_type": "UMLS",
    "source_id": "C0001430",
    "status": "OK",
    "UMLS_CUI": [
        {
            "id": "C0001430",
            "description": "Adenoma"
        },
        {
            "id": "C0001430",
            "description": "Adenoma, NOS"
        },
        {
            "id": "C0001430",
            "description": "[M]Adenoma NOS"
        },
        {
            "id": "C0001430",
            "description": "[M]Adenomas"
        },
        {
            "id": "C0001430",
            "description": "Benign adenoma"
        },
        {
            "id": "C0001430",
            "description": "[M]Adenoma NOS (morphologic abnormality)"
        },
        {
            "id": "C0001430",
            "description": "Adenoma, no subtype (morphologic abnormality)"
        },
        {
            "id": "C0001430",
            "description": "Adenoma, no subtype"
        },
        {
            "id": "C0001430",
            "description": "Benign adenomatous neoplasm (disorder)"
        },
        {
            "id": "C0001430",
            "description": "Benign adenomatous neoplasm"
        }
    ],
    "SNOMED_CT_EN": [
        {
            "id": "443416007",
            "description": "Benign adenomatous neoplasm (disorder) Benign
                adenomatous neoplasm Adenoma Benign adenoma"
        },
        {
            "id": "32048006",
            "description": "Adenoma Adenoma, NOS Adenoma, no subtype (morphologic
                abnormality) Adenoma, no subtype"
        },
        {
            "id": "189579004",
            "description": "[M]Adenoma NOS [M]Adenoma NOS (morphologic abnormality)"
        },
        {
            "id": "189578007",
            "description": "[M]Adenomas &/or adenocarcinomas [M]Adenomas and
                adenocarcinomas [M]Adenomas [M]Adenocarcinomas [M]Adenomas &/or
                adenocarcinomas (disorder)"
        }
```

```
    ],
    "SNOMED_CT_ES": [
        {
            "id": "32048006",
            "description": "adenoma"
        },
        {
            "id": "32048006",
            "description": "morfología: adenoma, no tipificado (anomalía morfológica
               )"
        }
    ],
    "ICD10CM_ES": [
        {
            "id": "D36.9",
            "description": "Neoplasia benigna, localización no especificada"
        }
    ],
    "ICD10PCS_ES": [],
    "MESH": [
        {
            "id": "D000236",
            "description": "Adenoma, Basal Cell"
        },
        {
            "id": "D000236",
            "description": "Adenoma, Follicular"
        },
        {
            "id": "D000236",
            "description": "Adenoma, Microcystic"
        }
    ],
    "wikidata_item_url": [
        "http://www.wikidata.org/entity/Q272741"
    ],

    "wikipedia_article_url": [
        {
            "arwiki": "https://ar.wikipedia.org/wiki/_>
            ...
            "zhwiki": "https://zh.wikipedia.org/wiki/"
        }
    ],
    "WordNet": [
        {
            "WordNet 3.1": "14259275-n",
            "WordNet 3.0": "14235793-n",
            "CSI": "HEALTH_AND_MEDICINE_",
            "WordNet Domain": "medicine",
            "sense": "adenoma%1:26:00::",
            "MCR synset": [
                {
                    "en": "a benign epithelial tumor of glandular origin",
                    "es": "tumor epitelial benigno de origen glandular",
                    "pt": "um tumor epitelial benigno de origem glandular",
                    "gl": "",
                    "eu": "",
                    "ca": ""
                }
            ]
        }
    ]
}
```

Connecting Multilingual Wordnets: Strategies for Improving ILI Classification in OdeNet

Johann Bergh
Lingolutions
Munich, Germany.
johann@lingolutions.com

Melanie Siegel
Darmstadt University
of Applied Science
melanie.siegel@h-da.de

Abstract

The Open Multilingual Wordnet (OMW) is an open source project that was launched with the goal to make it easy to use wordnets in multiple languages without having to pay expensive proprietary licensing costs. As OMW evolved, the interlingual indicator (ILI)[1] was used to allow semantically equivalent synsets in different languages to be linked to each other. OdeNet[2] is the German language wordnet which forms part of the OMW project. This paper analyses the shortcomings of the initial ILI classification in OdeNet and the consequent methods used to improve this classification.

1 Introduction

A wordnet is a lexical database of semantic relationships between words in a specific language. The first wordnet was created for the English language at Princeton University (also known as the Princeton WordNet, (Fellbaum, 1998)). As the usefulness of wordnets as lexical resources became apparent, the Princeton WordNet (PWN) was expanded and some wordnets were constructed from scratch in other languages.

The Princeton WordNet is distributed in electronic format as part of NLTK (Natural Language Processing Toolkit) and can be accessed with a corresponding Python library[3]. NLTK offers translations for synsets (groupings of synonyms) in various languages, although these translations are incomplete; meaning that not every synset in English has an equivalent translation in another language. There are also wordnets in other languages which were developed completely independent of the PWN, such as GermaNet (Hamp et al., 1997). Many of these wordnets contain high quality data which were constructed manually in a resource-intensive and time-consuming manner. Therefore, these wordnets are commercially licensed and not free to use, except for research and teaching. An example of a large Wordnet built independently from PWN and available on open-source licence is plWordNet (Piasecki et al., 2009; Dziob et al., 2019).

OMW is an open source project that was launched with the goal to make it easy to use wordnets in multiple languages with cc-by-sa-4.0 open-source licenses that include commercial and private use (Bond and Foster, 2013). OMW has the added benefit of connecting equivalent synsets in different languages by means of the ILI (Fellbaum and Vossen, 2008; Bond et al., 2016). The English version of OMW called EWN (McCrae et al., 2020) is basically a copy of the PWN with some enhancements and additions, most notably the addition of an ILI for each synset. Many of the OMW wordnets in other languages were developed by using the already existing translations in NLTK. These translations were extracted and packaged into new wordnets. Consequently, the equivalent synsets in the resulting wordnets were linked to each other via the ILI. Goodman and Bond (2021) developed the WN Python library that can be used to access the wordnets that form part of the OMW project. In Listing 1 we see how the translated lemmas of a synset in PWN can be accessed with NLTK Python library. Listing 2 on the other hand shows how to access these same synsets through the ILI or by searching directly for it in the other language.

Listing 1: Get French translation for EWN synset in NLTK

```
from nltk.corpus import wordnet as wn

s = wn.synsets('dog')
s[0].lemma_names()
['dog', 'domestic_dog', 'Canis_familiaris']

s[0].lemma_names('fra')
['chien', 'canis_familiaris']
```

[1]The next version was called CILI (Collaborative Interlingual Index), https://www.luismc.com/omw/ili

[2]https://github.com/hdaSprachtechnologie/odenet

[3]https://www.nltk.org

Listing 2: Get French synset via ILI or directly in WN

```
import wn
s = wn.synsets('dog')
s[0].lemmas()
['dog', 'Canis␣familiaris', 'domestic␣dog']

#Get equivalent French synset via ILI
ili = s[0].ili.id
s = wn.synsets(ili=ili, lang='fr')
s[0].lemmas()
['chien', 'canis␣familiaris']

#Search for French synset directly
s = wn.synsets('chien', lang='fr')
s[8].lemmas()
['chien', 'canis␣familiaris']
```

Though NLTK offers translations in many languages, German is so far not included. This means that a German wordnet for OMW could not easily be constructed with the exiting NLTK translations as a base, as was the case with many of the other languages. Therefore, an initiative was launched to create an open source German wordnet (OdeNet) which could form part of the OMW project. OdeNet was constructed from open source linguistic resources in combination with some manual and semi-manual corrections. Since OdeNet was constructed independently of existing resources in NLTK, it was not as easy to connect equivalent synsets in OMW via ILI. As an initial implementation, Google Translate[4] was used in combination with statistical methods as described by Siegel and Bond (2021). However, this implementation has some shortcomings, including:

- incorrect ILI classification for some synsets from a semantic perspective
- duplicate assignment of ILI's to multiple synsets
- Part of Speech (POS) for some ILI's is inconsistent between EWN and OdeNet

This paper describes these shortcomings and proposes solutions for improved ILI and POS classification in OdeNet.

2 Problem Description

A significant problem in using machine translation to connect equivalent synsets in different languages occurs, when translating homographs (words with similar spelling but different meanings) and polysemes. This is particularly noticeable when a word translated from a source language is a homograph or polyseme in the target language. As an example, we take the German word `Unterlegscheibe` from OdeNet. The corresponding English translation is `washer`. Searching for `washer` in EWN, we find three synsets containing the word:

- Name: `washer`
  EWN ID: `ewn-10788571-n`
  ILI: `i94042`
  Definition: `someone who washes things for a living`
- Name: `washer`
  EWN ID: `ewn-04562157-n`
  ILI: `i60971`
  Definition: `seal consisting of a flat disk placed to prevent leakage`
- Name: `washer`
  EWN ID: `ewn-04561970-n`
  ILI: `i60970`
  Definition: `a home appliance for washing clothes and linens automatically`

Our aim is to select the correct synset in EWN so that we can take the corresponding ILI and assign it to the synset in German. For somebody with knowledge of German, it is evident that the second synset in the list is the correct corresponding synset in EWN (i.e. we want to take the ILI from this synset and also use it in the corresponding OdeNet synset). It is difficult to do this assignment automatically, because of the missing context.

The usage of machine translation with Google Translate together with some statistical methods in the current OdeNet implementation (Siegel and Bond, 2021) also resulted in many of the synsets having duplicate ILIs, because the assignment of ILIs to synsets in OdeNet was not restricted to one ILI per synset. An example: The synsets `odenet-4330-n (Anzahl, Zahl)` and `odenet-688-n (Summe, Gesamtmenge)` both referred to `i35594 (measure, amount, quantity)`. Furthermore, Siegel and Bond (2021) used automatic methods for assigning the correct POS to synsets. However, they were only able to assign the correct POS to synsets in 93% of the cases. Often, multi-word lexemes were involved in problematic cases, as for example `postmortal, nach dem Tod, post mortem` was categorized as `pos "n"`, although it is `pos "a"`.

[4]`https://translate.google.de`

3 Proposed Solution

3.1 Basic Approach

Figure 1 depicts the complete algorithm for correcting ILI classification in OdeNet.

All synsets in EWN have a short, concise definition in the `Definition` field. We propose to use this definition to get more context for the disambiguation. First, we combine the word in the synset and the definition with a semicolon and do machine translations with DeepL[5]. Then, we extract the translated word from the machine translation and look for a corresponding match in OdeNet. These are the results for the `washer` example:

- EWN ID: `ewn-10788571-n`
  ILI: `i94042`
  Word-Definition combination:
  `washer: someone who washes things for a living`
  Machine translation:
  `Wäscher: jemand, der beruflich Dinge wäscht`
- EWN ID: `ewn-04562157-n`
  ILI: `i60971`
  Word-Definition combination:
  `washer: seal consisting of a flat disk placed to prevent leakage`
  Machine translation:
  `Unterlegscheibe: Dichtung, die aus einer flachen Scheibe besteht, um ein Auslaufen zu verhindern`
- EWN ID: `ewn-04561970-n`
  ILI: `i60970`
  Word-Definition combination:
  `washer: a home appliance for washing clothes and linens automatically`
  Machine translation:
  `Waschmaschine: ein Haushaltsgerät zum automatischen Waschen von Kleidung und Wäsche`

As is clearly evident, the machine translation of the second item now enables us to make the correct ILI classification (i60971) for the corresponding OdeNet synset.

3.2 Dealing with Ambiguity: ILI Classification Weight

Although we have obtained success with this simplified example, our aim is to construct a system whereby ILI classification for all synsets in OdeNet is possible. In order to achieve this, there are additional scenarios of ambiguity that we have to take into consideration:

Even with the context-based machine translation as described above, we could still find more than one possible candidate in OdeNet for the ILI of the synset we are evaluating in EWN. For example, consider the EWN synset with ILI `i66412`:

- ILI: `i66412`
  Word-Definition combination: `depth: the intellectual ability to penetrate deeply into ideas`
  Machine translation:
  `Tiefe: die intellektuelle Fähigkeit, tief in Ideen einzudringen`

If we now search for the translated lemma `Tiefe` in OdeNet, we will find three synsets (`odenet-847-n: ['Tiefe', 'Tiefsinn'];` `odenet-6615-n ['Abgrund', 'Tiefe', 'Schlund', 'Hölle'], odenet-16328-n ['Tiefe', 'Teufe']`). Which OdeNet synset do we assign the ILI to? Intellectually, this should be `odenet-847-n`, but this cannot be automatically decided.

More than one EWN synset can match a single OdeNet synset. For example, consider the Word-Definition combinations and translations of the EWN synsets with ILIs `i6124` and `i68929` below:

- ILI: `i6124`
  Word-Definition combination:
  `ethic: the principles of right and wrong that are accepted by an individual or a social group`
  Machine translation:
  `Ethik: die Grundsätze des Richtigen und Falschen, die von einem Individuum oder einer sozialen Gruppe akzeptiert werden`
- ILI: `i68929`
  Word-Definition combination:
  `ethics: the philosophical study of moral values and rules`
  Machine translation:
  `Ethik: das philosophische Studium der moralischen Werte und Regeln`

For both of the lemmas in the respective EWN synsets, the translated lemma in German is `Ethik` which is found in the OdeNet synsets `odenet-10-n ['Sittlichkeit', 'Wertvorstellungen',`

[5]`https://www.deepl.com` (After manual translation quality assessment, we chose DeepL for our implementation as it performed better on context-based translations than Google Translate)

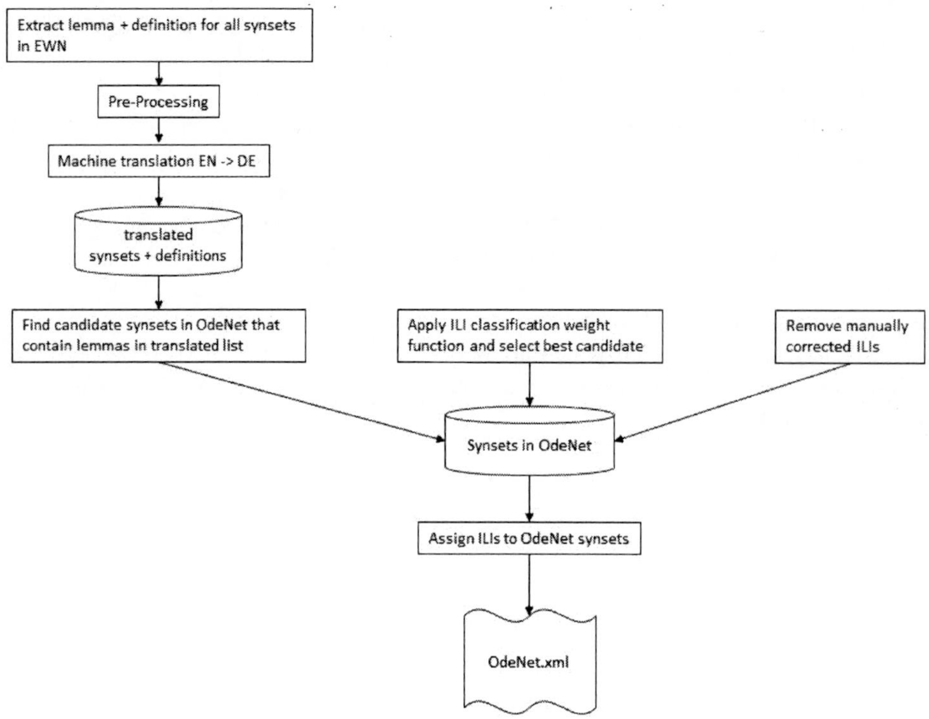

Figure 1: ILI classification

`'Wertmaßstäbe', 'Wertesystem', 'Moral', 'Moralvorstellungen', 'Ethik', 'sittliche Werte', 'moralische Werte']` and `odenet-4879-n ['Ethik', 'Morallehre', 'Sittenlehre', 'Tugendlehre']`. Which one of the EWN synsets' ILI do we assign to which one of the OdeNet synsets?

Since there could be multiple candidates in OdeNet synsets for ILI's in EWN synsets, it is necessary to write a classification function to assign weights to each of the candidates, so that the most optimal assignment can be made. Fortunately, OdeNet is very synonym rich (much more so than other wordnets), and we can use these synonyms in combination with a German spaCy[6] Word2Vec model to do the classification.

$$f(v_1, v_2) = \frac{\sum_i \sum_j dist(v_{1i}, v_{2j})}{|v_1| \times |v_2|} \quad (1)$$

First, we extract the Definition part of the translated Lemma and Definition translation. The content words in this translation are added to a vector (v_1). Only adjectives, adverbs, nouns and verbs are used. Function words, such as prepositions and articles, are discarded. Similarly, all the synonyms (lemmas in the candidate synset) are added to a vector (v_2). For each value in v_1 and v_2 a similarity value is computed. These values are summed and normalised to a value between 0 and 1, which is the weighted value for the candidate synset in OdeNet *competing* for the ILI in a specific EWN synset.

3.3 Optimising Machine Translation for POS by Pre-Processing

In English, there are many nouns and verbs that have the same spelling, such as `search`. Our idea is to use preprocessing in order to obtain better results from machine translation.

Experiments with DeepL machine translation indicated that translation results from English to German for verbs improve when adding `to` in front of the verb. In cases, where we have English nouns and verbs with the same spelling, it also helps the machine translation to distinguish the POS correctly. An example is the word `search`. In the case, where the synset refers to the verb

[6] `https://spacy.io/`

search, the machine translation performs better when adjusting the word to its infinitive form to search, and is also more likely to translate it as a verb in the target language. The EWN synset with ILI i28263 refers to the verb search. The Word-Definition combination is:

```
search: try to locate or discover, or try to establish the existence of
```

Pre-processing changes this to:

```
to search: try to locate or discover, or try to establish the existence of
```

Post-processing adjustments were also necessary in some instances for the machine-translated German text. For verbs, the machine translation added the word zu in front of the verb in some cases, as a result of the addition of to in front of the English verbs. Consequently, we removed zu from the translated text as a post-processing cleanup task, if the POS was a verb.

3.4 Correct POS classification in OdeNet

Siegel and Bond (2021) reported that the POS classification for the initial implementation of OdeNet was at 93.3%, with errors occurring mostly in cases where the lemma was a multi-word lexeme, which made correct POS classification difficult by automatic means. The data gathered in the table of translations can be leveraged to address this issue.

For each synset in OdeNet, we extract the first lemma of the synset. We then retrieve all records in the table of translations, where the first lemma from the synset is equal to the translated target lemma. If the POS of the lemma's synset is not equal to any POS's of the relevant records retrieved in the table, then there could be a POS misclassification in the OdeNet synset, since it would be reasonable to assume that the POS of the EWN synset translated to German should also have the same POS in the target language.

4 Results

Table 1 depicts the state of OdeNet, before and after the algorithm has been applied. It can be seen that there were 13,818 synsets with unique ILIs. Further, there were 5,965 synsets with duplicate ILIs; meaning that one unique ILI is assigned to more than one synset in OdeNet. The total number of unique duplicate ILIs were 3,703; meaning that on average, a duplicate ILI was assigned to 1.61 synsets.

The most noticeable difference after applying the algorithm is the complete elimination of duplicate ILIs. The number of synsets with unique ILIs has increased to 19,547 and all duplicate ILIs have been removed. The algorithm identified 361 synsets with possible POS errors. After manual evaluation, 325 of these synsets indeed ended up having a wrong POS. This means a successful identification of 90% of synsets with the wrong POS. Of the 36 false positives, most proposed an adjective for a noun or a verb and in many cases colloquial language was involved, such as in the case of odenet-19938-n (Tüftelei, Getüftel).

5 Concluding remarks

OdeNet is an open-source wordnet that was automatically compiled from an open thesaurus and connected to the multilingual wordnets in the OMW initiative by machine-translating synsets. The result of the machine translation was partly incorrect because the translation context was missing. Further, duplicate interlingual indicators (ILIs) were assigned in OdeNet. Additionally, there was a need to correct the automatically assigned POS.

In this paper, we described a solution for these problems by matching ILIs to OdeNet synsets, taking the English definitions into account. The results have shown that the algorithm is very effective in reducing duplication and improving the correctness of ILI classification.

The algorithm can potentially be improved by providing the ILI classification weight function, as described in section 3.2, with more context information. At the moment, we use synonyms to provide context, and these synonyms could be augmented with the hypernyms of the *candidate* synsets under evaluation. This should lead to higher classification accuracy, but is left for future research.

Although this algorithm was applied to improve the ILI classification for OdeNet, it can be used for any other language in theory. The success of the resulting classification will be dependent on factors such as how synonym-rich the language is and also how good the machine translation support is.

With some minor adjustments to the algorithm, we propose that it will also be possible to connect other lexical resources using the proposed method. For example, two thesauri, developed in two differ-

	EWN	OdeNet (before)	OdeNet (after)
Synsets	120053	36159	36159
Synsets with unique ILIs	117480	13818	19547
Synsets without ILIs	2573	16376	16612
Synsets with duplicate ILIs	0	5965	0
Duplicate ILIs	0	3703	0

Table 1: OdeNet after applying proposed algorithm

ent languages independently of each other, could be merged into a bilingual resource.

Since languages evolve independently of each other, it often happens that not all words in one language have a perfect equivalent in another language. It can happen that some semantic meaning is lost or added in the translation process. Even though you will mostly get the best possible match by applying an algorithm such as described in this paper, there can still be an extent of *fuzziness* or loss/addition of meaning. Currently, the OMW framework is modelled in such as way that a synset in one language can map to a single synset in another language via the ILI. This structure makes it difficult to model fuzzy matching or loss/addition of semantic meaning. This topic may be of interest for future research.

References

Francis Bond and Ryan Foster. 2013. Linking and extending an open multilingual wordnet. In *Proceedings of the 51st Annual Meeting of the Association for Computational Linguistics*, pages 1352–1362, Sofia.

Francis Bond, Piek Vossen, John P McCrae, and Christiane Fellbaum. 2016. CILI: The Collaborative Interlingual Index. In *Proceedings of the Global WordNet Conference*, volume 2016.

Agnieszka Dziob, Maciej Piasecki, and Ewa Rudnicka. 2019. plwordnet 4.1-a linguistically motivated, corpus-based bilingual resource. In *Proceedings of the 10th Global Wordnet Conference*, pages 353–362.

Christiane Fellbaum, editor. 1998. *WordNet: An Electronic Lexical Database*. MIT Press, Cambridge, MA.

Christiane Fellbaum and Piek Vossen. 2008. Challenges for a global Wordnet. In *Online Proceedings of the First International Workshop on Global Interoperability for Language Resources*, pages 75–82.

Michael Wayne Goodman and Francis Bond. 2021. Intrinsically interlingual: The Wn Python library for wordnets. In *11th International Global Wordnet Conference (GWC2021)*.

Birgit Hamp, Helmut Feldweg, et al. 1997. GermaNet-a lexical-semantic net for German. In *Proceedings of ACL workshop Automatic Information Extraction and Building of Lexical Semantic Resources for NLP Applications*, pages 9–15.

John Philip McCrae, Alexandre Rademaker, Ewa Rudnicka, and Francis Bond. 2020. English wordnet 2020: Improving and extending a wordnet for english using an open-source methodology. In *proceedings of the LREC 2020 workshop on multimodal WordNets (MMW2020)*, pages 14–19.

Maciej Piasecki, Bernd Broda, and Stanislaw Szpakowicz. 2009. *A wordnet from the ground up*. Oficyna Wydawnicza Politechniki Wrocławskiej Wrocław.

Melanie Siegel and Francis Bond. 2021. Compiling a German wordnet from other resources. In *11th International Global Wordnet Conference (GWC2021)*.

Association for Computational Linguistics
209 N. Eighth Street
Stroudsburg, Pennsylvania 18360

CURRAN ASSOCIATES INC.
proceedings.com

ISBN 978-1-7138-9088-1